Merleau-Ponty and Nishida

Merleau-Ponty and Nishida
Artistic Expression as Motor-Perceptual Faith

ADAM LOUGHNANE

Cover image: Sesshū Tōyō (1420–1506), Splashed Ink Landscape, 1495. Tokyo National Museum, Tokyo, Japan. (Wikimedia Commons)

Published by State University of New York Press, Albany

© 2019 State University of New York

All rights reserved

No part of this book may be used or reproduced in any manner whatsoever without written permission. No part of this book may be stored in a retrieval system or transmitted in any form or by any means including electronic, electrostatic, magnetic tape, mechanical, photocopying, recording, or otherwise without the prior permission in writing of the publisher.

For information, contact State University of New York Press, Albany, NY
www.sunypress.edu

Library of Congress Cataloging-in-Publication Data

Names: Loughnane, Adam, 1978– author.
Title: Merleau-Ponty and Nishida : artistic expression as motor-perceptual faith / Adam Loughnane.
Description: Albany : State University of New York Press, [2019] | Includes bibliographical references and index.
Identifiers: LCCN 2018048809 | ISBN 9781438476117 (hardcover) | ISBN 9781438476124 (pbk.) | ISBN 9781438476131 (ebook) Subjects: LCSH: Art and philosophy. | Phenomenology. | Philosophy and religion. | Nishida, Kitarō, 1870–1945. | Merleau-Ponty, Maurice, 1908–1961.
Classification: LCC BH39 .L68 2019 | DDC 181/.12—dc23
LC record available at https://lccn.loc.gov/2018048809

10 9 8 7 6 5 4 3 2 1

Contents

LIST OF ILLUSTRATIONS ... ix

ACKNOWLEDGMENTS ... xi

INTRODUCTION Faith, Flesh, and *Basho* ... xiii
   Nishida between Religion and Philosophy ... xxi
   Merleau-Ponty between Philosophy and Religion ... xxv
   Artistic Expression East and West ... xxviii
   Ambiguity, Negation, and Faith ... xxxvii

CHAPTER 1 Ontology, Ambiguity, and Negation ... 1
   Motor-Perceptual Fabric: Faith and Transitivity ... 1
   Nishida and Phenomenology ... 8
   Substance and Relation: Separation and Non-Obstruction ... 10
   Nishida's "Absolute Negation" ... 20
   Negation: Chiasm, "Continuity of Discontinuity" ... 24
   Merleau-Ponty Counter Sartre's *Nullité Absolue* ... 34
   Nishida: "Absolute Negation" and the "I-Thou" Relation ... 38
   Representation and Perceptual Negation: From Non-Subject
      to Non-Object ... 41

CHAPTER 2 Perceptual Fabric: Space, Time, and Light ... 51
   Vision and Multi-Perspectivalism: Seeing-Seen ... 51
      Representation, Ocularcentrism, and Multi-Perspectivalism ... 54
      Multi-Perspectival Perception ... 57
      The Three Graces ... 57
      Guo Xi: Angle of Totality ... 61
      "Dragon Veins": The Visible and Invisible in Daoism ... 65

Merleau-Ponty: Multi-Perspectivalism and "Depth"	72
Time and Negation I: Ecstatic Temporality	75
Nishida: "Eternal Now" and "Internal-qua-External Perception"	81
Skin and Bones in Rodin and Taiga	87
Multi-perspectivalism Creation and Obstruction	95
The Expanded Body: Vision and Touch	100
Tool as Non-Objective Bodily Extension	104
Space: Distance and Proximity	112
"Distanceless Distance"	116
Light, Tools, and the Aesthetics of Transparent Mediality	121
Molyneux's Problem: Obstruction and Light	125
Nishida: Full Reversibility and Expression	141
Everything Touching or Nothing at All	144
CHAPTER 3 Motor-Perceptual Fabric: Time and Motion	**149**
Sesshū Tōyō: Zen, Vision, and Motion	151
Cézanne's "Germinations" with the Landscape	163
Time: From Perception to Motor-Perception	169
Motion: Volitional Character of the World	170
Activity-Passivity	170
Ontologies of Expression	175
Motor-Background: "Solicitations" and "Unity of Act and Act"	178
Body and Expression in Time	193
Nishida's "Historical Body" and "Historical World"	193
Time and Negation II: "Deep Present" and "Absolute Present"	202
From Multi-Perspectival to Multi-Volitional	208
"Optimal Grip" and the Force of Tradition	213
New Art: Creating the Visible	219
Copy and Original	219
"New Art": Objectivity and Faith	223
Tradition as Historical-Volitional Ecstasis	228
New Solicitations, New Continuity of Act, and Act	230
From Creating the Conditions of Visibility to Creating the Conditions of Motor-Visibility	235
Vision as Motion	240
Motion as Vision	242
"Acting-Intuition"	244
Color(lessness) and Motion(lessness)	251
Motor-Chromaticity	252
The Color of Negation	259

CONTENTS

CHAPTER 4 Expression as "Motor-Perceptual Faith"	263
"Seeing without a Seer" and Moving without a Mover	263
Motor-Perceptual "Blind Spot" as Dynamic Obstruction	265
Nishida: "Seeing Without a Seer"	268
Mirroring, Mapping, and Seeing	270
History of Motor-Visibility	278
Klee: "End-Forms" and "Formative Forces"	278
The Invisibility of the Self as "Style" and the Temporality of Risk	281
Coherent Deformation and the Force of Tradition	285
Overcoming Reflection, Embracing Risk	290
Holography, Infinity, and Risk	290
Reflection and Faith	297
Spontaneity and Non-Willing	303
The Materiality of Spontaneous Expression: Bernard Leach and Pottery as Throwing-Thrown	307
The Fallacy of Motor-Perceptual Neutrality and Uni-Directional Expression	311
Spontaneity and the Temporality of Risk	317
The Limits of Reflection and Doubt: The Pre-Reflective and the Necessity of Faith	321
Faith, Negation, and Volition in the Pre-Reflective	324
Conclusion: Motor-Perceptual Faith between Philosophy, Religion, and Art	328
Secularizing the Spiritual: Nishida's "Inverse Polarity" and "Interexpression"	329
Spiritualizing the Secular: Merleau-Ponty and "Anatheism"	336
WORKS CITED AND BIBLIOGRAPHY	341
INDEX	355

Illustrations

1.1	Andreas Vesalius, "Optic chiasm," *De humani corporis fabrica*. 1543	29
1.2	"Muscle-tendon Chiasm" by the author	31
2.1	Raphael, *The Three Graces*. 1505 (Musée Condé, Chantilly, France)	58
2.2	Guo Xi, *Early Spring*. 1072 (National Palace Museum, Beijing)	63
2.3	Hasegawa Tōhaku, *Pine Trees*. 1595 (Tokyo National Museum)	68–69
2.4	Auguste Rodin, *The Three Shades*. 1886 (Musée Rodin, Paris)	88
2.5	Ike no Taiga, *True Views of Mt. Asama*. 1776 (Yabumoto Collection, Japan)	91
3.1	Sesshū Tōyō, *Splashed Ink Landscape*. 1495 (Tokyo National Museum)	152
3.2	Paul Cézanne, *Mont Sainte-Victoire*. 1904 (Philadelphia Museum of Art)	164
3.3	Méret Oppenheim, *Fur Lined Teacup*. 1936 (Museum of Modern Art, New York)	232
4.1	Eadweard Muybridge, *The Horse in Motion*. 1878 (Harry Ransom Center, Austin, Texas)	286
4.2	Théodore Géricault, *Epsom Derby*. 1821 (Musée du Louvre, Paris)	286

Acknowledgments

My deepest and most heartfelt gratitude goes to Graham Parkes for the immense support, which made this book possible. Most of this work took form while I was a graduate student under his supervision, and it was his encouragement to develop those ideas into a monograph that has eventually led to this book. As far as unrepayable debts go, I gladly remain indebted to one of the most humane and generous teachers, scholars, and mentors I have had the great luck to encounter within or outside academia.

I would also like to thank the staff, students, and administration in the Philosophy department at University College Cork for their support while carrying out this work. The earliest version of this research benefited greatly from the thoughtful commentary of my examining committee, including Julia Jansen and Brook Ziporyn. The impetus for this project actually began in 2010 with a set of questions provoked by Ziporyn's writings on Merleau-Ponty and Buddhist philosophy, which put me on a trajectory of research further influenced a year later by Lucy Schultz's illuminating presentation at the first East–West meeting of the Collegium Phaenomenologicum in Citta di Castello, Italy. My gratitude goes to both for initiating inquiry that has kept me busy for the good part of the last decade.

I must also extend a very special thanks to Professor Kazashi Nobuo for his contribution to my project and his gracious hosting while I worked on this book as a Japan Foundation Post-Doctoral researcher at Kobe University. While in Japan, I was also fortunate to receive the kind support of many whom I must thank, those being Oie Shinya, Okuburi Akiko, Katsube Naoki, and Motobayashi Yoshiaki, as well as the staff in the Graduate Department of Humanities.

I profited significantly from close readings of early drafts by Jason Dockstader and two anonymous readers of the manuscript originally submitted to SUNY. My gratitude also goes to anonymous reviewers from

Philosophy East and West and the *European Journal of Japanese Philosophy*, whose thoughtful readings and insightful criticism were immensely valuable in expanding and strengthening the content of my writing. Ralf Müller deserves special mention for his greatly-appreciated assistance in navigating the language of Nishida's *Zenshū*.

I would like to acknowledge the generous support without which I could not have had the time or freedom to complete this work. I thank the Irish Research Council for its patronage while undertaking the initial stages of this project during my Doctoral studies, and the Japan Foundation for a fellowship to continue this research in Japan, and finally to UCC for providing assistance to bring my original manuscript to completion through the CACSSS Research Publication Fund. Many thanks also go to *Philosophy East and West*, the *European Journal of Japanese Philosophy*, and *Performance Philosophy* for permission to reprint material from existing publications.

My thanks go to all others who contributed directly or indirectly to my work. For the many discussions and debates that began in person and continue throughout these pages, and for those who took care of me, offered residencies in their spare bedrooms and kitchen tables, friendship, inspiration, criticism, and support to see me through to the end of this endeavor; those include—but I'm sure not limited to—my parents Don and Anne Marie, my brother Ryan, Matt Miles, David Rafferty, Karen Houle, Scott Marratto, Alexandra Morrison, Alessandro Salice, Frank Chouraqui, Natalie Heller, Jason Dockstader, Alex Robins, Marco Pellitteri, Charis Eisen, and Sergei Gepshtein. Annette Loy deserves special mention for the love, support, and patience that helped see me through the final stages of this work. I would also like to thank my research assistants Ciara O'Mahony and Lauren Walsh-Dermody for their excellent work in helping to prepare the manuscript. Lastly, I thank the production team at SUNY, notably the acquisitions editor Christopher Ahn, senior production editor Eileen Nizer, editorial assistant Chelsea Miller, and language editors Sharon Green and John Wentworth for their greatly-appreciated enthusiasm, support, and patience.

Introduction

Faith, Flesh, and *Basho*

The fifteenth-century German philosopher and theologian Nicolaus de Cusa described God as an "infinite circle whose center is everywhere and whose circumference is nowhere." The origin of this saying is uncertain; it might have been spoken earlier by Empedocles or the mythical Hermes Trismegistus. A later religious philosopher, Pascal, as well as a staunch critic of religion, Voltaire, also invoke the dictum. So too do Nishida and Merleau-Ponty. The Kyoto School philosopher appeals to the notion throughout his writings to describe the "absolute present," and "absolute nothingness," whereas for the French thinker it is philosophy itself that is such a circumferenceless circle. Given the philosophic and religious appeals to this idea throughout history, its invocation at decisive moments of Nishida's and Merleau-Ponty's writings raises perplexing questions concerning the status of their philosophies in relation to religion, and the possible resonance between their projects. If their philosophies conform to this geometry, if they are circles whose circumferences are nowhere and centers everywhere, how might they overlap? And, if they do, how might we draw a comparative line from one project to the other, or conceive of the intercultural distance between East and West when the fields of philosophy are configured according to this enigmatic geometry?

The implications of this question are wide ranging for this dialogue in particular and for comparative philosophy in general. Certainly, they are much too broad for any single study, nevertheless, the provocative similarities between Nishida's and Merleau-Ponty's philosophies—only heightened by critical differences—call for a dialogue between the two, which embraces the challenges of intercultural encounter at a deep level. Nishida (西田幾多郎, 1870–1945) and Merleau-Ponty (1908–1961) lived in worlds with little overlap at the time, and despite not having spoken each other's languages or had access to each other's writings, there are, nonetheless, remarkable similarities and critical differences running throughout the entirety of their projects, presenting an exceptional opportunity for intercultural dialogue. Both of their far-reaching undertakings began as attempts to divert from Western metaphysical dualism. While they are by no means the only thinkers East or West to do so, they both strive to meet this challenge by exploring the moving and perceiving body, particularly as it can be studied in artistic expression. Beyond this shared point of departure, the terminus of their projects further motivates the encounter between the two: As their works culminate in their ontologies of flesh (*chair*) and *Basho* (場所), a philosophically curious concept comes to the fore in their late writings, namely the concept of faith, thus further invoking the question regarding religion. Neither would live to fully realize the implications of this notion, yet the extent to which faith confounds Western philosophy's self-conception compels a reading of their works in tandem. To that end, this study stages a dialogue between Merleau-Ponty and Nishida, to explore the similarities and differences between their conceptions of faith in hopes of expanding the problematics this concept poses for philosophic methodology that too easily distinguishes itself from religious and artistic practice.

Despite the intriguing affinities between the two philosophers, there are, of course, important, sometimes implacable differences that punctuate the encounter. We find one crucial point of divergence at the very outset: Nishida's is a religious faith (*shinnen* 信念), while Merleau-Ponty speaks of a perceptual form of faith (*foi perceptive*). This presents obvious challenges, nevertheless, neither of their conceptions of faith adhere to a strict sacred-secular binary, nor does either thinker interpret faith as the choice of a subject. By contrast, faith, for Nishida and Merleau-Ponty, is an orientation that negates the subject while affording a world beyond the sacred-secular opposition and philosophic methodology not categorically opposed to religion.

The philosophies of Nishida and Merleau-Ponty represent two distinct responses to a similar impulse. They pose a serious challenge to the philosophic method, not only in terms of its relation to faith and religion, but also regarding philosophy's relation to artistic expression. While their considerations of faith bring religious problematics into philosophy, they also suggest how the artist has developed more viable practices for enacting a version of faith that philosophy has neglected but must face. In reading their depictions of artistic expression along these lines, we can articulate new continuities between their earlier writings on artistic expression and their later works, as well as build conceptual bridges that enable the similarities and differences to circulate among their respective projects; bridges, which likewise, in one small way, span philosophy East and West.

Carrying out such a dialogue poses a substantial challenge to philosophy's self-conception, since it has historically been delineated in straightforward opposition to artistic expression and religious practices involving faith. Hoping to amplify this challenge, I explore Nishida's and Merleau-Ponty's theories of expression as motor-perceptual conceptions of faith. If it is meaningful to speak of the term I propose in this book's title, "motor-perceptual faith," it is only half neologistic since it derives from Merleau-Ponty's concept of "perceptual faith" (foi perceptive), or perhaps less than half neologistic since for him perception is always motor-perception. Thus, through a straightforward act of conceptual analysis, we might take perceptual faith to already be motor-perceptual faith. Nevertheless, if there might be a motor aspect that we can productively think alongside his concept of "perceptual faith," Merleau-Ponty does not appear to have explicitly drawn out these possibilities. This study is an attempt to do that work. What we find when unearthing the motor significance of "perceptual faith" is twofold. First, Merleau-Ponty's earlier depiction of artistic expression comes into focus as prefiguring the later concept. Looking back at "Cézanne's Doubt" from *The Visible and the Invisible*, the artist's work can, on my reading, be construed as a practice of "motor-perceptual faith." That is, his rendering of Cézanne's practice calls for the motor elements implicit to his later concept "perceptual faith." Second, when those motor implications come to light, intriguing pathways illumine that enable dialogue with Nishida's philosophy, whose theory of faith has comparable motor and perceptual features when considered in light of his theory of artistic expression. I thus propose to explore the possibilities of a sensorimotor faith as a provisional interpretive device derived from the encounter between the two thinkers, which, I must emphasize, is reducible to neither. I do not claim that there is a similar concept of motor-perceptual faith found in either of their projects. Rather, it is a meeting point where similarities and differences among their philosophies can circulate, sometimes productively, other times leading to irreconcilable differences. Certainly, one of the concerns I explore at greatest length (see chapter 4, "Seeing without a Seer" and Moving without a Mover) is a crucial variance between Nishida and Merleau-Ponty's ideas of the obstructions inherent to motion and perception. While the French thinker articulates explicit limits where perception is obstructed, the same question evokes possible inconsistencies in the writings of the Kyoto School philosopher. With this in mind, I seek to render this tension productive by elucidating similarities and differences between their notions of faith, hoping to discover new conceptual continuities and discontinuities among their projects and beyond any too-facile distinctions between art, religion, and philosophy East and West.

I will not in any way suggest that one should neglect the important qualities that distinguish philosophy, art, or religion East or West. Yet, in following Nishida and Merleau-Ponty's incitement to think beyond identity-difference binaries, we cannot take their philosophies seriously while applying the very logic they refute in service of upholding crude disciplinary or methodological boundaries. To think beyond rigid distinctions between philosophy, religion, and art might seem an appropriate approach to Nishida's philosophy, but not to Merleau-Ponty's. After all, historically speaking, Nishida's East Asian tradition has allowed greater fluidity in terms of delineating religious, aesthetic, and philosophic methodology. As I discuss in chapter 3 regarding the painter-priest Sesshū Tōyō, being a landscape artist was at once a religious as well as a philosophic practice. Whereas these boundaries tend to be more strictly enforced in the West, we must acknowledge how numerous critical features of Merleau-Ponty's understanding of philosophy—its relation to "non-philosophy"; the centrality of artistic expression in his writings; his explicit remarks about the ambiguity between religion and philosophy; and the unexplored implications of faith for his thought—when taken together, entice one to explore his project beyond simple disciplinary borders.

Nishida's project began as a deliberate attempt to establish a liminal position between disciplines and cultures. His philosophical undertaking was from its inception an explicit synthesis of Eastern and Western thought in what many have referred to as a "world philosophy." I discuss this feature of his thought at greater length throughout, yet his status as an intercultural philosopher is beyond dispute. Merleau-Ponty, on the other hand, is, of course, not known for having developed intercultural thought in any systematic way, nevertheless, one does not have to look far to see that he was, in fact, an unrecognized champion of intercultural thinking and a vocal critic of the Eurocentrism of his time, which demoted Asian thought to an inferior status. In his *Les Philosophes Célèbres* (1956) Merleau-Ponty proves a rare exception to encyclopedists who exclude the East from their compendia. That work of 1956 not only includes but *begins with* four chapters on Asian philosophers with a forward by Merleau-Ponty, "*L'Orient et la Philosophie.*" Three years earlier, in his essay "Everywhere and Nowhere," he works to redeem Western philosophy from its deeply rooted chauvinism by taking aim at the philosophers who did not flinch at excluding the East from "true" philosophy—primary among whom is Hegel, but also those who inherited his mistakes, which includes Husserl.[1] Against Husserl, who considered Chinese and Indian philosophy to be "empirical or anthropological specimens," Merleau-Ponty argues that "if Western thought is what it claims to be, it must prove it by understanding all 'life-worlds.' "[2] He further undermines any strict East–West distinction when he writes, "Pure or absolute philosophy, in the name of which Hegel excluded the Orient, also excludes a good part of the Western past."[3] Countering the Hegelian condemnation of Indian and Chinese philosophies to a state of "immaturity," philosophies never able to develop to the level of universality the West had, Merleau-Ponty proves uniquely sensitive for his time when he writes:

> Indian and Chinese philosophies have tried not so much to dominate existence as to be the echo or the sounding board of our relationship to being. Western philosophy can learn from them to rediscover the relationship to being and initial option which gave it birth, and to estimate the possibilities we have shut ourselves off from in becoming "Westerners" and perhaps reopen them.[4]

A significant thrust of "Everywhere and Nowhere" involves dismantling Hegel's "geographical frontier between philosophy and non-philosophy,"[5] the latter being the thinking of any tradition not progenitor or inheritor of the universalism of the Western Enlightenment. Rather than a single tradition at the top of the philosophical hierarchy, below which we find non-phi-

---

1. Husserl distinguished between the purely theoretical type of knowing characteristic of the European tradition, which carries that project from its Greek origin, and the "empirical anthropological type" of knowledge that is characteristic of China and India. Edmund Husserl, *The Crisis of European Sciences and Transcendental Phenomenology: An Introduction to Phenomenological Philosophy*. Merleau-Ponty, on the other hand, sees all thought traditions, including his own, as empirical or "ethnophilosophical" in the sense of being inescapably conditioned by their anthropological specificities. See Hwa Yol Jung, "Revolutionary Dialectics: Mao Tse-Tung and Maurice Merleau-Ponty."
2. Maurice Merleau-Ponty, *Les Philosophes Célèbres*.
3. Maurice Merleau-Ponty, *Signs*, 138.
4. Ibid., 139.
5. Ibid., 138.

losophy, Merleau-Ponty implores that "subordinating 'non-philosophy' to true philosophy will not create the unity of the human spirit. It already exists in each culture's lateral relationships to the others, in the echoes one awakes in the other."[6] Both Kwok-Ying Lau and Hwa Yol Jung see in Merleau-Ponty's concept of the "lateral universal" a paradigm for world philosophy.[7] He was a Western philosopher through and through, yet was not interested in excluding non-philosophy or demoting it to an inferior status; he rather sought the "Orient's secret, muted contribution to philosophy."[8] He wanted a lateral way of thinking that not only took into account the point of view on both ends of intercultural encounter, but also believed that "the mistaken views each has of the other can all find a place." What results is not a universal philosophy that shuns meaningful dialogue with other "particular" thought traditions, but what Merleau-Ponty describes as a "more comprehensive experience which becomes in principle accessible to men of a different time and country."[9] It is perhaps unfortunate that such an important thinker did not develop his inspiring intercultural openness into a more systematic facet of his philosophy, but the extent to which his thinking proves remarkably open and inviting to encounter with other thought traditions—in this study and a growing volume of scholarship that places him in dialogue with other non-Western traditions—might suggest that his cultural broad-mindedness and his refusal to peddle the Eurocentrism of his own tradition enabled a way of thinking that deserves attention and praise for its world-philosophical potential.

---

6. Ibid., 139.

7. Jung sees the concept as a "transversalist" alternative to the exclusionary universality the West upholds to distinguish itself from the thought of other cultures. He goes so far as to refer to Merleau-Ponty, as "unmistakably a consummate transversalist avant la letter." Hwa Yol Jung, *Transversal Rationality and Intercultural Texts: Essays in Phenomenology and Comparative Philosophy*, 23. Lau proposes that his "lateral" thinking is a viable way to disabuse Western medicine of its universal claims and to incorporate traditional Chinese medicine. Kwok-Ying, Lau, *Phenomenology and Intercultural Understanding: Toward a New Cultural Flesh*, 167–169.

8. Merleau-Ponty, *Signs*, 140.

9. Ibid., 120.

Despite Nishida's explicit intercultural approach, and Merleau-Ponty's openness to thinking beyond the constraints of his tradition, many good reasons endure for proceeding cautiously with this comparison. For instance, even between philosophers open to such dialogue, there are sometimes vastly divergent philosophical methodologies that have characterized the traditions out of which their thinking grows. The Western lineage we trace back to Greece has developed a set of practices and institutions that differ in fundamental ways from those that have evolved throughout East Asia. This leads many to question whether "philosophy" is even an appropriate term for the intellectual and spiritual traditions in this part of the world. The precursors to Nishida's philosophy, which include Buddhism, Daoism, Shintoism, and Confucianism, embrace religious, devotional, and meditative practices typically excluded from Western secular philosophy. A variety of practices originating in India and spreading through China, Korea, and Japan were legitimate sites for engaging in what amounted to philosophic-religious exercise. These included landscape painting, haiku poetry, rock gardening, calligraphy, tea ceremony, and—one of the most significant features that distinguishes the East Asian tradition from the Western tradition—the various bodily exercises of self-cultivation, including meditative and linguistic practices. Although exceptions exist, such practices are almost completely absent from Western philosophy, which has kept a strong hold on the distinctions between speculative, devotional, and artistic practices. No doubt there are good reasons to approach various studies according to distinct methodologies. Disciplinary specialization can achieve a great deal, and Western philosophy has made many advancements within this mode of inquiry. Yet, where the specialization of the Western tradition endures as an impediment to dialogue with a foreign tradition able to derive insights from a plethora of methodologies, a tacit and limiting commitment remains to a methodologically pure philosophy severed from non-Western philosophies, and detached from the insights available in religious and artistic practice. Yet, an honest look at the full breadth of the Western philosophical tradition, one that includes Heraclitus and Plotinus, Nietzsche and Wittgenstein and takes seriously the Asian influence on the ancient Peloponnese, shows that this position is untenable. Likewise, as I hope to show, simple distinctions between philosophy, religion, and art do not hold up in Nishida or Merleau-Ponty's thought considered separately; *a fortiori* if considered together. This is not to say that the philosopher is an artist or a person of faith, or that she should be. Rather, philosophy must acknowledge the limitations of two of its orthodox features that have enabled a too narrow self-conception, namely the methods of unrestricted doubt and reflection. Neither Nishida nor Merleau-Ponty calls for dismissing these methods outright, but both compel us to go beyond thinking about philosophy within simple identity-difference binaries that would underwrite its supposed distinctiveness. Nishida and Merleau-Ponty offer the possibility of seeing philosophy as an expressive practice not limited to reflection and doubt, a practice with generative continuities among the discontinuities with art and religion. Following this incitement in their thought, one can discern the constitutive role of faith within philosophy. Curiously, it seems that the artist's sensorimotor practices make this particularly visible.

Problematizing the definition of philosophy at this scale might sound like an audacious claim and one that is too broad for scholarly work. Rightly or wrongly, we are given to accept that academic philosophy operates on the micro-scale and cannot do serious work at the level of questions such as What is philosophy? or What is religion or art? or What are the relations among the three? Ultimately, I intend to explore a narrower and more specific concern arising between the philosophies of Nishida and Merleau-Ponty, but two things must be kept in mind. First, within Nishida's East-Asian tradition, one need not go out on a limb to defend such a transdisciplinary starting point, because philosophic practice in that milieu has always been hospitable to religion and art. By contrast, this starting point is deeply problematic in the Western intellectual tradition. Second, as one of the most celebrated thinkers of that tradition, Merleau-Ponty does explicitly call for thinking beyond religious and philosophic divisions. In the notes to his last work, *The Visible and the Invisible*, he is not far from basic East Asian orientations when he writes that nature and logos

> must be presented without any compromise with humanism, nor moreover with naturalism, nor finally with theology—Precisely what has to be done is to show that philosophy can no longer think according to this cleavage: God, man, creatures.

While Merleau-Ponty can by no means be considered a "religious" philosopher, his openness to "non-philosophy" provokes us to think beyond doubt and reflective intellection through what he called an "interrogation" of perceptual faith. This line of inquiry of his can both inform and learn a great deal from dialogue with Nishida, who likewise struggles to find a more complex methodology that remains philosophic yet thinks beyond the rigid confines of the discipline.

Nishida between Religion and Philosophy

The ambiguities between philosophic and religious thinking East and West are not an impediment to comparing these two thinkers; rather, it is an incitement to such inquiry. The writings of Merleau-Ponty and Nishida afford an exceedingly valuable intercultural dialogue between two formidable intellectuals. The dialogue is more complex and rich *because of* not despite the different ways both thinkers transcend major aspects of their respective traditions. For instance, we do not have the luxury of treating Nishida as a straightforward "Eastern" or religious philosopher.[10] Just as there is a deep-seated propensity to think about philosophy relative to art and religion within identity-difference binaries, likewise, we want to say Nishida is or is not a religious thinker or a Buddhist philosopher. Despite many scholars casting him as such, he was emphatic that his philosophy was not a "Zen philosophy." He does make abundant references to religious ideas and religious figures, yet the vast majority of those actually invoke Western religious traditions and Christian doctrine. It might be surprising to someone not familiar with his works that most allusions to religious ideas do not entreat his own East-Asian heritage. He scarcely refers to Buddhist literature or concepts, but more often and more directly to Christian orthodoxy of the Old and New Testaments, as well as Western religious thinkers such as Augustine, Boehme, Kierkegaard, Cusanus, and Eckhart with a particular affinity for the apophatic lineages of Christian mysticism. He appropriates their terminology to his own ends, invoking ideas of *kenosis, gratia,* "*Gotheit*," communion, faith, and salvation, as well as eschatological themes all inflected according to his intercultural ambitions.

While Nishida frustrates our desire to categorize thinkers as either religious or secular, neither can we label his thought—or the Kyoto School of Japanese philosophy he helped found—as "Eastern" as opposed to "Western" philosophy. Philosophy began as an academic discipline in Japan only after several Meiji-era thinkers returned in the late nineteenth century from Europe and North America inspired to establish a Western-style academic discipline. This was the beginning of the department of philosophy at Kyoto Imperial University, and eventually the "Kyoto School" of Japanese philosophy.

---

10. John Maraldo (1988, 2003, 2011) has engaged this issue extensively, approaching the question of Nishida's relation to Zen and religion from many angles. See also Davis (2004); Dilworth (1969, 1970); Heisig (1990); Kopf (2005); Krummel (2010).

Meanwhile, to this day, most departments in Japan consider themselves to be practicing Western-style philosophy. The explanatory strategy that casts Nishida as a straightforward "religious" or "Eastern" thinker is symptomatic, as many have noted, of a broader propensity toward essentialist treatments of Japanese thought, art, and culture.[11] More precisely, it is symptomatic of a propensity toward identity-difference thinking both Nishida and Merleau-Ponty strive to overcome.

Despite scarce references to his Buddhist lineage, we cannot ignore the influence of Nishida's background and education in Eastern religions. In exceeding his own tradition as a scholar, he does so as a Japanese man who for his entire life was deeply immersed in East-Asian thought, culture, and practice. Nishida grew up in a religious household and practiced Zen Buddhism for a significant period of his early adulthood. He was born in 1870 in the Ishikawa prefecture on the northwest coast of Japan where Pure Land Buddhism was widely adhered to. His father died when he was young, and Nishida was raised by his mother, who was a devotee of Pure Land. Despite growing up in a home and a homeland where Buddhist religious practice was part of everyday life, Nishida came to reject religion as superstition. Meanwhile, in high school the young Nishida studied the Confucian, Neo-Confucian, and Daoist classics. He became proficient in English and German, and studied Western philosophers including Hegel and Kant. Exposure to Western thought and Enlightenment ideas cast the Japanese schooling system as oppressive for Nishida, inciting him to protest and eventually drop out in 1890. He was later admitted to Tokyo Imperial

---

11. Despite Nishida often being labeled as the sole "originator" of the Kyoto School, there were several important Meiji-era precursors to the fully formed school, including Nishimura Shigeki (1828–1902), Nishi Amane (1829–1897), Fukuzawa Yukichi (1835–1901), Katō Hiroyuki (1836–1916), Inoue Tetsujirō (1855–1944), Inoue Enryō (1858–1919). For further elaboration, see Ōhashi (1990), Davis (2014), and especially Maraldo's (2017) "Framing the Place and Significance of Nishida's Philosophy in Europe and North America," where he charts five major interpretive contexts for reading Nishida outside of Japan. He challenges our labeling of Nishida as Japan's "first philosopher," or the "founder of the Kyoto School," since both contravene Nishida's own principle of "continuity of discontinuity." Maraldo further cautions that taking Nishida as a "philosopher of the East" or a "philosopher of Zen" ignores his substantial and persistent engagement with Western philosophy. Further, both estimations rely on an autobiographical determination that Nishida explicitly countered in his efforts to develop a philosophy irreducible to individual consciousness.

University, studied under the first Western-style philosophy professors in Japan, and graduated in 1894 with a thesis on Hume. While beginning his first forays into academic publishing, he became devoted to meditative discipline alongside his new friend, the popularizer of Zen Buddhism, D. T. Suzuki. Together they practiced seated meditation (*zazen*), undertook kōan training, and participated in several retreats (*sesshin*). Nishida would later give up these practices, leaving scholars to speculate about the measure to which his own religious experience influenced his philosophy.[12] While this will remain an open question, the status of Nishida's lifelong project as an endeavor to found a philosophy that embraced both Zen and Western thought, religion, and philosophy is beyond doubt.[13] For Nishida, philosophy was about seeing the self, and in his words, "this seeing means a transformation of the self, identical with the attainment of faith; this transformation or conversion must be in every kind of religion."[14] To foreshadow the later discussion, this vision and the faith it entails involves overcoming Western-style subjectivity, since, in Maraldo's words, "religious awareness, Nishida claims, arises out of the subject's knowledge of its own negation."[15]

Nishida's formal academic career began with his appointment to the department of philosophy at Kyoto Imperial University, and it took off in 1911 with the publication of his *An Inquiry into the Good* (*Zen no Kenkyū* 善の研究). Throughout his career, Nishida's studies focused almost exclusively on Western philosophers, including Hegel, Kant, Hume, the Neo-Kantians, Royce, Bergson, Lotze, and Husserl. He never wrote extensively on any of the forebearers of his Japanese tradition. Yet, as Bret Davis explains—in

---

12. See John Maraldo, "Nishida and the Individualization of Religion," *Zen Buddhism Today: Annual Report of the Kyoto Zen Symposium* (1988).

13. In a letter to his student Nishitani, Nishida writes, "You are absolutely right to say that something of Zen is in the background of my thought . . . It has been my dearest wish since my thirties to unite Zen and philosophy, even though that is impossible." But he claims that most do not understand what this entails and writes that "if ordinary uninformed people call my thought 'Zen,' I would strongly object because they do not understand either Zen or my thought. They simply bundle together x and y as the same thing, which is to misunderstand both my thought and Zen." Michiko Yusa, *Zen and Philosophy: An Intellectual Biography of Nishida Kitarô*, xx.

14. Nishida Kitarō, *Nishida Kitarō zenshū*, 2: 425, 445.

15. Maraldo, 150; "Nishida's Ontology of History," in *Japanese Philosophy in the Making: Crossing Paths with Nishida*.

an article dealing with the question of Japanese "philosophy of religion" (*shūkyōtetsugaku* 宗教哲学)—when asked regarding his first major publication, Nishida claimed that it was both his intellectual study and his religious experience as a Zen practitioner that had inspired the volume.[16] In the introduction to his maiden work, he writes that religion is "the consummation of philosophy"[17] and he later expresses that "great philosophies always arise out of a profound religious heart. Philosophies that forget religion are shallow . . . I think that all great philosophies are religious."[18]

Nearing the end of his career, Nishida concentrated increasingly on the relation between philosophy and religion. After becoming embroiled in the government's attempts to justify Japanese nationalism and its expansionist project, shortly before his death in 1945 he completed his last essay "The Logic of Place and the Religious Worldview" (*Bashoteki ronri to shūkyōteki sekaikan* 場所的論理と宗教的世界観). In this culmination of his life's work, he engages many Western religious ideas, but recasts them according to East-Asian principles, particularly according to the concept of nothingness (*mu* 無) as conceived in the Mahāyāna lineage that was the foundation of the Zen Buddhism he studied and practiced. Far from being a straightforward "Eastern" or "religious" philosopher, it was Nishida's stated goal to think beyond the East–West divide to establish a "world logic" (*sekai no ronri* 世界の論理) capable of reconciling the major Eastern and Western intellectual and religious traditions. As we delve into his writings throughout the next chapters, we will not find a resolution to the tensions between the sacred and the secular, or between philosophy East and West, but a deepening of his thought as he sustains those tensions that divide and unite various disciplines and cultures beyond identity-difference binaries. The question of the sacred and secular will be in the background throughout the first three chapters and reemerge in the last sections of the final chapter.

---

16. In his "Provocative Ambivalences in Japanese Philosophy of Religion: With a Focus on Nishida and Zen," Davis develops an intriguing framework for considering the relation between religion and philosophy in Nishida's thinking. He proposes understanding Japanese "philosophy of religion" as a double-genitive, which is "productively ambivalent" in that it instantiates the meaning of both the objective genitive (philosophy-of-religion: philosophical thinking about religion) and subjective genitive (philosophy-of-religion: the philosophical thinking that religion does).

17. Nishida, *An Inquiry into the Good*.

18. Nishida, *Nishida Kitarō zenshū. 18: 176*.

Merleau-Ponty between Philosophy and Religion

Just as Nishida's writings do not abide by a simple East–West dichotomy, neither does Merleau-Ponty's philosophy fit neatly within his own Western tradition where it thinks of philosophy, art, and religion as oppositional categories. Merleau-Ponty is well-known for his commentary on artistic expression, but much less so regarding religion. Yet, if one looks, one finds what I think is a quite unexpected measure of religious motifs and metaphor at critical moments of his writings, including ideas of "faith," "communion," "transubstantiation," "sacramentality," "grace," and he also refers to expression as a "miracle."

Like Nishida, Merleau-Ponty had a religious upbringing. He was born in 1908 and grew up in a devout Catholic household in Rochefort-sur-mer on the west coast of France. Although he would later turn away from his upbringing in the mid-1930s, his interest in religion persisted at least until his doctoral studies at the École Normale Supérieur. At that time, he was active in the Catholic socialist movement and wrote for several left-wing Catholic journals, including *Sept* and *Esprit*, edited by the Christian philosopher Emmanuel Mounier. Among his first publications were reviews of works by Max Scheler and Gabriel Marcel who were contemplating the relation between existentialism and Catholicism.[19] The decisive turn away from his religious upbringing was precipitated by what he viewed as the church's unjust support for several violent dictators.[20] In the late 1930s and early '40s, while forging a close friendship with Sartre, Merleau-Ponty departed from Catholicism toward Marxism and Gestalt psychology. He died in 1961 and received a Catholic burial. Shortly before his death, the last words he wrote—those quoted above, urging philosophy to think beyond the God-man-creatures "cleavage"—not only attest to how religion was a constant concern, but also show how his understanding of "non-philosophy" did not exclude religion. Indeed, far from it; he claimed that Christianity was of "enormous historical value"[21] and did not conceive of philosophy

---

19. Those works include Max Scheler's *Ressentiment* and Gabriel Marcel's *Être et avoir*.

20. Merleau-Ponty was shocked by the role the Catholic church played in supporting actions by Dollfus against workers in Austria. He was also disheartened by the church's support for violent dictators, which precipitated his turning away from religion toward Marxism and gestalt psychology in the late 1930s, leading to his thesis later published as *La structure du comportement* (1942).

21. Merleau-Ponty, *Signs*, 142.

as necessarily atheistic[22] because for him "there is no rivalry between faith and reason."[23]

That said, the French philosopher did not believe that the distinction between reason and faith should be passed over: "As soon as [philosophy and religion] are made identical," he writes, they "perpetually play the role of warring brothers in history."[24] They are neither simple friends nor adversaries; rather, they have a "hidden conflict of each with itself and with the other"[25] such that theism, naturalism, and humanism are not opposed but "ceaselessly pass into one another," not resulting in a philosophy-religion binary but a "nexus" or "vinculum 'Nature'—'Man'—'God.'"[26] This "hidden conflict"; how they "pass into one another"; the status of the "vinculum"; the question of their relation, as well as the question of relationality itself, compels us to take seriously the ambiguous logic underpinning Merleau-Ponty's philosophy—an ambiguity further emphasized through dialogue with Nishida. Philosophy is not distinct from religion, nor does it coincide. The two are related beyond identity and difference. Among Nishida's and Merleau-Ponty's many critical dissimilarities, they are aligned in complicating one's ability to hold faith and reason distinct. When considered together, these philosophers show how neither religious nor philosophic disciplines are purely different nor wholly identical with each other *nor with themselves*. If their boundaries are affirmed too strongly, if philosophy is held as absolutely distinct from faith, fully circumscribed by reflection and doubt, then it is questionable whether it is even conceivable as a discipline. Yet, if no distinction is upheld, then the rivalry Merleau-Ponty alludes to ensues. This position between identity and difference results in an ambiguity arrived at by a mutual form of negation, which is one of the persistent themes of this study. Where negation makes up one of the most basic features of Merleau-Ponty's and Nishida's ontologies, the similarities that do abide on this most abstract level enable dialogue on several concrete issues, regarding artistic expression, the artist's body, their motion, vision, the tools they use, and the traditions they inherit. The differences on the abstract level, on the other hand—the limits and obstructions of ambiguous relationality—invoke

---

22. Merleau-Ponty, *In Praise of Philosophy*, 46.
23. Merleau-Ponty, *Signs*, 143.
24. Ibid., 145–146.
25. Ibid., 143.
26. Merleau-Ponty, *Nature: Course Notes from the Collège De France*, 204.

a tension between the two thinker's projects, which nevertheless allows us to drive the study deeper into crucial issues concerning phenomenology, ontology, artistic expression, and ultimately regarding a bodily form of faith and its implications for philosophy.

The deep ambiguities in Nishida's and Merleau-Ponty's thought are an excellent occasion for dialogue between the two. While there are what Davis calls "productive ambivalences"[27] between philosophy and religion in Nishida's thought, those only expand when placed in dialogue with similar ambivalences in Merleau-Ponty's writings. Both arrive at a remarkably similar point between philosophy and religion where the ambiguity of that position is well illustrated.

If it is tenable to say our philosophers in dialogue reach a similar intercultural and interdisciplinary position, it is noteworthy that they arrive at this point from opposing directions. Nishida engages Western religious terminology and brings it down to earth, in effect, secularizing the spiritual terminology of Christianity. He speaks of the Christian God, but not as a transcendent being causing or judging activities on earth, not a personalistic deity, but as a principle immanent to the fabric of this world. His notion of God as "the absolute" (*zettai* 絶対), and related concepts of "absolute negation" (*zettai hitei* 絶対否定), and his over-arching theme of "absolute nothingness" (*zettai mu* 絶対無) instantiate his non-binary thinking as a feature of the fabric of reality. In other words, the highest spiritual principle is immanent, not a personalistic and transcendent God. The religious is the ontological. Merleau-Ponty, on the other hand, reaches a similar ambiguity between philosophy and religion by pushing the secular practice of phenomenology to its limits where he develops methodologies ("faith," "interrogation," "hyper-reflection") and terminology ("incarnation," "flesh," "communion," "sacramentality," "grace," "devotion," etc.) typically reserved for the sacred. In his case, the ontological is inflected with the religious. Further, when both philosophers reach this medial point—where philosophy as reflection and doubt is brought to its limits—they both recognize the necessity of faith. Although neither Merleau-Ponty's "perceptual faith" nor Nishida's "religious faith" are straightforwardly theistic, they are not straightforwardly secular.

---

27. Bret W. Davis, "Provocative Ambivalences in Japanese Philosophy of Religion: With a Focus on Nishida and Zen," in *Japanese Philosophy Abroad*, 250.

There is no God in whom to have faith, but there is a persistent demand to recognize elements of faith latent within the grounds of philosophy.

Of course, artistic expression and faith are part of Western philosophy insofar as we have philosophy of art, aesthetics, and philosophy of religion. Yet, I would argue, there is something different at stake in Nishida and Merleau-Ponty, something that calls into question philosophic methodology at a more foundational level. This is in part because faith is incorporated into their philosophic consideration, but it is also because there is a reading of their depictions of artistic practice, and this is the reading I develop in this book, which suggests that they share a belief that the artist has gone further toward cultivating a kind of faith that ought to inform philosophic methodology.

Their ontologies of flesh and *Basho* disclose limits to philosophic reflection and doubt and, I believe, compel their readers to consider forms of faith that are otherwise invisible within Western philosophy. The artist, the artwork, and the faithful person are not merely exemplars used to *illustrate* a philosophic position that would remain methodologically identical after simply appealing to "examples" from other disciplines for explanatory ends. Nishida and Merleau-Ponty articulate a demand immanent to philosophy itself to operate beyond itself, external to itself by taking up faith, not merely as an object of study, but as a procedure inherent to philosophy. Philosophy can only be philosophy if it is other than itself, if it exceeds itself. It must have a measure of "non-philosophy." Its self-identity lies in its being beyond itself, or not-itself, where it undergoes a productive disruption of its own domain. In this light, I explore the practices of artists such as Sesshū, Cézanne, Hasegawa, and Rodin, among others, to uncover how they enact a faithful bodily orientation within the motor-perceptual world. In so doing, they point the way to a more complex configuration between philosophy, religion, and art, East and West.

Artistic Expression East and West

The intercultural considerations and cautions noted above should also inform comparison between artists from different traditions. Scholars East and West have theorized about artists, artworks, and artistic expression in countless ways. While the art worlds in both traditions have often been closely linked to religious institutions, it is worth noting that in the East Asian traditions, it is much more likely that a painter or a calligrapher could be more than a *religious* artist—working with religious symbols, images, or motifs—but an actual religious figure *qua* artist: one whose works do not simply depict religious subjects, but whose practice of expression is itself a religious discipline. This is the case with Sesshū. As a Buddhist monk and landscape painter, he embodied aspects of philosophic, religious, and artistic practice. Cézanne, on the other hand, despite remaining a devout Roman Catholic throughout his life, is not considered a religious artist. Yet, for a nonreligious and nonrepresentational painter, he makes an interesting comment that should give us pause when rushing to place him in simple categories: "When I judge art, I take my painting and put it next to a God-made object like a tree or flower. If it clashes, it is not art."[28] Certainly, it would be wrong to consider his self-proclaimed "devotion" to the sensible world as religious (at least in a Western religious sense), yet the way he moved his body through intense meditation on the visible world might allow us to think about his highly idiosyncratic form of expression as a bodily practice of faith, a practice that affords dialogue with the great landscape painters of East Asia. Indeed, when Cézanne's works first appeared in Japan, artists and scholars saw them as a "doorway between East and West."[29]

Reading Merleau-Ponty's portrayal of Cézanne together with Nishida's conception of artistic expression reveals how the French philosopher comes into proximity of foundational East Asian frameworks for understanding expression. Considering Cézanne in this light, this study consciously reads Merleau-Ponty's later idea of faith retrospectively into his earlier writings, in particular "Cézanne's Doubt" ("*le doubt de Cézanne*"). My contention is that the earlier works—in which Merleau-Ponty focuses on the intricacies of artistic expression—actually prefigure the later concept of "perceptual faith," thus providing a new line of continuity between his early and late work. At the same time, this approach works in the other direction; taking from the early to give to the later works, thus proposing a new means for extending his unfinished project and expanding its concept of faith by reading it through his depiction of artistic expression. I suggest that Merleau-Ponty's portrayal of Cézanne's expressive practice is a practice of faith: not faith in a transcendent being, scripture, or event, but faith as a body whose possibilities are given and constrained by the way it is woven into the motor-perceptual world. In casting Cézanne as an exemplar of a

---

28. Natalia Brodskaya, *Cézanne*, 3.
29. Yanagi Soetsu, *The Unknown Craftsman: A Japanese Insight into Beauty*, 93.

non-theistic, bodily form of faith, we can then place him in dialogue with Japanese landscape painters whose expressive practices likewise provoke us to think beyond the rigid distinctions between philosophic, artistic, and religious methodology.

Another interesting East–West feature becomes prominent when comparing Nishida and Merleau-Ponty. Not only do both develop original theories of artistic expression, likewise, both strive at such a remove from the conventions of their respective traditions with their unique modes of philosophic expression. At times, Merleau-Ponty's idiom proves to be a strong exception to his Western heritage insofar as he uses provocative, enigmatic, and poetic descriptions more typical of East Asian philosophy. When he writes that "it is the mountain itself which from out there makes itself seen by the painter,"[30] he is not far from Nishida's claim that "the mountains and rivers must also be expressive."[31] He also says that "the artist sees through a fusion of eye and hand,"[32] not unlike Nishida's idea that "there is an eye at the tip of the artist's brush."[33] We find similar expressions throughout "Eye and Mind" (*L'Œil et l'Esprit*) where Merleau-Ponty quotes Malebranche saying that the "mind goes out through the eyes to wander among the things,"[34] and that the artist paints by "adding to what *they* could see of things at that moment, what *things* could see of them."[35] In these cases and many more, Merleau-Ponty's thought and language places him significantly at odds with the conventions of his Western heritage.

Such a poetic style with its underlying, sometimes paradoxical logic is not completely without precedent in the Western tradition, yet it is a mainstay of East Asian modes of expression. Interestingly, although Nishida comes out of that tradition, his style is also a significant exception to the modes of expression typical of his heritage. By adopting the terminology and style of European and North American academic philosophy, his prevailing idiom is closer to the conventions of Western philosophy. He seeks to cast

---

30. Merleau-Ponty, "Eye and Mind," in *The Merleau-Ponty Aesthetics Reader: Philosophy and Painting*, 128.

31. Nishida, *Fundamental Problems of Philosophy: The World of Action and the Dialectical World*, trans. D. A. Dilworth, 35.

32. Nishida, *Art and Morality*, 389.

33. Ibid., 156.

34. Merleau-Ponty, "Eye and Mind," 128.

35. Ibid., 130.

the enigmatic language of Zen experience in transparent terminology and arguments, in large measure eschewing the suggestive and poetic style typical of Buddhist writings. When he does employ paradoxical or poetic statements such as those above, he often clarifies them through plain-language exposition.

These expressive features of the philosophers' writings cannot be considered in isolation from their own theories of expression, as informed by artistic practice. Accordingly, Nishida writes that "just as art demands philosophy, so, too, does philosophy demand art."[36] Merleau-Ponty, likewise, looks to artists to challenge philosophic method as it is limited by reflection and doubt. Certainly, there are various reasons why each chose to focus on artistic expression. Yet, because they both maintain that the world is first disclosed through the body, not the reflective intellect, and that this is a moving and perceiving body, it is not surprising that the practices of the artists they studied informed their methods of philosophic expression. Where Nishida develops his ontology of *Basho* (場所), and Merleau-Ponty his ontology of flesh (*chair*), both are interested in commencing philosophic investigation at the moment when the body is first open to the world, prior to the intervention of the discriminating intellect.[37] This is the moment before ethical, epistemological, or metaphysical questions interpose, the moment of prior encounterability that precedes all question asking and position taking. This starting point for phenomenology, the body's pre-reflective openness onto the world is our first truth but it is not initially a philosophic, religious, or an aesthetic truth. The artist, especially the painter, Merleau-Ponty thinks is able to "draw upon this fabric of brute meaning," and "only art does so in full innocence." The "writer and philosopher" is hindered because from them

> we want opinions and advice. We will not allow them to hold the world suspended. We want them to take a stand; they cannot waive the responsibilities of [humans] who speak . . . Only the painter is entitled to look at everything without being obliged to appraise what he sees.[38]

---

36. Nishida, *Art and Morality*, 97.

37. Nishida explains how our "direct experience" (直接経験) of the world is like the experience of "one melodious sound," which we encounter before the discriminating intellect performs its abstractions analyzing the sound as physical vibrations (Nishida, *An Inquiry into the Good*).

38. Merleau-Ponty, "Eye and Mind," 123.

Opinions and advice, as they arise from philosophical reflection, can obstruct the openness to the realm of brute meaning. In developing approaches to explore this moment of experience, the philosopher's methodologies thus face the limits of doubt and reflection and the demands of faithful expression. Artists can teach us something about how to properly orient this pre-reflective moment, yet this raises a conundrum for philosophy: How do we reflect upon the pre-reflective without transforming it into reflection? How do we represent the nonrepresentational? These riddles intimate a series of contradictions and paradoxes that are not easily dealt with within the confines of Western philosophy strictly defined. The logic necessary for analyzing the artist's relation to the world, as an appropriate relation to the pre-reflective, in many respects exceeds the logic handed down by Merleau-Ponty's Western tradition, and its attendant grammar, which adheres to substance ontology and respects the laws of non-contradiction. Yet, this is why he turns to Cézanne: the artist has developed bodily practices, which overcome the logical impasse that plagues the philosopher. Describing the artist's practice therefore requires grammar outside of the laws of substance ontology. Artists have found a productive orientation to primordial experience not hindered by the self-undermining attempt to reach the pre-reflective through reflection. By embracing these problematics, artists such as Cézanne enable dialogue with those in China and Japan who grappled with similar paradoxes in striving toward comparable forms of expression.

I would like to be clear that I do not claim that Cézanne or any artist is better understood within another culture's art historical tradition, nonetheless regarding *Merleau-Ponty's interpretation of Cézanne's practice*, I suggest that his use of artistic expression as a philosophic exemplar, and as a site for questioning philosophic methodology, is exceedingly unique in his Western tradition. Moreover, in several instances, it is much closer to the long tradition of aesthetic theory and practice in East Asia, where it would not have been so unusual that artistic practice would inform philosophy or even ontology. Admittedly, this is a broad claim, but Merleau-Ponty's challenge to equally broad aspects of his Western tradition demands beginning at such a scale. As we will see, from this starting point we quickly arrive in more precise concerns regarding foundational principles of Nishida and Merleau-Ponty's ontologies, theories of expression, and concepts of faith.

In undertaking this dialogue, we must also be careful not to paint all of Japan with the same brush, nor assume that there is a monolithic aesthetic tradition spanning its long history.[39] We should also not ignore the profound differences that do characterize these traditions. It is not an inaccurate generalization that the Japanese have had widespread beliefs and practices adhered to with high levels of conformity that have led to culturally and aesthetically distinct forms of awareness. Of course, there is an ever-present danger in romanticizing or essentializing this aspect: Japan has certainly been colonized by the global aesthetics of capitalism just as much or even more than any other developed country. As much as countless tropes and essentializing narratives have been foisted upon the nation, Japan has itself been complicit in deliberately constructing various images for the outside world that cast it as the mysterious and exotic repository of "Eastern wisdom," as the land of the reclusive poet, the Bushidō warrior, and more recently as the world's technological utopia.

Despite how Japan has been misconstrued internally or externally, we should not ignore something quite tangible about a different aesthetic sensitivity that becomes visible when looking at the broad features of religious, philosophic, and artistic traditions that have evolved there over centuries. When looking to these traditions with Western eyes and categories, one sees elements of religion, aesthetics, and philosophy in their indigenous tradition of Shinto, and their imported traditions of Confucianism, Daoism, and Buddhism that cannot but bring cultural differences into relief when considered against the Judeo-Christian and Greek origins of Western culture. By comparison, Japanese culture has retained a unique orientation toward aesthetic concerns. The Ch'an school of Chinese Buddhism, in particular, and its Daoist influences are essential for understanding the amazing nuances of the Japanese appreciation for beauty. Once assimilated into Japanese culture, Ch'an became increasingly Japanese in character, evolving into what we now know as Zen Buddhism, and giving us, arguably, one of the world's most distinctive religious-philosophic aesthetics. While we must be careful to discern subtle differences between lineages, neither should we overlook how Zen developed a coherent aesthetic as it matured and distanced itself from Ch'an.

---

39. For a critical look at essentialist approaches to "Zen" art, see Yukio Lippit, "Of Modes and Manners in Japanese Ink Painting: Sesshū's 'Splashed Ink Landscape' of 1495"; Gregory Levine, "Two (or More) Truths Reconsidering Zen Art in the West," in *Awakenings: Zen Figure Painting in Medieval Japan*, ed. Greg Levine and Yukio Lippit.

Even if it is only a faint echo of a bygone tradition, in Japan it is palpable that there are "ways" to do most things and a general acceptance of the constraints of various everyday practices, which is quite distinct from Western culture where individualism has had longer to evolve. Instead of expressing *my* way of doing something, possibly in the hope of gaining recognition for my individuality or originality, in Japan it is more likely that one is willing to subordinate his or her own desires to the accepted way of doing something. One pours tea, greets colleagues, dresses, arranges flowers, or wraps gifts not simply to express one's individuality, but to *conform* (literally "with form") to a specific way of doing things. These often ritualized and repetitive forms—what the Japanese call Kata (方)—and the associated formalized "ways" of carrying out tasks were a central facet not just of Zen Buddhist practice, but of Japanese culture. In the Edo period (1600–1858), these practices became sedimented as foundational aspects of that culture. Various aesthetic practices (*geidō* 芸道)—of archery (*kyudō* 弓道) or the "way of the bow," martial arts (*judō* 柔道) or the "way of gentleness," calligraphy (*shodō* 書道) or the "way of the brush," flower arranging (*kadō* 華道) or the "way of flowers," "the way of tea" (*sadō* 茶道), and the "way of the sword" (*kendō* 剣道)—all included the Chinese character "Dao" (道) in their compound, indicating the philosophic-religious orientation of the practices. Of particular interest for this study is the Daoist orientation of non-action (*wuwei* 無爲): a spontaneous agency beyond activity and passivity that artists cultivated in all of the *dō* aesthetic practices.

Nishida himself was a calligrapher and wrote about his practice in his "Beauty of Calligraphy" (*Shonobi* 書の美). Elberfeld goes as far as to claim that Nishida's writing practice "combines philosophy and art in a way that cannot be found in Europe."[40] As we later proceed into his discussion of artistic expression, it is interesting to keep in mind that calligraphy, painting and the various *geidō* practices had much in common based on their shared Daoist principles. Among those practices were a common set of bodily movements, postures, and gestures that constituted a general legibility between them. As van Briessen explains in his *The Way of the Brush*, "a brush stroke resembles nothing so much as a sword stroke, the release of an arrow, the judo grip, the sumo throw, a karate chop."[41] The array of aesthetic relations among practices that had the most extraordinary profundity were those of

---

40. Elberfeld, "*Handelnde Anschauung (kōiteki chokkan): Nishida und die Praxis der Künste,*" 336.

41. Fritz van Briessen, *Way of the Brush: Painting Techniques of China and Japan*, 39.

the "Three Perfections" (*sanjue* 三绝): calligraphy, poetry, and landscape painting. The famous landscape paintings we often see with a calligraphed poem were collaborations between three practitioners skilled in their domains. Calligraphy was, in fact, the origin of this art form. Landscape painting later grew out of calligraphy, thus the axioms of brushwork, the codified gestures, the styles, and even the tools of landscape painting all evolved directly out of the written word.[42] Even the traditional Chinese term that referred to "written lines" (*hsieh* 寫) in calligraphy was used to describe what landscape painters did with their brushes. That a painter could "write" a landscape, is intriguing for various Buddhist lineages that understood the landscape as a sacred scripture.[43]

Japan emulated all aspects of Chinese culture for centuries, but increasingly infused them with a Japanese character. As early as the Heian period (794–1185) the Chinese tea ceremony and its associated aesthetics began to have a significant impact in Japan leading to the later formalization of the *geidō* practices. As the tea ceremony became articulated and refined according to Japanese tastes, the aesthetic and ethical principles of the ritual became central to the Japanese population. While not every citizen would practice tea or all of the various *geidō* art forms, the principles cultivated in these practices were widespread and recognized as a set of ideals definitive of what it meant to be Japanese, in a religious, philosophic, and aesthetic sense. These arts did not aim to prove a theory of beauty or truth. They do not exhibit something beyond their own enactment. *Geidō* practices were a means of being continuous with the movements, the "way" of nature: to "unify" (*tōitsusuru* 統一する) or undergo "communion" with the fabric of reality, to use Nishida and Merleau-Ponty's terms. This facet of body-world relationality is perpetually at issue, not only when ethical, epistemological, or metaphysical questions are at stake, but at every moment of mundane existence. This focus on the mundane, the "everyday," and the moment of pre-reflective contact with the world, brought into contemporary Western

---

42. The nomenclature for the main painting styles evolved directly out of calligraphy. Just as the calligrapher had three styles (c. *k'ai shu*; j. *kaisho* ["formal"], *hsing shu*, *gyōsho* ["semi-cursive"], *ts'ao shu*, *sōsho* ["cursive"])—ranging from the most controlled to the most spontaneous—likewise the landscape painter chose to "write" the landscape according to these styles.

43. For a discussion of how Dōgen develops his concept "*mujō-seppō*" (無情説法) as an amendment of Kūkai's earlier "*hosshin-seppō*" (法身説法) to describe *all* phenomenal reality as linguistic, see Graham Parkes, "Dōgen's 'Mountains and Waters as Sūtras."

philosophical imagination by Heidegger, has provided exciting possibilities for dialogue with the Asian philosophical tradition, which has derived philosophical insight from this moment of experience for millennia. The possibility of reflecting on the pre-reflective in some respects exceeds what is available within Merleau-Ponty's Western heritage, yet brings his thinking much closer to Nishida's tradition, wherein contemplating the paradoxes of "the form of the formless, the voice of the voiceless [has been] transmitted from our ancestors for thousands of years."[44]

When attempting to locate Merleau-Ponty within his own tradition, of course, at the most fundamental level, he is a Western philosopher. Yet, when one considers the challenges he articulates to conventional Western ideas of the subject, space, time, perception, motion, as well as the amendments he calls for in formulating his phenomenological methodology, and his interpretation of artistic expression, it becomes genuinely questionable why one would ignore how his thought concurs with basic Japanese orientations. Like Nishida, Merleau-Ponty does not elaborate the intricacies of the artist's expressive practice to develop a new theory of beauty, to say what is true about paintings, or to develop a refined way of making aesthetic judgments. In considering Cézanne's concentrated sensorimotor engagement with the landscape, Merleau-Ponty wants to draw attention to how the body can be continuous with the world, how it can "intertwine" (*entrelacs*) in a motor, perceptual, and expressive capacity. In this sense, artistic expression can inform philosophic methodology. A central thrust of Merleau-Ponty's phenomenology is to describe experience before it is thematized by the reflective intellect as philosophical, scientific, or aesthetic, but without completely ignoring reflection. This means that, like the Zen frame of reference, all mundane pre-reflective experience is a locus for engaging with the most primordial aspect of existence, with the flesh of the sensible. Although focus on this primordial level of existence is not absent from Western philosophy, it has been a central concern for Buddhist philosophy throughout thousands of years of its development. For Zen, "the way you do anything is the way you do everything," the saying goes. All actions, however prosaic, are moments for cultivating one's most important religious-philosophical relation to the world, and these practices tend to be highly ritualized, often in the most minimalist fashion. Likewise, Merleau-Ponty and Nishida focus on artistic practice precisely because it discloses aspects of our body's relation to the world that are always at issue, and the examination of which require the

---

44. Nishida, *Nishida Kitarō zenshū*, vol. 4.6.

deconstruction of old philosophical methodologies and the institution of new ones in their place.

The tradition of philosophic reflection assumed that, methodologically speaking, as philosophers we focus on the most important moments of one's existence: confronting an ethical dilemma, questioning the nature of truth or knowledge, examining a scientific object, or making an aesthetic judgment. Yet, one's existence is always at issue, not just in exalted or ethical situations, but in the everyday. One's continuity with the Dao is constantly at stake; one's "communion" with flesh or "unity" with *Basho* encompasses every moment of existence, hence the philosophic-religious importance of "ordinary mind" (*byōjōshin* 平常心) and the "depth of the ordinary" (*byōjōtei* 平常底) in Nishida's philosophy. This also explains the predominance of meditative practices in the Zen tradition. Clearly, it would be foolish to claim that Cézanne's expression is the same as Buddhist practice, yet given that he would sit meditating or "germinating" motionless with the landscape for many hours before marking a canvas, it would be equally questionable to ignore his idiosyncrasies and consider him uncritically as working within secular Western aesthetic conventions. Considering him and others such as Rodin in dialogue with Asian philosophy and art practice, along with Sesshū, Taiga, and other Asian artists is not without its dangers and interpretive risks, yet where any intercultural friction does arise is potentially just as illuminating as those instances where encounter appears more straightforward.

Ambiguity, Negation, and Faith

Considering Cézanne's expressive practice as read by Merleau-Ponty, and Sesshū's as interpreted through Nishida's philosophy and his Buddhist heritage arouses diverse philosophical and aesthetic questions worthy of focused research. I cannot engage all of these issues in this volume but touch on those that bear on my central theme: At its core, this study is an exploration of relationality: the body's relation to the world, the relation between motion and perception, the eye's relation to light, the hand's relation to the paint brush, the artist's relation to her landscape, and that landscape's relation to the tradition that has painted it. Together, these issues call for a foundational conception of relationality itself, which I explore in terms of negation. How do things, materials, space, time, bodies, and light relate? The answer throughout is that, on an ontological level, relations obtain as a structure of mutual negation.

The concepts surrounding negation, negativity, and nothingness are multifarious in Eastern and Western philosophy and can easily perplex. Before getting into a more direct consideration of this concept in the first chapter, allow me to provide a much too simple example to get the discussion off the ground. In the context of this study, negation is the overarching structure for describing relationality. And, because Nishida's and Merleau-Ponty's philosophies both have elements of relational ontology, negation is the most fundamental concern. Setting aside the ontological discussion at this point, we can consider relationality as negation with a simple example. We know that two hands can relate to each other in many ways. Let us consider *positive* relationality as two closed fists bumping against each other. They remain "posited" insofar as each hand's boundaries remain clearly drawn. This configuration keeps them separate and discontinuous with each other. Now, if one un-clenches their fists and spreads their fingers wide open, different kinds of relations can obtain between two hands. Let us imagine the hands intertwining together as *negative* relationality. By opening up, the hands can enter each other's space and interweave, achieving some continuity among the discontinuity. The entering/being-entered relation that obtains on both ends of the intertwinement gives us a visual to begin understanding negation. As opposed to the closed fists, where two hands remain posited, open hands allow one to negate the space of the other. Negation as an entering/being-entered type of relation is not hard to visualize with one's hands, but to describe how the same relation comes about between body and tool, eye and world, or artist and landscape requires a much more complex ontological explanation worked out throughout the entirety of this study.

As we delve further into the complexities of Nishida's and Merleau-Ponty's theories of negation, one of the central complications that arises is the question of the limits of relationality as negation. These limits, or "obstructions" represent the culminating tension of this dialogue. My proposition is that, despite the agonisms between the ontologies of flesh and *Basho*, both philosophers approach the question of relationality—including the artist's relation to the landscape—by deploying comparable theories of negation, which demand an embodied practice of faith. Yet, where the two philosophers diverge concerns how faith becomes necessary by virtue of the limits of relationality and obstruction. On this point, there is significant disagreement between the two.

Nishida's and Merleau-Ponty's ontologies are often referred to as ontologies of non-duality, yet I characterize them as instantiating a form of relational ambiguity. As a position between identity and difference, ambiguity arises from an irreducible tension between duality *and* non-duality. Rather than a stable binary, ambiguity captures the dynamics of negation as a multi-stable relation. Put more simply, this position embraces both duck and rabbit as well as the perceptual grounds that enables aspect-shifts between the two. A straightforward non-dualism misses several essential features of their theories of relationality as negation. I follow what Gereon Kopf calls a "non-dualism that does not reject dualism"[45] as an appropriate means of treating Nishida's and Merleau-Ponty's philosophies. Ambiguity captures a mode of relation beyond duality and non-duality and preserves the dynamic, sometimes dialectical, multi-stability of negation characterizing ontologies of flesh and *Basho*. While ambiguity is by no means the only way of framing their ontologies, it is a quite fruitful way to do so, and is my guiding interpretive principle throughout.

I should note that for those looking forward to considering the phenomenological interpretation of artistic expression and specific artworks, this part of the dialogue is delayed until the second chapter. While the aim of this study is primarily aesthetic, not ontological, for both Merleau-Ponty and Nishida, their concern with artistic expression is ontological, and basic features of their dense, thrilling, but often frustrating notions of flesh and *Basho* must be laid out before considering the expressive practices of Sesshū, Cézanne, and others. I have endeavored to delineate the features of their ontologies central to my study, and to do so for both specialists and nonspecialists alike, yet trying to please both inevitably means that neither reader's needs can be satisfied—the latter likely frustrated by the dense preparatory work, the former by the lack of density on issues that could easily fill a volume on their own. This is perhaps an unavoidable hazard of attempting comparative aesthetics for philosophers for whom ontology is central to their aesthetics. For those not as familiar with either philosopher, I have attempted to keep the ontological explanation to a minimum, however, the likelihood of misconstruing the discussion of artistic expression in the latter chapters will be high without the clarification in the opening chapter. The concepts of flesh and *Basho* do deserve dedicated studies of their own, and while I cannot pursue that project in this dialogue, I have endeavored to point to the works of scholars, many of whom I have relied on, who are better guides on the particularities of Nishida's and Merleau-Ponty's ontologies.

I begin exploring ontological ambiguity at an abstract level in the first chapter. Here, I make a case for ambiguity arising from the mutual form

---

45. Gereon Kopf, "Critical Comments on Nishida's Use of Chinese Buddhism," 319.

of negation both Nishida and Merleau-Ponty articulate in their late works. I consider Merleau-Ponty's understanding of negation as he develops it in contrast to Sartre's "absolute nothingness" (*nullité absolue*) in his 1968 *The Visible and the Invisible* (*Le Visible et L'Invisible*), and Nishida's understanding of "absolute negation" (*zettai hitei* 絶対否定) and "affirmation of absolute negation" (*zettai hitei no kōtei* 絶対否定の肯定) in relation to Mahāyāna accounts of emptiness, which culminate in his 1945 *The Logic of Place and the Religious Worldview* (*Bashoteki ronri to shūkyōteki sekaikan* 場所的論理と宗教的世界観). Merleau-Ponty's "chiasm" (*chiasme*) and Nishida's "continuity of discontinuity" (*hirenzoku no renzoku* 非連続の連続) are my main focus, for they are the principal concepts instantiating an unresolvable relational ambiguity. Exploring these ideas will help begin to pave an alternate route around "positivist" accounts of motion, perception, and expression, and most importantly, a non-positivist conception of faith.

In the second chapter, I take steps out of the abstract and advance from negation to *perceptual* negation. A critical ramification of a perceptually negated body is, I suggest, that human vision is multi-perspectival. In this chapter, I consider several artists whose art practice betrayed an awareness of such an expanded understanding of vision. Both Raphael and Guo Xi strive toward the multi-perspectival, yet, in exploring the metaphysics of vision implied by their works, we see that neither transcends the "positivist" uni-perspectival framework for visual perception. To explore this difference, I contrast "ocularcentric" assumptions in the Platonic and Daoist traditions, revealing intriguingly divergent routes to multi-perspectival vision in the classics of Greece and China. This difference persists and allows us to compare further artworks from the Eastern and Western traditions to uncover the divergent assumptions about vision. Considering the French sculptor August Rodin alongside the Japanese landscape painter Ike Taiga (as interpreted by art historians Rosalind Krauss and Malinda Takeuchi) allows us to ask the question of the multi-perspectival from another angle, this time regarding the ambiguity of surface and depth ("skin and bone") in vision. The theme of visual depth brings us to questions that lead nicely back to our philosophers in dialogue who ponder the issue throughout their writings. We thus consider Nishida's "internal perception-qua-external perception" (*naibu chikaku soku gaibu chikaku* 内部知覚即外部知覚) vis-à-vis Merleau-Ponty's notion of "depth" (*profundeur*), exploring these as theories of multi-perspectival vision that embrace the visible and invisible via spatial and temporal forms of negation. Despite similarities between their accounts, I argue that Nishida's account of vision as "seeing without a seer" (*mirumono nakushite miru koto* 見るものなくして見ること)⁴⁶ better resolves certain problematics of multi-perspectival vision by conveying a more thorough desubstantializing of the perceiving subject. Yet, that concept is not without its own complications. Indeed, this concept of Nishida's invokes the central tension in this dialogue regarding "obstruction" and limits to negation. That, however, is the subject of the final chapter. To conclude this second chapter, I make a more speculative attempt to expand the conception of light, which I suggest is a theoretical move immanent to but not fully worked out in either's account of vision. The claim I develop is that because of the ambiguous reversibility between the visible and the tactile, we can conceive of light as a tool, in some ways analogous to the blind person's cane or the painter's brush in terms of how it relates to the body through negation. Conceiving of light this way is a step that must be taken in order to fully appreciate a corporeal form of faith, and to see how artists embody that faith in their expressive practice.

The third chapter begins with an extended consideration of the Japanese landscape painter, Sesshū Tōyō, and the French painter, Paul Cézanne. Here, I seek to interpret facts we know about their expressive practices and read those in light of the earlier discussion of perceptual negation. But, their practices offer much more to help advance the study beyond the previous chapters. To do so, a further move is necessary. Regarding that advance, I would like to make a special note regarding a pattern I expect will become obvious at this point of the study. One might notice that from the second to the third chapter we proceed from "perception" to "*motor*-perception." Because the central aim of this study is to expand the concept "perceptual faith" toward "*motor*-perceptual faith," the third chapter establishes the groundwork for that move by augmenting several concepts from a perceptual to a *motor*-perceptual status. The first move necessary is the most fundamental one. The theory of negation has to be expanded to include motion. That is, we proceed from "perceptual negation" to "*motor*-perceptual negation." That move is partly realized by including Merleau-Ponty and Nishida's conceptions of time. In my view, this conceptual expansion is quite useful in explaining how both philosophers think about the moving body's relation to the world, particularly as exhibited in artistic expression. The practices of Sesshū and Cézanne exhibit this form of motor-negation, which ambiguates the distinctions between activity and passivity, motion and motionlessness. I propose Nishida's "unity of act and act" (*Sayō to sayō*

---

46. Nishida, *Nishida Kitarō zenshū*, 3: 255.

to no chokusetsu no naimen-teki ketsugō 作用と作用との直接の内面的結合) and Merleau-Ponty's "solicitations," (*sollicitations*) and "distant will"[47] as instances of such motor-negation. Once the artist's body emerges within a temporally expanded form of negation, the questions of history and tradition arise. The history of painting has a pull on the body, which complexifies the artist's relation to the landscape he paints. The central question of this chapter is how the painter can be continuous with a historically extended sensorimotor demand (tradition) in order to deform the visible in coherent ways. More simply put, how can the artist create new meaningful work when related to the landscape trough motor-perceptual negation? I close this chapter by exploring how the answer might lie in re-thinking the relation between color and motion: when thought of according to the structures of negation, this softens the opposition between color and colorless, motion and motionless, and helps us see how the artist moves in and is moved by the motor-chromatic world.

Having elucidated the ontologies of flesh and *Basho* in terms of the dynamics of motor- and perceptual-negation, the final chapter brings faith into the discussion casting it as an additional structure of the body's mutual negation with the world. Faith is part of this mediation because, as both Nishida and Merleau-Ponty claim, the world's motor-sensory demand on the body is "infinite," while the artist is constrained by her body's material limitations. Moving the body in the phenomenal world thus involves a motor and a perceptual obstruction or "blind spot" restricting what the artist can see and how she can move. It is on this point that the philosophies of flesh and *Basho* come up against the limits of the comparison. Nishida's "seeing without a seer" (*mirumono nakushite miru koto* 見るものなくして見ること) and the "self-seeing" (*Jiko jishin wo miru* 自己自身を見る) of *Basho* suggest a type of vision not obstructed by any such blind spots. This appears to go against Merleau-Ponty's philosophy and possibly beyond exceptions in the Huayan Buddhist conception of "non-obstruction" (c. *wuai* 無礙). I thus interrogate Nishida on this point at length, exploring how the lack of a concept of obstruction might undermine his ontology of *Basho* and his concept of faith.

Despite the ostensible tensions between Nishida and Merleau-Ponty regarding the limits of motion and vision, they align in imagining an artist who can embody an "infinite" form of expression. Enacting such expression,

---

47. Merleau-Ponty, "Eye and Mind," 147. Merleau-Ponty takes this term from an entry (#1104) in Paul Klee's diary: *The Diaries of Paul Klee: 1898–1918*, 387.

however, entails a motor-perceptual risk. It requires being out of control and allowing the world to move the body through a valence of one's own spontaneity. To work against the notion that spontaneous expression is a subjective form of agency, I make a brief intercultural excursus to consider the practice of pottery and specifically the British potter Bernard Leach, who facilitated artistic dialogue between East and West. The potter's body and its relation to the clay he turns is an excellent example of how spontaneous expression is not reducible to the subject but is granted by the materiality of the objective world. The long process of learning to turn clay properly leaves marks not just on the pot but also on the potter's body, and thus makes visible the mutual negation between body and world and the "inter-expressive" possibilities of bodily faith. To move spontaneously in expressive gesture without reducing this risk is *ipso facto* to move with a bodily form of faith. How the artist navigates the risks of motor-perceptual negation and responds with a sensorimotor form of faith discloses a viable means of abiding within the paradoxes that otherwise appear to thwart expression. Thus, artistic expression can inform philosophy, to the extent that it also seeks methodologies that tarry with similar paradoxes, particularly those involved in the struggle to overcome the snares of unrestricted reflection and doubt. In this context, I explore Merleau-Ponty's and Nishida's theories of expression for their implications not just for artistic, but also philosophic expression. I discuss how limited-yet-infinite forms of artistic expression, likewise constrain/enable philosophic methodologies compelling them to operate in excess of themselves, beyond methodologically pure disciplinarity where faithful expression becomes crucial. As such, philosophy faces its limits as a secular project. I bring the dialogue to an end by returning to Nishida and Merleau-Ponty to contemplate how their thought inhabits a liminal position between the sacred and the secular. Together, their philosophies permit the thought of a philosophic form of expression with more complex relations to art and religion as practiced and theorized in their Eastern and Western traditions.

Before setting off with the dialogue, I would like to make some final comments regarding the intended scope and audience of this undertaking. The reader will no doubt become aware that there are endless possible topics that emerge in an encounter between these two philosophers, many of which I cannot follow here. While I consider numerous issues in the first three chapters, my aim is that this preparatory work enables, later in chapter 4, a more narrowly focused look at a debate where I hope to contribute to specialist concerns in Nishida and Merleau-Ponty scholarship. Those concerns orbit around the uncertainties I have signaled regarding the limits ("obstructions") inherent to phenomenal encounter. To what extent there are obstructions and how they might affect motion and perception constitute the essential tension between Nishida and Merleau-Ponty in this dialogue. The position I work out looks to extend the debate by showing its implications for a bodily form of faith. It is on this point that I engage with specificities in contemporary scholarship in a more speculative fashion. That being said, this should not dissuade the novice reader. I have endeavored to write the first three chapters with the requisite background such that someone without specialization but with a good bit of curiosity will have what they need to engage meaningfully in the more specialized concerns upon reaching the final chapter.

A further remark I would like to make at the outset, so as to help readers avoid stepping off in an understandable but not entirely well-aimed trajectory, concerns expectations perhaps evoked by the book's cover or by the various artists whose names appear in the table of contents. What follows is purposefully distinct from philosophy of art and its historical or contemporary concepts and debates. It is distinct from the modern Western conception of aesthetics and the attendant concern for delineating judgments of the beautiful. The reader will not find discussions of beauty, aesthetic judgment, appreciation, taste, or definitions of art or artworks. My interest in building this dialogue regarding artistic expression is primarily ontological. That is, the various artists Nishida and Merleau-Ponty consider disclose embodiment beyond subject–object metaphysics. I thus engage their theories of artistic expression because of what they can show us about the motor-perceptual body and its relation to the world. Insofar as I concentrate on artists' expression throughout, this is a study in the classical sense of *aesthetikos*, a study of perception, yet given an expanded breadth by the innovations of two philosophers who have offered the great opportunity to contemplate artistic expression according to the phenomenological conception of the body.

The last consideration I would like to mention pertains to the meta-comparative methodology I employ. It is very important to keep in mind—especially for those new to intercultural or comparative philosophy—that none of the conceptual links I examine are intended to provide definitive statements that Nishida and Merleau-Ponty have "similar" ideas of x, y, or z. Further in-depth study of any issues I explore will reveal essential, possibly insurmountable differences. I cannot emphasize enough that in this dialogue I strive to follow the logic of both philosophers in going beyond identity-difference thinking.[48] My proposal to frame the comparison along the lines of motor-perceptual faith does not claim that this concept is found in either philosophy. In this sense, I follow Thomas Kasulis' conception of "constructive comparative philosophizing" where the goal is not to merely compare two philosophers or ideas, but to create a third concept from the encounter.[49] I intend "motor-perceptual faith" in this sense, merely as a provisional tool to place the two thinkers in dialogue; a bridge, no doubt shaky at times, whose goal is to smooth the way for interchange between two bodies of work in hopes of evoking not only similarities but also "productive ambivalences." Ultimately, what proves to be most productive are the incongruities between their ideas of faith as they arise by virtue of limits/obstructions to perception and motion. If productive, what I hope to attain is best articulated by Rolf Elberfeld in his call for a "dynamic concept of comparision," which he hopes will yield "a wide field of interculturally oriented sensuality research, through which the different ways of the sensory opening up of reality could be questioned about their structures." In placing these two in dialogue, my goal is not exclusively to accurately represent the philosophies, but through a productively ambivalent encounter I hope to "make it possible to break up and expand one's own perceptual habits through comparison."[50]

To conclude these prefatory remarks, I will say that what I take to be at stake in this dialogue, though not argued for explicitly, is one of many possible approaches to the perennial question, "What is philosophy?" But, an approach that does not presume to listen only to a single voice from a single tradition to formulate an answer. If we take seriously what these philosophers tell us separately regarding philosophical methodology—or *a fortiori*, what we hear from them when considered together—then we must seriously question aspects of the Western definition of philosophy at the most fundamental level, where it seeks to delineate itself strictly from non-Western thought and counter to those traditions that tolerate more complex internal and external disciplinary relations. My proposal, which I

---

48. Although Heidegger was skeptical regarding Western philosophy's relation to Eastern thought, we do find concepts in his thinking that are useful for intercultural comparative methodology. In theorizing the relation between poetry and thinking, he develops a framework for going beyond the identity-difference binary. The nuance is not always captured in translations of *"das Selbe"* and *"das Gleiche,"* which render them both as "the same." Heidegger distinguishes between what is straightforwardly equivalent or "merely identical" (*das Gleiche*) according to identity-difference thinking, and a form of sameness that embraces identity and difference (*das Selbe*). Martin Heidegger, ". . . Poetically Man Dwells . . ."
49. Kasulis, Thomas, "The Philosophical Truth: Comparatively Speaking."
50. Rolf Elberfeld, "Komparative Ästhetik Eine Hinführung," p. 20.

develop throughout these four chapters, is that a careful reading of Nishida's and Merleau-Ponty's philosophies on the concept of faith helps avoid the impairment of drawing too simple boundaries between philosophy, religion, and art, East and West.

Chapter 1

Ontology, Ambiguity, and Negation

In this chapter, I begin laying the grounds for the dialogue between Nishida and Merleau-Ponty regarding artistic expression by first establishing important features of their respective ontological positions; those being Nishida's ontology of *Basho* (場所) and Merleau-Ponty's ontology of flesh (*chair*). Once we proceed to consider several artists and their works in the following chapters, it should become clear that both thinkers depart from philosophy of art in the Western sense: instead of *first* developing an ontological position and then only *secondarily* applying that theory to artworks or artistic expression, Nishida and Merleau-Ponty invert the order. Artistic expression, or expression in general, actually informs key features of their ontologies. To be is to be expressive, thus the artist's practice is exceedingly more consequential than it would be in a restricted philosophy of art approach. These philosophers complicate the standard priority of ontology over expression. That being said, I begin this chapter considering their ontologies in the abstract, followed by closer inspection of artistic practice in the following chapters. There will be some conceptual heavy-lifting at the outset to establish the grounds of the comparison, but it is essential because the concept of negation discussed in this chapter is crucial for understanding artistic expression and the motor-perceptual forms of relationality discussed throughout.

Motor-Perceptual Fabric: Faith and Transitivity

Many ideas associated with taken-for-granted understandings of faith could impede dialogue between Nishida and Merleau-Ponty. Both philosophers invoke Judeo-Christian terminology throughout their writings, but neither of their conceptions of faith is theistic, and neither considers faith as a belief in God. One might then ask, what do they propose we have faith in? What is the *object* of religious or perceptual faith? This seems like a sensible starting point, but the problem lies in how our common sense, our metaphysics, and even our grammar expects there to be an object *to have faith in*. We presume there to be a deity, a leader, nature, fate, a promise, etc., in which one believes. Although the phrase "to have faith" is neither strictly grammatically transitive nor intransitive, our expectations cast it as metaphysically transitive: We imagine faith to be faith *in some thing*. As such, we tacitly accept that it is an orientation of a subject toward an object. Following this logic, we might approach Merleau-Ponty's "perceptual faith" (*foi perceptive*) as though it were faith *in perception*, or Nishida's faith as a belief in God or the "absolute." Without questioning this starting point, we reify metaphysical oppositions that both philosophers labored to overcome. To evade that danger, I read their concepts not as faith in a particular object, not as a subjective orientation, but instead as a non-transitive form of faith. To be precise, in their philosophies, faith is not a subject's belief in an object: *faith negates both subject and object*. If I were to sum up this entire study in a short sentence, I would say it is a comparison of two theories that strive to carve out a theory of artistic expression as a relation between a negated subject and object.

A great deal of scholarship on Nishida or Merleau-Ponty recognizes how important negation is for overcoming subject–object dualism. Yet, the link between negation and faith has not been explored in depth. While there are several crucial discrepancies in these philosopher's ideas of negation, the similarities are such that the differences become illuminating. For both philosophers, faith is a relation between a negated subject and a negated object, or as I will also refer to it, a relation between a non-subject and non-object. Although this nomenclature is typically associated with Nishida's East Asian heritage, Merleau-Ponty was also striving toward negated subjectivity and objectivity. In this chapter, I consider their ontologies of flesh and *Basho* in tandem on this specific issue to show how they formulate notions of faith based on comparable conceptions of negation. In doing so, I aim to achieve a picture of the artist as a non-subject, the landscape as a non-object, and artistic activity as non-transitive faith binding the body and world together in reciprocal expressive negation.

To consider faith as non-transitive—faith without a subject or object—means it is not faith *in* some thing, but is faith *as* some thing; faith as a feature of embodiment itself. This grounds the study at a more fundamental level than an approach that would cast faith as a belief, a mental state, something we can will, or an ethical or religious stance, that is, the disposition of a subject.[1] Faith in both Nishida's and Merleau-Ponty's philosophies is ontological, not an ontic choice one cannot decide for or against. It is not so much that one has faith *in the world*, but that *as woven into the fabric of the world* one is a faithful being. One can augment or diminish faith—indeed, on these grounds artistic practice is exemplary—but faith cannot be eliminated. I thus treat it as a sensorimotor faith where both the sensory and the motor are qualities of a perceptual field, not a subject.

Another shared aspect of Merleau-Ponty and Nishida's mature ontologies lies in their being what we might consider ontologies of expression.[2] That is, the relation between body and world, self and other, is a relation of mutual expression—of "making and being made" (*tsukuraretamono kara tsukurumono e* 作られたものから作るものえ) to use Nishida's term. When considering artists in this light, their expression is not individual creativity, originality, or genius (i.e., approaches that reify the subject). I explore the practices of Cézanne, Sesshū, Klee, Guo Xi, and others to show how these artists work far beyond these subjective orientations; rather, through motor-perceptual practices of faith they negate their own subjectivity to immerse in and harmonize with the demands of a world that is itself expressive. They seek to weave their bodies into the world's fabric not as expressions of their individuality, but as an expression of that field, of flesh and *Basho*. In this light, the moving and perceiving body expresses itself in what I investigate as a sensorimotor form of faith. While this is the character of all expression, of all our most mundane movements and gestures, artists such as Sesshū and

---

1. In "The Kyoto School and Reverse Orientalism," Bernard Faure criticizes Nishida's "pure experience" and "place of nothingness" as straying from philosophy and implying a form of faith. Despite Nishida proposing an *explicit* notion of faith, Faure's critique is epistemological and remains leveled at a subjective, transitive conception of faith, failing to appreciate its ontological implications in Nishida's philosophy. See Brubaker (2009) for a thorough critique of Faure's "epistemological" interpretation of Nishida.

2. Both Nishida and Merleau-Ponty explore Leibniz regarding the ontological implications of expression. Nishida is explicit about the ontological ramifications of his theory of expression, specifically regarding his concept "interexpression," which is the subject of chapter 4 of this study. For an extended consideration of Merleau-Ponty's philosophy as an ontology or "phenomenology of expression" see Renaud Barbaras, *The Being of the Phenomenon: Merleau-Ponty's Ontology*. Also see Veronique Fóti, *Tracing Expression in Merleau-Ponty: Aesthetics, Philosophy of Biology, and Ontology* and Donald A. Landes, *Merleau-Ponty and the Paradoxes of Expression: Philosophy, Aesthetics, and Cultural Theory*.

Cézanne are particularly adept at making motor-perceptual faith discernible. Their aesthetic practices present important challenges to assumptions that limit the scope in which we conceive of philosophic methodology. For their practices resist clean parsing within a sacred-secular binary.

Commentators have used a variety of metaphors to explain the ontologies of Nishida and Merleau-Ponty; characterizing flesh and *Basho* as perceptual fields, fields of forces, fields of consciousness, as *topoi*, place, and *chōra*. While each of these is helpful in portraying different aspects of their rich and complicated ontologies, I adopt a common metaphor used by both philosophers hoping to make concrete the multitude of abstractions in their systems. Both Merleau-Ponty and Nishida invoke the imagery and metaphorics associated with fabric throughout their writings. I would like to use the associated ideas of texture, weaving, wrapping, fibers, folding, lining, warp, and weft as provisional means for comparing their ontologies.[3] This imagery is apt for visualizing a non-transitive faith, and for distancing ourselves from the metaphysics, grammar, and the concepts that cast faith as a belief of a subject toward an object and, moreover, to move away from the account of expression as a painter-subject representing a landscape-object.

Merleau-Ponty makes use of fabric-related analogy throughout his writings. In his *Phenomenology of Perception*, he writes, "My body is the fabric into which all objects are woven,"[4] while later in *Eye and Mind* he refers to the body as being "caught in the fabric of the world."[5] In "What is Phenomenology?" he calls the real "a closely woven fabric,"[6] and we find references to tissue, strands, weaving, fibers and other fabric-related terminology throughout his writings. We must be careful, though. Fabric-related analogies and terms lend themselves to positivist assumptions because of their association with materiality and thus reify mind–matter opposition. It is important to keep in mind that for neither Nishida nor Merleau-Ponty is the fabric of phenomenal reality describable in positivist terms: the fabric metaphor is expedient where it helps us visualize the structure of negation. To this effect, Merleau-Ponty writes that the "closely woven fabric," of perception is the "locus of the simple or immediate nihilation."[7]

---

3. The Japanese word for experience, *"keiken"* (経験), has the idea (*kei* 経) of the longitudinal texture of woven material (warp).

4. Merleau-Ponty, *Phenomenology of Perception*, 273.

5. Merleau-Ponty, "Eye and Mind," 125.

6. *Phenomenology of Perception*, xi.

7. Merleau-Ponty, *The Visible and the Invisible*, 266.

As we get deeper into the analysis, we find a thoroughgoing negation of subject and object in Merleau-Ponty's philosophy invoking features suggested by the various fabric analogies. In *The Visible and the Invisible*, he refers to the visibility of flesh as having a "lining" of invisibility.[8] One of the French words Merleau-Ponty uses that is translated as "lining" is "*doublure*," which has the sense of a fabric where one material lines another, such as the way silk lines the inside of a suit.[9] When speaking of how flesh "envelops" visible and tangible things, he also uses the word "*tapiss*," which has fabric-related connotations too.[10] Meanwhile, we find him referring to flesh as an "ontological tissue," as the "the fabric of the visible," the "connective *tissue* of exterior and interior horizons"; he calls "wild being" (*l'être sauvage*) the "common *tissue* of which we are made," the "*fabric* of brute meaning"; The world for him is a "closely *woven fabric*," and our connection to it is by way of "intentional *threads*." There is a "*tissue* that lines" the visible and the seer, both of whom are "abstract[ed] from one sole *tissue*." Another important fabric-related term is "fold" (*pli*), but he cautions that "the field must not be conceived as a cloth in which object and consciousness would be cut out."[11] His appealing to the "fold" rather than the "cut out" is an important point to return to as we argue against the possibility of a position external to or "cut out of" the perceptual fabric of flesh. Galen Johnson proposes translating Merleau-Ponty's use of "*étoffe*" ("*l'étoffe ontologique*," "*une seule étoffe*") usually rendered as "stuff" instead as "fabric" or "cloth" to avoid the language of substance ontology, because, as he claims, "fabric has some life and movement as it folds, rustles, and moves together with the actions of the body."[12]

Turning to Nishida, we find provocative intimations of similar analogies when describing his idea of "nothingness" (*mu* 無). He quite remarkably uses a Japanese term that, among its various meanings, denotes the "cloth on the inside of clothes" or a material "lining" (裏付ける).[13] In an admittedly

---

8. He also uses "doublure" (*Le visible et l'invisible*, 193) when speaking of ideas "lining" the sensible (*The Visible and the Invisible*, 149). In other sections, when speaking of how flesh envelopes visible and tangible things, what is translated into English as "lining" is "tapiss" in French (*Le visible et l'invisible*, 162, 179, 195).

9. Merleau-Ponty, "Eye and Mind," 147.

10. Merleau-Ponty, *The Visible and the Invisible*, 123, 137.

11. Unpublished note: file 22 (1958–1959); quoted in Chouraqui (2013).

12. Galen A. Johnson, *The Retrieval of the Beautiful: Thinking through Merleau-Ponty's Aesthetics*, 32.

13. 裏 also has the meaning of "reverse side," "inside," and "backing."

liberal translation—yet one which Nishida himself oversaw—his collaborator-translator has rendered 裏付ける as the material "lining" of a kimono.[14] This resonates nicely with Merleau-Ponty's notion of the invisible lining the visible since the traditional Japanese belief was that the kimono's interior lining of silk is invisible yet imparts visible form and shape to the fabric's exterior. We find many other instances of the fabric metaphor running throughout Nishida's ontology. When unfolding the "peri-logical" (*hōronriteki*)[15] aspect of his *Basho* theory, he describes the "emplacement" of the various levels of *Basho* within each other, using the metaphor of "wrapping" (*tsutsumu* 包む) and "enveloping" (*fukumu* 含む). According to his ontology, beings visible on the level of the "place of being" (*yū no basho* 有の場所) are "enveloped" or "wrapped" within the "place of nothingness" (*mu no basho* 無の場所). Yet, we must be clear that among the layers of *Basho*, which overlap and envelop, the underlying layer is the "place of nothingness" (*mu no basho* 無の場所). This layer is reducible neither to pure materiality nor ideality but is the place embracing both and making their mediation possible.

Both thinkers have a propensity toward fabric metaphor while thwarting a "positivist" account that would link that terminology with materiality; in particular, materiality that would be unambiguously visible. Although the imagery associated with fabric lends itself to thinking of matter as straightforwardly visible, what is essential for deploying these analogies to help picture aspects of their complicated ontologies, is that both philosophers conceive of the fabric of reality as ambiguous regarding visibility and invisibility. The metaphor can be precarious because some of the most common associations of fabric are materialistic in a straightforward sense, such as in the fabric of one's clothes or sheets. But, we also use the terminology associated with fabric in ways distant from the association with fully visible material, such as in the "fabric of one's imagination," the "fabric of space-time," the "fabric of modern life," the "fabric of our community," etc. Neither these nor the

---

14. The passage in Robert Shinzinger's translation of "The Intelligible World" (*Eichiteki sekai* 叡智的世界) reads "wie mit einem Futter ausgeschlagen" (lined as a kimono is lined with a precious silk). The Japanese reads 判断的一般者の限定の過程に於て、主語と述語とが対立し、それが自覚的一般者に於て裏付けられる時、働くものと働かれるものとが対立するが、自覚的一般者に於ては、斯かる対立は知るものと知られるもの、即ち所謂主観客観の対立となる. Nishida Kitarō, "The Intelligible World," in *Intelligibility and the Philosophy of Nothingness*, 81.

15. Nishida, *Nishida Kitarō zenshū*, 3: 418.

previous set of associations on their own capture what is essential to the ontologies of flesh and *Basho*, but taken together, both the material and immaterial connotations associated with our notion of fabric might help us keep in mind throughout this study that we should strive to remain between the two, and between visibility and invisibility. Although there are key differences we arrive at in later chapters, we can get going with the dialogue by thinking about flesh and *Basho* as fabrics in a sense that embraces a quite diverse set of meanings—as the fabric reducible to neither the material nor the ideal, but that which holds the two realms together enabling their ambiguous multi-stability.

While this ambiguity is central to understanding their accounts of perception, it is likewise a principle that structures how Merleau-Ponty and Nishida think about all of the major topics I discuss; including, motion, expression, faith, touch, space, tools and time. Their ontologies embrace this principle of ambiguity all the way down to the most abstract level and all the way up to the most concrete: the way the invisible implicates itself into the visible is how the negative relates to the positive, being to non-being, hand to tool, eye to light, artist to landscape. This type of relationality is a recurrent theme throughout. As we work our way toward a more direct investigation of artistic expression and landscape painting, I explore how that same ambiguity obtains in motion, perception, and expression, such that distinctions between activity and passivity, seeing and seen, expressing and being expressed relate beyond duality and non-duality. Capturing this ambiguity within philosophic terminology—which amounts to articulating non-transitive accounts of motion, perception and expression—demands alternative grammatical structures, which helps explain the often enigmatic language Merleau-Ponty and Nishida use, such as "seeing-seen," "touching-touched," and "making-made."

One last note regarding the fabric metaphor: while exploring Nishida's *Basho* and Merleau-Ponty's flesh, I consider their various concepts as either describing the *texture* or *dynamics* of their underlying sensorimotor fabrics. The texture is how bodies woven into that fabric are related whereas the dynamics refer to how these bodies move. The main *textural* concepts in their writings—the warp and weft of the motor-perceptual fabric—are those that imply negation between bodies. In Merleau-Ponty's ontology, those are "chiasm" (*chiasm*) and "intertwining" (*entrelacs*). The *dynamic* aspects of his philosophy are "reversibility" (*reversibilité*), "institution" (*fundierung*), "perceptual faith" (*foi perceptive*), "hyper-dialectic" (*hyper-dialectique*) and "hyper-reflection" (*hyper-réflexion*). In Nishida's ontology, the *textural* elements of *Basho* are "absolute negation" (*zettai hitei* 絶対否定), "inverse polarity/correspondence" (*gyakutaiō* 逆対応), "continuity of discontinuity" (*hirenzoku no renzoku* 非連続の連続), and "self-identity of absolute contradictories" (*zettai mujunteki jikodōitsu* 絶対矛盾的自己同一); and the *dynamic* features are dialectic (*benshōhō* 弁証法), "interexpression" (*hyōgen-teki kankei* 表現的関係), and "created-creating/making-made" (*tsukurareta mono tsukuru mono* 作られたもの作るもの). This twofold textural-dynamic framework allows us to parse their concepts within the fabric metaphor. Yet, the binary itself does not escape the logic of ambiguity, thus neither pole exists as fully identical to or different from the other. In particular, motion, perception, and expression are aspects of the ontological fabrics that exhibit textural as well as dynamic features.

Nishida and Phenomenology

Before pursuing this dialogue, we must consider one possible comparative obstacle. In several of his works, Nishida repudiates phenomenology.[16] While this could present an obstacle for reading him alongside Merleau-Ponty, Nishida's claim relates to Kant and is based on disputed readings of Husserl that should not impede this dialogue.[17] If there were only one phenomenology and it was the classical version of Husserl, there could be difficulty including these two thinkers under its umbrella. Yet, with a less restricted definition, one that would include phenomenology's existential, historical, and linguistic turns, there is little difficulty counting Nishida. What I would take as a foundational concern of phenomenology, starting with Heidegger, is the project of describing the field of "encounter" (*Begegnung*) that exists

---

16. See Nishida, *Fundamental Problems*, 114, 122–126, 196–199; "The Intelligible World," 97–103.

17. For a discussion of Nishida in relation to the phenomenology of Husserl, see Maraldo, "Nishida's Ontology of History." Also see Bernard Stevens, "Self in Space: Nishida Philosophy and Phenomenology of Maurice Merleau-Ponty," in *Merleau-Ponty and Buddhism*; Ogawa Tadashi, "The Kyoto School of Philosophy and Phenomenology," *Analecta Husserliana: Japanese Phenomenology: Phenomenology as the Trans-cultural Philosophical Approach* VIII; Yuko Ishihara, "Later Nishida on Self-Awareness: Have I Lost Myself Yet?"; Elberfeld, "*Handelnde Anschauung (kōiteki chokkan): Nishida und die Praxis der Künste.*" For a discussion of the early, pre-Kyoto School reception of phenomenology in Japan see Keiichi Noe, "Phenomenology in Japan: Its Inception and Blossoming," in *The Bloomsbury Research Handbook of Contemporary Japanese Philosophy*.

prior to the discriminations of reflective intellection.[18] Merleau-Ponty is a phenomenologist in this sense as is Nishida. Furthermore, the method both philosophers use to reach this field is uniquely phenomenological. That is, they eschew objective or third-person descriptions of experience and focus on the "lived" first-person dimension. Taking this approach, both Nishida and Merleau-Ponty assume the phenomenological stance prior to all questioning: before epistemological, ethical, metaphysical, or aesthetic issues can be formulated as questions at all, before self can encounter other or world, the body is first woven into that world, and that is the locus of phenomenological investigation and insight. Despite Nishida's own claims, in this sense, in pursuing an account of the body's pre-reflective opening to the world, he is in line with Merleau-Ponty's orientation, as well as that of other phenomenologists, particularly Heidegger.[19]

A further aspect of their shared phenomenological orientation to the pre-reflective field that also begins with Heidegger, and one I find intriguing, is how these philosophers bend language in response to the demands of this field. All three develop a poetic idiom and make use of neologism that goes beyond the constraints of non-contradiction. Describing Being, *Ereignis*, flesh, or *Basho* invokes the paradox of employing the reflective intellect to describe what is prior to and evades reflection. Finding an orientation that does not seek to get around the paradox but works within it, demands a philosophical vocabulary and grammar that accommodates—and to a certain measure *performs*—the paradoxical nature of this pursuit. This raises an issue that is developed more in the coming chapters regarding the relation between language and ontology. While many philosophers innovate with language in order to *describe* the ontological, the thinkers we are considering are distinctive in that, for them, ontology also follows language. It is a bi-directional expressive relation. Many of the poetic formulations Nishida

---

18. Ishihara (2011) approaches the question of Nishida's relation to phenomenology by construing both the analytic "higher-order" theory (Rosenthal) and the phenomenological approach (Zahavi, Gallagher) as partial accounts (one objective, one non-objective) and claims that Nishida's "acting-intuition" encompasses both approaches, while articulating the dialectical relation between two forms of self-awareness, and is thus a more complete account.

19. See Elberfeld (1999, 2011) and Maraldo (2017) who suggests that a feature distinguishing Nishida from other phenomenologists is his belief that self-consciousness can manifest phenomena but that manifestation is not necessarily or exclusively channeled through an individuated self, whereas in Husserl and Heidegger there is an irreducible "mineness" to all experience.

and Merleau-Ponty use mirror the dynamics of "chiasm," "reversibility," "self-identity of absolute contradictories," and "interexpression." Likewise, along with these linguistic innovations Merleau-Ponty and Nishida turn to artistic expression as practices that also embrace the complex relations that obtain within the fabric of flesh and *Basho*.

This is not to say that no critical discrepancies distinguish their approaches. Indeed, this comparison leads directly to a major disparity between their philosophies regarding a classical phenomenological issue. Yet, just as we already accept that there are several sometimes different versions of empiricism, rationalism, or idealism, so too can we allow that there is not one single phenomenology, and rather than allowing the differences of the various brands to impede dialogue, our study can benefit from how they diverge on key issues.

Substance and Relation: Separation and Non-Obstruction

The concepts "substance ontology" and "relational ontology" are, to a large measure, retroactive scholarly terms employed to refer to philosophic traditions whose thinkers, in all likelihood, would not have used them. Nevertheless, when looking at thought traditions on a historical scale, the distinction does capture a difference among what we might tentatively consider divergent family resemblances between Eastern and Western philosophies. There are countless ways to construe this distinction, many trafficking in generality. Hoping to avoid that hazard, I would like to focus more specifically on the concepts of "separation" (*chōriston*) and "non-obstruction" (c. *wuai* 無礙; j. *muge*) as they serve as a more precise and meaningful distinction to capture what we refer to as substance and relational ontologies.

Envisioning an ontological fabric as the structure of relationality demands thinking beyond transitive metaphysics and grammar, and thus poses a serious challenge to the concepts and language of Western philosophy. Merleau-Ponty never departs from his own tradition, nevertheless, in seeking to innovate therein he moves toward relational ontological thinking that is standard in Asian philosophy.[20] Of course, we can engage his phi-

---

20. Galen Johnson claims that "the ontology of flesh is a logic of internal relations" (2010). Anya Daly pursues the question of relationality in Merleau-Ponty delineating "non-dual ontology" from "relational ontology" and arguing against the common tendency to ascribe monism to flesh. Daly, *Merleau-Ponty and the Ethics of Intersubjectivity*, 26.

losophy while remaining within the Western tradition. But we would have to provide reasons for ignoring how so many of his innovations distance him from his own substance tradition while bringing him into proximity with the philosophical concepts and language of relational ontologies of Sinitic traditions. Merleau-Ponty might even present valid challenges to Asian thinking on relationality if given the chance; indeed, regarding the obstructions that limit motor-perception, I believe he does. Nonetheless, the first step in posing these questions is to delineate assumptions that distinguish the substance tradition from the relational ontologies of Nishida's East-Asian heritage.

In the West, until recently, the substance ontological tradition has prioritized the isolated subject and object. The question of how entities relate has been secondary. "Primary substances" (*protai ousiai*) are, for Aristotle, individual objects, and those objects are ontologically independent of one another. In Book VIII of his *Categories* Aristotle posited independent beings as ontologically "separate" (*chōriston*) from each other, from sensible matter, and from their own accidental properties.[21] According to his hylomorphic theory, a thing is an *ens extensum*, an "extended thing." Later Aristotelian thought construed this extension as going only so far as the circumscribable (lt. *circumscribere*; gr. *perigraptos*), outer surface of the object.[22] Both the Latin and Greek insinuate that the object has a definite exterior limit (*circum-*, *peri-*) that can be "drawn" (*scribere*) or "grasped" (*graptos*). The form (*morphe*) is, then, like a wrapper that divides what is inside and constitutive of the object from what is external, incidental, and separate from it. Objects are knowable insofar as they are circumscribable, that is to say, where we can distinguish what an object is from what it is not by drawing a line around the object's perimeter. A point I would like to underscore is that here too language follows ontology: the law of non-contradiction precludes us from saying that something is both A and not-A, thus language respects

---

21. "By 'in a subject' I mean what is in something, not as a part, and cannot exist separately from what it is in." Aristotle also uses the term *chōrismos* (χωρισμός) to describe the "great divide" between ideas and objects, and between being and becoming, which he claims Plato's theory cannot overcome (Aristotle. Categories 1.1a24).

22. Appears in Ireneus and Nicephorus. (Despite substance ontological thinking to the contrary, the principle of inertia in Thomistic-Aristotelian metaphysics of the Middle Ages considered *ens extensum* as part of a heterogeneous continuum with the possibility of a mutual-penetrability between continua, which furnishes interesting possibilities for considering in relation to the structure of mutual-negation in Nishida and Merleau-Ponty.)

the circumscribable existence of substantial entities. It is thought-provoking that in later religious applications of Aristotelian thought, God himself was conceived of as *non*-circumscribable, which led to a different relation between language and ontology: various faith-based philosophies developed apophatic theories that extolled God's un-expressibility.[23] Neither Nishida nor Merleau-Ponty is an exception to linking language and ontology, but their distinctive ontologies demand distinctive language—that is, different philosophic expression—specifically language outside the bounds of non contradiction. Indeed, the ontologies of flesh and *Basho* call for contradiction. This is because, for these thinkers, the things we encounter in phenomenal experience are not best thought of as circumscribable objects. While we must take care to distinguish Nishida from apophatic traditions he engaged at a deep level, the obstructions that thwart circumscribability of objects (especially landscapes) creates a similar un-expressibility regarding all experience, thus implicating faith within philosophy in a much broader sense, which we discuss later.

Where substance ontological thinking has informed Western philosophy since Aristotle, we have, in the West, a deep-seated propensity toward distinguishing entities and individuals, saying where bodies begin and end, circumscribing an organism and defining it as separate from other objects and from its environment in order to eliminate ambiguity. Whether this way of thinking is the cause or the effect of a grammar based on non-contradiction is a fascinating question outside the scope of this study, nevertheless, this impulse toward circumscription might help explain the rigid tendency in Western academia to distinguish between disciplines, and the difficulty of fostering dialogue among them. If the objects of these disciplines are separate, and if they demand the use of distinct intellectual faculties (*epistêmonikon, doxasticon, technê,* or *theoria,* in Aristotle's scheme) it should not be surprising that proposals to think beyond philosophy-religion-art distinctions appear questionable in the West. When it comes to the East Asian tradition, the tendency toward blurring the lines between these disciplines might stem from a relational way of thinking and its tolerance, if not its demand, for ambiguous language and forms of expression. The Buddhist tradition that informs Nishida's philosophy avoids definitions of isolated objects or events

---

23. In chapter 1 of Dionysius the Areopagite's "The Mystical Theology," he explains that God dwells in divine darkness and is unknowable through both sensation and reason. He also discusses the limits of *Theoria* as knowledge of God and the necessity of *theosis* as unification with God.

in favor of the relational networks that sustain them. It is tempting to assert that Being (substantialism, positivity) is renounced for Nothingness (relationality, negativity), but what is essential for Nishida and Merleau-Ponty is that neither seeks to counter positivity by veering completely to the other end of the ontological spectrum to develop a philosophy of the strictly negative. Negation is precisely the ontological structure that allows for Being and Nothingness to relate; a structure that embraces the positive and the negative while holding ambiguous the more concrete binaries of visibility and invisibility, activity and passivity, creating and being created.

―◦―

Turning now to East Asia, we move from Aristotelian substance thinking to relational ontological thought as it arose in the Mahāyāna lineage of Indian Buddhism. In early Buddhism, one of the three marks of existence was the impermanence (*anicca*) of all phenomena as conditioned things (*saṅkhāra*), that is, things constituted by their external relations rather than by an internal, unchanging essence. Here, the relations among objects are more fundamental than the entities themselves. Nothing comes to be separately or independently. Thus, neither separateness (*chōriston*) nor circumscription is possible, neither with subjects nor objects. All things are "dependently originated" (*Pratītyasamutpāda*); in other words, they arise through a series of external causal relations. This explains not just beings, phenomena, or the interaction between them, but also the nature of reality itself. "Dependent origination" is an ontological theory grounded on a theory of causation, yet it is fundamentally distinct from Aristotelian causation. According to the principle of dependent origination, causation is not unidirectional. It does not issue from a single prior cause (or un-caused cause); instead, there is always a plurality of causes, visible and invisible, extending throughout a network of reciprocal determination. There are no independent or substantial subjects or objects with their own self-nature. To use the terminology we invoke in the next section, things are not characterized by their essence but by their "emptiness" (*Śūnyatā*) and are related to each other through "mutual negation." Thus, in speaking of things as empty, negated, and relational, we get the language of "non-self" (無我), "non-object" (無物), and "non-action" (無爲) within the various Asian Buddhist schools of the Mahāyāna lineage, and likewise in Daoism and in certain moments of Confucian philosophy.

These are some of the basic contours of Buddhist relational thinking. The account that affords a more in-depth concentration for the dialogue between

Nishida and Merleau-Ponty comes later in that tradition, as the Mahāyāna ("middle way") lineage evolved in the second century CE in Nāgārjuna's strand of Madhyamaka Buddhism. Touchstone of his philosophy is his equating "dependent origination" (*Pratītyasamutpāda*) and "emptiness" (*Śūnyatā*). Emptiness means that beings are devoid of independent essence (*sabhāva*). This is not straightforward annihilationism because to say that a thing is empty is not to say that it does not exist; rather, emptiness means that a thing exists but originates dependently, constituted by and non-separate from its relations. This raises one of three key points of Nāgārjuna's philosophy, which is central to our later discussion. Nāgārjuna seeks a "middle way" between essentialism/eternalism (*sastavadava*) and nihilism/annihilationism (*ucchedavada*). This standpoint bears similarities with the non-dual position beyond identity and difference sought by Nishida and Merleau-Ponty in their accounts of negation.

To go a little bit further with Madhyamaka, its idea of "emptiness" applies beyond sentient beings. Not only are humans or animals non-substantial, or selfless; further, all insentient beings and phenomena (*dhammas*) are also without essence (*svabhāva*), "own being," "self-nature," or "separate existence." All beings and phenomena are part of the causal network that sustains things in their emptiness. Granted, there are differences between humans, animals, and the material world, yet such differences are not fundamental and do not entail ontological "separateness" (*chōriston*) as they do in Greek thought. All entities and phenomena are, ontologically speaking, first constituted by emptiness and thus related, non-separate. Similarly, regarding flesh and *Basho*, things are not initially distinct based on their being mind or matter, sentient or insentient; rather, they are expressions of one common ontological fabric, where relationality comes by way of negation.

There is another aspect of Madhyamaka that proves relevant for our discussion of Nishida and Merleau-Ponty, that is, Nāgārjuna's theory of the "emptiness of emptiness" (*śūnyatāyāh Śūnyatā*). In his philosophy, emptiness is not a transcendent principle that regulates the world while being itself an exception to that principle. Like all things, the principle of emptiness is itself empty—it has no essence. What this means is that as a ground for philosophic methodology it is also in danger of reification. Nāgārjuna avoids this fate by conceiving of it as a groundless ground. As a principle it institutes limits on how we can speak of it or adhere to it in practice. It is not exhaustively effable nor are the practices that aim at embodying it permanent. This has vast implications not only for Buddhist ontology, but also for Buddhist practice and grammar. What I would like to signal now to foreshadow the later discussion is that emptying emptiness institutes a constitutive risk within philosophic expression and thus elicits a practice of faith. Without a stable metaphysical principle of pure externality to which one can refer with non-contradictory subject-verb-object grammar, the emptiness of emptiness demands a register of expression that, in embracing contradiction and paradox, elicits one's faith. In this sense, we find an ancient Indian predecessor to the theories of expression, which, on my reading, likewise risk speaking from a groundless ground that calls for faith. In Nishida and Merleau-Ponty's philosophies, we discern the need for a type of philosophic expression drastically at odds with that deriving from substance ontological thinking and its attendant law of non-contradiction, which does not recognize the limits to effability or the risk of expression. These are vital points for grasping both their theories of expression, and their own often poetic philosophical expression.

The nuances of Nishida's mode of expression would be difficult to grasp if we remained within substance ontology and the A/Not-A constraints of non-contradiction. Yet, it is tricky to discern how Nishida takes up an alternative Asian logic solely by way of textual analysis, since there are so few direct references to that tradition in his writings.[24] He does make occasional allusion to Buddhist concepts or lore, but the influence is discernible in the background of his thinking as a generalized Mahāyāna spirit traceable to Tiantai, Huayan, and Ch'an sources. Ch'an concepts, in particular, are important for understanding Nishida. Chinese Ch'an Buddhism (禅) is the school that later evolved into Zen Buddhism as it washed ashore in Japan. The Ch'an notion of *sokuhi* (c. *juédui* 即非) explains the contradictory logic underlying many of Nishida's neologisms.[25] The source of Nishida's refashioned "logic of *sokuhi*" (*sokuhi no ronri* 即非の論理) was more likely his lifelong friendship with D. T. Suzuki, as opposed to close readings of

---

24. See Kopf, 2005, 313–329, for a thorough discussion of Nishida's employment of Buddhist concepts and texts, and particularly the origin of his "one-and-yet-many" term, which, Kopf points out, Nishida finds in Hermann Cohen's "Einheit der vielheit" but does not acknowledge their occurrence in Tiantai or Huayan commentaries of the Avatamsaka Sūtras.

25. For a more detailed discussion see Nicholaos John Jones, "The Logic of Soku in the Kyoto School"; James Heisig, *Philosophers of Nothingness: An Essay on the Kyoto School*; David Dilworth, "Postscript: Nishida's Logic of the East in Last Writings," *Nothingness and the Religious Worldview*; Ha Tai Kim, "The Logic of the Illogical: Zen and Hegel"; Marcello Ghilardi, "Soku 即 and Analogy in Nishida's Thought," in *The Line of the Arch: Intercultural Issues between Aesthetics and Ethics*.

specific Buddhist texts.[26] *Sokuhi* could not be farther from Aristotelian logic, it is the logic of "neither A nor not-A" or "is *and* is not." Thus, it suggests an ambiguous position between positivity and negativity, belonging and separation. A position the painters we consider can sustain with the landscape. The main idea that Suzuki derives from the Diamond Sutra is that self-identity is only possible through self-negation. A can only be A if it is negated, if it is not-A. This logic reverberates throughout the entirety of Nishida's project and becomes pronounced in his last writings. No self exists without non-self, no being without non-being, no universal without particular, no conventional without the ultimate, no subject without object, no absolute without relative, no creating an image of a mountain without being created as an artist by that mountain. As I discuss later in the study, this is the implicit logic that governs Nishida's understanding of perception, motion, and expression, such that there is no unambiguous perception without perceptual-negation, no movement without stillness, and no external perception without it being negated by internal perception. Likewise, the making-made dynamic of "interexpression" obtains by virtue of the negation inherent to *sokuhi* logic.

There is also a meta-comparative implication to the logic of *sokuhi*. As Ghilardi suggests, the belonging/not-belonging aspect of *soku* is a helpful metaphor for describing the inter-cultural relation between East and West.[27] We later also contemplate how a great deal of Chinese painting terminology, practices, and even tools adopted in Japan are based on a similar *soku* coincidence of opposites. Indeed, movement and expressive gesture are only possible if one is part of but not entirely subsumed into the landscape.

I would like to now pay special attention to a later evolution of the logic of *sokuhi*, which evokes the central question of this chapter, and the central tension of this comparison; this concerns the limits of relationality, or the lack thereof. As Mahāyāna evolved within the Huayan (c. 華嚴; j. *kegon* 華厳宗) school of Buddhism, the question of emptiness was re-articulated within a fourfold structure that divided the world into (1) noumena (c. *li* 理), (2) phenomena (c. *shih* 事), (3) the non-obstruction between phenomena and noumena (c. *lishi wuai* 理事無礙), and (4) the non-obstruction between

---

26. See Cestari Matteo, "Between Emptiness and Absolute Nothingness: Reflections on Negation in Nishida and Buddhism," 320–346. Kopf (2005) questions the extent to which Buddhist classics directly influenced Nishida's thinking, whereas Cestari claims there is a more direct and discernible influence.

27. M. Ghilardi, *The Line of the Arch: Intercultural Issues between Aesthetics and Ethics*, 76.

phenomena and phenomena (c. *shishi wuai* 事事無礙). Despite few explicit references to Huayan in Nishida's philosophy,[28] several have noted that the idea of non-obstruction (c. *wuai* 無礙; j. *muge*) explains aspects of his thought.[29] The third level mentioned above—that between phenomena and noumena—is helpful for understanding how Nishida conceives of relations, such as that between the universal and the individual, between the "historical body" and "historical world," and the "interexpressive" relation between God and humans. But, I am less interested in this "vertical" relation between noumena and phenomena and more concerned with the "horizontal" relations among phenomena and phenomena referred to in the fourth level.[30]

Huayan is notable for resolving prior doctrinal disputes and claiming to have perfected the Buddhist lineage by returning its focus to the relations among phenomena. Yet, the fourth patriarch of Huayan Buddhism, Chengguan (澄觀) (738–839) amends the Huayan concept of non-obstruction in such a way that raises an important issue for our dialogue between Nishida and Merleau-Ponty. It will take until the last chapter to see the entire picture, but our philosophers in comparison do not agree about the limits of sensorimotor non-obstruction. Addressing this comparative discrepancy is the core of this study, and I propose my solution while setting

---

28. Nishida does use the Huayan phrase "non-obstruction between distinct phenomena" in his later writings, yet there is no strong evidence that he studied Huayan/Kegon philosophy in a systematic way. His use is more likely to derive from D. T. Suzuki, who did pursue focused research in this area of scholarship and also led a Kegon reading group including Nishitani and Kōyama.

29. See Krummel (2015); Kopf (2005); Dilworth (intro to "The Logic of Place and a Religious World-view"). There are very few critics in Huayan/Kegon scholarship of the idea of non-obstruction between phenomena (*shishi wuai fajie*). One of the few to take a stand against this concept was Kihira Tadayoshi (1874–1949), a student of Inoue Tetsujirō and a nationalist. He worried about the implications of non-obstruction at the political level, which would, he thought, advocate a principle of equality placing the common man and the emperor on a similar ethical level, thus undermining Japanese imperial rule. Nishida opposed Kihira and his followers, and during the war they became enemies (see Kōsei Ishii, "Kegon Philosophy and Nationalism in Modern Japan."

30. Krummel (2015) calls this the "horizontal interrelationships among those co-relative, interdependently originating beings" as opposed to the "vertical" relations between individuals and a universal principle. He discusses how in the writings of Chengguan emptiness is considered as a universal principle that is collapsed into the mutual non-obstruction and inter-penetration between phenomena, which fully de-transcendentalizes the principle of emptiness.

up a critical encounter on this issue between several readers of Nishida and Merleau-Ponty, including John Maraldo, John Krummel, Michel Dalissier, and David Brubaker among others.

In Chengguan's notion of the "non-obstruction of all phenomena" (*shishi wuai* 事事無礙), there is a limit to non-obstruction, which is very relevant for highlighting a critical discrepancy between Nishida and Merleau-Ponty. Let us first consider the third level where Chengguan describes the relation between noumena and phenomena. At this level, he describes the relation attained as a mutual form of negation. Phenomena can relate to noumena, or individuals to universals because "they interrelate and mutually negate each other, both affirming and denying, [this] is called non-interference." He further explains:

> Merging phenomena by noumenon, phenomena fuse with noumenon, two yet not two. The ten aspects have no interference because their meanings are the same. Furthermore these two, noumenon and phenomena, merging, each must pervade the other because mutually pervading they melt into each other.[31]

I characterize Nishida's and Merleau-Ponty's ontologies of *Basho* and flesh as being structured by various instantiations of mutual negation. Yet, the Huayan example muddies the waters between the two on the issue of negation as it relates to motion and perception. To render these discrepancies, we have to explore the abovementioned fourth level of Chengguan's account of relationality: the relation between phenomena and phenomena. In moving to this level, it might seem as if the noumenal realm has been sidelined. But throughout the intricate analysis of his *Mirror of the Mysteries of the Universe of the Hua-yen*, Chengguan employs *sokuhi* logic to thwart any simple distinction between phenomena and noumena. As Chengguan states, "Noumenon and phenomena are relative to each other; they are neither one nor different. Therefore, they can completely contain each other without destroying their original status."[32] Because each abides beyond full positivity or negativity, noumena and phenomena are able to interrelate non-obstructively. "[B]ecause phenomena are not one with noumenon," explains Chengguan, "they are restricted as individual phenomena,

---

31. Thomas F. Cleary, *Entry into the Inconceivable: An Introduction to Hua-Yen Buddhism*, 74.
32. Ibid., 42.

and because they are not different from noumenon they are extensive as all-pervasive noumenon."³³

Now, when we shift our focus to the fourth level—where phenomena relate to phenomena—we find the crucial limits to non-obstruction. Phenomena, as entities with an at least partially material form, are empty by nature; nevertheless, unlike the relation between phenomena and noumena, Chengguan writes, "If we see only in terms of phenomena, then they *obstruct* one another." While he claims that "phenomena have physical characteristics whereas noumenon has none," still he wants to maintain that the relation is neither unambiguous identity nor difference: "phenomena being neither one with noumenon nor different from noumenon."³⁴ Despite their being non-dual with noumena, and their being empty of nature, it appears that aspects of their materiality, spatial extension, their position and physical qualities impede full non-obstruction. In Chengguan's words, "phenomena basically obstruct each other" by virtue of their being "different in size and so forth." While "noumena" are "by nature undivided," this is not the case with "phenomena [which] are differentiated in division and position." Phenomena have an aspect of "boundaries," whereas noumena do not.³⁵ Non-obstruction does not fully obtain between phenomena. There are limits to phenomenal relationality through negation, as other commentators have noted.³⁶

In the final chapter, I argue that Nishida's theory of vision does not appear to acknowledge the kinds of phenomenal limits suggested in Chengguan's philosophy (and Merleau-Ponty's). In that absence, he might inadvertently

---

33. Ibid., 116.

34. Ibid., 119. Emphasis added.

35. Ibid., 92.

36. Jin Y Park maintains that phenomena are only fully non-obstructive from the point of view of noumena. While Huayan is known for being the school of Buddhism that resolves doctrinal disputes by returning the focus to the fourth level, the relations among phenomena, Park points to criticisms that the full mutual non-obstruction between phenomena is a "vision" that only a fully enlightened Buddha has, and otherwise can be seen only from the point of view of noumena (she suggests "non-interference among phenomenon seen from the perspective of noumenon"), thus contradicting the school's stated goal to focus on the fourth level of the relation between phenomena. Park proposes a different hermeneutical approach to the question that would redeem the fourth level for Huayan, which focuses on the Buddhist notion of compassion. This approach brings her to invoke Nishida (p. 185) and the religious consciousness that he believes arises when one accepts the self-contradiction at the foundation of the self and the world (Jin Y. Park, *Buddhism and Postmodernity: Zen, Huayan, and the Possibility of Buddhist Postmodern Ethics*).

posit a full non-obstruction between phenomena, which contradicts other important features of his late ontology, particularly with his concepts such as "seeing without a seer" (*mirumono nakushite miru koto* 見るものなくして見ること) and the "self-seeing" (*Jiko jishin wo miru* 自己自身を見る) of *Basho*. And while Merleau-Ponty also conceives of perceptual relationality as mutual negation, unlike Nishida, he does not endorse full "non-obstruction" between phenomena, or a full reversibility between motor-perceptual entities. Merleau-Ponty posits sensorimotor limits and obstructions, which in a curious East–West twist, might mean that he is, in some senses, closer to Chengguan than Nishida is. I engage these questions in more detail in the chapters to come, but first, now that we have established some of the background for Nishida and Merleau-Ponty's theories of negation, let us consider their own theories more directly.

Nishida's "Absolute Negation"

Many of the concepts in Nishida's philosophy that instantiate Buddhist forms of relationality center on his concept *Basho* (場所), also referred to as "place," "*topoi*," and sometimes "chōra" (χώρα). What began as an exploration of consciousness, later evolving into an epistemological project, eventually came to fruition in his final period as a philosophy deeply concerned with the "place" where bodies acted and interacted with the world according to what Nishida termed the "logic of place" (*basho no ronri* 場所の論理, *bashoteki ronri* 場所的論理). It is worth focusing on this aspect of his mature ontology in hopes of continuing a project initiated by Nobuo Kazashi, which places the ontology of *Basho* in dialogue with Merleau-Ponty's ontology of flesh.[37]

We should understand the ontology of *Basho* as part of Nishida's larger project of reconciling Eastern religious experience with Western philosophical systematics. Nishida attempted to think within Western metaphysics and epistemology, while going beyond its inherent subject–object dualism and its idealist–realist, monist–pluralist binaries. This theory grew out of his desire to escape from the psychologism of his earlier James-inspired account

---

37. Kazashi was among the first to propose dialogue between Nishida and Merleau-Ponty with his 1989 Merleau-Ponty Circle presentation, "Bodily Field of Experience as the Historical Horizon for Expressive Acts: An Essay toward a Comparative Study of Merleau-Ponty, James, and Nishida." A decade later this would be published as "Bodily Logos: James, Nishida, and Merleau-Ponty."

of "pure experience"[38] (*junsui keiken* 純粋経験) and "self-awareness" (*jikaku* 自覚). First appearing in 1929 in his "*Basho*" essay in *From the Acting to the Seeing* (*hataraku mono kara miru mono e* 働くものから見るものへ), the concept further evolves throughout the 1930s in his *The Self-Aware System of Universals* (*Ippansha no jikakuteki taikei* 一般者の自覚的体系) (1930–1932) and *The Self-Aware Determination of Nothing* (*Mu no jikakuteki gentei* 無の自覚的限定) (1933), and culminates in his final work, "The Logic of Place (*Basho*) and the Religious Worldview" (*Bashoteki ronri to shūkyōteki sekaikan* 場所的論理と宗教的世界観).

The epistemological project of the 1920s sought to overcome the Neo-Kantian framework that conceived of knowledge as the subject's imposition on an objective world. Nishida wanted to speak of an all-inclusive field of non-differentiation prior to subject–object opposition. He sought to explore the groundless ground for knowledge as an alternative to two versions of the epistemological subject arising from Aristotelianism, which reifies the object ("object logic" *taisho ronri* 対象論理), and Kantianism, which reifies the subject ("subject logic" *shugoteki ronri* 主語的論理). Primarily, Nishida pursued a "substratumless" (*mukiteiteki* 無基底的) philosophy of non-substantiality (*mukitei* 無期底) grounded in neither the subject nor the object, but in the prior grounds that allowed for their inter-determination. In the early stages, he conceived of this as the "field of consciousness" (*ishiki no ba* 意識の場). Rather than a foundational propositional truth on which other claims build according to a formal logic of non-contradiction, *à la* Aristotle, *Basho* is an empty ground. Nishida does not articulate a hierarchical logical structure where judgments are reduced to a more foundational truth, instead *Basho* comprises a circular relationality with a logic of nothingness (*mu no ronri* 無の論理) whereby contradiction is a necessary aspect of that ontology, similar to the Mahāyāna *sokuhi* logic.

His *Basho* theory underwent several significant revisions as Nishida responded to critiques (particularly, those of his colleagues who saw his theory as too far removed from social reality) and addressed his own dissatisfactions. Despite the concept undergoing modification, several elements consistently underpin the various uses. Some of these suggest paths for dialogue with Merleau-Ponty. The most notable example being the dynamics of negation.

---

38. For a discussion of the relation of Nishida's "pure experience" to James, see D. Brubaker, "'Place of Nothingness' and the Dimension of Visibility: Nishida, Merleau-Ponty and Huineng"; Kazashi (1999); David Dilworth, "The Initial Formations of 'Pure Experience' in Nishida Kitaro and William James."

While his early epistemological *Basho* theory is preoccupied with the relation between grammatical subject and object, as this project evolves throughout the 1930s he becomes increasingly concerned with the external world of relations among acting social-historical beings. Nishida progresses in this direction as he further refines the work of the early 1930s in the dual-volume *Fundamental Problems of Philosophy* (*Tetsugaku no konpon mondai* 哲学の根本問題 1933–1934), and in *Collected Philosophical Essays* (*Tetsugaku Ronbunshū* 哲学論文集 1930–1940).

For Nishida, neither the Kantian nor the Aristotelian frameworks can explain how beings relate, because they are constrained by the laws of non-contradiction inherent to positivist and substantialist accounts of objectivity. A circumscribed object defined in its positivity admitting of no negation precludes the possibility of inter-relation or inter-determination. (Think back to the interweaving fingers example. The positive objects are the enclosed fists. They remain separate.) To allow for the possibility of inter-determination (the open fists negating each other's space), Nishida conceives of the base of reality as the "place of true nothing" (*shin no mu no basho* 真の無の場所) or "place of absolute nothing" (*zettai mu no basho* 絶対無の場所) as the field wherein being and nothingness are non-dual and inter-penetration is the reality of entities related by way of negation. Things require a place in which they first exist between positivity and negativity to be able to encounter and inter-determine each other. Nishida posits *Basho* as a non-substantial medium, permitting non-obstructive (*wuai*) relationality in the Huayan sense, thus allowing entities to encounter and mediate one another. Within the fabric of *Basho*, beings and phenomena relate not as self-contained circumscribable entities, not as separate (*chōriston*) in the Aristotelian sense, but through self-negation (*jiko hitei* 自己否定). The character of relationality as mutual self-negation, which I explore in more detail below, reflects the Huayan idea of "mutual identity and penetration" (c. *xiāng jí xiāng rù*; j. *sōsoku-sōnyū* 相即相入). Co-constituted through mutual negation, entities are neither fully substantial nor fully desubstantialized, neither fully posited nor fully negated. This kind of relation beyond affirmation and negation is, therefore, beyond the logic and grammar of substance ontologies. Aristotle's law of non-contradiction dictates that A and not-A cannot both be true.[39] Rather than follow this law—appropriate for describing positive objects—Nishida develops a "logic of absolutely contradictory self-identity" (*zettai mujunteki jikodōitsu no ronri* 絶対矛盾的自己同一の論理). This, Nishida will propose,

---

39. Aristotle, "Metaphysics: Book 4."

is the appropriate way of describing entities related through mutual negation. Again, language (expression) follows ontology. Objects, the self, phenomena, these do have identity, but that identity is contradictory: at once A and not-A. I am constituted in relation to thou, and that encounter is enabled as mutual negation by a phenomenal field (*Basho*) ambiguous regarding positivity and negativity. Nishida develops several other principles that deploy a similar contradictory logic, including his principle of "self-identity of opposites" (*sōhansurumono no-teki jikodōitsu* 相反するものの的自己同一),[40] "affirmation of absolute negation"[41] (*zettai hitei no kōtei* 絶対否定の肯定), and "absolute negation-qua-affirmation"[42] (*zettai no hitei soku kōtei* 絶対の否定即肯定). This contradictory mutual negation allows for inter-determination between subject and object beyond the binaries of positivity and negativity. Contradiction and ambiguity are necessary conditions for things to be encounterable as non-separate beings, for them to interact and inter-determine one another. *Basho*, as a groundless ground accommodates these contradictory dynamics according to the *sokuhi* logic of Nishida's Zen heritage. As we examine in the following chapters, the logic underpinning these various principles of Nishida's governs not only how reality can be spoken of in language, but how it can express itself in paint.

To return to the earlier analogy, if mutual negation is the *texture* of the relational fabric, we must clarify the *dynamic* ways in which entities relate as part of that fabric. In enabling body–body and body–world relations, *Basho* does not function as an underlying substratum "standing under" allowing entities to determine one another. This substance manner of thinking conceives of determination in one direction. It is essential in understanding Nishida's philosophy that there is a two-way, reciprocal determination operating at several levels (between universal and particular, body and world, humans and god). This is the essence of many of his concepts, including "dialectic," "inverse-determination," and "mutual negation." I continue to discuss this in the abstract, but in the next chapters we see how this two-way determination is the decisive quality enabling the body–world relation as a reciprocal "making-made" determination crucial for artistic expression as motor-perceptual faith.

---

40. Nishida, *Nishida Kitarō zenshū*, 8: 84
41. Nishida, *Fundamental Problems*, 112.
42. Ibid., 109.

Let us recap and collect our thoughts before moving on. Nishida developed his *Basho* theory as an alternative to Aristotelian logic and grammar. *Basho* is a non-substantial, relational, and non-obstructive field within which entities are emplaced and can encounter one another through mutual negation. Returning to Merleau-Ponty below, we see that his ontology of flesh also goes beyond substance thought and conceives of phenomenal encounter as a mutual form of negation. Starting in the next section, we look at how both philosophers conceive of the structure of that negation as a chiasmatic relation, or in Nishida's language, continuous-discontinuity (*hirenzoku no renzoku* 非連続の 連続). Yet, let me signal that this is where the critical divergence I have been alluding to begins. Both thinkers develop their ontologies to describe the pre-reflective plane of experience, and more importantly, they appeal to artistic expression as a way of perceiving and acting in accord with the dynamic motor-perceptual demand of this locus. In my view, both conceive of faith as an orientation that risks going along with this directive—a motorsensory directive—from the fabric in which one is enmeshed; but this is to get slightly ahead of ourselves at this point. Yet, the critical divergence to signal in this chapter is that Nishida does not appear to articulate explicit limits to non-obstruction with his account of "absolute negation" (*zettai hitei* 絶対否定) and "absolute nothing" (*zettai mu* 絶対無), whereas Merleau-Ponty will do so. Put another way, Nishida contravenes the Huayan restrictions regarding the fourth level of non-obstruction (*shishi wuai* 事事無礙), whereas, remarkably, the Western philosopher might recognize those limits. This difference is crucial for their notions of faith.

Before exploring this point of contention further, I want to dig farther back into their texts to gain a precise understanding of negation at work in their philosophies. This will prepare the way for a more direct consideration of negation as a motor-perceptual determination, one that helps us get a grip on the artistic practice of Cézanne and Sesshū discussed in chapters 2 and 3 where I frame faith in terms of a motorsensory negation between the artist's body and the landscape. Now, let us re-engage with Merleau-Ponty and Nishida to spell out with more precision how they develop theories of negation.

Negation: Chiasm, "Continuity of Discontinuity"

Because Nishida and Merleau-Ponty both use such enigmatic and complex language to articulate their ontologies, deciphering their individual writings poses a challenge. Placing them in dialogue amplifies that challenge. One way to make the comparison more concrete—and to make it more visual—is to focus on a common structure underlying flesh and *Basho*, that is, the structure of chiasm. While Merleau-Ponty is well known for this term, several commentators have noted that aspects of its etymology are also apt for describing Nishida's account of relationality,[43] most notably, his concept "continuity of discontinuity" (*hirenzoku no renzoku* 非連続の連続).[44]

Throughout the 1930s Nishida experiments with several formulations to describe the mediation that obtains between body and world, self and other, body and tools, etc. Of course, Nishida sought to capture their mediation beyond the dualities of substance-based logic. Neither identity nor difference can describe how things relate to each other or through time. In substance thought, a *continuous* self-identity underwrites subjects and objects thought to be separate (*chōriston*), that is, *discontinuous*. Personhood endures by virtue of one's self-identical mind or soul persisting throughout time. But, while my soul, essence, nature, etc., enables my continuity, it is the basis for discontinuity with others. To give an account of relationality in substance ontological terms is an attempt to overcome discontinuity. But, because it remains positivist, it is like wanting to interweave one's fingers while keeping one's fists clenched. Nishida takes a different approach. For the self, objects, landscapes, or tools to encounter requires an intertwining (mutual negation) of continuity *and* discontinuity.

---

43. Several commentators, including Maraldo (2014, 2017), Krummel (2015), Krummel and Nagatomo (2012), Kazashi (1999), Stevens (2009), Brubaker (2009), and Cipriani (2009), have pointed out how many of Nishida's concepts are based on the same chiasmatic structure Merleau-Ponty employs in that they instantiate various aspects of the ambiguity between identity and difference. Nishida does so regarding temporality with his concept "continuity of discontinuity" (*hirenzoku no renzoku* 非連続の連続), regarding the relation of the "historical body" (*rekishiteki shintai* 歴史的身体) to the "historical world" (*rekishiteki sekai* 歴史的世界), regarding logic with his "self-identity of absolute contradictories" (*zettai mujunteki jikodōitsu* 絶対矛盾的自己同一), regarding motor-perception with his concept "acting-intuition" (*kōiteki chokkan* 行為的直観), and regarding expression with "interexpression" (*zettai ni aihan suru mono no sōgo kankei wa, hyōgen-teki denakereba naranai* 絶対に相反するものの相互関係は、表現的でなければならない).

44. While Nishida uses this term mostly regarding time, Krummel and Nagatomo read it more broadly as a general ontological principle arrived at through self-negation. They write: "self-negation (*jiko hitei*), which [Nishida] also considers a "continuity of discontinuity" (*hirenzoku no renzoku*) . . . We find that this dialectic [of self-negation] involves a chiasma of vertical and horizontal interrelations manifest in various types of relations—such as individual-environment, person-person, subject-object, etc." (*Place and Dialectic*, 2012, 236)

If two things were wholly *continuous*, if there were no difference between you and I, or myself and a mountain, there would not be separate entities, and thus nothing to relate. If, on the other hand, myself and another were entirely *discontinuous*, then relation would be impossible, because mere encounter requires sharing something, minimally the fact of being emplaced in a common phenomenal field. Yet, because we do encounter things and beings that are distinct from ourselves, they must be partially discontinuous to even appear, but they also have to be embedded within a continuous field that enables encounter. *Basho* is that field whose texture is continuously discontinuous. This is the structure of negation as Nishida understands it. To encounter things, we must be negated by them; we must be a non-self to achieve continuity. They must enter into our definition, but they cannot negate us without remainder—all positivity is not reduced. Likewise, the other, the object, or the paint or the paper is negated by me; they must be available for encounter as non-objects. We see in the coming chapter how the temporal orders likewise negate each other for time and motion to transpire. Continuous-discontinuity is also central to Nishida's theory of expression as "making-made." In all cases, mediation is possible because of an interweaving of positivity and negativity, or, to bring in Merleau-Ponty's terminology, what Krummel calls a "crisscrossing chiasma of continuities of discontinuities both in time and in space."[45]

Merleau-Ponty's use of the concept "chiasm" (*chiasme*) throughout *The Visible and the Invisible* is pivotal in his late ontology, and the main term instantiating the ambiguous structure of negation. As I explore in the section below, its imagery, morphology, and even etymology are essential for understanding the complex motor-perceptual relation Cézanne achieves to the landscape. There are many ways to interpret this concept, but I consider it for the texture of relationality it specifies, which echoes that of Nishida's continuous-discontinuity. When encountering anything, Merleau-Ponty writes, "we situate ourselves in ourselves and in the things, in ourselves and in the other," whereby, through "a sort of chiasm, we become the others and we become world."[46]

---

45. Krummel, *Nishida's Chiasmatic Chorology*, 104.
46. Merleau-Ponty, *The Visible and the Invisible*, 160.

To unravel his enigmatic language and grasp what Merleau-Ponty is putting forth with this concept, I analyze chiasm as a structure of mutual negation, which sustains ambiguous relationality without resolving into duality or non-duality. While visualizing aspects of their ontologies is useful, as I have cautioned already, a proper understanding of chiasmatic relationality requires thinking beyond the visible-invisible binary. This is where the earlier hand-interweaving example proves inadequate, since it only helps us grasp the visual aspect of negation. The fabric metaphor including its invisible "lining," however, gets closer to a more complex idea of mutual negation since for both Nishida and Merleau-Ponty it is essential that negation embraces the visible and the invisible. Before unpacking Merleau-Ponty's provocative statements and considering them in dialogue with Nishida, let us reflect in this section on the idea of chiasm itself and later move toward chiasm as mutual negation on the ontological level.

The notion of chiasm is rich in meaning, accruing linguistic, perceptual, anatomical, religious, and grammatical senses through its use in various cultures. In the West, its etymology goes back to the 22nd letter of the ancient Greek alphabet X (*chi*), which is the root of the terms "chiasmus" and "chiastic structure." The letter's morphology, its crisscross x shape, had various meanings in early Greek and Roman times.[47] The "chiasmic" sense associated with the letter also has assorted grammatical and rhetorical uses throughout Eastern and Western oral and literary history. A grammatical structure known as the "chiasmus" in classical Greek rhetoric derived from the x-shape of its root. Through what they called "inverted parallelism," one writes two clauses in reciprocal and inverse relation. A modern instance of grammatical chiasmus is Heidegger's "the being of language is the language of being," but the same structure is also found in Sumero-Akkadian literature, early Hebrew literature, Aramaic contracts, Talmudic narrative, the New Testament, and in the Book of Mormon. Most studies of this

---

47. In Plato's *Timeaus* the two parts of the world soul cross each other, forming an X shape. This same configuration was also used in the Chi-Rho symbol ☧ in medieval art and Roman symbolism. The first two Greek letters of the word "Christ" (Greek: ΧΡΙΣΤΟΣ, or Χριστός), Chi (χ) and Rho (ρ), were employed to symbolize the crucifixion in Roman symbolism. It was also used in the most celebrated page of the Book of Kells, the Chi-Rho page.

structure focus on Western and Near-Eastern sources, but as a grammatical technique, its historical roots also extend to Buddhist literature, early Prajñāpāramitā sūtras, and Buddhist hagiography. One of the most famous *apadānas* (biographical stories of the Buddha's life) of the Theravādin tradition, the *Vessantara Jātaka* is noted for its chiastic structure.[48] There are famous examples throughout Buddhist literature, most notably the *Heart Sutra*'s most enduring maxim, "form is emptiness, emptiness is form." The chiasmatic structure also turns up in later Kyōto School philosophy when Tanabe Hajime writes about "the self-awareness of nothingness constitutes the nothingness of self-awareness," and recently in John Krummel's book on Nishida, where he frames the ontology of *Basho* in terms of chiasmatic relationality, playing on its grammar in the work's subtitle, "place of dialectic, dialectic of place." Merleau-Ponty employs the structure when he asserts that there cannot be any "consciousness of ambiguity without some ambiguity of consciousness."[49]

Another linguistic derivation, the "chiastic structure" is a narrative device that applies a crisscrossing structure on a macro level to longer passages. We find it in Homer, the Hebrew Bible, and the New Testament, among others. Some Mahāyāna sūtras previously believed fragmentary were found to be sophisticated wholes when analyzed according to this structure.[50]

These grammatical and rhetorical configurations are fascinating, but it is important to appreciate that their significance is not merely poetic, or, we might say, the poetic use of chiasmatic structures has a deeper significance in that they are apt for describing a world that is itself chiasmatically structured, a world that calls for such unorthodox grammatical and literary constructions. Again, ontology and language meet. What chiasmatic structures show us is that subject-verb-object grammar might be inappropriate and at odds with the texture and dynamics of phenomenal reality. If people and things encounter through chiasmatic negation, then the language of substance ontology will prove unsuitable for describing relationality.

In the examples above, grammar and narrative structure follow character morphology, and in the following examples, we see how language also follows

---

48. Shi Huifeng, "Chiastic Structure of the Vessantara Jātaka: Textual Criticism and Interpretation through Inverted Parallelism."

49. Merleau-Ponty, *Parcours Deux: 1951–1961*, 331.

50. M. B. Orsborn, "Chiasmus in the Early Prajñāpāramitā: Literary Parallelism Connecting Criticism & Hermeneutics in an Early Mahāyāna Sūtra."

human physiology. This is something to keep in mind as we engage in greater depth with the difficult language and the various neologisms Nishida and Merleau-Ponty use to describe the world, the body, and artistic expression.

Since Merleau-Ponty and Nishida depart from the law of non-contradiction to describe the various ambiguities that characterize perceptual encounter, it is very interesting to discover that human visual anatomy instantiates more than one chiasmatic form of ambiguity. The part of the brain below the hypothalamus where the optic nerves partially cross is called the "optic chiasm" (figure 1.1). It is pertinent to note that—in keeping with the configuration of ambiguity as mutual negation—these passageways only partially cross. The brain's visual apparatus divides the nerve stimulus arriving from each eye, and channels visual data from left and right pupils to both hemispheres of the brain. The juncture where the nerves meet from both eyes allows right and left visual data to go to both the right and left

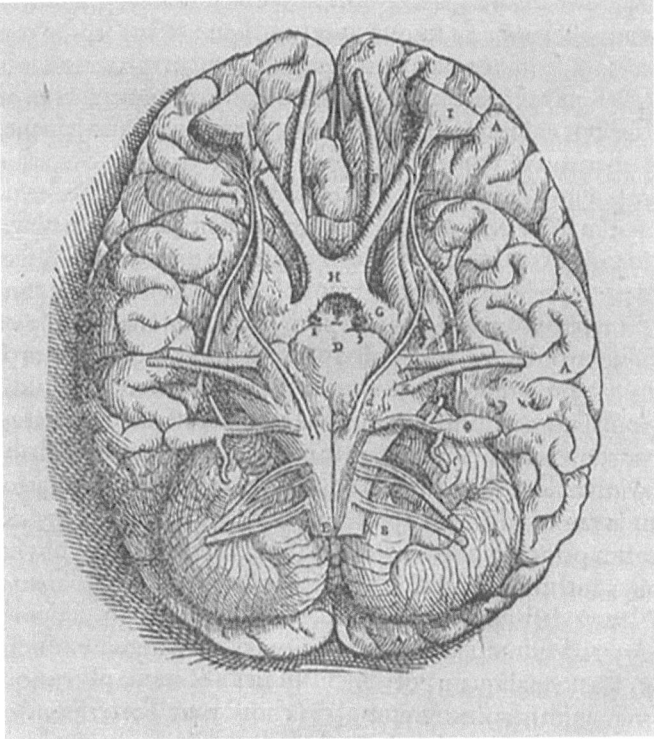

Figure 1.1. Andreas Vesalius, "Optic chiasm," *De humani corporis fabrica*, 1543.

hemispheres. Although there are dual pathways, they are ambiguous regarding left and right visual content as enabled by the chiasmatic juncture. There is a second type of chiasmatic structure at this intersection. Not only is the information sent through this physiology ambiguous, so too is the physiology itself. There is an anatomical chiasm in the juncture where fibers of the nervous system and visual system intertwine, where electro-magnetic impulses become mental images. Taken together, these various instances of chiasmatic relationality in optical physiology and function are the texture of "flesh" as Merleau-Ponty understands it. Thus, we find this ambiguity not just in the optic, but throughout the body and in how it relates to other bodies. As Galen Johnson writes, "The optic chiasm may serve as a paradigm for other more figurative bodily chiasms, the crisscrossings of touching and being touched, seeing and being seen, feeling and being felt, hearing and being heard."[51]

To make chiasmatic relationality more concrete and visual (eventually we need to grasp it beyond the visible) we can consider this depiction of a rotator cuff, muscle, and tendon (figure 1.2). The image shows that although there appear to be two different tissues, there is no localizable point where the fibers of the muscle definitively changes into the tissue of the tendon. Chiasmatic relationality, be it between different tissues in one body, or between different bodies, confounds the identity-difference binary. If we look at this image from a faraway perspective, one notices a *continuity* of form uniting muscle and tendon. If we take a close-up perspective, one can notice the *discontinuity* where two tissues gradually weave one into the other. As in the fabric analogy, here too the entire configuration is, at once, continuous and discontinuous such that one cannot conclude that there are simply one or two structures. It must be both at once. Helen Fielding captures this ambiguity: "in the chiasm there is ultimately no fusion—the two sides remain distinct—there is, however, no limit between the one and an other."[52] This indeterminacy undermines our desire to circumscribe body parts and define them as "separate" according to substance ontological thinking. We want to say A or not-A, tendon or not-tendon, muscle or not-muscle, according to the law of non-contradiction. To describe a body related to itself beyond these binaries demands the unorthodox grammar

---

51. Johnson, *The Retrieval of the Beautiful*, 31.

52. Helen A. Fielding, "A Phenomenology of 'the Other World': On Irigaray's 'To Paint the Invisible,'" 225.

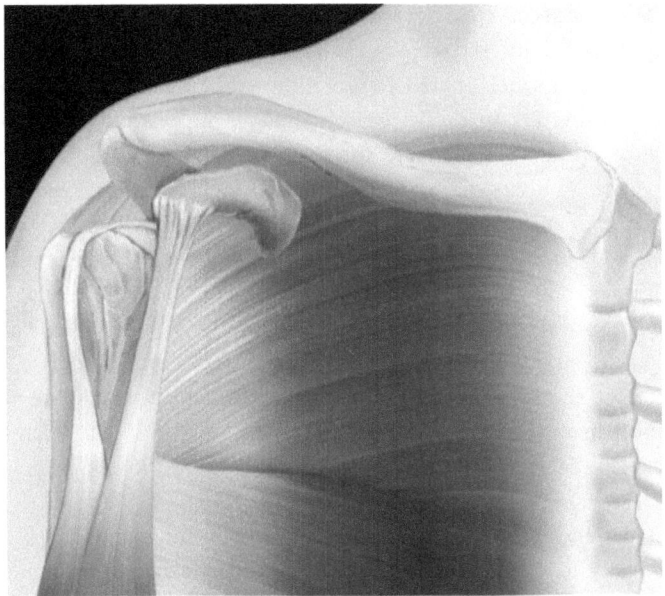

Figure 1.2. "Muscle-tendon chiasm" (image by the author).

and logic of the various chiasmatic structures. Thus, language too becomes chiasmatic to describe a body that is related to itself in this way. Later, to appreciate the painter's relation to the landscape, we have to expand this description and show how the body also relates to what is outside of itself through a similar chiasmatic continuous-discontinuity.

To foreshadow the coming discussion on artistic practice, we might consider how Japanese aesthetic theorists and practitioners had a sense of continuously-discontinuous forms of relationality. The structure of chiasmatic interweaving shows up in areas of Japanese thought on aesthetics prior to Nishida. As early as the eighteenth century in the Rinzai School of Buddhism, one of the many notions of beauty as *kire* (切 "cutting") became prominent in the teachings of Hakuin. This aesthetic principle describes how artists cut away part of a scene and exclude what is absent while skillfully suggesting it through the use of negative space. Thus, what is made discontinuous by the cutting is brought into continuity beyond positive-negative binaries. While commonly referred to as a "cut" aesthetic, which suggests division and separation á la Aristotle, the more complete rendering is "cut-continuance" (*kire-tsuzuki* 切れ続き): something that both divides and connects, creating a chiasmatic continuity and a discontinuity. The play of positivity and negativity, visibility and invisibility that the cut deploys produces a heightened beauty as it enables the viewer to enter the definition of the art work by actively imagining what is absent and cut away. Once one develops an eye for *kire* it is remarkable how prevalent it is in Japanese architecture, painting, cinema, rock gardening, haiku poetry, Nō drama and, of course, the art of "cutting" flowers, *ikebana*.[53]

Ma (間) is another important principle instantiating continuous-discontinuous ambiguity. It is often visible in the quintessentially Japanese negative space of landscape paintings. *Ma* is translated variously as "interval," "gap," "pause," and "the space between two parts." Yet, as with *kire*, a closer inspection of the term reveals an ambiguity much more in line with the continuous-discontinuity of chiasm. *Ma* does not denote an unambiguous distance between separate objects. As Ghilardi writes, it is a principle that

> divides-and-links two dimensions, two discourses, two figures . . . *Ma* is a sort of aesthetic (perceptive and emotional) awareness coming up from a fissure, and implies a cut, a discontinuity . . . yet it involves or creates a link, a passage, a gateway or continuity, otherwise there would not be any recognition of this difference. So, *ma* allows the appearing of a continuity of discontinuity, in Nishida's words.[54]

Perception, for Merleau-Ponty is an instance of a similar relation: as Frank Chouraqui writes, "perception [i]s a relation in both senses of the term, that of link and that of distance."[55] The concepts of *kire* and *ma* will prove apt for grasping the ambiguous relations between the visible and invisible, between sky and mountains, trees and clouds, and between positive and negative space in paintings such as Hasegawa's "Pine Trees" (see figure 2.3 in chapter 2). The ambiguous connecting-dividing relation might also provide an answer for the question posed in the introduction

---

53. For an illuminating discussion of *kire* and its relation to the Japanese dry landscape gardens, see Parkes (2000) and in relation to the cinema of Ozu, see Graham; Parkes and Adam; Loughnane, "Japanese Aesthetics," *Stanford Encyclopedia of Philosophy*.
54. Ghilardi, *The Line of the Arch*, 81.
55. Frank Chouraqui, *Ambiguity and the Absolute: Nietzsche and Merleau-Ponty on the Question of Truth*, 130.

regarding the intercultural distance between philosophies inhabiting a field that is all center and no circumference.

Having reflected on the various ways phenomenal, aesthetic, and linguistic reality instantiate relational ambiguity, we can now further articulate these ideas moving one step closer to the ontological implications of chiasm and continuous-discontinuity. Specifically, we need to consider the mutuality of negation. As we discuss below, negation obtains on both ends of phenomenal encounter. Considering this feature will aid in filling out the picture of flesh and *Basho* as ontological fabrics, and later shed light on the enigmatic description of artistic expression Nishida and Merleau-Ponty deploy. Before ending this section, let us return briefly to the fabric analogy to explore why negation must be mutual and manifest on both ends of phenomenal encounter.

Any piece of fabric requires both a set of threads called the warp, which provides the scaffolding for the material, and lateral threads called the weft, which weave into the spaces between the warp. If we think of the warp and the weft as longitudinal and latitudinal planes, we can begin to see negation as a type of mutual interweaving, or "intertwining" (*entrelacs*) to use Merleau-Ponty's term. If the longitudinal plane disallowed negation by the latitudinal plane, we would simply have two layers, one lying on top of the other, with no possibility of the textures or dynamics of properly woven fabric. In a sense, they would be mutually obstructive: if you pushed one against the other it would move away, not sharing the same space, or field. (They would be two continuities that are discontinuous, i.e., non-chiasmatic.) Making fabric involves weaving two discontinuous planes into a single plane. This is to mutually negate one plane with the other: to make two discontinuous planes, continuous (i.e., chiasmatic). This shows the need for a *mutual* negation. If only one plane negated no interpenetration would occur. When interwoven, what results is a mutually supporting set of strands that make up a single plane, a fabric that allows for a whole set of dynamics, contours, torsions, and relations to other fabrics that would not be possible if the interweaving did not happen by a reciprocal negation. When it does, the single plane of a woven fabric instantiates a spatial and material ambiguity. That is, chiasmatic continuous-discontinuity is visible: from one perspective it simply appears to be a single piece of fabric, a continuous plane of a scarf, a tablecloth or bed sheet. From another perspective, if we look closer, we can discern two discontinuous planes, one lateral, one longitudinal. Thus, it is at once a single, non-dual, continuous plane, and two dual, discontinuous planes. Only in this way can a woven fabric be fabric. The chiasmatic negation maintains this ambiguity. Although the example is still too simple, in order to make use of it for our purposes we must expand the idea such that it explains not just objects or body's relations to each other, but those entities' relations to the phenomenal field they inhabit. As bodies, we are woven into the perceptual fabric of flesh and *Basho*, as are all objects and phenomena. The further step we must take is to expand this analogy beyond a positivist framework and think of the fabric beyond the visible-invisible binary as a non-substantial scaffold for being and nothingness.

Before moving on, it is important to remember that chiasmatic texture is not only indicative of the relation between the body's tissues, but is also the character of the relation between the body and the ontological fabric of flesh and *Basho*. Thus, it is also the nature of the artist's motor and perceptual relations to the landscape he paints. The body ambiguously intertwines with the world and the point of demarcation between the two is, like the demarcation between muscle and tendon, cloud and mountain, warp and weft, difficult, perhaps impossible to fully circumscribe. To grasp this constitutive indeterminacy demands looking further into Nishida and Merleau-Ponty's notions of mutual negation. To bring this section to an end, I might also mention that the chiasmatic structure of continuous-discontinuity can serve as a model structure for the relations that we attempt to build in carrying out inquiry through intercultural philosophy. Hwa Yol Jung is thinking along these lines when he proposes "transversality" as a paradigm for comparative methodology. The concept comes from geometry where it refers to the crossing of two diagonal lines. As a framework for intercultural encounter, "transversality" thus invokes the structure of chiasm to instantiate what Jung calls a "middle voiced" approach to comparison.[56]

Merleau-Ponty Counter Sartre's *Nullité Absolue*

In these last sections of the chapter I look more closely at the conceptions of negation in Nishida and Merleau-Ponty's writings, focusing on the common feature of mutuality, which both insist upon regarding negation.

---

56. Jung, *Transversal Rationality and Intercultural Texts: Essays in Phenomenology and Comparative Philosophy*, 21.

The self-identical, fully determinate, fully positive subject cannot encounter beings or objects within the perceptual fabric. Yet, neither can a subject without any determination or positivity. To perceive is to be a perceptual non-self, yet not a complete non-self. Perceptual encounter is not possible for a thoroughly negated consciousness, nor is it conceivable within a context of straightforward positivity. Seeking to avoid either extremity, Merleau-Ponty positions himself counter to the positivism he reads in Bergson and the negativism of Sartre. For the purposes of this dialogue with Nishida, I focus on Merleau-Ponty's critique of the latter. We find hints at various forms of negation throughout his writings, but the most explicit articulation is at the beginning of his final work. A critical aspect of Merleau-Ponty's discussion of negation in *The Visible and the Invisible* involves a critique of Sartre's notion of "absolute nothingness" (*nullité absolue*), which frames consciousness as wholly negated.[57] Thus, Sartre's description of the relation between being and nothingness remains within the logic of identity and difference. In his words:

> . . . the being which I am not represents the absolute plenitude of the in-itself. And I, on the contrary, am the nothingness, the absence which determines itself in existence from the standpoint of this fullness.[58]

For Sartre, being-in-itself is "full positivity," "absolute presence,"[59] whereas consciousness, "Being-for-itself is defined . . . as being what it is not and not being what it is."[60] Although Sartre sometimes approaches this issue in an epistemological sense, he is pondering the question of the encounterability of the other. When Merleau-Ponty critiques his friend's approach, he focuses more directly on the ontological aspects of perceptual encounter with the other.

---

57. For a comprehensive look at the philosophical, as well as personal, and political relation between Merleau-Ponty and Sartre, and their eventual break, see Jon Stewart, *The Debate between Sartre and Merleau-Ponty*. Also see the chapter "Being and Nothingness: Dialectic" in Barbaras, and the chapter "Sartre and the Problem of Mediation" in M. C. Dillon's *Merleau-Ponty's Ontology*.
58. Jean-Paul Sartre, *Being and Nothingness: An Essay on Phenomenological Ontology*, 177.
59. Ibid.
60. Ibid., lxv.

Sartre wants to think outside of the positivist framework to explain how the self meets the other, but with binary opposition remaining as the underlying logic, he goes to the opposite extreme and construes phenomenal relation as requiring not a partial but a complete negation of the subject. For Merleau-Ponty, if the perceiving subject is pure nothingness, then the perceptual object would have to be pure positivity. This is unacceptable for him, because "from the moment that I conceive of myself as negativity and the world as positivity, there is no longer any interaction."[61] Interaction and perception are only possible in an ambiguous relation where there is neither pure negativity nor pure positivity, because "our relationship with Being is ignored in the same way in both cases,"[62] writes Merleau-Ponty. Accordingly, negation cannot be absolute. On these grounds, Merleau-Ponty labels Sartre's absolute negation as a positivist philosophy disguised as a negativist philosophy.[63] To conjecture an absolute negativity for consciousness is to uphold a stable duality between positivity and negativity; a duality precluding the possibility of encounterability altogether.[64] To use a term that comes up later in this chapter, the purely negative or purely positive are "mutually obstructing." They do not permit phenomenal encounter since neither allows for

---

61. Merleau-Ponty, *The Visible and the Invisible*, 52.

62. Ibid., 127.

63. For Merleau-Ponty, the body's perceptual openness onto the world cannot be captured in a philosophy of full negativity or positivity. The body is neither at a "simple distance (n)or absolute proximity" to the world. Both of these alternatives rely on full "negation or identification" (*The Visible and the Invisible*, 127).

64. "But there is no self-mediation either if the mediator is the simple or absolute negation of the mediated: the absolute negation would simply annihilate the mediated and, turning against itself, would annihilate itself also, so that there would still be no mediation, but a pure and simple retreat toward positivity. It is therefore ruled out that the mediation have its origin in the positive term, as though it were one of its *properties*—but it is likewise precluded that the mediation come to the positive term from an abyss of exterior negativity, which would have no hold on it and would leave it intact. Yet it is in this second manner that the dialectic is translated when it ceases to be a way of deciphering the being with which we are in contact, the being in the process of manifesting itself, the situational being, and when it wishes to formulate itself once and for all, without anything left over, state itself as a doctrine, sum itself up. Then, to get to the end, the negation is carried to the absolute, becomes negation of itself; at the same time being sinks back to the pure positive, the negation concentrates itself beyond it as absolute subjectivity-and the dialectical movement becomes pure identity of the opposites, ambivalence" (*The Visible and the Invisible*, 92–93).

continuous-discontinuity. As we will see, negation is necessary for perceptual encounter, but as Renaud Barbaras explains, "subjective negativity includes some positivity in the sense that it is a *concrete* subjectivity." He follows this with a question that helps focus our study, asking, "what does the kind of positivity of subjective negativity consist, what is the concrete way of existing of a consciousness defined as absence of Self?"[65] As we delve deeper into the complexities of negation, negativity, and nothingness throughout this study, keeping a firm grip on the irreducible "positivity of subjective negativity" will prove decisive, not only concerning Merleau-Ponty, but particularly with Nishida and his Asian tradition where it is perhaps an even greater danger that we stray into the utterly negative. For Merleau-Ponty, perceptual encounter is not possible for Sartrean consciousness as "absolute negation," since, as he writes, if I perceive, "then I am no longer the *pure negative*":

> [T]o see is no longer simply to nihilate, the relation between what I see and I who see is not one of immediate or frontal contradiction; the things attract my look, my gaze caresses the things, it espouses their contours and their reliefs, between it and them we catch sight of a complicity. As for being, I can no longer define it as a hard core of positivity under the negative properties that would come to it from my vision.[66]

Perception is an event between positivity and negativity, between perceptual self and non-self, achieved through a negation taking hold on both ends of the encounter. In Nishida words, "[I]ntuition is that which negates us while affirming us and affirms us while negating us."[67] One cannot be a pure seer; nor can one ever be seen in full determinacy. Vision is always "seeing-seen," as Merleau-Ponty puts it. Nishida foreshadows this realization by more than twenty years when he writes in his *Fundamental Problems of Philosophy*, "[i]f seeing and the seen are merely one, there is no intuition."[68] The two cannot collapse or else there is no vision. Thus, a gap is necessary, but not simple discontinuity. While ambiguity is necessary for perception, both philosophers claim that consciousness itself is not possible

---

65. Renaud Barbaras, "Perception and Movement: The End of the Metaphysical Approach," in *Chiasms: Merleau-Ponty's Notion of Flesh*, 85.
66. Merleau-Ponty, *The Visible and the Invisible*, 76, 77. Emphasis added.
67. Nishida, "Logic and Life" in *Place and Dialectic*, 322.
68. Nishida, *Fundamental Problems*, 1.

without mutual negation. For Merleau-Ponty, "The absolute positing of a single object would be the death of consciousness."[69] Meanwhile, Nishida speaks of the same "death" in his 1933 *Fundamental Problems* (*Tetsugaku no konpon mondai* 哲学の根本問題) when he writes:

> Negation as self-negation, i.e., absolute negation, would be a self-death. The self would ultimately be nothing. There is no meaning to such an inclusion of absolute negation within the self . . . For in order for there to be the mutual determination of individuals, the external must be internal and the internal must be external.[70]

Both of our thinkers in dialogue conceive of the relation with the other, and relationality itself, as a two-way, partial, and mutual negation. Flesh and *Basho* are the perceptual fabrics whose chiasmatic continuous-discontinuity enables perceptual encounter. The other does not present itself as separate from oneself, but "by a sort of *chiasm*, we become the others."[71] On both of their accounts, when perceiving objects, we become those objects, because our partially negative consciousness accommodates the presence of the partially positive object, not unlike the Chinese painter who, in order to paint bamboo, must learn to grow bamboo inside himself.[72] Without grasping the mutuality of negation on the ontological level, such claims appear as little more than poetic embellishments, yet when we see phenomenal encounter beyond mutually obstructing positivity or negativity, as a relation between a non-subject and non-object, what rings of linguistic indulgence can be heard as an appropriate description of encounter between beings and objects that are themselves between full determinacy and indeterminacy.

Nishida: "Absolute Negation" and the "I-Thou" Relation

The tradition in which Nishida lived and wrote has a long history of contemplating the negative. Although he rarely avows that tradition explicitly,

---

69. Merleau-Ponty, *Phenomenology of Perception*, 82.
70. Nishida, *Fundamental Problems*, 47.
71. Merleau-Ponty, *The Visible and the Invisible*, 160.
72. This is an ancient Chinese saying, which Jacques Taminiaux also refers to in his commentary on Merleau-Ponty, in Jacques Taminiaux, "The Thinker and the Painter," 287.

Mahāyāna concepts of nothingness and negation are unmistakable in his writings.[73] The Japanese term he uses for "negation" is *hitei* (否定). This character appears on its own and also in his terms *jiko hitei* ("self-negation" 自己否定), "*zettai hitei*" (絶対否定), and "*zettai no hitei*" (絶対の否定), these last two most important instances being translated as "absolute negation." These latter concepts are most pertinent, for they betray striking parallels with Merleau-Ponty's thought on negation, corroborating the dialogue between the two philosophers on ontological grounds. The immediate difficulty, however, is that an "absolute" negation would seem to be a valid target for the critique Merleau-Ponty levels at Sartre's absolute nothingness, thereby making the comparison untenable. Yet, when considering its etymology, we see that Nishida's "absolute" negation actually points to the same mutual form of negation Merleau-Ponty embraces contra Sartre.

Without looking into the etymology of Nishida's "absolute" it would be easy to interpret it as the opposite of the many meanings associated with negation and ambiguity. Nevertheless, Nishida plays on an intriguing etymological twist in the Japanese word for "absolute" (*zettai* 絶対), which places it very much in line with Merleau-Ponty's understanding of negation. The term comprises two characters, 絶 (*zetsu*), which means "to sever, to go beyond, to cut through, to vanish, break or overcome" and 対 (*tai*), referring to "opposition," "to oppose," or "to face."[74] The compound 絶対 (*zettai*) is distinct, if not the opposite of what we generally take as "absolute." In placing these two Chinese characters together, it refers to severing opposition, or "transcending opposition." *Zettai hitei* is an absolute negation in the sense that it *absolutely undoes opposition*, that is to say, it undoes duality. Yet, if the outcome were non-duality, this would simply reify it as a concept. As Maraldo writes, "that which merely breaks through opposition is not truly absolute either. The true absolute, Nishida says, must negate itself."[75] Absolute negation "severs" binaries while also going one step further to sever the binary between binary and non-binary.[76] Thus, Absolute

---

73. For an excellent and comprehensive discussion of the relation between Nishida's philosophy and Mahayana, and Hegelian ideas of negation and dialectic, see Krummel (2015).

74. See Maraldo's, "Nishida's Ontology of History," 253; Krummel (2015); Ghilardi (2015); Michel Dalissier, *Anfractuosité Et Unification: La Philosophie De Nishida Kitarō*, 64, 394.

75. Maraldo, "Nishida's Ontology of History," 253.

76. See also Krummel (2015) and Gereon Kopf, "Is Dialectical Philosophy Tenable? Revisiting Hegel, Nishida, and Takahashi."

negation in Nishida's philosophy is a nothingness of nothingness (無の無 *mu no mu*), or a negation of negation along the lines of the Mahāyāna idea of emptiness of emptiness (*śūnyatāyāh Śūnyatā*) where everything said of the concept, including its name itself must be continually negated such that no final grounds are tenable for building a foundational philosophical system. A similar anti-foundationalism is discernible in Nishida's dialectics, which resist the final synthesis of Hegel's system. What Lucy Schultz refers to as Nishida's "dialectic of dialectics"[77] resonates with a similar resistance to finality in Merleau Ponty's thought. He also sees the need for a non foundational openness in philosophical interrogation and develops his idea of "hyper-dialectic" (*hyper-dialectique*) as a form of thought resisting the finality of synthesis in Hegelian dialectics.[78]

Unlike Sartre's *nullité absolue*, which upholds the positive-negative binary, Nishida's *zettai hitei* invokes a mutual negation that does not set up an opposition between being and nothingness. "Absolute nothing" (絶対無 *zettai mu*) does not oppose Being; it is the field where being and nothingness are neither dual nor non-dual. Applying this concept to the issue of encountering the other, we have a "mutual-negation"[79] where "[e]ach negates the other for the sake of self-affirmation."[80] Nishida echoes Merleau-Ponty's similar insight, that if it were not for the mutuality of negation, no encounter would be possible with the world, or with the other. Things in their full positivity *or full negativity* are mutually obstructive. This is essential for Nishida's theory of expression, because if negation were "pure inexistence," "that which is nothing" (*mu no dōzen* 無の同然), *nihil negativum*, or what Dalissier calls "sterile, pure"[81] negation, not even God could create anything.

Like Merleau-Ponty, Nishida theorizes inter-subjective encounterability beyond a stable self-other binary. Only non-selves can encounter one another. His term "I and thou" (*watashi to nanji* 私と汝) suggests a way of being related that involves mutual negation on both sides of the encounter, that is, both the self and other negating such that the other can be. Again, he

---

77. Lucy Schultz, "Nishida Kitarō, G.W.F. Hegel, and the Pursuit of the Concrete: A Dialectic of Dialectics."

78. For an in-depth discussion of Nishida's dialectics in relation to Hegel and Mahāyāna non-dualism, see Krummel, 13–49.

79. Krummel and Nagatomo (2012) refer to Nishida's absolute negation as "mutual negation."

80. Nishida, *Nishida Kitarō zenshū*, 8: 58; Krummel and Nagatomo, *Place and Dialectic*, 51.

81. Dalissier, *Anfractuosité et unification*, 68.

uses the concept of *zettai*, and its non-dual connotations, this time regarding the other as "absolute other" (*zettai ta* 絶対他). This term invokes the other not in full positivity, but to suggest a duality that is severed, a continuous-discontinuity between self and other arrived at through mutual negation. But where it is even possible to encounter this other as other, there must be a place within which the two are encounterable. This enveloping field is *Basho*. Woven *into* and *out of Basho*—the ontological fabric that enables encounter between mutually negated beings—the other overcomes the obstructions of the self and is available for genuine encounter not constrained by the obstructions of positive selfhood.

The decisive point for Nishida is that affirmation and negation are not mutually exclusive ontological principles; they are simply the binaries we arrive at if we submit ambiguity to reflective intellection. A pivotal aspect of Nishida's late ontology is his principle of "affirmation of absolute negation" (*zettai hitei no kōtei* 絶対否定の肯定), which, like Merleau-Ponty's refutation of Sartre, precludes a one-sided negation. One cannot affirm oneself counter to or in the absence of another or the world without at the same time being negated by them. Chouraqui explains that Merleau-Ponty was of a similar mind; he writes that "negintuition as the primary determination of the subject applies to the object in the same way."[82] The mutuality of negation calls for a non-subject *and* non-object. Thus, encounter is possible when, Nishida writes, "the objective is the subjective, or rather subjectivity can be seen in the very depth of the objective . . . it has the meaning of determining and negating the person." And to further anticipate our later discussion, he claims, "this is especially so in aesthetic creation."[83] In the next chapter, I discuss how mutual negation allows us to see how when an artist paints the landscape, a multi-valent negation obtains between the painter, her tradition, and the "mountains, rivers, trees and rocks" she paints.

Representation and Perceptual Negation: From Non-Subject to Non-Object

As we consider the negated subject and object in more detail throughout this study, an insight of Chouraqui's that would be illuminating to keep

---

82. Chouraqui, *Ambiguity and the Absolute*, 144.
83. Translation based on Nishida, *Fundamental Problems*, 65, with minor revisions by the author.

in mind whenever either is referred to is his description of the asymptotic tendency toward the poles of subjectivity and objectivity. Like the geometric asymptote, which approaches the X or Y axes infinitely without ever reaching them, similarly, even though it is unattainable we nevertheless strive toward being fully posited subjects or perceiving fully posited objects. As the Greek word *asumptōtos* (ἀσύμπτωτος, "not falling together") suggests, the asymptote and the axis sustain a relation without ever collapsing the distance between the two. Likewise, regarding attaining subjective or objective determinacy, "the impossibility of attaining either pole," Chouraqui writes, is expressed as "the impossibility of self-identity."[84] While negation is the structure of relationality that ensures that the poles remain related without "falling together," our desire for determinacy sends us on a trajectory toward the "inexistent" possibility of self-identity. While success is impossible, we nevertheless "operate in our lives as if the objects around us (as well as ourselves) were totally self-identical and determinate."[85] This craving for determinacy on either pole is, I believe, a desire to reduce an existential risk associated with the negative. A risk, I will argue, certain artists have accepted and thus shown new ways of being bodies related to the world. I do not think it is a stretch to say that our Western philosophic tradition has given us to see negation or the idea of negated selfhood as a threat. Evading this threat is to deny the structure of negation that renders subject and object indeterminate but encounterable. And thus, avoiding the risk of indeterminacy ignores or possibly suppresses a form of bodily faith elicited by the world we are negating and negated by. By not accepting the risk, we end up putting ourselves in danger by conducting our projects according to a mistaken conception of the self, the object, and the relation between the two. The representational framework of perception and its attendant metaphysics is one such mistake that misconstrues the body's mediation with the world and thus endangers both poles of the relation.

The "representational" model (also called "indirect perception"), as one of the prevailing frameworks for theorizing about perception, ignores negativity and seeks to bridge the gap between fully determinate subjects and objects. We

---

84. Chouraqui, *Ambiguity and the Absolute*, 144.
85. Ibid., 17.

use this term as a somewhat retroactive appellation for a set of assumptions that constrained thinking about knowledge, perception, and language, often without being argued for explicitly. Features of what we now call "representationalism" extend all the way back to Aristotle and continue throughout Western philosophy in the writings of Locke, Malebranche, Descartes, and Kant, among others. The problem with this framework, for our purposes, is that it tends to re-affirm separateness or an unambiguous distance between perceiver and thing perceived: a spectator at a distance from what she sees. The Greek way of knowing referred to as *theoria* (θεωρία) meaning "contemplation, speculation, things looked at," and *theoros* (θεωρός)—as derived from the root *thea* (θέα) "a view" and *horan* (ὁρᾶν) "to see"—perpetuates the idea of a "spectatorial" distance. Whether understood as literally seeing with the eyes, or metaphorically as "seeing" with the mind, theoretical knowledge implies a separation between the subject and the perceptual or epistemological object: a decidedly non-chiasmatic discontinuous relation.

While there is no single "representational" theory, the offspring of this framework share assumptions that posit a metaphysical discontinuity between the perceiver and the perceived. Whether explicitly stated or not, representationalism construes vision as the reception of sensory data that bounces off of objects and travels through a non-perceptual medium only to become perceptual when received and processed by the human visual apparatus. Those who follow this assumption understand perception as delivering not the real external world, but only a replica, which becomes housed in the mind as an internal representation. Thus, a major preoccupation of those adhering to the model is epistemological: How can we have true knowledge of the external world if the perceiving subject distorts, rearranges, or synthesizes data emanating from the perceptual object? My concern is not epistemological but the perceptual assumptions that give rise to its problematics. The hitch is that the representational model takes the perceptual object to be un-ambiguously separate from the subject and ignores negation. Thus, the seer, her mental image, the object seen, and the medium through which images travel are discontinuous. Most of our taken-for-granted ideas, and some of the most sophisticated philosophical and scientific frameworks for understanding perception, are representational in this sense. This positivist account of perception gains traction from how well it explains how visual technologies function, but as Merleau-Ponty asserts, we lose what is human about vision when we "substitute for perception what we would see if we were cameras."[86]

---

86. Merleau-Ponty, "Cézanne's Doubt," 64.

The various representational assumptions fail to grasp many important aspects of perceptual experience because of their underlying positivist ontology. I use "positivist" in the sense that perception is explained only by what is observable, measurable, quantifiable, etc., which in this case means it is reduced to the effects of sense data reflecting off of circumscribed objects and the various processes that data undergoes upon entering the human perceptual apparatus.[87] Positivist accounts do not consider negativity, absence, or invisibility as constitutive aspects of perception, and, therefore, fail to notice how the negative is bound up with and complexifies positivity, presence, and visibility. According to representational assumptions, what is invisible, absent, or unseen is secondary, non-essential, non-visual, or is simply ignored. Objects are perceived but are not themselves perceptual, not part of an underlying fabric that enables encounter. Moreover, memories, projections, meaning, or imaginings that impinge upon vision *relate to* but not considered part of the visible, because they do not remain after the object is perceived, and they do not survive circumscription. A positivist might agree that negative elements are *related to* or *impinge upon* the perceptual, but because they are not part of the positive representation, they do not count as part of the visual or perceptual itself. Following from the various binaries of the representational model, a rigid distinction arises between the perceptual and the non-perceptual. Further sets of binaries between mind and matter, proximity and distance, activity and passivity, vision and touch ensue. Oppositions such as these impede a full understanding of the phenomena of perception because philosophies built thereupon remain confined by various conceptual instantiations of the identity-difference dichotomy. Both Nishida and Merleau-Ponty are emphatic that perception cannot be submitted to this logic less we reduce perception to its purely positive aspects, those mere features human perceptual physiology share with cameras and other visual technologies. Grasping what is human about perceptual encounter requires going beyond positivity to a framework that embraces mutual negation. Flesh and *Basho* are perceptual ontologies and, as a result, a non-perceptual entity cannot exist. To see things is not to have a representation of a circumscribed object at a distance. I cannot perceive an "object." Positive objectivity was only ever a fiction that ensued because we first wanted to know what things were before we asked how they appeared. I cannot encounter "hard-core" positivity. It would obstruct my vision. A negated object on the other hand,

---

87. Nishida has a detailed analysis of the "physiological" understanding of vision in *Intuition and Reflection in Self-Consciousness*, 114–116, and in *Ishiki no Mondai*, 185

a non-object with "fissures and gaps"[88] is something I can see insofar as I meet it as a negated subject. I can have it as long as it, at the same time, has me. As Merleau-Ponty writes, one "cannot possess the visible unless he is possessed by it."[89] Expanding this insight to its full ontological extent, he further notes that, when I perceive, I not only belong to the thing, "I belong, through my point of view, to the world as a whole."[90] Similarly, for Nishida, to see is not to represent a positive object: "[T]o view a thing aesthetically . . . must mean to submerge the self within the thing in itself."[91] This language of Nishida's and Merleau-Ponty's would be inconceivable within a positivist representational framework, but they would say that so too would perceptual encounter be unthinkable. Only through perceptual negation can visual encounter take place, and this requires going beyond the positivity of the representational model.

Because representationalism chops up the perceptual world, making subject and object separate, in order to describe perceptual encounter it must find some way to put it back together. Taking an array of positivist assumptions as the starting point for theorizing about perception, it is then incumbent upon such theories to explain how perceptually discontinuous entities can encounter each other. How would the perceptual and non-perceptual interact? On this essential point Nishida and Merleau-Ponty are in agreement: if a perceiving subject were absolutely *discontinuous* from an object, the subject would overwhelm and ultimately supplant the object, subsuming it as the perceptual relation obtains. Thus, the subject–object distinction would collapse and there would be no perception because perception is a relation between two things. *Thus, discontinuity alone cannot explain perception.* (To go back to our fabric example, if two planes of material try to relate without interweaving, they have no option but to remain discontinuous lest one cancels out the other.) Conversely, if the visual subject were wholly *continuous* with the object it perceives, there would cease to be a relation between two things and there would be no possibility of coming into any relation, perceptual or otherwise. There would be a complete lack of obstruction because there wouldn't be two things to obstruct each other. *Thus, continuity alone cannot explain perception.* (In the

---

88. Merleau-Ponty, *Phenomenology of Perception*, 389.
89. Merleau-Ponty, *The Visible and the Invisible*, 134.
90. Ibid., 384.
91. Nishida, *Art and Morality*.

case of fabric, encounter would turn two planes into one.) Perception is a relation that must sustain identity-difference, continuity and discontinuity. A subject cannot perceive an object. What perception needs is a non-subject and a non-object related by way of mutual negation. As Nishida states, "[i]f seeing and the seen are merely one, there is no intuition."[92] Human perception is an event *between* identity and difference. It is a *soku* relation. The perceiving subject must be partly *continuous* with the object seen, while remaining partly *discontinuous*, as suggested by Nishida's term "continuity of discontinuity" (*hirenzoku no renzoku* 非連続の連続), and Merleau-Ponty's "intertwining" (*entrelacs*). Perceptual encounter is not the relation between objects with a clearly demarcated separation (*chōriston*) between insides and outsides or self and other. The relation is ambiguous, between determinacy and indeterminacy, as alluded to in the *ma* idea of space, *the kire* notion of cut-continuance, and *chiasm* as mutual negation. As determinations of a common perceptual fabric, through perceptual encounter the self enters the other and the other enters the self. As Merleau-Ponty writes, "there is not identity, nor non-identity, or non-coincidence, there is inside and outside turning about one another."[93] Similarly, in Nishida's words: "in order for there to be the mutual determination of individuals, the external must be internal and the internal must be external."[94] Because mutual negation is the texture of the perceptual fabric uniting the perceiving subject and perceived object, a perceptual form of negation obtains on *both* ends of the perceptual act. Thus, the negated self demands the negated object, the object with "fissures and gaps" sustaining the self beyond itself.

The question we must now face is, how do we get from the negated subject to a negated object? While a negated self is by no means common currency, it is not completely without precedent in the Western tradition. The idea of a negated object, however, is more difficult to put forth. How can we construe the non-object? There is something about the supposed immateriality of consciousness or selfhood that makes it easier to conceive how they have a valence of negativity. But, for neither Nishida nor Merleau-Ponty is there a strict distinction between consciousness and objects. Merleau-Ponty claims that "what begins as a thing ends as consciousness of the thing, what begins as a 'state of consciousness' ends as a thing."[95]

---

92. Nishida, *Fundamental Problems*, 1.
93. Merleau-Ponty, *The Visible and the Invisible*, 264.
94. Nishida, *Fundamental Problems*, 47.
95. Merleau-Ponty, *The Visible and the Invisible*, 215.

Likewise, Nishida argues that we "see by becoming things, and hear by becoming things."[96]

Whether we remain within the representational framework or not, it seems intuitive that in perceiving objects some aspect of them enter consciousness and are contained there. It is less intuitive to think that objects themselves can be so negated, that in being perceived they sustain the existence of the perceiving self. However, without *mutual* negation, we are left with Sartre's object-as-pure-positivity against consciousness-as-pure-negativity. Merleau-Ponty is not far from Nishida when he writes that,

> the world, in the full sense of the word, is not an object, for though it has an envelope of objective and determinate attributes, it has also fissures and gaps into which subjectivities slip and lodge themselves, or rather which are those subjectivities themselves.[97]

When contemplating the negativity of the object, one must be on guard from following Sartre in absolutizing that negation. This would merely reinforce the positive-negative binary, from the opposite direction, rather than ambiguating the distinction. Merleau-Ponty is sensitive to this. He does not propose erasing all aspects of positivity:

> In reality, this glass, this table, this room can be sensibly present to me only if nothing separates me from them, only if I am in them and not in myself, in my representations or my thoughts, only if I am nothing. Yet (one will say) inasmuch as I have this before myself I am not an absolute nothing, I am a determined nothing: not this glass, nor this table, nor this room; my emptiness is not indefinite, and to this extent at least my nothingness is filled or nullified.[98]

Similarly, Nishida suggests that the negated object has a place for the perceiver: "[T]o view a thing artistically," he maintains, "must mean to submerge the self within the thing in itself. In abandoning the self, one conforms to the objective itself."[99] To perceive is therefore not simply for

---

96. Nishida, *Last Writings: Nothingness and the Religious Worldview*, 102.
97. Merleau-Ponty, *Phenomenology of Perception*, 389; ibid.
98. Merleau-Ponty, *The Visible and the Invisible*, 53.
99. Translation based on Nishida, *Art and Morality*, 101, with minor revisions by the author.

a subject to receive sense data from an object, both conceived as positively circumscribed entities.[100] The object itself must have negativity, to render itself as a perceptual object. I not only make space for the object to inhabit; there is a place, a "depth" in the object itself, which my perceptual self inhabits.

Part of what motivates Merleau-Ponty's concept "depth" (*profondeur*) is an attempt to describe a perceptual relation beyond objecthood. While he does not use the language of "non-object" or "negated object" we cannot ignore the provocation to think in this direction when he says "a certain hollow opened up within the [object] in-itself, a certain constitutive emptiness—an emptiness which . . . sustains the supposed positivity of things,"[101] and later when he writes that for objects to be perceived "one sole condition is laid down for their coming on the scene . . . that they could present themselves to me as *other* focuses of negativity."[102] I italicize "other" here because it shows he is thinking about both ends of the perceptual relation as negated.

Although objects, others, and the world are available for perception through this structure of negation, later we will see how certain artworks make this more visible than others. Paintings of Cézanne, as well as several Chinese and Japanese landscapes, manifest their non-objecthood to such an extent that they help make visible the ambiguous relation between the perceiving subject and perceived artwork. To achieve this wondrous effect, the artist does not simply represent the landscape. Rather, to foreshadow the coming discussion, the painter moves their body in artistic expression from a motor-perceptual continuity with the landscape. They do not merely represent or copy what is out there but participate in the constituting of the landscape as a visible non-object. As Ghilardi puts it, great paintings show that "the landscape is not *something to represent*, but rather *a way to see*."[103]

Moving forward, in the coming chapter I discuss four further consequences following from the representational assumption. These include (1) upholding a strict dichotomy between the perceptual and non-perceptual,

---

100. For a discussion of the difference between "l'énergie de la lumière" (*hikari no enerugi* 光のエネルギー) and "sensations du lumière" in Nishida, see Dalissier (2009), 271–272, where he explains that Nishida takes it that there is a correspondence between these two levels, between light "en soi" and as it is experienced "entre le sens et l'existence de la lumière."

101. Merleau-Ponty, "Eye and Mind," 144.

102. Merleau-Ponty, *The Visible and the Invisible*, 59.

103. Ghilardi, *The Line of the Arch*, 103.

(2) affirming an unambiguous distinction between distance and touch, (3) understanding vision's reach as being limited to the surface of objects, and (4) explaining vision as constituted by a uni-perspectival and frontal vantage point. Contrary to these, I show how Nishida and Merleau-Ponty, as well as several artists, challenge these assumptions as they overturn representational positivism. In so doing, they affirm that (1) there is no non-perceptual anything, (2) distance and touch are ambiguous, (3) visual experience exceeds surfaces to include depth, and (4) vision is always multi-perspectival.

Chapter 2

Perceptual Fabric

Space, Time, and Light

Vision and Multi-Perspectivalism: Seeing-Seen

The complexities and the wonders of the human body are a perennial subject of inquiry in Eastern and Western art history, art theory, and practice. The countless ways of studying the body, its flesh, anatomy, perception, and movement remain foundational aspects of art practice to this day. Yet, the techniques and conventions for representing the body are not uniform across cultures. For example, the body as studied by way of the nude is rare throughout East Asian art history. If there is a more prevalent tendency in Japan and China, it is to minimize the body's presence in favor of depicting its surroundings, its natural environment of mountains, trees, and waters.

The philosophies associated with different ways of representing the body are likewise geographically and historically diverse. For instance, attempts to depict the ideal human body were not a major preoccupation of all cultures. Whether the artistic impulse came from or motivated various philosophies, the propensity toward enamoring the perfect body was bound up with notions of transcendence, belief in an ideal realm, permanence, and perfect forms—ideas associated with Greek culture and Platonism in particular. The relative lack of depictions of idealized human bodies in East Asian art makes sense in its philosophic tradition where ideas of immanence, impermanence, asymmetry, and imperfection were more likely to inform art practice.

Although artists such as Cézanne, Guo Xi, Hasegawa, or Raphael might have had similar aims, they were immersed in different intellectual backgrounds and would have thought about their practices along appreciably different theoretical lines. These artist's innovations are intelligible within the cultural, intellectual, and religious contexts in which they worked and conducted their experiments. Throughout history, some artistic movements were relatively self-contained, making it appropriate to theorize or historicize them within clear-cut regional boundaries. Yet, when it comes to understanding the depictions of artists Nishida and Merleau-Ponty articulate, it is not so easy to interpret their theoretical works as characteristic of their respective traditions. Nishida arrives at his vision of the artist, in part, by going beyond Eastern thought and adopting Western concepts and terminology. Meanwhile, Merleau-Ponty also intended to break with conventions in his own Western tradition, and although he did not engage significantly with East Asian thought, he proffers conceptions of artistic expression that are highly idiosyncratic within his Western heritage while fitting well with Eastern orientations for theorizing artworks. Transcending founding principles of their traditions, Nishida and Merleau-Ponty arrive at intriguing common grounds, albeit from opposite directions. In placing these two philosophers in dialogue, we have a unique possibility for considering artistic expression and philosophy in an inter-cultural context. In this chapter, I continue to explore their ontologies of *Basho* and flesh while beginning to include several artists in the dialogue.

In line with my overarching effort to develop an ontological account of motion, perception, and expression, this chapter examines these not as human activities but as dynamic features of a general motor-perceptual fabric in which the body is interwoven. To do so requires a significant expansion of our conception of the body. Moreover, it requires challenging the idea that casts space between bodies as a *non-perceptual* interval. One of the most significant impediments to rethinking space is a positivist conception of light. By conceiving of light's relation to the body within the ontology of negation I have been developing, we see that light not only enables vision but also limits it in important ways. Yes, vision is our most vivid sensory modality, and only through it do we uncover the amazing detail of the macroscopic, the microscopic, and everything in between. We achieve an astonishing intimacy with the world, objects, other bodies, and our own bodies through light-based perception. But, we have to ask, why does light not distort our access to the world the way other mediums do? Why does it not get in the way and limit the body's expansion throughout the perceptual fabric? Ultimately, we must ask, is light always non-obstructive? With few exceptions,[1] light has been treated as a fully transparent medium, not itself discernible, only rendering things it illuminates visible. All of these issues raise pertinent questions regarding the representational model and positivist assumptions for understanding light. When considering our visual relation to objects, we do not often ask about the prior relation of the body to light. Yet, a central preoccupation of this chapter is to show that there are ways in which our relation to light is not unlike the hand's relation to a paintbrush or the blind person's relation to the world through her cane. Nishida and Merleau-Ponty use these examples to go beyond subject–object metaphysics to describe the body's relation to tools. This chapter endeavors to expand these examples to produce a similar picture regarding the body's relation to light. What I find, counter to most philosophies, psychology, science, and even counter to Merleau-Ponty and Nishida, is that light is not an ever-transparent medium. Articulating the limits of light-based vision allows us to expand the limits of the body, its motion and perception.

Neither Nishida nor Merleau-Ponty dwell to a large extent on the subject of light, but I would like to develop some of the intriguing remarks they do make by reading these in tandem with two themes about which they have a great deal to say, namely (1) the body's relation to tools, and (2) the ambiguity of the visual and the tactile. Interpreting their analysis of light alongside these themes affords a much wider conception of the body whereby its motion, perception, and expression pervades the entirety of flesh and *Basho*, where part of that expansion is enabled by light. This expansion is crucial since one impediment to grasping their perceptual ontologies is that representational assumptions lead us to think of the space between subject and object as carrying sense data while itself remaining a non-perceptual medium. On my reading, neither Nishida nor Merleau-Ponty entirely avoid this fate, because of not having maintained a thoroughgoing ontology of negation regarding light. Nevertheless, there are resources in their philosophies, which if applied to this question of light, can, I believe,

---

1. In the Cave Allegory in Plato's *Republic*, when the prisoner is first freed and sees the fire in the cave the light hurts his eyes and does not allow him to see the objects it illuminates. Later, upon emerging from the cave the sun's light obstructs his sight: "Suppose . . . that someone should drag him . . . by force, up the rough ascent, the steep way up, and never stop until he could drag him out into the light of the sun. The prisoner would be angry and in pain, and this would only worsen when the radiant light of the sun overwhelms his eyes and blinds him" (*Republic*, Book VII).

establish all space as perceptual without any non-perceptual space intervening between bodies. To establish *Basho* and flesh as thoroughly perceptual (and later, motor-perceptual), this space between must be accounted for as part of an underlying ontological fabric: not as a non-perceptual interval or gap, but as a continuity of discontinuity similar to chiasm, *ma* (間), and *kire* (切). Light is one key for realizing the full implications of flesh and *Basho* whereby they are fabrics out of which the body is woven. A second major point I establish in this chapter is that when we understand light within the texture of mutual negation between bodies, our idea of touch undergoes an expansion. Touch obtains at a much greater distance than the outer reaches of the body. It manifests not only at the end of the blind person's cane or painter's brush—a claim explicit in both Nishida and Merleau-Ponty—but at the distal end of one's visual reach—a claim implicit in their writings, which I seek to develop in this chapter.

REPRESENTATION, OCULARCENTRISM, AND MULTI-PERSPECTIVALISM

Both the Eastern and Western philosophic traditions have a long history of prioritizing the visual. Ancient Greek thought as well as the Indian origins of Mahāyāna Buddhism were, broadly speaking, "ocularcentrist" insofar as vision was the most philosophically and religiously significant of the body's perceptual modalities.[2] When vision-based metaphor reaches the level of a philosophical obsession, this tendency has been referred to as "scoptophilia." Certainly, if we look back throughout Eastern and Western history, until very recently, an overwhelming majority of the most vital aspects of philosophies and religions, the highest truths, the deepest knowledge, understanding, enlightenment, and compassion demanded strengthening, improving, and deepening one's vision.[3] Accompanying the rich visual symbolism in both traditions is an equally rich use of light-related metaphor. To overcome

---

2. See Martin Jay, *Downcast Eyes: The Denigration of Vision in Twentieth-Century French Thought*. And D. M. Levin, *Sites of Vision: The Discursive Construction of Sight in the History of Philosophy*.

3. Various Buddhist terms associate vision and wisdom, including enlightenment as *kenshō* ("to see rightly," "seeing into one's true nature"), "the knowledge and vision (*jiiana-dar-sana*) of the Buddha," the divine eye (*divya-caksus*), the wisdom eye (*jñāna-caksus*), the Buddha eye (*Buddha-caksus*), and the Dharma eye (*Dharma-caksus*), as well as, "having limitless vision" (*Samantadarśin*) and being "one with the universal eye" (*Samantacak*). See David McMahan, *Empty Vision: Metaphor and Visionary Imagery in Mahayana Buddhism*.

philosophic or religious blindness was to "come out of the darkness," to "see the light," to "mirror the truth," to attain en*light*enment, illumination, or luminosity. Nishida himself plays on the ocular and mirror metaphors when speaking of "speculation" (*shisaku* 思索) and "reflection" (*hansei* 反省)." And, to nicely foreshadow the later discussion regarding the proximity of vision and touch, we can cite Dalissier, who writes, "to speculate, then, is to think in closer and closer '*contact*' (*sesshoku* 接触) with absolute nothingness, to '*touch*' (*sawaru* 触る) it in our meditations."[4]

An ocularcentrist bias could, it would seem, lend itself quite well to a study of vision and the visual arts, yet as the central epistemic and sometimes ontological metaphor, it underwrites representational theories of knowledge and perception with potentially hazardous implications. Vision gives what appears to be the most detailed and un-mediated access to the world and its objects, but epistemologies that take it as a metaphor for a specific kind of knowledge also emphasize detached observation, distance, dispassionate reflection, and lead to subject–object metaphysics where truth is understood as "correspondence" between an image in the mind and the separate visual object. Hwa Yol Jung calls this Descartes' "epistemological panopticon."[5] This representational framework and its suppositions regarding distance and separation (*chōriston*) have been linked to destructive attitudes toward the world, objects, and fellow humans, not to mention motivating Eurocentric attitudes. As Elberfeld explains, there are exceptions to ocularcentrist distance-based sensory metaphor in Chinese and Japanese culture where the sense of hearing and even smell have been the dominant sensory modality. These modalities, he explains, "evelop one completely and swallow one" thus eliminating the precarious distance reinforced by visual metaphor and epistemology based thereupon.[6] Ranking vision as the highest of the senses and as the only universal model for knowledge also served as a substantial impediment for intercultural thought where other cultures were understood (most prominently by Hegel) as unable to reach the universality of knowledge allied with the visual. This bias is the foundation for some of Western philosophy's most humiliating moments, where the paragons of the Enlightenment, Hume, Kant, and Hegel, allow overt racism to seep

---

4. Michel Dalissier, "The Idea of the Mirror in Nishida and Dōgen," 120. Emphasis added.

5. Jung, *Transversal Rationality and Intercultural Texts: Essays in Phenomenology and Comparative Philosophy*, 215.

6. Elberfeld, Rolf. "Sensory Dimensions in Intercultural Perspective and the Problem of Modern Media and Technology," 481.

into their projects.[7] One lone voice of dissent was Herder who recognized the potential damage of Enlightenment rationalism and its visual metaphor. Skeptical of how colonialism threatens to level cultural differences, and for the overriding epistemological visual metaphorics, he asks "is the whole body just one big eye?"[8] If the whole body were merely one eye, then that body would always be at an unambiguous distance from the world and its objects, providing little respite from the peril that attends the detached position. Merleau-Ponty and Nishida can, on my reading, offer a way around these dangers by showing that vision is not detached, to see is not to be at a distance from the world or the object, but is what Marjorie Green calls a "distanceless distance."[9] Making the case for this understanding of vision, (which I undertake in the below section, "light as tool") helps us reconceptualize light and its relation to the eye and grasp vision as a kind of touch not unlike the body's way of touching objects and using tools.

While ancient Greek and the philosophies originating from the Indian Mahāyāna tradition lean heavily on vision and light-based metaphors, they are by no means ocularcentrist in the same way. The key difference being that Indian visionary literature and practices were not based on subject–object metaphysics, representational epistemologies, or positivist theories of perception. This explains why Nishida was predisposed to think beyond subject–object metaphysics when taking up the questions of knowledge, perception, and action. It also helps us appreciate the extent to which Merleau-Ponty departs from his Western heritage with his theory of perception.

Studying Nishida and Merleau-Ponty's nonrepresentational approaches to vision discloses the limitations with everyday and many philosophic depictions of vision. Yet, I will advance a line of thinking proposing that

---

7. Hume considered all non-white races as "naturally inferior," Kant declared that black man was "stupid," but of all three, Eurocentric chauvinism is the most systematic in Hegel's project. He dismisses Oriental thought as "immature," never able to attain the rationality associated with sight, always particular, never universal, and thus not partaking in the movement of world history that Western philosophy contributes to because of its ability to attain universal knowledge through pure intellection.

8. J. G. Herder, *J. G. Herder on Social and Political Culture*, 199

9. Green, Marjorie. "The Aesthetic Dialogue of Sartre and Merleau-Ponty" in *The Debate between Sartre and Merleau-Ponty* (1998), 301.

the ocularcentrist problem is not limited, but rather stems from positivist assumptions regarding light. In this chapter, I therefore seek to expand upon Nishida and Merleau-Ponty's conceptions of vision and the body to reveal aspects of their philosophies that provide a new understanding of light and its relation to the body.

Multi-Perspectival Perception

Several twentieth-century philosophers have contributed to the project of rethinking the body's relation to the world. But, artists might have started earlier and went farther not just in considering perception beyond representational positivity, but also in experimenting with ways of representing the nonrepresentational. The artists I consider in this chapter, starting with Raphael and Guo Xi, work beyond assumptions philosophers continue to grapple with. One of their techniques is to explore the multi-perspectival aspects of vision.

While Cézanne is Merleau-Ponty's exemplar because he signals a path beyond representational conventions, his expressive practice is particularly illuminating concerning motion and will enter the discussion in the following chapter on motor-perception. To begin the dialogue on multi-perspectivalism, I consider two artworks, Guo Xi's *Early Spring* (早春图) and Raphael's *The Three Graces* (*Le Tre Grazie*), so as to draw a contrast between some of the Eastern and Western philosophical suppositions about perception and their application in art practice. Although both artists utilize multi-perspectival strategies to transgress the limits of representationalism and positivism, the different philosophical principles underlying those attempts result in varying levels of success.

The Three Graces

Let us begin by looking at Greek conceptions of perception to appreciate how Merleau-Ponty challenges aspects of his Western philosophical heritage. Neither Plato nor Aristotle argued explicitly for a "representational" theory, but both set Western philosophy on that path for thinking about perception. Plato's understanding of vision as derived from his epistemology and metaphysics is particularly relevant for appreciating how bodies have been represented in the Western world. According to him, true knowledge of an entity was non-spatial; that is, not knowledge of an object from a single perspective, but a view, in a sense, from everywhere and nowhere. For

Figure 2.1. Raphael, *The Three Graces*, 1505. Musée Condé, Chantilly, France.

Plato, to know something is to know its form, and Platonic forms are non-perspectival, which, for obvious reasons, precludes bodily vision as a source of knowledge. The type of thinking that assumes such a non-perspectival position Merleau-Ponty called *pensée de survol* "high-altitude thinking"; one of Western philosophy's longest standing blunders. Nevertheless, theoretical contemplation was for Plato a disembodied practice. To know reality the philosopher must, as repeated throughout the *Republic*, become blind to the material world. Philosophic education is a "turning around" of the soul from "a day that is like night" where they learn to look toward "the true light of day" (521c), which is the vision of the other world of forms. The philosopher must return to the cave and habituate himself to the way of seeing there, but the soul's eye is "destroyed and blinded by [non-theoretical] pursuits" (527e). The philosopher's kind of "vision" was, therefore, not bodily vision at all. To know something is to know it through *theoria* or theoretical "vision," which is to overcome the body's limited perspective and to "see" without spatial, visual, or bodily limitation. This gives rise to what Hans Jonas calls a "spectatorial distance," which interprets the world as made of fixed objective things observable for detached, theoretical contemplation; in effect, giving rise to subject–object dualism.[10] Nietzsche will later develop his perspectivism in direct contrast to this "spectator" theory of knowledge and its non-perspectival, non-bodily assumptions.[11] We should note, however, that while Platonic ideas of vision filtered down, giving rise to modern representational metaphysics, there are intriguing and overlooked exceptions in Plato's and Aristotle's accounts of perception that are quite at odds with the representational model.[12]

---

10. See Martin Jay (1994) and David Levin (1999) on the distancing and objectifying tendencies of ocularcentrist metaphysics.

11. In book three of *Genealogy of Morality* Nietzsche warns us to be on guard against thinking of "an eye that is completely unthinkable, an eye turned in no particular direction, in which the active and interpreting forces, through which alone seeing becomes seeing something, are supposed to be lacking; these always demand of the eye an absurdity and a nonsense. There is only a perspective seeing, only a perspective 'knowing' . . . But to eliminate the will altogether, to suspect each and every affect, supposing we were capable of this—what would that mean but to castrate the intellect?" Friedrich Nietzsche, *On the Genealogy of Morals*, 119.

12. In his *Theatetus*, Plato develops his "activist" theory of perception where vision is considered with such vividness and complexity, so bound up as an essential way of world-revealing that he struggles to avoid the unacceptable conclusion that knowledge could be perception. Far from conceiving perception as the mere passive reception of sensory data, his activist model has it that vision extends out through the eyes into the perceptual field to meet the object. Perception is a "birth" not in the head, but at the juncture of the emanations arising from both the perceived object and perceiving subject (156 a–e, 160 a–b.). This model put forth in the *Theatetus*, also called an "emission" theory of vision, holds that it is not just the fire outside the head that is responsible for vision but that there is fire inside the eyes themselves that goes out to meet the world. This notion of perception is far removed from the modern empiricists' representational assumptions, in that, like Merleau-Ponty and Nishida, Plato did not conceive of perception as the reception of mere sensory data, but involved the body extending into the visual world. In *Timaeus*, Plato refers to one's "light-bearing eyes," which contain a "pure fire which is akin to the light of day" (45b) that "[f]lows through the eyes in a smooth and dense stream . . . and whenever the stream of vision is surrounded by daylight, it flows out like unto like, and by coalescing with this it forms a single body along the eyes' visual path, wherever the fire which streams out from within makes contact with that which meets it from without" (45c–d). In Plato's theory one does not simply receive light but sends light contained in the eye beyond the boundaries of the body into the world to meet the objects in the world. When one's own visual light contacts things in the world, it "distributes the motions of every object." I am indebted to Paul Bogaard for advising on these topics. See A. W. Nightingale, *Spectacles of Truth in Classical Greek Philosophy: Theoria in Its Cultural Context* and McMahan, *Empty Vision: Metaphor and Visionary Imagery in Mahayana Buddhism*.

Throughout Western art history, several important figures have taken on representational assumptions and, like Plato, might have implicitly conceived of the body's situated visual perspective as deficient. Cubism is one of the most well-known examples. Artists such as Picasso, Braque, and Léger fragmented the object to achieve a better representation of a thing or person by incorporating additional perspectives. Their technique tells us something very interesting about the understanding of vision that governs their experiments. To break up the object is, at least implicitly, to assume that multiple perspectives were not part of normal situated vision. This implies that the multi-perspectival was *achieved*, rather than *given* in the original perception. (As we turn to Guo Xi in the following section, we see how his mode of depiction and the principles that inform it understand the multi-perspectival as *given* in normal vision.) It is unlikely that artists such as the Cubists wanted to demote the body's vision to an inferior status to prioritize the mind's way of seeing, the opposite is more likely the case. Yet, they might have been perpetuating certain positivist and uni-perspectival assumptions about vision that run counter to their artistic aims.

Prior to Cubism, several Western artists also sought to go beyond the uni-perspectival. But, instead of breaking up and fragmenting the object, these artists multiplied it. They did not depict a single body fragmented into several perspectives but represented several non-fragmented bodies. This is the case with the "*Three Graces*" motif. As classical learning reemerged in the Renaissance, theoreticians debated and artists held competitions (*paragone*) where they vied to determine which medium (sculpture or painting) offered the best representation of the body, judged primarily on how many different points of view could be represented. In this period, the *Three Graces* motif became pervasive in art practice. Although its exact origins are unknown, one of the earliest examples is Raphael's (figure 2.1). This particular arrangement of bodies in space—employed by, among others, Boccioni, Rubens, Cranach, Botticelli, Canova, and Rodin—intends to overcome the poverty of a single and incomplete point of view. There is a gesture here beyond positivism. Sculptures or paintings that use this motif do not depict three different people. Yes, three bodies do appear, yet they are, in a sense, a single body modulated in space to offer three different perspectives. The Graces stand together but in various angles such that any one perspective an onlooker takes transcends the singularity of their vantage point offering a more comprehensive grasp of the body being depicted. An onlooker standing in any position can see not only the front of the torso, its flesh, and curves, but also how these relate to the tightness of muscles in the back, the weight bearing on the skeleture, and the flexing tendons in the neck and legs. The viewer can stand face-to-face meeting one of the body's gazes head-on, while from the same position seeing another body from profile staring out at a distant onlooker. The *Three Graces* technique was used in many important works of art, and still is to this day, yet the understanding of perception informing the experiments remains tied to representational assumptions, which might not exploit the full breadth of human perception as Nishida, Merleau-Ponty, or Guo Xi have. The "Graces" motif is limited, to a great extent, because it remains positivist because it does not consider the perceptual object within the context of negation. Thus, its positivist and representational conventions imply that situated vision is uni-perspectival and the multi-perspectival is available only by multiplying the object.

The *Three Graces* arrangement does offer more perspectives on the body being depicted, nevertheless, its assumption regarding perception falls short of multi-perspectival vision as articulated by later philosophers and artists. The painter or sculptor using this motif wants multiple perspectives, yet, in triplicating the body, the underlying theory of vision actually remains uni-perspectival. That is, they believe that one must break up or multiply the body to *achieve* multiple perspectives. Vision is not multi-perspectival, they must have thought, but scenes and objects can be manipulated to approximate the effect. The additional perspectives are not *given* in the singular vantage point, but are achieved by adding different vantage points. Multiple perspectives are the result of a trick. There is no evidence the artist thought normal vision was multi-perspectival. In fact, the technique asserts the opposite. The *Three Graces* realizes extra perspectives by accumulating singular, discrete, positive, uni-perspectival views. Instead of finding the many perspectives within the single vantage point—as we will see with Nishida and Merleau-Ponty as well as Guo Xi—the *Three Graces* gives multiple perspectives through many vantage points. Its metaphysics of vision, therefore, remains uni-perspectival according to positivist and representational assumptions. In this case, the visible is in no way lined by the invisible; instead it is beside it, and there is, therefore, no ambiguity between the seen and the unseen that would allow us to think of the artist, the artwork, or the perception that unites them as part of a common perceptual fabric.

Guo Xi: Angle of Totality

In the Mayāyāna Buddhist tradition, and in Daoist philosophy, there are similar attempts to go beyond uni-perspectival vision in philosophy and art, but the theoretical foundations of those efforts differed significantly from

Western techniques. Eastern intellectual and aesthetic traditions developed fascinating means for creating artworks and theorizing about them beyond representational positivism. In Nishida's case, unlike Merleau-Ponty, to think along nonrepresentational lines did not require rejecting a tradition of aesthetic theory that had conceived of perception otherwise. The Buddhist tradition and its Chinese roots, which formed the background for Nishida's thinking, inspired art movements that grasped the various ambiguities between the visible and the invisible, interpreting multi-perspectival vision in a different way than those who employed the *Three Graces* experiment.

To explore the aesthetic principles of Zen Buddhism influencing Nishida's thinking, it is worth recalling the Chinese roots of Zen, and particularly the Daoist influence on Zen aesthetics. Daoism was a strong influence of Zen, and one of the main frameworks for the Chinese landscape painters who Japanese artists would emulate. China had an enormous and lasting impact on all areas of Japanese artistic, philosophical, political, and religious life. As late as the Japanese Muromachi Period (1333–1573), Chinese painting techniques and aesthetic principles still set the standard by which Japanese artists would learn. The influence of the greatest master of landscape painting, Guo Xi (郭熙) (c. 1020–c. 1090), is felt throughout China and Japan. His *Early Spring* (早春图) (figure 2.2) is arguably the masterpiece of Chinese landscape painting. Daoist aesthetic principles—and particularly where they were brought to their highest articulation in the Song Chinese landscape painting tradition—aimed at multi-perspectival depiction. Unlike Platonic and representational attempts, Guo Xi's working principles are much more in line with the understanding of perception developed by Nishida and Merleau-Ponty.

One of Guo Xi's strategies was the "angle of totality," or "floating perspective." This technique depicted the landscape in multiple perspectives not by breaking up or multiplying the object—as the *Three Graces* motif demanded—but by negating it, treating it as a non-object. The painter would not represent the mountains and rivers as though sight were constituted solely by the perspective given through visual data received while standing in one position while painting. Instead, he would depict the landscape as it appeared through time, as it would look to a monk wandering through its paths, a fisherman docked on its banks, a farmer examining the minute features of the ground, or a surveyor taking the perspective of the whole. In his seminal work *The Great Image Has No Form, or The Non-object Through Painting*, Francois Jullien describes this multi-perspectivalism as follows:

Figure 2.2. Guo Xi, *Early Spring*, 1072. National Palace Museum, Beijing, China.

To paint the mountain will be to paint it as a "total" (hun) image, in its plenitude and compossibility: "high-low," "great-small," "turning toward-turning its back," and so on, rather than to paint merely 'three or five mountaintops' scarcely filling the page. . . . To paint is not to apprehend the mountain "in one locale" and from a "single corner." . . . It is to paint the mountain after climbing many a hill and sketching many a varied mountaintop, after having one's fill of hikes and vistas, after letting the infinite forms and resources of the mountain ripen in one's spirit.[13]

Prefiguring Cubism—as well as Merleau-Ponty's critique of the representational understanding of perception—by almost 900 years, Guo Xi already understood that vision was greater than the singular perspective and includes the aspects of multiple vantage points. Guo Xi himself writes, "it is the form of one mountain and, at the same time, of tens and hundreds of mountains . . . A single mountain unites within itself the aspect of several tens or hundreds of mountains."[14] Thus, Guo Xi did not have to fragment or multiply the object to give us additional perspectives. Even from the single vantage point we see many different valences of the landscape because of the ambiguity of positive and negative features, because we do not perceive the landscape as a circumscribed object. Although it comes centuries later, Merleau-Ponty elaborates a similar perceptual logic, explaining that when we see one landscape it does not make us *recall* another which we then import into the present to expand the single into multiple perspectives: "I do not *visualize* anything; all these landscapes are already there in the harmonious sequence and infinite unfolding of their perspectives," writes Merleau-Ponty.[15]

The contrast between Guo Xi and Raphael regarding multi-perspectivalism leads us to further discussion of Nishida and Merleau-Ponty's unorthodox understanding of perception. Although there is a drive toward overcoming a limited singular perspective in the Western-style, Platonic, *Three Graces* attempt as exemplified by Raphael, he could only strive toward his objective by disavowing bodily vision and choosing an arrangement that ignored the full breadth of visual experience. Raphael denies the body's situatedness

---

13. Francois Jullien, *The Great Image Has No Form, or on the Nonobject through Painting*, 55.
14. Ibid., 3.
15. Merleau-Ponty, *Phenomenology of Perception*, 384.

through his technique. The Eastern attempt, as exemplified by Guo Xi, also goes beyond the uni-perspectival, yet it does so by affirming the body, its perception, and its spatial situatedness. The difference is essential: The *Three Graces* is a multi-perspectival *technique* for representation. It wants to expand the uni-perspectival to the multi-perspectival. On the other hand, with the "angle of totality" approach, the painter immerses himself in the visual world that is originally multi-perspectival. (To foreshadow the coming discussion, what he finds is not simply a perceptual, but a motor-perceptual complexity.) The former is positivist, whereas the latter is in line with an account of perception that includes negation and sees the ambiguity between the visible and invisible. Guo Xi is thus much closer to the account of perception in both Nishida's and Merleau-Ponty's philosophies. As we delve further into this account, considering Merleau-Ponty's "depth" and Nishida's distinction between "internal perception" and "external perception," we find a theoretical explanation disclosing all perception as multi-perspectival.

"Dragon Veins": The Visible and Invisible in Daoism

As we have seen with the *Three Graces* motif, if one wants to enable a multi-perspectival experience but remains tied to a positivist framework that assumes vision is originally given as uni-perspectival, that attempt involves adding more visible to the visible. If vision were reducible to positive visual data, the only way to truly expand one's perspective would be to add other positive visual streams from other sources depicting other perspectives. Since this is impossible in strictly human vision, it seems that our only way to go beyond the uni-perspectival is by positivist tricks that attempt to *simulate* multi-perspectivalism. Merleau-Ponty and Nishida are able to think beyond these limitations and expand perspectives not by adding more of the positively visible, but by expanding it through the negative and the invisible, which both thinkers refer to as "lining" the visible. Such an expansion is not attained by adding more positive visual streams, angles, or sense data to the visible; rather, "the hallmark of the visible is to have a lining of invisibility . . . which it makes present as a certain absence."[16] Merleau-Ponty makes this expansion with his concept "depth" (*profondeur*), while Nishida makes a similar move through the ambiguity he discerns between "internal perception" (*naibu chikaku* 内部知覚) and "external perception" (*gaibu chikaku* 外部知覚), which he combines

---

16. Merleau-Ponty, "Eye and Mind," 147.

with the connecting-separating *soku* term to give us "internal perception-*soku*-external perception" (*naibu chikaku soku gaibu chikaku* 内部知覚即外部知覚).

Before looking at these concepts of Nishida's in more depth, let us consider a Daoist treatment of the relation between the visible and invisible. Both Nishida and Merleau-Ponty are, on this matter, much more in line with Daoist principles than they are with the Platonic tradition, and their thinking finds more in common with the works of Chinese and Japanese painters such as Guo Xi and Hasegawa than with Cubism or with works employing the *Three Graces* motif. Prefiguring Merleau Ponty's formulation by almost a millennium, Guo Xi demonstrates an appreciation of the complex relation between the visible and the invisible. As Jullien writes, Chinese painters knew long ago that "presence must give way to absence, that the visible turns inside out to become the invisible."[17] Like Merleau-Ponty, Daoist aesthetic principles take the relation between the visible and the invisible not as duality, where one stands beside or opposed to the other, not as visible here and invisible there, but rather as an ambiguous intertwining where the invisible permeates the visible. Jullien writes that Chinese landscape artists

> do not paint distinctive, much less disjunctive, aspects. In reality, they do not paint things to show them better and, by displaying them before our eyes, to bring forth their presence. Rather, they paint them between "there is" and "there is not," present-absent, half-light, half-dark, at once light-at once dark.[18]

This aesthetic orientation toward ambiguous visibility and invisibility is consonant with one of the most basic tenets of Daoist philosophy, derived from the well-known *yin yang* (阴阳) structure and its iconography. Traditional Chinese philosophy, medicine, martial arts, and science are based on this structure, which describes all of nature, as well as the social and political systems that follow its rhythms, as a dynamic and ambiguous relation between presence and absence. The complementary black-and-white forms of the *yin yang* symbol refer to "shadow and light" and seem to suggest duality, or an absolute distinction between presence and absence, light and dark. However, the small dot of the opposing shade in each shape

---

17. Jullien, *The Great Image Has No Form*, 14.
18. Ibid., 4.

de-substantializes that form, negates it, permeates it with its opposite, and sets up an ambiguous dynamic between the two. The white is not simply white, nor is the black exclusively black. The positivity of either shade is interrupted by the presence of their opposites within, but neither sublates them into a higher or more final order. *Yang*, the world's visible features that are bright and present (later in Daoist thought associated with the masculine) were not absolutely opposed to *yin*, the dark, invisible features that are absent (associated with the feminine). Yin and yang are not opposing forces but are in a "complementary opposition" that represents the movement and harmony of nature. As Hans-Georg Moeller writes, "non-presence and presence, belong to each other and depend on one another,"[19] but he explains that this interrelation between opposites does not involve one being more primordial or the causal source of the other: "The relation is not a diachronic chain of causation and origination, but is rather a pattern of synchronicity and co-evolution."[20] Thus, in finding a relation to the visible *within* the invisible, we do not look at one time at one part and another time at another part. The invisible is not beside or behind the visible, but augments the visible from within.

Hasegawa's famous *Pine Trees* (1593) (figure 2.3) is an exceptional work for visualizing the ambiguity between visibility and invisibility postulated in Daoist philosophy. As with the *yin yang* dynamic, the empty parts of the screen should not be thought of as pure absence, invisibility, or negative space, while the trees and branches stand in un-ambiguous presence, visibility and positivity. The fullness (c. *you* 有) is not separate from the emptiness (c. *wu* 無), any more than the emptiness is divided away and remains opposed to the fullness: rather, both "co-evolve" according to a mutual interpenetration and negation. Duality is neither upheld nor entirely overcome. Returning to Jullien, he notes, "presence and absence mingle continually, and that presence, far from aspiring to stand apart from absence, extends further and becomes distilled by virtue of it."[21] Therefore, the painter "does not aspire to immobilize [the landscape] as Being and to determine it as object. He paints it between 'there is' and 'there is not,' *you* and *wu*."[22] To do so is not

---

19. Hans-Georg Moeller, *Daoism Explained: From the Dream of the Butterfly to the Fishnet Allegory*, 26.
20. Ibid., 135.
21. Jullien, *The Great Image Has No Form*, 11.
22. Ibid., 2.

Figure 2.3 (left). Hasegawa Tōhaku, *Pine Trees*, 1595. Tokyo National Museum, Tokyo, Japan.

simply to represent both "there is" (being) on one part of the silk and "there is not" (nothing) on another part. The master painter, "paints his landscape in the tonality of as if, in the mode of appearing-disappearing, at once 'as if there were' and 'as if there were not.'"[23] Similarly, the Chinese landscape painter Shitao is said to capture the moment between "merging-emerging, between being-there and not-being-there."[24] The unity achieved is not "synthetic" in the sense of two perspectives being fused together, but is "daoic" in the sense of retaining the indeterminacy between presence and absence.

There is a great deal more to appreciate in a painting such as Hasegawa's if we refrain from treating it according to positivist assumptions, which describe it by way of its material objectivity and uphold visible-invisible binaries. Painting as Hasegawa did is to create a non-object, which through its negating-negated availability—to itself and to us—is continuous with the perceptual fabric in which it adheres and in which we see it. To experience this work is not to have one's sight stopped at its surface as though vision and what it palpates were of a different substance: as though vision were exhaustively explained by sense data reflecting off the painting's surface. To engage with this painting is to extend perception into and throughout its depth and all of its valences of co-constitution. In Ghilardi's words, "the onlooker must merge in the image, completing the empty spaces, making it

---

23. Ibid., 8.
24. Ghilardi, *The Line of the Arch*, 101.

Figure 2.3 (right). Hasegawa Tōhaku, *Pine Trees*, 1595. Tokyo National Museum, Tokyo, Japan.

a lively element of nature itself, 'between' visible and invisible."[25] Or as the art historian Yukio Lippit remarks, "the viewer is forced to meet the image halfway in order to complete it."[26] Within a positivist framework, it would be quite understandable to scoff at such language, thus "merging" with the image could be at most metaphorical. Yet, in an ontology of negation—a framework that can actually explain perceptual encounter—one cannot perceive anything without a reciprocal merging that negates subject and object.

To return to Möller's insight regarding Daoism, the important point to keep in mind is that the invisible is not beside, before, or behind the visible. When considering the provocative empty spaces of Hasegawa's painting, one is not seeing merely the invisible or the negative, while the visible and positive are the other areas covered with ink. We do not merge with the empty ink-less regions while the ink-filled areas obstruct our attempts to assimilate into the image's fibers. This would be to uphold too stable of a binary between the negative and positive, presence and absence. What is negative does not simply separate the positive forms, but connects to the degree that it divides. Hasegawa's empty spaces are better understood according to the idea of space as *ma* (間) and the aesthetic principle of cut-continuance (*kire-tsuzuki* 切れ続き), both of which instantiate Nishida's idea of continuous-discontinuity and Merleau-Ponty's "distanceless distance,"

---

25. Ibid., 99.
26. Lippit, "Of Modes and Manners in Japanese Ink Painting," 56.

to be discussed below. As with the black and white of the *yin yang* symbol, the visible and the invisible are not binaries sitting side by side, mutually excluding the other; they intertwine and mutually penetrate each other. The dramatic negative spaces of his "Pine Trees" might appear circumscribable, but the negativity in Hasegawa's painting permeates the entire work. The areas painted, the pine trees themselves are half way between determinacy and indeterminacy, and as such our perceptual encounter with them is enabled.

In the Chinese tradition this invisible aspect, often taken to be the dimension that imparts a wondrous feeling to the observer, was known as the painting's "Dragon veins" (龙脉 *lung mo*). This term had a straightforward geophysical meaning, referring to the various articulations of peaks that ran along the upper ridge of mountain ranges forming vein-like patterns. Dragon metaphor was commonly used to describe the lay of the land. A typical feature of the Chinese painting tradition is that almost all aspects of the natural world, be it specific tree branches, a bird's wing, bamboo leaves, or the various ways water takes shape in rivers, streams, or waterfalls, all of their minute configurations were codified and specific brush techniques developed for rendering them properly. This was, of course, especially true for mountains, which were sacred spaces of Buddhist worship and among the most important elements of landscape painting. Thus, the terrain of different mountain formations suggested an "emerging dragon," "receding dragon," "crouching dragon," "prosperity dragon," etc., and each had laws dictating how they should be painted as per the conventions of the various schools.

For our discussion, the important use of the term "dragon veins" was the one that referred to the invisible internal relations that bound the elements of a painting together. "Dragon veins" were not only the physical patterns of mountains, but also the web of aesthetic interdependence that straddled the visible and the invisible. Thus, Chinese painters and the Japanese who emulated them strove to capture the vitality of the landscape by attending to this aspect that weaves together the forms of the visible world without itself being visible. Yet, just as *yin* is never without *yang*, these veins cannot be pure invisibility because if there were no visible forms, no positivity in a work, there would be nothing to bind. Conversely, if the veins were fully visible, the painter would forfeit painting at the limit of "there is and there is not," and settle for "there is," thus losing the generativity of the identity of opposites. When a landscape painting comes to life, the Chinese claim that "the dragon veins have been stretched properly," and a painting thus has the "cohesive strength which draws the observer irresistibly into the depths of the painting."²⁷ When stretched properly, a work becomes a magical perceptual phenomenon not just to behold but also to merge with through perceptual negation.

If I can recall my earlier note, I mentioned that the movement from this chapter to the next involves proceeding from the perceptual to the motor-perceptual. As we progress, we see that the notion of "dragon veins" helps facilitate that advance because it actually has significance not just for vision but also for motion. When the artist is searching for the veins, she is not simply looking to depict something that the observer will later enjoy through *perceptual* engagement, but is searching for an invisible pull within the landscape that will move the sensorimotor body and solicit the artist's gestures while painting and the viewer's body while beholding their work.

———◆———

At this point in the discussion, one might like to ask, if all objects are perceived with the reversibility of the visible and the invisible and are continuous with a single ontological fabric, why is a painting better than any other object at exhibiting these features? Certainly, both Nishida and Merleau-Ponty would claim that paintings are an especially good site for disclosing our perceptual relation with the world, yet this leaves an important question open. How is it that some artists are better than others at engaging with the visual world such that they can make a work of art that becomes expedient for showing our body's continuity with flesh or *Basho*? It is interesting to note that artworks that seek to represent the world accurately, naturalistic or hyper-realistic works that purport to depict the world so perfectly do not necessarily make this continuity palpable. An issue I consider in chapter 4 when discussing "coherent deformation" relates to naturalistic or hyper-realistic works, which purport to depict the world so perfectly yet are perhaps not good at exhibiting the discontinuous-continuity we are looking for. That discussion is yet to come, but at this point we can slightly amend the above question: in what follows we will ask, how does the artist gear into the perceptual fabric such that her body interweaves and is guided by its motions thus producing works that are *continuously-discontinuous with* but do not *represent* the world? Soon, this question will move the study beyond the perceptual to the motor-perceptual, bringing us closer to thinking of a bodily form of faith.

---

27. van Briessen, *Way of the Brush*, 57.

Merleau-Ponty: Multi-Perspectivalism and "Depth"

As mentioned in the previous chapter, a major obstacle in conceiving of a general perceptual fabric is that it is much easier to understand consciousness as negated than it is to grasp how an object could be negated. However, an illuminating passage from Merleau-Ponty's early work *The Phenomenology of Perception* shows how he believes that multi-perspectival vision obtains not just between the perspective of humans, but also between the perspective objects have on the world and on us.

> When I look at the lamp on my table, I attribute to it not only the qualities visible from where I am, but also those which the chimney, the walls, the table can "see"; but back of my lamp is nothing but the face which it "shows" to the chimney. I can therefore see an object insofar as objects form a system or a world, and insofar as each one treats the others round it as spectators of its hidden aspects and as guarantee of the permanence of those aspects. Any seeing of an object by me is instantaneously reiterated among all those objects in the world which are apprehended as co-existent, because each of them is all that the others "see" of it. Our previous formula must therefore be modified; the house itself is not the house seen from nowhere, but the house seen from everywhere. The completed object is translucent, being shot through from all sides by an infinite number of present scrutinies, which intersect in its depths leaving nothing hidden . . .
>
> To see is to enter a universe of beings, which display themselves, and they would not do this if they could not be hidden behind each other or behind me. In other words: to look at an object is to inhabit it, and from this habitation to grasp all things in terms of the aspect which they present to it. But insofar as I see those things too, they remain abodes open to my gaze, and, being potentially lodged in them, I already perceive from various angles the central object of my present vision. Thus every object is the mirror of all others.[28]

While the term "depth" (*profondeur*) is not thematized extensively in his early work, it grows into a central concept by the time Merleau-Ponty composes his last writings. In those works, Merleau-Ponty develops his

---

28. Merleau-Ponty, *Phenomenology of Perception*, 79.

concept of "Depth" primarily regarding a lived form of spatiality, yet at this time multi-perspectival reversibility is also becoming an increasingly central feature of his ontology. While most scholarship on this concept focuses on the account of space, I consider "Depth" regarding its implications for a form of multi-perspectival vision. As Merleau-Ponty writes, "Depth" is "either nothing, or else it is my participation in a Being without restriction, first and foremost a participation in the being of space beyond every particular point of view."[29]

Vision becomes multi-perspectival because the vantage point of others insinuate into our own, with that vantage point echoing throughout objects in the visual fabric. By contrast, the representational model would only consider vision in terms of how positive data enters our own *single* perceptual openness. Yet, for Merleau-Ponty, "The other's gaze on things is a *second openness*."[30] While we see bodies or objects inflected by the other's point of view, we do not have to imagine that perspective, as though we needed to have a second visual input added to our own. The multi-perspectival given by "Depth" does not arrive by adding additional representations to our own. The other's or the object's perspective is *representationally absent*; nevertheless, it counts in our perception. I do not receive the data that reaches your eyes, but if we are both looking at an object, your thoughts, desires, and emotions factor in to how I see it. If you are starving and I am full, the apple we both see looks different to both of us. Further, my own distance to the apple would also look different depending on our relative proximities to it. If I am within easy reach, the perceived distance between you and the apple will be "lined" with a sense of urgency because it is inflected by your perception of my closer proximity. My vision is impacted by the other's perspective, despite that perspective being representationally absent, or invisible to me, and I likewise impact the vision of others. "The invisible of my body can invest its psychic energy in the other bodies I see. Hence my body can include elements drawn from the body of another, just as my substance passes into them; man is a mirror for man."[31] To signal our later discussion, Merleau-Ponty writes that this fact of our "having access to the very world the others perceive" is the other "certitude of the perceptual faith."[32]

---

29. Merleau-Ponty, "Eye and Mind," 134.
30. Merleau-Ponty, *The Visible and the Invisible*, 59. Emphasis added.
31. Merleau-Ponty, "Eye and Mind," 130.
32. Merleau-Ponty, *The Visible and the Invisible*, 57.

Vision is never entirely my own, nor another's. As sighted beings, we are woven into a plenum where vision is dispersed throughout, not localizable in a discrete visual entity. What I see is always co-constituted through self-other, self-object, self-world perceptual negations resulting in the ambiguity of the visible and the invisible. Merleau-Ponty alludes to this ambiguity when in the same paragraph in *The Visible and the Invisible*, he describes perception as having an "anonymity innate to Myself" (*anonymat inné de Moi-même*) as well as a "fundamental narcissism" (*narcissisme fundamental*).[33] One never encounters a pure and simple other, because according to the logic of chiasmatic negation, not only does the other enter my consciousness by way of the negation I have for him, a place where I am non-self, a place of alterity where I am absent and *anonymous* to myself, but the other's body is also disclosed with a perceptual opening in which my own body abides: a negation where I invest their body with my own *narcissistic* perception. "Thus since the seer is caught up in what he sees, it is still himself he sees: there is a fundamental narcissism of all vision."[34] The ambiguity of narcissism and anonymity means one never simply sees: seeing is always implicated in being-seen, thus Merleau-Ponty refers to human vision as "seeing-seen." This ambiguity is true both of our encounter with other perceptual beings, and of our perception of things. Later in his last work, Merleau-Ponty describes how the artist feels a reversible anonymity and narcissism in relation to the object they paint.

> And thus, for the same reason, the vision he exercises, he also undergoes from the things, such that, as many painters have said, I feel myself looked at by the things, my activity is equally passivity—which is the second and more profound sense of the narcissism: not to see in the outside, as the others see it, the contour of a body one inhabits, but especially to be seen by the outside, to exist within it, to emigrate into it, to be seduced, captivated, alienated by the phantom, so that the seer and the visible reciprocate one another and we no longer know which sees and which is seen. It is this Visibility; this generality of the Sensible in itself, this anonymity innate to myself that we

---

33. Ibid., 139; *Le Visible et L'invisible: Suivi De Notes De Travail*, Collection Tel 36, 181.
34. Merleau-Ponty, *The Visible and the Invisible*, 139.

have previously called flesh, and one knows there is no name in traditional philosophy to designate it.³⁵

The notion of flesh goes beyond conceptualizing things as confined to their material objectivity and perception reduced to sensory data; it also transcends the confines of positivism toward a negated non-object. That is to say, the object is not solid and positive, but "shot through from all sides"; not a closed off terminus of my vision but "abodes open to my gaze"; I do not stand over-against objects but am "potentially lodged in them" and thus "perceive from various angles the central object of my present vision."³⁶ Once again, this language could easily be taken as indulgent according to a theory of perception constrained by positivist and representational assumptions, yet reads as a straightforward description of perception in a context of negation, where both the perceive subject and object relate by way of their shared indeterminacy.

Time and Negation I: Ecstatic Temporality

Merleau-Ponty does not elaborate to a great extent on the possible connections between his theory of time and negation, yet in a working note in *The Visible and the Invisible* where he ruminates on his concept "*Stiftung*," he writes that we must understand "time as Chiasm," chiasm being a structure we have already explored for its character of mutual negation. In his early work he even uses the chiasmatic grammatical structure to refer to time's relation to the self: "We must understand time as the subject and the subject as time."³⁷ The self is not in time as an object is in a container, nor do the different temporal orders follow each other in an unambiguous succession: Merleau-Ponty writes that "past and present are *Ineinander*, each *enveloping-enveloped*—and that itself is the flesh."³⁸ Time is not an interval that separates events. Similar to the dividing-connecting dynamics of *ma* (間) and *kire* (切), primordial temporality "holds [events] together while keeping them apart,"³⁹ writes Merleau-Ponty. Time moves by way of a

---

35. Ibid.
36. Merleau-Ponty, *Phenomenology of Perception*, 79.
37. Ibid., 490.
38. Merleau-Ponty, *The Visible and the Invisible*, 268. Emphasis added
39. Merleau-Ponty, *Phenomenology of Perception*, 490.

continuous-discontinuity between temporal orders. Grasping the movement of time as enabled by such a chiasmatic temporal negation affords greater expansion of vision as multi-perspectival.

In further comparing Merleau-Ponty and Nishida, it becomes evident that part of the multi-perspectival aspect of vision they argue for follows from their conception of time's passing as enabled by mutual negation. Not only does perception have a spatial depth whereby vision is multi-perspectival, but it also has a temporal depth that is chiasmatically ambiguous, continuously-discontinuous among the past, present, and future.

One might attempt to explain away the complexity of a multi-perspectival depth by asserting that the perceptual object is in fact not temporally negated. The argument could be that multiple perspectives come from one's remembering past experiences and importing them into present consciousness. I know what it felt like to be burned by a candle in the past so I impute those feelings to my present experience of fire. The important thing to keep in mind—and in this sense both Nishida and Merleau-Ponty follow Husserl—is that there is a temporal "horizon" to all experience, which inflects the present with the past and future without having to actively recall extraneous temporal orders into present consciousness. We do not add one onto the other. The present is originally disclosed with a horizon that includes past experiences and expectations for the future. This is Husserl's "ecstatic time consciousness," which is taken up by Merleau-Ponty:

> [T]he object is seen at all times as it is seen from all directions and by the same means, namely the structure imposed by a horizon. The present still holds on to the immediate past without positing it as an object, and since the immediate past similarly holds its immediate predecessor, past time is wholly collected up and grasped in the present.[40]

The "horizon of intentionality" is not *re*-presented or re-called into consciousness in order to gain a fuller multi-perspectival picture of what initially hits the eye as a single perspective. Perception originally embraces multiple vantage points, not as a concatenation of previously disparate moments of experience. Visual data are not simply given, with the multi-perspectival being a later construction. It is the other way around: the multi-perspectival

---

40. Ibid., 80.

is given, is the original perception, and the single perspective is what we get when we pull apart the original unity through acts of cognition and abstraction. The negated aspects of perception are not supplementary or brought in from outside; they are the horizons of the original perception.[41] Those who employ the *Three Graces* motif would not, it would seem, assume this form of temporality regarding perception. It is not enough for them that the past and future inflect one's present vision. In adding additional bodies in various perspectives they tacitly cut the temporal horizon away from the present that would otherwise instantiate that moment as multi-perspectival.

Husserl's phenomenological account of time inspired Merleau-Ponty's own work on temporality, and, in addition, it also proves useful in explaining parts of Nishida's approach to time. For Husserl, intentional objects are perceived with what he referred to as their "retended" past and "protended" future.[42] When we view an object, see a body in motion, or hear a song, we intend it in terms of what it has been and what it will be. The positive sensory data received in the present comes "lined" with this temporal horizon. Therefore, the perspective I take on any object includes my own plus other perspectives I have had or might have in the future. If I have lost the race to the apple in the past, my distance to it will be tempered by this retended past. Likewise, if I have not eaten all day, the speed of my movements quicken where they are inflected by the anticipated hunger that comes into my present motions by way of the protended future.

According to Husserl, there is no unambiguous, pure present. Present time consciousness—what he calls "primal impression"—is always constituted by the "horizon" of temporality. The point I would like to underscore is that this horizon is independent of any willful reflective acts such as remembering or anticipating. There is no denying that we *can* reflect on the past through acts of remembrance, or on the future through acts of anticipation, projection, and imagining, but these are acts of reflection. Husserl sees a different relation between the temporal orders, which obtains even when one is not reflecting on the past or the future. The key point here is that

---

41. Brook Ziporyn has a helpful elaboration of this point relative to conceptions of multi-perspectivalism in Merleau-Ponty and Tiantai Buddhism. He writes: "these non-X elements which are present here as X are revealed simply by closer attention to X itself; they are not brought in from outside." Ziporyn, "How the Tree Sees Me: Sentience and Insentience in Tiantai and Merleau-Ponty," 63.

42. Husserl, Edmund, *On the Phenomenology of the Consciousness of Internal Time (1893–1917)*. Trans. John B. Brough. Dordrecht: Kluwer. Sec. 40.

retention and protention are not willed acts. Merleau-Ponty elaborates on this point in his *Phenomenology of Perception*.

> It is particularly true that my present vision is not restricted to what my visual field actually presents to me, for the next room, the landscape behind that hill and the inside or the back of that object are not recalled or represented. My point of view is for me not so much a limitation of my experience as a way I have of infiltrating into the world in its entirety.[43]

We do not need to will retention or protention, as though there were a pure present accessible to experience when one is not actively reflecting on the past or the future. The "primordial now" has a horizon and internal reference before and after itself. As such, the present is, in a sense, outside or beyond itself: the present is "ecstatic," literally "standing outside itself" as the etymology of this term suggests.[44] (We might overcome the "triplification" problem with the *Three Graces* motif if we take it as depicting a single body in a temporally ecstatic iteration. But then, it is still *displaying* ecstatic temporality rather than being satisfied with instantiating it.) This ecstatic present, with its horizon of temporality, is the basic unit of time consciousness. Husserl thus reverses the conventional assumption: it is not through willful, reflective acts that we expand the present by adding the past and future; rather, it is through such acts that we subtract the horizon of past and future forming an original part of the ecstatic present, and we do so in order to attain an abstract, unambiguous present.

This model of temporality has significant implications for motor-perception. Remembering and imagining are acts that give the mind representations of how things were in the past or how they might be. Retention and protention are not representational in this sense. When encountering objects, people, or events, certain features might prompt us to imagine how they used to be or how they might be in the future. But even when nothing prompts such representations, objects are nevertheless experienced with a non-representational horizon, which includes references before and beyond the present. These past and future aspects are representationally

---

43. Merleau-Ponty, *Phenomenology of Perception*, 384.

44. Merleau-Ponty employs Heidegger's term "*ek-stase*" when describing the "ecstatic" conception of the perceptual body (*Phenomenology of Perception*, 81, 100, 430) as well as "ecstatic temporality" (*Phenomenology of Perception*, 487, 491).

absent, they are invisible, yet they are no less real, and no less constitutive of the visible. Retention and protention are thus not re-presentations but presentations of a temporally ecstatic object constituted by the visible and the invisible. Guo Xi's achievement is more in line with multi-perspectivism as it follows from this notion of temporality. A painting need not resort to representing a perspective from time t1 and then another from time t2, etc., to depict multiple perspectives. The single mountain already embraces a temporal expanse and therefore does not need to be multiplied.

While Husserl's account opens an initial way for understanding Merleau-Ponty's and Nishida's notions of temporality, it does not go so far as to conceive of a temporal form of negation. Early on, Merleau-Ponty follows Husserl's framework, yet he later criticizes that account for its inability to explain the past or future as anything other than an element of the positivity of the present. By contrast, Merleau-Ponty seeks an ecstatic account that recognizes the "circumscribed negativity"[45] of the past and future, which is nonetheless part of the present, without which the movement of time itself would be impossible. (I elaborate the divergence between Merleau-Ponty and Husserl on this issue in a second section on "Time and Negation" in the following chapter.)

While this conception of time might be thought of as an innovation of contemporary Western thought, Dōgen (道元 1200–1253) had a theory close to what we now consider an "ecstatic" account of time more than 700 years earlier. Like Husserl, Dōgen saw the sequential account of time—with three isolated and discrete temporal phases "flying away" in a linear fashion—as an ontologically deficient and soteriologically dangerous one. His poetic rendering of "being-time"/"existence-time" (*uji* 有時) suggests an ambiguity between the temporal orders of past, present, and future. The common belief, he writes, is that "the past life has already perished, the future is yet to come, and the present does not stay." By contrast, Dōgen claims:

> The past did not necessarily already perish, the future is not inevitably yet to come, and the present is not inexorably impermanent. If you learn the not-staying, the not-yet, and the no-longer as present, future, and past, respectively, you should certainly understand the reason that the not-yet is the past,

---

45. Bettina Bergo in Maurice Merleau-Ponty, *Husserl at the Limits of Phenomenology*, 165.

present, and future. [The same holds true of the no-longer and the not-staying.]⁴⁶

If the present were not related to the past and the future this way, it would be impossible to conceive of the existence of the present. Time consciousness does not travel a linear path from the past, through the present toward the future. In Dōgen's enigmatic words: "[t]here is (totalistic) passage from today to tomorrow, passage from today to yesterday, passage from yesterday to today, passage from today to today, and passage from tomorrow to tomorrow."⁴⁷

As with the body's different tissues, the ecstatic model of time consciousness depicts the temporal orders as related beyond the identity-difference binary, and both Nishida and Merleau-Ponty explain the relation between past, present, and future in terms of a chiasmatic form of continuously-discontinuous negation. The present does not stand as a discrete moment following a wholly exhausted past and before a not-yet realized future. If the present moment had to end entirely before the next followed, temporal orders would be discontinuous and temporal flow would be impossible. On the other hand, if there were no distinction between past and present, if they were continuous, all that would exist would be the present moment. Change through time is only conceivable as a continuous-discontinuity. Temporal orders must intertwine chiasmatically. The past and present are not beside each other but are "*Ineinander*." Past and future line the present just as the invisible lines the visible. Further, the ambiguity of the temporal orders gives rise to the ambiguity of the visible and the invisible.

To recap, let us recall that what we are aiming at is a theory of expression where artists are not seeking to represent the world but want to find a motor-perceptual continuity with the landscape they paint. We have considered the relation between artist and landscape as an intertwining within a single perceptual fabric, and have described the spatial and temporal relations in that fabric as chiasmatically negating, thus enabling a multi-per-

---

46. Dōgen, *Moon in a Dewdrop: Writings of Zen Master Dōgen*, trans. K. Tanahashi, 57.
47. G. W. Nishijima and C. Cross, *Shōbōgenzō: The True Dharma-Eye Treasury: Volume 1*, 258.

spectival form of perception. The many perspectives are one aspect of the "Depth" inherent to the world we perceive. Turning now to Nishida, we find a similarly ecstatic account of time in his theory of the "eternal now," also resulting in a multi-perspectivalism given by the ambiguity of "internal perception" and "external perception."

Nishida: "Eternal Now" and "Internal-qua-External Perception"

Nishida explains the relation between past, present, and future as a temporal form of negation on several levels, including the temporality of perception.[48] The "eternal now" (*eien no ima* 永遠の今)[49] is not the present moment over against what has been or will be, but encompasses all three temporal orders.[50] When discussing the dialectical process through which one's identity achieves unity, Nishida refers to the I's relation to its past selves as a relation of negation. Like the chiasmatic relation, the temporal orders are neither fully continuous nor discontinuous. Temporal flow does not proceed by one moment following another; rather, it is by way of a reciprocal determination whereby one negates itself such that the next can be. We thus cannot live as a fully present, fully identical self, as substantialist views of time claim. We must, Nishida believes, "live by dying." That is to say, not to first live and then die, but instead appreciate that in each and every moment life is "lined" by death insofar as movement through time requires the negation of each moment, the negation of life for life to continue.[51] Each present moment continuously dies, continuously gives way to what is not itself, to what is past and future in order for time to move. The present moment must be its own negation, it must be not-present in order to be present.

This form of temporal negation also obtains between different historical periods; a point that we return to later in addressing how Nishida and Merleau-Ponty conceive of the painter's relation to her tradition. The painter's stance toward the great artists who have come before calls for a

---

48. See Krummel (2015) pp. 101–103 for a discussion of this form of temporal negation and its relation to creativity as "making-made."
49. Nishida, *Nishida Kitarō zenshū*, 1: 146, 3: 172, 6: 48.
50. Ibid., 9: 45, 7: 57.
51. Ibid., 9: 231.

temporal negation within visible conditions that have a temporal depth. Of course, the artist does not seek to represent what has been made visible in the past, but pursues a motor-demand within the temporal expanse of the present that can guide their expressive gestures.

We can extend the comparison with Merleau-Ponty regarding negation and multi-perspectivalism by considering Nishida's concept of "internal *qua* external perception." Because we are never unambiguously subject or object, but always subjective-as-objective, we never see purely as a subject nor are we ever seen purely as an object. For Nishida, like Merleau-Ponty, vision is seeing-seen.[52] He echoes one of the French philosophers well-known formulations when writing that "even our own bodies are seen from the outside [. . .] our body is that which sees as well as that which is seen."[53] Although some point to differences between how the two philosophers prioritize the poles of this relation, Nishida and Merleau-Ponty are in agreement concerning the ambiguous position of the perceptual body as situated between seeing and being seen.[54]

Like Merleau-Ponty, Nishida does not conceive of various conscious features—such as feelings, memories, volition, or desires—as *non*-perceptual but "connectable" to perception through acts of cognition or reflection. For Nishida, there is a single, continuous perceptual flow: "Concrete consciousness is not a union of independent sensations, but is rather continuous. This kind of continuous unity is precisely the activity of visual perception."[55] As his ontology matures and the concept of *Basho* becomes more central, he further emphasizes this unity of perception. *Basho* is an ontological fabric

---

52. Steve Odin, *The Social Self in Zen and American Pragmatism*, 371. "Similarity between the concept of the lived body in both Nishida and Merleau-Ponty as that which both sees and is seen: 'Merleau-Ponty also defined the body as both 'the seeing' (le voyant) and 'the visible' (le visible)' (1987, 51). For both Nishida and Merleau-Ponty, then, insofar as the body is both that which sees and that which is seen, the embodied self has the reflexive character of being both subject and object at the same time."

53. Nishida, *Nishida Kitarō zenshū*, 8: 328.

54. Yuasa (1987, 51) claims that Merleau-Ponty prioritizes one's own body and its-being-seen, whereas with Nishida there is no necessary distinction or prioritization between one's own body and other objects in the visual field.

55. Nishida, *Nishida Kitarō zenshū*, 2: 163.

that includes perception, volition, intellect, emotion, memory, and projection. Although these elements can be examined independently through acts of reflection, for Nishida they are all perceptual and valences of an originally unified *Basho*.

As with Merleau-Ponty, so with Nishida perception is much richer than what the positivist reduces to the single vantage point. Like the French philosopher, he too achieves an expansion of the perceptual by questioning the parsing of the visible from the invisible, and ambiguates the distinction between depth and surface by challenging the distinction between what he calls "internal perception" (*naibu chikaku* 内部知覚) and "external perception" (*gaibu chikaku* 外部知覚). One's life is not disclosed in pure presence. An aspect always lies out of reach, in the negative. The experience of the exterior is infused and heightened by the anticipation of the interior. To foreshadow the coming discussion of Rodin and Ike Taiga, we never see just the skin of a body or landscape without that vision being inflected by the bones. Vision does not abide a strict internal/external binary. It does not respect the surface-depth distinction. It might if visual experience were reducible to the visible. Nishida's detailed consideration of this issue is developed later in *Fundamental Problems of Philosophy* (1934), where he claims: "there is no internal perception apart from external perception . . . the world of perception exists as internal-qua-external perception and vice versa."[56] Nishida approaches this issue of interiority and exteriority from the perspective of what he believes to be an invalid distinction between "direct experience" (*chokusetsu keiken* 直接経験) and "indirect experience" (*kansetsu keiken* 間接経験). Traditionally, he thinks, we have conceived of perception as *direct* while memory and anticipations are only *indirectly* perceptual. Nishida illustrates the problem with these assumptions by considering the simple case of looking at a box. This quote below is a counter-example meant to demonstrate a positivist assumption that he later refutes:

> [W]e can think that when I see a certain box from outside, I am conscious of its exterior but I am not conscious of its interior. At least we can think that its interior is not manifested in consciousness and that it is not directly an object of consciousness. But in such a case the fact that it is not directly

---

56. Nishida, *Fundamental Problems*, 189.

an object of consciousness must mean that it is not directly in sensory consciousness.[57]

This example shows how representational assumptions cast the interior of the object as non-perceptual (by way of memory, anticipation) while the exterior is perceptual (by way of sensory data). Nishida wants to dismantle this opposition, and so he further questions the distinction between "direct consciousness" (*chokusetsu ni ishiki* 直接に意識) and "indirect consciousness" (*Kankaku-teki ishiki ni chokusetsudenai* 感覚的意識に直接でない).[58] Extending the above counter-example, he describes how "psychologists" define consciousness of the inside of the box, the "invisible" aspect, as being "indirect."

> If mental states are states which accompany the activity of the brain aroused by external stimuli, then the interior of the box which cannot directly stimulate the sense organs must be thought of as indirect for our consciousness. We are only able to represent it indirectly by means of past experience. The psychologist thinks that the consciousness of the "interior of the box" is established by revival of the impressions of the past, which are stored in the brain. In this way it is not illogical to think that the consciousness of thought is indirect.[59]

This common "psychological" understanding is positivist and representational in that it makes the mistake of describing visual experience only with present visual data (similar to what Merleau-Ponty calls the "sensationalist" prejudice), whereas other aspects can *relate* but are not themselves perceptual. Yet, since *Basho* is a relational perceptual fabric—encompassing all that can impinge upon the visual, including past experiences—this means that the memory of the interior of the box is not less direct or inferior to the perception of the outside of the box. Nishida argues that we are conscious of the "absent things" though they are not present to the senses. The inside,

---

57. Nishida, *Nishida Kitarō zenshū*, 2: 439.

58. To draw this contrast, in *Ishiki no Mondai* Nishida uses the term "indirect for our consciousness" (感覚的意識に直接でない) and several instances of contrasting terms such as "direct experience" (直接経験) "direct perception" (直接的経験), and "direct consciousness" (直接に意識).

59. Nishida, *Nishida Kitarō zenshū*, 2: 439.

although invisible and absent in a positivist sense, still impacts upon what is visible and therefore is directly perceptual.

> Perhaps it may be thought that only sensory consciousness is direct for us, and that consciousness of thought is not direct. But there is no way for consciousness, which is not direct to exist. For thought too, as the activity of consciousness, must be direct for us. The fact that it is thought that the consciousness of thought, differing from sensation, is indirect does not mean that the activity itself can be thought as indirect, but that its object can be thought of as indirect.[60]

Like Merleau-Ponty, Nishida arrives at this ambiguity by a similar understanding of temporality as it relates to perception. The conviction that thoughts, impressions, or emotions of the past are "indirect" results from the prior assumption that perception is present, visible, and positively sensual. Yet, by contrast, Nishida's elaboration culminates in a very Merleau-Pontean point: "if present consciousness can be completely analyzed into its sensory qualities, there would be no way to represent the non-present content of consciousness."[61] If the present were "perceptual" and the past "non-perceptual," when invoking the past it would obstruct the present rather than "line" and inflect it. Likewise, with the future. But, we know from our own experience that the past and future do not obstruct the present but mingle with it, thicken it, and multiply its possibilities. We clearly do experience the non-present from within the present. If it were not the case, "if we consider that our consciousness is determined in the present," writes Nishida, then "there is no way of knowing about non-present things." But we cannot deny that we have consciousness of non-present things: As Nishida asserts, "We possess consciousness such as memory, imagination, and judgment."[62]

Without including the non-present, we would be at pains to count the invisible and absent with little to help us grasp why a candle looks different after being burned, or why food and space look different depending on whether one is starving or full. Yet, our experience tells us that the non-present, the invisible, influences perception. Like Merleau-Ponty and Husserl, Nishida

---

60. Ibid., 210.
61. Ibid., 440.
62. Ibid.

is not of the mind that the non-present is a separate representation tacked onto visual stimuli. He explains that we tend to "think that consciousness of the past exists in the present in our consciousness as a representation of memory. We say that sensory consciousness of the present represents consciousness of the past."[63] All aspects of present consciousness are part of the sensible; in this way, the distinction between "direct perceptual" content and "indirect perceptual" or remembered/anticipated content does not hold. When Nishida writes that "present consciousness is entirely sensation," it could sound as though he is thinking counter to Merleau-Ponty's critique of the "sensationalist" fallacy. But, in saying this Nishida does not mean that "present consciousness" is only *present* sensation. What he intends conforms to Merleau-Ponty's expansion beyond sensationalism: he means that even when the past and future are experienced these are part of present sensation. Remembering anticipated events is "direct" and perceptual. The past experience of the inside of the box continues to be "sensation" even while looking at the outside of the box. The representationally absent counts as sensation for Nishida. Vision is thus ambiguous regarding internality and externality because of its being ambiguous regarding the past, present, and future. Because perception is never limited to the visual data given in the present from a single vantage point, because it always has a temporal depth spanning past and future perceptions, direct consciousness of the outside of the box includes an equally direct yet non-present aspect of the interior of the box.

> [W]hen we see the exterior of a box it cannot be said that its interior is not directly an object of consciousness. For it cannot be said that in the present the facts of the past are not manifested in consciousness. Of course, they are not manifested as sensation, but it cannot be said that thought objects are not manifested in the consciousness of thought. Moreover, it cannot be said that the consciousness of thought, in comparison to sensory consciousness, is necessarily indirect sensation.[64]

---

63. Ibid.

64. Nishida approaches this issue of interiority and exteriority from the point of view of what he believes to be an invalid distinction between "direct" and "indirect" perception: a distinction wrongly indexed to perception and memory, respectively. He argues against the belief that when perceptions are stored in memory they cease to be perceptual. The perceptual reality of memory is vividly illustrated in Nishida's account of the fragrance of the rose: "It is not the case that one smells the fragrance and then the past memory of a rose occurs, but in the midst of the rose's fragrance one smells the past memory" (*Nishida Kitarō zenshū*, 3: 116).

On the question of vision and surfaces Nishida is in agreement with Merleau-Ponty, who says that we do not " 'see' [the object] according to its exterior envelope; I live it from the inside; I am immersed in it. After all, the world is around me, not in front of me."[65] Vision is not an internal representation of an external object, it is a "straits between exterior horizons and interior horizons ever gaping open."[66] Just as Merleau-Ponty views the visible as lined by the invisible, so Nishida understands our seeing the object as lined by its internal view point. For both thinkers, the non-present or representationally invisible aspects impinge upon the visual and are both directly perceptual because of perception embracing all temporal orders through an ambiguous, continuously-discontinuous negation.

Skin and Bones in Rodin and Taiga

Let us now apply what we know about multi-perspectival vision from Merleau-Ponty and Nishida and appraise two artists, both of whom seek to produce works that complicate the distinction between surface and depth. Artists have proven adept at disclosing the expansiveness of human vision. Rodin is one such artist whose brutally contorted and broken bodies afford new ways of understanding the body, vision, skin and bones. In her masterful work *Passages in Modern Sculpture*, Rosalind Krauss, one of the twenty-first century's most celebrated art historians, traces the history of sculpture with Rodin at the center of her analysis. She claims that one of the major concerns preoccupying artists up until Rodin was the attempt to depict bodies with a balanced internal-external relation. Sculptors wanted to make the outside surface of the body evince a properly proportioned internal structure. "Surface," writes Krauss, "in traditional sculpture is understood to be a reflection of a pre-existent, internal armature or structure."[67] We might see only skin, but we take this as indicative of the underlying bones. She alleges that although there is no actual skeletal morphology, bones, or musculature under the surface of sculptures depicting the human form, the perfection of the external surface is, nevertheless, judged based on how it suggests proper proportion, symmetry, and harmony between the internal and external structures. Krauss situates Rodin as a turning point in this tradition insofar as his works depart from this convention and present

---

65. Merleau-Ponty, "Eye and Mind," 138.
66. Merleau-Ponty, *The Visible and the Invisible*, 132.
67. Rosalind Krauss, *Passages in Modern Sculpture*.

Figure 2.4. Auguste Rodin, *The Three Shades*, 1886. Musée Rodin, Paris, France.

bodies whose surfaces are distorted to deliberately challenge the way vision operates in relation to interiority and exteriority, skin and bones. Rodin's *Three Shades* (figure 2.4)—a further instance of the *Three Graces* motif—is her central example. On Krauss's reading, "It is this communication between the surface and the anatomical depths that Rodin aborts."[68] Her claim is that by doing so, Rodin is able to have vision dwell on the surface of the

---

68. Ibid., 27.

bodies rather than being concerned for the inner structure, and in this way his work marks a major innovation in Western sculpture. Our vision of the Shades' bodies, she claims, "is stopped at the surface."[69] She goes on to interpret a great deal of those Western artists working in the wake of Rodin—from Brancusi, the Futurists, to Picasso, Philip King, Robert Morris, and Richard Serra—as exploiting a "unitary volume which dispenses with an internal armature, forcing all attention on the elaboration of its surface."[70] The forces these artists work with, she writes, act "over the surface of matter. Shaping those substances from the outside, these forces act with no regard to the intrinsic structure of the material on which they work."[71] However, Krauss's claims are in unequivocal quite straightforward disagreement with how Rodin himself thought about the relation between surface and depth. For instance, he explains that

> [i]nstead of imagining the various parts of the body as more or less flat surfaces, I represented them as projections of *interior volumes*. I endeavored to express in each swelling of the torso or the limbs the presence of a muscle or a bone that continued deep beneath the skin.[72]

Rodin's understanding of his work is much more in line with the notion of Interiority and exteriority found in Merleau-Ponty's and Nishida's writings. To be fair, Krauss need not be constrained by the artist's conception of his work and her argument might not stand or fall thereupon. Nor is an art historian required to enter into the complexities of ontology as it relates to perception. Yet, while her art historical credentials are beyond question, her claims about vision, and her invoking Merleau-Ponty, bring this work into the realm of phenomenology. Krauss might be right in an art historical frame that Rodin or others worked toward vision "stopped at the surface" of the skin. Yet, where she alleges that they succeed in this attempt, the argument contravenes Merleau-Ponty and Nishida's philosophies, or possibly what we could refer to even broadly as a phenomenological position regarding perception. A sculptor could only "abort" the communication

---

69. Ibid., 28.
70. Ibid., 181.
71. Ibid., 33.
72. Auguste Rodin and Paul Gsell, *Art: Conversations with Paul Gsell*, 25. Emphasis added.

between skin and bones if vision were merely positive; if it were a relation entirely reducible to sensory data reflecting off of surfaces; and if the artist's project were simply representational. One could only "force all attention on the elaboration of the surface" if the visible were not saturated with the invisible, or if there were a strict distinction between "internal" and "external perception." The visible (skin) does not obstruct the invisible (bones), nor can an artist achieve this by any particular aesthetic technique. Skin and bones are visible within a chiasmatic continuity of discontinuity. The artist cannot isolate surface to the exclusion of depth. Moreover, if Merleau-Ponty and Nishida have anything to show us it is that no artist can succeed in such an attempt, and furthermore, it has been the principal aim of many important painters and sculptors to demonstrate how that project is neither possible nor desirable. Despite her invoking Merleau-Ponty, the claims Krauss develops in relation to vision do not consider the implications of his notion of "Depth," nor the co-constitution of the visible and invisible, which takes an unequivocal stance on the ambiguity of the relation between surface and depth, skin and bones.

Ike Taiga (池大雅, 1723–1776) was an Edo-period Japanese "literati" (文人畫 *wenrenhua*) painter and calligrapher of the Nanga school (南画). He worked in a moment when Japanese artists were grappling with their Chinese inheritance, striving to carve out a distinct national style. Debates regarding realism and naturalism were prominent throughout the art world in Japan. One of these debates invoked the question of surface and depth, cast at the time as the "skin" and "bones" not of the human body, but of the landscape. Taiga's approach, we will see, was contrary to the one Krauss puts forth and more in line with Nishida and Merleau-Ponty's understanding of vision. Taiga and the members of the Nanga school were convinced that for a painting to be "true" that the artist must strive toward "realism," but one that was not positivist or excessively devoted to the reality of the surface of things, to their "skin." Taiga sought to overcome the surface-depth binary by divulging the landscape's "bones" into its depiction.

An approach in the late eighteenth century that sought to achieve this complexity was known as "*shinkeizu*" (真景図) or "true view paintings." Although this movement only took root after his death, I discuss in the next chapter how Sesshū was its progenitor. Contrary to the slavish devotion to copying Chinese masterworks, which was widespread throughout Japan, Taiga and his fellow Nanga painters placed greater emphasis on painting from actual scenes. Within the vibrant circles of artists and theoreticians in Edo-period Japan, a distinction between *shai*, or "painting the idea" (learning the styles of past masters) and *shasei* "sketching from life" (connecting

Figure 2.5. Ike no Taiga, *True Views of Mt. Asama*, 1776. Yabumoto collection, Japan.

with the "spirit resonance" of actual landscapes) had currency. The former granted the artist certain latitude to interpret Chinese masterworks while the later prized deep *in situ* perceptual engagement with actual landscapes referred to as "famous spots" (*meisho* 名所), these were vistas heralded for their beauty often depicted in celebrated literature and poetry. *Shasei* study included meticulous attention to the natural world, but did not aim to represent its "skin." Instead, the painter who had reached such facility with their practice that they could go beyond technique and beyond the constraints of devotion would consume themselves to such a degree with the visual world before them that their painterly gestures would be solicited by the landscape itself. While the *shinkeizu* practice does not yet carry this study to where we can discuss faith, it does invoke the form of motor-perceptual continuity we are looking for regarding artistic expression. Chinese and Japanese painters considered the relation that embraced painter and landscape as a "spirit resonance" (c. *ch'i yun*; j. *kiin*). This term, originating in fifth-century China in the *Guhua Pinlu* (*Old Record of the Classification of Painters*) was used by "literati" painters to refer to the indescribable beauty of paintings unattainable by those with mere technical mastery who sought to accurately depict the landscape or to copy previous works.[73] Striving toward continuity through this form of resonance, the painter's practice accrued

---

73. Aida-Yuen Wong, "A New Life for Literati Painting in the Early Twentieth Century: Eastern Art and Modernity, a Transcultural Narrative?"

meaning beyond the strictly artistic. The root of the Japanese term for "spirit resonance" is "*ki*" (j. 気; c. 氣), an important Daoist term referring to "life energy," and "vitality." *Ki* was the most basic energy animating all reality and the fundamental principle of motion and change in nature. Thus, where a painter strives to attain resonance with *ki*, their artistic practice accrues religious and philosophical significance. Artists who pursued the *Shasei* ideal sought this resonance with the actual landscape, rather than with the brushstrokes of the great Chinese masters they copy. As Takeuchi writes, *shinkeizu* according to Taiga expressed "the artist's profound apprehension of nature's truths and his expression of something beyond the mere visual morphology of a given landscape."[74]

The most well-known of *shinkeizu* paintings, and the work used to popularize this approach in Edo-period Japan, was Taiga's "True View of Mr. Asama" (*Asamadake shinkei-zu* 朝熊嶽真景図) (figure 2.5). This masterpiece is not "true" or an example of "realism" in the sense of being an accurate representation of a landscape. In fact, no such landscape exists as depicted in the work. As Guo Xi had before him, Taiga amalgamated vistas from several different vantage points to compose his work. Like the *Three Graces* motif, it comprises several perspectives not visible from any single vantage point. But, unlike that motif, it does not multiply the subject depicted. The single landscape includes multitudes of vistas. The multiple unfold from within the singular. While this engagement with the actual landscape brought the *shasei* element into the painting, Taiga did not ignore the conventions of Chinese painting. Evidence of both Northern and Southern Song brushwork are present in the work. *Shasei* demands that the artist goes beyond mere copying of previous masters, yet the *shai* is still present in *shinkeizu* work.

How was Taiga's painting "true" if it does not depict an actual scene? This decisive issue demands that we consider the third element of *shinkeizu* style, which was the artist's own character. Unlike Taiga's contemporary Ōkyo who took the "objective" (*fūkeiga*) approach focusing on the "skin" of the landscape, and thus constrained himself to the visually positive, Taiga sought a realism that encompassed the visible skin as it is inflected by the invisible bones. As Takeuchi writes,

> Taiga probed the structure of nature's "bones"; Ōkyo pursued the fleeting visual effects on its "skin." From the perspective of a

---

74. Melinda Takeuchi, " 'True' Views: Taiga's Shinkeizu and the Evolution of Literati Painting Theory in Japan," *The Journal of Asian Studies* 48, no. 1 (1989): 11.

Nanga painter, Ōkyo busied himself with the transitory appearance of the surface aspects of reality, whereas Taiga pursued its eternal underlying essence.

How do you find the bones if the landscape conceals them from view? If it were the case that painter and landscape were cut out of two separate ontological fabrics, finding the landscape's bones would involve a subject going deeper into an object. Going beneath *its* surface. Yet, because painter and landscape are part of a single continuous motor-perceptual fabric, because they are woven together through a chiasmatic continuous-discontinuity, to go deeper into the landscape is to go deeper into a valence of the self as it extends throughout the perceptual field. Thus, the third element enters the *shinkeizu* method—the artist's personality as expressed through the poetic deformations he performs in his work. The expressiveness or "emotional tone" (*seishu*), which was part of the overall reception of paintings included the invisible aspect added to the work by the observer's sense of the artist's personality. The better the work the more present the artist would be while otherwise representationally absent.

In pursuing all three ideals of *shinkeizu*, Taiga thus discovered a way beyond the surface/depth, skin/bones alternatives. Describing this approach, Ghilardi is in stark opposition to Krauss when he writes, "The surface of things is *one* with the profundity they conceal. Surface is profundity itself, surface *qua* (*soku* 即) profundity."[75] Taiga's work reaches beyond these binaries because his devotion was at the intersection of the visible and the invisible, and he recognized how his own body, his vision and his expressive gestures were implicated in that relation.

Returning to Rodin, and putting art history aside momentarily, having seen the *Three Shades* in person, it strikes me that one of the most strongly arresting sensations is precisely how Rodin makes us feel beyond the Shade's skin to their bones. This is palpable in the crippling contortions of their bones and musculature. But the relation is more complex. Rodin does not simply pull one's vision below the Shade's skin, but onlookers are also afforded the opportunity to feel below their own skin where their bodies are contorted as an echo of the Shades'. Far from halting vision on the outside of the figures he sculpted, Rodin's style supports the claim that vision always entails far more than an apprehension of external surfaces. The discomfort one feels when seeing the distorted bodies invokes Nishida's understanding

---

75. Ghilardi, *The Line of the Arch*, 76.

of "internal-*qua*-external" perception and the narcissism-anonymity of vision Merleau-Ponty posits. I do not simply see the necks painfully elongated as though their pain were situated only in those bodies, without any implications for my own. Even inanimate sculpted bodies have a negation for narcissistic perception in which we feel our bodies. Certainly, we cannot grasp Rodin's innovations while ignoring how the distinction between the Shades' skin and bones does not hold, but further: it is not simply that there is an ambiguity between skin and bones on the side of the sculpted flesh and a separate ambiguity on the side of our bodies that view the sculpture. My insides are felt below the depths of their skin. The internal distortions I see impel me to feel those crippling deformations inside my own body. Thus, our ambiguities are ambiguous. To enter into the depths of the flesh of *The Three Shades* is at the same time to enter into a valence of our own bodies, projected into theirs through perceptual negation. "My body can include elements drawn from the body of another, just as my substance passes into them; man is a mirror for man."[76] Neither my body nor others are perceived exclusively in their own positivity. When viewing any body, I feel them through the negation that accepts my "narcissistic" infusion as internal-external perception, yet also with the "anonymity" that denies my experience being reduced completely to my own. I sense other bodies not just from the outside-in, but also from the inside-out. I have previously seen the inside of boxes, and this memory lines my perception of every outside of a box I will see. Likewise, the pain suggested by the Shades' contortions evokes the pain that has cut below my own skin, or where broken bones have been visible on the surface of my flesh. While these might be distant memories now, nevertheless they are directly perceptual, not separate from their appearance in other bodies, sculpted or real. Thus, when taking in the convolutions of skin and bone in Rodin's *Shades* in the present, that moment swells from within to embrace my past sufferings and my future attempts to avoid them. Vision does not rest on the surface of the *Shade's* skin indifferent to how their flesh discloses its depths, not in the sculpted bodies, and not in our own as they are constituted by such great works of art.

What Rodin and Taiga help us see is that the visual experience we have is much richer and more complex than the positivist or representational frameworks allow. The lessons they offer are of great use, they illuminate features of visual experience operative in all perceptual encounter. For example, if vision could rest on surfaces we might not have feelings of discomfort or strength when seeing other differently abled bodies. The ambiguity of

---

76. Merleau-Ponty, "Eye and Mind," 130.

surface and depth also explains why a building that initially seems to have enormous density and weight looks thinner, lighter, and less substantial the instant it is revealed to be a façade, even though the exact same perceptual data touched the eyes before and after one reaches the vantage point that undoes the illusion. Likewise, in a more universal and sophisticated illustration that corroborates this perceptual logic: even though the bodily data we receive is exactly the same before and after, a chocolate Easter bunny looks lighter and disappointingly less substantial when the news is broken that our gift is a hollow rather than solid version—a feeling that is sadly palpable without our having to break the surface (change the visual data) to overcome the internal/external divide, because that divide between skin and bones is already ambiguous without our having to do so.

MULTI-PERSPECTIVALISM: CREATION AND OBSTRUCTION

At this point in the dialogue, I would like to consider a discrepancy between our philosophers, which raises an important question regarding the body, its perception and motion. Both Nishida and Merleau-Ponty suggest that the landscape "sees" and even paints itself. While a focused discussion of these points is yet to come, we can begin considering in more detail the question of the world's implication in human vision. While Nishida and Merleau-Ponty agree on some of the broad features of how perception is ambiguous regarding internality and externality, that it has a depth whereby the skin and bones of bodies and landscapes inflect each other, there is a potential incongruity regarding the extent to which the world is implicated in human vision. Nishida is not typically regarded as having gone as far as Merleau-Ponty has in terms of developing the ontological implications of perception. He does posit that external vision of an object includes a non-present but nonetheless perceptual experience of its interior, and asserts that "even our own bodies are seen from the outside."[77] But, it appears that Merleau-Ponty goes a measure further, particularly as we discern his ontology from suggestions that vision does not just *intertwine with* but actually *emanates from* objects. He intimates as much in "Eye and Mind" when quoting Marchand who describes the painter's feeling of being looked back upon by the forest, and when he notes that "since things and my body are made of the same stuff, vision must somehow come about *in them*."[78] Merleau-Ponty wants a non-internalist conception of perception where vision is a worldly

---

77. Nishida, *Nishida Kitarō zenshū*, 8:328.
78. Merleau-Ponty, "Eye and Mind," 125. Emphasis added.

phenomenon not reducible to the subject. This is also Nishida's wish, but there are important differences that motivate some reservation regarding the measure to which the two thinkers can be compared.

While Nishida's formulation does not posit specific objects in the perceptual field from which vision emanates, as Merleau-Ponty suggests, it might be that this absence actually stems from the Japanese philosopher's attempt to push multi-perspectivalism—and the perceptual ontology that would back it—to a deeper level. Put another way, it might not be that he neglects the objects from which vision would arise, but that his conception of negation regarding perception is so thorough that no objects remain. Certainly, when we consider what transpires on the human end of perceptual encounter, we find negation approaching this degree.

In Nishida's later writings, vision becomes increasingly central. In the late 1920s he develops his concepts of "seeing without a seer" (*mirumono nakushite miru koto* 見るものなくして見ること)[79] and later the "self-seeing" of *Basho* is part of his continued effort to advance a radically non-internalist account of perception, where vision arises in the world but is not localizable in either subject or object. In this account, vision is not a human action but an event of a broader perceptual fabric. It is the "self-seeing" of *Basho* itself. To posit "seeing without a seer" is to retain the event of vision (seeing), and the fabric in which it circulates, but to drop the individuated subject (seer) as the exclusive node to which vision is attributed. In their commentary on Nishida's concept of vision, Krummel and Nagatomo note that "here the meaning of 'seeing' extends beyond merely humans to encompass life or world in general."[80] In this sense, it appears that Nishida is in fact ontologizing a type of vision that could, in principle, be fully non-obstructed, where vision could be the world's own and not reducible to the point of view of a subject. When we conceive of vision without a seer, this absence implies a thorough de-substantialization and de-localization of the perceiving subject. This suggests an extreme multi-perspectivalism without discrete visual entities or any fixed locale from which sight arises, which reveals something of a departure from Merleau-Ponty on this issue. Perhaps because of the pervasiveness of his writings, Merleau-Ponty is better known for having developed an account of seeing without a subjective seer. While Nishida is not as well known for having done so, it is hard to imagine how vision could be any more de-subjectivized, or as alluded to just above, de-objectified. In

---

79. Nishida, *Nishida Kitarō zenshū*, 3:255.
80. Krummel and Nagatomo, *Place and Dialectic*, 360.

my view, there is no question that Nishida goes as far as Merleau-Ponty in developing an ontological account of vision, the question is: does he go farther, and if so, can we reconcile their positions? If not, if they disagree, how does one appraise their divergent formulations? Taking a stance on this crucial matter requires delving further into their thought and the works of commentators who have engaged this very question.

Reverting to Merleau-Ponty on this issue, we find that he does retain a minimal localization or subjective point of view. Neither the perceptual subject nor the object is fully negated. He goes far toward removing the obstructions that reify the subject as an individuated visual locus, invoking a "vision that we do not make but is made in us,"[81] as Lawlor writes. Yet, unlike Nishida, Merleau-Ponty is explicit in maintaining an irreducible "mineness" to perception, a point of view, which implies that vision cannot be fully non-obstructed, reversibility cannot be fully reversible. As he says in *The Visible and the Invisible*, "I am always on the same side of my own body."[82] Turning back to Nishida, it could be that in the absence of articulating explicit limits to visual obstruction that his multi-perspectivalism inches close to a "view from nowhere" non-perspectivalism.[83] Sorting out this issue requires careful consideration of Nishida's philosophy, but it is quite clear regarding Merleau-Ponty that his project, from its very beginning, explicitly countered what he called the "perspectiveless"[84] position, or what amounts to the same thing, the *"pensée de survole"* ("high altitude thinking") that assumes a God's-eye view on the world. Although Merleau-Ponty struggled to carve out an understanding of vision that is not reducible to the human subject, he does not allow the human point of view to dissolve completely. To be fair, it is unlikely that Nishida would have disagreed on this point or explicitly posited "perspectivaless" vision. Yet, without articulating explicit limits to non-obstruction, Nishida's theories of "seeing-without-a-seer" and *Basho*'s "self-seeing" do not explicitly preclude this possibility and thus demand further consideration within this conversation with Merleau-Ponty.

---

81. Leonard Lawlor, *Early Twentieth-Century Continental Philosophy*, 151.

82. Merleau-Ponty, *The Visible and the Invisible*, 148.

83. I agree with Davis (2004) that Nishida should not be read as proposing a "view from nowhere" position, but in Chapter 4 I explore how a lack of visual/ontological "obstructions" in his philosophy leaves his notion of "seeing without a seer" open to this interpretation, contrary to his broader ontology indicating otherwise.

84. Merleau-Ponty, *Phenomenology of Perception*, 77.

Brook Ziporyn further reinforces the argument that Merleau-Ponty's theory of vision has limits, but he is critical of the French philosopher in this respect. He refers to another line of Marchand's quoted in "Eye and Mind," namely that the painter wants to be "penetrated by the universe, and not want to penetrate it,"[85] as evidence that the reversibility of Merleau-Ponty's account of vision stops short of a full "reversibility of reversibility."[86] For Ziporyn this is a shortfall since it prioritizes the subject of vision. To put this in the context of the Huayan concept of non-obstruction, (or Ziporyn's Tiantai concept of "intersubsumption") obstruction remains as the subject's point of view. By conceiving of vision as "seeing without a seer," Nishida might satisfy Ziporyn's desire for full non-obstructed reversibility. Yet, let me underscore that if he does, if there is a complete negation of the perceptual subject and object, this might clash with other foundational aspects of Nishida's philosophy, forcing us to choose which we follow in order to take a stand on this key question. How the body intertwines with the perceptual fabric—in ways that Nishida's *Basho* theory is committed—might imply limits to reversibility that invoke inconsistencies in his philosophy because of un-acknowledged obstructions where a minimal subjective point of view constrains vision to being at least partially perspectival and never completely worldly, that is, the visual subject retains at minimum some measure of positivity. Specifically, in chapter 4, I consider the pivotal implications of Merleau-Ponty's *punctum caecum*, or "blind spot," a constitutive perceptual obstruction, which when considered in dialogue with Nishida raises questions regarding the comparability of their notions of faith.

Before developing this point of contention between the two, the discussion can proceed one small step closer to considering how the landscape paints itself, and thus begin the movement beyond the perceptual to the motor-perceptual. We are led further in this direction by a shared contention among Nishida and Merleau-Ponty that how the world insinuates itself in the body implies that as vision evolves it becomes a creative way of moving. In Nishida's words, the world "at its root, is also a world whereby historical

---

85. Merleau-Ponty, "Eye and Mind," 129.

86. Brook Ziporyn, "How the Tree Sees Me: Sentience and Insentience in Tiantai and Merleau-Ponty," 80.

nature sees by making."[87] Further, not only does the historical world see by making, but in the other direction, the world "makes continuously via seeing; to make is simultaneously to see. Life in this sense," according to Nishida, "must be formatively (*zōkei*) artistic."[88] As Nishida expresses in "The Standpoint of Active Intuition," the world is not inert, non-perceptual matter: its seeing and its acting are wrapped up in each other.

> The historical world is what itself constantly determines itself in the manner of forming activity; it is what constantly itself sees itself. Thus we are able to say that it itself determines itself in custom. What, being passive, is dynamic is custom. All things are inert. But in the historical world, the concrete is not merely inert; it is what actively forms things, what sees things.[89]

The movements of the world—of which the painter's body and its expressive motions are one instance—are exemplary of this type of seeing. For Nishida, one way of being an artist is to engage the world as it determines itself through its own self-seeing. Similarly, in Merleau-Ponty's philosophy, Cézanne is exemplary because his expressive gestures enact a de-localized perception occasioning a form of expression where "it becomes impossible to distinguish between who sees and who is seen, who paints and what is painted."[90] But, how are we to interpret such assertions? Does the world actually paint? How do we understand the ontology that underwrites these poetic formulations? Perhaps one of the difficulties comes from our being hardwired to assume that the human type of seeing and motion are the standard measure in light of which all other instances are merely "metaphorical." This would be the case if there were a strict distinction between the substances in which body and mountain inhere. But, since on Nishida and Merleau-Ponty's account this is decidedly not the case, attributing vision or motion to a human as opposed to a mountain is neither more nor less metaphorical. Human vision is importantly different from any of its other manifestations. If the tree sees me, as Ziporyn affirms, it surely

---

87. Nishida, "Logic and Life," in *Place and Dialectic*, 255.
88. Ibid.
89. Nishida Kitarō, "The Standpoint of Active Intuition," in *Ontology of Production: Three Essays*, 135.
90. Merleau-Ponty, "Eye and Mind," 129.

does so in a way that is different from (and expands) our assumptions about human vision.

———◁○▷———

Before moving on to the next section, let us recap. So far in this chapter, I have considered multi-perspectivalism from various angles, and shown how the ambiguous negation between bodies, objects, landscapes, etc., implies that vision is much more subtle and complex than a positivist or representational account allows. Our vision is tempered by the perspective of others, even of objects, and does not abide by the distinction between surface and depth. The works of Rodin and Taiga have disclosed these aspects of perception and have helped evoke a critical divergence between Nishida and Merleau-Ponty regarding the full extent of multi-perspectival vision and the possible limits to negation that undergird it. In the following sections, before proceeding to consider motion in the next chapter, I fill out the account of vision I have been developing by examining three more features that further widen the scope within which we think about perceptual experience such that vision is seen as more comprehensively pervading the perceptual fabrics of flesh and *Basho*. Those are (1) the relation between vision and touch, (2) the body's relation to tools, and (3) the body's relation to light. This fuller account of vision brings the dialogue a step closer to considering the contention between Nishida and Merleau-Ponty regarding the obstructions inherent to perception and their implications for artistic expression and faith.

The Expanded Body: Vision and Touch

This second section of the chapter seeks to broaden several intuitions regarding the perceptual body and the relation between vision and touch. This is carried out in view of appreciating innovations that great landscape painters such as Cézanne and Sesshū attain, as well as the phenomenological depiction thereof. To run the full gamut of implications that come through visual-tactile ambiguity we begin by reworking basic ideas regarding touch itself, which also demands reconceptualizing the space normally assumed to divide bodies that appear to be separate, that is, not touching. Carrying out the analysis in the chapter's remainder expands our apprehension about touch as it relates to tools—an important consideration for later grasping the artist's relation to his implements—and shows how similar forms of touch obtain through the visual, specifically, through light's tool-like mediation between body and world.

———◆———

It might seem quite un-problematic to begin with the idea that bodies are touching when there is no space between them and separate when space or some object intervenes to obstruct that contact. The remaining sections of the chapter endeavor to overturn these seemingly un-problematic suppositions. Even if one takes on-board the idea of a perceptually negated non-subject and non-object, the question remains as to the area that appears to separate the two: the space, the light, and the air that divides bodies away from each other. What we have to be on guard against is assuming that that space is neutral regarding perception, or a non-perceptual void that merely allows vision to traverse it. To avoid these common representational suppositions means countering deeply held convictions that cast vision as a strictly human faculty. No doubt the human knot in the perceptual fabric is exceedingly more intricate than others; however, the mistake is to assume on this basis that human vision is exhaustively definitive of the sensible, rather than one expression of a more general perceptual reality, which includes all bodies, objects, and phenomena, as well as the space between them. By challenging these assumptions, our philosophers want to elevate perception to an ontological status, while divesting the human of its monopoly over the sensible. Far from a conception where vision originates in the seer and shoots out into the world in the direction of merely receptive objects, Nishida writes, "[t]he actual visual perception of living things is determined by things."[91] For Merleau-Ponty, Lawlor writes, we do not make vision, "it is made in us."[92] Taking this a step further, in *The Visible and the Invisible* we read that "he who sees cannot possess the visible unless he is possessed by it, unless he *is of it*."[93] Likewise with the tactile, it is a phenomenal realm, not simply what we feel inside our bodies when we make contact with things, because, as Merleau-Ponty writes, "Everything said about the sensed body pertains to the whole of the sensible of which it is a part, and to the world." For what it tells us regarding the intricacies of tactile experience, it is worth

---

91. Nishida, *Art and Morality*, 25.
92. Lawlor, *Early Twentieth-Century Continental Philosophy*, 151.
93. Merleau-Ponty, *The Visible and the Invisible*, 134.

quoting at length this later description of the body's relation to the sensible as "Intertwining":

> If the body is one sole body in its two phases, it incorporates into itself the whole of the sensible and with the same movement incorporates itself into a "Sensible in itself." We have to reject the age-old assumptions that put the body in the world and the seer in the body, or, conversely, the world and the body in the seer as in a box. Where are we to put the limit between the body and the world, since the world is flesh? Where in the body are we to put the seer, since evidently there is in the body only "shadows stuffed with organs," that is, more of the visible? The world seen is not "in" my body, and my body is not "in" the visible world ultimately: as flesh applied to a flesh, the world neither surrounds it nor is surrounded by it. A participation in and a kinship with the visible, the vision neither envelops it nor is enveloped by it definitively. The superficial pellicle of the visible is only for my vision and for my body. But the depth beneath this surface contains my body and hence contains my vision. My body as a visible thing is contained within the full spectacle. But my seeing body subtends this visible body, and all the visibles with it. There is reciprocal insertion and intertwining of one in the other.[94]

To circumvent broad features of the representational account, a simple reversal is necessary: perception is not, strictly speaking, a human faculty, nor is the object a completely *non*-perceptual entity. Allowing that the body is only one part of a greater sensible fabric, and not the origin of the perceptual, might seem like a deflationary account. However, a perceptual ontology that decenters the human is not only a more accurate phenomenological description of how we experience the visible world; it is also a considerably richer portrayal of the body and its perceptual faculties. Displacing the human body, doing away with the individuated substantial seer, is, in fact, a highly *inflationary* move, one that can explain the extraordinary achievements of artists, not to mention our everyday, embodied experience. The possibilities and complexities for appreciating and enjoying the body are multiplied exponentially in a relational account of perception, which is, on

---

94. Ibid., 138.

my reading, inherent to *Basho* and flesh. Taking this step requires grasping how the space between bodies is itself perceptual. We can then appreciate how touch extends through vision, that is, the way that the visual and tactile are intertwined—a position endorsed by both Nishida and Merleau-Ponty. I first explore this visual-tactile relation in terms of how vision expands through the use of tools. Approaching the end of the chapter, in a more speculative section, I attempt to push certain implications further regarding tools to consider new ways of conceiving of the body's relation to light. Specifically, I consider how, contrary to prevailing philosophic and scientific doctrine, light, is not inherently a transparent medium but always includes a valence of perceptual obstruction. That is, light has a moment of opacity. This aspect of the body's relation to light is not commonly recognized in philosophy, East or West, nor in Nishida's or Merleau-Ponty's writings, but can nevertheless be established by extending other features of their thought. If viable, a tool-use analogy describing light-based vision provides a way of seeing the perceptual field as fully saturated not just by vision but by touch. The tactile will, as it were, extend as far as the eye can see.

―◦―

It is difficult to grasp the works and techniques of artists such as Guo Xi or Rodin using conventional understandings of space and distance confined by representational assumptions about perception or positivist notions of objectivity. Merleau-Ponty and Nishida propose a much more intimate relation between the artist than the one that would construe them as subjects standing over against objects they paint. A serious revision is needed to appreciate the artist's motor-perceptual practices and the works themselves. Conceptualizing vision and motion in an ontological context frees us from the positivist definition of the body, providing a more complex and intriguing portrayal of artistic practice.

Part of the difficulty of understanding vision as an event that exceeds the human body is that its object appears to be at such an obvious remove from the body. Unlike touch, where distance between bodies is by (positivist) definition eliminated, when considering the visual, one has to account for the distance between bodies and objects, or the body and the world. Going deeper into Merleau-Ponty and Nishida's thought, their theories of perception demand rethinking of common intuitions regarding distance and space. It seems relatively straightforward to think of the body as located at various distances from objects in the world. Some are far away, while others are closer. I can see the ones far away but can only touch them if I eliminate the intervening distance between myself and them. Nothing could appear more self-evident. But by extending our previous discussion of negation, it is possible to construct an entirely different understanding of space—one that shows how vision and touch do not line up so easily with a simple distance–proximity binary.

The insubstantial nature of vision lends itself to a belief that it could span the divide between the inside and outside of the body and predisposes us to think beyond that dichotomy. But in moving from the visual to the tactile, that expansion is more difficult to achieve. The body that touches appears to have a clear demarcation between its inside and outside. What could be more obvious than the fact that the body ends at the outer extremity of the skin, and touch happens when something contacts that surface? If this were the case, then relationality as negation would apply only to the visual while the physical body itself would endure as a circumscribed entity separate from the objects in the world, and on that basis the visual and the tactile would remain distinct. But to follow Nishida and Merleau-Ponty's more enigmatic depictions of artistic practice requires challenging these assumptions that distinguish vision and touch. For example, in his "Artistic Creation and Historically Formative Act," Nishida writes, "When painting our body becomes the tip of the brush, when sculpting, the grip of the chisel."[95] Later, in *Art and Morality*, he extends this idea to include vision, where "there is an eye at the tip of the artist's brush or the sculptor's chisel."[96] Even Chinese artists thought about the relation to their tools this way. When painters became adept with their brush, they were said to "have brush" (*yu pi*), and when they had mastered ink, to "have ink" (*yu mo*). Although these sayings can come across as dangerously steeped in figurative language, we might nonetheless interpret them literally according to a conception of the body where the visual and tactile enjoy greater possible intertwinings.

Tool as Non-Objective Bodily Extension

Of all the aesthetic elements codified and strictly controlled in the Asian landscape painting traditions, the artist's tools were among the most wonderfully elaborate. The particularities of the Japanese artist's brushes (*fude*,

---

95. Nishida, "歴史的形成作用としての芸術的創作 *Rekishi-Teki Keiseisayō Toshite No Geijutsu-Teki Sōsaku*," in *Nishida Kitarō Zenshū*, 9: 177–264.

96. Nishida, *Art and Morality*, 156.

筆), its length, weight, its center of balance, the color of its lacquer, and the materials used to make them were meticulously crafted for specific effect. Early in this tradition when writing Chinese characters was the main determinant of brush design, mulberry stems were used, later replaced by heavier woods and ivory as that practice evolved into landscape painting. When rendering mountains and waters, vegetation and animals, the artist had an array of decisions regarding which brushes were best. If they needed to depict exacting details, the feelers from around the rat's nose, or the hairs from the beak of the kingfisher were preferred. Coloring demanded the coarse absorbent hair of the badger, whereas shading was best achieved with a more pliable rabbit hair.[97] The sharp and soft fibers of the marten's coat were ideal for elegant and clean outlining, whereas goat hair was better suited for the spontaneous "boneless" style painting Sesshū practiced. If one prefers to accentuate the "bones" of a landscape, the stiff unabsorbant hair of bear or fox were the finest for strong outlining. Badger, fox, wild horse, goat, weasel, or squirrel hair each had its own suitability for rendering bamboo leaves, plum blossoms, rice plants, chrysanthemum, orchids, pine, etc. The multitude of forms one might paint—flowers, birds, humans, mountains, water, clothing, faces, bodies, leaves, not to mention their modulating demands depending on the changing seasons—demanded specific tools made from materials enabling the artist to capture the world with an extraordinary degree of precision: this is even more remarkable in that the tool's specificity almost entirely disappears in making the world visible. Brushmakers were thus essential for carrying forward the tradition of landscape painting in Asia, and were considered master craftsmen in their own right, and brushmaking an artform in itself.

To understand the artist's tools merely as objects, all of these particularities of the brush appear to be curious eccentricities, but perhaps not consequential to how we think of our body's relation to the world. Yet, for the purposes of this study, and for undertaking a phenomenology of landscape painting, just as we have done regarding the body, I want to continue thinking beyond positivity as the analysis proceeds to consider the perceptual and motor-perceptual features of objectivity. Considering the material specificities of tools as non-objects helps develop our study by disclosing important aspects of body-world relationality. Looked at in the context of mutual negation, the material features of the artist's tools are not

---

97. H. P. Bowie, *On the Laws of Japanese Painting*, 34; Maria CHENG, *Essential Terms of Chinese Painting*, 299.

simply the invention of those who craft them, or those who use them, but are features that become necessary as dictated by an intersection of motion and perception—the motion and perception of the body *and* the landscape. If a new or meaningful disclosure of the landscape is possible through a spontaneity afforded by certain materials and not others, this means that there is a network of material constraints obtaining between artist, landscape and the world of wood, animal hair, and brush maker, which compels the artist's practice, that is, limits it while also enabling its possibilities. Artists thus do not just choose rabbit or badger hair because *they* prefer those materials for depicting objects the way *they* desire. The brush only takes on its form when the brushmaker conforms to a set of demands given by the landscape itself: its materials, shapes, weight, bristles are what the landscape needs in order to express itself through the artist's body. The brushmaker thus learns to read the necessities of a network of constraints when making the brush: landscape painters situate themselves in this milieu enabled by their tools when using them. To practice either art seriously means actuating a set of relations (body-tool-landscape) that tell us much more about those practices if construed in terms of mutual negation. Turning to Nishida and Merleau-Ponty to examine the phenomenological implications of tool use, we find they too conceive of this relation in terms of negation. Let us now look at their discussion of tool use, and in later sections ("The Materiality of Spontaneous Expression," in chapter 4) return to consider in more depth how the material world both constrains and enables artistic expression.

When grasping any tool, be it kitchen utensil or a paint brush, it would seem simple enough to think that the surface of our animate body ends at a definite limit and that inanimate, non-sentient matter, wood or ivory, begins on the other side. As such, bodies are in contact but are mutually obstructive, not mutually negating. For the most part, this idea of relationality is sufficient; however, it is not so useful an assumption for explaining complexities of tool use, especially according to Nishida's or Merleau-Ponty's depiction of artistic expression. The intricacies of the relation between body and tool are more appropriately understood within a framework that challenges this taken-for-granted positivist understanding of bodies, objects, and relationality.

Building on Heidegger's portrayal of tool use as "equipmentality" (*Zeughaft*), Merleau-Ponty's oft-cited example of the blind man's cane illustrates the phenomenological understanding of tools and their relation to the body in a way that bears similarities with how Nishida takes it that the eye manifests at the tip of the paintbrush or chisel. When a blind person first learns to use a cane, it feels foreign to the body. One has to think about it, negotiate and fiddle with the implement, and to the extent that it occupies consciousness as a thought, it is an impediment to properly sensing the world. It does not aid or extend perception. It obstructs. It is an opaque object at this stage, and it limits the body rather than expanding it. At this point, it might seem appropriate to retain a positivist, circumscribed, non-ecstatic notion of corporeity and treat the cane as a non-negated object. Yet, as a blind person becomes more proficient, this definition and the attendant subject–object dualism become less suitable.

After a period of learning and adjusting to its features, a tool ceases to be *thought about* as an object and becomes something *thought through*; ceases to be seen and is *seen through*; ceases to be touched, and becomes something the world is *touched through*. At this point, for all phenomenological intents and purposes, a tool is part of the body. In Merleau-Ponty's terms,

> [t]o get used to a hat, a car or a stick is to be transplanted into them, or conversely, to incorporate them into the bulk of our own body. Habit expresses our power of dilating our being-in-the-world, or changing our existence by appropriating fresh instruments.[98]

Once a certain adeptness is attained, the cane itself begins to fade from consciousness. It becomes transparent. No longer an object of thought. The blind person stops focusing on the cane or negotiating with *it*. Now, the point where the cane meets the hand is no longer the locus of attention. It is not thought about because obstruction between hand and handle fades away and the tool is no longer felt as an alien, material object separate (*chōriston*) from the body. The point of sensitivity is no longer between hand and the cane's handle, but between the outer tip of the cane and the ground. To use the language of Gestalt psychology, a previously "distal stimulus" becomes a "proximal stimulus."[99] As these collapse, body and tool intertwine in such a way that subject–object metaphysics is no longer appropriate for capturing the quality of the relation. Yet, body and tool do

---

98. Merleau-Ponty, *Phenomenology of Perception*, 166.
99. Kurt Koffka, *Principles of Gestalt Psychology*.

not blend into each other, they are discontinuous in their continuity, just as we are when we touch anything without a tool. But, with the cane, once it fades from consciousness, the blind person's sentient range is extended as she can sense the world touched at the cane's extremity. Merleau-Ponty explains, at this point, that using the tool

> does not consist in interpreting the pressures of the stick on the hand as indications of certain positions of the stick, and these as signs of an external object, since it relieves us of the necessity of doing so. The pressures on the hand and the stick are no longer given; the stick is no longer an object perceived by the blind man, but an instrument with which he perceives.[100]

When the blind person becomes familiar with his tool, or the artist her paintbrush, it is not inherently different than any other body part. When using our hand, we do not attend to the feeling of our shoulder plus upper arm, plus elbow, plus wrist, plus hand and then manipulate a tool or object. With the cane, "the length of the stick does not enter expressly as a middle term,"[101] writes Merleau-Ponty. Yes, there is a division between body and world mediated through the tool, but it is not a cut between body and world, but a cut-continuance. It is chiasmatic. The tool's mediation is not that of a positive object. All of the intervening connections between hand and cane make themselves absent so that one can feel the texture and contours of the world in more detail because *their* qualities—not the cane's—can have one's full attention. In Merleau-Ponty words, "The blind man's stick has ceased to be an object for him, and is no longer perceived for itself; its point has become an area of sensitivity."[102] The cane becomes absent, it no longer obstructs, but enables the ground to be read with more precise attention. The cane hides so that sentience can manifest at its distal point. This experience, which we all have with our hats, pens, hammers, and keyboards points the way beyond a strict distinction between vision and touch. As Merleau-Ponty writes, when the cane has "extend[ed] the scope and active radius of touch," this experience "provid[es] a parallel to sight."[103]

---

100. Merleau-Ponty, *Phenomenology of Perception*, 176.
101. Ibid., 165.
102. Ibid.
103. Ibid.

Our most common everyday phenomenal encounter with tools has this dynamic. Whether a bicycle, coffee maker, or computer, until they cease functioning, they recede from conscious attention. They are not objects for us. We do not think about them, and their getting-out-of-the-way allows us to accomplish tasks with more expansive attention and dexterity. For the practiced artist, where hand meets brush is not a concern. They feel at the point where the brush touches canvas (and as we discuss later, where eye "palpates" landscape). This body-tool dynamic is enabled by perceptual negation. Because phenomenal entities are open to each other and enter into each other. As Nishida writes, "[t]he fact that human beings possess tools must already be made possible through affirmation *via* the world's self-negation."[104] If the tool were not available through negation—if it were an object in the classical sense, fully circumscribed—it would obstruct the body and sentience would not circulate through it. To the extent that tools function as body auxiliaries, mutual phenomenal negation obtains between them. This intertwining makes it possible to experience things as bodily extensions: not wholly continuous with the body, but neither is it entirely discontinuous as positivist metaphysics would have it. For tools such as the blind person's cane, the artist's brush, or most of the things we deal with on a daily basis, there is a dimension of our experience of them that is best understood, possibly can only be understood, when we bring them into view as negated objects, as non-objects, which present in how they extend the body's possibilities while absent from consciousness. Our cars, coffee mugs, sunglasses, none of these stand over-against the body as a "hard core" of positivity, as an object over-against a subject. The continuously-discontinuous relations that obtain through negation are better captured in philosophies that go beyond substance thinking and deal with non-subjects and non-objects and, as is the case with Huayan Buddhism, philosophies that explain the non-obstruction between phenomena and phenomena. While such an approach is more prevalent in Asian philosophy, Merleau-Ponty brings this thinking into Western philosophy through his innovations: innovations that are intriguing insofar as they place him in line (possibly more than Nishida) with Chengguan's departure from Huayan orthodoxy regarding the limits of non-obstruction.

---

104. Nishida, "Logic and Life," in *Place and Dialectic: Two Essays*, 237.

The phenomenal character of tool use illustrates two important points in the philosophies of Nishida and Merleau-Ponty. First, it expands the tactile by extending the body's sentience beyond the point at which skin touches objects to include the point at which tools touch the world. Second, as the body's tactile reach expands so too does the body itself. The phenomenal body does not end at the outer limits of the skin but encompasses any implement through which sentience extends. The expansion of the phenomenal body through the incorporation of tools is an expansion of the visual into the tactile. Of course, the blind person does not receive positive visual data from the cane's end. But this would only be a necessary condition for defining vision or touch within the representational model. The visual is infused with the tactile, and vice versa. Through their ambiguity, and that between the visible and the invisible, the body extends through the cane to touch the world and to see the world from an expanded perspective. In this way, tools become part of the phenomenological definition of the body. As Merleau-Ponty puts it, tools are "a bodily auxiliary, an extension of the bodily synthesis."[105] Similarly with Nishida:

> While as a biological life our existence is bodily to the end, we have the possibility of possessing all things as tools. And this in turn means that things become our body. In its paramount sense, we can say that our self enters the world of tools.[106]

An insight common to both philosophers is that the body extends beyond its material objectivity. Nishida argues that "[w]e cannot conceive of the human body as analogous to the biological body."[107] His thinking and his language suggest a comparable extended conception of corporeity: "Hence while the existence of a human being is bodily, we always think of it as that which transcends the so-called body."[108] These philosophers work with what has come to be referred to as an ecstatic model of the body. The body stands (*stasis*) outside (*ek-*) of itself, that is, it stands outside the enclosure of skin normally thought to be its outer limit. Accordingly, the body can incorporate tools into its flesh because they too are woven into the

---

105. Merleau-Ponty, *Phenomenology of Perception*, 176.
106. Nishida, "Logic and Life," in *Place and Dialectic*, 257.
107. Ibid., 246.
108. Ibid.

same perceptual fabric we are. According to Merleau-Ponty, non-obstructive relationality arises because "[m]y body is the fabric into which all objects are woven."[109]

Because of how body and tool intertwine, representational models and their reification of subject–object binaries are doubly unhelpful. To perceive is not to represent, not to "receive [a structure] into oneself passively: it is to live it, to take it up, assume it and discover its immanent significance," writes Merleau-Ponty.[110] The body is ambiguously subject and object, and far from a monism, idealism, or even materialism, participation in the world does not require making the entire world exclusively into mind or matter. Both subjectivity and objectivity are essential to reversible interactions with the world. And, we should not forget that the body's objectivity is essential for its commerce with the world. Merleau-Ponty explains as much in a striking passage from "Eye and Mind," where he emphasizes that we are not just subjects, but are also "a thing among things," also "one of them." He continues, explaining how the objective body is

> caught in the fabric of the world, and its cohesion is *that of a thing*. But because it moves itself and sees, it holds things in a circle around itself. Things are an annex or prolongation of itself; they are incrusted in its flesh, they are part of its full definition; the world is made of the very stuff of the body. These reversals, these antinomies, are different ways of saying that vision is caught or comes to be in things—in that place where something visible undertakes to see, becomes visible to itself and in the sight of all things, in that place where there persists, like the original solution still present within crystal, the undividedness of the sensing and the sensed.[111]

That tools extend the body's tactility might not be an overly mystifying proposition since most of us have experienced becoming familiar with a new tool, a keyboard, sports equipment, or a musical instrument and felt how an initially foreign and obstructive object recedes from consciousness extending the body's sentience and capabilities as one gains proficiency. Our

---

109. Merleau-Ponty, *Phenomenology of Perception*, 273.
110. Ibid., 301.
111. Merleau-Ponty, "Eye and Mind," 125. Emphasis added.

philosophers in dialogue want us to think of the artist's relation to her tools in this light, but they want a greater expansion that might not be so easily verified in one's own experience. What they claim, and what is pivotal to the argument I develop, is that touch manifests at a much vaster remove than the distal point of the paint brush or the chisel: tactility obtains at the outer reach of vision, where the artist's sight touches the distant features of the landscape. In effect, this gives us a body that extends not just through the incorporation of tools, but through vision. Establishing this point will show how the artist receives a motor perceptual directive from the landscape that extends miles from the body. To continue expanding the definition of the body to include a visual ecstasis requires rethinking the relation of vision and touch as well as distance and proximity.

Space: Distance and Proximity

For the most part, the tools we use every day tend to have an unambiguous proximity to the body. While touch obtains in a complex way, objects also seem to touch the body in a straightforward way. Thus, we do not tend to notice how even things that appear to be at a distance from the body retain a tactile relation to it. For the purposes of this study, to understand how the artist receives a motor-perceptual directive from the landscape he paints—a landscape that extends miles and miles away from the body—we have to go much further to show how touch manifests at the outer reach of vision, where the painter's sight touches the distant features of the landscape. To continue expanding the definition of the body to include this possibility requires rethinking our conception of space and distance in relation to perception.

Merleau-Ponty is more explicit about a visually ecstatic body. He is well known for enticing passages such as when he claims that "to see is *to have at a distance*" and that vision is "action by contact"[112] or "palpation with the look."[113] On his account, to see is not simply to receive data but is "a hold taken by my eye upon the object."[114] Here again it is easy to read these passages of Merleau-Ponty's as merely metaphorical. To avoid that reading, we must re-think the notion of space that renders the visual and

---

112. Ibid., 127, 131.
113. Merleau-Ponty, *The Visible and the Invisible*, 134, 177.
114. Merleau-Ponty, *Phenomenology of Perception*, 325.

tactile as entirely distinct perceptual modalities. To say that we hold, have, or palpate objects with our hands is no more or less metaphorical than to say we do so with our eyes. As I argue in what follows, a visually ecstatic body, a body that extends into the perceptual field undoes the common ideas of space and distance that impede understanding how a painter like Cézanne touches Mt. Sainte Victoire despite it seeming to be at an unambiguous distance. (It might also explain how the Japanese modal painter, even when copying Chinese masterpieces in the studio, touches the landscapes in a country he has never set foot on. But this demands considerations of history and tradition we consider in the next chapter.) My primary approach for explaining a visually extended body, where touch obtains at the outer reaches of one's gaze, requires re-conceptualizing the space between body and landscape, and that involves exploring tool-like aspects of the body's relation to light.

We might think of tool use as an element of *the visual manifesting through the tactile*, vision as inflected by sensitivity at the outer extremity of the tool's reach. But what of the *tactile manifesting through the visual*, that is, feeling at the outer edge of vision? Because of the vast reach of the body's vision, this presents far greater opportunities for expanding its range throughout the perceptual fabric.

When one's skin makes contact with an object, the need to account for an intervening space is obviated. We do not need a representational model to explain how to run one's hand along a sculpture to feel its contours or to explain how to leaf through the pages of a book. But with vision, it is more complicated because of the supposed non-perceptual rift that divides the eye from what it sees. Touch is proximal, whereas vision is distal. Vision never actually touches the objects in the world. To see is not to touch. The visible and the tactile are distinct, and the body ends at its skin's outer extremity.

If we stick with these assumptions and the representational assumptions that support them, the concept of touch would actually disappear altogether. Rather than refuting them, I would like to push these positivist assumptions to their extreme but nonetheless logical conclusion, which is that bodies defined in their positivity never touch. This is, I propose, an implication of positivist thinking about bodies and perception. If my body is a circumscribed object and touch only occurs when my hand traverses *all* the space separating it from its object, then nothing ever touches. If the body ends at the outer extremity of the skin, I am always distant from things in the world because, according to Coulomb's Law, there is a microscopic electrostatic repulsion that separates all bodies by 10^{-8} meters. In a handshake, skin never truly touches skin. Tire never touches road. What we feel when we grasp something is a deformation of the skin caused not by actual contact but by an electrostatic repulsion that stimulates nerve endings. It is a truth of physics that atoms repel one another, and that, for example, when riding a bike, the cyclist actually hovers over the seat while the bike is also hovering over the pavement made up of atoms likewise repelling each other. Even the densest materials on earth are composed of mutually repellent particles such that they are 99.99% empty space. The material world is more empty than substantial, yet, despite these scientific facts, and despite the enormous empty space *within* bodies, our beliefs about the distance *between* bodies admit far less ambiguity regarding distance and touch.

Although this microscopic repulsion exists, jettisoning our idea of touch altogether obviously does not sit well with our philosophic or everyday intuitions. It is a useful concept and it makes more sense to change our definition of the body to include its electrostatic outer layer and thus retain the idea of touch. But a positivist definition of the body disallows this accommodation. According to a strict definition, if the body ends at the skin's surface, anything that exceeds the skin might be related to the body, but it is not what the body *is*, and therefore the body proper would never truly touch anything. But to change our language about touch on such a basis would be foolish. All bodies maintain their thin sheath of electrostatics. There is no scientific or philosophic reason to not make the leap to include this extra 10^{-8} meters within our definition of the body. It is what we do every time we use the idea of touching. And while most would easily grant such an inclusion, what we have to recognize is that in doing so we are, however microscopically, endorsing an expanded definition of the body beyond its material circumscribability. Thus, to use any conception of touch is to define the body beyond the skin. We undertake such endorsements every day for scientific, legal, physiological, and philosophic purposes. There is no reason to revise our definition of tactility or to limit our definition of the body such that its circumscription excludes its electromagnetic coat. Our everyday understanding of the tactile body includes this microscopic layer. To retain the possibility of the tactile, despite the supposed empty space between bodies, is to take a small step toward a larger body defined beyond the outer edge of the skin and beyond a positivist ontology. Now, to return to our concerns, this small step, an infinitesimal electrostatic expansion of the body, might seem insignificant, but it has wider implications as we expand the tactile toward the visual in hopes of re-thinking the space between us and our visual objects. It would be easy enough to dismiss this microscopic space when thinking about or trying to define touch, but considering that it is essentially a phenomena that involves electrically charged particles allows us to further develop the ambiguity with vision, which is also a relation between electrically charged particles (in this case, electromagnetics),[115] albeit there is an implication here we cannot ignore. Thinking of vision and light in this context allows us to see that just as the tactile body expands, so too can the visual body. This expansion, with the help of Nishida and Merleau-Ponty, invokes a conception of the perceptual body without *any* discernible outer extremity, a body always in proximity to objects it sees. Such a definition is necessary for conceiving of flesh and *Basho* as ontological fabrics fully pervaded by the visual and tactile without any non-perceptual space dividing bodies away from each other. To achieve this demands re-conceiving light and its relation to the body.

I anticipate that construing the ecstatic body as extended by way of electromagnetics/statics might strike some as naturalistic.[116] Yet, it is neither more nor less so with the example of the blind person's cane. If we were to treat the cane as non-perceptual matter, then that phenomenal description would likewise rely on naturalistic assumptions. Merleau-Ponty had more to say on this matter, since it was a challenge he faced directly.[117] But it is

---

115. There are important differences between electromagnetics and electrostatics, but from the point of view of embodied experience regarding how different electrical charges produce touch and vision as body-world relational phenomena, they are not significantly dissimilar: With touch, mechanoreceptors are impacted by electrostatic repulsion and undergo a chemical change that generates an action potential, which sends an electric impulse through nerve fibers to the brain. With vision, photoreceptors are impacted by electromagnetism and likewise undergo a chemical change inducing an action potential that sends electric impulses through optical nerves to the brain. While there are variances at the interface of the different receptors and either electromagnetic or electrostatic charges, vision and touch are not reducible to what happens at this locus and includes the entire visual and tactile physiology. What is decisive is not the difference at the interface, but the similar structure of relationality, which in both cases, and according to both Nishida and Merleau-Ponty, would be mutual negation.

116. For an account of the various dangers of "naturalizing" phenomenology, see Gary Madison, "Did Merleau-Ponty have a Theory of Perception?" (1992) and Sebastian Gardner, "Merleau-Ponty's Transcendental Theory of Perception" (2015), both of whom argue against the possibility of Merleau-Ponty providing a theory of perception employable in philosophy of mind or cognitive science.

117. Merleau-Ponty referred to the kind of thinking that assumed a fully determinate realm of objects as "préjugé du monde" and the "natural attitude." In *Phenomenology of Perception* he puts forth his unambiguous support for Husserl's rejection of naturalism.

fundamental to how both he and Nishida understand the body's relation to tools that neither the subject nor the object can be taken as straightforward *res cogitans* or *res extensa*. The body is subjective-qua-objective and has a "double belonging" that intertwines with the world because it finds the same ambiguity there. We can include the electromagnetic/static in a phenomenological description of the body because the body's material dimension is irreducible. The material aspect of bodies or tools, and the electric dynamics between them can be contemplated and the danger of naturalism only arises if we forget the ambiguity that comes by way of mutual negation. Neither Nishida nor Merleau-Ponty deny the reality of objective features of the world; they merely deny a pure objectivity not intertwined with the sensual. The fabric of reality, including matter and the physical forces that constrain them, are pervaded by a general sensibility. To explain how the body extends through tools already means accounting for, however tacitly, the materiality of the body magnetism of the intervening space.

If the body is at an electromagnetic "distanceless distance" from tools, then it is worth considering how the interval between myself as a sighted being, and the landscape as a visual object, is also mediated by electromagnetics by way of a similarly ambiguous distance. To take this next step regarding a visually expanded body means we can achieve the more difficult of the two ambiguities alluded to above, that is, we proceed from the relatively easy case where vision obtains at the end of a tool (the visual inflecting the tactile), and take steps toward the more difficult question of how touch manifests at the outer edge of vision (tactile inflecting the visual). The further argument I propose below is that, when considered in this way, light shows up as remarkably tool-like and, like tools, extends the body's perceptual reach while also limiting it—not fully transparent or invisible, but also obstructive, opaque, and visible as light.

"DISTANCELESS DISTANCE"

The dynamics of magnetism should be accounted for regarding vision to the same extent that matter cannot be ignored when understanding the body's relation to a cane, or any tool. My hat or my glasses do become part of the "full definition" of the body, but they are never fully continuous. Their materiality obstructs and insinuates a discontinuity with the body. Remaining vigilant to keep negation in mind as the character of all relationality—including its material or electromagnetic aspect—allows us to avoid positivism while discussing in a strong non-metaphorical sense, how Nishida believes vision manifests at the end of the painter's brush, and how Merleau-Ponty believes vision to be "action by contact" and "palpation with the look."

How does the ambiguity of the visual and the tactile obtain when a visual object could be miles away, as Mt. Sainte Victoire was from Cézanne or the mountains of Japan were for Sesshū? It seems intuitively correct to preserve the concept of touch and accept a microscopic expansion of the body. Touch is still touch even if there is a microscopic repulsion between body and object. But if the distance were greater, at what point would the language of touch become less tenable? If we can accept a 10^{-8}m, expansion, what about 10^{-4} or 10^{-2}? What about a millimeter or a centimeter? Could we still consider it touch? There is a distance at which we exit the tactile and speak of objects as distant. Thus, they cross a threshold from tactile to visual availability. But, if we must distinguish vision from touch then we would have to be precise regarding how far we can divide bodies before we stop referring to them as touching and speak of them as remote, separate, and unavailable for touch. If there is always an empty space between bodies, why should a microscopic electrostatic divide be thought of as touch, while a larger electromagnetic divide, such as is the case with vision, should not be? Even in an electromagnetic separation, there is division, but there is also a connection insofar as things remain encounterable and we can feel their features despite the interval. The electromagnetic interval enabling vision is thus better thought of as a cut continuance, space as *ma* and chiasm, rather than a simple cleavage or non-perceptual void.

There are meaningful similarities between vision and touch despite the significant differences of distance between the body and visual or tactile object. Good and intuitive reasons might remain for having different words (visual and tactile) to refer to different manifestations of a similar physical phenomenon, yet, when we consider how we parse these, the logic of the distinction is not consistent with how we divide all perceptual modalities. Hearing is a good example. Whether we hear the sound waves traveling from a stage 200 meters away or hear the exact same soundwaves coming through headphones in contact with our body, despite the vast differences in intervening space, we still refer to both as hearing. We do not distinguish between different types of aural experience based on the distance or proximity to the source. It is the same sense and is referred to with the same language regardless of distance from the lips of someone whispering in your ear, an orchestra, or a thunder bolt. We do not change the definition of the *quality* of the relation (i.e., it remains aural) depending on the *quantity* of distance that divides us from the emitter of sound. If there is always an electrically mediated distance with both touch and vision, why is an irreducible microscopic divide considered touch and a greater distance non-tactile vision? If the type of relationality remains *qualitatively* the same, why switch to an entirely different and incommensurable framework (from touching to vision) to explain that relation when it spans more distance? We might grasp Merleau-Ponty and Nishida's descriptions of visual-tactile ambiguity as resulting from their maintaining the same account of relationality despite that vastly different distances between subject and object that would otherwise distinguish perceptual modalities. Indeed, they both complicate the very idea of distance itself, which can be used to substantiate a strong sense of ambiguity between vision and touch, such that we should say that touch obtains at the distal end of one's visual reach.

There is a much more intimate and complex relation between perceptual subject and object. If to see something is not to stand at an unambiguous distance from it, if vision is a way of "palpating" the object, then a whole realm of intimacy opens up for visual experience. "In order to perceive things, we need to live them,"[118] Merleau-Ponty writes. Similarly, Nishida notes that the artist "immersed itself within pure objectivity"[119] (different from "natural objectivity"). To see something is not to stand at a remove from it. Because perception is a mutual negation of the perceiver and the thing perceived, and if the intervening space between me and a visual object both divides and connects, then to see is to inhabit and to be inhabited, as Merleau-Ponty expresses in his early work:

> My eye for me is a certain power of making contact with things, and not a screen on which they are projected. The relation of my eye to the object is not given to me in the form of a geometrical projection of the object in the eye, but as it were a hold taken by my eye upon the object, indistinct in marginal vision, but closer and more definite when I focus upon the object.[120]

In *The Visible and the Invisible,* he argues that the object of perception is "much more than the correlative of my vision, such that it imposes my vision upon me as a continuation of its own sovereign existence."[121] These

---

118. Merleau-Ponty, *Phenomenology of Perception*, 379.
119. Nishida, *Nishida Kitarō zenshū*, 2: 363.
120. Merleau-Ponty, *Phenomenology of Perception*, 325.
121. Merleau-Ponty, *The Visible and the Invisible*, 131.

passages suggest that, contrary to the representational model, vision is an ontological concern. It is not a strictly human faculty that somehow traverses non-perceptual distance. To see is to be woven into the fabric of that which is visible. "When seeing," Bernard Flynn writes, "I do not hold an object at the terminus of my gaze, rather I am delivered over to a field of the sensible." Extending this logic, Flynn further claims that to see "is not to pose a thing as the object pole, much less a *noema* (Husserl), of my act of seeing. Rather seeing is being drawn into a dimension of Being, a tissue of sensible being to which the perceiving body is not foreign."[122]

In this framework, it becomes clearer how the notion of distance and proximity normally used to distinguish the visual from the tactile needs to be recast. We do not grasp what is essential about perception when we define it as a representation of things separated by an unambiguous distance; rather, that interval is a "distanceless distance," as Marjorie Green calls it.[123] Things appear at a remove, yet, as woven into the same perceptual fabric, there is an element of distancelessness. Neither distance nor proximity on their own can properly capture the relation between bodies as part of a common perceptual fabric. As with a scarf for example, it neither makes sense to say that both ends are at a distance or simply distancelessness from each other. The right and left ends, where they are part of a single piece of fabric, are distanceless from each other. There is no other intervening material that distinguishes them, no definitive point at which the left side ceases to be the left as you make your way to the right side. Yet, at the same time, the two ends are not coterminous. Even for what appears to be a continuity, there is a discontinuity. As perceptual beings woven into the texture of a perceptual fabric, no outside of that fabric exists from which we could inhabit a view of unambiguous distance or proximity.

Because there is a "distanceless distance" between ourselves and the things in the world, to see them is to inhabit them, to mingle with their bodies and, ultimately, to see is to touch. The visible and the tactile are not distinct when the self and world consist of the same fabric. As Merleau-Ponty notes:

> We must habituate ourselves to think that every visible is cut out in the tangible, every tactile being in some manner promised to visibility, and that there is encroachment, infringement, not only

---

122. Flynn, "Maurice Merleau-Ponty," *Stanford Encyclopedia of Philosophy*.
123. Green, Marjorie. "The Aesthetic Dialogue of Sartre and Merleau-Ponty," 301.

between the touched and the touching, but also between the tangible and the visible, which is encrusted in it, as, conversely, the tangible itself is not a nothingness of visibility, is not without visual existence. Since the same body sees and touches, visible and tangible belong to the same world.[124]

Merleau-Ponty and Nishida agree that while the visual is more expansive than the tactile, they are neither entirely identical, nor distinct.[125] The French philosopher refers to them along the lines of a chiasmatic ambiguity when he says that "there is double and crossed situating of the visible in the tangible and of the tangible in the visible; the two maps are complete, and yet they do not merge into one."[126] Nishida also hints at such a chiasmatic relation between the two when, in *Art and Morality*, he states: "[t]he world of visual perception represents the world of tactile perception, and vice versa."

For both philosophers, the artist's expressive gestures exemplify this ambiguity between seeing and touching. A key reason why Merleau-Ponty focuses on Cézanne is because his experiments with perception and expressive movement demonstrate the intertwinement of the visual and the tactile: "The painter's world is a visible world, nothing but visible: a world almost mad, because it is complete though only partial. Painting awakens and carries to its highest pitch a delirium which is vision itself, for to see is *to have at a distance*."[127] He goes on to claim that "painting extends this strange possession to all aspects of Being."[128] Nishida writes that to "truly to unite [the visual and the tactile] successfully is the task of the artist . . . The artist must always follow the laws that obtain between the visual and the tactile elements."[129] One way to understand what the artist achieves when she follows these laws is to transfer what we know about her relation to her tools and to conceive of her ecstasis throughout the visual field through light along the same lines—that is, to conceive of light not as an essentially transparent medium, but as a tool with an ineliminable obstructive valence.

---

124. Merleau-Ponty, *The Visible and the Invisible*, 134.

125. Both Nishida (*Art and Morality*, 136) and Merleau-Ponty (*Phenomenology of Perception*, 260) state that while the visual and tactile are ambiguously intertwined, the visual is more expansive than the tactile.

126. Merleau-Ponty, *The Visible and the Invisible*, 134.

127. Merleau-Ponty, "Eye and Mind," 127.

128. Ibid.

129. Nishida, *Art and Morality*, 99.

Light, Tools, and the Aesthetics of Transparent Mediality

In the previous section we saw how the body expands through the use of tools, how non-obstruction obtains between body and instrument, and how the distance-proximity binary is destabilized by way of the ambiguity of the visual and the tactile. I would like to revisit some of these issues in this section, but with the further aim of extending the insights regarding tool use to challenge intuitions regarding light. Reconsidering light within an expanded phenomenological framework is essential for the account of expression I am developing. If artists feel *Basho* and flesh as ontological fabrics entirely saturated with their body's motion and perception, if they cultivate a kind of vision that is a "palpation," then we must question any assumption that casts the interval between objects as mere empty, non-perceptual space. In this section, concentrating mostly on Merleau-Ponty, I explore how we can surpass the notion of space as non-perceptual interval by challenging the notion that light is always and essentially a transparent medium. Overturning this prejudice affords a better appreciation of how the artist feels the landscape through vision, and how that landscape reaches through light to express itself from within the painter's gestures.

The interval that divides the body of the blind person from the ground, where a simple and unambiguous distance appears, is rendered ambiguous by the cane. Likewise, the paintbrush becomes part of the definition of the artist's body such that her contact is with the canvas, not just the brush. But, to palpate something with the look; there is no tool intervening between the seeing artist and the remote objects in the landscape she paints. There are only light, air, and space. But, among these media, the landscape is visible to the eye only if light is present. Illumination is the enabling feature of that contact where the visual and the tactile intertwine. To palpate the distant mountain, no physical implement or tool spans the distance, and what fills that prevailing space, light in particular, seems too ephemeral as to have anything in common with the tools that span smaller distances. Nevertheless, Merleau-Ponty insists that vision is "action by contact"[130] and "not unlike the action of things on a blind man's cane."[131] In what follows,

---

130. Merleau-Ponty, "Eye and Mind," 131.
131. Ibid.

I propose reading these claims in a strong sense. In so doing, we find that light relates to the artist's body in remarkably similar ways as tools do. Establishing the tool-like dynamics of the body's relation to light discloses features of the performative aspect of the artist's sensorimotor practice that might otherwise remain unnoticed. Recasting light in this way affords new exciting possibilities for grasping the astonishing feats of sensorimotor intertwinement great landscape painters realize.

To think of artistic expression beyond the prevailing context that construes light as a transparent medium is to think counter not only to a great deal of the Western philosophic and scientific tradition and against recent trends in Western art history, but also, as I attempt, it is to use one aspect of Merleau-Ponty's phenomenology (tool use) to challenge his own conception of light as non-objective transparency. Occidental philosophy has been cast as a tradition of "ocularcentrism" based on vision's supposed supremacy over all other senses for enabling the most detailed and immediate access to the world. This tendency is only heightened early in the twentieth century with modernist literary and artistic projects, which go beyond privileging vision toward fetishizing the notion of transparent mediation between body and world. As Dalmasso elaborates, this project culminates with "mediality in the epoch of the post-medial," which seeks to refine "non-mimetic immersivity" through virtual and augmented reality technology, where the question of the appearance or disappearance of media comes to the fore.[132] Counter to this trend toward transparency, as several important Merleau-Ponty scholars have insisted, his philosophy and its associated aesthetics assert the "resistance of the sensible."[133] Following Merleau-Ponty leads us from what Dalmasso calls a "philosophy of mediality" to an "aesthetics of mediality," which acknowledges the obstruction that attends all perceptual relationality, but also, and more importantly, sees the generative potential of the resistance inherent to perceptual obstruction. Following Merleau-Ponty allows us to go beyond the aesthetics of transparent mediality where this generative locus can be brought into relief. Such a framework considerably expands the interpretive possibilities for the motor-perceptual relations achieved by artists such as Cézanne or Sesshū.

---

132. Anna Caterina Dalmasso, "Le Médium Visible. Interface Opaque Et Immersivité Non Mimétique," 114.

133. See Emmanuel Alloa, *Resistance of the Sensible World: An Introduction to Merleau-Ponty*.

To begin thinking beyond the aesthetics of transparent mediality, the first step must be to dispel the notion that light is a wholly invisible medium. If light has anything in common with material implements, it must have a similar revealing *and* obstructing quality. But, because light appears as the most see-through of any medium, it is not obvious that it shares this feature with tools, which can achieve a certain degree of transparency, but remain irreducibly obstructive, never fully transparent. Merleau-Ponty writes, "Lighting and reflection . . . play their part only if they remain in the background as discreet intermediaries, and lead our gaze instead of arresting it." Light makes other things visible but is not itself visible.[134] Light opens up the world to be perceived, it enables the aesthetic while itself persists as anaesthetic. Aristotle set the Western intellectual tradition on a long-enduring path that has construed light as transparent (*diaphanés* διαφανής or "visible through").[135] For him, light is a medium,[136] but as opposed to the potential transparency of air, water, or other translucent solid bodies, light is, in his words, "Transparent *qua* transparent."[137]

Other than when light is at such an intensity that it blinds us, we typically experience it as a see-through intermediary, not occluding objects but sustaining them in their greatest possible detail. The inclination might be to assume there is an absence of anything like a tool when we are in visual contact with a mountain or a still life, but this is to ignore aspects of the body's relation to light, not to mention crucial elements

---

134. Merleau-Ponty, *Phenomenology of Perception*, 361. J. J. Gibson is one of the few who questions whether light is itself visible. He asks "Do we ever see light as such?" and claims that "the only way we see illumination . . . is by way of that which is illuminated." Thus, light itself is not visible and, according to him, only becomes so when it reflects off of a surface or particles in the air. Gibson, *The Ecological Approach to Visual Perception*, 55.

135. It is noteworthy for this discussion that the etymology of Aristotle's conception of "transparency" as "diaphanous" (*dia* "through" + *phainestai* "bring to light, cause to appear, show") employs the same "middle voiced" root as the term "phenomenology," that is, *phainestai*, intimating that illumination through a transparent medium is an event not fully reducible to a subject or object.

136. Aristotle argues against Democritus's belief that the space between eye and object must be empty, and asserts that vision "must be affected by what comes between. Hence it is indispensable that there be something in between—if there were nothing, so far from seeing with greater distinctness, we should see nothing at all" (*de Anima* 419a1).

137. Ibid., 418b1.

of Nishida's and Merleau-Ponty's theories of visual experience. Emmanel Alloa's *Resistance of the Sensible World* is perhaps the definitive study on the topic of transparency in Merleau-Ponty's philosophy. Alloa highlights the importance of the opacity and the "resistance" that attends the mediality of air, water, as well as the body, the other, and even ideas. He writes that perception

> is a relationship only by virtue of a medium that connects things and separates them at the same time, a milieu that, rather than being a neutral space, is an operator of spacing. The medium forms a screen of sorts, allowing for something inaccessible or absent to be present.[138]

This mediating screen, far from a straightforward limitation to perception is the source of its latent potential: "There is no vision without the screen,"[139] writes Merleau-Ponty. Similarly, for Nishida, light does not fully anesthetize itself, the eye does not only feel the naked visual object but, "the eye feels the light rays." And, "Without this vital unity," Nishida writes, "the eye could not see light."[140]

Alloa's project is outstanding in terms of underscoring the value and effect of the obstructive features of mediality throughout Merleau-Ponty's project. The obstructive (-and-thus-expansive) aspects of various media he highlights helps this study to proceed from the resistance easily discernible with tool use to consider the more ephemeral mediality through air and water. Of course, for our purposes, the medium in question is light; however, light is curiously absent from Alloa's analysis. Nevertheless, we can use his insights to challenge orthodox views that cast light as fully transparent, and thus establish further similarities with material media such as the artist's tools and light as the medium through which the landscape becomes visible.

In seeking to establish the analogy between light-based and material-based obstructive mediality, what might first come to mind are several

---

138. Emmanuel Alloa, *Resistance of the Sensible World: An Introduction to Merleau-Ponty*, 100.
139. Merleau-Ponty, *The Visible and the Invisible*, 150.
140. Nishida, *Intuition and Reflection in Self-Consciousness*, 121.

light-*related* tools we are familiar with. We extend our visual capabilities through the use of eyeglasses, telescopes, or microscopes, X-rays, and MRI imaging to see deeper, farther, and with more precision into the micro- and macroscopic worlds. Such tools operate through a similar ecstatic mutual negating dynamic as the cane or paintbrush. They extend the body's capacities, making themselves inconspicuous to consciousness, but only partially. These tools and technologies expand our visual potential but never to the exclusion of a certain resistant obstructive dimension. While such light-related implements are interesting examples for contemplating the associations between light and tools, the line of thinking I would like to pursue is more basic in that it looks to establish that relation for all visual experience, not just when using any particular tool. Light itself, in normal visual engagement, seems to show up in similar ways in relation to the body as tools do. If the analogy holds, the obstructing-revealing dynamic of light-based mediation should be discernible as operative in all visual experience. Part of the difficulty of noticing the visually obstructive features of light is that they are exceedingly short-lived so as not to be noticed. Nevertheless, there are decisive ways that light-based mediation is not immediate. Exploring various moments of obstruction—and the process through which obstruction is modulated—invokes a classical debate I would like to focus on regarding the separability of the visual and the tactile, known as "Molyneux's Problem." My suggested approach to this long standing philosophical challenge helps us see how light-based mediation is similar to material mediation in tool use, and thereupon affords an enhanced appreciation of how artists act on and are acted upon by the landscape.

Molyneux's Problem: Obstruction and Light

There is a centuries-old precedent regarding conceptualizing vision that would refute the idea that light relates to the body in similar ways as do tools. A tradition of thinking on this topic began with the seventeenth-century Irish philosopher William Molyneux. He formulated a problem that would remain an open philosophic and scientific question until very recently. Motivated by his wife's blindness, Molyneux explored the perceptual implications of her deprivation and came to initiate what would later be referred to as "Molyneux's Problem." The "problem" raised the question as to whether a blind person who recognized objects on the basis of how they felt in their hands while still blind would be able to recognize them visually should they regain their sight.[141] In line with Molyneux, his contemporaries Locke and Berkeley both asserted that the visual and the tactile were distinct perceptual modalities, and thereupon claimed that a newly sighted person could not recognize previously felt objects, but would require further learning to equate the newly visual with the previously tactile.[142] The ostensible necessity of a period of learning was the basis for positing vision and touch as distinct sensory domains. This conclusion is, of course, in direct contradiction to the ambiguity Nishida and Merleau-Ponty posit between the visual and the tactile, and could undermine any analogy that sought to elucidate tool-like features of light. In his *Phenomenology of Perception,* Merleau-Ponty considers the case of the blind man regaining sight and argues against the empiricist "proofs" that the confusion that ensues evinces the separation of the senses. While his discussion is mostly regarding the issue of the spatiality of the tactile and the visual,[143] I would like to take a different angle looking at the relation between sensory modalities by focusing on his notion of tool use.

At the time Molyneux and his counterparts were investigating this problem, there were very few cases[144] of patients having regained sight fol-

---

141. William Molyneux, a seventeenth-century Irish natural philosopher, initially submitted his "problem" to John Locke, who refers to it in his *An Essay Concerning Human Understanding.* The question reads as follows: "Suppose a man born blind, and now adult, and taught by his touch to distinguish between a cube and a sphere of the same metal, and nightly of the same bigness, so as to tell, when he felt one and the other, which is the cube, which is the sphere. Suppose then the cube and the sphere placed on a table, and the blind man made to see: query, whether by his sight, before he touched them, he could now distinguish and tell which is the globe, which the cube? To which the acute and judicious proposer answers: 'Not. For though he has obtained the experience of how a globe, and how a cube, affects his touch; yet he has not yet attained the experience, that what affects his touch so or so, must affect his sight so or so." John Locke, *An Essay Concerning Human Understanding.*

142. Locke's response to Molyneux reads: "I agree with this thinking gentleman, whom I am proud to call my friend, in his answer to this problem; and am of opinion that the blind man, at first sight, would not be able with certainty to say which was the globe, which the cube, whilst he only saw them; though he could unerringly name them by his touch, and certainly distinguish them by the difference of their figures felt." Locke (1836), Book 2, Ch. 9.

143. Merleau-Ponty, *Phenomenology of Perception,* 253–262.

144. Valvo et al. estimated that less than twenty cases had been known in the last thousand years. Alberto Valvo et al., *Sight Restoration after Long-Term Blindness: The Problems and Behavior Patterns of Visual Rehabilitation.*

lowing congenital blindness; however, the scientific consensus based on now contemporary research follows suit and upholds the distinction between the visual and the tactile.[145] The main argument for keeping these distinct is that establishing a connection between a newly-visible object and one previously identifiable by touch requires a period of learning once sight is regained. For a visual object to translate from the tactile to the visual is not given, it is accomplished. On this point, if we recall the above discussion regarding the blind person's cane, and think of light along the lines of how tools are incorporated into the phenomenal body—if we think of light as a tool—this pivotal feature of the argument, the period of learning required to identify a visual object, might in fact substantiate the claim that the visual and the tactile are not two inherently distinct perceptual modalities and allow us to articulate tool-like features of light-based vision.

To test the analogy let us consider the introduction of light to the newly sighted person according to how Merleau-Ponty describes the introduction of the cane to the newly blind. When light is first presented to the newly sighted it initially appears opaque: it obstructs vision. Research has shown that given the gift of light-based sight for the first time, there is an initial clumsiness, sometimes lasting for months or years, concerning how one sees objects and navigates the newly visual environment. Patients experience considerable "agnosia" (from the ancient Greek ἀγνωσία: "ignorance," "absence of knowledge") involving an inability to identify objects, sounds, shapes, track movement, or locate smells in space. There is a stage in which they do not yet see the world, but are learning to get a handle on the new intermediary of light. Merleau-Ponty alludes to a similar period of learning: "Everything is at first confused and apparently in motion. Discrimination between colored surfaces and the correct apprehension of movement do not come until later, when the subject has *learned* 'what it is to see.' "[146] Also recall that a similar lack of dexterity attends the first moments of the blind person taking up their cane. It initially appears as an almost fully opaque and obstructive object until its obstructive valence eventually diminishes.

---

145. Pawan Sinha, "The Newly Sighted Fail to Match Seen with Felt." MIT professor Sinha conducted experiments where he took patients from total blindness to full sight. Based on the findings of the experiment he determined that the answer to Molyneux's problem was "no." Because of the time needed to learn to identify visual objects previously known only by touch, he concluded there was no connection where information is sent directly between the visual and the tactile.

146. Merleau-Ponty, *Phenomenology of Perception*, 259. Emphasis added.

Let us consider tool use in more detail. We already know that a newly blind person requires a period to adjust to the cane. With vision, because most of us get used to the intermediary of light long before we are self-conscious, we do not experience the period of learning. Yet, just as when the blind person first takes up a cane and must make gradual physical and psychological adjustments in order to intertwine with this new implement, likewise, the newly sighted person or the newborn goes through their own adjustments: there is a period or learning to fine-tune optical muscles, dilate pupils, focus properly, cultivate a new set of muscle movements not just in the ocular tracts but in the neck and the whole body, and one must also train new neural and nerve pathways that will eventually enable visual experience.

To further substantiate the similarities between the bodily incorporation of light and physical implements, we can also see that there is a similar shift regarding the point of sensitivity as the blind person gets to know the cane, or the newly sighted person learns to see with light: a shift from a proximal to a distal sensitivity. With the cane, it is initially an opaque, obstructive object and attention is first manifest at the proximal point where hand grasps tool; only later does this specific point of sensitivity recede into the background allowing touch to manifest at the outer extremity of the tool, at the distal point where cane touches ground. Now, turning to sight, following the idea that vision is palpation, we can see that a similar shift from the proximal to the distal is achieved through light.

When sight is initially restored to the blind, light does not immediately offer the opportunity to sense the world at its distal reach. The world is initially occluded. This is perhaps why Merleau-Ponty says that to see an object "it was necessary *not* to see the play of shadows and light around it."[147] If vision were camera-like, we could simply say that the period of agnosia is a stage where vision has not yet been properly "turned on." Perhaps, though, what is happening is that *light* is what one sees, and the point of sensitivity is proximal, manifesting where light-touches-eye—not yet distal, where eye-touches-world. That is, visual sensitivity has not yet traveled through the medium of light and extended sentience from its proximal to the distal end. At this stage the eye palpates light, but it does not yet palpate objects in the world. Thus, what the newly sighted see is light; it is obstructive, not yet transparent. And, since light does not have any particular form, we might say that we are blind insofar as we seek form through vision. Alternatively,

---

147. Merleau-Ponty, "Eye and Mind," 128.

we might say at this stage—when the visual physiology is turned on but vision has not yet learned to proliferate through the medium of light, that we actually do have vision, but a vision of formlessness. Thus, we might ask why seeing formless light should be essentially different from seeing the world of form *through light*. Similarly, we still have tactile sensation of the handle before sentience extends through the cane.

The cane is not initially semi-transparent, nor is light. Light does accomplish transparency but for the newly sighted person it is originally obstructive, it does not immediately hide to allow for vision to manifest at its distal extremity, where it touches the world, because the eye has yet to become adept at interacting with it: it has not yet intertwined. Mutual negation that would minimize obstruction does not obtain instantly with the tool, not with the cane or the paintbrush, why should we expect it to do so instantly with light? Contrary to Molyneux, we *should* expect a period of learning to intertwine with the new medium of light: this amounts to a period of the body working its way to a continuous-discontinuity with light through mutual negation.

At the outset, prior to intertwinement, light, just like a physical instrument, is partially obstructive, thus the visual and tactile appear distinct because of the moment of disjunction, but that disjunction is temporary. It can be overcome. The initial clumsiness and learning period for a newly sighted person is similar to the initial period of a newly blind person growing accustomed to a cane, or to someone picking up a paintbrush for the first time. In the first stage of tool use, attention is on the relation between body and tool, and the world the implement will eventually disclose is absent from consciousness. Initially, the cane is not transparent. Likewise, we should expect that light first presents itself as obstructive, rather than as a wholly transparent medium through which we see and touch objects. Vision is palpation with the look, but not at the very first moment that the visual physiology is turned on. Likewise, the cane does not manifest touch at its outer edge in the very first moments a blind person starts fiddling with it. It takes time for the distal stimuli to migrate into a proximal stimuli and the cane is the medium that enables this eventual accomplishment. In the case of vision, light is the medium, and, as I have argued, it becomes incorporated into the body with a similar obstructive-revealing accomplishment as tools. Thus, when this moment of visual learning is considered according to the gradual intertwinement of body-tool relationality, it is no ground for claiming, as Molyneux and others do, that the visual and tactile are inherently distinct. The fact that it takes time to acquire the visual capacity to identify objects actually lends further support to the notion of the reversibility of the visible and tactile: A reversibility that would not be possible if they were not both determinations of a common perceptual fabric.

When the blind is newly sighted, or when a newborn first experiences light, at this point *light itself is visible*, not the world—just as the cane, not the ground, is initially tangible. (Similarly, the person emerging from Plato's cave is initially blinded by the sun's light.) The world is first occluded when one gains or regains sight. The same way that the blind person is first concerned with the point at which hand touches tool, a newly sighted person would be concerned with the point where light touches the eyes. Before proficiency is gained, a curious mingling of the visual and the tactile occurs, as Merleau-Ponty notes, "a patient operated upon after being blind for eighteen years tries to touch a ray of sunlight."[148] Sentience has not yet extended through the medium to its outer end, but it is possible. When proficiency is gained, when the body learns to adjust itself to what light demands of it, light and eye enter into a relation where sentience manifests at its distal point, where eye palpates the world. Now, there is a shift in the locus of sentience: The *body-light* locus of touch becomes absent from consciousness, light *becomes* increasingly transparent, and the body-object locus is a site for tactility. Light now achieves partial transparency, it gets out of the way just as the cane eventually does, and the world can then come to bodily presence through the illumination. Light converts from opacity very close to full transparency, from being obstructive to almost fully non-obstructive. According to Merleau-Ponty, light hid[es] to make the object visible.[149] But, because light is related to the body with varying degrees of transparency and obstruction, we must think of light's hiding as a partial achievement not as originally and always given.

According to the above reasoning, we have a way to think about the more difficult of the two visual-tactile reversals: As one learns to feel at the outer extremity of the cane (once *visual*-tactility is achieved) so one learns to feel at the outer extremity of light (once *tactile*-visuality is made possible). Touch thus manifests through light, vision can now be "action at a distance,"[150] and the entire illuminated field becomes part of the body's ecstasis, just as the cane or any other tool extends the phenomenal body. In

---

148. Merleau-Ponty, *Phenomenology of Perception*, 261
149. Ibid.
150. Merleau-Ponty, "Eye and Mind," 131.

this way, vision obtains as touch: vision is now truly "palpation." As such, wherever vision extends throughout the perceptual fabric, because it does so by way of the body's expansion through/as light, the body pervades that fabric. There is no non-perceptual interval between myself and any object that otherwise appears to be distant. Through visual-ecstasis, a light-based ecstasis, we are at a distanceless-distance from the object—simultaneously continuous and discontinuous with it through a mutual light-based negation.

There is more in Nishida and Merleau-Ponty to disclose how light is not an inherently transparent, or invisible, medium. As with any intertwinement, continuous-discontinuity remains. The visible remains chiasmatically lined by the invisible. What a viewer receives when an object is illuminated is not the object fully naked, but as it is clothed according to the particular way that light reveals the world and objects in it. The assumption I am arguing against, that light is transparent-qua-transparent, maintains that light does not clothe the object in any specific style, that as a non-obstructive medium it is somehow neutral in how it illuminates the world. If light were entirely transparent, its various manifestations would not have a signature of any sort. But, we know from astronomy that we learn the character of planets and stars by their light signature. Similarly, many have remarked on the different quality of light in the Mediterranean or the Arctic. The experience of seeing the world in infrared, as a thermal image, by x-ray or night vision also reveals different ways that light discloses itself (i.e., is not completely transparent) while illuminating the world. Seeing things in these various forms of illumination reveal objects, color, depth, and movement in different ways than light-based illumination does, and because they are *particular* ways of revealing, because they mediate according to different qualities, they partially obstruct the object. They do so because they disclose more than the object *in itself*, they also reveal something of themselves *as ways of revealing*. If light were completely transparent it would disclose nothing of itself when illuminating objects. In Kalderon's words, "we see the character of the illumination by seeing the way objects are illuminated," and that "the transparent, understood as a condition on the visibility of a thing, is experienced *along with* that thing as what it appears through."[151] More precisely expressed, Dalmasso writes that

> at every moment I can turn my look in the direction of the presence of the medium, see it appear . . . the medium can at

---

151. Mark Eli Kalderon, "Aristotle on Transparency," 9, 11. Emphasis added.

any time cease to be an incarnation of meaning, to emerge in its opacity, to detach itself from the depths of our experience and to become the intentional object of a thematization.[152]

Thus, any of the various forms of illumination can be brought into relief as particular kinds of illumination, not entirely transparent because they reveal something of themselves in rendering the object visible. The more decisive point for this project is that neither does the light we are accustomed to fully hide. The illumination considered "normal," daylight illumination, which we can easily take as "non-stylized" illumination, even this light shows something of itself and thus partially obstructs the object. Yet, this "thickness" is not a simple detractor, it is not a "minus." Human vision is born from the obstructing-revealing ambiguity of the visual world.

To illustrate this point regarding the obstruction inherent to daylight vision, let us consider a hypothetical example where someone only ever saw the world through thermal vision. Such a person would assume that that way of disclosing the world constitutes a transparent medium for seeing objects; a neutral, non-stylized conduit that hides in order to make objects or the world visible. But, if we were to introduce someone to what we consider normal illumination, he would not only notice the objects, he would then notice the particularities of light itself and how it clothes or stylizes the world with its own character. Light would not hide, it would make itself conspicuous as a particular kind of illumination, an odd or uncomfortable one perhaps, but nevertheless as one way of revealing the world's details, which is semi-obstructive, not wholly transparent. By virtue of light-based illumination being the only kind most of us experience, it is easily taken to be a fully transparent and invisible medium. It is not easy to notice its obstructive valence. That aspect might be noticeable only as one shifts between different forms of illumination, and, even if one notices these differences, this might not lead one to recognize the obstructive aspect of all visual encounter.

Let us return to Molyneux and consider some potential problems with these speculations. I have asserted that seer and the thing seen are both determinations of a common perceptual fabric where the visible and tactile

---

152. Anna Caterina Dalmasso, "Le Médium Visible. Interface Opaque Et Immersivité Non Mimétique," 112.

are reversible. The prevailing stance on Molyneux's problem argues that if touch and vision were united, a moment of learning should not be necessary in order to connect the previously tactile with the newly visible. While a scientist might look to the initial period of learning to prove the distinction between the visual and the tactile, within the context of a phenomenological analysis, we should focus on their prior encounterability. The visual and the tactile could not even come to intertwine through a period of learning if they were not already determinations of a common perceptual fabric, and already partaking of an ontological continuity such that neither is a discrete perceptual modality independent of any other.

To recall Molyneux's position, the conclusion that the visual and the tactile are two distinct perceptual modalities relies on a "camera model" of perception that says nothing about the inter-determination of seer and seen, or their mode of encounterability. We should not expect that the non-obstructive visual encounter Molyneux's conclusion demands can simply be achieved when visual physiology is "switched on."[153] No doubt photons impact the photoreceptors of those who experience agnosia, and there may be different degrees of nerve processing occurring at different rates. But we must go beyond the positivist camera model of perception if we want to ask about the relation between the visual and tactile. Human vision is much more than a uni-directional impact of light stimuli on the retina. Vision is the reversible mutual negation of body, light, and object. It is achieved, not given. Human vision is seeing and being seen, but also touching and being touched. The period after sensitivity is restored to the visual apparatus is not the point at which human vision all of a sudden "clicks on" as a fully operational perceptual system, just as the moment we give the blind person a cane is not yet the moment they can navigate through crowds with the use of their cane. One can turn on the switch to the part of our physiology that is camera-like, but it takes time for the body to inter-determine in tandem with a tool or with light to render it transparent enough to feel the

---

153. In his 1995 book *An Anthropologist on Mars*, Oliver Sacks, a neurologist and acclaimed author, tells the story of Virgil, a man who regains his sight, and despite his eyes receiving light waves he is not able to decipher what he sees and thus remains blind. This, perhaps not unwittingly, illustrates the difference between a positivist account of perception that would be constituted purely by "visual data" and a phenomenological account of human perception where perceiver and thing perceived are in a relation of mutual negation and intertwinement. Virgil is an example of someone who has "vision" as a camera would, but not yet as a human can. Human vision within a perceptual fabric is the achievement of a mutual negation between the perceiver and thing perceived as well as between the visual and the tactile.

world through it. It would not make sense to put a cane in the hand of a newly blinded person, expecting them to immediately identify objects they had previously differentiated through sight alone, and to then claim from their temporary inability that vision and touch are distinct. The period of learning needed does not prove visual-tactile independence. Non-obstruction between phenomena is possible, the semi-transparency of a tool or light is possible, but it is an accomplishment. The period of learning is necessary because we enter *new* visual-tactile relations where inter-determination takes time, not because the visual and tactile are distinct. In a philosophy of mutual negation, obstruction can be minimized but never eliminated. A phenomenological theory of vision cannot locate the precise moment when intertwinement is fully realized. But in my view, the theory can adequately demonstrate, counter Molyneux, that the period of learning to identify previously tactile objects in vision should be expected upon regaining sight. The fact that obstruction can be overcome with both perceptual modalities according to the same obstructing-revealing progression evinces rather than refutes the reversibility of vision and touch. Relatedly, this period of learning also shows that the relation light achieves to the body is similar on several counts to the relation achieved with tools.

We should keep in mind that while the visual and the tactile are part of an undivided sensation, they do not overlap perfectly. In Merleau-Ponty's words:

> The very fact that the way is paved to true vision through a phase of transition and through a sort of touch effected by the eyes would be incomprehensible unless there were a quasi-spatial tactile field, into which the first visual perceptions may be inserted. Sight would never communicate directly with touch, as it in fact does in the normal adult, if the sense of touch, even when artificially isolated, were not so organized as to make co-existences possible.[154]

We can therefore recognize "without any threat to the unity of the senses" that "the senses are distinct from each other . . . insofar as each one of them brings with it a structure of being which can never be exactly transposed."[155] Instead of refuting the relation of the visible and the tactile, the

---

154. Merleau-Ponty, *Phenomenology of Perception*, 259–262.
155. Ibid., 261.

period of learning necessary bespeaks an underlying ambiguity between the two: a relation that is fragile and disruptable, but also one that can be learned and rebuilt. In presenting an alternative approach to Molyneux's problem, this solution offers good reason to think of light in its obstructing-enabling dynamic as similar to the cane or any tool we learn to integrate into the phenomenal body. And, if the above account is viable, then it offers good reason to think of light, in its obstructing-enabling extension throughout the perceptual world as similar to the cane or the paintbrush or any other tool we learn to integrate into the phenomenal body.

―――◆―――

If the analogy between light-based vision and tool use is plausible, then we have part of what we need to grasp how visibility and tactility permeate the entirety of the perceptual fabrics of flesh and *Basho*. Before concluding this line of argumentation, there is one further consideration that can help elucidate the tool-like features of light. Let us consider this by staging a final anticipated counter-argument.

Although Merleau-Ponty explains how reversibility obtains with a cane or a painter's brush, it is not immediately clear how one ought to think about reversibility in the case of light. With the cane, I have the dual abilities of being able to push on it as well as feeling how the world pushes back through the tool. All tactile experience has this twofold aspect of touching and being touched. While I can push things around by touching them, the reversibility of vision does not seem to have the same mechanical causality. Yet, if we continue reading Merleau-Ponty's claims in a strong sense when he asserts that light is a kind of "action by contact," or "action at a distance"—and if action is inherently causal—then we must ask what kind of causation obtains through the medium of light such that one can palpate objects through vision.[156]

---

156. In his work on Aristotle where he discusses Merleau-Ponty's claim of vision as "action at a distance," Kalderon takes up the question of vision and causation and claims, "If causation requires contact, there is no action at a distance." Yet, he reads Merleau-Ponty's notion of distal contact in a more than deflationary sense. He writes that when Merleau-Ponty speaks of "action at a distance," he is merely referring to the fact that "vision *presents us* with objects located at a distance"; thus, in my estimation, ignoring central tenets of Merleau-Ponty's phenomenology, including the reversibility of the visible and the tactile as well as the body's ecstatic dispersion into the perceptual field. Emphasis added.

Of course, the major difference is that the hand or tool allows for the exertion of mechanical force on the world in a manner that is not imaginable through vision. Whereas it is quite easy to knock over an object with a cane, we cannot push over a glass simply by looking at it with varying degrees of strength or focus. Objects in the perceptual field stay where they are regardless of one's visual movements. That said, maintaining a strict delineation of sight and touch regarding causal force might rely on the idea of space as non-perceptual interval and light taken as fully transparent. Further consideration of the tool-like features of light-based vision disclose how the gaze can exert causal force in the world, and possibly a much more complex causality, which makes it possible to elaborate further analogies between physical and illuminative mediality.

I propose that we can remain within a phenomenological framework and conceive of a type of causation that becomes discernible in moments of heightened intensity of visual encounter. I began this section claiming that seeing the tool-like features of light-based vision offers new ways of appreciating the amazing performative quality of artistic expression. Let us consider performance itself.

Any art practice can become performative as soon as one is conscious of being watched while expressing themselves. If a painter is being watched, their expressive gestures might be inflected with a performative aspect that would not be present in the same way in the absence of onlookers. Yet, let us consider cases where the performer would be more likely to be in a field populated by more gazes. Anyone who has acted, performed, danced, or given a recital in front of an audience knows the effects of being immersed in a perceptual field with a great deal of force on the body: how movements change and become restricted, breathing fluctuates, the heart beats faster, and one's brow might sweat when performing in a perceptual field permeated by the sight of many spectators. If we remain within the representational framework, and ignore the intermediary of light, it would be easy enough to construe these effects as arising from the performer simply being *conscious of* being seen by so many. If one can become more comfortable with such circumstances, they simply *think differently* or *ignore* the presence of the audience. The body is affected by being watched, and of course we can attempt to ignore the fact of being watched. But, perhaps the ability to think in these ways does not *result in* more controlled bodily movements, perhaps it is the other way around. One first learns to move the body in different ways in response to the force of the audience's gaze and only then is given the freedom to think those thoughts.

There are strong intuitions regarding perception that prevent us from thinking about visual "touch" in anything other than a metaphorical sense. If we do consider *being seen* as *being touched* it is not likely that we understand this touch as having the kind of causal force possible when we push things with our hands or knock into things with our bodies. Clearly, we do not have this sort of causality with vision. Light is not a conduit for mechanical causation, but that is not to say that there are no causal similarities between the visual and tactile. To compare vision and touch at this level is admittedly challenging, however, I would argue that the difficulty stems from deeply seated positivist notions of perception and light. To grasp the causal similarities between the visual and tactile demands that we go beyond thinking of vision or touch as *mere contact*. Contact between two bodies does not give us what is distinctive about the phenomena of human vision or touch. Touch is not mere contact. Visual and tactile experience are much broader and more complex events, and in that complexity they bear interesting similarities to each other not easy to notice in a positivist account.

One intuition that divides the visual from the tactile based on causality is, I believe, that if there is any causal relation with vision we take this to be a mediated relation at a distance, light being the medium, whereas with touch, the relation is not mediated and no distance separates the tactile body and object. If someone pushes me and to remain upright I contract certain muscle groups, the touching part that initiated the reaction seems to be immediate. If, on the other hand, I tense up when performing, the contraction of muscles seems to be the effect of a mediated cause. To feel "touched" in this sense, to feel the gaze of an onlooker or an audience includes the intermediaries of light, mechanoreceptors, chemical changes, the creation of action potentials within the nerve, electrical signals moving through nerve fibers, and then all the complex mediation of the brain, which finally produces the bodily reactions by sending impulses out to the body's extremities, to tighten muscles, possibly producing sweat and quickening one's breathing. All of this mediation does certainly obtain in vision. Yet, the important point is that none of this distinguishes vision from touch. The phenomenon of human touch is also a highly mediated relation. Human touch, as opposed to mere contact, also includes nerve fibers being impacted, chemical changes being produced, action potentials, and signals travelling along nerve fibers to the brain. Mere contact at the skin's surface would not produce the reactions we find typical of human's being touched in particular ways. If the entirety of the tactile physiology from the skin to the brain were not functioning properly, if there were a short-circuit anywhere, when pushed I might not react as a human does but as objects do. My physiology and cognition might not coordinate to tighten muscles in the proper ways to protect my body from harm. In this case, touch does not obtain, and my reaction to being pushed would be of the order of objects undergoing mere contact, not a human body undergoing the phenomenon of touch. Neither the visual nor the tactile are *mere contact*. Vision does not obtain solely by way of photoreceptors being impacted by lightwaves, nor does human touch obtain just because something makes contact with the skin. Thus, even though we react to the causal force of being seen or touched by someone's vision in a wide variety of ways depending on our own personal physiology and history, the bodily reactions we have are no less causal, no less tactile, and no more mediated than those we typically associate with being touched. The fact of vision being mediated does not distinguish it from touch, and the processes through which the visual and the tactile do manifest as body-world phenomena, exhibit several striking similarities.

If the starting point is the latter of these two possibilities and the fact of the performer sharing a common motor-perceptual space with her audience is kept in mind, then we cannot ignore the medium that binds us. After all, vision is not only palpation when *I* am seeing. When I am *being seen*, others are palpating my body. If the dancer can control her breathing while feeling the tactility of an audience's vision, and if she can find a way to perform gracefully within the motor-perceptual field, she has not eliminated the causal force of the audience's gaze any more than the blind person has eliminated the forces he feels jutting up through the cane. Taking into account the medium of light, we can construe the adjustments the dancer makes in her mouth, throat, lungs, and diaphragm in analogy with those adjustments the blind person learns with his fingers, hands, forearms, upper arms, shoulders, and most likely throughout his body as he learns to move in tandem with his cane.

One could argue that there is no such causal relation taking hold through the intermediary of light since some people feel the effects of being watched acutely, while others can move elegantly as though they were not being watched at all. Physical causation always obtains in the same way; the same force on a cane pushes an object over in the same way, whereas different people in the same motor-perceptual field respond differently to the same audience. Thus, the fact that our bodies are impacted by other's gazes would not necessarily help establish the analogy with the reversible causal forces possible with physical media such as the artist's tools. Yet, thinking back to the cane, the period of learning in which it transforms from separate object to intertwined non-object does not in any way call into question the material reality of the tool. Different people would take differing amounts of time and learning to intertwine with it. Nevertheless, the cane's physical, causal, mechanical valences remain the same. By analogy, the absence or variability of struggle in performing while being watched does not disprove that certain tool-like relations are operative and that causal forces obtain between those bodies that share a common motor-perceptual fabric. The comfort one can achieve comes by learning to move within a field where the audience's gaze arrives through the intermediary of light. One learns to respond to the force of that gaze but does not eliminate that force. A performer dances *in* that field but also dances *with it*. A musician performs with their instrument, but also plays the motor-perceptual strands that bind them to their audience in reciprocal determination through the medium of light. Becoming adept as a performer is to learn to orchestrate the forces of light on one's body. Irrespective of how one might become more proficient in dealing with a performative situation, the fact that we can learn to move our bodies skillfully in a field permeated by an audience's gaze does not negate the causal force of vision. Thus, the performer always has at least two instruments: the body and light.

Moving gracefully as a performer is not to overcome the determinative forces of the medium, but rather results from learning to move according to its demands. Those demands significantly augment if one is in an expressive relation with a visual field filled with people one hopes to impress. If light is action by contact, then the skill of acting, performing, or dancing might be understood as cultivating dexterity with light as the visible-invisible instrument of all performance. To become skilled with the intermediary of a cane or light is to reduce its obstructive valence, but not to eliminate it. If obstruction could be completely reduced, light would no longer function as a binding-at-a-distance medium between performer and audience. Performers learn to move and express themselves gracefully in the face of their audience through the intermediary of light. And, because it is an inter-determinative relation, the impact the great dancer or actor has on the audience, the way that arresting expressive gestures can change how we as a member of an audience breathes, likewise relies on a determination in our direction as audience that manifests through the medium that binds us together. None of these complex inter-determinations is visible within an aesthetics of transparent mediality.

There are, no doubt, other examples wherein the continuous-discontinuity possible with tools is not entirely analogous with the relation that obtains with light. However, there does appear to be a version of causal reversibility in both cases. Such reversibility in the cane-as-a-tool, or light-as-a-tool, demonstrates how the body can extend through the perceptual fabric to manifest visual-tactile ambiguity at any point in the phenomenal field. We do not tend to think of the way the body extends through light because its tool-like effects are exceedingly insubstantial. In most cases our body's intertwinement with light achieves such an almost perfect transparency at an early age that the contingency of that transparency is not discernible. From a scientific standpoint, its invisibility precludes its being considered a tool at all. By contrast, phenomenologically speaking, its (partial) invisibility in no way excludes it from being thought of as a tool-like extension of the body. Certainly, the way light achieves near complete transparency bespeaks an incorporation into the body's definition so perfect that it should be the model of ecstatic corporeality, with material objects such as hammers, canes, or paintbrushes being slightly less perfect examples.

If this reasoning holds up, then similar thinking with any/all of the senses can show how the relatively unnoticed but partially opaque perceptual medium between bodies, the supposed non-perceptual space, is better understood as a feature of a general perceptual fabric wholly permeated by tactility and visuality. There are no gaps or positions external to these fabrics. That means no points in space persist as non-visual or non-tactile, and the body extends throughout space as it does through the tools that extend its definition. The further implication I consider in the following chapters is that there is no position of full non-obstruction, no vision without inherent limitations nor bodily action with complete freedom of motion.

According to the reasoning in this section, we can imagine our sentient bodies not as originally separate (*chōriston*) from the world of circumscribed objects, in need of an elaborate theory to explain our contact with them, but rather as primordially woven into the perceptual fabric, even through the most insubstantial-appearing medium of light, and thereupon always in a relation of touching and being touched, seeing and being seen, even by the most remote objects throughout the landscape. Conceiving of light according to its tool-like features gives us what we need to grasp space as distanceless-distance or as the Japanese conception of *ma*. If vision can partially manifest through a cane or paintbrush, and if our phenomenal body includes that tool in its definition, then we can also appreciate light for the tool-like way that it relates to the body and extends the ambiguity of its vision and touch. If vision is palpation, then light is a tool that makes this visual-tactile ambiguity possible. And, when pervading the perceptual field through a visual form of ecstasis, we do not simply see by way of light, but because we are in a relation of mutual-determination, as Nishida notes (citing Condillac): "It is not so much that we see it, but rather that we are the light itself."[157]

As we move in the coming discussion to further ponder the expressive practice of landscape painters, we might note the difference that they do not usually perform in front of an audience. Although their practice does not tend to be subject to the pressures of the gaze, it is perhaps worth keeping in mind Merleau-Ponty quoting Paul Klee who expresses that he sometimes felt as though the trees looked back upon him. Just because there is only one node of human visuality in the painter-landscape relation does not necessarily mean that that relation is one-way or non-reversible. Painters such as Sesshū and Cézanne, who I consider in the next chapter, might be thought of as artists who have achieved an amazing dexterity not just with their paintbrushes and paint, but with light itself, where, according to its tool-like qualities, it allows not just for a perceptual, but a *motor*-perceptual transfer from the distal to the proximal end of its mediality. What comes through this transfer is more than a way of seeing or touching at a distance, but a way of being moved according to the demands of the landscape itself.

Nishida: Full Reversibility and Expression

These speculations regarding light further invoke the issue of phenomenal obstruction. If light were an ever-transparent medium, this would not be necessary, but just as tools do not become 100% continuous with the body, the constitutive discontinuity that remains instantiates an obstruction between body and tools, body and light. Let us take up this issue now and bring into relief a divergence that emerges between Merleau-Ponty and Nishida, which we deal with in various ways throughout the remainder of this study.

Nishida and Merleau-Ponty agree that the reversibility of the visual and tactile is most discernible in the artist's expressive practice. While it is the latter who turns out a great deal more pages exploring the complexities of the visual and the tactile, Nishida is not far behind—some of his ideas might push the reversibility of the visual and the tactile even further than his counterpart's thinking. Although Merleau-Ponty never explicitly references Conrad Fiedler, while Nishida does so at some length, it is possible that aspects of their agreement on this issue is derived from their mutual

---

157. Nishida, *An Inquiry into the Good*, 151.

study of Fiedler's work and the relation he puts forth between the visual and the tactile.¹⁵⁸ Nishida's concern with the artist is also motivated by the salience of her expressive movements for disclosing the intimacy between the visual and the tactile. In his early work *Art and Morality*, Nishida says that the "artist must always follow the laws that obtain between visual and tactile elements . . . ,"¹⁵⁹ and in his essay "Logic and Life," written thirteen years later, Nishida still holds that "[w]e can probably consider the tactile, however, to be what is most real to us. Our world of sensory perception is constituted where visual and tactile sensations come together."¹⁶⁰

Merleau-Ponty and Nishida understand the relation between the visual and the tactile as ambiguous, and see the artist as benefitting from the quality of this relation in their expressive practice. But how far can this similarity be sustained? Although both thinkers are in agreement concerning basic features on this issue, neither discusses longstanding artistic practices that could help illustrate this ambiguity. Life drawing is one of the oldest and most enduring practices in Western art education. Anyone who has trained according to its conventions will likely have practiced what is called hand-eye synchronicity. The technique involves looking only at the model—not where hand and paper touch, but where eye and the model's body touch—and imagining that one's eye is palpating the contours of the subject. Unless the instructor is a trained phenomenologist, she might tell students to "pretend as if" one's eye is touching the contours, thus exposing a representational bias. The idea with hand-eye synchronicity is that hand movements are supposed to be geared into eye movements such that they become harmonized: part of a single motor-perceptual continuity. The alternative would be to first store a representation in the mind and in the next moment execute the hand movements needed to create a likeness corresponding to the model. These examples allow a preliminary way into some of the philosophers' more elusive and poetic references. For instance, when Nishida writes:

---

158. Nishida comments extensively on Fiedler in his *Art and Morality*. See also Michael Marra, *Essays on Japan: Between Aesthetics and Literature*. Although, Merleau-Ponty did not cite Fiedler in any of his published works, several have noted his influence on the French philosopher. See Simone Frangi, "La Matrice Morphologique De La Pensée Esthétique De Maurice Merleau-Ponty"; Valentina Flak, "Dal Modello All'archetipo! Natura E Morfologia Fra Klee E Merleau-Ponty."
159. Nishida, *Art and Morality*, 99.
160. Nishida, "Logic and Life," in *Place and Dialectic*, 234.

Here the hand of the artist assists at those places where the eye is unable to function. Fiedler also states that the hand, taking over after the work of the eye is finished, causes further development. At this time, the hand becomes one with the eye; the entire body becomes the eye, as it were. The world of visual perception that has been perfected in this way is the objective world of art. Sculpture and painting are realities that have been disclosed by the eyes and hands of the artist becoming one.[161]

Meditating on this issue of the artist's vision and movement, Nishida goes one step further than Merleau-Ponty. He writes: "Artistic creation is not mere creation; it is a productive seeing . . . An artist's vision involves his seeing things in the perspective of expressive movement; he sees things through his hand."[162] A subtle distinction is needed to explain this particular passage of Nishida's. The example of hand-eye synchronicity illustrates how the hand's movements can be guided by the visual. Nishida's thinking addresses the opposite end of the ambiguity obtaining between the visual and the tactile. He not only posits, as Merleau-Ponty does, that *hand movements are geared into vision*, but also reverses the synchronicity to suggest that *vision is determined by hand movements*. This is, again, the part of the reversible mutual negation between the visible and the tactile that is more difficult to account for. It might be conceivable that the hand learns to synchronize with the eye, that it moves the brush while the eye palpates the object. But if the visual and tactile are truly in a relation of ambiguous determination, then vision should also be determined by hand movements. How we move should also determine how we see. (This brings up the question as to whether highly trained athletes, dancers, or artists might actually see the world differently by way of cultivating significantly different ways of moving the body.) Nishida alludes to this reversibility: "the artist sees through a fusion of eye and hand."[163] Later in *Art and Morality*, he writes:

> [T]he intuition of the artist is a vision of things in such a horizon. It is not vision only of the eye, but of the eye and hand as one experience. In this way we must also interpret a creative

---

161. Nishida, *Art and Morality*, 27.
162. Ibid., 35.
163. Ibid., 206.

act in the plastic arts as an expressive movement accompanying the development of pure visual perception.[164]

That hand movements could fuse with eye movements is plausible if not possible to verify in one's own art practice; however, to account for how hand movements constitute vision is another matter. Can the way that we move in the world influence how we see that world? Responding to this particular implication is a major concern of this study and involves a fuller account of bodily movement and expression carried out in the fourth and final chapter. Although Merleau-Ponty is less direct than Nishida in his allusions to how movement affects vision, we can glean his view from other moments in his writings. Chapter 4 extends the dialogue further on this issue by considering the type of spontaneous movement that yields what the Merleau-Ponty calls "coherent deformation."

Everything Touching or Nothing at All

Before closing this chapter, I would like to address several issues that the reader might have noticed were bubbling beneath the surface. The persistence of many strongly counter-intuitive positions these philosophers develop, not to mention the unorthodox language used to articulate them, calls for straightening out exactly what kind of ontological position is being established in comparing the two. What is at stake is the question of how their ontologies of ambiguity by-way-of mutual negation—and all of the motor-perceptual doors these open—avoid the extremes of substance dualism or monism.

Because the representational model and the dualism that motivates it are so fundamental to our worldview, it is not a small task to meaningfully expand the notion of the body, its vision and touch, to the extent suggested by the examples given above. One might fear that in attempting to overcome the hazards of dualism we have strayed into an everything-goes, everything-connects form of monism. If the expanded understanding of the body means that I touch everything I see, we might lose the ability to distinguish the body from the world and from the objects it perceives. To posit relationality as unambiguous proximity would be to collapse all distinction between distance and distancelessness, and to maintain a simple non-dualism without ambiguity. Not only is such an idea undesirable, moreover, the concept of "touch" itself would lose its meaning. The more the phenomenal body expands through vision, the farther away bodies

---

164. Ibid., 158.

could be while still being considered as "touching," the thinner the notion of the tactile becomes.

On the opposite end of the metaphysical extreme is the notion that nothing touches anything, this is the idea already considered where even the notion of touch is revised because of a microscopic non-perceptual space that divides bodies from each other. In this framework, both to see or to touch something is to remain separate from it, not continuous in any way. This particular assumption of distance—arguably the dominant assumption handed down from the Western substance ontological tradition—upholds the extreme position that all bodies are absolutely discrete, separate (*chōriston*), and not touching.

When taken to their logical conclusions, both of these extreme metaphysical perspectives go too far and neither allows us to understand vision or touch where both of them obtain as a chiasmatic continuous-discontinuity. Although visual and tactile relations render ambiguous the body's relation to tools, to objects, to light, and the world, there is nevertheless a reality to these distinctions. Discontinuity remains as a constitutive obstructing aspect. Merleau-Ponty is sensitive to this problem and brings negation into his account of perception without erasing all aspects of positivity, which depend upon the constitutive role of negativity. As quoted above, "I am not an absolute nothing, I am a determined nothing: not this glass, nor this table, nor this room; my emptiness is not indefinite, and to this extent at least my nothingness is filled or nullified."[165]

Because our relation to the world is one of a "distanceless distance," the aim is to problematize both ends of the extreme views of monism or dualism: namely that we are either completely in touch with the world (distancelessness), or entirely separate from it (distance). By treating light as a transparent medium, the dominant philosophic paradigm, however, treats vision unproblematically as a relation at a distance. The examples and experiments of this chapter are meant to show that, as part of a mutually negating perceptual fabric, visual and tactile experience are relations that can only be properly understood beyond identity-difference binaries. Krummel and Nagatomo sum up this ambiguity nicely regarding Nishida's understanding of the body-tool relation:

> Nishida adds that through the use of one's body as tool one incorporates other things into the body as its extension (Z8 31), while conversely the body itself in its interaction with

---

165. Merleau-Ponty, *The Visible and the Invisible*, 53.

things becomes a thing of the world. This also means that the world, as a realm of instruments, itself becomes a tool as well as becoming an extension of the bodily self . . . The body mediates our relation to other tools and tools mediate our relation to the environment of things. Through body and tool, self and environment are thus interconnected. And yet the very things that we make and use still stand-apart from us. To that extent there is a severance in this interconnection between humanity and world. This is the reason behind Nishida's characterization of "technics" or technē (*gijitsu*) as a "continuity of discontinuity" (*hirenzoku no renzoku*) between body, tool, thing, and world.[166]

Neither Merleau-Ponty nor Nishida promotes the notion of everything-touching-everything, nor do they support the idea of nothing-touching-anything. Continuity and distancelessness are both necessary for encountering an object, yet without discontinuity and distance there would be no perception. Human perception is only possible at the ambiguity between these two extremes. This is a key characteristic of flesh and *Basho*. It is the character of the relation between the visual and the tactile as deployed in their writings and the foundation upon which they build their understanding of artistic expression.

In this chapter and the previous one, I have endeavored to lay the ground for grasping the complex ways that the artist's body pervades the phenomenal field. Now that their bodies, their tools, and the light that pervades this field of relations have a place within their ontologies of mutual negation, the next step is the one I have been signaling throughout: that is, to proceed from the *texture* of the ontological fabric to its *dynamics*, from the perceptual to the *motor*-perceptual. I have mostly considered the spatial implications for perceptual negation up to this point, now by including time and motion, we can take that step, going from perceptual negation to motor-perceptual negation, from perceptual ecstasis to motor-perceptual ecstasis. In other words, to show how the body is, as in perception, beyond itself as a moving body, a body whose motions are not merely a feature exclusive to the

---

166. Krummel, Nagatomo in *Place and Dialectic*, 46.

human body, but a dynamic aspect of a larger motorsensory fabric. Flesh and *Basho*, then, are not just perceptual fabrics, but motor-perceptual fabrics, whose textures and dynamics constrain the artist's movements, while at the same time affording expanded expressive possibilities.

Chapter 3

Motor-Perceptual Fabric

Time and Motion

Having considered numerous ways the artist's body extends throughout the perceptual field, through vision, through tools, and by way of light, the dialogue can now move from the perceptual to the *motor*-perceptual, attending to the ways artists move within their perceptual ecstasis. This is to proceed from considering the textural features of the sensorimotor fabrics to contemplating their dynamics. Taking this next step in this dialogue brings us closer to reflecting more directly upon the highly original, and in some cases remarkably comparable theories of expression put forth by Nishida and Merleau-Ponty.

To enable this next step, time and motion are brought into the discussion. Just as we considered perception in the framework of relationality as mutual negation, now we will do the same for time and motion. Negation is key to answering the central question of this chapter, namely, if the body is woven into an all-pervasive sensorimotor fabric, how is it possible to create great new artworks? How did Cézanne and Sesshū move their bodies and find the gestures and alignments with the landscape such that their paintings now endure not just as great artworks, but as punctuations of the motor-perceptual field? Negation is thus explored in a wider scope encompassing the artist's body, movement, time, as well as the tradition of previous great works that have established the conditions of visibility in which artists strive toward creating something truly new and meaningful.

Presumably, one reason we value great artworks such as Rodin's "Three Shades" or Hasegawa's "Pine Trees" is because, among the many things they offer, they help us to see something not previously visible. Achieving such an aim is complicated because the artist's body and the artwork created are embedded in a motor-perceptual fabric with a temporal depth that must be reckoned with. The enormous weight of tradition looms over the bodies of all great artists. How does one see and move within a world whose visibility is constituted by a tradition of towering artistic figures whose works push and pull and obstruct the body's expressive possibilities? How is innovation possible such that something new and previously invisible comes into existence? If the artist's body is intertwined throughout the warp and weft of flesh and *Basho*, if there is no position of motorsensory externality, why does this fabric not obstruct the artist's bodily motions? To explore these questions, this chapter considers important motor-perceptual features discernible in Cézanne's and Sesshū Tōyō's art works and practices. While Nishida did not consider Sesshū in depth, as Merleau-Ponty did Cézanne, the religious, philosophic, and aesthetic practices of the great Japanese painter are, nevertheless, apt for illuminating how Nishida conceives of a non-obstructive relation between moving body and moving world.

Before exploring how Cézanne and Sesshū moved their bodies, we should dwell on what immediately appears to be a meaningful disparity. As mentioned, Sesshū was a religious figure as well as an artist, a monk-painter. Whether you construe his Buddhist lineage as religious and/or philosophic, there is a marked difference as compared to Cézanne whose biographical details do not cast his religious beliefs as directly impinging upon his artistic practice. These questions culminate in the final chapter where I follow Nishida and Merleau-Ponty seeking to destabilize the sacred-secular binary. It will be useful to keep in mind as we consider Sesshū and Cézanne that their forms of expression accomplish a destabilization such that the corporeal form of faith they enact is neither strictly secular nor sacred.

There are countless ways of moving the body, gesturing or even constraining movement that are religious. Some might make the sign of the cross, create mandalas, bow, genuflect, walk to Mecca, or whirl continuously. On the other hand, some sit motionless in prayer and meditation to express their religious devotion. These ways of moving the body are typically reserved for special times and places: during Ramadan or Kwanza, when in a mosque or church, during prayer time, or at a wedding or funeral, for instance. However, for the purposes of this dialogue, one could think of all bodily motion—not just those that happen at specific times or places—as having philosophic and religious significance. Such a view of the body, space, and time is typical of Zen Buddhism. As such, mundane, everyday bodily practices—such as drinking tea, cooking, cleaning, and walking—comprise a set of movements that seek continuity with the most basic animating principle of the world. Zen aesthetic practices such as calligraphy, flower arranging, and painting aim at nurturing a harmonious continuity as part of the world's fabric. This is why such mundane practices are elevated in its worldview to the most profoundly religious expressions. All practices are ways of moving the body in time and through space, and as a result they offer the possibility of uncovering the deep religious and philosophic significance of all embodied experience. Priest-painters such as Sesshū did not paint or meditate to cultivate a conscious comportment solely when engaged in those activities. Zen practice, whether mundane or aesthetic, was meant to nurture a compassionate and enlightened mind in all activities. Thus, the sacred-secular binary is not appropriate for understanding its practices. When we turn to consider Cézanne we cannot help but acknowledge that he suffered a great deal and was not able to achieve a peaceful mind outside of his artistic practice. He did, however, develop ways of engaging with the landscape, becoming continuous with it through perception and motion, which give us reason to also think of his distinctive practice beyond the sacred-secular binary.

Sesshū Tōyō: Zen, Vision, and Motion

Sesshu Tōyō (雪舟等楊, 1420–1506) was a celebrated Japanese painter, poet, calligrapher, and gardener who produced paintings in all of the major Chinese genres and styles, from bird and flower paintings, to portraiture, hanging scrolls, screens, and fans. It was his landscapes, however, particularly his "Splashed Ink Landscape" *Hatsuboku Sansui* (figure 3.1)[1] for which he has been immortalized. Nishida ranks him among Japan's

---

1. Although this work is commonly referred to as *Haboku Sansui* (Broken-Ink Landscape) it is more properly called *Hatsuboku Sansui* (Splashed-ink Landscape). The confusion arises from the spoken form of the two words (both *p'o mo*), which in Chinese are homophonous but written with different characters. See Ichimatsu Tanaka, *Japanese Ink Painting: Shubun to Sesshu*, 127, 73. Sesshū learned the *Hatsuboku* style from Yu Chien and *Haboku* from Chang Yu-sheng and Li Tsai, while traveling in China. Furthermore, "ink" is somewhat of a misnomer since it is an acid and liquid, giving a shinier finish, whereas what Japanese painters used was *sumi* (墨) a solid obtained from the charcoal of certain plants, which tended more toward a dull, matte finish.

Figure 3.1. Sesshū Tōyō, *Splashed Ink Landscape*, 1495. Tokyo National Museum, Tokyo, Japan.

greatest artists of all times, and in the passage below invokes his name while pre-figuring a concept of his that will be central to our later analysis, that is, "interexpression":

> We reach the quintessence of good conduct only when subject and object merge, self and things forget each other, and all that exists is the activity of the sole reality of the universe. At that point we can say that things move the self or that the self moves things, that Sesshū painted nature or that nature painted itself through Sesshū. There is no fundamental distinction between things and the self, for just as the objective world is a reflection of the self, so is the self a reflection of the objective world.[2]

Moving back in time from the Edo period of Taiga and the Nanga school, Sesshū's historical circumstances in late Muromachi Japan (1336–1573) look appreciably different. For centuries, Japanese artists had been emulating styles, themes, and techniques of various Chinese schools, particularly those of Sung and Yuan painting (*sougenga* 宋元画). Beginning in the fourteenth century when a renaissance of Chinese culture was underway in Kyoto, its court had attained one of history's greatest aesthetic cultures, but only for a brief period before descending into civil war. During this period, and long after, the works of the masters from the "Continent" were the standard by which Japanese arts were measured. The Chinese painting traditions so venerated in Japan were heavily codified, dictating the minutia of brushwork, compositional technique, and thematics, as well as the rituals of patronage, bestowal, and reception of artworks. Practices were handed down through manuals dictating the intricacies of the bodily movements appropriate for depicting all the various features of the natural world. Numerous lengthy manuals authorized the precise gestures and tools considered best suited to painting particular leaves, clouds, mountains, and animals. Among the many techniques and themes, some were deemed "learned" and others "vulgar." An entire nomenclature evolved to classify brushstrokes, to dictate the materials to make ink, how heavy it should weigh on the brush, the precise quantity of water to use, the pressure with which to execute a line at the beginning, middle, and end of a stroke, and the bodily postures to assume while diminishing or augmenting pressure, etc. Likewise, wonderfully vivid terminology helped the painter visualize the sixteen different strokes,

---

2. Nishida, *An Inquiry into the Good*, 135.

including: "lines like tangled hemp stalks," "like veins of lotus leaves, "like torn net," "lines like the big/small axe cuts," "lines like nails pulled out of mud," "lines like spread-out hemp fibers," "lines like lumps of alum," "like bands dragged through mud," etc.[3] All of these wonderful peculiarities, of which these are but a tiny sample, meant the Chinese art world was able to maintain its tradition with amazing continuity over centuries. What it meant on the side of the artist was that there was an enormous weight bearing upon their practice to conform to the dictates of that tradition, thus rendering the question of innovation in China and Japan along vastly different lines than it has been in the West.

While Sesshū was known as a painter "outside of the academy,"[4] his innovations were by no means a rebellious departure from Chinese restrictions. Nevertheless, he had a complex relation to the Continent that set him apart from his contemporaries. In the late Muromachi Period, the time in Japan corresponding to the Ming Dynasty in China, almost no artists had actually traveled to China to see the landscapes depicted in the works some spent a lifetime copying. Sesshū distinguished himself since he did travel to China, visited its monasteries, trained at T'ient'ung, one of the Five Great Temples of China where he received Zen instruction, and was able to sketch the legendary vistas depicted in the works of Chinese masters. While these travels contributed to Sesshū's reputation as Japan's preeminent artist, he was disappointed with what he saw in China.[5] On returning to Japan he left the cultural capital of Kyoto, retreated to the Japanese provinces, and began to depart ever so slightly from Chinese influences originating a painting style that would become uniquely Japanese. At the time a shift was underway from *kara-e* (唐絵 "Chinese painting") to *yamato-e* (大和絵 "Japanese painting"), where representations of deities for devotional purposes, and paintings of Daoist and Buddhist themes (*Doshakuga*) were being supplanted as the heart of aesthetic practice. Fourteenth-century Japan saw its first movements toward initiating an art tradition seeking purely aesthetic ideals. As one of

---

3. See van Briessen, *Way of the Brush*, 46, 51–52.

4. Tanaka (1974) explains that his endeavor was to master a realism derived not from other paintings but from directly observing the actual world around him. It was in this way that Sesshū escaped from the academic bonds and proceeded to create his own personal artistic realm.

5. Although the distinction between the Northern and Southern Song landscape traditions was not well known in Japan at the time, Sesshū's work upon returning from China is said to betray influences of both schools; see Lippit, "Of Modes and Manners in Japanese Ink Painting."

the foremost masters of ink painting (*shigajiku* 詩画軸) at the time, Sesshū was instrumental in this movement without which the later innovations of Taiga and the Nanga school would have been unimaginable. The distinctive painting style he developed came not just from a different way of seeing that departed from Chinese conventions, but by new ways of moving his body. Thus, studying the particularities of Sesshū's practice helps take this study from the perceptual to the motor-perceptual.

———◆———

There is ongoing debate regarding the extent to which Sesshū should be considered a "zen" or religious artist (*ebushi*),[6] yet what we can be certain of is that he was a devoted Rinzai Buddhist practitioner known to have

---

6. We must be careful not to overstate the extent to which Sesshū can be considered an exemplar of Zen principles. There is debate in the literature as to whether his works evince the unmediated, natural, and spontaneous experience typical of Zen practice. Sesshū historiography is split on casting the artist as the prototypical Zen artist (Covell [1975], Haga, Tapié [1962]), and those who take his Zen status as a trope generated in part by the artist's own "strategies of self-fashioning." In his twenty-four-part series on the painter, Ōnishi Hiroshi (1976–1978) initiated the critical approach to this question. (See also Lippit [2012] and Shimao Arata [1992, 2002]). Shimao is the most articulate countervoice in the discourse that takes for granted the image of Sesshū as Zen painter. For a voice that counters Shimao's, see Watada Minoru, "*Sesshū Nyūmin-Hitori No Gasō Ni Okotta Tokushu Na Jiken*." Lippit is especially emphatic that the image we have of Sesshū was a carefully crafted narrative that aggrandized those aspects of the painter's story that fit the Zen image. A great deal of Lippit's skepticism regarding Sesshū's Zen authenticity stems from his active self-narrativizing. We might consider, however, Melinda Takeuchi's (1989) work, which points out that personality was an essential part of what animated a painting, not extraneous to the work. While her argument invokes the Japanese tradition in the eighteenth century, the art world of Sesshū's time followed a Chinese tradition that took very seriously the need to cultivate a character that would infuse artwork with the same "spirit-resonance" (c. *ch'i-yun*; j. *kiin*), a spirit that animated the artist, the artwork, and those beholding the work. Cultivating one's personality was necessary because "the force of their personality [was] a requisite component of spirit-resonance, that spills over into their work," writes Takeuchi. Nishida puts forth a similar sentiment in his "The Beauty of Calligraphy" (*Sho no bi* 書の美), where he claims that the value of art "derives not so much from the technical merit as from the *personality* of the artist. Certainly, every art in one way or other is an expression of the artist as a person" (emphasis added). For a related discussion of the extent to which Kyoto School philosophers influenced our view of Japanese Zen that led to seeing artists such as Sesshū as "Zen" artists, see Sharf (1995). Also see Levine (2007) for a discussion of what is "Zen" about Zen art, and what the role of the Western, post-war, "non-practitioner" art historian can be (including analysis of the "Suzuki effect" and the "counterhistory" of Zen art).

painted and practiced Zen every day of his life between twelve years of age and his death at eighty-six. We know that he signed his paintings as "Tōyō, Japanese Zen priest," that he was a monk at Sōkoku-ji monastery, the epicenter of Japanese intellectual and artistic life, and was later given an official monastic title. However we construe his religious affiliation, Sesshū was a practicing Buddhist and his art practice would have been one element of that devotion. Thus, just as Zen does not abide a strict sacred-secular binary, neither should we choose one end of that opposition to define his artistic practice.

Sesshū helped initiate an indigenous artistic tradition at a time when philosophic-religious practices were departing from Chinese influence, as Chan Buddhism gave rise to Zen Buddhism in Japan. Japanese religious and philosophic learning, like artistic learning, was previously based almost exclusively on imported teachings. Along with monks such as Kūkai, Dōgen, Eisai, and Saichō, Sesshū was part of a grand historic movement toward establishing a Japanese form of Buddhism that would become a lasting feature of the country's religious, philosophic, and aesthetic identity. During his life, Zen was reaching its height as a religious discipline, as were the related arts under Ashikaga patronage. The Muromachi Period was the time of Zen aesthetics: not only monochrome ink paintings, but all artistic "ways" (*michi* 道), including calligraphy, tea ceremony, Nō drama, and dry landscape gardening flourished as expressions of the Zen spirit of the time.

To the extent that religion and art have met throughout history, the aesthetic tradition of Zen Buddhism is one of the world's richest and most recognizable. Artworks created according to Zen principles are simple, austere, and unadorned. Paintings, calligraphy, rock gardens, and tea-ware are striking yet understated; they appear natural, as though they came to be with minimal human effort. The severe beauty of a Zen garden, a hanging scroll, a tea hut, is heightened by their appearing as if almost nothing was done to bring them into existence. Often reaching their perfection through years, possibly centuries of wear, erosion, and rusting, Zen artifacts look as though they were crafted by the gentle hand of the elements, the passing of time, the erosion of water, and the pull of gravity. Their beauty refers equally to the human bodies that fashion them as it does to the weather and natural processes that bring them to perfection. The practitioners of Zen arts—the tea host, the swordsman, the Nō actor, the archer—seem to expend minimal effort in bringing forth highly refined movements that appear natural and effortless. After years of dedicated practice, the master tea host moves through the room with the same ease with which her shadow traces the walls. An ink landscape, such as Sesshū's *Hatsuboku Sansui*, looks as if it came to be with the same spontaneity as leaves blowing across grass. The haiku poet's sparse portrayal of nature reads as though the trees and the rivers are describing themselves in the absence of human observation. Artworks created in the Zen spirit look, read, or sound untouched, as if the creators had erased themselves in the act of creation. Erasing the "self" was, after all, one of the main goals of Zen religious and aesthetic practice.

While these aesthetic principles are discernible in many great Zen artworks, certainly, all of the above risks indulging in the ever-present hazard of romanticizing the Zen artist and essentializing the art movement. One must be careful in this regard, yet in equal measure it would be naïve to ignore vast differences that distinguish aesthetic and philosophic ideals between Zen and Western art traditions. It might very well be that few Zen artists, if any, achieved a full erasure of the self, but that is beside the point: insofar as erasing the self was one of the abiding goals of art practice, we can distinguish this aim from those of the traditions that had equally unattainable and easily essentializable aesthetic ideals, which tended toward reifying the self, displaying it as the individual creator, producing the self as an artistic genius or re-producing the self through birth in the soul. If we drew these distinctions at the historical scale they demand, we would no doubt find exceptions on both sides East and West, nevertheless general tendencies toward distinct ideals would be visible, particularly regarding whether aesthetic practice sought to build up or tear down the self. We need not take a stance on Sesshū's religious status based on whether he actually achieved a full negation of his self, any more than we could revoke the title of "Renaissance" artist from Michelangelo because of his not having fully attained the forms of freedom theorized in the fifteenth century. As a priest and painter, Sesshū pursued his Zen discipline while motionless in meditation and while in motion painting a landscape. Both are motor-perceptual disciplines we can speak of as religious. They are not religious because they represent important Buddhist figures or events, or because they depict states of enlightened mind. Indeed, painters such as Sesshū do not represent anything. The framework of mimesis has no place in discerning what is essential about his work. Painting is an occasion to move one's body in non-dual relation with the world. Sesshū's paintings are not representations of nature, but traces of the painter's moving perceiving body having been discontinuously-continuous with nature, an expressive relation impeded by the interference of the self.

For Zen practitioners the self was an obstruction to be forgotten so that the brush, bow, or sword could manifest, rather than represent, objectify, or interfere with nature. Zen aesthetic practice recognized nature as the consummate artist, not the self. Artists such as Sesshū wanted to learn nature's language and above all become continuous with its motions, which brings up an important theme of this chapter: human motion and its relation to the motions of nature. The central paradox I explore with reference to Cézanne and Sesshū is as follows: becoming continuous with nature's *motions* involves a rigorous practice of *motionlessness*. More specifically, it entails a form of expression that goes beyond the distinction between that binary. Advancing the discussion of flesh and *Basho* from perceptual fabrics to motor-perceptual fabrics will afford such a view.

Let us now consider what we know about Zen artistic and religious practice to understand further aspects of Sesshū as a painter-priest. More than any Buddhist sect, the various Zen lineages maintained the strictest orientation toward meditative practice. The Chinese word *Chan* (禅), from which the Japanese term "Zen" derives, means "meditation," or "meditative state." As a priest, Sesshū would have sat motionless in meditation daily. One goal of Zen practitioners is to overcome the dichotomies that the reflective intellect imposes on experience, which divide the self from the fabric of nature. Dualisms such as subject and object, self and world, activity and passivity, distort reality and impede the realization of enlightenment. Sitting motionless for long periods helps the practitioner circumvent these dualities, which otherwise obstruct one's becoming continuous with the motions of nature.

Unlike many Buddhist meditative disciplines, a noteworthy particularity of Zen dictates that meditation is practiced with open eyes, thus bringing a visual element into the practice. Although practitioners stare at a blank wall and resist grasping anything as they would in normal visual experience, this aspect of the practice has interesting philosophic and aesthetic implications worthy of consideration in this study. As noted, in Zen Buddhism various artistic practices were extensions of religious practice. Painting is, therefore, among many paths for cultivating an enlightened mind. It is neither more nor less problematic to consider Sesshū's artistic practice religious, or his religious practice artistic. Being an artist and monk in the Zen tradition, his practice and works afford speculation regarding the visual elements of Buddhist practice and their relation to movement and painting.

Sesshū was a disciple of master priest-painter, Shūbun (周文, died c. 1444–1450). Shūbun's school of Japanese artists, the so-called "academic" painters, so venerated the Chinese masters that most training entailed copying Chinese masterpieces. Although greatly influenced by Shūbun, as acknowledged by inscriptions on his own works, Sesshū was considered by his peers to be less constrained by the dictates of the Ashikaga academy. In the provinces (Bungo, present Oita Prefecture in Kyushu) where he established his *Tenkai Togaro* studio ("The Heaven-Created Painting Pavilion"), Sesshū developed his own discipline that advanced beyond his school's conventions, partly by developing a practice of prolonged visual observation. "In contrast to other members of the Shūbun School, Sesshū looked more often at nature than did his contemporaries . . . he was following nature, nature was his teacher, and his mode of engagement was more visual than his contemporaries," writes Covell.[7] It sounds less groundbreaking today than it would have at the time, but he began to *paint landscapes*, rather than *painting paintings of* landscapes (more on this below in the section "Copy and Original.") In choosing to paint "from nature"—what later evolved into the "true view pictures"[8] (真景図 *shinkeizu*) style and its "drawing from life" (写生 *shasei*) component employed by Taiga—Sesshū pursued a uniquely visual aesthetic discipline that led to his original mode of expression and to some of the greatest Japanese art ever created.

Even the few painters who had mastered Chinese techniques and were permitted to paint from nature would seldom finish an entire painting *in situ*. Chinese painting was predominantly a studio art. After completing a number of drafts of the landscape, painters would return to the studio to compose the work over a period of weeks, months, or even years. In sharp contrast, Sesshū was noted for completing entire works *in situ* in a single sitting. This is germane for our discussion not only because of the percep-

---

7. Jon Carter Covell, *Under the Seal of Sesshū*, 53.

8. The *shinkeizu* approach, prefigured by Sesshū and Sōami, is only later codified in Kawamura Minsetsu's *Hyaku Fuji* (One Hundred [pictures of] Fuji), and popularized by the Japanese landscape painter Taiga (池大雅) and members of the Nanga (南画) school of painting, if not more so by way of the efforts of their contemporary critic Kuwayama Gyokushū (1746–1799). Despite its being a Japanese term, the practice of painting actual locations (*meisho* 名所絵) originates in Chinese painting as far back as the Song dynasty and in Li Song's (李嵩) depiction of the West Lake at Hangzhou, and with the late Ming dynasty painter Zhang Hong (張宏). Both Sesshū's *Ama no hashidate-zu* (天橋立図) and his *Toufukuji* (東福寺) are renditions of actual places, which prefigure later Nanga *shinkeizu* tendencies (Japanese Architecture and Art Net Users System, 2001). See also Takeuchi.

tual engagement Sesshū had cultivated, but because of the motor-perceptual demands his idiosyncrasies would have required. His proto-*shinkeizu* approach was much more than an innovative visual technique: to complete works in one sitting demanded that he cultivate new ways of *moving*. He thus developed an original set of gestures and a highly cultivated form of spontaneous expression not entirely constrained by the dictates of the Chinese tradition.[9] Thus, one can interpret Sesshū's inventive ways of seeing as unique ways of moving, which has implications not just for his artworks, but also for philosophy and religion.

While we must remain on guard from essentializing Zen arts and romanticizing Sesshū's attempt to embody that image, what he strove toward enables us to think about art practice, as well as art's relation to religion and philosophy in new and exciting ways. Highly trained spontaneous forms of expression seek the continuity with the sensorimotor world we have been considering. Now that motion is part of the discussion, we can consider the motor aspects of flesh and *Basho* and construe them as motorsensory fabrics. As with perceptual negation, the self must be a partial non-self to perceive in continuity with the perceptual fabric. Now, moving to motor-perception, we can consider the artist as non-self concerning his moving body, and spontaneous movement is one aspect of expression that approaches a moving form of negation. While Lippit is skeptical of the Zen trope in relation to Sesshū, nevertheless, he frames the artist's spontaneous practice as evincing Zen's central precept of self-negation: "The subject [Sesshū's painting] posits, however, is a self-negating one, perpetually under erasure, imagined in the Zen literati discursive nexus as an ideal of selflessness."[10] He further describes it as an "evacuation of subjectivity" where

> the brush-wielding artist [is]transformed into a medium through which creation occurs. Strokelessness enhances author function to such a degree that presence becomes absence. Splashed Ink Landscape thus showcases a mode of ink painting that projects both cultivated artistic agency and a state of subjectlessness. This

---

9. See Joseph D. Parker, *Zen Buddhist Landscape Arts of Early Muromachi Japan (1336–1573)*, SUNY Series in Buddhist Studies.

10. Lippit, 68.

condition of the permeable subject would prove pitch-perfect for the Japanese monk painter of the late medieval period.[11]

To contemplate Sesshū's religious practice as a pursuit of negated subjectivity is quite straightforward. If he strove toward similar goals through artistic means, considering that practice in relation to Zen ideals calls for inquiry regarding the motorsensory dimensions of his expressive practice, specifically regarding spontaneity and negation. Thus, the analysis moves from negated perceptual selfhood to negated *motor*-perceptual selfhood. What then does it mean to be negated as a moving body? To begin approaching this critical issue, we can return to some of the fundamental ontological principles the dialogue began with. The grounds for comparison between Nishida and Merleau-Ponty were established by comparing their common appeal to negation as mutual. The form of relationality that obtains between phenomena within flesh and *Basho* is a reciprocal form of negation. Both subject and object, self and other, painter and landscape, can only encounter one another through a continuously-discontinuous, chiasmatic negation, otherwise they would mutually obstruct. Thus, if Sesshū is able to achieve negation with the landscape as a non-self, its mountains and rivers must be encounterable as negated objects. Further, because the analysis is coming closer to focusing on artistic expression, we must investigate those negated objects for the implications they harbor for movement. Let us now look in more detail at Sesshū's art practice and his art works to see how they do indeed suggest the form of motor-perceptual negation we are searching for and how his art work is best appreciated not as a representational object, but as a negated non-object.

---◦---

Sesshū painted "Splashed Ink Landscape" in his seventy-sixth year, a time when he claimed that his eyes "were growing misty" and Daoism was exerting increased influence on his life and work. He had gifted the painting to his close disciple Josui Sōen as a farewell gift for his student who had faithfully accompanied him on his many travels and hikes throughout the sacred mountains of Japan. According to the Zen conventions of dharma

---

11. Ibid., 71.

transmission, the painting was a "transmissive object" that established Sōen within Sesshū's lineage.

Sesshū was known in Japan as the father of broken ink landscape painting and the works he executed in this style were emulated for centuries. His masterwork "Splashed Ink Landscape" was composed according to Chinese *p'o mo* (j. *sōsho*)[12] conventions, more specifically in the *Yujian* style.[13] Paintings executed according to that style were referred to as "boneless" since they departed from the rules otherwise prescribing that object's forms were to be outlined. By contrast, painting in the splashed ink style did not involve circumscribing objects to reveal their "bones" by way of controlled modeling. Instead, painters' techniques ranged from spontaneous washes and splashes to actual ink-flinging and dripping. While this technique sounds reckless and was associated with an "aesthetics of inebriation" and "aesthetics of accident," it is in fact the most demanding style, regarded as the highest form of expression and the most severe test of the artist's skill. Likewise, it tested the observer's sensitivity like no other genre. The aim was to give only a suggestion or a trace of trees, mountains, or waters, rather than the "bones" that would isolate and circumscribe their forms. Works such as Sesshū's "Splashed Ink Landscape" offer the impression of a poetic immediacy rather than representational verisimilitude. The landscape is captured with extreme abbreviation and abstraction where any form, if even discernible, is driven as far as possible from objecthood without disappearing completely into non-objecthood as unmitigated negation. The tree occupying the central position appears somewhere between taking on form and disappearing into formlessness: somewhere between "there is" and there is not." The trees, the inn blending into its trunk, and the tiny boatsman all appear, but feel as though they are on the verge of being lost, maybe already transitioning into memory, only a brushstroke away from disappearing completely. Nothing might have even emerged had the ink dried differently.

---

12. Sesshū was one of the only Japanese painters of the time to master all three Chinese painting styles (derived from calligraphy), including *shinsho* (真書, accurate, angular, "standing"), *gyōsho* (行書, moving, rounded, "walking"), and *sōsho* (草書, cursive, indistinct, "running").

13. Lippit, 58. In mid-fifteenth century Japan there were six major modes of painting associated with the Chinese painters: Xia Gui, Muqi, Liang Kai, *Yujian*, Ma Yuan, and Sun junze. The styles range from the most formal and legible (Xia Gui) to the most poetic and obscure (*Yujian*).

One simply cannot capture what is remarkable about Sesshū's painting if the starting point is to construe its trees and mountains within a framework of objectivity. But, we must ask, is depicting a negated object achieved simply by rendering less of it, by abstracting and hinting at forms rather than circumscribing them? Clearly not, but it is more important that we dwell upon the problem inherent to the question itself. To ask in this way is to assume that features of an artwork or a style are reducible to artist's choices. But, the spontaneity and abbreviation are not a choice. The mode of engagement with the world through spontaneous expression negates the self and releases the artist from the burden of an ego that must choose one way or another. Marks on paper or silk are the trace of a mutual-expression that obtains between painter and landscape, not a record of decisions of a painter-subject who sought to accurately represent a landscape-object. The mountains and waters, bamboo and birds of a work done in the splashed ink idiom appear between visibility and invisibility because that is what happens when a painter risks engaging their motor-perceptual body with the world such that it responds to the expressive desires of the landscape itself. This leads to another difficult question: if the expressive relation between artist and landscape comes about through this form of negation, in what sense does the landscape move the artist's body? How does the non-object have a motor demand? Facing this question is crucial for delineating the negated object and the artist's movements relative to it, and must be approached from several different angles in the following sections. As we now turn to Cézanne, and Merleau-Ponty's depiction of his work, we see that the French philosopher also construes the artist as striving beyond objectivity—without fully losing the object—and portrays Mont Sainte Victoire with a motor pull on Cézanne's body, which the artist responds to with his own idiosyncratic motor-perceptually ecstatic gestures.

Cézanne's "Germinations" with the Landscape

Paul Cézanne's paintings were not religious in any straightforward sense. Yet, like Sesshū, he too developed unique ways of looking and moving, which also sought continuity with the movements of nature at the intersection of motion and motionlessness. Cézanne would often sit for hours, "germinating" with the landscape: not moving, just looking. (Nishida makes a similar remark: "Matisse, according to Max Raphael, would look at the same object

Figure 3.2. Paul Cézanne, *Mont Sainte-Victoire*, 1904. Philadelphia Museum of Art, Philadelphia, Pennsylvania.

for weeks or months until it compelled him to create it.")[14] When he finally stirred, his gestures came spontaneously, yet this was not an untrained spontaneity. He had previously drawn hundreds of sketches and researched the landscape's geological features. When his gestures did begin, all of *his* knowledge and *his* thoughts were left behind: "[t]he landscape thinks itself in me, and I am its consciousness," said Cézanne.[15] His works were not merely a product of his motions; the landscape spontaneously organized *itself* through his body. "Motivating all the movements from which a picture gradually emerges," writes Merleau-Ponty, "there can be only one thing: the landscape in its totality and in its absolute fullness."[16] For the landscape to motivate anything in any way other than a metaphorical sense would be difficult to conceive within the confines of objectivist metaphysics or aesthet-

---

14. Nishida, *Intuition and Reflection in Self-Consciousness*, 62.
15. Merleau-Ponty, "Cézanne's Doubt," 67.
16. Ibid.

ics informed thereby. Cézanne's practice, particularly as Merleau-Ponty casts it, allows one to theorize artistic expression far beyond those constraints.

Like Sesshū, Cézanne's expressive practice did not aim at representing the landscape taken to be a motor-perceptually inert object, but instead sought continuity with its motions and its "nature." The French painter believed that his approach distinguished him from the Impressionists who were still caught within the representational paradigm. "[T]hey created pictures," he exclaimed, "we are attempting a piece of nature."[17] When his friend Emile Bernard asked "aren't nature and art different?," Cézanne responded: "I want to make them the same."[18] This meant much more than that he painted *real* landscapes as opposed to copying others; rather, instead of representing the world, he sought to develop a unique way of being related to it as a source of motion. "Of nature," Cézanne said, "the artist must conform to this perfect work of art. Everything comes to us from nature; we exist through it; nothing else is worth remembering."[19] To achieve conformity with the natural world, Cézanne originated gestures but not simply out of his subjective aspiration to do so, or from a desire to be original. He moved his body in ways that the visual world demanded, he "len[t] his body to the world";[20] and thus his movements could arise partly from the field into which his body extends. Merleau-Ponty explains that this "extremely close attention to nature and to colour"[21] brought Cézanne to the brink of his own humanity, to the point where his motions were so continuous with the world's that almost nothing distinguished the two, where it became "impossible to distinguish between who sees and who is seen, who paints and what is painted."[22]

What then is depicted between the indistinguishable seers and painters? Is Mont Sainte Victoire the same kind of object as those famous Chinese and Japanese vistas depicted by Sesshū or Guo Xi? To accord with the overarching theme of this study, Cézanne's mountains would have to be somewhere between "there is" and "there is not" for any dialogue to be meaningful. And, indeed, Merleau-Ponty's incisive portrayal of the French painter's studies, his

---

17. Merleau-Ponty, "Cézanne's Doubt," 62.
18. Ibid., 63.
19. Ibid., 62.
20. Merleau-Ponty, "Eye and Mind," 123.
21. Merleau-Ponty, "Cézanne's Doubt," 61.
22. Merleau-Ponty, "Eye and Mind," 129.

palette, his outlining, and the eccentricities of his expressive practice, reveals a mode of depicting objects between unambiguous positivity and negativity. At first glance, Merleau-Ponty's language appears to suggest that Cézanne diverges from the Impressionists in seeking to re-institute the object, indeed he uses that language, but a closer look reveals that what the artist aimed for is a long way from a positive object *in itself*. Yes, Cézanne counters the Impressionists who were willing to forsake almost all substantiality allowing for the near complete dissolution of the object, but Cézanne's rejoinder is more nuanced than a simple reversal that would reinstate substantiality. To do so would be a meek inversion of "there is not" in favor of "there is," but following Nishida and Merleau-Ponty we know that overturning absolute positivity only reproduces the same problems within pure negativity, that is, both lack the ambiguity that makes vision and motion possible. As it is with Nishida, so with Merleau-Ponty, the "target is not negativism or positivism, it is the very alternative they both posit."[23]

Merleau-Ponty writes that the Impressionist palette led to objects being "lost in its relationships to the atmosphere"[24] whereas the painter from Aix's use of "warm colors and blacks shows that Cézanne wants to represent the object, to find it again behind the atmosphere."[25] He pulls back from a full negation of the object, a full loss to its atmospheric relations, but the outlining he uses is not that which would reinstate a positive object by circumscribing it. As opposed to the "prosaic conception of the line as a positive attribute and property of object in itself,"[26] Merleau-Ponty appeals to

---

23. Chouraqui, "*Ambiguity and the Absolute*," 183.

24. Merleau-Ponty's critique of Modernist painting and Abstract Expressionism was likewise based on their not using any outlining to define their shapes.

25. Merleau-Ponty, "Cézanne's Doubt," 62.

26. Merleau-Ponty, "Eye and Mind," 142. The full quote explains beautifully and incisively how we experience lines beyond positivity: "Bergson scarcely looked for the 'sinuous outline' [*serpentement*] outside living beings, and he rather timidly advanced the idea that the undulating line 'could be no one of the visible lines of the figure,' that it is 'no more here than there,' and yet 'gives the key to the whole.' He was on the threshold of that gripping discovery, already familiar to the painters, that there are no lines visible in themselves, that neither the contour of the apple nor the border between field and meadow is in this place or that, that they are always on the near or the far side of the point we look at. They are always between or behind whatever we fix our eyes upon; they are indicated, implicated, and even very imperiously demanded by the things, but they themselves are not things. They were thought to circumscribe the apple or the meadow, but the apple and the meadow 'form themselves' from themselves, and come into the visible as if they had come from a pre-spatial world behind the scenes."

Leonardo's "flexous line."[27] Cézanne's outlines are broken, thus the language of substance ontology, *perigraptos* and *circumscribere* are not fitting to describe how he paints the world.[28] Color rather than dark outlining achieves solidity, but there is "no outline to enclose the color."[29] Merleau-Ponty further explains that "[i]n giving up the outline Cézanne was abandoning himself to the chaos of sensation, which would upset the objects and constantly suggest illusions."[30] Looking closely at the quote below, one can discern that Merleau-Ponty understands Cézanne's outlining as struggling between the dual hazards of either losing or reifying the object:

> If one outlines the shape of an apple with a continuous line, one makes an object of the shape, whereas the contour is rather the ideal limit toward which the sides of the apple recede in depth. Not to indicate any shape would be to deprive the objects of their identity. To trace just a single outline sacrifices depth—that is, the dimension in which the thing is presented not as spread out before us but as an inexhaustible reality full of reserves.[31]

Further nuances of Merleau-Ponty's depiction reveal that Cézanne's "suicide" was his striving to paint the object between positivity and negativity. If the "feeling" of the Impressionists tended toward the wholly negated object,[32] and the properly perspectival *object* was the desire of "thought," Cézanne took the middle way, not "choos[ing] between *feeling* and *thought*, as if he were deciding between chaos and order. He did not want to separate the stable things which we see and the shifting way in which they appear; he wanted

---

27. Leonardo was also well known for using another technique that undermined the positivity of the line. "Sfumato," which means to "turn into smoke," is a technique that blurs outlines through a gradated blending of colors. Realism is achieved by eliminating hard edges and achieving a "soft focus" effect.

28. In "Eye and Mind" (p. 143) Merleau-Ponty offers a beautiful explanation regarding how we experience the line in drawing beyond its positivity.

29. Merleau-Ponty, "Cézanne's Doubt," 63.

30. Ibid.

31. Ibid., 65.

32. Another line in Merleau-Ponty to pursue the idea of a non-object is regarding his notion of the "pre-objective." See Michael Schreyach, "Pre-Objective Depth in Merleau-Ponty and Jackson Pollock," *Research in Phenomenology*; Michael Kullman and Charles Taylor, "The Pre-Objective World"; Thomas N. Munson, "The Pre-Objective Reconsidered." For a discussion of how the "pre-objective" becomes objective, see Chouraqui, 132.

to depict matter as it takes on form, the birth of order through spontaneous organization."[33] Thus, he brings the object back from its complete suspension, but not so far as to affirm it completely. His cups and saucers are not rendered according to the geometry that would dictate how an object should look to the intellect, but their ellipses are "swollen and expanded" to depict how they appear in "lived perspective." Meanwhile, when it came to the landscape, like Guo Xi's "floating perspective" Cézanne's "lived perspective" gave up the singular vantage point; to capture the "landscape as an emerging organism" he painted it by "all partial views one catches sight of must be welded together; all that the eye's versatility disperses must be reunited."[34] Accordingly, the multi-perspectival comes into Cézanne's painting by virtue of the demands of the negated object. Furthermore, the artist who heeds that demand is not the individuated subject: the position between positivity and negativity obtains on both ends of the painter-landscape continuum. Merleau-Ponty's project began as an attempt to overcome the object in-itself, as well as the subject as "pure consciousness"[35] and Cézanne is his exemplar for having developed an expressive practice that strives toward just that. He studied intensely every day only so he could learn how to paint what the landscape and the objects demanded.

Cézanne might not have disrupted the Western art canon, yet Merleau-Ponty's depiction of his practice sets him apart from other painters of his tradition. How was Cézanne able to arrive at such a unique mode of expression? With Sesshū, seeking motor-perceptual continuity the way he did might not have been explicitly prescribed by his aesthetic tradition, yet, it is nonetheless intelligible within the context of Zen artistic practice and the broader historical circumstances of Muromachi Japan. For Cézanne, by contrast, despite his practice arising from a serious engagement with European art history, it is not so easy to explain his particular motor-perceptual innovations in relation to major figures of that tradition. To return to our question of the relation between art, religion, and philosophy, Cézanne's techniques do not fit so neatly into any Western religious or philosophic

---

33. Merleau-Ponty, "Cézanne's Doubt," 63. Emphasis added.

34. Ibid., 67.

35. ". . . reduce all phenomena which bear witness to the union of subject and world, putting in their place the clear idea of the object as in itself and of the subject as pure consciousness. [Objective thinking] therefore severs the links [that] unite the thing and the embodied subject" *Phenomenology of Perception*, 373.

context. When asking where exactly he does fit, or how to understand what he has taught us about art, perception, or motion, Cézanne's innovations can inform the Western phenomenological project of describing a body beyond positivist metaphysics, while also enabling productive dialogue with Japanese aesthetic principles and Nishida's understanding of artistic expression.

Time: From Perception to Motor-Perception

Having discussed the practices of Cézanne and Sesshū in greater detail, in the coming sections I consider movement more directly, now regarding the theories of time in Nishida and Merleau-Ponty.

A painter might consider temporal aspects of her expression and wonder, for example, when is the right time to paint a landscape: in the morning, when the mist clears and soft, diffuse colors blend into each other; in the afternoon, when the sun spreads its light indiscriminately across the landscape; or at dusk, when shadows lengthen and the bright sides of trees and mountains facing the low-lying sun contrast with the darkening sides that face away. To ask *when* to paint a landscape is to ask regarding time and movement. Of course, there are enumerable subtle temporal elements to consider. Insofar as a specific moment will be depicted on canvas, and later seen by human eyes, this implicates a multitude of components that must be taken into account, including the relations between light, landscape, the painter's motion, and her vision.

To choose the appropriate moment to paint, or the right instant to make the next brushstroke, involves temporal concerns that seem incalculable, possibly infinite. Not only do bodily gestures move through space, and are therefore temporal, but also as the sun travels across the sky, the landscape never appears exactly the same in any two moments. Similarly, the paint on a brush dries slightly in every passing instant, while the artist's expressive capabilities are modulated by a body constantly metabolizing its fuel, offering at every moment increasing or decreasing amounts of energy, precision, and dexterity. All the body's parts, as well as the painting materials and the landscape itself, are temporal and in constant motion, and none can be fully seen, represented, or controlled by the painter who is caught up in their fabric. Nor can this continuity of movement be grasped with conventional, linear, or positivist views of time, which consider motion and motionlessness as a stable binary or view motion and perception as separate bodily phenomena. To grasp the artist's astonishing ability to engage all of the above temporal intricacies calls for a complex, phenomenological account of time and motion.

The enormous complexity of the relation between the moving body and moving world might explain the desire to arrest change, and to give a simplified account of time and motion that does not take into account the negative. Artists are indispensable for phenomenology because their gestures reveal qualities of the body and the world that would otherwise remain unseen. Their form of embodiment calls for equally complex frameworks for understanding time and motion. Artistic practice is exemplary for Nishida and Merleau-Ponty where it counteracts the overly simplified understanding of motion and time handed down by positivist philosophies or sciences—an understanding further reinforced by technologies that perpetuate positivist assumptions. After almost a century of innovations in visual and motor technologies, there is a tendency to think of motion and perception according to those models. But just as the "camera" model of perception is inadequate for understanding human perception, so too a "motion camera" model proves insufficient for describing human motor-perception.[36] A camera's relation to light lacks those features of human motion and perception that phenomenology underlines. Visual technologies do not achieve reversibility between the visible and the invisible, nor does a motion camera record movement within the ambiguity between motion and motionlessness. Among the many reasons camera technology metaphor is incapable of describing human motion and perception is that they operate within a different temporality than the human motorsensory body, and thus reify distinctions between activity and passivity that block us from noticing what is most important in Cézanne and Sesshū's expressive practices. In light of this, let us examine various temporal attributes discussed by Nishida and Merleau-Ponty, revealing the implications for creating those artworks that disclose otherwise unnoticeable features of the body and its relation to the world.

Motion: Volitional Character of the World

ACTIVITY-PASSIVITY

In the introduction, and throughout this study, I have returned to a number of enigmatic lines of Nishida and Merleau-Ponty's referring to the world or

---

36. Bergson makes a similar point regarding the "cinematographical mechanism" in chapter 4 of *Creative Evolution*.

the landscape itself as having vision, thought, as demanding movements and colors, and as expressing itself through the artist's body, tools with eyes at their tip, seeing through a fusion of eye and hand, and bamboo growing inside the painter's body. Interpreting these passages in a strong sense, that is, as more than merely metaphorical, is possible if one grasps the bi-directional determination between body and world that obtains at a motor and perceptual level. It is worth going further here to demonstrate how these philosophers challenge assumptions about the body to establish flesh and *Basho* as motor-perceptual and expressive fabrics in which reciprocal determination takes place. Understanding their philosophies demands significant rethinking of many assumptions about movement and expression. For example, when we imagine an artist's motions and gestures, we might consider how limbs move through space, the different directions, speeds, weights, and pressures that the hand exerts in tandem with a drawing instrument, a brush, or a chisel. Imagining the body this way, our motions could—theoretically at least—be broken down, in their most abstract sense, to modifications from one spatial point to another in a given amount of time. No doubt, these are overly simplified examples, but where these sort of assumptions are the building blocks of theories that extend much further, I would like to highlight that they reify several dichotomies that are potentially un-productive for understanding bodily motion, not to mention artistic expression. The main opposition I focus on in the coming sections is that which arises between motion—usually thought to be objectively visible—and the motionlessness that punctuates the artist's gestures whose dynamics are not so easily visible. Motionlessness in particular is prone to being ignored whereas what is important are those gestures we can see and trace through time and space. Those moments when an artist is either still or contemplating her next set of movements are generally not thematized or commented on: the positive gesture is what we look at when exploring the artist's activity. We will have to challenge and recast the binaries of motion and motionlessness (and by implication activity and passivity) to appreciate artists such as Sesshū and Cézanne, as well as the expressive theories of Nishida and Merleau-Ponty.

Just as we should estimate artworks in their positive *and* negative features, in what they offer through visibility and invisibility, so the artist's expressive movements should be seen in the full light of activity and passivity, where expression is constituted by both positively visible gestures alongside inactivity and motionlessness. The moments of inactivity are not inconsequential to motion. The negative aspect of expressive motion—the instant of hesitation, calculation, or indecision—is equally constitutive of the artistic gesture. To pursue this line of thinking, we have to find a way to conceptualize a period of inactivity—the negative of motion lining the positive—where motionlessness lasts much longer than a fleeting hesitation. How is motionlessness understood when it extends over hours, or even days, as with Cézanne and Sesshū's meditations?

Both Nishida and Merleau-Ponty formulate accounts of motion whereby activity and passivity are held ambiguous. In his earliest writings, Nishida asks: "from what does the distinction between active and passive derive?"[37] This opposition does not exist in an absolute sense for any phenomena in the world. Moreover, to maintain this distinction, the subject would have to be distinct from the object, and not related by mutual negation with the field that allows for the encounter between the two. However, Nishida insists that "[t]here is no distinction between active and passive in reality, for they are the two sides of one reality; the unifier is always active and the unified is always passive."[38] Similarly, consider Merleau-Ponty's words, "my activity is equally passivity."[39] The flesh is the "fact that my body is active-passive."[40] Yet, as entangled within a pervasive motorsensory fabric, a fabric with a temporal depth, one's activities are never strictly one's own. Being active can simply be to go along with what the world elicits from us, whereas passivity sometimes requires that we fight hard against the ways the world pulls on the body. Accordingly, Merleau-Ponty is of the belief that "there can be no question of fitting together passivity before a transcendent with an activity of impermanent thought. It is a question of reconsidering the interdependent notions of the active and the passive in such a way that they no longer "place us before the antinomy" of a "philosophy of reflection."[41] Otherwise put, his depiction of Cézanne shows an expressive practice that accepts and is productive within such an antinomy.

Where our philosophers in dialogue strive to give an account of artistic expression without the substantive, anthropocentric, individuated subject/artist as such, they too embrace the antinomy. Artistic expression cannot be reduced to artistic activity. Both philosophers look to do away with the

---

37. Nishida, *An Inquiry into the Good*, 65; Nishida, "Logic and Life," 252; Merleau-Ponty, *The Visible and the Invisible*, 139, 142, 221, 271.
38. Nishida, *An Inquiry into the Good*, 65.
39. Merleau-Ponty, *The Visible and the Invisible*, 139.
40. Ibid., 271.
41. Ibid., 43.

substantive subject/artist and—along the lines of Nishida's "seeing without a seer"—both thinkers explore artistic expression without an artist.[42] Of course, the artist plays a significant role in expression; however, despite their differences, Nishida and Merleau-Ponty both want to displace the traditional notion of the active subject and its agency, in service of a philosophy in which expression is a more expansive event than one permitting tidy parsing between the poles of activity and passivity. Because motion and perception are phenomena that cut across the body-world distinction, because they straddle temporal modalities, and because human movement is not an exclusively human event, artistic expression cannot be exhaustively described by the activity of a self. The question of how the artist offers up their passivity such that the landscape's activity can work from inside the body brings us back, again, to the issue of negation and later to the risk met with a motor-perceptual form of faith.

Both Sesshū and Cézanne brought about significant advances to their aesthetic traditions through their innovations. It is difficult to speculate about what exactly motivated their experiments, but if we were to start anywhere, it seems apt to assume that the artists themselves were the ones who initiated and were responsible for their practices. One assumes that they decided what their projects were and how they would be fulfilled. Whether their advancements are framed in terms of a desire for originality, novelty, progress, or evolution, or merely for the sake of art itself, what could be more straightforward than presuming that the painters themselves are the agents behind their expressive projects? With this as our guiding principle, we scour their history, psychology, physiology, beliefs, obsessions, and neuroses for answers to our questions about their art. Amid all this foraging, we tend to ignore the landscape itself. For it is not immediately obvious how the natural world has a part to play in dictating the particularities of an artist's practice. The object painted is thought to be only minimally consequential in relation to the particular bodily and perceptual orientation taken toward it. If I were a positivist, I would tend to consider the artist as the active expressive agent, and although the landscape no doubt has its own kind of

---

42. In Nishida's case this can be understood based on the type of inter-determination that obtains as a "determination without determiner" (*genteisurumononaki gentei* 限定するものなき限定).

movement and activity, growth and decay, I would not typically consider these motions as having any expressive agency through the painting that results. In this restricted framework, I might allow that the landscape *inspires* an artist's activity, but in general this will not include the possibility that it has any causal force regarding the actual movements of the artist's body. The artist is expressive, not the landscape.

Following this conventional framework, the human has access to the full breadth of the active-passive spectrum, whereas the world is limited to a passive (or at least volitionally neutral) role. By contrast, Nishida and Merleau-Ponty hold the active-passive distinction to be ambiguous, and not only with respect to the human; the landscape too exists beyond this binary. If this were not the case, there would be grounds to maintain a subject–object distinction where volition is concerned, whereby the artist would be fully active and the landscape passive. The implications of such an incongruity would raise serious issues for the ontological foundations of Nishida's and Merleau-Ponty's philosophies that require a mutual motor-perceptual negation between body and world. If only the artist enjoyed the ambiguity of activity and passivity, then this would present as an obstruction, a mere discontinuity with the landscape reduced to the limited kind of motion positivist metaphysics expects. As such, expression would remain a strictly human affair, the result of artistic activity. This would be to posit a position external to or "cut out" of the motorsensory fabric. Not a chiasm or a continuous-discontinuity, but a simple discontinuity between an active-passive subject and a passive object. In Nishida and Merleau-Ponty's concepts of expression, however, the landscape partakes in the full reversibility of activity and passivity. Merleau-Ponty is unequivocal: "Why would not the synergy exist among different organisms, if it is possible within each? Their landscapes interweave, their actions and their passions fit together exactly."[43] Artistic expression cannot be entirely appreciated within an ontology that conceives of the world as inert matter volitionally inconsequential to human movement. Bodily motion must be understood, Marratto writes, "as movement discriminatingly allowing 'itself' to be moved."[44] Just as vision is seeing-seen, so too bodily movement is moving-moved. Delving further into the ontologies of flesh and *Basho*, as the active-passive binary is ambiguated, the distinction between expressing and being expressed, making and

---

43. Merleau-Ponty, *The Visible and the Invisible*, 142.
44. Scott Marratto, *The Intercorporeal Self: Merleau-Ponty on Subjectivity*, 153.

being-made is likewise destabilized. To reach this point requires rethinking deeply held assumptions about the body, movement, time, and negation.

Ontologies of Expression

The distinction between motion and motionlessness tends to be strictly upheld in Western philosophy, and is one way of distinguishing animate from inanimate beings especially within the context of substance dualism. According to common sense and a great deal of the history of Western philosophy, the world, landscapes, or objects may have a kind of movement, but this is distinct from the movement of animate bodies, which have an internal principle of motion. Objects have motion imposed upon them from outside. After Aristotle, philosophers in the West developed a notion of objectivity as passive or "inert" matter, that is, matter governed strictly by external principles of mechanical motion, with human movement being seen as essentially different from the motion of the objective world of nature. Where these are grounding principles, a dichotomy arises between internal and external sources of motion motivating later distinctions between subjectivity and objectivity. Neither Merleau-Ponty nor Nishida conceives of motion along these lines. Their concepts of "objectivity" and "nature," discussed below, are more in line with earlier ideas of a basic principle of motion and change common to the world and to all beings.

Precursors to Merleau-Ponty and Nishida's ontologies do exist in both the Western and Eastern traditions. The ability to conceive of "objectivity" as inanimate matter is a product of Western philosophical modernity, before which ontologies were not necessarily founded on an absolute distinction between animate and inanimate nature. Some of these ontological principles would include Platonic "eros," Daoist "way," Empedocles's "love" as a cosmic force, Spinoza's "Conatus," Dōgen's "Buddha-Nature," and of course Nietzsche's "Will to Power." The early Greek notion of *physis* was an animating principle that pervaded the entirety of the natural world—human bodies as much as mountains and rivers. Aristotle focused on a more fundamental type of motion, shared between all beings by virtue of their *energeia*. Even material objects, in actualizing their potential, "act" toward an end (*telos*)— in their case, forming matter—and in this way participate in motion.[45] In Aristotle's philosophy, while there are distinct features of animal motion,

---

45. Aristotle, "Physics," 201a 10–11, 27–29, b 4–5.

the most basic source of motion is not grounds for bifurcating the world into animate and inanimate beings. Of course, all these various ontologies achieve different aims in their respective philosophical systems, yet each postulates a general animating or energetic principle prior to the human-world divide. Examining each one in detail would no doubt reveal that the movements of nature and the cosmos are thought differently within each, but they share the feature of postulating a common principle of motion for both animate and inanimate nature, which is, in the broadest terms, also the case for *Basho* and flesh.

While the philosophers that approach motion on the ontological level might prefigure or inform Nishida or Merleau-Ponty, what we need is a connection between ontology and expression: more precisely, an ontology where expression is not exclusive to the human world. This is not as easily found in either tradition, yet Dōgen—a philosopher whose traces are felt throughout Nishida's writings—does anticipate later ontologies of expression. Dōgen identified a tendency still prevalent in the thirteenth century toward treating animate and inanimate nature separately, where only the former was animated by Buddha-Nature. All the phenomenal world is, according to Dōgen, Buddha-Nature: rocks, waters, and artists alike. This ontological extension had vast implications for Buddhist thinking and practice, and his particular way of overcoming the animate-inanimate distinction raises the question of how the world is itself expressive. Dōgen revises Kūkai's earlier concept "*hosshin-seppō*" (法身説法), "the Dharmakāya expounds the Dharma," which only attributed expression to sentient beings. According to this idea, all humans and animals expound the Buddha Dharma at all times and in all of their actions. Dōgen enlarges this idea with his concept "*mujō-seppō*" (無情説法), "insentient beings (*mujō*) expound the Dharma," where all sentient *and* non-sentient beings express the Buddha Dharma. As such, the language of expression extends beyond humans to include the entire phenomenal world. How this prefigures our discussion is that Dōgen conceives of a continuity between the expression of human beings, and all entities in the natural world. As Graham Parkes writes in the introduction to his translation of Dōgen's "Mountains and Waters as Sūtras": "the natural world can be experienced and understood as a spiritual sermon and sacred scripture, as a spoken and written expression of Buddhist teachings."[46] Dōgen's writings articulate a notion of expression that applies equally to the entire world as a single expressive fabric, as a sūtra that can be read across time

---

46. Parkes, *Dōgen's Mountains and Waters as Sūtras*, 83.

and space. The fundamental constituents of reality, according to Dōgen, speak. "The Buddhist teaching is all the phenomenal world before us."[47] Buddhist sūtras are not only texts or verbal teachings: all objects, rocks, stones, mountains, and trees express the Buddha Dharma. The Buddha's mouth, Dōgen writes, "is hanging on all the walls—every mouth is on all the walls."[48] Merleau-Ponty is not far off when he writes that Cézanne learned that "expression is the language of the thing itself and springs from its configuration."[49] Barbaras follows this line of thinking and formulates the task of philosophy as "a way of speaking that reaches the world again as mute expression," and in so doing finds not the speech of the subject, but "the speech of the *things themselves*."[50]

Human language surely has many distinguishing features that make it difficult to conceive of the world as engaging in a similar form of expression. It would be foolish to ignore those differences. Yet, it is interesting to consider that human motion is likewise much more complex than most worldly motion, but we still call the motion of objects "motion." We have more difficulty saying that the world has language or is expressive. Why can we not allow that humans are perhaps expressive in much more intricate ways while also allowing that what happens in the natural world is likewise expressive, or that the natural world has its own language. The ontological positions Nishida and Merleau-Ponty establish move beyond the human monopoly over language and instead look at expression precisely for how it connects us with nature, rather than how we are divided away from it. By focusing on elements of expression shared among all beings, we see an infinite complexity not visible within the limited anthropocentric notion of language. So too with motion, perception, and volition: if we insist that these features divide humans from nature, we forsake the ability to appreciate the astonishing ways the moving body intertwines with the moving world. I would argue that we lose the ability to appreciate what is most significant about the works of Sesshū, Cézanne, and many other important artists whose works can help disabuse us of our dangerous anthropocentrism.

Flesh and *Basho* are in line with the above-mentioned ontologies in that they do not ascribe different sources of motion or expression to animate

---

47. Dōgen, *Flowers of Emptiness: Selections from Dōgen's Shōbōgenzō*, 22.
48. Ibid., 80.
49. Merleau-Ponty, *Phenomenology of Perception*, 376.
50. Barbaras, "*The Being of the Phenomena: Merleau-Ponty's Ontology,*" 66. Emphasis added.

and inanimate entities. By attributing expressive activity to the landscape, it might seem like Nishida and Merleau-Ponty are stripping the artist of her due agency, or reallocating agency from subject to object, animate to inanimate. Indeed, Nishida and Merleau-Ponty's often obscure language does seem to over-ascribe passivity to the artist, ostensibly giving more to the world than seems appropriate. Yet, perhaps in a world still dominated by a Western scientific worldview, with philosophies still grounded in substance ontological thinking and material reductionism, attributing any agency to the world or passivity to the subject is liable to sound somewhat suspect. And yet we must recognize the broad historical tendency in Western philosophy to anthropocentric conceptions of motion, language, and expression. Both Nishida and Merleau-Ponty seek to challenge this tendency at the most fundamental level by decentering the subject and articulating ontologies that rectify the conceptual misallocation of various forms of agency within binary metaphysics. Neither thinker wanted to completely erase all distinctions between the human and nonhuman world. However, those differences have been pushed to such an extreme form of anthropocentrism, the subject has been so reified, and the attendant binaries so solidified in Western thinking that these philosopher's works can indeed come across as obscure, or poetic gestures toward passivity. The project of decentering the subject is inevitably a project that disabuses humankind not just of the mistaken and dangerous idea of its own autonomous existence, but also of the illusion of full control of its motion, perception, and expression. To counter the foundation of modern subjectivity will inevitably risk overemphasizing passivity and robbing the subject of agency. Thus, the act of decentering they articulate is not merely a descriptive project; it is also a soteriological one. Humans suffer less when they conceive of themselves as part of the world rather than separate (*chōriston*) from it, and there is no doubt that one of the primary sources of suffering in our time stems from the illusion of our being detached from the world. Although the soteriological part is more explicit in the East-Asian tradition, one could argue that for Merleau-Ponty, at least one reason for articulating a new conception of the body's relation to the world is that living one's life according to that non-dual picture leads to increased health, flourishing, and well-being.

Motor-Background: "Solicitations" and "Unity of Act and Act"

Among the diverse positions in Western philosophy, none but a few would cast human action as related in any appreciable way to the kind of movement that occurs within the landscape. The idea of all reality being a continuity of "act and act"—as we consider in this section—is not one that finds a great deal of purchase in the West. Yet, in ancient China, various ways of thinking about landscape were much more in line with how Nishida and Merleau-Ponty conceive of its motions. In this context we can revisit the idea of "dragon veins." We discussed this idea previously regarding the invisible network weaving together the visible elements, the trees, mountains, and rivers in a painting. Now, moving from the sensory to the sensorimotor, we can consider dragon veins not only for their perceptual but also their motor implications. The term originated with the Chinese practice known as *fengshui* (風水). *Fengshui*, often derogatively called "geomancy" but more literally translated as "wind and waters,"[51] is a practice of harmonizing the spaces and objects within houses, gardens, one's workspace, or ancestral burial grounds. Hwa Yol Jung calls it an "eco art" or sometimes "geophilosophy," a term also used to refer to Daoism and to the thought of Merleau-Ponty and Deleuze.[52]

The physics of *fengshui* casts the world as animated by patterns of energy known as *qi* (氣). This energy did not respect distinctions between the animate and inanimate world, it permeated humans as much as stones. Indeed, it was one of the fundamental principles governing Chinese and Japanese rock garden design.[53] More generally, "dragon veins" were patterns of energy that could be read by the fengshui practitioner. Where their reading would guide the practitioner's motions in the environment in which they worked, the dragon veins served as invisible motor solicitations. The practitioner geared his body into the patterns of energy such that he could design harmonious spaces their bodies would live, move, and meditate within. Chinese painters would have also understood their attempts to achieve "resonance" with the landscape according to these principles. Thus, expression was not the imposition of the artist's creative idea so much as a translation of energy from one state to another. As Parkes explains regarding Northern Song painting: "A traditional condition for successful landscape painting in

---

51. As Field explains, a more precise translation would be "(hinder the) wind (and hoard the) water." This is because wind was known to disperse qi energy, whereas water collects qi. Because qi energy is the source of one's vitality, they should thus hinder the wind and hoard the water. S. L. Field, *Ancient Chinese Divination*.

52. Jung, *Transversal Rationality and Intercultural Texts: Essays in Phenomenology and Comparative Philosophy*, 224.

53. For a more in-depth discussion of fengshui in relation to rock gardens, see Graham Parkes, "The Role of Rock in the Japanese Dry Landscape Garden," in *Reading Zen in the Rocks: The Japanese Dry Landscape Garden*.

China is *qi yun sheng tong*, which refers to the artist's ability to let his work be animated by the same *qi* that produces the natural phenomena he is painting. So rather than attempting to reproduce the visual appearance of the natural world, the artist lets the brushstrokes flow from the common source that produces both natural phenomena and his own activity."[54] The artist's expression, therefore, was a conduit for the invisible energy coursing through the landscape.

While this might sound intriguing yet scientifically unfounded, and while there are astrological frameworks in *fengshui* that are clearly pseudoscientific, other principles are quite easy to verify in our own experience. The example of stringed instruments resonating together, for example—also an enduring metaphor in Western philosophy—is one way that resonance was described in *fengshui*. Nevertheless, to take the step from the body-landscape relationality posited in *fengshui* into the phenomenological realm, we can construe resonance as obtaining through the mutual-negation that is the foundation of both Nishida and Merleau-Ponty's ontologies.

By taking this step, we achieve for motricity what we have already established for perception. Here, we make another pivotal expansion as we move from the perceptual to the motor-perceptual. That is, we advance from multi-*perspectival* vision to multi-*volitional* action. To prefigure how we get from there to here in the coming sections: we have already described perception as ambiguous regarding subject and object, internality and externality, by virtue of a mutual *perceptual-negation* between non-self and non-object. This has given us multi-perspectival vision. Moving to the motor-perceptual level now requires extending that same structure to see how a mutual *motor-negation* obtains between body and world, such that the activity-passivity, motion-motionless binaries are ambiguated. The further symmetry that becomes discernible as we make this move is that just as the perceptual negation gave us a *multi-perspectival* form of vision, motor-perceptual negation yields a *multi-volitional* form of motion: movement that is diffuse, spread throughout the landscape and not reducible to any single node in the motor-perceptual fabric. Motor-negation helps make contemporary the redeemable elements from the *fengshui* notion of "resonance," while also filling out the missing parts to the theory introduced above regarding the non-object in Cézanne and Sesshū; that is, it offers us a phenomenological route to approach the question of how the landscape moves the body.

---

54. Ibid., 102.

With Merleau-Ponty's "depth" and Nishida's "internal/external perception" we have already noted how vision pervades into objects' unseen valences. Similarly, these philosophers suggest that we also project our motion into things and have motion projected into us. Seeing a body move includes an echo of how we would feel our own bodies amid those movements. When we witness a contortionist or somebody bound in a shibari pose, for example, we do not have a representation of their discomfort. We do not merely see other bodies and their limbs, flesh, and muscles. As Nishida puts it, the "visual act [is] accompanied by its own muscular sensation."[55] I never have a representation of another body as entirely separate from my own. The feeling I have in my body when I see a painfully constricted body is not just a visual experience; it also inflects the experience I have of my own body. This is another reason my encountering Rodin's "Three Shades" inflicts a painless-pain in my body somewhere beyond both our skin and bones. Even if those feelings of my own body do not arrive as positive sensory data to my skin or retina, as unseen, and nonrepresentational, they nonetheless "line" the visible sense data I do receive. The motor-possibilities of my body affect those I see, because "the invisible in my body," writes Merleau-Ponty, "invest[s] the other bodies that I see. Hence my body can include segments drawn from the body of another, just as my substance passes into them; man is a mirror for man."[56] Because the experience of one's own body always passes through and is given back by the bodies of others, visual encounter includes invisible motor elements in the perceptual field that are not mere representations.

The motor-body's constitution is given not only by other human bodies, but also by way of objects in my perceptual field. This is crucial for my interpretation of landscape painters. Vision and motion are in a relation of reversible intertwinement; thus, just as we do not experience non-perceptual objects, so we never experience non-*motor*-perceptual objects; for, as Merleau-Ponty claims, they "present themselves to the subject as poles of action . . . call[ing] for a certain mode of resolution, a certain kind of work."[57] I can't help but to encounter Rodin's "Shades" as demanding an adjustment of my own neck even though it is not contorted as theirs are. Through their devotion to the visible world, painters such as Cézanne and

---

55. Nishida, *Art and Morality*, 26.

56. Merleau-Ponty, "Eye and Mind," 130.

57. *The Structure of Behavior*, 87. Also, see Al-Saji, "The Temporality of Life: Merleau-Ponty, Bergson, and the Immemorial Past," 180.

Sesshū find a much more subtle motor demand in the landscape, one that comes by way of mutual motor-perceptual negation.

When I see the sculpted bodies of Rodin, what I receive is much more than an intellectual estimation of their size and mass: I also feel my own body's possibilities and limitations relative to them. I do not just cognize these, I also sense a corporeal anticipation of the motions, energy, and postures required to touch them, or move them, to relieve myself from their painful postures, the memories and anticipations they provoke, all of which "line" the original perception. In a similar but more nuanced sense, the artist learns the expressive gestures needed to paint a landscape from how she feels her visual-tactile body projecting out into the motor-perceptual field. The moving body is postured by the way objects limit or enable motion. These objects, to use Merleau-Ponty's language, are "solicitations" (*sollicitation*)[58] that motivate one's movements.

> The body is no more than an element in the system of the subject and his world, and the task to be performed elicits the necessary movements from him by a sort of remote attraction, as the phenomenal forces at work in my visual field elicit from me, without any calculation on my part, the motor reactions which establish the most effective balance between them, or as the conventions of our social group, or our set of listeners, immediately elicit from us the words, attitudes and tone which are fitting. Not that we are trying to conceal our thoughts or to please others, but because we are literally what others think of us and what our world is.[59]

One might take on the idea that bodies and objects solicit one's movements while maintaining that in some circumstances the body is motor-neutral regarding its surroundings. However, this would perpetuate the notion that there is space outside of flesh or *Basho*, which the body can inhabit, where it could instantiate a non-solicited posture—either in motion or motionlessness. That is, a non-negated position. But the background of motor-solicitations is not an addition that is sometimes present and other times not. "The

---

58. Merleau-Ponty believes that our thoughts have a "motor-accompaniment" that "solicit" our movements (see *The Structure of Behavior*, 74, 189. *Primacy of Perception*, 5) and even posits a linguistic form of "solicitation" (see *Primacy of Perception*, 88).

59. Merleau-Ponty, *Phenomenology of Perception*, 122.

background to the movement is not a representation associated or linked externally with the movement itself," according to Merleau-Ponty, "but is immanent in the movement inspiring and sustaining it at every moment."[60]

To describe the body in isolation from a worldly set of background solicitations is to hold a positivist conception of motion that does not take seriously the intertwining of perception and movement. Because the two are intertwined, and because we project our perceptual bodies into a world that is always in motion, our *motor*sensory bodies are always inflected by the motions within the perceptual field. One's perceptual experience always entails a certain bodily posture, whether or not one is confronted with specific objects. There is no autonomous non-solicited position to occupy. The body is always first available according to its being constituted by its projection into the world, as a body moving beyond itself in what we might consider a motor form of ecstasis.[61] That world does not come to presence as passive matter, but as a perceptual *and* a motor world. The idea of a motor-neutral body or world is an abstraction. The body is forever enmeshed in what both Nishida and Merleau-Ponty understand as a "background" of motor-demands. As Merleau-Ponty notes:

> Each voluntary movement takes place in a setting, against a background which is determined by the movement itself . . . We perform our movements in a space which is not "empty" or unrelated to them, but which on the contrary, bears a highly determinate relation to them: movement and background are, in fact, only artificially separated stages of a unique totality.[62]

Returning to Merleau-Ponty's poetic depiction of Cézanne's practice, we can grasp the relation between the painter and the landscape as describing a body that is woven into a background of motor-solicitations. Cézanne is successful to the extent that he gives himself over to the landscape's demands (To signal later discussions, this demand does not arise from an unambiguous present moment, but includes the history of other artist's responses to it). In answering how the landscape's features summon the artist's body,

---

60. Ibid., 127.

61. For a discussion of the theme of "ecstasis" in Merleau-Ponty's writings, see J. A. Gosetti-Ferencei, *The Ecstatic Quotidian: Phenomenological Sightings in Modern Art and Literature*.

62. Merleau-Ponty, *Phenomenology of Perception*, 159.

Cézanne "lends" himself to the visible world such that it expresses itself through his body and his gestures. Similarly, regarding Nishida, Heisig states that "if there is any judgment of what distinguishes good art from bad . . . it is a function of the degree to which the artist is given over to this background."[63] Nishida also uses a term translated as "background" (背後)[64] to refer to the way the world's motions insinuate into human motion. In *Art and Morality*, he writes that "we must recognize an independent force in the background of experiential content."[65] In his philosophy, it is this background that mobilizes the artist's body. "Art discovers the life of the self in the background of nature."[66]

Motion and motionlessness are not strictly human events; they cannot be accounted for by a focus limited to the circumscribable contours of the human body. We might want to retain some distinction between motion and motionlessness, yet because the self is part of an "infinite continuity of acts," (*sayō no mugen renzoku* 作用の無限連続)[67] and because my motor-body is negated by that world, even an attempt to remain motionless or passive is still an act within the motor-perceptual fabric, which is always in motion. As in Einsteinian physics, when the entire universe is in constant motion, there is no point of motionlessness, no origin or fixed reference point where an entity could remain unambiguously motionless: all movement is relative to the background of general motion. In Merleau-Ponty's words: "every movement has a background, and . . . the movement and its background are 'moments of a unique totality.' "[68] If we limit our scope to the body as divided away from that totality, we can certainly talk about motionlessness. But to perform such an abstraction is to squander the amazing complexity and beauty of the type of expressive motion artists achieve.

Although it is not clear whether Nishida was influenced by Husserl's notion of "motor-intentionality" to the same extent as Merleau-Ponty was, nevertheless he also conceives of the world as a background of motor-solicitations. While Merleau-Ponty's concept of "solicitations" are, on my

---

63. Heisig, *Philosophers of Nothingness: An Essay on the Kyoto School*, 59.
64. Nishida, *Nishida Kitarō zenshū*, 3: 302.
65. Nishida, *Art and Morality*, 54.
66. Ibid., 45.
67. Ibid., 126.
68. Merleau-Ponty, *Phenomenology of Perception*, 127.

account, tacit in his depiction of artistic expression, Nishida makes a more explicit connection between the two. As Nishida's concept of *Basho* becomes increasingly central, he describes action as a complex event at the juncture of body and world. Bodily movement is not an event that occurs within a passive or motor-neutral container. *Basho* is itself an active "volitional" reality silently implicated in the body's movements—motion that is equally moving and being moved, making while being made. Like Merleau-Ponty's "solicitations," Nishida explains how the world "beckons" the body's movements. As he writes in *Fundamental Problems*:

> [I]n artistic intuition, seeing must be a kind of acting and vice versa. Artistic intuition must be an infinite activity. In artistic activity we neither structure things conceptually nor imitate things merely passively. Things beckon and move us. Things become the self and vice versa. Moreover, it is an infinite process of self-determination as the activity of the unity of subject and object.[69]

For Nishida, the artist discloses the common source of motion underlying all existence. "[R]eality is not static but must be dynamic," he writes. To establish this point, he claims that "the essence of matter does not lie in 'extension' but rather lies in 'activity.'"[70] We do not experience inert material objects but what Nishida calls "volitional objects" (*ishitaishō*, 意志対象).[71] To see this aspect of the world of things we have to overcome the assumption that *we* are volitional and meet passive things, whereupon we impose our movements according to our expressive desires. Rather, objects are themselves volitional and beyond the active-passive distinction.[72] In his earlier thinking, Nishida was already contemplating "the true objective world (as) the objective world of the will."[73] Although he would later disavow the voluntarism of his early period, it should be noted that even in those writings he is not speaking of the autonomous will of the individuated subject. When he speaks

---

69. Nishida, *Fundamental Problems*, 179.

70. Nishida, *Nishida Kitarō zenshū*, 2: 366

71. Nishida, *Art and Morality*, 3, 22, 126.

72. As Dalissier explains, the distinction between matter and form only arises on the plane of "oppositional nothingness," whereas on the plane of "absolute nothingness" it appears as a "animating matter" arising from "creative nothingness" (*sōzōteki mu* 創造的無). Dalissier, "The Idea of the Mirror in Nishida and Dōgen," 117–119.

73. Nishida, *Art and Morality*, 141.

of an "objective will," he is referring to an aspect of the human body and of the world. "[J]ust as we can think of things as carrying force," Nishida notes, "we can further think of intelligible reality as possessing will."[74] Reality is volitional and the human will is one manifestation of this ontological source of motion. The world, according to Nishida, moves with a "volitional character."[75] As many have pointed out (including Nishida himself), his early works succumb to a psychologism,[76] and what some have called a form of "hyper-voluntarism."[77] These writings and his concept of "pure activity" were based on Fichte's understanding of the "absolutely free will." Despite the ostensible voluntarism, Nishida's "pure objectivity," "pure will," or "pure activity" are not "pure" in the sense of an agency located strictly within the confines of the human body, unadulterated by the world. Even in his early writings, he does not envision an active subject in opposition to a passive world. He eventually abandons the voluntarism of his early works, yet what continues into the later writings is an approach to bodily movement that cuts across the distinction between simple binaries whereby motion would be held as separate from the world as background. To portray action in its fullness entails showing how motion arises in a continuity of discontinuity within the volitional background Nishida would later refer to as "*Basho*." In his "The Historical Body" essay of 1936, he writes:

> [T]he world is a living world, and in one aspect it moves itself; that is, in the world there is the aspect of the world moving itself in and through itself. Our human existence has its being in bodily existence through its functions which are related to that aspect of the self-moving world, functions that various parts of the body have in relation to the world's movements.[78]

As his mature ontology becomes more refined, Nishida is explicit about the type of action that is ambiguous with respect to subject and object. The

---

74. Nishida, "Basho," in *Place and Dialectic*, 124.

75. *Last Writings: Nothingness and the Religious Worldview*, 64.

76. See Maseo Abe, "Nishida's Philosophy of Place."

77. As Ken'ichi Iwaki points out, behind this "'Fichtean voluntarism' [is] the absolute self as 'pure activity,' where 'behind pure experience there must be included the will' but he came to find this inadequate and then he turned later to a kind of 'intuitionism' and the logic of place, where the will itself is formed." Ken'ichi Iwaki, "Nishida Kitarō and Art," in *A History of Modern Japanese Aesthetics*, 271.

78. Nishida, "The Historical Body," in *Sourcebook for Modern Japanese Philosophy*, 48.

earlier voluntarism is attenuated to such an extent that almost all substantial agents of motion are effaced. He wants to show how action can happen without an actor. Rather than simply thinking of certain objects and their particular solicitations, Nishida imagines the entire world as a "unity of act and act" (*sayō to sayō to no chokusetsu no naimen-teki ketsugō* 作用と作用との直接の內面的結合).⁷⁹ According to this thinking, the world is not matter, nor is it characterized primarily by extension: the fundamental quality of the world and objects is that they are "acts."⁸⁰ As woven into *Basho*, the self is not over-against inert objects, but intertwines with them as an "infinite continuity of acts." An artwork is not an exception, it is interlaced within this infinite continuity and is likewise an act. As Nishida writes in *Art and Morality*, "In this horizon, both the artist and his work become one inseparable act."⁸¹ This vein of thinking continues throughout his later work, his 1936 "The Historical Body":

> An artwork combines both—subjective activity and objective result. It is not that the artist just acts subjectively; rather, from the objective side, he is also acted upon by the thing. If one speaks of an opposition of subject and object, the artist acts out of his subjectivity and at the same time he is acted upon from the side of the object. The artwork is realized from a mutual interaction—or reciprocal transaction—of subjectivity and objectivity. An artistic production in this transaction becomes an objective work independent of the artist himself.⁸²

One can choose where to look, or what to focus on, and it seems easy enough to distinguish one's body from objects in the world; nevertheless, regarding movement, it is a much more diffuse phenomena, especially problematic, maybe impossible to neatly parse between body and world. "There is no action," Nishida conjectures, "in the strict sense when an individual simply determines itself."⁸³ We are not active merely as human bodies: "[w]e are active bodily as the world's own self-transformations."⁸⁴ The passivity lining our activity is the body's volitional negation that allows

---

79. Nishida, *Art and Morality*, 36, 43.
80. Nishida, *Nishida Kitarō zenshū*, 2: 366.
81. Nishida, *Art and Morality*, 26.
82. Nishida, "The Historical Body," 40.
83. Nishida, *Fundamental Problems*, 29.
84. Nishida "World as Identity of Absolute Contradiction," 58.

objects and other bodies to affect our actions. As Iwaki Ken'ichi writes, *Basho* is the "background of all acts . . . the place that includes the entirety of acts within itself."[85] It is the motor-perceptual fabric that embraces—not subjects acting on objects—but both subjective and objective dimensions of all acts. The essence of movement is wider than the subject's acts, it is a network of actions, some visible some invisible, and this event, the "unity of act and act," according to Nishida's thinking, is particularly discernible in artistic expression: "The immediate union of act and act in the transcognitive standpoint is the essence of these acts, and thereby each act can be conceived of as the locus of aesthetic content."[86] The origin of the act of artistic expression is not the "pure" free will operating in exclusion from the volitional demands of the expressive world; rather, artistic expression unites the acts of the self and the acts of the world. The "acts of the world" are the invisible background of acts toward which the artist must intertwine herself. The background is much more than a set of meanings; it is an array of acts and motor-demands, which pull on the artist's body, and to which she can respond in ways that might deepen the continuous-discontinuity such that artistic expression is born from the relation itself.

If we consider the meditative motionlessness of Sesshū and Cézanne in this context we can appreciate the importance of their aesthetic practice for reconceiving of the body and its motion. Our tendency is to describe bodily movement as independent from the background of motor-solicitations, as an act in *discontinuity* with the world's acts. As a Western thinker steeped in substance ontological thinking, I have an instinct to circumscribe not just bodies or objects, but also their motion, thus I want to find a starting point and an endpoint for the body's trajectories and gestures. Yet, the body is not just in a perceptual negation but a motor-perceptual negation with the world. Motion is an event of the motorsensory fabric, which subtends the body-world distinction. When Cézanne sits staring out on the landscape of Mt. Sainte Victoire, or Sesshū sits in meditative stillness, even these are not as straightforward passive motionlessness. One's vision is not the only aspect of the body that extends out into the perceptual field; likewise one's gestures and movements are inflected by the particularity of the world's demands and are therefore events beyond the body-world distinction. Bodily movements are undulations within the perceptual fabric which does, of course, include the

---

85. Ken'ichi Iwaki, "Nishida Kitarō and Art," 275.
86. Nishida, *Art and Morality*, 21.

artist's body, but is not reducible to it. Our gestures, our attempts to express meaning with our bodies are confined by the contexts in which we move, and are solicited by the outside as much as the inside, thus undermining the legitimacy of that binary for describing bodily motion. For this reason, it would be a struggle to remain motionless as these artists did. When the background of motor-solicitations is in view, sitting still is an action, often the most difficult to sustain. The motor-body is negated by a motor-world that is always pulling on it, a world whose demands are much older and much more powerful, especially given their invisibility. Neither Nishida nor Merleau-Ponty wants to describe this world as one of indiscriminate flux in which no entities are discernible. Subject and object are never completely eliminated, nor are activity and passivity. They remain present as a striving toward a positivity that can never be accomplished, a tension between act and act that is multi-stable and irresolvable. As Chouraqui explains, we strive asymptotically toward positive subjectivity and objectivity, without ever reaching full determinacy on either pole. As such, our movements as partial subjects striving toward partial objects remain in a continuously-discontinuous relation between body and world. Otherwise, if the asymptote collapsed and positive subjectivity and objectivity obtained, movement could ensue as unambiguous activity or passivity, motion or motionlessness, but then the question of relationality and encounter would intrude. The world's motions would either be wholly inconsequential to those of the body, or they would fully obstruct the body's ability to move. Motion is, however, a chiasmatic intertwining that allows for more or less passivity or activity, but never one to the full exclusion of the other. The meditator and/or the painter never have the luxury of unambiguous passivity, nor do they enjoy the full control of unambiguous activity. Within this tension they negotiate their expressive movements, including those times of heightened activity when they do not engage in any readily visible motion, which might explain why holding oneself still in meditation even for a short period can be so difficult.

To appreciate the artist's movements is to appreciate the world in which those movements are possible and meaningful. Creating a work that is new and potentially great is not to have created an original way of moving the body. Rather, it is to have worked out a new continuity of act and act within the motor-perceptual world into which the body is woven. For the sake of description, we can always abstract bodies from that world and consider their motions in isolation, yet this is to break apart an event previously united as a more basic continuity. What is more, it is to lose the beauty and intricacy of the gestural negotiations artists perform in tandem with the landscape, and also puts out of view the negotiations a painter enacts with a tradition of great artists who have contributed to the worldly solicitations that must be grappled with in order to bring a landscape to presence in a novel way. Motion—including the type where the body's limbs do not move—always produces, in a subtle way, a change in the environment in which the movement obtains. Some movements, no doubt, have more of a lasting effect on the history of motion that will follow. If one wants to create an artwork that will be a meaningful component of art history to come, one must engage with the great works of the tradition. They are great insofar as they have established the warp and weft of the perceptual fields the artist now deals with. If I want to paint landscapes, if I want my work to reveal something new, I need to know how earlier painters have determined the present conditions of visibility; and such conditions persist as motor and perceptual determinations that act on my actions in the present. To make great artworks is to learn those conditions. It is not to find where I am free to express myself; rather, it is to search within the motor-perceptual fabric for the solicitations that will appropriately constrain my expressive gestures. Both Cézanne and Sesshū responded to the motorsensory reality given by their traditions and, where they created great works, those works remain within the present motor-perceptual world as a set of solicitations that are still available as attractions for bodies and gestures long after those artists' bodies have ceased moving. Great artists throughout history have found a way of inflecting the motor-perceptual fabric with their textures and dynamics thus constituting the background set of motions we are now in a relation of continuous-discontinuity with. As woven into the background, every movement pulls and tugs in one direction while manifesting tension, torque, and movement throughout the fabric in which other bodies and objects are enmeshed. Some of those actions will have a long-term effect on the world's fabric. The devotion of artists such as Sesshū and Cézanne, their experimenting beyond motion and motionlessness, and ultimately their faith in the motor-perceptual world have constituted the background in such a way that will be available for bodily intertwinement for some time to come for anyone who seeks to understand bodily motion or move the body in artistic expression.

    These artists teach us that the body is not an autonomous motor-neutral entity only secondarily adjusted to accommodate and respond to various intentional objects and their motor-solicitations. The body is an act, even when motionless; it is interlaced within a motorsensory fabric as an "infinite continuity of acts." Only in this way do we experience our bodies or objects within their ecstatic reach. There is no pure or prior motionlessness to movement. When the motor-background is included in our account of motion, to stop moving could actually be described as shifting from passivity to activity. Remaining completely still in a meditation hall or facing Mt. Sainte Victoire is a certain way of responding within a background of the world's motor solicitations. Although it is tempting to assume that remaining stationary should be the easiest thing to do—possibly because of a naïve idea of an unambiguous form of passivity—in practice it can be excruciatingly difficult and sometimes painful. Why is it so difficult to do nothing? This is because there is no sensorimotor externality that frees us from the world's motor demands. There is no position outside to the fabric of flesh or *Basho* where the body is free from the pull of history, that is, the pervasion of what Nishida calls the "historical body" throughout the "historical world." The body is always embedded in a set of solicitations, always an act within an infinite continuity of acts. As such, it is never unambiguously passive. One cannot simply let go and sit still for long periods of time; one must constrain one's actions, which is itself an action, sometimes the most strenuous action. If we include all action within a background—a temporally extended background—the efforts that counter one's own actions likewise obtain within a setting of motor-solicitations. Even in remaining ostensibly motionless and passive, one has to exert significant force against the background that pulls the body into its habitual (temporally ecstatic) set of motions and postures. To endure motionlessness is to counter those temporally distal solicitations, which can require heightened activity. Heidegger was aware of this where he construed "non-willing" as a higher form of willing,[87] and "letting beings be" (*seinlassen*) beyond passivity. "(As I propose regarding motor-perceptual faith, Heidegger also sees an inherent risk to poetic enunciation, insofar as it leaves one "unshielded" (*schutzlos*) and outside of protection.)[88] Our motor-intentional postures toward beings, sedimented beyond our lifetimes, constrained by our traditions and cultures, disclose our own bodies and the environments we live in as permeated with motor demands that are not easily countered. To sit motionless in a motor-perceptual field, in front of a landscape that is similarly motor-perceptual, is not to cease moving so much as it is one particular modification of the body's being already moving with the world. (Interestingly, a particular strand of contemporary dance

---

87. Martin Heidegger, *Discourse on Thinking*.
88. Martin Heidegger, "What Are Poets For?," 100.

theory and practice questions the need to define dance as bodily "movement," so as to give motionlessness a constitutive role in performance.)[89] There is no access to a "pure" or unmoved body experienced outside of a relational network of motor-demands. Motionlessness is a particular way of orienting oneself as woven into a background with constantly evolving motor desires for the body, thus expressive movement is beyond the distinction of motion and motionlessness. Returning to ponder Cézanne and Sesshū and the earlier account that construes their movement as responses to negated objects, we can understand how the different trees, mountains, and rivers in their paintings move the body by virtue of a demand that issues from the encounter. Trees and bamboo, boats and tigers, are non-objects, or motor-negated objects insofar as the encounter with them involves the interweaving of our activity and passivity, motion and motionlessness, and theirs. Of course, this would have been true of Cézanne, but it is particularly interesting to think of Chinese landscape painting and the enormous weight of that tradition that determined the minutiae of sanctioned bodily orientations and specific gestures, tools, and brushstrokes appropriate for depicting specific objects. We might understand the hundreds of detailed manuals as attempts to read and perpetuate the motor-solicitations set in the landscape by the great painters of that tradition. Otherwise put, these manuals are part of the *texture* of the motorsensory fabric and thus determine the *dynamics* of bodily movements for painters seeking to express themselves in tandem with the landscape whose temporal depth has been determined by a history of artists.

To collect our thoughts, let us sum up what we have discussed thus far in this chapter. Picking up from the previous chapter, which described the various forms of multi-perspectivalism achieved by perceptual negation, now we further extend the ecstatic definition of the body by considering how it moves throughout time. The artistic practices of Sesshū and Cézanne are exemplary for disclosing how the body is woven into the perceptual field's texture of motor negation. Their artworks show how the landscape moves the body; that is, because part of the mutual negation binding artist and

---

89. See N. S. Smith and L. Nelson, *Contact Quarterly's Contact Improvisation Sourcebook: Collected Writings and Graphics from Contact Quarterly Dance Journal, 1975–1992.*

landscape has a motor valence. Our bodies pervade the perceptual field not only in terms of vision but also motion. This raises the question of how exactly negated objects move the body, which brought us to Merleau-Ponty's notion of "solicitations" and Nishida's "unity of act and act." In the last sections above, I have hinted at how the landscape's motor demand does not issue from a circumscribed present moment, but has a historical depth. Objects pull on the body and inflect its postures and gestures not only based on the solicitations in the present moment, but according to how those objects have been entangled with motor-perceptual fabric throughout time. Thus, Taiga's movements, for example, are potentiated by contours of a topography, which Sesshū inflected several hundred years earlier. To understand these temporal dimensions of the landscape's historical depth more fully, let us now turn to Nishida's account of the relation between the "historical body" (*rekishiteki shintai* 歴史的身体) and the "historical world" (*rekishiteki sekai* 歴史的世界) and Merleau-Ponty's "deep present."

Body and Expression in Time

If the artist's body is cut from an ontological fabric with a historical depth, many questions arise concerning how or to what measure they are free to move. How are we situated within the causation of time, limited by the past, by our own or other's actions, or free for our futures, able to move our bodies in new or creative ways? What is the artist's relation to his past, to his tradition, to those who have labored to create/modify/deform the visible, and how does he institute a new visibility for the future? We also have to reconsider what it means to be "new," or a "copy" or "original" when artworks rely on conditions of visibility instituted by past artists. Meanwhile, all of these issues ask for clarity regarding the type of relation binding temporal orders. How does the past and future impinge upon the present moment when the artist puts brush to paper?

Nishida's "Historical Body" and "Historical World"

Nishida asks whether "Sesshū painted nature or that nature painted itself through Sesshū."[90] We might find Merleau-Ponty's unwitting rejoinder when he writes that it is "impossible to distinguish between . . . who paints and

---

90. Nishida, *An Inquiry into the Good*, 135.

what is painted."⁹¹ Clearly, the conception of time we glean from their theories of expression is not one where the artist first paints and then at a later point the landscape expresses itself. To put it in the context of the fabric analogy, we might consider the artist's gestures as "lined" by the landscape's motor-demand. But, what if that demand issues from punctuations in the motor-perceptual world given by artists hundreds or thousands of years old, by epoch-making painters, poets, or by those who left marks on the caves at Lascaux? How do we understand how the landscape's expression impinges upon the artist's at this scale? To approach this question requires filling out the notion of expression with a theory of time that accommodates the complexities of such historical determination.

Nishida's understanding of time is neither realist—which would frame time as a feature of the world external to the mind—nor transcendental—where time is imposed upon the world by the synthesizing intellect. We might go farther to say that Nishida's theory of time is ontological insofar as it is a feature of relationality itself. Moving beyond the mid-1930s Nishida frames temporality as an ambiguous relation at the intersection of what he calls a "historical body" (*rekishiteki shintai* 歴史的身体) and a "historical world" (*rekishiteki sekai* 歴史的世界).

In his 1936 "Logic and Life" (*ronri to seimei* 論理と生命), he writes that "[o]ur bodily self is not merely born through the biological species but born also through the historical species."⁹² What does it mean for the body to be "historical"? The relation between historical body and historical world is a mutually expressive relation. The body is not simply the *product of* history; it also produces history. Time, as a relation between historical body and world follows the reciprocal determination that characterizes expression. To capture this, we could modify the above quote to read: "it is impossible to know if time determined the painter or the painter determined time." The historical body's temporality entails a reversible mode of expression with the historical world. Thus, Nishida's theory of time is grounded in his theory of expression: The relation between body and world is an expressive relation, but it is not just the case that humans make the world, or are made by it. All activity is ambiguously situated between "making and being made" (*tsukuraretamono kara tsukurumono e* 作られたものから作るものえ). Maraldo invokes Merleau-Ponty when describing this interrelation between "two poles of creativity" as a "chiasm or cross-over between the historical

---

91. Merleau-Ponty, "Eye and Mind," 129.
92. Nishida, "Logic and Life," in *Place and Dialectic*, 272.

body and the historical world."[93] Again, this kind of expression is rooted in the relation of mutual negation. In Nishida's words:

> [I]f we are to conceive the relationship between life and environment in light of the foregoing, true life would have to thoroughly include negation within itself. That is what historical life is. It is upon this world of historical reality that we endlessly confront the environment and face the world of death.[94]

How exactly does time impinge upon expression? Nishida's temporality has, embedded within it, an account of a bidirectional expressive determination between body and world, which he refers to as "interexpression" (*hyōgen-teki kankei* 表現的関係).[95] I focus on this in greater depth in the final chapter. On Nishida's account, one does not simply observe the time of the external world, nor does the body undergo change in that world. Rather, body and world express themselves reciprocally throughout time. Following Nishida's rationale, it is impossible to explain the historical body independently of the historical world within which it is a relation of identity of contradiction.[96] The body does not receive time but determines it. To return to our example, the temporal punctuation brought about by great artists might be difficult for anyone to discern other than those such as Chinese painters who were profoundly devoted to the aesthetic constraints instituted by their forebears. To the extent that any artist could succeed in creating great works within the massive constraints of the Chinese art world attests to a measure of freedom for the historical body within the determinations of the historical world.

---

93. Maraldo, "Nishida's Ontology of History," 426.

94. Nishida, "Logic and Life," in *Place and Dialectic*, 240.

95. I use David Dilworth's translation of "表現的関係" (*Nishida Kitarō zenshū*, 10:347) as "Interexpression." Both this translation as well as a more literal, expanded translation ("the mutual relationship between absolutely opposed things must be expressive)" (*zettai ni aihan suru mono no sōgo kankei wa, hyōgen-teki denakereba naranai* 絶対に相反するものの相互関係は、表現的でなければならない) would accord with this study's overall proposition that expression is the encounter and reciprocal determination of mutually negating entities.

96. See Brubaker in Park, *Merleau-Ponty and Buddhism*: ". . . the self is unable to determine its own existence from within itself; it is the objective social and historical environment that confers meaning and self-identities upon the individual," 157.

Nevertheless, for those who seek freedom of expression to create new artworks as a body woven into a world, the constraints can appear insurmountable. "The historical world forms itself by means of our bodies,"[97] writes Yuasa Yasuo, and its expressive desires are much greater than one's own. But, how can we speak of the world as having expressive "desires" of any sort? In his "Logic and Life" Nishida writes: "Our bodily self realizes itself as a creative element in the historical world, and historical life realizes itself through our body. The historical world forms itself through our body."[98] The historical world has expressive desire insofar as it is constituted by the sum total of motor-perceptual demands impressed upon its fabric by all those who have previously expressed themselves. We all have historical bodies and thus move and perceive according to constraints of the sensorimotor world, but most of us do not need to be aware of that level of determination. Artists, on the other hand, if they are to create works legible (or create a new legibility), must be aware of that level of determination which presents itself as what the motor-perceptual world desires for artworks to be novel.

We have our own expressive desires as we attempt to affect history, but so does the historical world. It is much more likely that any of our actions go along with the world's demand and dissolve into the great current of history rather than making determinations that are discernible for others at that scale. All of our actions are historically formative because our bodies are historical, yet to punctuate the visible in a lasting way such that one's determinations solicit the movements of artist's in the future is exceedingly difficult. The caveat is that one cannot achieve such a determination out of their own artistic agency. The artist must give herself over to the world in order to implicate her own historicity into flesh or *Basho*. Along the lines of Nietzsche's "objective artist" in *The Birth of Tragedy*, the artist is the medium through which the world expresses itself. Or, as Nishida puts it, "a work of art is therefore less my work than a work of the world's logos."[99] Similarly, Merleau-Ponty writes that the subject "is nothing but a project of the world."[100] But, as a historical body one is never fully passive

---

97. Yasuo Yuasa, *The Body: Toward an Eastern Mind-Body Theory*, trans. T. P. Kasulis, 71.
98. Nishida, "Logic and Life," in *Place and Dialectic*, 277.
99. Nishida, *Nishida Kitarō zenshū*, 9: 121.
100. Merleau-Ponty, *Phenomenology of Perception*, 499.

without one's own expressive desires. For if negation is to remain mutual, one cannot be merely a medium. The artist does not entirely renounce her own creativity; yet it is certainly attenuated in the face of much larger, more powerful desires embedded within the motor-perceptual fabric by those previous great artists who have torn apart and re-woven some region of the visible world as a new continuity of act and act.

Nishida recognizes that the idea of an expressive world, and an artist as its medium runs counter to many deeply held Western philosophic tenets. He locates the hitch with Aristotelian logic. It is worth pondering in this section how he proposes to intervene in this thinking by importing the Eastern logic that underwrites his theories of time and expression. Nishida proposes an inversion of Aristotelian subject-based logic, by what he calls a predicate-based logic.[101] This framework provides an interesting and potentially viable logical scaffold for the project of "decentering" the subject, which many philosophers have attempted in the twentieth century.

Aristotle's logic maintains that a person, as substance, is always subject and can never be predicate. Whereas an arm, a foot or eyes are all predicated of the subject, of *this* human (primary substance), and a person can be further predicated of the species human being (secondary substance), this is the upper limit of predication: human life cannot be further subsumed under a more encompassing substance or being. As subject, the human is, Aristotle writes, "that of which everything else is predicated, while it is itself not predicated of anything else."[102] The world is not a greater substance of

---

101. Nishida's idea of *Basho* was significantly influenced by the Neo-Kantian philosopher Emile Lask who attempted to discover a unity or non-duality underlying Kantian mainstay dualisms of subject and object, sensible and intelligible, being and becoming, activity and passivity, etc. These are unified in lived experience as an "oppositionless object" (*gegensatzlozer Gegenstand*) before we theorize or make judgments about the world. Lask understood the locus of this undifferentiation to be a "place" or "domain" of the predicate, which inspired Nishida's theory of *Basho*, as evinced by the multiple references to Lask's "oppositionless object" in his "*Basho*" essay. See Emil Lask, *Die Logic der Philosophie und die Kategorienlehre* and *Die Lehre vom Urteil*. For a discussion of the relation of Lask's philosophy to Nishida, see Krummel and Nagatomo (2012), 24, 25, 86–96, and Krummel (2015), 86.

102. Aristotle. *Metaphysics* 1028b36.

which the human species is a lower order predication. Insofar as substance is the cause of the being of an entity, the world is not the cause of human beings. As such, while one's human nature determines one's being, the world does not do so in any "substantial" way. The human subject is substantially autonomous in this sense: the self as subject can never be predicated of the world. Further, in a decidedly non-ecological sense, as mentioned earlier, this subject, as a "determinate individual," is "separate" (*chōriston*) and able to exist on its own.[103] For Aristotle, causation with respect to the substance of self and world is a non-reversible one-way ontological street. To place this in the context of the foregoing, the artist makes things in the world but is not made by the world. Accordingly, obstructions might impede artistic expression, but these would be subjective, not ontological obstructions. Contrary to this, in Nishida's philosophy, the body is caused by and predicated of the world, thus artistic expression (and all movement) is impeded (and expanded) by a constitutive ontological obstruction.

Now, let us consider Nishida's turn away from Aristotelian subject-based logic to what he calls a predicate-based logic. He inverts Aristotle's framework, positing the self as always predicate of the world, meaning the self can never be an autonomous subject or substance. This takes his philosophy beyond Aristotle's uni-directional determination to a two-way street where a reciprocal, or "interexpressive," making-made relation between body and world manifests.[104] Just as a body has various parts that constitute it as an

---

103. Ibid. 1029a28.

104. In this sense, Nishida's understanding of mutual negation appears to accord with the Neo-Tiantai understanding of ambiguity. One of the requirements Ziporyn articulates for "intersubsumption" is that there is a quite radical "reversibility between substance and attribute" (p. 60) where any "coherence" (his term for any possible being, object, event, phenomena) can subsume any other. He explains that in all relations anything "can function as the primary, the subject, and the other as the derivative, the predicate" (p. 174). "The predicate can equally be the substance of the substance, that the roles can always be reversed" (p. 175). While this "omnicentrism" seems to be in line with Nishida's "predicate logic," intersubsumptive ambiguity is quite significantly more radical in that anything can subsume any other "coherence," such that the human could literally be the predicate of a coffee cup, the tire of a car, a memory of a distant relative, a landscape to be painted, or even a hypothetical object or thought. Nishida does not explicitly state that humans can undergo such intersubsumption with any object, yet his discussion of perceptual reversibility as pertains to artistic expression, and as "seeing without a seer" where the seer/artist achieves such reversals with paint brushes and perceptual objects, would seem to allow us to extend his notion of reversibility to all objects.

organism, so the world is viewed as an organism of which humans and their bodies are parts. Furthermore, because both the individual subject and the world have their own histories, these form part of the body-world interdetermination, or what Nishida later calls "inverse determination" (*gyakugentei* 逆限定). As Heisig writes, the relation between the historical body and historical world "works in two directions . . . the body gives concreteness to historical life, and that the historical world gives the body an arena in which to work."[105] To conceive of body-world relationality this way is to think outside of the confines of Aristotelian subject-based logic, thus opening up new foundations for thinking in appreciably innovative ways about art practice than has been afforded by our Western inheritance.

Nishida does not just make body-world causation a two-way determination; he also expands it throughout time and describes it as reversible where bodily activity is concerned. Here we see how it connects to the theory of expression elaborated above. It is not only that the body makes the world and the world makes the body, but that the "making" is always ambiguous regarding body and world. Thus, he refers to the "making-made" (*tsukuraretamono kara tsukurumono e* 作られたものから作るものえ) form of action. While Merleau-Ponty does not directly take up Aristotle on this matter, his theory of expression might demand the logic Nishida develops. His concept of expression as put forth through his analysis of Cézanne has a similar making-made dynamic that would be precluded by subject-based logic. Indeed, commentators have described the bidirectional making-made element in Merleau-Ponty's philosophy as "expressing-expressed."[106] Conceiving of artistic activity according to this "paradox of expression" entails that there are constitutive obstructions to creativity. Because one's movements are predications of the moving world, one is never free to move as he desires, nor is the full topography that determines the artist's motor projects ever fully visible. Nevertheless, faithfully submitting to these obstructions can enable meaningful deformations of the visible.

We can, of course, abstract a body and a world from any action, to see them as separate and un-obstructing, yet any action is first a twist or a fold of the motor-perceptual fabric. An individuated body or world is a secondary abstraction. On this account, nothing the historical body does is purely traceable to an autonomous subject. Thus, Nishida claims that

---

105. Heisig, *Philosophers of Nothingness*, 68.
106. Landes (2013); Marratto (2012).

the work of art is "less my work" than that of the world's logos. Because the individual is a predicate of the world, the movements of the body *are* the movements of the world, just as the movements of my arm *are* the movements of my body, even if the rest of my body appears otherwise still. Further, to act on the world is at the same time to create a world that acts upon oneself. In the same way that seeing is reversibly seeing and being seen, and touching is always touching-touched, so action as a historical body in a historical world is ambiguously located between acting and being acted upon, making and being made. In Nishida's words, expression is "a productive transaction; and so in productivity subjectivity becomes objectivity and makes things, and at the same time that which is made makes that which makes."[107] This is not two reciprocating processes following each other in time: one does not first see and then is later seen. One does not touch and then, in the next instant, is touched. We do not find two distinct events, but "one transactional process."[108] We sometimes mistakenly "conceptualize the historical world . . . as produced out of nature by human work and activity, sometimes as producing the individuals who interact in it;" however, Maraldo explains, "we should think of it primarily as the mediating place of interactive creation. Individuals create their identities through their interactions in the world, and that world is continually created with them."[109] Neither the creating nor the being created is primary.

Merleau-Ponty echoes the Nishidean understanding of expression when he claims that "[w]e choose our world and the world chooses us."[110] Cézanne does not simply decide to act on Mont Sainte Victoire now, later to be acted upon by the mountain, but his actions are *at once* an ambiguous attunement between himself as a body determined by the historical circumstance current in Aix in the last century, in the art world of France at the time, as well as the topography that surrounded him. Not even one's very first action would escape such temporal determination: "to be born," writes Merleau-Ponty, "is both to be born of the world and to be born into the world. The world is already constituted, but also never completely constituted; in the first case we are acted upon, in the second we are open to an infinite number of possibilities."[111] Action cannot be parsed neatly

---

107. Nishida, "World as Identity of Absolute Contradiction," 41.
108. Ibid.
109. John Maraldo, "Nishida Kitarō," plato.stanford.edu/entries/nishida-kitaro/.
110. Merleau-Ponty, *Phenomenology of Perception*, 527.
111. Ibid.

between what comes from us and what comes from the landscape, what is bodily and what is worldly, because "we exist in both ways at once."[112] Likewise, all the movements that follow from one's having been born flow with this same ambiguity between creating and being created, between giving and receiving meaning. "[A]ll explanations of my conduct in terms of my past are . . . true, provided that they be regarded not as separable contributions, but as moments of my total being."[113] This temporality entails that my conduct is never entirely explicable by my past or my environment. It is impossible to say "whether I confer their meaning upon them or receive it from them."[114] As for Nishida, so it is with Merleau-Ponty: "I am a psychological *and* historical structure."[115]

In this framework of action, the question of artistic expression is posed in a unique register. When approaching a landscape, my historical body does not act alone, separate (*chōriston*) from a world that will act upon the canvas or the silk; the landscape itself, as a temporal phenomenon depicted throughout history, constrains the ways in which it can itself be brought to presence. If Sesshū or Taiga engage with the landscape at this order of its visible-invisible temporality, including its historical motor-perceptual solicitations, these constraints act upon their actions, and in this sense, the historical world expresses itself through their historical bodies. Nishida sums up the foregoing:

> That we act with the "historical body" means that the self immerses itself in the historical world; insofar as it is the expressive world's self-determination, we can say that we act or function . . . [a]s the creative element in the historical world, our bodily self and the historical life actualize themselves through our bodies. The historical world forms itself by means of our body.[116]

To move the body while complying with the expressive constraints of the visible world involves a partial negation of one's own desires, but a negation that does not lead to an all-out relinquishing of one's own

---

112. Ibid.
113. Ibid., 529.
114. Ibid.
115. Ibid., 529. Emphasis added.
116. Nishida, *Nishida Kitarō zenshū*, 8: 324 (1965). (Translation in Yuasa, 70.)

creativity in untrained spontaneity or unambiguous passivity. In a later section below, we discuss this orientation toward the world in terms of Nishida's "acting-intuition."

Time and Negation II: "Deep Present" and "Absolute Present"

I have followed Nishida's thinking to show how a mutual form of expression obtains between the historical body and historical world. There are hints in Merleau-Ponty's philosophy and his depiction of Cézanne's practice that he also construes the artist's relation to the landscape with a similar historical depth. Now, I would like to look in more detail at the movement between past, present, and future, as our two philosophers in dialogue convey it. This involves further deploying the concept of negation to understand the passage of time within a chiasmatic relational structure.[117]

If we were to ask Nishida what the nature of the moment is when a historical body is productively continuous with a historical world, he might suggest that we consider his 1930s idea of "absolute present" (*zettai genzai* 絶対現在). Although Nishida said very little about this temporal order, we can clarify and expand it by reading it alongside concepts we have already discussed. It would be quite understandable to assume that if there were an absolutely present moment that it would be *absolutely not the past* and *absolutely not the future*. Yet, as in "absolute negation" (*zettai hitei*) the absolute points beyond opposition, in this case, beyond the opposition between the temporal orders. Further, as was the case with *zettai hitei*, the relation to what is beyond itself is included in itself by mutual negation. As Maraldo explains, "the 'self-negation' at work here is twofold: an indeterminate absolute present negates itself by perpetually instantiating itself in determinate moments and each moment negates itself in its passing away and giving way to the next moment."[118] Just like the self, which lives by dying, the present presences by continually negating, simultaneously dying and being born to what is outside of itself, to the past and future.[119]

In the section on "Time and Negation" in the second chapter, I discussed Merleau-Ponty's relation to Husserl to convey his conception of temporality within the framework of negation and signaled that I would re-engage with that discussion to consider the ways Merleau-Ponty criti-

---

117. See Maraldo, "Nishida's Ontology of History," 262; Krummel (2015), 112–118.
118. Maraldo, "Nishida's Ontology of History," 253.
119. Krummel, *Nishida Kitarō's Chiasmatic Chorology*, 114.

cizes and departs from Husserl. This departure brings him in even closer proximity to Nishida. In *The Visible and the Invisible*, Merleau-Ponty refers to "time as chiasm,"[120] thus invoking the form of mutual negation already discussed regarding the body, now in terms of the relations between the three temporal orders. As mentioned, his early conception of temporality takes on several key aspects of the Husserlian account whose influence can be felt throughout the *Phenomenology of Perception*.[121] From its inception, Merleau-Ponty's philosophy was an attempt to articulate an alternative to the in-itself/for-itself binary. His notion of time follows this path giving an account that is neither a subjective, transcendental imposition, nor a realist account. Time is not a property exclusive to either the body or the world. Merleau-Ponty takes up Husserl's terminology of "protentions" and "retentions," but these are not features of a "central I"; instead, they "anchor me to an environment," they come from "perceptual field itself, so to speak, which draws along in its wake its own horizon of retentions, and bites into the future with its protentions."[122] An insistence on ambiguity between past, present, and future is discernible throughout Merleau-Ponty's writings. However, as several authors[123] have pointed out, he later embarks on a re-reading of Husserl concerning his account of temporality. His revisions—not entirely finished in the working notes of *The Visible and the Invisible*—critique Husserl's conception of temporality as privileging the present moment of experience, and lacking "thickness." It is this thickness that Merleau-Ponty revisits with his concept of the "Deep Present," and by conceiving of flesh as a perceptual fabric with a temporal "depth."[124]

---

120. Merleau-Ponty, *The Visible and the Invisible*, 267.

121. "[T]he present still holds on to the immediate past without positing it as an object, and since the immediate past similarly holds its immediate predecessor, past time is wholly collected up and grasped in the present. The same is true of the imminent future which will also have its horizon of imminence. But with my immediate past I have also the horizon of futurity which surrounded it, and thus I have my actual present seen as the future of that past. With the imminent future, I have the horizon of past which will surround it, and therefore my actual present as the past of that future. Thus, through the double horizon of retention and protention, my present may cease to be a factual present quickly carried away and abolished by the flow of duration . . ." (*Phenomenology of Perception*, 80).

122. Merleau-Ponty, *Phenomenology of Perception*, 484.

123. Cf. Barbaras, 218–223. Mauro Carbone, *The Thinking of the Sensible: Merleau-Ponty's a-Philosophy*, 1–13; Alia Al-Saji, "The Temporality of Life: Merleau-Ponty, Bergson, and the Immemorial Past."

124. Cf. Dylan Trigg, "The Role of the Earth in Merleau-Ponty's Archaeological Phenomenology," *Chiasmi International* 16 (2014).

Merleau-Ponty modifies Husserl's account of temporality by conceiving of time as chiasm. In this way, he moves closer to the type of negation between the temporal phases advanced by Nishida. Merleau-Ponty believes that Husserl could not account for the past or future as anything other than an element of the positivity of the present. What Merleau-Ponty seeks is an ecstatic account capable of recognizing the "circumscribed negativity" of the past and future, which is nonetheless part of the present, without which the movement of time itself would be impossible. According to Merleau-Ponty, Husserl still adhered to time as a succession of positive "now" moments. Alia Al-Saji insists on a temporal form of negation in Merleau-Ponty's philosophy, when she notes that he "has come to understand time differently in *Le visible et l'invisible*: not as succession, but as a structure requiring the negativity of pastness to make possible the existence and passage of the present."[125] One moment does not extinguish itself completely so that the next one can fill its place. Time is not a serial succession. If this were the case, no passage from the past to the present and the future would be possible because the temporal orders would mutually obstruct one another. Merleau-Ponty focuses on what he calls a "time before time" that does not move in a linear direction, but is instead "pregnant" and moves by "piling up, by proliferation, by encroachment, by promiscuity."[126] In his mature ontology, the relation between temporal orders is a chiasmic relation of mutual negation. The "flesh of time"[127] is the temporal fabric that spans both body and world. As in Nishida's thinking, rather than a succession of now moments, according to Merleau-Ponty, temporal orders mutually negate each other. The "past and present are *Ineinander*, each enveloping-enveloped—and that itself is the flesh."[128] Glen Mazis comments on this part of Merleau-Ponty's philosophy, referring to the "reversibility of flesh [a]s the reversibility of past and present,"[129] and goes on to explain that the envelopments of flesh are temporal insofar as they have a "memory." The "enveloped-enveloping" temporal relation brings us into the "memory of the

---

125. Al-Saji, "The Temporality of Life: Merleau-Ponty, Bergson, and the Immemorial Past," 190.

126. Merleau-Ponty, *The Visible and the Invisible*, 115.

127. Ibid., 111.

128. Ibid., 268.

129. Glen Mazis, "Merleau-Ponty and the Backward Flow of Time: The Reversibility of Temporality and the Temporality of Reversibility," 58.

World," and, as Mazis puts it, "comes to re-member us, taking us into its body as our body, opening depths of time. It is a heightened coming forth of the reversibility of flesh."[130] The temporal body is not closed in on itself in opposition to the world. The body is, in Merleau-Ponty's words, "openness upon a natural and historical world."[131] The world itself is likewise an opening unto the body: an opening modulated by temporality. All the body's movements and the meanings it confers upon the world are movements that are at the same time given by the objects and constrained by their history. There is therefore an "anonymous" or "pre-personal" agent underlying one's actions. As Merleau-Ponty explains in his early work:

> My first perception and my first hold upon the world must appear to me as action in accordance with an earlier agreement reached between x and the world in general, my history must be the continuation of a prehistory and must utilize the latter's acquired results. My personal existence must be the resumption of a prepersonal tradition. There is, therefore, another subject beneath me, for whom a world exists before I am here, and who marks out my place in it. This captive or natural spirit is my body, not that momentary body which is the instrument of my personal choices and which fastens upon this or that world, but the system of anonymous "functions" which draw every particular focus into a general project.[132]

As volitionally continuous and discontinuous with the world, the artist has no choice but to lend an aspect of his motions to the expressive desires of this anonymous agent. And it is, as Merleau-Ponty provocatively states, "by lending his body to the world that the artist changes the world into paintings."[133] This way of portraying the relation between the historical body and historical world is essential for discerning the motorsensory expression of faith cultivated by the artist. The artist's body is not only motor-perceptually negated by the landscape, but this negation also has a historical depth. In *The Visible and The Invisible*, Merleau-Ponty writes, "the visible landscape under

---

130. Ibid., 59.
131. Merleau-Ponty, *The Visible and the Invisible*, 85.
132. Merleau-Ponty, *Phenomenology of Perception*, 296.
133. Merleau-Ponty, "Eye and Mind," 123.

my eyes is not exterior to, and bound synthetically to . . . other moments of time and the past, but has them really behind itself in simultaneity, inside itself and not it and they side by side 'in' time."[134] The landscape is not temporal all by itself; it is implicated in the temporality of the body through which it comes to presence. There are "chiasms of temporality as held by the landscape."[135] Mazis beautifully frames this temporality in terms of the body's ecstasis—or what he calls a "re-membering" of the body into the landscape that holds time:

> The landscape, its things, are not mute: memory is "lodged" there, held, housed, kept, and in the "membering" openness of perceiving-perceived, where the landscape and its things become one's limbs or elongations, one is suddenly re-membered through the landscape to upheavals in time. These "burstings" of time, or "chiasmatic leaps," these "reversings" outside unfolding are of another possibility of time held within the landscape.[136]

Facing such a landscape, without having to thematize its temporality, the artist's vision is inflected by its historical depths. The landscape comes to presence through more than light-waves reflecting off of its surface; it is also co-constituted by the non-representational presence of all other landscapes painted throughout history. The artist does not merely "continue the task instituted by their own beginnings, they also inscribe themselves within a tradition of painting that overlaps on their work, just as their work is intertwined within that tradition."[137] To attempt to bring the landscape to visibility is to engage with a tradition that has been doing so for centuries in the West and for millennia in Asia. The landscape the artist sees, the way it is visible, and the way it solicits the painter's gestures are the ways the tradition presences. Finding the landscape's directives entails discovering "a presence that is richer than what is visible of it."[138] We might consider one way the visible is richer is that it includes motor-solicitations with a

---

134. Merleau-Ponty, *The Visible and the Invisible*, 267.

135. Mazis, "Merleau-Ponty and the Backward Flow of Time: The Reversibility of Temporality and the Temporality of Reversibility," 60.

136. Ibid., 59.

137. M. C. Dillon, *Merleau-Ponty Vivant*, 210.

138. Merleau-Ponty, *Husserl at the Limits of Phenomenology*, 27.

historical thickness. To be an artist, to see a landscape, is not merely to re-present what is positively visible, or even to re-present what is invisible. It is to respond to the invisibility lining what is visible, which includes the motor-perceptual demands embedded in the landscape by others' responses to it.

As in Nishida's philosophy, where the account of temporality implies a bidirectional form of expression, similarly Merleau-Ponty sees time and expression as linked. He alludes to this when he writes that "each expression is closely connected within one single order to every other expression."[139] Any painting is implicated with all others.[140] The world is historical. There is a "memory of the world,"[141] writes Merleau-Ponty. To gear one's body into this order of expression is a "commitment to a historical sense that appears as the depth of the visible," writes Darian Meacham, who quotes Merleau-Ponty claiming that "faith in things unseen."[142] The artist must have faith because the landscape moves her body according to its historicity. This is "the power of the reversibility with the landscape, within temporality"[143] and for this reason, painting is, as Jacques Taminiaux writes, "always to paint more than one paints. As soon as there was painting, it was in excess of itself. At the time as it offers a field of visibility that goes beyond the given picture, the perceptual power of the painter is doubled with a prospective power."[144] Painting is in excess of itself because the movements that bring it about are not simply the expressive power of a body, but are likewise this

---

139. Merleau-Ponty, "Indirect Language and the Voices of Silence," 110.

140. See Haar in Véronique Fóti, ed., *Merleau-Ponty: Difference, Materiality, Painting*, 183. "Every gesture of expression is not an absolute commencement or re-commencement. Every expression inserts itself into a painter's particular itinerary and, responding to the gestures of other painters, inserts itself thereby into a tradition and history of painting. The empirical historicity of gestures, always doubled by a historiality (which is to say, an epochal determination), brings about that the gesture of expression does not come to pass, as Merleau-Ponty believes, at the heart of a simple, naive, and ever new presence, such as perceptual presence is taken to be. Merleau-Ponty understands the unity of painting across history as the fact that every gesture of pictorial expression refers to every other across time and distance by drawing upon the living present."

141. Merleau-Ponty, *The Visible and the Invisible*, 194.

142. Darian Meacham, "'Faith Is in Things Not Seen': Merleau-Ponty on Faith, Virtù, and the Perception of Style," 189.

143. T. W. Busch and S. Gallagher, *Merleau-Ponty, Hermeneutics, and Postmodernism*, 61.

144. Jacques Taminiaux, "The Thinker and the Painter," in *The Merleau-Ponty Aesthetics Reader: Philosophy and Painting*, ed. Galen Johnson, 292.

"prospective power" beyond the body. As Nobuo Kazashi affirms, "expressive 'acts' are grounded in, and originate from, the sociohistorical horizon of being; in this sense, expression is not so much the product of a particular individual as that of the field of sociohistorical being."[145] Finding a posture and gestures that allow these complex temporal determinations to impinge upon one's expressive movements demands a motor-perceptual attunement to the ambiguity of the body's active and passive aspects as they span the past, present, and future at the intersection of historical body and historical world.

Artistic activity is grander than the work of an individual creative artist who represents the positive features of the visual world. Expression, on the order that Cézanne achieved, is an intimate relation between a motorsensory body and a world, both of which have a complex history and a set of expressive desires evolving throughout time. To engage with the landscape as an historical field involves an infinite number of variables that cannot be represented or accounted for reflectively, yet because expression is always making as well as allowing oneself to be made, the body can become involved in a "silent calculus" that enables meaningful expression. Because both Nishida and Merleau-Ponty describe this as an infinite task, it is beyond the control of the reflective intellect, and insofar as expressive movements arise from the body's being negated, that task demands a bodily form of faith.

From Multi-Perspectival to Multi-Volitional

In the previous chapter, by considering perception within a context of negation, we expanded the context for understanding vision beyond the standpoint reducible to an individuated seer. Thus, we had multi-perspectival vision: a type of seeing that embraces the (representationally absent but no less constitutive) perspectives of other people and objects in one's present visual field, and the field as it had been visible in the past. Now a similar expansion occurs with bodily movement such that we arrive at an account of motion where its causes are diffused throughout the motor-perceptual fabric.

I have tried to show that motor-solicitations are not simply immediate; they do not issue unambiguously from a discrete present moment. The demands the world places on the artist's body include the present observable features of the landscape, while being "lined" by a temporally expanded set of invisible solicitations. Thus, the painter paints not just what she sees, but also what others have seen, while contributing to how others will see the world in the future. In doing so, she does not move as an autonomous

---

145. Kazashi, "Bodily Logos: James, Merleau-Ponty, Nishida," 117.

body. Rather, her gestures mark a continuation of a "pre-personal" tradition that has constituted the visibility of the world. Solicitations are, therefore, historical. The "unity of act and act" includes all past acts that impinge upon the present. That previous gestures of one's tradition can inflect one's own is possible via a temporal form of negation between past, present, and future. In this sense, there is no past, present, or future motor-neutrality within the motor-perceptual fabric into which the body is woven. Motion, then, cannot be reduced to the individuated body, nor can it be attributed to a self-contained volitional subject. As Schultz argues, "our actions are determined simultaneously by our own volition and the world in which we live. . . . Thus, volitional action and intuitive receptivity come together to form one continuous circuit of exchange between the self and world during the creative process."[146] If there is anything like volition, it must be thought of as a dispersed feature of the general sensorimotor fabric, which cuts across the body-world, active-passive dichotomies.

Through my reading of Nishida and Merleau-Ponty, I have attempted to establish how there is a dispersion of vantage points throughout a *perceptual* field, resulting in a multi-perspectival form of vision. Following the implications of a temporally expanded form of solicitation within a world whose texture is a continuity of "act and act," I now want to consider how there is a dispersion of agency or volition throughout the motorsensory field, resulting in what we might call a "multi volitional" field, or what David Dilworth calls "pantheistic voluntarism."[147] Just as there is seeing without a substantial seer, we might consider action without an actor.

Analyzing our everyday gestures shows us some of the ways that our volition is impacted by the historical world. For example, I might wave goodbye to my friend, and without even thinking about it, I will draw upon a wider volitional context that is my pre-history. The gesture's specific inflection, the duration of the movement, the lengthening of the spine, the corresponding tightening of muscles in the mouth and eyes, none of which I have to think about, all come from a background of motor-particularities determined by the sociohistoric world my movements draw upon. Of course, not all cultures perpetuate the same set of gestures to say "hello" or "goodbye." The body might display different patterns at different times

---

146. Lucy Schultz, "Creative Climate Expressive Media in the Aesthetics of Watsuji, Nishida, and Merleau-Ponty," 72–74.
147. David Dilworth, "Nishida's Early Pantheistic Voluntarism" (1970).

or in different parts of the world. Background motivations attract one's body into these specific movements because all movements are part of a continuity of act and act. We can certainly act against these attractions, we can act in strange and unrecognizable ways, we can march to the sound of a waltz,[148] yet it might take slightly more effort to will forth any gesture that diverges from the generally accepted one within one's culture. This is because, as Marratto writes, actions "make sense precisely insofar as they *make* sense."[149] To allow oneself to be partly determined by the prevailing motor values takes comparatively less effort than *making* new senses. All movement has a making-made expressive dynamic, but to institute the sense of new movements is a risk that requires a different form of effort, one that is essential for the artist to create a work that is truly new in a meaningful way. Nevertheless, in most of our everyday motions we are happy to enact what has already been *made* meaningful. I need not think about *how* I wave in a context where my gestures appear already natural to me: I simply initiate the movement, and through passivity—the motor-negation I offer the world—that historic world manifests the particularities of the movement of my historical body. This aspect of human movement is the world's movement. Through my body's ecstatically temporal dimension, my gestures are related to all those who have taken them up in the past and have entrenched them within the motor-perceptual fabric as a set of solicitations. Because of what Ziporyn calls the "temporal pre-situatedness of our actions,"[150] I receive the particularity of the movement and perpetuate that motor-particularity as a set of culturally specific gestures that will act on the actions of others in the future. According to Merleau-Ponty, this ambiguity of activity and passivity means that it is not "possible to say whether I confer their meaning upon them or receive it from them."[151] It goes both ways. Every gesture is, therefore, not just volitionally ecstatic, but also temporally ecstatic: every time I wave, I passively take from history, while also further entrenching motorsensory attractions that will intertwine with the movements of those who will passively take up the gesture in the future. Every one of my movements is "moved by some impact of the world which [they] then restore to the visible through the traces of a

---

148. Joel Krueger, "Affordances and the Musically Extended Mind."

149. Marratto, The Intercorporeal Self: Merleau-Ponty on Subjectivity, 97.

150. Ziporyn, "How the Tree Sees Me: Sentience and Insentience in Tiantai and Merleau-Ponty," 71.

151. Merleau-Ponty, *Phenomenology of Perception*, 529.

hand."[152] In performing any simple movement, I am, Merleau-Ponty writes, "receiving and giving in the same gesture."[153] I am making and being made in Nishida's words.

Let us take up two objections to the above reasoning that should be addressed before making any conclusions regarding the historical depth of the solicitations that constrain-enable the artist's body. First, one might argue that what motivates the particularities of one's gestures supposedly evoked by an object or its background are simply subjective, and say nothing about the objects themselves. One could make a case that knowing how to touch any object, perhaps a sculpture for example, involves conventions handed down as bits of information from one person to another in specific socio-historical contexts. We know not to smash our hand up against a sculpture's hard surface to appreciate its features because we have been told not to do so in the context determined by the norms of behavior in art institutions. But, we could ask, couldn't unconventional gestures also give access to the sculpture's features? No doubt such movements might allow us to assess the sculpture's character, but they would not do so in a way appreciably different from any other sculpture. Punching a Michelangelo would not be significantly different from punching a Rodin or any lesser-known artist's work. For the particularities of the sculptures to be palpable, before even thinking about them, one's motor-possibilities and potential gestures are already dictated by its specific features, and it is likely these movements would be evoked independently of historical or cultural context. Before any decisions are made, the pressure exerted on the marble, the speed at which the hand runs across its surface, and the parts of the hand used to feel are, partially at least, pre-given and elicited by the visual form and texture of the object. It is not just highly refined statues that demand such specific gestures. All objects have a size and form, as well as a weight, color, and texture. These temporal dimensions demand certain movements from the body if they are to be perceived and felt in their specificity.

The further objection I can foresee could appeal to the experience of encountering a new or foreign object, something one had never seen or handled before. It is conceivable that one could encounter an object whose purpose is not clear, whose textures are not discernible, whose mass or weight is not apparent, and further, one that is not disclosed in a context that helps determine our appropriate bodily comportment toward it. The argument

---

152. Merleau-Ponty, "Eye and Mind," 127.
153. Merleau-Ponty, *Prose of the World*, 11.

could be that such objects would appear without a historically determined set of solicitations. The continuity of acts in which the objects inhere is not clear, or perhaps, one could argue that the indeterminacy of that object evinces the possibility of a position external to the motor-perceptual fabric, insofar as the new or foreign object does not appear as an "act," because it does not solicit movements that reveal its use or its properties. It would seem that such encounters support the argument that solicitations are merely a subjective overlay to an objective world of motor-neutral objects: objects that remain external to the motorsensory fabric.

This objection is, in a sense, a phenomenological non-starter, since there are no truly "new" objects for experience. If consciousness began all at once, with the flick of a switch, and motor-intentionality went from zero to fully functional in an instant, then there would only be one single opportunity to experience a completely new object. After this first experience, all subsequent experiences of objects would never be "new" in the manner of the first one. Even the most foreign, confusing, and unrecognizable object is familiar insofar as we know how to treat unrecognizable objects. Dreyfus writes: "we each experience a constant readiness to cope with things in general that goes beyond our readiness to cope with any specific thing."[154] Without the specific intellectual or motor handle on an object, it still presents itself as already in dialogue with the body's motor-intentionality. In the absence of specific solicitations based on prior experience, the ostensibly "new" object is not motor-neutral, it still calls for a set of postures and movements from the body—namely those that we have used for new objects in the past. Thus, the unrecognizable object discloses our own bodies as already patterned with a specific set of appropriate movements: they demand a carefulness, an exploratory touch, they call for the motions that will determine their weight, the tools that measure the qualities of their materials, and the function of their parts. The new object draws us to different vantage points, to see the back- and under-side, to open them up, to smell them and taste them. The key point here is that once we finally determine what the object is, we do not progress from motor-neutrality to motor-intertwinement; we simply exit one exploratory horizon with its solicitations and enter another horizon that is more indicative of the object in its specificity. But we never engage the object without such a horizon, without motor-directives with an historical depth as a background of solicitations. Thus, as Nishida teaches us, objects are always acts. Even completely foreign objects are always encountered within a motor-perceptual continuity of act and act and thus constrain and enable our movements toward them.

---

154. H.L. Dreyfus, *On the Internet*, 57.

"Optimal Grip" and the Force of Tradition

Another important question arises as we apply this thinking to the great artists such as Cézanne and Sesshū who distinguish themselves and create the artworks that endure within their art historical traditions. If all objects, including landscapes, are acts that partially determine one's gestures, why are some artists better than others at responding to what the landscape commands? This is, essentially, to ask regarding how to define creativity within the account I have been building. The idea that the artist creates something ex-nihilo out of their artistic genius and simply throws it into the world that awaits their next masterpiece is clearly as far removed as possible from what creativity means for Nishida and Merleau-Ponty. The artist who stands outside of history and works from a position unentangled with the motor-perceptual fabric their art work will determine would be enacting a one-way determination of that fabric. This is the notion of creativity derived from the similar notion of uni-directional determination associated with divine creation. It is creation as *making* rather than the *making-made* bidirectional determination underlying Nishida and Merleau-Ponty's notions of expression.

In this section, we can take the first steps toward answering the question regarding creativity that will pre-occupy us throughout this chapter and into the next. Looking now at Merleau-Ponty and his commentators, I would like to consider some of the nuances of the motor-solicitations that come from objects and the latitude one has in responding in different ways to them.

Objects do not just dictate random body movements, they solicit the motions that nudge the body into gestures and positions that tend toward the best perspective to apprehend their form, texture, and function. The dialogue between body and world includes these directives, which elicit movements and bring the object into what Merleau-Ponty calls "maximum sharpness" or "clarity," or what Hubert Dreyfus calls "optimal grip."[155] My body does not simply calculate on the basis of the features of objects in the world, "my body is geared onto the world" and I move until I achieve

---

155. "I run through appearances and reach to the real colour or the real shape when my experience is at its maximum of clarity . . . these different appearances are for me appearances of a certain true spectacle, that in which the perceived configuration, for a sufficient degree of clarity, reaches its maximum richness. I have visual objects because I have a visual field in which richness and clarity are in inverse proportion to each other, and because these two demands, either of which taken separately might be carried to infinity, when brought together, produce a certain culmination and optimum balance in the perceptual process" (Merleau-Ponty, *Phenomenology of Perception*, 371).

a "maximum sharpness of perception and action," which arises when "my perception presents me with a spectacle as varied and as clearly articulated as possible, and when my motor intentions, as they unfold, receive the responses they expect from the world."[156] This seems simple enough when we think of a new tool or piece of technology, but becomes exceedingly more complex when we consider a landscape and the solicitations that arise from its invisible valences that have been determined by great painters of the past. Before getting to that level of complexity, let us keep it simple for now and further contemplate some of the dynamics of our everyday encounters.

An onlooker need not represent a skyscraper's form to know that they do not press their nose against it to appreciate its form with maximum sharpness, nor do they step back ten feet to see the details on the back of a coin. "Our motor intentions already seek the optimal without mental contents of what the optimal could be."[157] The best vantage point is often reached by relinquishing deliberation and releasing the body to respond to the demands of the object or environment—allowing the body to touch the world, while being touched by it. The form of an object solicits the proper movements that reveal its qualities, just as different materials evoke different palpitations. More often than not, we find ourselves enacting those movements or inhabiting the positions of maximum sharpness without having deliberated on them or represented the appropriate position or gestures. Before thinking about it, a soft piece of fur evokes a gentle stroke, whereas a punching bag solicits a jab, and a button, a poke. We do not make typing finger motions to stay afloat in water, nor do we wave our arms to stay upright while walking down stairs. Environments, architecture, materials, and forms as they appear to vision shape the body's motor-perceptual infrastructure and stimulate appropriate movements. To this effect, Merleau-Ponty contends:

> The object which presents itself to the gaze or the touch arouses a certain motor intention which aims not at the movements of one's own body, but at the thing itself from which they are, as it were, suspended . . . Hardness and softness, roughness and smoothness, moonlight and sunlight, present themselves in our

---

156. Merleau-Ponty, *Phenomenology of Perception*, 292.
157. Dilan Mahendran, "Optimal Grip, Préjujé Du Monde, and the Colonization of Being."

recollection, not pre-eminently as sensory contents, but as certain kinds of symbiosis, certain ways the outside has of invading us and certain ways we have of meeting this invasion.[158]

But, we should acknowledge that we often meet this invasion in drastically different ways. Because our bodies—not just the world of objects—are historical, we carry our own particular backgrounds into any encounter, which means that what attracts me might repel you. In the *Phenomenology of Perception*, Merleau-Ponty describes how, in the absence of deliberating over where to stand in an art gallery, the painting silently pushes one's body into the optimal position from which to perceive its form and its most salient features.

> For each object, as for each picture in an art gallery, there is an optimum distance from which it requires to be seen, a direction viewed from which it vouchsafes most of itself. . . . The distance from me to the object is not [experienced as] a size which increases or decreases, but [as] a tension which fluctuates round a norm.[159]

But what if instead of being attracted to the position of maximum clarity, a viewer is terrified by the painting, and retreats from any viable vantage point? It seems possible that a painting could evoke such a reaction, while soliciting the opposite reaction in others, yet I do not think that this drastic difference undermines the notion of a body-soliciting motor-background or allows us to speak of a position external to the sensorimotor fabric. Even in retreating, the viewer would nevertheless seek the optimal position from which to *not* see the work. In doing so, she would not only employ the painting, but moreover, in withdrawing to the least sharp vantage point relative to it, she would respond to the solicitations of a room that constrains and affords certain movements. Thus, we never escape the grip of background motor-solicitations; we simply shift the horizons in which we move. When the woman decides to evade the painting, she performs an "aspect shift," or a figure-ground shift, between the internal and external

---

158. Merleau-Ponty, *Phenomenology of Perception*, 370.
159. Ibid., 352.

horizons.[160] In maneuvering her body into the right position, she makes the external horizon of the painting (i.e., the room) the new internal horizon, using the floor, lighting, walls, gravity, etc. to navigate. All of this is achieved spontaneously, that is to say, without the need to represent that optimal position or deliberately shift aspects.

The perfection with which most movements are evoked, their appropriateness to the background, and the ease with which we slide effortlessly into optimal positions, points to a shared motor-perceptual background, which exists in silent dialogue with the body through the passivity lining its activity. But, we want to understand the artist's creative relation to her landscape. This differs from coins and skyscrapers. Although he does not use such language when speaking of Cézanne, Merleau-Ponty employs the logic of "solicitations" when conceiving of the painter's relation to Mont Sainte Victoire. In intertwining with the mountain, Cézanne partially empties his own volitional body to permit the mountain to guide his brushstrokes into the optimal gestures that bring the mountain to presence. Likewise, the choice of colors is not simply the prerogative of the painter; the landscape "demands" particular tones that eventually bring it to visibility. As Merleau-Ponty writes in "Indirect Language and the Voices of Silence," the landscape is "capable of demanding *that* colour . . . in preference to all others."[161] Similarly, in the inscriptions that adorn his "Splashed Ink Landscape," Sesshū attributes agency to the ink and the cosmos. Lippit puts this aspect of his painting in the context of the agency inherent to the artist's materials:

> Splashed ink revealed inner nature in a particular and remarkable way, by inverting the manner in which brushstrokes are typically read as indexes of an artistic subject. In the *Yujian* mode, the almost total lack of brushwork, conventionally understood as the somatic trace that most legibly registered a painter's character, conveyed transparency of person. In Splashed Ink Landscape,

---

160. See Mahendran, "Optimal Grip, Préjujé du Monde, and the Colonization of Being": "the painting standing out is never an in-itself as discrete object but always in referential relation to the wall behind it, floor, ceiling, building, people, collection of objects within the gallery and so on. These set of referential relations appear on the outer horizon of the painting."

161. Merleau-Ponty, "Indirect Language and the Voices of Silence," 92.

uninscribed ink is viewed as an extension of Sesshū's unconstrained and refined disposition. This transparency, in turn, leads to a heightened attention to ink's own agency in the formation of the image. Thus, the commentary on Splashed Ink Landscape is interspersed with direct acknowledgments of the inkwork itself, such as in Gettō's description of "ink [gushing] out to form a wineshop banner on the bay."[162]

If the motor-solicitations of any particular landscape completely determined the painter's gestures, there would be no latitude permitting new ways of responding to the world, and no difference between the works of an untrained painter and those of Cézanne. To put it another way, there would be no possibility of making a truly new painting and creativity might cease being a meaningful concept. This is perhaps the consequence of a positivist conception of action. If the world demanded the full range of our expressive movements, its solicitations would obstruct rather than line the body's movements; the continuity between act and act would collapse into one single undifferentiated act. If we were, as Sartre has it, absolute negativity and the world full positivity, this would be the nature of bodily movement. By contrast, in an ontology of mutual negation, the body is solicited, but never entirely constrained by the acts that permeate the perceptual field. Because negation remains mutual, bodies do have a certain freedom to move in previously unexpressed ways. Yet, because the same world can actually solicit drastically different movements in different bodies, we have to account for the possibility of this difference without going too far in the other direction where the world would only randomly solicit movements or not solicit them at all, thus enabling the various unhelpful myths of originality and individual creative genius. The idea of an optimal orientation solicited by objects themselves might explain how we use everyday objects, but it is a trickier line of thinking to speculate about the optimal orientation an artist should take in the face of a landscape. To grasp how the artist can create a new artwork by folding and twisting the motor-perceptual fabric; to appreciate their mode of response within a landscape whose solicitations are invisible and hundreds or thousands of years old; to define creativity in this context requires considering the body's historicity at the scale of

---

162. Lippit, "Of Modes and Manners in Japanese Ink Painting," 71.

the artist's tradition. At this scale, the artist's task is colossal, since, as van Briessen puts it regarding Chinese landscape painting, "a tradition must indeed exert a tremendous power if a painter, deliberately trying to break away from it, is caught . . . in its invisible pull."[163]

If Cézanne sought to grip and be gripped by Mont Sainte Victoire, he did so in relation not to a landscape positively visible in the present, but rather to a mountain that comes to visibility within a temporal expanse embracing echoes of how the world has been depicted in his tradition all the way back to Lascaux. Yet, Cézanne must go beyond those punctuations of the sensorimotor. He must respond with some minimal form of novelty to the world's solicitations, not by escaping the pull of the motorsensory fabric, not by moving from a position of non-intertwined motor-perceptual freedom, but *by finding a new constellation of constraints as yet unseen* and allowing those to guide his gestures. The painter's tradition "overlaps" on the work, yet, as Taminiaux writes, artists do not just "respond to what the visible world elicits in them,"[164] nor do they simply "continue the task instituted by their own beginnings, they also inscribe themselves within a tradition of painting."[165] The painter is always constrained by a temporally extended set of solicitations, and never creates from outside the historical continuity of acts. Her task is to discover a new intertwinement within the demands of the tradition in which she finds herself, but an intertwinement that is not wholly new. If one did not allow for "overlap" with what has come before, the work would not be intelligible within the tradition in which the artist seeks to innovate. A work's legibility is constrained by the painting conventions and the prevailing conditions of visibility of a tradition. To ignore these constraints is to paint as a self, to paint "there is," which amounts to rendering what the artist wants, not what a tradition calls for. This mode of creativity licenses subjective flights of fancy and is underwritten by the goal of displaying one's own self and its originality, rather than negating the self and allowing expression to arise as an attunement with something beyond the confines of that self. Only with the latter approach, one that demand a corporeal faith, is new artwork possible.

---

163. van Briessen, *Way of the Brush*, 275.
164. Taminiaux, "The Thinker and the Painter," 292.
165. Ibid.

New Art: Creating the Visible

Copy and Original

Placing Cézanne and Sesshū in dialogue regarding the question of artistic expression invokes intercultural road-blocks because of their respective artistic and philosophic traditions having significantly different metaphysics of copy and original. I have looked to delineate how artists can be creative and move their bodies in new or original ways when those movements are constrained and enabled by the world's sensorimotor pull. Before returning to develop that line of thinking, we must first acknowledge a drastically different notion of originality as it undergirds notions of creativity East and West.

The Chinese landscape painting tradition and its continuation in Japan were predominantly studio-based practices until around the eighteenth century when Taiga and other Nanga painters in Japan initiated the *shinkeizu* movement. Before this time many works would have never seen the light of day. An artist might spend months or the better part of a year in his studio learning the various brushstrokes and techniques of a Guo Xi or a Wang Wei. The various schools were so extremely convention-laden in ways near unimaginable in the West. Before landscape painting even appeared in a significant form in the West, the Chinese art world already had deeply established critical and theoretical coteries that set out the prevailing codes of the different art currents, deciding how works adhered to the various manners, and castigating, often bitterly, heterodox artists who deviated from accepted norms. This meant that innovation was exceedingly slow in China to the extent that even trained historians now have difficulty distinguishing between works from different epochs. Things are further complicated—especially for the Western interpreter who wants to define creativity as somehow indexed to originality—because Chinese artists could stake their entire career on copying the works of the masters.[166] All of these peculiarities of Asian landscape painting raise intriguing questions when brought into our discussion regarding how the volitional body communicates with the great works of a tradition. Moreover, the Chinese orientation to its past masters

---

166. There were important heterodox Chinese landscape painters who rejected this approach, such as Mi Fei and Shih T'ao.

seriously complicates assumptions regarding copy and original that are upheld in Western aesthetic discourse.

Although Sesshū was thought to have brought revolutionary innovations to Japanese painting, he was nevertheless a "modal" painter as his predecessors Shūbun and Josetsu were before him. As a modal painter he would have studied and copied the Chinese works that were part of the Ashikaga Shogunate's collection, the foundation of Five Mountain Art Academy. While he was considered a painter "outside of the academy," in no way did he throw out the rule book. Like all other serious Japanese painters of his time, Sesshū devoted a significant amount of his study to practicing the strokes of the masters of the Continent. Sesshū himself is quoted as saying that "in painting landscapes . . . [t]he best practice is to copy with easy strokes (freely, not slavishly) the brush work of Bayen (Ma Yuan) and Kakei (Hsia Kuei) and others." Nevertheless, he frustrates our desire to maintain a simple binary between copy and original when he continues: " 'Painting is not imitation of other things,' yet real landscape, or everything seen before one's eyes, is the proper teacher in painting."[167]

Part of the difficulty of appreciating how Asian landscape painters innovated, and what this meant for notions of time, motor-perception, the body, etc., is that we in the West have very different ideas of the aesthetic—not to mention the metaphysical—distinctions between copy and original. We have been given to believe in a metaphysical discontinuity between the art work and that which it depicts. As Plato taught us, that discontinuity is accentuated if we have a copy of a copy. Thus, art works are less real than that which they represent. Doubly so if they represent a representation. Yet, in the Chinese art world, "painting is not imitating objects, persons, landscapes, giving the illusion of a new reality; image itself is already admitted to the realm of natural entities, it belongs to the same reality." Even if I copy a painting, it was alive and my image "will be really alive, not a copy or imitation, but a fragment of life, part of nature itself." To paint a great landscape work in the studio is not to be once or even doubly removed from reality. We might even consider that a painting of one of the famous scenes in China gives better access to the natural world than an unremarkable scene we could paint *in situ* somewhere else.

In Western art history we refer to a work as "painterly" when the artist's brushstrokes are discernible. While we appreciate this aspect of certain works, and while it is part of an almost completely bygone art practice to copy the brushwork of the masters, copying remains a preparation for

---

167. Covell, *Under the Seal of Sesshū*, 53.

one's own original works. The output of one's copying might later inform original works but those copies are never considered authentic works in and of themselves. If we appreciate how a painterly image suggests some charming aspect of the artist's personality, the gracefulness or spontaneity of her movements, this can augment our feelings toward a work or an artist, but copying those gestures is not highly prized in the West. By contrast, in Asian landscape painting, where the brushwork is discernible, those markings serve as solicitations for the copyist who does not simply learn to *appreciate* the kind of expression they disclose: the artists devote themselves to learning the motor-perceptual performance that those marks intimate. This is another way that a great painting or work of calligraphy is not limited to its objectivity. The artwork is not a static object but is a performance, and like performances in other artistic realms, there is greater latitude for repetition. Van Briessen has a compelling analogy to describe this performative aspect of Chinese painting. He suggests that we consider a great masterwork along the lines of a musical score.[168] To copy it is to perform the piece, to give a rendition or an interpretation. Just as Glenn Gould's performances of Bach's compositions are considered artworks in their own right, so too could the renditions of those who copy/perform a Dong Yuan or a Ni Zan. To copy is to seek resonance with a motorsensory event that can still solicit movements in the phenomenal field in which the artist paints. The master artist might "originate" a particular motor-perceptual score, but that performance can be brought to life again and again. If the performance is equally compelling, it is just as worthy as an artwork, just as good at soliciting later renditions in the future. Painting a landscape or painting the painting of a landscape are both "natural acts," writes Ghilardi: "Only a spontaneous, natural painting can be vital and authentic as well, not a simple copy of the visible but an enhancement of the animating character of the world."[169]

In submitting to their traditions, Asian landscape painters gained a facility with their craft that is almost unfathomable. They no doubt had the skill to innovate if that had been their goal, but they were more likely to suppress their impulse to be original or to vaunt the self.[170] This would have been the case if any painter departed too far from the masters they

---

168. van Briessen, *Way of the Brush*, 35.
169. Ghilardi, *The Line of the Arch*, 93.
170. Displays of virtuosity were considered in bad taste, particularly because that approach could call into question disciples' devotion to their master after whom their work was modeled.

emulated. This explains why it is so difficult to accurately locate a Chinese landscape painting in its historical period. The Western propensity toward progress and the "shock of the new" is as far away from the Chinese mindset as possible. Whereas for the greater part of the past half-millennia Western artists have sought uninhibited innovation and originality under the myth of progress we invented, Chinese culture has been oriented toward maintaining their vast tradition and solidifying their history rather than changing or improving it. Emphasis was on preservation rather than progress. Thus, the changes that do transpire in the art world were miniscule, and this is the speed of progress we should expect from art practices whose foundation were a negation of the self. These peculiarities of the Chinese art world have implications for the self-awareness cultivated in its art tradition. As Van Briessen says:

> Whenever in the history of Chinese art a new style emerged, it was usually without any conscious idea of breaking away from tradition. Innovations in style were sometimes made so gradually—deriving as they did from the conditions of the period and education—that neither the age nor the individual painters were aware of them. It was not until later that these developments could be recognized in their proper perspective.[171]

No doubt Chinese artists and the Japanese painters who venerated them cultivated self-awareness in their practices, and of course art historians do identify innovations throughout the tradition, which disclose the individuality of the artists. There are more than enough stories of hostile clashes between artists and critics to disabuse us of the notion that Asian painters had overcome the trappings of the ego. The "untrammeled" (*yipin* 逸品) personality that was said to be above worldly concerns and petty squabbles was a narrative used to construct the artist's image in Tang and Song China and later in Japan. Yet, we also have ample biographical and anecdotal matter recounting how artists were caught up in personality cults, how they competed aggressively for commissions, argued to distinguish their school as the dominant art institution, and fought to be included in the catalogues of great artists of the time. Nevertheless, when we hold up the Chinese landscape tradition and its innovations against those in the West to determine what distinguishes them at the scale of centuries, in

---

171. van Briessen, *Way of the Brush*, 34.

hopes of delineating their notions of creativity, the distinctive features that do appear from this standpoint are undeniable. What becomes visible is that significantly different foundational beliefs governed the art worlds. To appreciate the practices handed down from generation to generation, what was depicted and how, the pace of innovation, attitudes toward copying, systems of apprenticeship, theories of expression, all of these demand that we consider the Buddhist and Daoist frameworks that distinguished the Asian artworld from the world that arose out of Judeo-Christian and Greek traditions. We could certainly find artists in the West who conceived of their practice along the lines of a negation of self-hood, but that approach would have more than likely put them at odds with the philosophic or religious principles of their tradition, and the practices formulated to achieve its ideals. I consider Cézanne as an exception to his tradition in this sense, particularly as he is depicted by Merleau-Ponty.

"New Art": Objectivity and Faith

If it is so exceedingly difficult to discern what is novel in Chinese art, and a challenge to distinguish copy from original, what drove painters in that tradition to make new works? As Westerners we might assume that a work is more original to the extent that the artist's subjectivity shines through. Indexing subjectivity to novelty in this way does not help us understand Chinese painting, nor Nishida's conception of art. For him, art is not new in the sense of its being concocted out of the artist's imagination. In fact, Nishida appears to go some way in the opposite direction. For him new art has nothing to do with subjectivity, but "[T]he direct object and the content of art is the objective world which is reproduced through the language of art."[172] The concepts of "objectivity" (*kyakkansei* 客観性) and "becoming object" (*kyakkanteki naru* 客観的なる), are central to Nishida's understanding of artistic expression.

If a painting or a sculpture are to be historically and philosophically relevant, the artist should discard the individual pursuit of subjective expression, and immerse himself in the objective world.[173] The meaning of "new art," he writes in *Ishiki no mondai*, "lies in that it strictly departed from

---

172. Nishida, *Nishida Kitarō zenshū*, 2: 374.
173. See Maraldo (2017, 219–220) for a discussion of Nishida's own misgivings with the "absorption" model. He also juxtaposes this model with that of new cognitive sciences who use the metaphor of "interaction" rather than "immersion" or "absorption."

the confusion of conceptual subjectivity, and immerse[s] itself within pure objectivity."[174] The measure to which the artist is able to perform such a negation of their own subjective desires will determine the quality of the work and where it will be located in its tradition. To put it in the language of the earlier discussion, what distinguishes good from bad art is not the degree to which an artist achieves a subjective form of freedom, but rather "the degree to which the artist is given over to [the] background."[175] The artist "as free person finds the true self through submerging itself in objectivity."[176] As Nishida elaborates, we do not attain to the true self through subjectivity: "Truly creative free will is active when it has destroyed conceptual consciousness, and becomes purely objective, i.e., when it has become the fusion of subject and object. At this time we can see true individuality, the true self."[177] In our study, one means of becoming objective could be allowing the background of motor-solicitations, the artist's tradition as it is embedded in the landscape, to move the body.

Both of our philosophers in dialogue frame the task of the artist as rooting oneself in the motor-perceptual world. While Nishida conceives this as "becoming object," Merleau-Ponty is not far when speaking of Cézanne's devotion to "nature." He also reads Klee's practice according to a similar conception of nature:

> Through vision, then, the painter touches both extremities. In the immemorial depth of the visible, something has moved, caught fire, which engulfs his body; everything he paints is an answer to this incitement, and his hand is "nothing but the instrument of a distant will." Vision is the meeting, as at a crossroads, of all aspects of Being. "A certain fire wills to live; it wakes. Working its way along the hand's conductor, it reaches the canvas and invades it; then, a leaping spark, it arcs the gap in the circle it was to trace: the return to the eye, and beyond." There is no break at all in this circuit; it is impossible to say that here nature ends and the human being or expression begins.[178]

---

174. Nishida, *Nishida Kitarō zenshū*, 2:363.
175. Nishida, *Art and Morality*, 59.
176. Nishida, *Fundamental Problems*, 69.
177. Nishida, *Nishida Kitarō zenshū*, 2: 366.
178. Merleau-Ponty, "Eye and Mind," 147.

Because the world is volitional and beckons one's movements, the artist must lend his body to the world, by way of negation, such that the movements of nature manifest. In *Phenomenology of Perception*, Merleau-Ponty claims that "[i]n order to perceive things, we need to live them."[179] Nishida too conceives of a similar giving over to perceptual objects in artistic activity: "[T]o view a thing aesthetically must mean to submerge the self within the thing in itself. In abandoning the self, one conforms to objectivity itself."[180] But how far can these particular claims be taken? It could seem as though these philosophers suggest the artist completely relinquishes all agency, especially with Nishida's concept of "pure objectivity" (*jun naru kyakkan* 純なる客観). Yet, his use of the term "pure" is potentially misleading, since it lends itself to a mistaken dualist interpretation, whereby objectivity would be pure in the sense of not being mixed into subjectivity. However, if the world were unambiguously objective and the human subjective, encounter between the two would be impossible. Positive non-negated subjects and objects are mutually obstructive. The body, however, is not purely subjective: the body has an irreducible objectivity. With his terminology, Nishida is not suggesting an objectivity that belongs to things in the world as opposed to the body; rather, he means to invoke a valence of objectivity that cuts across the body–world divide: objectivity as one of the ways that the body shares itself with the world. The "external world," Nishida conjectures, "refers both to our bodies and to other material things."[181] As such, "in expression objectivity is subjectivity or rather subjectivity can be seen in the very midst of objectivity."[182] To become purely objective is not to discard subjectivity or to passively submit to the world's solicitations, but is to attune oneself with one aspect of the body's own nature: to become objective is equally a reorientation of subjectivity. It signals the "new art" of which Nishida speaks, "which advanced in the direction of objective purification, having been carried through completely, attained a new subjectivity."[183]

Another potential mis-construal of Nishida's "pure objectivity" could interpret it as implying that the artist fully negates its own will and passively "goes with the flow" of nature. Becoming objective, Nishida writes,

---

179. Merleau-Ponty, *Phenomenology of Perception*, 379.
180. Nishida, *Art and Morality*, 101.
181. Nishida, *An Inquiry into the Good*, 24.
182 Nishida, *Fundamental Problems*, 65.
183. Nishida, *Nishida Kitarō zenshū*, 2: 364.

does "ha[ve] the meaning of determining and negating the person," yet at the same time, "the person finds his true self therein. This is especially so in aesthetic creation."[184] The volitional negation is always a partial negation: only in this way can movement arise through a non-obstructive relation between body and world. Nishida states that "motion must contain self-negation within itself,"[185] yet this negation is never outright negation. "The unity of contradictions must be sought in activity. But even if it is said that affirmation is negation, activity cannot be said to include *absolute self-negation*."[186] We are able to become objective through bodily motion because, like the perceptual body, the *motor*-perceptual body has a negation, in this case a volitional negation, which allows it to intertwine with the volitional world. "For the self to move things," writes Nishida, "things must be within the self, and for things to move the self, the self must be within things."[187] Volitional negation is always a mutual negation; otherwise, the self-identity of contradictories would not be maintained—the chiasm would cease to be the texture of relationality, subject and object would be discontinuous, not continuously-discontinuous, and would therefore mutually obstruct. Nishida continues: "[h]istorical generation [*seisei*] must be the contradictory self-identity of active and passive."[188] This objective aspect of the body (like the past and future in the ecstatic present, which give the present its ecstatic reach) gives the body access to the world. In *Art and Morality* Nishida writes:

> [I]n the body, subjectivity and objectivity are internally united . . . As our self is the fusion point of various worlds, so, too, is our body the fusion point of various worlds, and we are able to enter into various worlds by taking [the objective body] as a point of departure. When we enter into the objective world of the will through the body, which, because it is the foundation of the self, must be recognized as the condition of the establishment of the self and at the same time an unknowable by us, then the world of the self and the world of things are in opposition.[189]

---

184. Nishida, *Fundamental Problems*, 65.
185. Ibid., 3.
186. Nishida, *Nishida Kitarō zenshū*, 6: 37.
187. Nishida, *Art and Morality*, 40.
188. Nishida, "Logic and Life," in *Place and Dialectic*, 252.
189. Nishida, *Art and Morality*, 205.

Among the many features pointed to, which distinguish the subjective and objective realms, volition is typically thought to be a quality of the former and not the latter. In stark contrast, for Nishida, "[O]ur will is *not subjective* in essence."[190] To understand human motion and activity we must overcome the bifurcation of the subjective and objective, because, as Nishida provocatively claims: "[i]f we are purely subjective, we can do nothing. The will is able to realize itself only by according with objective nature."[191] This is, of course, true of the artist's will. To immerse oneself in copying a great artist of one's tradition is to deepen one's sensorimotor embeddedness in the landscape and in a tradition. Such a practice constrains one's own expressive desires, but the restrictions do not simply limit artistic expression, far from it, it is by negating the self and gearing into the world's expressive desires that the wonders of artistic expression become possible.

We now come to a turning point in the discussion that puts us on track to look more closely at the central theme of the study. If artistic expression involves negating the self as subject such that it immerses itself in objectivity, I propose that this demands a bodily form of faith. Artists who strive to create "new art" risk moving their bodies beyond the subjective will where the objective world of "volitional objects" calls on and patterns its infrastructure in ways that the subject cannot control. To express oneself artistically among the world's solicitations requires faith because it is a risk to surrender control of one's movements. The will is never completely one's own; it is never entirely under one's control because it does not obey the confines of a positively circumscribable body. One is outside of oneself in willing. As Ziporyn puts it: "however much I am able to control my world, there is always something beyond it; at the very least, my controlling act itself is spontaneous and not done by me. My will is not willed by me."[192] How the world is depicted, therefore, is never simply the artist's choice. In Merleau-Ponty's words, "we choose our world and the world chooses us."[193] Expression is inherently risky because motion is an attunement between the body and a network of invisible forces that manifest in the body's visible motions that accept their motor-demands. All motion, expressive motion in particular, includes an implicit motor-perceptual risk. To move as a negated

---

190. Ibid., 141. Emphasis added

191. Nishida, *An Inquiry into the Good*, 77.

192. Brook Ziporyn, *Being and Ambiguity: Philosophical Experiments with Tiantai Buddhism*, 164.

193. Merleau-Ponty, *Phenomenology of Perception*, 527.

body is a risk because the complete control we desire would be possible only for a body that was fully circumscribable and motion that would be external to the "infinite continuity of acts." Both are fictions of positivist metaphysics and enable the illusion of control and safety we desire. Without that possibility of control, there is a constitutive risk impinging upon all expressive motion whether we acknowledge the body's negation or not. Where the origins of motion extend beyond one's circumscribable body and one's control, all movements, however insignificant, accrue various levels of risk. Because creating is "making and being made," because we "receiv[e] and giv[e] in the same gesture,"[194] because we are between what Ziporyn calls the "pusher and the pushed,"[195] or what Dōgen alludes to as "turning things while being turned by them"—all bodily action exceeds one's control, includes an inherent risk, and thus if one does accept these risks, their expression enacts a bodily form of faith.[196] When motionlessness too is an active patterning of a motor-perceptual background, refraining from moving the body does not evade the necessity of faith.

Tradition as Historical-Volitional Ecstasis

If the will were an internal, subjective faculty at a remove from the world, and the origin of motion could be traced to a circumscribable locus, one could still *choose* to engage in risky endeavors, but this would not entail that there is a constitutive risk to all movement. Risk, as something we can choose to take up or not, would be merely ontic. Yet as entangled within a general motorsensory fabric, the origin of one's movements is not localizable as such. Merleau-Ponty alludes to this idea when quoting Paul Klee's idea

---

194. Merleau-Ponty, *Prose of the World*, 11.

195. Ziporyn, *Being and Ambiguity: Philosophical Experiments with Tiantai Buddhism*, 236.

196. The Dōgen quotation is from "Instructions for the Tenzo" (*Tenzo kyōkun*) in *Moon in a Dewdrop*, 56. Hyong-Hyo Kim sums up this Yogācāra logic of giving-receiving: "[T]he objective world does not remain as completely passive reality in relation to the subject but reacts to the body which the subject projects to the world. The world suggests something to the body, attracts its attention, and enthralls it. This also suggests that the world, as much as the body, is standing upright and talking to the perceptions of the body. To make a reference again to Yogācāra concepts, it is said 'The seed is giving a birth to the current action' . . . and 'the current action is shaping the seed' . . . The mutual influence and bridge-making of the transcendence and projection of the body to the world, and the world's introjection into the body, are what Merleau-Ponty refers to as the flesh." *Merleau-Ponty and Buddhism* (Lexington Books, 2009), 26.

of a "distant will."[197] Volition, if we can even use the word in this context, is a force that cuts across the body-world divide. Motion is a multistable phenomenon negotiated between internal and external forces. Accordingly, it is not only when we choose to take on risk, but all movement goes forth with a tacit acceptance of what we might consider an ontological element of risk. Thus, moving the body in any way enacts a corporeal form of faith.

In the previous chapter we considered how the ecstatic body pervaded the perceptual field, through vision and by way of tool use. Now, having explored a motor-ecstasis in this chapter, the idea of solicitations, "unity of act and act," and "optimal grip," let us consider the human will as it is implicated in the account of expression being developed, bringing the discussion closer to answering not only how the landscape moves the body, but how all phenomenal reality is expressive.

Because the artist is embedded in a world whose motions are intertwined with their own, whatever the status of the individual's volition might be, motion cannot be exhaustively reduced to the will of an individual. Just as one's vision pervades the perceptual fabric, so too does volition. On Ziporyn's account, "this will hence pervades the field completely by appearing nowhere simpliciter within it."[198] Bodily action includes but is not reducible to the contractions of one's own muscles and the directives given by a supposed autonomous agent, nor is it limited within the confines of the body's visible outer shell. Nishida provocatively claims that "to know the change of an external thing through one's vision is the same as feeling the movements of one's own body through muscular sensation."[199]

We have already discussed how vision is seeing-seen. How objects appear in the world is not reducible to one's singular point of view. Vision is multi-perspectival. Now, consider motion: when the body is not the sole origin of action, movement can be considered multi-volitional. Action manifests beyond any single volitional node in the sensorimotor fabric. It is a diffuse phenomenon. As such, a body that seems to be still, once regarded in the broader context of its motor-background, is rendered ambiguous regarding motion and motionlessness. The full contours of moving phenomena are never visible, since the background is infinite and the distal and invisible sources of motion implicate themselves in the motion we see. Just as we

---

197. Merleau-Ponty, "Eye and Mind," 147. Merleau-Ponty takes this term from an entry (# 1104) in Paul Klee's diary.

198. Ziporyn, *Being and Ambiguity: Philosophical Experiments with Tiantai Buddhism*, 284.

199. Nishida, *An Inquiry into the Good*, 24.

should not forget that what we do see is "lined" by so much more, likewise, we might consider motion as lined with motionlessness and vice versa.

Defining artistic expression within a restricted positivist account of motion and volition not only misses the beautiful complexity that obtains between artist and landscape, but the insightfulness of many of Nishida's and Merleau-Ponty's most important locutions is too easily dismissed as merely poetic or suggestive. However, now that we have framed expression in terms of a volitionally ecstatic body, we can appreciate Nishida's claim that "the mountains and rivers must also be expressive"[200] or Merleau-Ponty's suggestion that "landscape thinking itself in me . . . and I am its consciousness," as intelligible and profound insights. In a similar light, we can appreciate a much earlier Chinese saying that "to paint a bamboo, one must first be able to grow it inside oneself."[201]

New Solicitations, New Continuity of Act and Act

It is essential that the artist accept his immersion within the volitional world, without losing himself completely to its demands. To relinquish one's agency or creative desires to nature of objectivity would suppress alternative, experimental, or interventionist responses to the world of objects, and thus limit the possibility for new artworks. Given that such a limitation would surely be in direct contradiction to Merleau-Ponty's and Nishida's depictions of artistic expression, I consider this at some length.

One could argue that the movements we say are solicited by the world are simply a set of habitual conventions accumulated over time. Nishida and Merleau-Ponty both speak of motor-perception in terms of habituation. And yet their understandings of artistic expression are clearly based on the need to transcend habitual movement. While the artist learns to respond to the world's solicitations, he or she must go beyond them. Whereas the movements that constitute an appropriate wave are given to me without my having to think about them, the artist's gestures are not automatic to the same extent: the artist faces a world he must transform into a new set of gestures *motivated but not entirely given by* that background. Otherwise, the painter would engage with his tradition, but would not carry it forward in any meaningful sense.

---

200. Nishida, *Fundamental Problems*, 35.
201. Taminiaux, "The Thinker and the Painter," 287.

Both philosophers allow for the object to exert a motor-perceptual pull on the body, while also allowing for the body to modify those responses to counter the force of habit. By working against the sedimented set of background solicitations, they do not go from a motor-entwined position to a motor-neutral one. Un-entangled motor-neutrality is not accessible. Artists do not exit the motorsensory fabric when their motions seek to counter solicitations; they find a previously invisible set of motor-demands, a new intertwinement with the landscape. For Nishida and Merleau-Ponty, artists are exemplary in this regard because they discover new ways of intertwining with the motor-perceptual world.

There is a line in Merleau-Ponty's "Indirect Language and the Voices of Silence" that beautifully describes the bidirectional relation between the painter and her tradition: "this is the historicity which lives in the painter at work when with a single gesture he links the tradition that he carries on and the tradition that he founds."[202] Similarly, even the tightly constrained Chinese landscape painting tradition has this reciprocal expressive structure where an art work is "two things at the same time: a new composition and a creative rendering."[203]

Any familiar object in a given sociohistoric context accrues a set of motorsensory specificities, which determine how it patterns the bodies that come into contact with it. Because an object is regularly treated in a particular way, we experience that object with the force of its historicity. We have always seen people waving or holding cups in a particular way, so we are attracted to these gestures and find it easier to follow suit. This is the "made" part of the "making-made" relation, or the "tradition" that the artist "carries on." If movements only included this aspect of historicity, there would be no means of intervening or behaving toward them that would counter the accumulated set of inflections they solicit. This might render artistic innovation impossible. Yet, because actions also include the "making" part of the "making-made" relation, or the "tradition" the artist "founds," that historicity manifests simultaneously in the same gesture as being always open to modification. If these interventions are strong enough, if they come to inhabit a significant amount of that object's historicity, they will loosen old knots and tie new ones within the motorsensory fabric such that future expressive bodies will move and perceive according to newly

---

202. Maurice Merleau-Ponty, "Indirect Language and the Voices of Silence"; ibid., 100.
203. van Briessen, *Way of the Brush*, 260.

determined constraints. Thus, for example, it might be a long time before an artist can paint any Japanese mountain without responding to Hokusai's depictions in his *Thirty-Six Views of Mount Fuji*. So it is with Cézanne and oranges, Hasegawa and pine trees.

While we can act against the accumulated set of historical solicitations, this does not negate the fact that objects always appear with a horizon of motorsensory demands. We can decide to gesture in a new way, or use an object for an unforeseen purpose, or paint landscapes with innovative means, yet when we do so, the extra effort needed—however infinitesimal—to overcome routine ways of moving, or to work at variance with solicitations, supplements that historicity in new ways, rather than stripping away the temporal layers that would arrive at a motor-neutral nonhistorical object. Because the historical aspect is never entirely closed off, because it is perpetually available for further determination—never fully made but always open by way of the making-made dynamic—there is an abiding possibility of intervening in the historicity of an object, a material, or an

Figure 3.3. Méret Oppenheim, *Fur Lined Teacup*, 1936. Museum of Modern Art, New York. © Estate of Méret Oppenheim, Pro Litteris, Zurich/IVARO, Dublin, 2018. Digital image © The Museum of Modern Art/Licensed by SCALA/Art Resource, New York.

event. Interventions can re-orient the motor-perceptual historicity of objects; they do not erase that historicity or overcome the pull it has on the body.

Discerning how Japanese or Chinese artists intervened in the motor-perceptual fabric of their time is difficult to appreciate in our time and culture since those works are not part of a general legibility or, for all but a few, they do not have great philosophic or religious significance. Looking from the outside into any Japanese aesthetic practice, be it calligraphy, archery, poetry, tea ceremony, etc., discerning what is aesthetically decisive is near impossible for those of us not trained in those practices and who cannot notice the nuanced minutiae of the art form or the tools and implements used in their performance. For example, it might be almost impossible for someone like myself to appreciate the profound meaning that accrues within the implements of the tea ceremony. I can *understand* the significance of a 500-year-old tea cup, I might have a cerebral appreciation, but its profound religious significance might have brought an eleventh-century tea master to his knees. That is, it would seize upon their sensorimotor body, not simply their intellect. It is unlikely that the nuances of the tea ceremony could shock us to the extent of intervening in the sensorimotor relations between ourselves and a tea cup, this intercultural impediment is not entirely insurmountable. Unfortunately, landscape painting itself is not as crucial in our culture, but we can turn to other everyday practices to find a locus where we are invested in objects in comparable ways. It is an unexpected intercultural example, but consider Méret Oppenheim's more contemporary intervention into the phenomena of the tea cup. Although her surrealist intentions and how they are taken up in art history do not tend to focus on this aspect of her work, her *Fur Lined Teacup* (1936) is nevertheless an intriguing piece for disclosing motor aspects of the historical body's intertwinement with historical objects, which might give us a glimpse into the profound effect the various *Geidō* practices would have had in their time.

We do not merely *know* the type of movements that fur or a teacup solicit; we feel our body patterned by these objects and materials. We can take many different orientations toward fur, but there is a particular set that we find our body already predisposed toward, as with a teacup. Effortlessly we slide into the demands that these everyday objects place on our bodies. However, when two objects with quite different arrays of motor-perceptual solicitations are deployed in a single art object, as in Oppenheim's, our usual set of responses is confused by an intervention into their motor-perceptual historicity. Again, it is not that we necessarily cognize this confusion or have a representation of the two sets of divergent historical solicitations.

Instead, Oppenheim's work prompts us to acknowledge that we find our body already drawn into this confusion. I want to drink from the cup but already cannot help but feel the fur in my teeth, as one set of solicitations piggybacks on another by virtue of their having been combined in one object. I am provoked to stroke the fur as I would a pet, and without having to touch the object I already feel the discomfort of the hardness and curvature of the porcelain underlying the pelt. That we feel this set of discomforts so palpably demonstrates the extent to which our bodies are already in a "silent dialogue" with the historically accumulated set of attractions with which objects come to presence. Yet, having intervened so acutely in dissonant solicitations, Oppenheim shows the ever-present possibility of modifying the body's orientation to the object's historicity, as well as the possibility of inventing new movements that will pull on future bodies and create novel continuities of act and acts. But, in having gone so far, such works might not endure as punctuations in the visible field.

Let us shift back to the example of landscape painting and imagine the highly aestheticized court life of Heian-period Japan or Song China where the conventions surrounding depicting landscapes would have been part of a general legibility. Artists, as well as the cultivated citizenry, had fluency regarding how mountains and rivers had been depicted in the visual arts, in famous scenes in poetry, in rock gardens, and especially from their own travels through sacred mountains. In traditions where so little innovation was permitted, if an artist were to challenge the expectations of the informed onlooker, this could, like Oppenheim's piece, intervene not just in one's *knowledge about* landscapes, but in an accumulation of pre-reflective bodily expectations regarding mountains and rivers as phenomena, as continuities of act and act within which their bodies would have been intertwined. It is difficult to imagine in our time what it might have been like in an era where an artistic genre could be so important to a citizenry as landscape painting was in China and Japan during certain periods. That importance was grander than the merely aesthetic: landscape painting was a philosophic and a religious practice and the Buddhist and Daoist lay populations would have found significance at this order in the artworks of the great painters they venerated. Certainly, in our time, we might appreciate the innovations of Taiga, Cézanne, or Sesshū, we might be amazed by the beauty of their works, but it is less likely that our bodies could be invested in the context of legibility or background sensorimotor relations such that we feel a visceral shock when beholding them. Put differently, we are not as deeply enmeshed acts within those continuity of acts that are the paintings; yet, nor are we completely discontinuous insofar as we can still discern innovations. But, what is crucial is not whether we can discern exactly what is beautiful or where innovation might lie. We might appreciate the innovations, but it is another thing altogether to feel the sensorimotor torsion given by works that would have been stunning in the time and context of their creation. To appreciate this in our own time, a work such as Oppenheim's might help us understand what was at stake in China and Japan when great works came on the scene. The palpable discomfort we experience when our everyday expectations (our sensorimotor intertwinement) are disrupted, shows us what it might have been like to behold the innovations of important painters such as Sesshū or Taiga. Although it would have been an exceedingly more nuanced shock enabled by heightened aesthetic awareness of an educated population, yet, like the tea cup, if one feels a bodily impact when beholding the innovations of Sesshū, it is felt not because he simply *represents* something in a new or different way: what is crucial is that his having made the landscape visible how he did would have impacted his audience in a more profound bodily way at the level of sensorimotor expectations at play when seeing paintings, but also when reading poetry, wandering through rock gardens, or climbing mountains or navigating rivers. That is, the impact is not representational, it is motor-perceptual. Further, as a punctuation in the motorsensory fabric of the time, it is not localizable: changing the conditions within which mountains are (visible as) mountains reverberates throughout that fabric and impacts the phenomena of mountains in any of its possible disclosures, be they artistic, literary, or everyday. Moving on to the next section, let us consider in more detail how artists go beyond determining the conditions of *visibility* and affect the conditions of *motor*-visibility.

From Creating the Conditions of Visibility to Creating the Conditions of Motor-Visibility

While Nishida and Merleau-Ponty have common ground in terms of theorizing how the artist determines the conditions of visibility in which their art work is seen, the latter thinker has more to offer on the subject. He alludes to this possibility when stating that we do not just see the great work but "see according to it or with it."[204] While this is a common refrain in Merleau-Ponty scholarship, I attempt to advance his thinking on this

---

204. Merleau-Ponty, "Eye and Mind," 126.

point by exploring how those ways of seeing include the possibility of new ways of moving.

If an artist is familiar with an object—be it a body or a landscape—she would tend to know how to look at it, the best vantage point to see it from, and the techniques for depicting it that produce the optimal representation of its features. Where the artist takes up these various orientations more or less automatically when depicting an object, that object's solicitations have become embedded in her body, and she, in a sense, gives the object partial reign through volitional negation to her sensorimotor body. We can imagine Taiga who was said to have filled three 200-page sketchbooks in one visit to Mt. Fuji as allowing for a similar occupation of his sensorimotor body. Likewise, Cézanne did innumerable sketches of Mont Sainte Victoire and studied its geological foundations, its "bones." Once the movements the objects solicit have functioned well for long enough, it becomes easy and natural to represent a person, trees, or a mountain. Cézanne did not move into expressive gesture at the moment he was able to represent the mountain: Merleau-Ponty writes that he began to move when something "caught fire, which engulfs his body."[205] The crucial point is that the artist, in rendering endless sketches, even in copying another work, must go beyond the motor-continuity that enables accurate representation. For they do not simply want to *represent the visible* but strive to *create visibility*. For this, a break, a discontinuity in the motor-continuity is needed.

The artist wants to allow her body to be guided by the visible, but she cannot simply rely on the habitual set of solicitations dictated by an aesthetic tradition or school of painting. Certainly, the Chinese tradition was noted for its slavish devotion to convention that all too often produced mere copies in the bad sense of the term. Both Cézanne and Sesshū are celebrated artists because they invented not just a new way of representing the landscape, but a new way of seeing the world. For Merleau-Ponty, the "painter's role" is not to reproduce what has historically been visible, it is, rather more complex: the artist must "circumscribe and project what is making itself seen within himself." What was previously invisible enters the visible but not strictly through the artist. The newly visible "emanate[s] from

---

205. Ibid., 147.

the things themselves, like figures emanating from the constellations."²⁰⁶ Capturing these constellations as they emerge from the invisible constitutes a type of creativity that is inherently risky.

How does one orient oneself, one's body, and gestures within a motor-constellation that encompasses the landscape and the pull given by the great artists who have depicted it throughout history? The painter wants to achieve what seems impossible, namely to make the motor-perceptual object into a newly visible object, and therefore a newly motor-soliciting object, but not strictly out of her own individual faculties. A tie that binds Cézanne and Sesshū (but might distinguish the latter slightly from his Chinese heritage) is that they are not wholly satisfied with the visibility that is given to them by their tradition, and are thus not comfortable being fully constrained by the operative set of solicitations and motor-responses. These artists want to forge a new visibility, but it is a negotiation more than a creation. What they want can only be arrived at in tandem with the landscape. Since both are in motion, the search for a new visibility is a search for new constellations of bodily movements, for new gestures that come from but are not reducible to those that came before. Rendering the world according to how it has already become sedimented in the body does not renew the landscape's visibility, but only reproduces the prevailing conditions of visibility. This would result in works that might look novel in a restricted sense, not new in the sense we are looking for.²⁰⁷ To be more precise, the former creates within the prevailing conditions of visibility, whereas the latter creates the conditions of visibility within which it will be seen.

---

206. Merleau-Ponty, "Eye and Mind," 129.

207. There is an intriguing parallel here with Maurice Blanchot's theory of literary expression in his "Literature and the Right to Death" in his *The Work of Fire*. Blanchot explains how if the author represents his or her reader that their work will inevitably fail. The author cannot give the reader what they want because, just as the conditions of visibility are in the future for the painter, likewise, the conditions of readability are in the future for the author: "Because the reader has no use for a work written for him, what he wants is precisely an alien work in which he can discover something unknown, a different reality; a separate mind capable of transforming him and which he can transform into himself. An author who is writing specifically for a public is not really writing: it is the public that is writing, and for this reason the public can no longer be a reader; reading only appears to exist, actually it is nothing. This is why works created to be read are meaningless: no one reads them. This is why it is dangerous to write for other people, in order to evoke the speech of others and reveal them to themselves: the fact is that other people do not want to hear their own voices; they want to hear someone else's voice, a voice that is real, profound, troubling like the truth."

To avoid reproducing the visible, an artist does not simply choose to take flight into subjective creative fancy, attempting to be "original" for the sake of originality. Neither Nishida nor Merleau-Ponty defends a distinctly modern idea of "creativity," which would reify the conception of the subject and give license to the myth of the artistic genius. If the artist wishes to alter the conditions of visibility, there are two constraints she must accept—one objective, another subjective. On one hand she cannot reproduce the "objective" features of the landscape: for this would be the appropriate aim if the artist were entirely passive and expressive movements were fully dictated by what the landscape solicits. In this case, obstruction would originate in the subjective. On the other hand, the artist does not want to create works that are completely "subjective": for this would be the artist working out of intertwinement with the landscape, whereby her movements would not be constrained in any way by the object's motor-perceptual demands. In this case, obstruction would originate in the objective. The prerequisite for creating good art, according to Nishida, involves going beyond these subject–object binaries where non-obstruction can obtain between body and world at a point where "the artist[s] medium takes over, releasing the mind from its subjectivity and reality from its objectivity."[208] Released as such, artistic expression that ensues within the ambiguity of a world not-fully-objective and self not-fully-subjective opens the possibility for creation where motor-visibility can be modified.

In contemplating how the conditions of visibility can be altered, possible new motor-orientations within the world can be discovered; we can articulate a further aspect of risk that implicates itself into artistic expression, and thus, another instance of faith. If the conditions of motor-visibility were fixed, once an artist discovers them and attunes her body to its motor valence, she could then create a positive technique for proper representation. Certainly, this is one reason for adhering to the copious amounts of technical manuals in the Chinese tradition: specifically, to not disturb the conditions of visibility. Following technique reduces the risks an artist takes. To do so is to operate according to the visible as it is determined in the present. In this sense, we might say, painting comes before painting. But, because artworks always do have the possibility of shifting the conditions within which they are seen, to attempt to affect the conditions of motor-visibility is to work beyond what can be made into technique. That is, it is to work at the level of the invisible. It is to risk working in the dark, without the objective

---

208. Nishida, *Art and Morality*, 59.

criteria of a manual or a technique to underwrite the risk. To do so is to exercise a motor-perceptual form of faith. The artist *does not* set out on the impossible task with a fully visible image he then applies to canvas: rather, visibility is created *in the process of painting* and moving the body. In this case, "painting does not come before painting."[209] If the work succeeds, it should surprise or shock the painter as much as any other observer. When the artist reworks the visible through expressive activity, he has rewoven the sensorimotor fabric into an orientation that did not previously exist in that particular pattern. Moreover, the reconstitution is not limited to visibility: because motion and perception are intertwined, when an artist re-orients the conditions of visibility within the perceptual, he likewise reconstitutes the conditions of *movability* within the *motor*-perceptual.

Having established a context for understanding a perceptually *and* volitionally ecstatic body, the last sections of this chapter consider in more detail some of the intricate ways in which Nishida and Merleau-Ponty depict the relation between vision and movement. Both thinkers approach this issue from different angles and with different concepts but share a comparable orientation where they explore the relation between motion and vision in terms of their ambiguity and mutual co-implication. To properly understand the "actual body," Merleau-Ponty argues that we must look "not [at] the body as a chunk of space or a bundle of functions but that body which is an intertwining of *vision and movement*."[210] In a similar vein, Nishida quotes the German aesthetician who also influenced Merleau-Ponty: "As Fiedler states, the development of pure visual perception is spontaneously accompanied by expressive movement and becomes the act of artistic creation."[211] While the intertwinement of vision and motion can afford myriad possibilities when thinking about artistic expression, I consider these in two broad categories: *vision as a way of moving the body*, and the related but more complicated issue of *moving the body as a way of seeing*. Following this, I close the chapter by exploring the fascinating ways that color can be thought within a context of negation.

---

209. Merleau-Ponty, "Indirect Language and the Voices of Silence," 91.
210. Merleau-Ponty, "Eye and Mind," 124. Emphasis added.
211. Nishida, *Art and Morality*, 52.

Vision as Motion

I want to take up the question further regarding how the artist attunes her body to the expressive impulse embedded within the landscape, to further establish how this yields an expansion of the conditions of the body's movability.

Nishida explores the relation between vision and motion with some of his more intriguing terminology of his earlier period. In his 1923 *Art and Morality*, he invokes a distinction between the body's internal organs and what he calls its "external organs" (*gaibu kikan* 外部機関). Here, we shift slightly from considering one end of mutual negation where the artist's body is inflected by things to the other end where that body infuses objects in the world with aspects of its corporeity. The body's "external organs" are the objects in the motor-perceptual field that are permeated with one's motion and perception as they extend out beyond one's body and pervade that field. The artist is able to tune into the world's movements not just because she is receptive, but because her body's "organs" are out there among the mountains and rivers, trees and animals.

One might argue that the distance between internal organs and external organs is potentially too vast to consider them as part of the same body. Yet, this is to invoke the binaries of vision and touch Nishida and Merleau-Ponty have helped us overcome, as well as maintaining too simple conceptions of space and distance. That my internal and external organs are part of my body is enabled by vision. Because the body extends throughout light, there is no unambiguous distance between oneself and one's distal organs. The ambiguity between the visual and the tactile means that even far-off organs are within my body and inflect its movements. In a remarkable line, Nishida explains that we do not simply represent distant objects in the perceptual field: "[t]o know the change of an external thing through one's vision is the same as feeling the movements of one's own body through muscular sensation."[212] Later, in *Art and Morality*, Nishida explains that visual experience is more than ocular, it also yields a change in the external organs of the body.[213] To move in the phenomenal field is to move one's internal organs and to modulate those objects encountered through motor-negation. One is not divided away from the world because one's organs and muscles are in here and not out there. "That which unites the artist and his work," writes

---

212. Nishida, *An Inquiry into the Good*, 24.
213. Nishida, *Art and Morality*, 25.

Nishida, "is internal muscular perception, and a single life force courses through the two."[214] Thus, Nishida believes that we can

> look upon an artistic work as the development of muscular sensation. . . . Fiedler states that the eye not only gives sensation and perception, but that it also moves the external organs of the body, thus causing what is immanent to be developed into external expressive movement.[215]

Nishida follows Fiedler in further elaborating the artistic implications of what obtains between the body and its motor-visually expanded instance. In his 1941 "Artistic Creation as Historically Formative Act," Nishida writes that "Fiedler argues that when our self becomes one with the sense of sight . . . then a world of infinite visual developments unfolds and the sense of sight becomes one with the bodily movements in the outer world."[216] He continues following Fiedler to illustrate how the artist proceeds from passive to active vision, where "our active behavior directly associates with action in the outside world, and action in the outside world immediately becomes a continuation of our active behavior."[217]

Because of the way that the body invests the things in the world it encounters, even while the artist is completely still, the body is set in motion through one's visual modulations. To meditate on the landscape is to engage visually with a variety of objects that give and receive movement. I feel the motion in the rivers and the trees as though they were my own external organs and muscles. "[P]erception is a form of action"[218] because the body is never indifferent to the objects with which vision intertwines. Sight is not just the passive reception of sensory data: choosing different objects to concentrate on is to choose different orientations of the volitionally ecstatic body. It is to modulate the ambiguity of one's activity and passivity in ways corresponding to the motions of those objects, mountains, or other bodies. While the world reaches into our motor-perceptual negation, we at the same time reach out and inhabit the negation where the world accepts our

---

214. Ibid.
215. Ibid.
216. Nishida, *Nishida Kitarō zenshū*, 9: 234.
217. Ibid.
218. Nishida, *Fundamental Problems*, 74.

body's extension into that field. Nishida goes so far as to say that "there is no seeing when faced with things lacking any sort of connection with our movement."[219] Thus, a further feature of the non-object is that we encounter it visually and always with a motor-demand.

Because the phenomenal body is dispersed throughout the landscape, one must exert oneself to not change when the world changes. The motionless artists, Cézanne or Sesshū meditating on the mountains and rivers, do not just passively receive neutral visual information: their motionlessness affords a vantage point on a world pulling them in other directions. Thus, it is a struggle to maintain but it might afford a differently visual object. A body visually open to the world is never neutral as far as motion is concerned.[220] There is no way to arrest the motor-perceptual reversibility between internal and external organs; motionlessness is a modification of motion, not its opposite. And, because the conduit through which we give and take motion is vision, establishing new conditions of visibility likewise creates new conditions of movability.

MOTION AS VISION

Let us now make the shift signaled above, from considering *vision as a way of moving the body*, to the more complicated issue of *moving the body as a way of seeing*. There is a straightforward sense in which moving the body is a visual act. If we move things around to see their different sides, or move our bodies into different vantage points relative to objects, these movements entail changes in visual perspectives. Merleau-Ponty says as much when he writes that "[a]ll my changes of place figure in principle in an area of my landscape," but he goes further when he continues, explaining that these movements are "carried over onto the map of the visible."[221] This brings us to the more subtle sense in which vision and motion are intertwined. Yes, I can move my body to see different aspects of an object that already

---

219. Nishida, "Logic and Life," in *Place and Dialectic*, 251.

220. As Zahavi writes in relation to Husserl, "a stationary point of view is only the limiting case of a mobile point of view." D. Zahavi, *Husserl's Phenomenology*, 99. Along similar lines, Mahendran (2010) explains that "[p]erception is for the most part always a kinaesthetic relation to the world even at times of motionlessness. Wakeful perception is actively optimal in that my body is actively engaged even while seemingly still."

221. Merleau-Ponty, "Eye and Mind," 124.

appears in my visual field, but more importantly, and more difficult to discern is how certain movements can make things visible in new and different ways. This is the more complicated of the two intertwinements of vision and motion alluded to above. Anyone can move around to the other sides of an object, yet it is an entirely different and much more difficult task to create new visibility through particular ways of moving the body. This is why Merleau-Ponty and Nishida look to the artist. As Nishida writes in his "Logic and Life" essay, the artist "makes continuously via seeing; to make is simultaneously to see. Life in this sense," according to Nishida, "must be formatively (*zōkei*) artistic."[222]

Merleau-Ponty's rendering of Cézanne's practice illustrates this latter type of reversibility. Cézanne did not first have a representation of the landscape, fully formed and worked out, which he then simply placed on his canvas. He was not copying the visible, as though it already existed once and for all; instead, he sought to change the very conditions of visibility as he developed new ways of moving. This might also have been the case for Sesshū or any other artist who departs from their tradition to create new artworks through new ways of moving the body. Artistic gesture can show the painter herself a world that was not previously visible before the painting made it so.

Let us consider an example to illustrate what is at stake. If most of us painted, although our works would be distinct, we would still most likely rely on conventions of representation that would not impact the conditions of visibility themselves. Cézanne, in Merleau-Ponty's view, was able to break conventions and work beyond those conditions. To achieve this type of relation to the landscape through painting sounds like an impossible task; it is, in fact, an "infinite" task, as we discuss in the next chapter. Nevertheless, the artist cannot take on this task alone. Because the landscape moves Cézanne's body and is partially responsible for the artist's gestures, it is not possible for Cézanne to know ahead of time what the painting will ultimately look like. Only as the work comes to completion could Cézanne appreciate how the landscape was making itself seen within him, how it was patterning his body and inflecting his brushstrokes. The final work will be new to Cézanne as well; new insofar as he will see for the first time with his own eyes what the result was from the intertwinement between his body and the landscape. If the deformation can remain

---

222. Nishida, "Logic and Life," in *Place and Dialectic*, 255.

coherent, then the painting can offer a new way of seeing not just itself, but all perceptual phenomena. Thus, moving the body in the way Mont Sainte Victoire demanded presented a new vision. Something previously unseen. The expressive approach that achieves this outcome can never be codified, it could never be fully articulated in a manual. It is beyond technique. To invoke a term that is later pivotal for the dialogue, there is a "blind spot" inherent to this approach and thus the achievements of earlier painters of a tradition must constrain one's expression but cannot do so by way of representations of techniques that would reduce the inherent risk in attempting to change the visual at this level. Moving the body as the visible constitutes itself, without a representation or a manual to guide one's actions, is a risk that demands faith. It demands faith because the body is geared into a motor-perceptual demand that can only guide one's gestures if it is not represented, if it remains in the invisible while it works through the body to eventually change visibility itself. Lending one's body to the landscape as such unlocks the possibility of making the world differently visible and the body differently movable. Movement constitutes vision. In other words, movement creates visibility *in motion*. Or, as Merleau-Ponty put it, movement arises "by some impact of the world, which it then restores to the visible through the traces of the hand."[223]

To paint as Cézanne did is to have faith in the motorsensory world that gave his body and its gestures their specific style, and to risk a type of expression that could not come from an individuated body working out of intertwinement with the landscape. Artists who engage in the motor-perceptual world in this key, who immerse their body in its fabric, can uncover a new world made visible by the expressive movements that he or she allows to arise in their body only if they have faith to be moved by a mover that cannot be positively represented, and to be a body expressing itself partially beyond one's ability to control. This ability of motion to impact vision as enabled through a sensorimotor form of faith is the aspect of expression most relevant to this dialogue. For Nishida, this mode of visibility/movability is developed in artistic expression, through what he calls "acting-intuition."

"Acting-Intuition"

In his 1934 *Fundamental Problems of Philosophy*, Nishida writes that "our action is not merely movement. Action must have the significance that

---

223. Merleau-Ponty, "Eye and Mind," 127.

we see something through it."²²⁴ In this work, he develops his concept of "Acting-intuition" (*kōi-teki chokkan* 行為的直観) in part to describe the reversibility of motion and vision. As with Merleau-Ponty, artistic activity is particularly apt for manifesting this reversibility, thus active intuition has implications for Nishida's theory of expression.²²⁵ I discuss this aspect of his idea below, but first let us discuss the background of the concept whose etymology is relevant to previous discussions of volitional ecstasis and the ambiguity of activity and passivity.

As Nishida developed his account of the "historical body" and "historical world" throughout the 1930s, he sought an account of action, which in overcoming the subject–object distinction, likewise went beyond the active-passive binary. Heisig frames this well, particularly regarding the ambiguity maintained with a "non-subject" and "non-object":

> In all knowing, there is not only one's active, reflective grasp of things but a passive intuition in which one is grasped by things. The problem is, this ordinary, spontaneous knowing is kept out of reach because of a prior commitment to the idea that one must either be subjective or objective about things, but never both at the same time. Nishida wants a conversion to a new standpoint of awareness in which one sees through the falsehood of this dichotomy . . . a new relationship must be cultivated in which self and world inter-act and inter-intuit each other. Self has to be understood as a subject that is not a non-object, and world has to be understood as an object that is not a non-subject. As Nishida says, one needs to awaken to "a seeing without a seer."²²⁶

The key point for this concept is that acting-intuition does not just describe the way the body moves; it is not just the character of human

---

224. Nishida, *Fundamental Problems*, 181.
225. Maraldo suggests that *kōiteki chokkan* can be translated as "performative intuition" to suggest the way in which this orientation within the world is expressive. He also suggests "enactive intuition," "acting intuition," "active intuition," and "action-intuition" as other possible translations (John Maraldo, "Enaction in Cognitive Science and Nishida's Turn of Intuition into Action").
226. Heisig, *Philosophers of Nothingness*, 55.

motion. It is also the character of the world's own motion, how it lets things be seen, and how it sees itself. Neither the self nor the world preexists in a static form before their mutual formation through acting-intuition. Both world and self are co-constituted in their expressive reciprocity of acting intuition.

Nishida chooses both terms of his concept *kōi-teki chokkan* carefully in order to suggest the mutual negation between self and world and a related ambiguity between activity and passivity. The non-verbal, substantive term, for "intuition" (*chokkan* 直観) is neither, strictly speaking, the intuition of the active subject or the *being intuited* of a passive object. Accordingly, Krummel and Nagatomo write: "Intuition in this context is not simply a human doing but simultaneously refers to the activity of the world forming itself through our human acting and intuiting."[227] To intuit is not to passively receive sense data from the phenomenal world. In true intuition, the self does not simply receive the world, but instead becomes a creative agent within it. One lends one's body to the world while the world becomes the body of the self.[228] When one intuits the world, he is at the same time acting *on* the world and *as* the world. Indeed, Nishida uses the term "active self" (*hataraku jiko* 働く自己), which would seem to reify the subject, yet, as Krummel and Nagatomo further explain, the word Nishida uses for "action" is derived from the Japanese *hataraku* and refers not to the agency of an individuated self, but rather to a more general movement of the world. His choice of *hataraku* is similar to the German verb *wirken*, which means to "work," "act," or "have an effect," but is also related to the noun *Wirklichkeit*, which means "reality" or "actuality."[229] *Hataraku*, thus, invokes motion as a general feature of phenomenal reality, as a bidirectional making-made reciprocity that obtains between the body and world. To return to the question of the relation between ontology and language discussed above, Maraldo suggests that along with the chiasmatic relation Nishida's neologism describes, the term itself is also a grammatical chiasm where vision is inflected by motion and motion inflected by vision.[230]

---

227. Krummel and Nagatomo, *Place and Dialectic*, 375.
228. Nishida, *Nishida Kitarō Zenshū*, 8, 328, as translated in Kazashi "The World Becomes the Self's Body: James, Merleau-Ponty and Nishida."
229. Krummel and Nagatomo, *Place and Dialectic*, 337.
230. Maraldo, "Nishida's Ontology of History," 199.

Acting-intuition is the volitional orientation exemplified by the artist who in the same gesture makes and is made by the world, and in so doing maintains ambiguity between an active subject and an active object. If the artist merely ridded herself of agency in a form of passive intuition, this would culminate in an utterly negated non-self, yet, as both Merleau-Ponty and Nishida contend, such a self would have no means of interacting with the world. A full negation of the body would be the historical world's self-formation working independently of—and thereby obstructing—the historical body, but this is not movement as it obtains within the motor-perceptual world of *Basho*.

Having articulated how Nishida's acting-intuition corresponds to a similar reversibility in Merleau-Ponty's thought, the discussion can now return again to further elaborate the second of the two forms of reversibility—namely how moving the body can reveal new aspects of the visual world. For both philosophers, artists and their work are the paradigms of a type of expression that creates new visibility through motion. In his *Fundamental Problems*, Nishida writes that "[w]e act through seeing, and we see through acting . . . Indeed, artistic creativity is a kind of action in such a sense."[231] The artist's expressive movement is the locus of reversibility. This entails a very specific way of orienting the motor-perceptual body in what Nishida calls "pure visual perception" (*junsui shikaku* 純粋視覚): "In this way we must also interpret a creative act in the plastic arts as an expressive movement accompanying the development of pure visual perception."[232] As previously noted, Nishida's use of the world "pure" (*junsui* 純粋) can easily confound his intended meaning. Referring to visual perception as "pure" seems to suggest a type of vision independent of other sensory modalities, separate from the body's motion or the motions of other bodies in the motorsensory fabric past or present. Of course, this would run counter to how Nishida and Merleau-Ponty understand the visual body. Vision is not "pure" in the sense of being a human faculty that distinguishes the body from a non-perceptual world of objectivity. It is pure precisely insofar as it is a feature of the world, which exists prior to any bifurcation that would define vision as separate from the world. Nishida is clear on this point: "pure visual perception is spontaneously accompanied by action."[233] He looks to

---

231. Nishida, *Fundamental Problems*, 193.
232. Nishida, *Art and Morality*, 158.
233. Nishida, *Nishida Kitarō zenshū*, 2: 368.

artistic expression as the locus of this relation between vision and motion: "As the act of pure visual perception develops into language, it naturally moves our body and develops into a kind of expressive movement. This is the creative act of the artist (*künstlerische Tätigkeit*)."[234] In this sense, it is not just the hand that works in intertwinement with the eye, but "the entire body becomes the eye;"[235] Further, "it is not vision only of the eye, but of the eye and hand as one experience."[236] Vision is pure in its being a phenomena of a general motor-perceptual fabric. A vision Nishida refers to as "seeing without a seer." Accordingly, the vision of the hand, or of the world itself, is no less "pure" than that of the human eye.

Intuition is therefore creative because it is always implicated in the moving body that makes the world. One is receptive to that world and, in this way, expression is not a uni-directional form of production whereby an idea is born in the head and launched out into the external world. Nishida describes the kind of creative expression issuing from active-intuition as "from the created to the creating"[237] (*tsukuraretamono kara tsukurumono e* 作られたものから作るものえ). Despite being able to isolate the human side of creation, all action is part of a broader motor-perceptual fabric, and acting-intuition is the character of this motion. Intuition is not passive, it is an action, and because action is diffused throughout the world's moving fabric, our movements constitute our own lives while giving the world itself form. According to Nishida's predicate logic, my body is partly the world's body, and vice versa. Nishida insists that this is not a monism, but rather a "dynamic dialectic."[238] The body and world interact creatively due to the volitional negation that allows them to respond to one another. Active-intuition describes a non-obstructive moving-seeing relation through which the artist simultaneously penetrates and is penetrated by the world.

We can try to isolate the human will from the broader volitional fabric, and believe that we have located the locus of creativity, yet because body and world are related by mutual negation, this only gives us half the

---

234. Nishida, *Art and Morality*, 24.

235. Ibid., 27.

236. Ibid., 158.

237. Nishida, *Nishida Kitarō zenshū*, 9: 305; Nishida, "World as Identity of Absolute Contradiction"; "The Logic of the Place of Nothingness and the Religious Worldview," in *Last Writings: Nothingness and the Religious Worldview*.

238. Krummel and Nagatomo, *Place and Dialectic*, 44.

picture, if not less. As Krummel and Nagatomo note, "In the passivity of receiving information, we are negated, but in our volitional acts, we affirm ourselves, in both cases vis-à-vis the environment. "Seeing" and "acting" represent these contradictory moments as in fact complementary, interdependent, and inseparable."[239]

Without the accounts of motion and perception developed by our philosophers in dialogue, Sesshū and Cézanne's prolonged periods of visual and meditative stillness could suggest a way of thinking about vision and bodily action as separate. In such narratives, it is as though the artists were purely receptive and non-motile only until they had sufficiently absorbed their landscapes visually and then only later acted and expressed the fruits of their meditations in their works. Along these lines, Maraldo writes: "we might ordinarily conceive of the artist as a pre-given entity who views, is inspired by, and utilizes pre-given things in the world around her as she then goes about making her work."[240] Yet, he goes on to explain that it is not such a "causative process," and that the temporality of reversible action and perception is not necessarily sequential. Action does not necessarily follow vision in time. As Maraldo explains, "Nishida envisioned an alternative":

> Whereas this mutual formation can be described in terms of a causative process taking time, with the person first intuiting or internalizing and then acting or externalizing, Nishida described it in terms of the place or *topos* wherein intuiting entails acting and acting intuiting, and wherein the difference between internal and external collapses . . . the artist takes in or intuits the world and transforms or enacts it, both of which are but two moments in a single unfolding—not only of the world but of the artist as well. Both artist and work are formed mutually and are reflected in one another.[241]

Action and intuition are not sequential, but are simultaneous and reversible. Thus, to impact the conditions of visibility is at the same time to change the conditions of movability. I am visually formative as a moving body and motor-formative as a seeing body. There is never a purely physical

---

239. Ibid., 42.
240. Maraldo, "Nishida Kitarō," 2015: plato.stanford.edu/entries/nishida-kitaro/notes.html
241. Ibid.

action, nor is there unambiguous vision to the exclusion of motion. The idea of an artist painting strictly out of her own active motor-perceptual faculties might be conceivable if motion were distinct from vision, yet this amounts to a fictional body in a motor-perceptual vacuum, not the body as it exists as part of a larger motorsensory continuum of *Basho* or flesh. Because the artist can—or perhaps must—create visibility as she moves, and does not have a positive representation of those conditions at hand before expressing herself, she moves in creative gesture with the faith that the risk of allowing the world to move her body will result in something new.

Because acting-intuition is the character of the motor-perceptual world, we must not only acknowledge how the world acts and moves, we must also understand how the *world* intuits and sees. This brings us to Nishida's notions of "seeing without a seer" (*mirumono nakushite miru koto* 見るものなくして見ること) and the "self-seeing" (*Jiko jishin wo miru* 自己自身を見る) of *Basho*. These concepts are further instances that are tempting to read as merely poetic or metaphorical; however, in the context of the mutual perceptual and volitional negation outlined above, these can be taken as phenomenological descriptions whose idiom captures the body's continuously-discontinuously intertwinement with the visual world. Nishida is clear that the world itself has a way of seeing: "[T]he world of historical reality expressively determines itself and goes on seeing itself through acting-intuition. This is the formation of historical nature."[242] The "world's self-seeing," which Nishida invokes, is not another seeing above and beyond human vision; rather, because the body is inextricably worldly, there is an aspect of its seeing that is the world's seeing. Nishida's "seeing without a seer" resonates with what Merleau-Ponty calls "anonymous" vision. This vision is not strictly speaking human, because it is enacted at the intersection of a mutually formative body and world.[243] To what extent vision is anonymous,

---

242. Nishida, "Logic and Life," 301. Heisig articulates this further: "His idea is that action and intuition, the seer and the seen, can be seen as jointed at the roots in the body, which both sees the world and is the receptacle for the world's making itself seen—so that neither can ever be abstracted from the other." Heisig, *Philosophers of Nothingness: An Essay on the Kyoto School*, 54.

243. See Krummel and Nagatomo, *Place and Dialectic*, 362. "Again this refers to acting-intuition that has been extended or broadened in meaning beyond the acting-intuition of mere human beings. Rather the world or reality itself creates and determines itself through acting-intuition. As it makes itself, it 'sees' itself within itself. It designates a shift in stance from the human perspective to that of the world or reality."

and how the world "sees" are questions that invoke the central issue in this confrontation to come between Nishida and Merleau-Ponty. These issues bring us back to the initial discrepancy signaled in the opening chapter between the extent to which obstruction obtains in phenomenal encounter. We come to these questions in the final chapter. Before proceeding to that crucial discussion, let us finish this chapter by returning to consider how color fits into the discussion of vision, motion, and faithful expression.

Color(lessness) and Motion(lessness)

Having worked our way from perception to motor-perception, from perceptual negation to motor-perceptual negation, I would like to consider one last comparative issue regarding Sesshū and Cézanne, namely, color, where we find an important divergence between Nishida and Merleau-Ponty regarding their portraits of the artist.

Merleau-Ponty is emphatic about the importance of color, not just in Cézanne's artworks but in the artist's life too. He depicts the painter as obsessed with the colored world. He goes so far as to claim that Cézanne developed a metaphysics of color. There is no way to reflect upon the French painter's works without taking very seriously his relation to the colored world, for that relation sheds light on how Cézanne perceived nature and how he moved as part of it. However, this presents a challenge when comparing his works with those of Sesshū, Guo Xi or other East-Asian landscape painters, since they worked almost exclusively in black ink. Despite his having faced a world colored with the same intensity and vivacity as Cézanne's, Sesshū depicted that world with a single tone. Sesshū painted his "Splashed Ink Landscape" in the *gyō* style of Chinese painting, which foreswears color altogether, considering it to be a base form of expression. He continued the monochrome landscape painting tradition (*sansuiga* 山水画), which began in China as an extension of calligraphy. Given what appears to be a fundamental discrepancy that could not be more straightforward, we must ask whether these choices about color are fundamentally divergent ideas about the visual world, about art, metaphysics, or about the materials used to bring the landscape to presence in painting.

What is hopefully clear already is that to set up an opposition like this between Cézanne and Sesshū is to maintain a binary opposition between the chromatic and non-chromatic, not to mention an implicit binary between the visible and the invisible, which we should expect neither Nishida nor

Merleau-Ponty would abide. Long before either wrote about painting, Chinese artists and theorists had thought deeply about these questions concerning color and representation. As far back as T'ang and Song China, those who painted and wrote about painting saw no simple opposition between color and monochrome. The Chinese believed that all colors could be expressed in black and white. "Whoever masters the use of ink can paint it in all five colors" the saying goes.[244] While Chinese landscape painters might not have had the phenomenological explanation to support this conviction, for that we can turn to Nishida and Merleau-Ponty. By further developing their ontologies of negation, this time regarding a theory of color, all obstacles are removed for comparing the monochrome works of Sesshū with the vibrantly colored landscapes of Cézanne.

To advance this issue, let us bring the problematics of color into the context of relationality as mutual negation. If we were to treat color as a straightforwardly positive feature of the objective world, as a non-negated quality not woven into the motorsensory fabric, there would be impediments to comparing Sesshū and Cézanne. Yet, when considered as a *textural* feature of the motor-perceptual fabric of flesh and *Basho*, color is shown to impinge upon the body in relation to mutual negation, thus eliciting *dynamics* within that fabric. As such, color is not simply an inert perceptual quality; rather, it is a motor-perceptual feature of the world—another way the world pulls on and configures the body, its postures, and gestures. Color has a motor-reality, it solicits one's motions. It is better understood as an act within a continuity of acts than as secondary features coating the circumscribed surface of objects. Approaching color in this manner enables and expands the dialogue between Cézanne and Sesshū, while also bringing out important differences between motor-aspects of Nishida and Merleau-Ponty's theories of color.

Motor-Chromaticity

It would seem that Sesshū and Cézanne must have taken significantly different orientations toward the colored world, and by extension must have thought about painting and the world in fundamentally different ways.

---

244. The Chinese landscape master Chang Yen-yüan was one of the first to suggest that ink could invoke "all five colors." While this belief is not as prevalent in the Western art world, the French print-maker Honoré Daumier was said to believe in the chromatic possibilities within black and white.

Cézanne's practice, and the innovations he brought to European painting, can be largely explained by his devotion to the colored world. Like the Impressionists, he wanted to remain true to experience by not outlining objects. Yet, unlike the impressionists, he sought to restore some of the solidity of the object. These two desires—which may strike one as mutually exclusive—taken together constituted what Cézanne's friend Emile Bernard called Cézanne's "suicide." Nevertheless, the French painter's objects overcome the seeming paradox: without outlines that would circumscribe and thus distinguish one absolutely from the other, his mountains, trees, and fruit appear "illumined from within," not fully lost in the background. He chose his palette in such a way that color itself could manifest the outline of the objects he painted: "When the colour is at its richest, the form has reached plenitude,"[245] Cézanne wrote. Through his experiments with color, he attains solidity without absolute distinction between objects, thus engendering substantiality within relationality, "there is" within "there is not," and a mode of depiction between positivity and negation.

One might assume that monochrome is simply like chromatic painting minus the color. Though intuitive, such a simple distinction between color and colorlessness is a result of overly simplified assumptions about representation that do not begin to consider the complex ways in which colors reach into the motor-perceptual body as that body reaches out into the colored world it seeks to paint. If we see color as a feature of the motor-perceptual fabric into which the body is woven, then we can complicate the division between color and monochrome. This distinction cannot be upheld precisely because by talking about color(lessness) we are already talking about motion(lessness).

That color has implications for bodily movement is a relatively uncontroversial point that has been well established in mainstream science. Prefiguring what is now a generally accepted standpoint, in *The Phenomenology of Perception*, Merleau-Ponty outlines how color affects motion. The body's movements are, he writes, "differently modified in [their] sweep and [their] direction according as the visual field is red, yellow, blue or green."[246] He elaborates the different motor-reactions enacted by the body within different color fields:

> With a green visual field the assessment is accurate, with a red one the subject errs on the side of excess. Movements outwards

---

245. Merleau-Ponty, "Cézanne's Doubt," 65.
246. Merleau-Ponty, *Phenomenology of Perception*, 242.

are accelerated by green and slowed down by red. Localization of stimuli on the skin is modified by red in the direction of abduction. Yellow and red emphasize errors in judging weight and time, though in the case of cerebellar patients blue and particularly green have a compensating effect. In these various experiments each color always acts with the same tendency, with the result that a definite motor value can be assigned to it.[247]

Later in *Sense and Non-Sense*, he places his thinking about color and bodily motion in the context of his earlier concept of "solicitations": "red or blue are nothing other than my different ways of running my eyes over what is offered to me and of responding to its solicitation."[248]

While color is already associated with bodily motion, even in the representational model, it is not so obvious how color itself could have its own kind of motion. For a great deal of the history of Western philosophy, color has been ignored or treated as a secondary attribute of objects. If objects are in motion, it is not because of their color attributes. Color is inert and motionless. It only moves insofar as the thing it is stuck to moves and has no obvious relation to the motion of the body that perceives it. Yet, we have already shown how perception is persistently implicated in motion. And if visual perception is always—in chromatically sighted individuals—saturated with color, we cannot help but enquire into the relation between motion and color. In so doing, one can extend Nishida's and Merleau-Ponty's philosophy to speak of what we might consider a theory of motor-chromaticity. Because motion is always modulated by the color field within which it obtains, just as there is no simple motor-neutral visual position, we can challenge the idea of an unambiguous chromatic neutrality that would serve to distinguish color from colorlessness. Thus, in reflecting on the motor-dynamics of color, we find the means for extending the dialogue between landscape painters who appear to make vastly different commitments regarding how to depict the natural world.

Color is in motion in an obvious sense in most of our visual experience. Even in sitting motionless in front of a landscape, the slowly fluctuating

---

247. Ibid., 243.
248. *Sense and Non-Sense*, 93.

shades we see are ever modulated by the intensity of the sun, the movements of clouds, the varying degrees of particles in the atmosphere, etc., meaning that one's visual field always has various degrees of color saturation, as a result, finely tuning the body's movements, postures, and possibilities. We can acknowledge how, in a straightforward sense, the apparently motionless painter can be conceptualized as in motion: as part of a visual field whose color is constantly changing, the aspect of one's body that extends into that field and inflected by its colors is likewise always in motion. Because perception is always motor-perception, a still body in a field of moving and changing color cannot be absolutely motionless.

While Merleau-Ponty's insights that certain colors determine one's moods or behaviors is a rather uncontroversial idea, what might not be so straightforward is the ontological explanation that accounts for this phenomenon. If conceived along the lines of the representational framework, the effect color has on the body could be construed simply as a subject registering certain qualities of a distinct object or color field, and then adjusting their motions in response. However, to think of color-inflected motion merely as an effect of color does not capture the underlying relation between the body, motion, and color. If it were merely an effect, this would imply that there is an originally non-color-inflected body, or motor-neutrality regarding one's visual ecstasis, and only once one perceives a certain color does the body assume its various color-determined postures, moods, and motor possibilities. But the body is always in a color field. (If Chinese theorists are right that black and white contains the full spectrum of colors, this might also be true of the blind.) It is not that motor-possibilities exist and then are modified by the body being introduced to color: motor-possibilities themselves have a color dimension insofar as they are given partly by the body's visual ecstasis into a colored world. As Merleau-Ponty explains:

> When we say that red increases the compass of our reactions, we are not to be understood as having in mind two distinct facts, a sensation of redness and motor reactions—we must be understood as meaning that red, by its texture as followed and adhered to by our gaze, is already the amplification of our motor being.[249]

One does not first see an object and then secondarily cognize its color attributes. An object or a room first comes to presence as colored and as

---

249. Merleau-Ponty, *Phenomenology of Perception*, 245.

having already elicited a facet of one's postures, moods, or movements. While the influence might be exceedingly subtle, colors inflect the body's gestures, if only by the smallest measure. Of course, one can easily overstep these constraints, or resolve to work against them: one can put effort toward acting blue in a red room, for instance.[250] As Marratto points out, the "motor value" of color's solicitation is information, and value, not law: "When Merleau-Ponty says that a definite motor value can be assigned to the color, he does not mean that a fixed law governs the structure of relations between sensory information and movement; rather he means that perception, as movement, is itself the assignment of a value." Thus, while all reds solicit movement, they might do so differently depending on how that color has accrued motor-perceptual value in my past and in the past of the tradition within which one moves and expresses themselves. The crucial finer point Marratto makes is that "motor *values* of colors only reveal themselves within acts of *evaluation*, and those acts will themselves take the form of movement."[251] Thus, countering the color-based solicitations that permeate the perceptual field is possible, but this would involve an effort to assign value, rather than allowing what is already sedimented in that field to inflect the body pre-reflectively. This is possible because determination is always bidirectional. There might be an optimal grip partly determined by an object's or a room's color, but this is not to say that we cannot exert ourselves against it. To actively counter a solicitation, the person would slightly skew the active-passive balance that would normally obtain without our having to think about it. In order to counter the influence of color on the body, one becomes marginally more active, thus lessening the extent to which motions arise through negation and acting never with full but slightly more individuated agency. One does not step outside of the motorsensory fabric in doing so, but one can command slightly more control of the body.

Because volition is dispersed throughout the perceptual field whether we counter solicitations or not, and because color makes a difference to how movements are solicited, motor-intentionality is never neutral in respect of

---

250. See Krueger (2013) for an intriguing example of what we might consider counter-solicational movement: "while the triple meter of the waltz is not experienced as affording marching—trying to march to a waltz feels somehow odd, as though the music is working against us and our bodily gestures are not 'fitting into' the appropriate musical cues—a duple meter at the correct tempo would establish a different entrainment context, one in which marching responses do feel more appropriate."

251. Marratto, *The Intercorporeal Self: Merleau-Ponty on Subjectivity*, 83.

color. The "distant will" is color-inflected. This has important implications for the commonly accepted distinction between color and colorlessness—an implication that might have been recognized by medieval Japanese artists and aestheticians.

While Sesshū's paintings lack any positive reference to specific colors, this absence might bring chromaticity to phenomenal presence in a more significant way than the presence of color. If perceptual experience is indeed always intentional regarding color, then colorlessness, the absence of color, is not a straightforward absence. Because humans reach into the perceptual world with an intentionality motor-tuned to color, when there is an absence, as in the case of viewing a monochrome painting, one is not motor-neutral regarding color. As Thomas Hoover explains, because "the palette of the mind is richer than that of the brush," the lack of positive color does not preclude the *phenomenon* of color, which manifests beyond the visible-invisible binary. Thus, even with the visible absence of color, viewing a monochrome work is not without a chromatic relation. Ashikaga artists knew, Hoover explains, that

> black ink, carefully applied to suggest all the tones of light and shade, could be more expressive and profound than a rainbow of colours . . . Eastern artists use ink to produce the illusion of colour—an illusion so perfect that viewers must at times remind themselves that a scene is not in full polychrome. And just as the seemingly unfinished artistic statement nudges the viewer into participating in a work, the suggestive medium of monochrome with its implied rather than explicit hues tricks the viewer into unwittingly supplying his own colours.[252]

This elucidation helps us grasp a more complex relation of the body to color, but for our purposes we should not consider what happens as an "illusion" or "trick" as though vision functions this way only when viewing certain paintings. Even in the absence of color, part of the body's perceptual ecstasis into the world has a color valence. Just as our reaching into the volitional world from a position of apparent stillness ambiguates the body in respect of motion and motionlessness, so our *perceptual* ecstasis into the *visual* world involves a color-determination, regardless of whether the objects we reach into are colored or colorless. This is a further implication

---

252. Thomas Hoover, "Of Modes and Manners in Japanese Ink Painting," *Zen Culture*.

of perception being irreducible to sensory data: even the imagined presence of color lines our experience of the monochrome. Sesshū's landscapes do not display a simple absence of color. Its shades solicit the body according to how they echo throughout one's past experiences of fully chromatic rivers and mountains. If the absence of color prompts a viewer to supply her own color, through how the past presences, then it would seem that the negation between body and world has a colored aspect: a colored reaching into the world and being reached into. In her work *Artistry in Ink*, Seiroku Noma details this possibility while alluding to the superiority of monochrome painting. She claims that artists "armed with pigments" have attempted for centuries to "reproduce the colours of nature" without success.[253] But Japanese *sumi-e* painters, she claims, "recognize that the real colors of nature cannot be reproduced exactly," and as such they have "grasped one of the most fundamental truths of nature."[254] To paint is not to copy nature, but rather to create a work that is continuous with nature. Instead of reproducing what is thought to exist as a stable set of chromatic qualities, the *sumi-e* artist reduces all colors to shades of black. As a result, Noma claims, the *sumi-e* artist is able to "paradoxically, make one feel their genuine nuances."[255] If perception was only reception of visual data in the present, the monochrome artist could not elicit such a response, but within a perceptual fabric whose temporal depth has valences of chromaticity, these inflect present experience whether it is colored or colorless. This helps us to appreciate how Nishida speaks of the calligrapher's vision, which sees the "tendency towards black and white in all the colors."[256]

---

253. Seiroku Noma, *Artistry in Ink*, 3.

254. Ibid.

255. Ibid.

256. Nishida, *Intuition and Reflection in Self-Consciousness*, 64. Dalissier expands on this insight of Nishida's: "Toutefois, il est possible d'étendre son exemple, dans une certain mesure, à la peinture en couleurs, si l'on évoque les analyses de Fiedler. Notre «vision,» «puissance devoir» (視力 *shiryoku*), «distingue» (*kubetsu suru*) extérieurement le «bleu» du «rouge» de manière grossière: en revanche, l'oeil du calligraphe distingue de manière «differentielle» (微分的 *bibunteki*) l'infinité des nuances de gris qui reconstitue un spectre entier de couleurs «entre» le blanc et le noir; il distingue tout aussi bien dans le lavis l'infinité des nuances de rouge et de bleu que l'infinité des nuances de rouge déployée en direction du blanc dans un sens et en direction du noir dans l'autre . . . En un sens, on peut dire que nous n'en avons jamais fini avec la couleur, par example le bleu (Klein)" (2009), 158.

The practice of monochrome painters is, on this account, a quite remarkable refutation of a representational and positivist understanding of perception, and its dichotomies of presence and absence, color and colorlessness. Insofar as our motions are inflected by the color of the perceptual fields we move in, if that world is never exclusively experienced as mono- or poly-chromatic, then the distinction between motion and motionless is similarly ambiguated. The practice of ink painters such as Sesshū is, thus, a medieval Eastern antecedent to features of contemporary Western phenomenological accounts of motor-perception. It is also an understanding of color that Merleau-Ponty recognized in Paul Valéry's coinage "the secret blackness of milk"[257] and in Ziporyn's claim that we can even imagine "'whiteness' being expressed by 'blackness.'"[258]

The Color of Negation

The intricacies of chromatic experience, as demonstrated by black-and-white painting, problematize the distinction between color and colorlessness. Monochrome is not the simple absence of color because perception is never determined only by visibly present sensory data. We gain much more understanding of artworks, as well as our bodies and the world, if we think of color as an event that arises through negation thus undoing binaries of chromatic-non-chromatic, visible-invisible, motion-stillness, making-being made. Moreover, just as a negation implies a non-subject and non-object, the chromatic relation requires what we might consider a negated color, a "non-color," or colorlessness as a constitutive aspect of color experience. Nishida conceives of color along these lines. In order for a red object to be encounterable, he postulates, there must be an aspect of "non-red," both in the perceiver and thing perceived. As he explains in his *Ishiki no Mondai*, the sensation of red is unified with the sensation of non-red.[259] Like bodies to the world, a painter to their tradition, or the temporal orders in relation to each other, color also achieves visible presence through negation with other colors and with the color aspect of the perceptual negation that is human openness to the world.[260]

---

257. Merleau-Ponty, *The Visible and the Invisible*, 150.
258. Ziporyn, *Being and Ambiguity: Philosophical Experiments with Tiantai Buddhism*, 103.
259. Nishida, *Ishiki No Mondai* (unpublished translation), 45, 75.
260. For a more in-depth discussion of Nishida's understanding of color in relation to negation and his ontology of absolute nothingness, see Dalissier (2009), 65, 70, 450.

Although Merleau-Ponty does not frame his discussion of color explicitly in terms of negation, his thinking bears similarities to Nishida's on this point. He contends that we never experience color in pure positivity. "[A] naked colour, and in general a visible, is not a chunk of absolutely hard, indivisible being, offered all naked to a vision which could be only total or null."[261] Color experience is not a relation between a subject and a colored object both walled up in their own positivity: the relation is a "straits between exterior horizons and interior horizons ever gaping open."[262] Color is, then, not a positive feature, but a "certain differentiation, an ephemeral modulation of this world—less a colour or a thing, therefore, than a difference between things, and colours, a momentary crystallization of coloured being or of visibility."[263] To experience a red is to experience *this* red, and its *thisness* is the contribution that one makes to the phenomenon, as well as what is given by the sociohistoric world one is woven into. Red is experienced as invested with its relational peculiarities. It is a certain texture of a motorsensory fabric given by other events that have impinged upon it. As Merleau-Ponty states, "red literally is not the same as it appears in one constellation or in the other."[264] Earlier in *The Phenomenology of Perception* he writes that "[T]his red would literally not be the same if it were not the 'woolly red' of a carpet."[265] Depending on one's orientation within various constellations, red appears as a different "punctuation in the field of red things."[266] One's experience of red is therefore less determined by pigments and wavelengths, and more so by "tiles of rooftops; the flags of gatekeepers and of the Revolution; of certain terrains near Aix or in Madagascar. It is also a punctuation in the field of red garments, which includes, along with the dresses of women, the robes of professors, bishops and advocates generals."[267]

The experience of color is not a determination of the objective world; instead, it is an event at the intersection of negated subjects and objects. Color is such that it receives what we put into it through mutual investment, and for this reason it is always experienced as infused with subjectivity, but

---

261. Merleau-Ponty, *The Visible and the Invisible*, 132.

262. Ibid.

263. Ibid.

264. Ibid.

265. Merleau-Ponty, *Phenomenology of Perception*, 5.

266. Merleau-Ponty, *The Visible and the Invisible*, 132.

267. Ibid.

never to the complete exclusion of its objectivity. A major punctuation in the constellation of red, seeing one's own blood, for example, might pull the phenomena of red down the asymptote as far as possible toward full objective determination, but like all other phenomena it never reaches full positivity such that it would be sealed off from counter-determinations from other events or our subjective inflection. The relation between a color and oneself is ever open to reciprocal expression, of "interexpression," as making and being made. Conversely, one can certainly attempt to contemplate an abstract color or redness in itself, but this is to force something relational into something substantial or objective. To ponder color in-itself, or a color-neutral body, is a second-order modification of an original chromatically negated continuum.

The color aspect of the body's mutual negation with the world does not yet explain how color is itself in motion. Colored objects move, yet color itself is thought to be motionless. By contrast, both Nishida and Merleau-Ponty conceive of color as a type of activity. Again, speaking of red, Nishida notes that the "type of red becomes a force and an activity."[268] For Merleau-Ponty too, color is a way of "vibrating and filling space,"[269] and light, which always arrives as color, is not the reception of passive sense data, but is "action by contact."[270] Musing on Cézanne's practice, he writes that the "world is a mass without gaps, a system of colours across which the receding perspectives, the outlines, angles, and curves are inscribed like lines of force; the spatial structure vibrates as it is formed."[271]

In prolonged engagement with the landscape, the artist is not a color-neutral agent standing over against a motor-neutral world, representing objects and choosing which colors to use and the bodily gestures that would best capture them on canvas. The painter does not just choose colors, but allows bodily movements to be chosen by the colors of the world. As a color-perceiving being I am not in control of my body, I "surrender a part of my body, even my whole body, to this particular manner of vibrating and filling space known as blue or red."[272] The artist is in motor-perceptual ecstasis in the chromatic world, thus color is a further dimension of the

---

268. Nishida, *Nishida Kitarō zenshū*, 2: 357
269. Merleau-Ponty, *Phenomenology of Perception*, 246.
270. Merleau-Ponty, "Eye and Mind," 131.
271. Merleau-Ponty, "Cézanne's Doubt," 65.
272. Merleau-Ponty, *Phenomenology of Perception*, 246.

risk the painter accepts, it is one of the ways they are beyond control, a quality of a "surrender" that demands faith.

We do not see color's more subtle incitements to motion the way we see the volition of an animal manifest in its movements, or the action of a flower blooming or a volcano erupting. Color could be taken to be motionless if one had access to a position external to the motor-perceptual fabric. It is questionable whether we could think of a color without becoming entangled in the relations it has accrued throughout history, or any of its subtle sensorimotor forces, because when visually engaged with red or green or blue, that color is always in motion, always soliciting the body's movements with a temporal expanse that embraces its history of determinations. Although partly an invisible motion, it makes itself visible through the passivity that is the human body's perceptual and volitional negation. The part of one's gestures solicited by the color of objects is the chromatic world's movement making itself seen through one's body. Color paintings—which include monochrome paintings—are, like the rest of the world, an act. A motor-perceptual act. The chromatic world is motor and perceptual, and is thus "capable of demanding *that* colour and *that* object in preference to all others, and since it commands the arrangement of a painting just as imperiously as a syntax or a logic."[273] Whether the artist meets this demand with a palette-full of colored pigments or black ink alone, all painters respond to a world that solicits the body according to its chromaticity: artistic creativity is an act within a continuity of motor-chromatic acts. Despite their disparities, because Sesshū and Cézanne move their expressive bodies beyond the motion-motionless binary, their artworks invoke experiences beyond the color-colorless opposition.

---

273. Merleau-Ponty, "Indirect Language and the Voices of Silence," 92. Emphasis added.

Chapter 4

Expression as "Motor-Perceptual Faith"

"Seeing without a Seer" and Movement without a Mover

To carry out this dialogue between Merleau-Ponty and Nishida, I have sought to highlight similarities between their ontologies of flesh and *Basho*. Despite some striking parallels, their philosophies diverge on decisive issues, some of which I discuss further in this chapter. My main concern has been to explore how great artworks can be created in a context where the body intertwines with and pervades a wider motor-perceptual fabric. How is it that the motion and perception, which manifest through negation, do not obstruct the artist? On this point, we return to a contention raised in the second chapter. While both philosophers construe the body–world relation, as well as expression, motion, and perception within an ontology of mutual negation, there is, however, a discrepancy between the two concerning the limits of non-obstruction, which has implications for their philosophies, and for important questions in phenomenology. As previously intimated, Nishida appears to go farther than Merleau-Ponty and in ways suggests a full de-substantialization or full negation of the visual subject by positing "seeing without a seer" (*mirumono nakushite miru koto* 見るものなくして見ること), the world's "self-seeing" (*Jiko jishin wo miru* 自己自身を見る), and the "self-seeing" of *Basho*. The implication we must now engage is that if vision is not limited by the point of view of an individuated seer, if it can be wholly worldly, then it would seem that the phenomenon of vision could transpire without its being minimally localized in a perceiving subject. If this were the case, it would be more than a diffuse phenomenon, it might suggest the possibility of vision as a standpointless standpoint. Because of

263

the co-implication of vision and movement, we cannot help but ask about the related possibilities of movement without a mover. Certainly, these resonate with ideas in Asian philosophy and aesthetics, but might present incomensurabilities in the dialogue with Merleau-Ponty. If Nishida's "seeing without a seer" involved a fully de-substantialized seer or mover, this would exceed the already-discussed Huayan limits to non-obstruction that obtain at the phenomenal level. The French philosopher posits definite limits to the reversibility of motion and perception.[1] Indeed, Merleau-Ponty is critical of the ideal positionless "view from nowhere" he reads in Leibniz, whereas Nishida is more ambivalent in this regard.[2] In Merleau-Ponty's system, phenomenal bodies are partially obstructing by virtue of their being intertwined within the motor-perceptual fabric of flesh. This obstruction does not come about because of a reification of the perceptual subject: the limitation to reversibility arises by virtue of negation being mutual, never fully accomplished but always hovering between identity and difference. As Kaushik writes, "at no point does this vision function to collapse or absorb their differences, even if it is productive of differences of all kinds."[3] Thus, seer and seen encounter one another through negation, implicating not a full but a partial obstruction between the two, which limits the seer and localizes both to some however minimal point of view on the world. Merleau-Ponty's term that invokes these limitations is "blind spot" (*punctum caecum*); a constitutive limit to reversibility between seer and seen. Exploring further reversals between vision and motion in this chapter, I continue in my attempt to expand the perceptual to the motor-perceptual and search

---

1. Brook Ziporyn points to Merleau-Ponty's claims in "Eye and Mind" (p. 167) that the painter wants to be "penetrated by the universe, and not want to penetrate it" and in *The Visible and the Invisible* (p. 148) that "I am always on the same side of my own body."

2. In *The Phenomenology of Perception*, he refers to Leibniz's formulation as the "geometrized [géométral] projection of . . . all possible perspectives, that is, the perspectiveless position." We should keep in mind that while Merleau-Ponty is critical of this "view from nowhere" (p. 67) he is, nevertheless, open to the idea of the "view from everywhere" (p. 69). As opposed to a "perspectiveless" viewpoint that would grasp the object in its positive totality, the "view from everywhere" is a situated and a perspectival form of vision. It does not grasp the object from everywhere by virtue of a totality of positive sensations, but because of the multi-perspectival perspectives available through the ambiguity of the visually positive and negative, the visible and the invisible.

3. Ravi Kaushik, "Lighten Up: Merleau-Ponty and Nancy on Light, Form and Intelligibility," 186.

for the motor possibilities within Merleau-Ponty's idea of a perceptual blind spot. If a motor-perceptual blind spot were part of the *texture* of the sensorimotor fabric, this would instantiate a *dynamic* obstruction limiting the artist's expressive movements while also making them possible in the first place. Far from a straightforward set of constraints, these limitations are what ground the artist's possibilities, which, in being constrained, are far more expansive than those associated with theories of "creative freedom," which do not acknowledge negativity. Indeed, the artist's possibilities are given through a faithful body–world coordination of their mutual limits. By discovering the necessity of faith directly within the structure of mutual negation, as a texture of the motorsensory fabric itself, we find the sacred within the secular and can explore artistic expression beyond that binary. Precisely here—*because of phenomenal obstruction*, because of a perceptual and a motor-blindness—artists express (themselves) faith(fully). Pursuing these issues will bring us back to our opening questions regarding philosophy, religion, and art.

Motor-Perceptual "Blind Spot" as Dynamic Obstruction

In the working notes of *The Visible and the Invisible* Merleau-Ponty explains how invisibility is produced by a blind spot (*punctum caecum*), which cannot be "treat[ed] as a simple state of non-vision,"[4] but is essential to the coming into being of the visible. He elaborates: "[t]o this structure is bound the ambiguity of the consciousness, and even a sort of blindness of the consciousness, of imperception in perception—To see is to not see."[5] The significance of this blind spot is not limited to the eye's vision; this physiological fact is the manifestation of a more fundamental ontological principle that determines all of the body's relations. What is beyond the visible is not a simple lack, but is our "tie to Being, is [our] corporeity, are the existentials by which the world becomes visible, is the flesh wherein the *object* is born."[6] Where vision is limited is not mere invisibility or barren perceptual void. Here, all of the artist's possibilities are born because of, what Carbone calls the "pregnancy of the invisible in the visible."[7]

---

4. Merleau-Ponty, *The Visible and the Invisible*, 133.

5. Ibid., 225.

6. Ibid., 248.

7. Mauro Carbone, *The Flesh of Images: Merleau-Ponty between Painting and Cinema*.

The term "blind spot" can be misleading if we understand it in a positivist and representational sense. The blind spot is not a circumscribed area here or there, which can be brought into sight by moving the body into a different position. It is a limit to vision that cannot be overcome. There is a dynamic and elusive quality to the blind spot. Unlike a blind spot in a car where one can move one's body into a position to see; instead, what Merleau-Ponty speaks of is an invisibility that responds to the body's movements and perpetually evades one's attempts to eliminate it. When one tries to shift into a different vantage point to change one's perspective on the invisible, it changes, it undergoes an aspect-shift from background to figure. If we try to represent the invisible we lose it as we transform it to the visible. This inevitability arises because visibility does not manifest in one place and invisibility in another; rather, as we have already seen, the visible is "lined" with the invisible. The blind spot cannot be eradicated or circumvented because its invisibility is not elsewhere; it is *within* the visible. All our perceptions—even those we think we receive in full positivity—include an irreducible blind spot. In this sense, it should be thought of along the lines of a constitutive incompleteness that limits all perception while furnishing it with its latent potential, since, as Merleau-Ponty writes, "[w]hat it does not see is what makes it see."[8] The invisible is the aspect that turns from our attention, withdraws and evades our motion, perception, and knowledge, but also makes all of these possible as body–world determinations. This blind spot is not the result of inaccuracy, error, or miscalculation; it is an ineradicable feature of the body's being continuous-discontinuously woven into the perceptual fabric in which we seek to move and perceive. If one were wholly continuous (i.e., non-chiasmatic) there would be no blind spot, but neither would there be motion or perception.

Now, making our familiar jump from the perceptual to the motor-perceptual, when searching in Merleau-Ponty's works for indications regarding similar blind spots for the moving body, we do not find an explicit connection between the two. Barbaras has conjectured that Merleau-Ponty was moving in this direction. He writes, "it is impossible for perception to witness movement because it is essentially movement: movement cannot be an object of perception because it is the ultimate subject of perception."[9] Thus, because of the co-implication of perception and motion, one's movements are never fully transparent to oneself. As Merleau-Ponty writes in his working notes,

---

8. Merleau-Ponty, *The Visible and the Invisible*, 248.
9. Barbaras, "Perception and Movement: The End of the Metaphysical Approach," 87.

I cannot see myself in movement, witness my own movement. But this *de jure* invisible signifies in reality that *Wahrnehmen* and *Sich bewegen* are synonymous: it is for this reason that the *Wahrnehmen* never rejoins the *Sich bewegen* it wishes to apprehend.[10]

Because perception and motion or synonymous, the perceptual blind spot is already a *motor*-perceptual blind spot. It is an evasive impossibility that grounds all bodily movement: One that limits but is nevertheless "pregnant." Just as the visible cannot be circumscribed because it is lined with the invisible, so activity cannot be strictly demarcated because it is lined with passivity, that is, activity is worldly, given by something that transcends the body and is thus never fully visible or under one's control. If I try to control or represent the visible, it perpetually evades my efforts insofar as my body remains partially determinate, with a positivity that grounds me and limits me to a determinate point of view. Movement is no different. If I act to try to fully control my movements, I prompt a shift in the motorsensory fabric my body pervades. I might become more active in one sense, but I am always caught up in an invisible set of background solicitations, which interweave with my motions. As such, despite my attempts to fully control my own actions, because of a motor-obstruction, a motor blind spot, as my body proliferates throughout the sensorimotor fabric it is always partially beyond my control. The negative of motion always includes an irreducible positivity. As an event in a general ontological fabric, one's actions are never visible in their entirety and, therefore, never controllable. It is only by attempting to limit the body to its circumscribed visibility, by cutting it out of its fabric, that we think we can say "that is my action." But, within an account of phenomena that includes the ontologically negative, one cannot identify specific features of the visible field that invisibly inflect one's actions, nor can one isolate the part of one's motions that comes from one's own body or that which derives from the world and its background. As part of an infinite continuity of acts, one's movements evade full control, passivity is irreducible, just as the blind spot avoids being turned into visibility. Accordingly, one never sees in full clarity nor moves in full control of the body.

The visible undergoes an aspect-shift (figure-ground shift) to maintain the visible-invisible ambiguity; similarly, the *motor*-blind spot maintains

---

10. Merleau-Ponty, *The Visible and the Invisible*.

active-passive ambiguity. The distinction between activity and passivity is multistable, ever vacillating between the two, never one to the exclusion of the other, never without a draw and repulsion to the other. Faith is implicated in all motion because one can never fully control one's actions insofar as they are a diffuse phenomenon. Attempting to have a circumscriptive grasp of one's actions would be like trying to measure the surface of one's bedsheets while wrapped up in them. All movements would be self-defeating because the attempt to measure the surface topography changes the topography, because that topography contains everything, including those movements. Only a position exterior to the phenomenal fabric could successfully make such an estimation, but such a motor-neutral position—much to the vexation of the positivist—is a fantasy. The blind spot therefore maintains itself by virtue of the body being entangled within the motor-perceptual fabric it seeks to comprehend, represent, or control. All of our most basic movements and attempts to reduce the invisible or to fully control the body's movements (i.e., eliminate passivity) arise as modifications of the motorsensory fabric, as modifications of flesh. Consequently, they are subject to its dynamic limitations, its obstructions. We pull in one way and are pulled on in myriad other lateral and horizontal directions. Because all motion is beyond one's control by virtue of the motor-blind spot, a constitutive lack of control, that obstruction infuses all motion with risk. To search for new ways to move, to find new gestures to connect with the world, as Cézanne and Sesshū did, is to augment this risk in the hope of re-patterning the fabric of flesh or *Basho* with new possibilities for the moving-perceiving body.

Nishida: "Seeing without a Seer"

A great deal is at stake in Nishida's theory of vision for his wider ontology. The questions of whether the world actually sees, is self-aware, or expressive, all have implications for the status of philosophy and religion in his thought, not to mention the problems of mysticism and his stance toward phenomenology. In taking up these problematics we can also reconnect with the issue of multi-perspectival vision we began with in the first chapter. All of these crucial issues are implicated, in one way or another, in how Nishida conceives of the visible as well as related concepts of "reflection," (*hansei* 反省, *utsusu* 写す) and "self-mirroring" (*jiko shazō* 自己写像).

Let us recall that for Nishida vision is a phenomenon wider than one's own seeing. Vision is ontological insofar as it is a negated mediation between seeing and seen. When one "negate[s] the self *absolutely*," he writes, "there is seeing without a seer."[11] We have already considered Nishida's expansion of the visual through multi-perspectival vision, but this concept is something more and demands closer attention for understanding his philosophy and for finding the limits of the dialogue with Merleau-Ponty. To delve deeper into Nishida's thinking on this issue, we must be careful to read more closely because while some of his terminology seems to suggest a "view from nowhere" position, this is not consistent with several of his most important concepts, which if scrutinized regarding the question of obstruction, suggest that he too would agree that there are limits inherent to negation that obtain on either end of the subject–object relation; in vision and in motion. Indeed, Davis claims that "seeing without a seer does not entail a view from nowhere,"[12] while other scholars remain divided.[13] To place this question in the context of where this study began, if "seeing without a seer" were a "view from nowhere," this would be tantamount to a full negation or full indeterminacy of the visual subject. The problems should be clear, since, as I claimed in the first chapter, perceptual encounter cannot obtain for a fully posited or a fully negated subject. While Nishida otherwise retains an aspect of determination and positivity as an essential aspect of negation, the question is nevertheless complicated by ambivalences in his writings regarding this concept as well as his often-repeated notion of "becoming one with sight." In "Artistic Creativity and Historically Formative Act," he boldly asserts:

> When we cut off all associations and become one with the sense of sight, we see things on a flattened level of history. In contrast to the world of concepts, here opens up a world expressive of infinite views.[14]

---

11. Nishida, *Nishida Kitarō zenshū*, (1978–1998) 5: 179. Emphasis added.
12. Davis, "Provocative Ambivalences in Japanese Philosophy of Religion," 263.
13. Several scholars, including Krummel (2012, 2015), Stevens (2009), Maraldo (2006), and Ishihara (2011) comment, implicitly or explicitly, on the idea of non-obstruction for Nishida regarding his concepts of "seeing without a seer" and the world's "self-seeing." A more directed consideration of limitations to visual reversibility and obstructive perceptual blind spots is found in Brubaker (2009) and Maraldo (2006).
14. Nishida, *Nishida Kitarō zenshū*, 9: 234.

This provocative statement of his mature writing makes it difficult to avoid the "view from nowhere" allegation. Let us also recall that on the question of Leibniz's "view from nowhere," Nishida is more comfortable than Merleau-Ponty. In his final work he invokes Leibniz while also referring to de Cusa's "infinite sphere with no circumference."[15] It is worth noting that de Cusa also proposes a mystical union of seeing and being seen and refers to God's view as an "infinite angle."[16] In the absence of clear declarations otherwise, and with a great deal of ambivalence on the issue, we must seek answers to these crucial problems by looking wider in Nishida's works. Although he does not appear to disavow the type of seeing, which would constitute a full negation of the visual subject, many of his later concepts seem to preclude that possibility. Let us now take up the matter in dialogue with Royce, and Ueda, and conclude this section by exploring "seeing without a seer" and visual negation as read against the background of Nishida's later concepts of "historical body," "continuity-of-discontinuity," and the maintenance of subject–object ambiguity he insists on between vision and motion.

Mirroring, Mapping, and Seeing

Maraldo discusses Nishida's formulation of self-awareness (*jikaku* 自覚) as a system of infinitely reflecting mirrors, which through its "self-mirroring" (*jiko shazō* 自己写像) reflects the whole of existence in each of its parts. As we should expect, this form of relationality is not only the structure of the self, the world also "represents self within itself."[17] The world or *Basho* is able to "see itself" because, according to Nishida's predicate logic, human consciousness is predicated of the world. Since I am part of the world, woven into its fabric, when I see, the world sees itself through my eyes. Counter to what Aristotelian subject-based logic would allow, my eyes are part of the world's body. Thus, as Stevens puts it,

---

15. Nishida, *Last Writings: Nothingness and the Religious Worldview*, 53.

16. In his *The Vision of God* (1453) de Cusa expounds upon visual practices for monks meant to achieve a mystical union between seeing from the circumference and being seen from the center. Later, in *Complementary Theological Considerations (1454)* his God is a mathematician whose divine creativity is grounded on un-restricted vision encompassing "infinite angles."

17. Nishida, *Nishida Kitarō zenshū*, 3: 255.

[w]hen consciousness experiences itself, the world experiences itself at the same time. The historical body constitutes the self-expression of the world itself. This self-expression or self-determination of the historical world is located in a particular human body.[18]

Maraldo analyzes the limits to the various metaphors of self-mirroring in ways that help us further explore the question of obstruction and blind spots in Nishida's philosophy. He explains how mirrors reflecting each other have an inherent visual limit insofar as, for a seer, there will always be a vantage point that will not be reflected in the mirror: "The image (real or reflected) is seen from the vantage point that is itself never reflected in the mirrors."[19] This is, from the point of view of self-consciousness, an obstruction that prevents one's achieving full self-awareness as self-mirroring. Neither one's self-awareness nor the world's "self-seeing" can have a full non-obstructed representation of itself. A seer always remains, and this determination obstructs one's ability to see oneself or the world from a positionless vantage point.

To develop this contention, Maraldo considers Josiah Royce's idea of a "perfect map." This hypothetical map is supposed to represent all of England point for point in perfect detail and can only be complete if it also represents the map itself, which is being drafted within the country's borders. But, the complication with this "self-representational" system is that it would need to represent the place from which the person renders the map, but this is impossible since that position will always evade depiction. Thus, it is a dynamic motor-perceptual blind spot: visual, because it refers to an attempt to see something, motor insofar as making a map involves bodily movement. If one wanted to represent the position of the mapmaker, he would have to step out of the map and occupy another position from which to draw, and

---

18. Stevens, "Self in Space: Nishida Philosophy and Phenomenology of Maurice Merleau-Ponty," 139.

19. John Maraldo, "Self-Mirroring and Self-Awareness: Dedekind, Royce, and Nishida," in *Frontiers of Japanese Philosophy*, ed. James Heisig (Nanzan Institute of Religion and Culture, 2006). Maraldo further explores how in knowing and judging there is an "incompleteness" that arises between knowing and the act of knowing, judgment and the act of judging. He suggests that Nishida is able to overcome this aspect, otherwise evident in Royce and Dedekind through his *Basho* theory, because in it self-awareness is not posited as the ultimate place, that is, of course, the status of *Basho*. In the early work, the will is the more embracing place. Later, Nishida moves away from the idea of "places within places" and focuses more on the "self-contradictory identity" of relations between places, which allows for self-mirroring to obtain fully.

that newly occupied locus of depiction would then need to be vacated in order to be depicted, and so on *ad infinitum*. This implies that there is a dynamic obstruction to self-representation that impedes full visual disclosure according to the similar dynamically evasive blind spot in Merleau-Ponty's philosophy. The metaphorical attempt to defend non-obstructive vision reproduces the problems it is meant to overcome. Exhaustive representation or unobstructed visibility are not possible. When we apply these insights to Nishida it would seem to suggest that there is no possibility of seeing without the presence of a minimal seer. The seer remains as a determined point of view. According to Maraldo's interpretation of Royce's metaphor, a position always remains, which hides itself because the mapmaker has no choice but to inhabit a determinate viewpoint and drawing point, just as, physiologically, in vision there is always a seer situated in and constrained by their vantage point.

Maraldo invokes Ueda Shizuteru's attempt to overcome the problem of the unseeable position—and by extension the problem of "seeing without a seer"—by positing a map without a mapmaker. Ueda entertains the possibility of England mapping itself. Maraldo's rejoinder is that territory outside of England will still need to be excluded and therefore total representation remains elusive. Despite the infinite reflection, or the world's self-depiction, the decisive point regarding the question of Nishida's "seeing without a seer" is that, as Maraldo writes "a 'seer' to whom things appear is needed,"[20] and thus a non-perspectival seeing is thwarted by an obstructive blind spot that is the irreducible perspectival nature of vision. (Although I cannot pursue this line of thinking here, it is worth considering whether the multi-perspectivalism that Nishida posits as the ambiguity "internal perception-qua-external perception" [*naibu chikaku soku gaibu chikaku* 内部知覚即外部知覚] might be applied to the inside-England/outside-England binary such that the mapmaker could actually achieve what Ueda proposes.)

Despite pointing out the limits in the various metaphors, and despite suggesting what I understand as several irreducible obstructive aspects to vision, Maraldo does, nevertheless, consider a way out for Nishida. Exploring his unpublished lecture notes of 1926, he quotes Nishida as saying that in the ultimate, in the "place" of "absolute nothingness" (*mu no basho* 無の場所), "there is nothing that mirrors." Self-mirroring is, then, not inherent to that "place" but is a second-order determination thereof. Thus, in attaining to this level, in attaining the absolute as no-self there is "no seeing or

---

20. Ibid., 154.

knowing self"[21] and one can thus achieve "seeing without a seer." I would like to consider this contention in detail.

If there is a seeing that would be "first-order," a seeing as part of the texture of perceptual fabric itself, not yet a determination indexable to an individual seer, then the question we might ask is, does that vision as it obtains in the place of absolute nothingness escape the mutual negation or the sociohistoric determination of the world, which Nishida's later ontology otherwise endorses? For one to overcome one's limited (yet multi-perspectival) perspective to see without being a seer would require a full negation of themselves as visual subjects. This would be to transcend the body's (at least partial) objective determination, which limits its vision to its particular vantage[22] point and precludes one's seeing entirely from the point of view of the world. Yet, Nishida is otherwise unequivocal in defining the body, even as negated, as constituted by physical and objective qualities.[23] Indeed, without this aspect of embodiment there would be no possibility of interdetermination between body and world. The "true self" in Nishida's late philosophy, Brubaker writes is "the self-less individual who acts personally, with a physical body, in the objective place of social and historical interactions."[24] To transcend the aspect of vision that is bodily—and thus obstructive—would require a full negation, but that, according to Nishida, is not a conceivable option for the embodied self. To achieve "seeing without a seer" as a complete negation would require the elimination of the physical body from the field of absolute nothingness and leave us asking where vision would arise. But, this goes counter to Nishida's otherwise pervasive insistence on subjectivity-*qua*-objectivity; it ignores his claim that seeing arises through negation (because there would be no bodies to be negated); and moreover, such a position, if brought about on the field of absolute nothingness, has no fidelity to the meaning of "absolute" as *zettai* whose etymology precludes both the straightforward maintenance or obliteration of oppositions.

---

21. Nishida, *Nishida Kitarō zenshū*, 5: 427.

22. As limited to one's own perspective, that inherently "viewpointerly" viewpoint is still multi-perspectival. The "mineness" of experience does not reduce perception to a single "me"—it remains multi-perspectival.

23. In his *Fundamental Problems*, Nishida writes, "We determine and oppose one another by being separated by our bodies and through absolute negation, i.e., physical qualities." Also, see Brubaker (2009) for an in-depth discussion of the problematics of Nishida's definition of the body as "physical actions in the objective world."

24. Brubaker "Place of Nothingness' and the Dimension of Visibility," 165.

Let us look at the problem from another point of view assuming that it might be possible to make a transition from our limited visual perspective as *seeing as an at least minimal seer* to "seeing without a seer." In doing so, we find further problems in squaring Nishida's ontology of vision with his philosophy of history. Negation is not simply the way bodies relate in the present moment, there is likewise a temporal aspect to negation, the one we have been discussing between the "historical body" (*rekishiteki shintai* 歴史的身体) and the "historical world" (*rekishiteki sekai* 歴史的世界). We must ask, in attaining to the ultimate, in achieving absolute nothingness as no-self, does the structure of the historical relation remain? What this question amounts to is whether mutual negation is the texture of *Basho* itself, or is it simply a second-order determination that can be overcome, for example, in achieving no-self or seeing without a seer. If the latter, then comparison with Merleau-Ponty's ontology of flesh is significantly limited, since he is clear that mutual-negation is an irreducible texture of flesh itself: Even in achieving continuity with the motor-perceptual fabric, one remains subjective *and* objective, negated and negating. Thus, vision is a relation of partial negation, never a full negation, which would erase the seer. If, however, the former were the case, and mutual-negation remains at the level of the absolute, then, the possibility of unobstructed seeing as "seeing without a seer" is problematic in relation to Nishida's philosophy of history. Let me venture an attempt to show why this is the case.

Hypothetically speaking, if an artist could achieve a full negation of himself as a seer, this would be an event with a before and an after. There would be an initial period where one was a visual subject (seeing of a seer) and a period that follows where one would achieve full visual negation (seeing without a seer). The catch is that to proceed from one state to another would involve wiping out the historical nature of the body. Because the body is an "historical body" and the world an "historical world," both related through negation, even if one could see from the perspective of the world, one would still do so as someone with a history before that achievement: a history that ties oneself to one's body as at least a partially individuated seer. If one could achieve the world's "self-seeing," one would always do so as one who previously saw as an individuated seer, and that historical depth of the visual would inflect all of one's seeing in the present, thus making it perspectival where the past impinges upon the presently visual. The historical continuity with our previous self as a partially temporally negated (and thus partially posited) self, would impede a full transcendence of myself as an individuated seer. To see as the world's self-seeing would require removing the body's historical aspect. Yet, it is one of the pivotal arguments of Nishida's later philosophy that the body as a determination of the place of nothingness is irreducibly sociohistorical. Even at the level of the absolute and the non-self, this "selfless place of personal existence is the sociohistorical world," writes Brubaker.[25]

Let us take this line of argumentation one step further. If we could achieve a full break with our seeing self and its history, there would be a radical *discontinuity* with our previous self, but we know that it is crucial for Nishida's thinking that history proceeds by way of a continuous-discontinuity (*hirenzoku no renzoku* 非連続の連続). To achieve the viewpoint of the world would require a severance from one way of being a self to a completely other way: from a form of relationality based on negation to a different way of relating, which might not be relational at all since, as described above, that move would entail overcoming one's physical determination. Going beyond one's viewpoint implies such a radical break in self-identity, or more precisely: the full dissolution of the self that would be necessary is an extreme form of negativism, which, following Merleau-Ponty's critique of Sartre, only reproduces the problems of positivism. The disillusion of the seer is the reduction of self-identity rather than the maintenance that Nishida insists on as "absolute contradictory self-identity" (*zettai mujunteki jikodōitsu* 絶対矛盾的自己同一).

Following Nishida's own philosophy of history, if I am able to transcend my individual view point in some way and achieve a partial discontinuity to my previous visual state, there is always a continuity with my previous self that remains because of the irreducible historical nature of the body and the world. That element of continuity means that I am always partly a seer. "Seeing without a seer" would require a full historical discontinuity and is thus not consistent with Nishida's wider notion of historical body–world relation. A full negation of my own visual subjectivity is untenable; therefore, I am always partially bodily and historical and thus obstructed-obstructing the visual world. I propose that a reading of Nishida's "seeing without a seer" is only tenable if precedence is given to his philosophy of history and its implied temporal relationality as continuously-continuous negation. Merleau-Ponty might simply say, relation between temporal orders must remain chiasmatic.

Partial obstruction is inherent to an ontology of mutual negation. To recall a point from chapter 1 regarding perception and negation: if subject

---

25. Ibid., 171.

and object were unambiguous positivity, they would be fully obstructive; if, on the other hand, they were fully negated, no interaction is possible. Where we relate to other entities, perceive them and encounter them, we are in a relation that involves a partial obstruction. Nishida's ontology is based on mutual negation but insofar as his "seeing without a seer" does not articulate the limits that hold it back from the full negation implied, the idea transgresses some of his own more basic ontological commitments. We can, therefore, question this part of Nishida's philosophy of vision, while remaining immanent to his own thought. Certainly, the reading that prioritizes his philosophy of history affords closer dialogue with Merleau-Ponty.

To challenge the possibility of a wholly negated visual subject as "seeing without a seer," of course, does not imply that vision entails a substantial seeing subject. Perception is a relation and requires relata, which are otherwise lost if either the subject or the object is nullified. Insofar as the perceptual relation obtains through negation—as Nishida believes it does—this means that there is always a minimal seer, a negated seer to be sure, but not a fully negated seer. However minimal, there is always a "mineness" to phenomenal experience.[26] Therefore, an obstruction abides as a limitation to *my* visual experience. Likewise, with motion, since the body's movements are also in a relation of mutual negation with the background of motion, they are not discrete actions of an individuated agent, but are acts within an infinite continuity of acts. Non-action is never "go with the flow" passivity. That would be a full negation of the volitional self. One is not overwhelmed by the infinite continuity of acts, but is an act among them: negated and negating. Within this ambiguity, it can be true that motion and perception are events of a basic motor-perceptual fabric, while it is also true that there are limits to full reversibility between all points within that fabric, which manifest as motor and perceptual obstructions. You and I are both embedded within *Basho*, and my vision and my motion do count in yours, but you will never see from my vantage point nor move my body, and thus there is at least minimal obstruction on both a motor and a perceptual level.

One last point I will make on this issue: Just as obstruction arises in the Huayan context because of the physical features of phenomena, so too in Nishida's philosophy, his own insistence on subjectivity-*qua*-objectivity should preclude a full negation of the visual subject and thus

---

26. In "Nishida's Ontology of History," Maraldo develops this idea relative to Heidegger's idea of "*jemeinigkeit*" ("mineness") and discusses ways in which this might go against Nishida's "absorption model" of "becoming the thing."

raise questions regarding the limits to "seeing without a seer." Nishida and Merleau-Ponty agree that one is always subjective and objective, never one to the exclusion of the other. While the artist strives toward what Nishida calls "pure objectivity," (*jun naru kyakkan* 純なる客観) she never does so to the full exclusion of subjectivity. To fully transcend that visual subjectivity, to wholly erase the seer would be to collapse the subjective-*qua*-objective relation to which Nishida is otherwise committed. If the artist achieves a different, possibly a heightened visual state, she might see something of the world's perspective. She may immerse herself in pure objectivity, but never to the full exclusion of the "mineness" of her visual subjectivity, and never beyond the objectivity of her body that roots her in a determined point of view, however minimal that might become. Inherent to the maintenance of subjective–objective ambiguity is a blind spot and motor-visual obstructions that impede full erasure of the seer or mover.

For the purposes of this inquiry into artistic expression, because of the irreducibility of an obstructive blind spot, the artist's motor-perception should not aim at full negation or non-obstruction. To do so would reduce the risk of expression, but because that risk is irreducible, it is not a productive goal for artists to strive toward. Maintaining an ambiguity between the visual aspect of the historical body and historical world is one of the limitations the artist must accept and work with, but it is here, in the "pregnant" tension between the two that the artist's possibilities are born. Indeed, the relation to tradition, be it European or Chinese, is one vital source for the artist to gear their body into to find truly novel conditions of visibility and movability. It is essential for the artist to both negate and be negated, and for the creation to be expressing-expressed. To do so is to risk expressing oneself with a blindness that is both motor and perceptual and that demands a bodily form of faith.

As we consider in greater detail what kind of faith accepts the constitutive risk of expression, further implications are revealed for challenging the methodologies of reflection and doubt that typically keep philosophy distinct from religious and artistic forms of expression. Let us now examine the obstructions *and the possibilities* given by the way the seer is embedded within and obstructed by his historical tradition.

Having explored the wider view, considering the foundational concepts of Nishida's later thought, I would argue that those concepts do preclude reading "seeing without a seer," the "Self-seeing" of *Basho*, or "becoming one with sight" as implying a full negation of the visual subject. Fully non-obstructed relationality—visual or otherwise—goes contrary to Nishida's most fundamental ontological commitments.[27] Most, if not all of his late concepts posit a mutual-negation as the structure of relationality, which would be collapsed if the seer dissolved fully into the visual world. Nevertheless, while none of his enigmatic concepts *should* entail a "view from nowhere," in the absence of articulating clear limits to visual negation, we are left to guess how or to what extent "infinite vision" remains short of full reversibility, or a multi-perspectivalism so extreme as to be an omni perspectivalism. What are the obstructions or blind spots that would redeem his concept of "seeing without a seer"? I have not, thus far, found clear answers to these perplexing issues, but as open questions they complicate but also render "productively ambivalent" the dialogue with Merleau-Ponty.

History of Motor-Visibility

Klee: "End-Forms" and "Formative Forces"

A decisive element of the dialogue between Nishida and Merleau-Ponty regarding phenomenal encounter hangs on the question of the body's historical determination. Limits to visual and motor-reversibility are instantiated by virtue of one's present sensorimotor projects being determined by the past. The artists we have been contemplating appear to cultivate a deep engagement with their traditions, yet, artistic creativity must also work out an equally complex orientation to the future. To continue pressing forward with the dialogue in this section, we consider the importance of the artist's tradition while inching our way toward articulating how he can cultivate a forward-looking orientation to the past.

To create new important works, artists accept a form of risk instituted by the contingency of the conditions of motor-visibility. The risk the artist accepts today is different than it would have been a hundred years ago. We neither see the world nor move our bodies to depict it as people did during the Renaissance, for example. The development of linear perspective and theories of advancing and receding colors exemplify how—through artistic and scientific innovation—a different orientation within the perceptual

---

27. See John Krummel, "Embodied Implacement in Kūkai and Nishida"; Maraldo, "Self-Mirroring and Self-Awareness: Dedekind, Royce, and Nishida."

fabric appeared quite abruptly and made a discernible punctuation in the motor-visible. The works of Leonardo, Brunelleschi, Raphael, and other practitioners employing the techniques of foreshortening and perspective did not just represent a world that was already visible, but rather made the world visible in a new way, which ultimately came about through new bodily gestures. One could certainly adopt one's techniques in the present, but those innovations are already taken for granted, already so well established as part of the sensorimotor fabric that we now move and see so completely according to those determinations that they are invisible as determinations and simply appear "the way things are." Thus, we perpetually require new experiments to make visibility visible. This marks the importance of new artworks, as well as the risks taken by those who create them.

Although his works might not have achieved a complete reorientation of the motor-perceptual fabric to the level attained by artists during the Renaissance, Paul Klee appears to have had a clear grasp of the possibility of art to effect such a change. In one of his most enduring quotes, he says that "art does not reproduce the visible, but makes visible."[28] Echoing this sentiment in a later diary entry, he writes: "in art vision is not so essential as making-visible."[29] Gerald Cipriani places this line of thinking in the context of Merleau-Ponty and Nishida's *Basho*:

> [P]ainting does not therefore imitate the objective real world as if it were an already visible world that painting strived to look like. Painting, or art in general, is rather a form of "expression" in the sense that it expresses what could not have been seen without it. The artist makes us discover a world to which we belong without seeing it. Artists for Merleau-Ponty and for Cézanne, do not provide an illustration of the world, but make the world appear as such from an invisible *Basho* that becomes slightly different with each perceptual experience.[30]

If the conditions of the motor-visible did not have this mutability, creating artworks would be markedly simpler, less risky; moreover, there would

---

28. John Sallis, *Paul Klee: Philosophical Vision: From Nature to Art*, 8.
29. Paul Klee, *The Diaries of Paul Klee: 1898–1918*, 410.
30. Gerald Cipriani, "Merleau-Panty, Cézanne, and the *Basho* of the Visible," in *Merleau-Ponty and Buddhism*, ed. Park, Kopf, & Gereon, 153.

be little need for new artworks to challenge and renew our ways of seeing. The prevailing conditions would lend themselves very nicely to being heavily codified as they were in the Chinese painting manual tradition. But, the visible does change. If its conditions were stable, an artwork could be judged by way of a correspondence-based aesthetic logic. A painting of a landscape, a chrysanthemum, or a group of persimmons could be appraised based on how it matched the object's static visible features. Yet, Merleau-Ponty in particular works outside of the representation-correspondence model, precisely because of the instability of the visible. There is no unchanging visual world to which an artwork can correspond, nor is there a set of gestures that can bring that world or its objects to a presence that would be stable for all times. This contingency manifests as a further instantiation of the motor-perceptual blind spot: the visibility that will be brought about and the bodily movements that will achieve it are not pre-given or discernible in the present. A painting cannot come before painting. This is a further aspect of the risk the artist takes on, since they are constrained to move in the present. An artist who accepts this contingency can do more than simply "respond in an original way to the situation," but, in Dreyfus's words, he can "respond in a way that changes people's perceptions of the situation."[31] But to do so one must not be fully constrained by the visible, that is, by the past.

Since they admit of so little noticeable change, the conditions of motor-visibility according to which we see and move in the world might appear immutable. Yet, those conditions have been determined by contingent events throughout history: artistic, scientific, religious or numerous other forces dye the fabric and weave it into new patterns, giving it new textures and folds. The fabric into which we are woven in contemporary Western life, while it might admit of varying degrees of deviation, is nevertheless broadly determined by a set of events that comprise the particular conditions of motor-visibility at this moment. The very way we see the world would not be the same if mirrors had not been invented, if the caves at Lascaux had never been discovered, if Renaissance innovations had never appeared, if cameras were not so ubiquitous, if we had not seen war on television, the inside of our bodies through X-rays, or the planet from space. Although none of these events makes a difference we explicitly notice, they change the conditions of noticeability itself. Some artists have dedicated themselves

---

31. "Meaning, Relevance, and the Limits of Technology." An interview with Richard Dreyfus. Conversations with History; Institute of International Studies, UC Berkeley. globetrotter.berkeley.edu/people5/Dreyfus/dreyfus-con5.html

to seeing the contingency of the visible. Artists such as Klee, Cézanne, and Sesshū are able to make an almost imperceptible aspect of the visible the focus of their practice, yet it must be an oblique focus, because what they strive toward has never been visible. As John Sallis explains, the artist focuses on the creative forces that alter the visible fabric rather than the present state or "end-forms" of visibility; as such, the artist is "not bound to these appearances."[32] It is in making "the shift from the end-forms (the natural appearances) to the formative forces behind them," writes Sallis, "that the artist is perhaps a philosopher."[33] Klee was particularly well-known for aiming at this level of expression.

We can now articulate one criterion for artworks within a context that acknowledges the ambiguity of the visible and the invisible: the great artwork changes the present conditions of visibility within which it is seen, thus creating a new visibility for the future. To invoke Merleau-Ponty's line again, "[r]ather than seeing [the artwork], I see according to, or with it."[34] The artist can create new artworks by looking beyond the end-forms of the present state of visibility and risk moving with the formative forces of the visible despite the motor-blind spot that makes the task feel impossible. Risk is an integral aspect of being oriented toward the future in expression. Accordingly, Klee was a great artist because he was able to see beyond the givenness of the visible forms, and instead of representing these he worked on the formative forces of the visible fabric itself. Heidegger was struck by this aspect of Klee's work. In a letter sent to his friend after seeing an exhibition, he writes: "[i]n Klee something has happened that none of us grasps yet."[35] Heidegger, as well as countless other philosophers—including Merleau-Ponty, Nishida, Benjamin, Adorno, Deleuze, Blanchot, Derrida, Foucault, and Gadamer—turn to Klee's work because his future-oriented commitment to the visible has something important to offer to philosophy.

The Invisibility of the Self as "Style" and the Temporality of Risk

The tradition of Chinese painting manuals and the practices that followed its dictates might appear to be quite counter to Klee's approach, possibly

---

32. Sallis, *Paul Klee: Philosophical Vision: From Nature to Art*, 15.
33. Ibid.
34. Merleau-Ponty, "Eye and Mind," 126.
35. Sallis, *Paul Klee: Philosophical Vision: From Nature to Art*, 21.

appearing to be purely past-oriented. Insofar as the more famous guide books such as the *Mustard Seed Garden Manual of Painting* determined practice in China and Japan for centuries, this would suggest that those who followed its codes and rules would not have assumed that the conditions of visibility changed appreciably over time, if at all, and thereupon closed themselves off from the futural possibilities of expression. Yet, there is a persistent exhortation to go beyond blind devotion to the techniques elaborated in the Mustard Seed manual's hundreds of pages. The truly skilled practitioner learns the rules until they are second nature, such that he can depart from them and cultivate a practice that goes beyond their constraints.

If artists simply followed the rules set out in manuals, or even sought to copy the innovations of Klee or Cézanne, they might attempt new works, but the underlying assumption takes for granted that how the world appears is the only way it can appear. Works would be much less risky to create, expressive practices far more circumscribable. To represent the world or even to distort or abstract from it would be much less of a gamble by virtue of a stable form of visibility. However, this would only be possible if artworks were not themselves part of the visible fabric they depict, not continuous with flesh or *Basho*. Because all works are part of this fabric, because there is no motor-perceptual externality, however insignificant their impact might be, great works can affect the conditions in which they are seen. Cézanne's "Mont Sainte Victoire" or Sesshū's "Splashed Ink Landscape" are not simply made *in the world*, they also *make that world*. This relation between artwork and nature dictates a specific temporality for expression, which necessitates a risk and therefore faith on the part of the artist. It is a risk because before visibility comes into being through the work, it has never existed in that exact form, and therefore, the artist cannot have a representation of it ahead of time. Alphonse de Waehlens argues that the real issue is "how to express, by the use of signs (new ones, to be sure, but old ones as well), that which heretofore, while included in the world, has never intentionally appeared," and while all artworks might do this, great ones, he thinks, are able to "express it in such a way that everyone will henceforth be able to see it."[36]

If the conditions of visibility were stable they would precede the artist's work in time, and she could be oriented strictly toward the past in representing the world. The temporality would be such that painting would come before painting, and correspondence measures would function appro-

---

36. Alphonse de Waehlens, "Merleau-Ponty: Philosopher of Painting," in *The Merleau-Ponty Aesthetics Reader: Philosophy and Painting*, ed. Galen A. Johnson, 188.

priately for judging and comparing works within this temporality. Because the visible is contingent, always being made, it lies ahead of the artist, in the not-yet represented future, and thus, even an exhaustive cataloguing of all of the innovations that have so far determined the present state of visibility cannot be relied upon as a set of conventions that produce the same meaning now as they did in the past. The artist's task is to take a stance toward this not-yet visible future in order to affect the visible fabric itself. To make something truly new, something not yet seen, this temporality implies a risk, a working in the dark, and a temporal blind spot where one cannot rely on the present conditions of visibility and the bodily movements needed to reproduce them. It is as though one has to navigate through terrain that is always changing and whose maps are thus always getting older, always representing a slightly earlier instance of the land's form. The average artist follows the conventions of the earlier versions of the map to reduce risk, whereas the great artist wants to make a new map, but not only that, he is also willing to hazard composing that map as he is running through the terrain. This is the temporal risk of expression for one who accepts the motor-perceptual blind spot constraining creativity that aims to change the conditions of motor-visibility for the future.

This dilemma does not just manifest in the visibility of the landscape to be painted; there is a further temporal blind spot in the artist's ability to see him- or herself. De Wachlens articulates this in reference to Merleau Ponty's concept of "style." He elevates the artist's risk by showing how it is not only the world's visibility that lies in the future; in addition, the artist's style is always out of reach, never visible or graspable for oneself.

> And he cannot know his style for himself. Others will make it become fully significant. For himself or herself, style is the very modality of access to reality—as is our body for each of us. He cannot possess it "reflectively," and can but perceive in its texture a vague allusion to himself or herself. To himself or herself, style is the way what is to be painted must be painted. The painter's style is his painterly body. He brings it to perfection in using it . . . But the painter is lost if he "sees" this style for itself and makes an object of "delectation" of it. At the moment he begins copying himself and exhibiting himself. Style then has ceased being what it is.[37]

---

37. Ibid.

The artist's style is forever invisible to himself because it is not a self that paints but a non-self, one dispersed throughout the perceptual fabric and therefore not localizable or controllable, not even seeable at some circumscribed spatial-temporal location. Style is not a set of gestures one chooses from among several options readily available as one might choose the clothes that complement one's body. Style includes but transcends the body. It is not a set of actions, but an event that happens in the motor-perceptual fabric that is always an ambiguous relation extending far beyond that body. This style is not given purely by the artist, but instead, following Wachlens, style must be "wrested from the world, the work of others, and 'his own attempts.'"[38] If one could represent a style and choose it, that choice would be self-defeating since believing that one can even see the self so clearly and know the gestures needed to reproduce the effects of its style, already means that one is not properly oriented to the history of other's expressions, because that world and the self are always partially occluded because of being mutually negating. Expression is thus indirect and oblique by virtue of constitutive motor-perceptual obstructions. We might prefer the safety of proceeding directly but, as Johnson writes, "no one makes beauty directly, and if we attempted to do so it would only mar the work."[39] It mars the work because it goes against the nature of the relational world it seeks to make visible. The fully determinate subject could work directly if their goal of creating a fully determinate object were attainable. Merleau-Ponty invokes the fabric metaphor to describe the indirect nature of expression, he writes that "like the weaver" in creating, one "works on the wrong side of his material."[40] To be an artist and to have a style is not to be a substantial self with a visible identity and self-grounded agency, but to allow artistic expression to happen by negating one's self, one's identity, and one's agency, becoming partly anonymous to one's body and expressive self. Style is invisible, it is a feature of the blind spot that obtains between negated subject and object, not the possession of a creative individual. Accordingly, it is not only the case that painting does not exist before painting; moreover, the painter does not exist before painting. As soon as there is a painter, the risk of negation has been reduced. To engage in expression, accepting the obstructions that hinder it, puts the visibility of the self as well as the

---

38. Ibid.
39. Johnson, *The Retrieval of the Beautiful*, 40.
40. Merleau-Ponty, "Indirect Language and the Voices of Silence," 82.

visibility of the world within risk. Yet if one's actions succeed, through an act of faith, expression can arise in the body in tandem with a world that has much greater expressive resources than the individuated self would have working on a style it mistakenly believes could be entirely visible and representable. In order to work at this level, the artist risks deforming the present conditions of visibility, which is doubly risky since the artist himself is woven into the visible fabric and any experiments therein venture his own visibility to himself, venture having his self-seeing descend into incoherence. Nevertheless, great artists, Merleau-Ponty believes, can succeed in deforming the visible in a way he calls "coherent."

Coherent Deformation and the Force of Tradition

I expect that some questions might be forming throughout the preceding sections that deserve attention. Questions regarding what the expressive approach could be that avoids the sterility of perpetuating the prevailing conditions of visibility, or how exactly does one experiment beyond what is already representable to contribute to the evolution of the visible? The coming sections delve more closely into these particularities to take a few steps closer to filling out the account of expression being developed. Let me begin by considering Merleau-Ponty's notion of "coherent deformation" (*déformation cohérente*).

Despite the critique of the representational framework inherent to both Nishida and Merleau-Ponty's theories of expression, there are artworks that are quite striking in their ability to correspond with the visible world. Nineteenth-century European realist works, or more recent "hyper-realist" paintings or drawings, for example, have an immediate and sometimes wondrous impact on the senses because they seem to depict the visual world so faithfully. Putting aside for now the question of what creates this feeling, we can ask why other kinds of works, those that seem to distort the world, can also produce intense feelings. How is it that highly stylized or abstract renditions of a tree, a landscape, or an animal can be so fascinating, while they appear at the same time to be a distortion of what we would consider the "real" visible world? Sesshū's *Hatsuboku landscape* departs so utterly from the conventions of how trees can be depicted that hardly any discernible reference remains that corresponds to our ideas of a tree, yet his version impacts with more intensity than a straightforward representation could. If the artist's task is to make the world visible, then we must explore the logic of deformation employed by Sesshū and Cézanne in their paintings.

Figure 4.1. Eadweard Muybridge, *The Horse in Motion*, 1878. Library of Congress Prints and Photographic Division, Washington, DC, United States.

Figure 4.2. Théodore Géricault, *Epsom Derby*, 1821. Musée du Louvre, Paris, France.

As Merleau-Ponty explains, while looking at photos of Eadweard Muybridge (figure 4.1), one can have the peculiar sensation of knowing that the horses' bodies are in motion, while feeling as though they are oddly static. There seems to be a discrepancy between seeing these photos and having seen animals in real motion. A snapshot of a horse registers all the light that bounces off of the animal's body and hits the celluloid, and perfectly accounts for all the objective features of that particular instant. Nevertheless, the image still lacks an element of motion as we know it. One explanation might have to do with the materiality of representation. To paint, photograph, or draw a moving body is to depict motion on a static material support. It would seem reasonable that something is lost in the process; however, Merleau-Ponty believed that through "coherent deformation," Gericault was able to overcome this obstacle, and properly depict movement on canvas.

To paint a horse in motion, the artist does not have the safety that his or her representation can simply correspond with a photographic depiction, since the photo is not entirely true to the visual experience of motion. Since correspondence and representation fall short, one way to depict motion is to deform the body to give the viewer the feeling that real motion obtains on a motionless canvas. Gericault therefore elongates his horses in *Epsom Derby*, and although the distortion is obvious and does not seem to correspond with photographic reality, at the same time we do feel that movement is happening on the canvas in a way we do not with Muybridge's representations.

We call what Gericault did a "distortion" because we assume that there is a stable visual world "out there," and that the camera captures it more perfectly than our eyes do, or better than artworks can. Yet, because human perception is constituted by the visible as well as the invisible, because our vision finds depth in the world, the camera is actually a distortion of human vision, not a model for it. Deformation—although never "representationally" perfect—is necessary to approximate human vision on a material medium that is motionless.

Another reason camera technology fails to approximate human vision has to do with a further aspect of its relation to time. When the camera model is taken as the archetype for human perception, we assume that vision is made up of discrete snapshots of the world that combine in a linear fashion to give the appearance of moving bodies. This is what Gibson calls the "stimulus sequence theory."[41] Yet, as discussed, the visual

---

41. Gibson, *The Ecological Approach to Visual Perception*, 209.

world is perceived not according to linear temporality, but with an ecstatic horizon. Every instant is experienced as spanning past and future. We do not see the horse at time T_1 and space S_1, and then T_2 and S_2, and so on. The materiality associated with the camera model gives the mistaken idea that we can actually experience an indivisible instant of discrete time or space, which would correspond to a single frame of film. By contrast, if we could hypothetically isolate the unit of visual experience, it would not really be "isolated" or even a "unit," but would rather be something like a "span," where T_1 has an internal reference to $T_{-1, -2, -3 \ldots}$ and $T_{+1, +2, +3 \ldots}$. The "unit" of visual experience embraces the past, present, and future, whereas the material of the snapshot performs a temporal dislocation. In making a representation on static canvas or piece of paper, an image is cut off from its ecstatic range. No doubt it is useful for many reasons to be able to isolate an instant in this way, but the danger is that the camera is so convincing that we become seduced by its realism—and our own commitment to the correspondence notion of truth—and together these over-determine our understanding of vision in general. An even greater danger is that when our artistic works do not match photographic representations, we assume that the camera model is the better visual apparatus, and deviations from its way of portraying the world need to be rectified to achieve representational accuracy. The paintings of Cézanne, Sesshū and others, do not make this mistake. While these artists also use material other than that of the human visual apparatus, their engagements nevertheless maintain a relation to human vision. Coherent deformation is what the artist has to do in order to depict the experience of motion on a motionless material. To do so successfully depends on working within further constraints set down by the body's sociohistoric determination.

If one accepts the challenge of coherently deforming a scene, the artist cannot attempt to affect visibility with unconstrained "originality" or "creativity." One way that an artist remains coherent in deforming the world is through a grasp of the history of expression that determines the present conditions of visibility. An artist cannot deform an object or a body beyond the constraints determined by how it has been depicted in the past, yet neither does she want to simply reproduce these conditions. Picasso's abstract horses in his *Guernica*, for example, might not have been a meaningful punctuation in the visible fabric forty years earlier. Intermediary steps by other artists must be acknowledged in order for it to be a *coherent* deformation. Likewise, other events weaving and dying the visible fabric were necessary: the rise of photojournalism through advancements in technology, making cameras smaller and more portable, making the atrocities of war visible to Picasso and the general public in an unprecedented manner. These technological advancements radically reoriented the visible fabric in which Picasso worked and in which his viewers saw the world. His *Guernica* is an event that would not have been meaningful prior to these innovations, (it would have deformed the visual too much) nor would it be meaningful in the same way now that our present conditions of visibility have been so radically changed by various art movements, and by other technological innovations that have made the brutalities of war even more readily available on television, personal computers, and smartphones. All of the new visual technologies that make this possible are also advancements in the material of visual representation, and therefore change the fabric in which things become visible. These events, even though they do not appear specifically related to the art world, nevertheless determine how vision operates. They enable, if not demand certain deformations. And one cannot gloss over the previous intermediary deformations that made artistic innovations visible and yet "coherent." This might explain why depictions of the future almost always appear to have failed so blatantly when we look back on them from the time they were meant to depict. This is because there is a temporal blind spot facing forward. To depict the future is different than working to deform the conditions of visibility in the present for the present. When we try to represent what the future will look like, we do not have access to the intermediary deformations that would make that attempt coherent. In this case, the temporal blind spot is too great because there is not yet any access to unforeseen technological, political, material, social, or religious events that will determine the visible fabric between the time when one paints and the arrival of the time period that one attempts to depict. Hence, in working without being determined by the necessary intermediary developments of the visible, in deforming objects, one goes beyond their constraints and loses coherence. But, the constraints are essential, either when looking forward to depict the future, or when looking back to engage with art's tradition. To go too far forward in an act of aesthetic prediction exceeds what is available in the current conditions of visibility. To go too far back is to remain constrained by those conditions. In the former we find no meaningful solicitations, no traction within a field of act and act. In the latter the solicitations are too heavy and practice is too convention-laden. One reaches too far into the not-yet representable future (takes on too much risk), whereas the other relies too heavily on the already-represented past (takes on almost no risk); one tends too impatiently toward deformation the other too conservatively toward coherence; one toward unadulterated difference, the other to stale repetition: neither is able to productively reorient the visible. For deformation to remain coherent, these are its temporal constraints.

Overcoming Reflection, Embracing Risk

Let us imagine that one recognizes all of the impossibilities that complicate expression; that they acknowledge the obstructions impinging upon the motor-perceptual body; appreciate the paradoxes, the aporia, the need for coherent deformation; know that their body pervades not just the present motorsensory field but one with vast historical depth; they accede to the limits on motion and perception instituted by phenomenal blind spots that fasten them to their tradition while making that tradition's innovations ineffective in the present—what then? It seems like painting would be a near impossible task, where an infinite set of considerations would present themselves before one even began. While both Nishida and Merleau-Ponty describe artistic expression as "infinite," neither renders it as impossible. How artists accept the challenges of expression can inform philosophy, but to truly take up what they imply might be unimaginable for philosophies that see no possibilities beyond methodologies of doubt and reflection.

Holography, Infinity, and Risk

Because obstructions limit perception, we never obtain a full picture of the world, an object, the landscape, even our own bodies. We cannot bring all invisibility to visibility, nor can we extract ourselves from the motor-background and transform all passivity into activity to achieve the control we desire. Since elements of the body's motions are solicited by a world lined by an irreducible invisibility, there is no mechanism of full control of (one's own) movements. To move is to always be partly beyond one's own control and is therefore a risk that demands motor-perceptual faith. Perhaps "demand" is not the right term since it implies that we could choose otherwise. As I mentioned in the very beginning of this study, Merleau-Ponty's "perceptual faith" is intransitive, it is not a subject's faith in relation to an object. We need not decide to exercise faith. Faith is not an act added to one's actions. Insofar as one moves the body, one is—however minimally—

motor-perceptually faithful. The fact that we lack full control but nevertheless move implies a constitutive element of bodily faith.

Despite there being no position of motorsensory externality, no autonomous agency, nevertheless, many deeply entrenched intellectual commitments determine practices that go against these features of embodiment. Those practices might aim to eliminate risk and to reduce the need for faith. But, Nishida is unequivocal, and we can read Merleau-Ponty this way too; faith obtains by virtue of the world's various ways of negating the body. Thus, while we cannot get outside of the motor-perceptual continuity of *Basho* or flesh, our assumptions that inform our methodologies can go counter to the facts of our determination therein, impeding the ability to attune properly in practice. Some of those assumptions and practices include methodological doubt, over-reliance on reflective intellection, and as we explore now, part-whole metaphysics.

If asked, I believe that many artists would find it relatively unproblematic that their finished work could be considered a whole composed of parts. Although this might seem relatively straightforward, the temporality dictated by this part-whole dichotomy could be at odds with the artist's desired expressive outcome. What could be more obvious than the fact that the parts come first, and the whole emerges later? I sculpt this part of a leg, not the whole tendon, just a particular area and its corresponding muscle and tissue, and the whole leg and then the body follow in time. The entire form does eventually emerge, but my artistic gestures aim at parts and never does any single movement sculpt the whole body at one time. Despite what seem like reasonable assumptions about entities and movement, both Nishida and Merleau-Ponty conceive of artistic gesture beyond this part-whole metaphysics and temporality. For Nishida, "each of the artist's exquisite brush strokes expresses the true meaning of the whole."[42] Echoing this view, Merleau-Ponty contends that Cézanne's gestures contained the whole of the painting: "[E]ach stroke must contain the air, the light, the object, the composition, the character, the outline and the style."[43] Similarly, Sesshū's gestures were said to "encompass four hundred provinces with one stroke"[44] and when reading Shitao's account of his own expressive practice, we see that he too thought beyond part-whole metaphysics:

---

42. Nishida, An Inquiry into the Good, 33.
43. Merleau-Ponty, "Cézanne's Doubt," 66.
44. Asaoka; Ōta, *Zōtei Koga Bikō*, 4 vols., vol. 2, 671.

"Mountain as sea, sea as mountain": This is what really counts to feel. The identical in the different, the different in the identical. Every phenomenon is an unceasing movement that evolves and changes in another one. On the sea we get the element of the mountain—by the shapes of the waves, in its mass and strength—and in the mountain we perceive the dimension of sea—by the water of springs, the torrents, the mists and clouds, the humidity on the cliffs. "I perceive in the modality of mountain-sea."[45]

Grasping how artistic gestures can overcome part-whole configurations requires some unpacking. If this does not contradict a great deal of Western philosophy, then it at least goes against common sense. And yet, an important part of modern Japanese philosophy, as well as its Buddhist (*Kegon, Tiantai*) and Shintō roots, is based on a "holographic" model, which is an interesting alternative to part-whole metaphysics.[46] As Thomas Kasulis explains in his seminal work *Intimacy and Integrity*, the nature of relations—not only in painting but with all objects and throughout existence—is such that the whole (*holo*-) is inscribed (-*graph*) in each of the parts. To illustrate this, Kasulis appeals to the example of DNA, where each infinitesimally small body part, every molecule, hair, or drop of blood, contains the blueprint for the entire body. While rare, this way of thinking is not completely foreign to Western thought; it inspires Borges' *Aleph* where the so-called "object" is a point in space that contains all other points. Of course, the holographic model makes its most enduring appearance in the West in William Blake's "Auguries of innocence," where he writes "To see a world in a grain of sand / And a heaven in a wild flower / Hold infinity in the palm of your hand / And eternity in an hour."[47] Most would agree that this is a beautiful poem,

---

45. Han Linde, *Shítāo Yǔ "Huà Yǔlù" Yánjiū* 石涛与"画语录"研究.

46. In his discussion of mandalas, Kasulis explains the "holographic" relation where each element of the design fully manifests Dainichi Buddha. While the innermost features represent the highest spiritual/mental attainment, this region is not hierarchically above the outermost features. Each level is internally related to all others. To approach enlightened mind is not to travel from the outermost to the innermost regions of the mandala. One can find direct access to all features of the "esoteric" Buddhist mindset from within any of the Mandala's features (Thomas Kasulis, *Intimacy or Integrity: Philosophy and Cultural Difference*).

47. It is possible that Blake's familiarity with Sir William Charles's (1785) translation of the *Bhagavad ghita* explains his use of "holographic" logic in his writings.

but few would argue for its logic, which undermines fundamental elements of Western philosophy and science. Likely fewer still would recognize that the holographic logic inspiring Blake's poem existed many centuries earlier as put forth in the Huayan Buddhist dictum, "one particle of dust contains the entire world."[48]

Returning to the issue of risk, we can see that when part-whole assumptions enter art practice, they can feed a desire to reduce a type of risk that should rather be engaged. If it were the case that paintings were straightforward wholes composed of parts, the artist could work with a confidence not otherwise available. If the artist were painting only this branch or sculpting this arm, and not at the same time all the relations that bring them into their particular visibility—the air, light, smell, wind, etc.—he could proceed with his work assuming a finite correspondence between the marks he makes and the objects in the world. But, as Merleau-Ponty and Nishida argue, each stroke (-*graph*) must contain *all* (*holo-*) of the elements that bring any particular part to visibility. Yet, this is exceedingly complicated, since the visible is lined by the invisible. If expressive movements seek to represent only the visible, then they cannot include the whole, they cannot have a relation to the infinite, which Nishida and Merleau-Ponty believe the artists must attain. Accordingly, the painter has to work in two temporal directions at once: working on the parts building up the whole, while also working from the not-yet visible whole toward the parts. Such is the complex temporality of parts and wholes impinging upon expressive gesture. While this appears like an impossible task for the self, it is conceivable for a self negated by the world and working in conjunction with its motor demands.

An image of the whole guides the artist's brushstrokes, yet until the painting is complete, until every color, shading, and contour has been made, no matter how well planned the painting, the artist never has complete access to a positively visible representation of the whole. "What he expresses cannot, therefore, be the translation of a clearly defined thought, since such clear thoughts are those that have already been said within ourselves or by others,"[49] writes Merleau-Ponty. Those clear thoughts are constrained by the conditions of visibility as they are determined by the past. To change

---

48. See Park's discussion of the part-whole metaphysics of Huayan Buddhism, as well as the related concepts of "mutual containment" (c. *xiangru*) and "simultaneous containment" (c. *tongshi dunqi*) (2008), 163–166.

49. Merleau-Ponty, "Cézanne's Doubt," 69.

those conditions, artists thus work only with "a vague fever, and only the work itself, completed and understood, will prove that there was *something* rather than *nothing* to be found there."[50] Expression is "like a step taken in the fog—no one can say where, if anywhere, it will lead."[51] Although Merleau-Ponty does not thematize the notion of risk, as we see here, that idea is inherent to the various ways expression accepts its own partial blindness. To move the body while occluded by sensorimotor fog, the visual obstruction implicates a motor risk. Each of the artist's gestures thus ventures a partially blind endeavor that might result in something or nothing, being or non-being. Nishida's account of expression implies a similar constitutive blindness, which also implicates risk, for him, the risk of life or death.

> [W]e take risks at each and every step. We face towards death and enter into non-being. Death always lies in wait for us. But as long as we can form things objectively we are alive. In such a case the objective world is a world of expression. As long as we are creative, and as long as the thing expressed and the act of expression are one, we are alive.[52]

The unity of the act of expression and the thing expressed is a key feature of Nishida's theory of expression as "from the made to the making." While the artist can represent discrete visible forms, he must find a way to gear the body into the invisible continuity of acts of the whole landscape. The whole operates as a motor-perceptual solicitation that is, in a sense, prior to the parts insofar as they are visible and circumscribable, while the landscape is neither. Allowing the body to follow the impetus of the whole is a risk because it exceeds the ability of artists to exercise a type of control they can mistakenly assume they possess—a mistake enabled by representationalism and its attendant part-whole metaphysical assumptions. Going with solicitations is a risk because the temporality of the holographic model of relations is incommensurate with the temporality of representation and correspondence. Put more simply, for correspondence-based expectations to be truly useful, the final image expressed would have to be positively visible before the parts that build up to represent it. In operating within the ambiguity of the visible and the invisible, and within the indeterminacy of parts

---

50. Ibid.

51. *Sense and Non-Sense*, 3.

52. Nishida, *Fundamental Problems*, 148.

and wholes, the artist departs from the representational model; therefore, she risks operating based on a truth—and reveals a truth—which cannot be accounted for by that model. More precisely, when she has faith to allow her movements to be solicited by the landscape, her gestures overcome the seeming paradox of the whole being co-extensive with the parts.

The problem that reemerges now is that there are potentially endless calculations that need to enter into each stroke that would embrace the whole and parts. A painting would never begin if the artist had to grasp all the features of the entire visual field before painting. As alluded to, rather than diminishing this dilemma, both Nishida and Merleau-Ponty conceive of the artist's gestures as "infinite." According to what he called an "infinite logos," Merleau-Ponty argues that because every one of the artist's movements must overcome what appears to be infinite conditions "expressing what *exists* is an endless task."[53] Regarding Matisse, he claims that "[b]y a simple gesture he resolved the problem which in retrospect seemed to imply an infinite number of data."[54] And when discussing Cézanne:

> [I]f the painter is to express the world, the arrangement of his colors must bear within this indivisible whole, or else the painting will only hint at things and will not give them in the imperious unity, the presence, the insurpassable plenitude which is for us the definition of the real. That is why each brushstroke must satisfy an infinite number of conditions.[55]

Nishida also conceives of the visual world as infinite.[56] In a footnote from his 1917 *Intuition and Reflection in Self-Consciousness* (*Jikaku ni okeru chokkan to hansei* 自覚における直観と反省) Nishida quotes Conrad Fiedler, who writes: "there is an infinity which has nothing to do with the realm of thought, and which reveals itself purely as an infinity of the visible world."[57]

---

53. Merleau-Ponty, "Cézanne's Doubt," 66.
54. "Indirect Language and the Voices of Silence," 83.
For a discussion of Nishida's idea of infinity and unification in relation to Matisse, see Dalissier (2009), 163.
55. Merleau-Ponty, "Cézanne's Doubt," 66.
56. For a discussion of the philosophical and mathematical predecessors of Nishida's conception of infinity, see Maraldo, "Self-Mirroring and Self-Awareness: Dedekind, Royce, and Nishida"; Michel Dalissier, "The Idea of the Mirror in Nishida and Dōgen."
57. Nishida, *Intuition and Reflection in Self-Consciousness*, 186.

It is not the philosopher, but rather "the artist and those who can follow him [who] stand before this infinity."[58] This thought persists appearing later in his *Fundamental Problems* where he writes that "artistic intuition must be an infinite activity."[59] The beauty of Nishida's formulation is that it brings together his wider theory of vision-inflected action and his theory of expression within a conception of infinity: "pure visual perception," is not simply visual, it is more; it "naturally moves our body and develops into a kind of expressive movement."[60] Because the visual world is infinite, to meet it in expression requires that one have faith in the body's ability to engage beyond doubt and reflection. This is why philosophy cannot only be philosophy, why there is an element of faith shown to us by our experience within the motor-perceptual world. And, if this calls into question the relation between philosophy and religion, then the artist is also implicated since it is "the creative act of the artist," through which the "prospect of a world of infinite visual perception opens up."[61]

To express oneself, the artist needs to find a way to engage with the infinite. To understand this order of expression, we must face the difficult question of how one does so with one's body and its gestures, which are finite. The answer is that "one" cannot. That is to say, one cannot if she is understood as an autonomous expressive self working purely within the control of her own deliberative reflection, that is, not giving up part of her expressive control to the world and thus achieving the infinity beyond representation. The reflective intellect cannot represent or calculate the infinite. As Merleau-Ponty states, "our corrections would never be rapid and precise enough if they had to be based upon an actual calculation of effects."[62] The infinite nature of the part-whole dilemma cannot be reckoned with by reflection, and therefore presents a constraint that the body easily overcomes by way of faith. The artist does not attain the infinite by calculating or by taking control. There is a type of visual absorption where the body is given over to the "outer world" where the infinite is possible. As Nishida alleges, when our "self becomes one with the sense of sight . . . then a world of infinite visual developments unfolds and the sense of sight becomes one with

---

58. Nishida, *Fundamental Problems*, 179.

59. Ibid.

60. Nishida, *Art and Morality*, 24.

61. Ibid.

62. Merleau-Ponty, "Indirect Language and the Voices of Silence," 103.

the bodily movements in the outer world."[63] This way of seeing is a way of moving. But, one must exercise faith to allow the negation between body and world to obtain without impeding it through reflective intellection or methodological doubt. The artist has no choice but to have faith in their body's ability to overcome its finite nature because the proof the reflective intellect seeks is not simply unavailable to the artist; moreover, the attempt to seek that assurance thought to alleviate doubt actually closes the body off from the infinity of the motor-perceptual world. As Merleau-Ponty notes, the philosophy of reflection "renders impossible that *openness upon being* which is the perceptual faith."[64]

Reflection and Faith

For Nishida, all of the world, including bodies and artworks, are an "infinite" unity of act and act. Reflection is also an act, yet in being inherently dualistic, it disturbs the unity that binds body and world.[65] As Nishida writes in *Art and Morality*, "[w]hen such an immediate experience has been reflected upon, the distinction between act and object emerges."[66] The problem is that a subject cannot paint an object, not the way Cézanne and Sesshū did. Unity is only possible where subject and object are united in risking their own coherence. Because "independent, self-sufficient true reality manifests itself in the form of this union [of subject/object]," Nishida asserts that we must "realize the true state of this reality with our entire being rather than reflect on it, analyze it, or express it in words."[67] To reflect is to add thought onto action already underway, to seek to understand a gesture

---

63. Nishida, "歴史的形成作用としての芸術的創作 *Rekishi-Teki Keiseisayō Toshite No Geijutsu-Teki Sōsaku*."

64. Merleau-Ponty, *The Visible and the Invisible*, 88.

65. "Reflection" is an important concept Nishida uses in two—not always well delineated—senses. The sense of reflection Nishida is critical of, and the one I focus on here, is an intellectual form of reflection, *hansei suru* (反省する), which implies a retroactive look back upon something or oneself at an earlier moment. The other term for "reflection" he uses more often is *utsusu* (写す), which means to reflect in the sense of mirroring, copying or duplicating. This is an important dynamic in the self-mirroring of *Basho*, but not the concept I focus on in this study. See Maraldo (2017) for a discussion of the implications of the various uses for Nishida's relation to phenomenology.

66. Nishida, *Art and Morality*, 123.

67. Nishida, *An Inquiry into the Good*, 51.

rather than simply making the next brushstroke, or to endeavor to know in full clarity what one is going to do before one begins doing it. Meanwhile, Merleau-Ponty also recognizes the perils of a philosophy based solely on reflection and cautions that when I "adopt a critical attitude toward [the perceptual] when I ask 'what I am really seeing,'" that we "break away from the primary *faith* inspired by perception."[68] His project was from the beginning an attempt to recuperate contact with the sensible world, not by discarding reflection outright, but by developing broader methodologies such that philosophy remains true to what the perceptual world demands. There is no question of ignoring the aspect of our world that is properly governed by reflection, but as Merleau-Ponty writes, "[a] philosophy of reflection, if it is not to be ignorant of itself, is led to question itself about what precedes itself, about our contact with being within ourselves and outside of ourselves."[69] His critique aims not at reflection per se but at a philosophy that does not see the prior pre-reflective grounds out of which reflection arises. The question of exactly how the reflective emerges from out of the pre-reflective is a vast issue in Merleau-Ponty scholarship, which I cannot develop here. What I focus on in the section below, is the question of how the pre-reflective moment becomes a locus that can bear great philosophical and artistic fruit. Indeed, phenomenology is premised on the fecundity of this very moment, which offers a greatly expanded framework for understanding artistic expression. Reflection only gives us a tiny corner of the world, because it "objectifies points of view of perspectives, whereas when I perceive, I belong, through my point of view, to the world as a whole."[70] Merleau-Ponty and Nishida want philosophic methodologies that feed off of the entire sensible world to this extent.

Yes, reflective thought is necessary and appropriate in many situations. And yet, in terms of creative expression, it can interfere in the process by adding an extraneous act that obstructs the exchange between body and world where the infinite is appropriately dealt with. In our perceptual openness onto the world, which is in place before reflection insinuates itself, Merleau-Ponty writes, "[W]e do not think the object and we do not think ourselves thinking it;" instead, he explains, "we are given over to the object and we merge into this body which is better informed than we are about

---

68. Merleau-Ponty, *Phenomenology of Perception*, 280. Emphasis added.
69. Merleau-Ponty, *The Visible and the Invisible*, 73.
70. Merleau-Ponty, *Phenomenology of Perception*, 384.

the world, and about the motives we have and the means at our disposal for synthesizing it."[71] Our prejudice in the West has been the unquestioned belief that the reflective intellect is "better informed" to direct our actions. Of course, certain circumstances might demand more focused reflection and less "giving oneself over" to the world. But, even when in deep intellection, the body is still in silent dialogue with the world. What Merleau-Ponty calls this "muted relationship with the world . . . [is] always already accomplished when the reflective return intervenes."[72] His critique of reflection brings our attention to this moment of pre-reflective carnal belonging in the world, so that we can care for a primordial aspect of our embodiment, which is perpetually at stake. At this level, we find that the body is, as he says, "better informed" at dialoguing with the world, however, to let action arise from what is a blind spot of the reflective intellect is inherently risky. Reflection aims at control, hence, to delegate actions to a body–world interchange that is invisible and elusive demands faith.

Returning to the example of art practice, when one does not have faith in the body–world dialogue, when reflection is relied upon too heavily, the artist aims at *making* rather than the ambiguity of *making-made*. The reflective intellect wants to eliminate this ambiguity in order to have a kind of certainty that expression will turn out as hoped. Instead of simply acting we seek to "comprehend our natal bond with the world only by *undoing it in order to remake* it, only by constituting it, by fabricating it."[73] In reflection, I do not adhere to the world but rather "suspend my adhesion to the world in order to make of it a thought of the world."[74] Of course, the artist must think deeply. Cézanne is Merleau-Ponty's exemplar because of his having found a means of expression that does not choose between intellection and sensation. One needs both because to side too much with the former is "not to coincide with the flux from its source unto its last ramifications,"[75] and if there is anything that Merleau-Ponty wants to teach us it is what philosophy can learn by developing rigorous methods that coincide with the flux of sensation.

---

71. Ibid., 277.
72. Merleau-Ponty, *The Visible and the Invisible*, 35.
73. Ibid., 32.
74. Ibid., 65.
75. Ibid., 45.

The reflective intellect is necessary for moving in the complex ways we do, but it cannot exhaustively account for, control, or even understand our most basic movements. Even our everyday actions would never succeed if all of the calculations that occur to enable them had to be reflected upon. What we do is not enabled by exhaustive knowledge, but through a "naïve frequenting of the world," which Merleau-Ponty believes obtains "before the reflection, and in order to make it possible."[76] Reflection tends more toward extending one's *understanding of action* rather than *extending the scope of action*. To nourish one's action, as Cézanne or Sesshū did, requires not that one allows the body to move as negated by the world rather than trying to capture it, because "the moment that the reflective effort tries to capture it," we miss the relationship, "which we shall here call the openness upon the world (*ouverture au monde*)."[77] As Merleau-Ponty claims, being open, coinciding with the flux requires faith. What is key to remember is that the faith that allows the body to intertwine with the world is not a choice but the openness operative before any choices become discernible. This is not a faith in the religious sense of belief in a deity that we can opt into or out of; instead, Nishida writes, it is "a faith we cannot lose:"[78] In his very last work, he writes:

> People often confuse religious faith with subjective belief. [. . .] [T]hey even consider faith to be grounded in the subjective power of the will. I maintain, however, that religious faith pertains to something objective, some absolute fact of the self . . . Religious faith involves precisely this dimension wherein the self discovers itself as bottomlessly contradictory identity.[79]

Likewise, Merleau-Ponty thinks of faith not in terms of an option that a subject can take up, or even argue for or against, but as an ineradicable element of the body's relation to the world. Before the philosopher conjectures what the body or the world is, the two are already in dialogue, already open to one another, independent of what the conclusions of reflection might be. In Merleau-Ponty's words:

---

76. Ibid., 51.
77. Ibid., 35–36.
78. Nishida, *An Inquiry into the Good*, 157.
79. Nishida, *Last Writings: Nothingness and the Religious Worldview*, 85.

beneath affirmation and negation, beneath judgment . . . it is our experience, prior to every opinion, of inhabiting the world by our body, of inhabiting the truth by our whole selves, without there being need to choose nor even to distinguish between the assurance of seeing and the assurance of seeing the true, because in principle they are one and the same thing—faith, therefore, and not knowledge, since the world is here not separated from our hold on it, since, rather than affirmed, it is taken for granted, rather than disclosed, it is non-dissimulated, non-refuted.[80]

Faith is a feature of the body's being related through mutual negation with the world. The motor-perceptual body exists outside of itself. Vision, perception, motion, and also faith are ecstatic dimensions of which the human manifestation is but one aspect. To see or to move is not to *decide* to be partly out of control, but is an ongoing relinquishing of control. Merleau-Ponty writes that the "self to which one returns is preceded by an alienated Self or a Self in ec-stasy in Being."[81] An alienated self, a negated or non-self; we can reflect on these but our vision must be indirect, oblique, because when we do focus on these blind spots appear that obstruct the reflective intellect. Thus, we do not abandon reflection but follow Merleau-Ponty in cultivating hyper-reflection (*sur-réflection*) that is "carried outside itself," a reflection that is true "only if it knows itself as reflection on an unreflective experience, and consequently as a change in structure of our existence."[82] To carry reflection outside oneself, beyond the self, as a non-self, this is the change in the structure of existence—from a subject with the illusion of its difference from the object to a negated self at a distanceless-distance with all the phenomenal world. The issue is not whether the outcomes of reflective calculation are accurate or not, but that the reflective intellect is the mode of engagement of the subject, which performs calculations based on finite resources. The body also calculates, but because its dialogue with the world does not invoke binaries that frustrate communication between the two, it has the benefit of drawing on the calculative sway of a much larger and formless volitional and historical agency. To prioritize reflective thought, or to limit philosophy to its principles is to deny the "natural

---

80. Merleau-Ponty, *The Visible and the Invisible*, 28.
81. Ibid., 51.
82. Merleau-Ponty, *Phenomenology of Perception*, 72.

marvels" available when one faithfully allows mutual negation to obtain, and permits the world to move the body. Reading Merleau-Ponty's words below, we get a sense of why granting the world this range is so important for his philosophy:

> These simple acts already enclose the secret of expressive action. As the artist makes his style radiate into the very fibers of the material he is working on, I move my body without even knowing which muscles and nerve paths should intervene, nor where I must look for the instruments of that action. I want to go over there, and here I am, without having entered into the inhuman secret of the bodily mechanism or having adjusted that mechanism to the givens of the problem. For example: without having adjusted the bodily mechanism to the position of a goal defined by its relation to some system of coordinates, I look at the goal, I am drawn by it, and the bodily apparatus does what must be done in order for me to be there. For me, everything happens in the human world of perception and gesture, but my "geographical" or "physical" body submits to the demands of this little drama which does not cease to bring about a thousand natural marvels in it.[83]

The artist does not have to will a special kind of modification into her movements to enact these marvels: this mode of intertwinement is the everyday state of bodily activity, and, by contrast, it is through willing that one constricts their possibilities to the realm of the acting self. These marvels obtain in all movements, yet given the Western propensity toward conceiving of autonomous forms of agency and the world as motor-neutral, the ways the body can interact with and express the world become severely constrained. Cézanne is important because he exhibits a heightened form of the expressive reciprocity that typifies all movement. The many paintings of Mont Sainte Victoire cannot be attributed solely to Cézanne: the mountain expressed itself through the artist's body. It is a risk to allow one's expressive gestures and one's artworks to be co-authored by an invisible source of agency, but the alternative is to remain within the poverty of a strictly

---

83. Merleau-Ponty, "Indirect Language and the Voices of Silence," 103.

subjective orientation to the world. "A sculpture sculpted merely by the eye or a painting painted merely by the eye is incomplete,"[84] writes Nishida. Only by intertwining with the "élan vital" can the artist respond to the "demands infinite development as the basic act underlying all acts."[85] The infinite is reckoned with by a "silent calculus," not the calculation of the reflective intellect.

A phenomenologically expanded context for bodily movement, one that accounts for what is possible when faith enters expression, helps one appreciate the otherwise inexplicable graceful naturalness of Japanese aesthetic practitioners. Yet, difficulties emerge for absorbing these insights into philosophic methodology. Nishida's Eastern forebears were well aware of the paradoxical nature of negating action; certainly, Daoism and Buddhism were traditions founded on facing these quandaries head on. Theory and practice were formulated to address the paradoxical dynamics of a self striving to negate itself, of willing not to will, or of the active attempt to cultivate the various forms of passivity that religious, philosophical, and artistic practice demanded. These concerns are not completely absent from the Western philosophical tradition, but aside from the few exceptions, its thinkers have mostly maneuvered around the paradoxical, contradictory, and tautological. Our French philosopher is an important exception: regarding the central theme of our study, he writes, "[W]hat is strange about this faith is that if we seek to articulate it into theses or statements, if we ask ourselves what is this we, what seeing is, and what thing or world is, we enter into a labyrinth of difficulties and contradictions."[86] Rather than evade these complications, particularly as he approached his last writings, Merleau-Ponty develops a philosophy that embraces these problematics. One such complication is the enigma of willfully attempting to enact a kind of faith that is beyond the reach of the human will.

SPONTANEITY AND NON-WILLING

The paradox of actively willing passivity often arises regarding the subject of spontaneous expression. There is an inherent spontaneity to even the most

---

84. Nishida, *Art and Morality*, 26.
85. Ibid.
86. Merleau-Ponty, *The Visible and the Invisible*, 3.

thought-out and controlled action. Because the body's activity is lined by passivity, and because the world inflects every one of my gestures by way of background solicitations, there is always a spontaneous element even to my most deliberative movements. This notion of spontaneity is not that of the German idealists who were at pains to redeem human freedom in a world where material determination was being made increasingly evident by the physical sciences. What I refer to here in terms of spontaneity might be the opposite, a spontaneity that comes precisely *because of* our being immersed in materiality/objectivity: in the case of the artist, a freedom of expression that comes not in spite of but through one's determination.

Part of being well oriented as an act within an infinite continuity of acts is to relinquish enough control to allow spontaneity to take hold. The paradox is, however, that to will spontaneity is self-defeating.[87] The more one exercises independent volition, the more he obstructs the world's solicitations. If we will too hard, what we strive toward eludes us. As Merleau-Ponty writes, "[v]alues and ideas come forth abundantly for him who, in his meditative life, has learned to free their spontaneity."[88] Nishida also considers the artist in this light: "When inspiration arises in a painter . . . the brush moves spontaneously."[89]

Nothing seems strange about saying "he acted spontaneously," or "she spontaneously did this or that." And yet, as the grammar suggests, this is to predicate action to a subject. This grammatical convention discloses a metaphysical supposition that spontaneity is an act of a human agent. If asked, most people might say that acting spontaneously is one among a variety of forms of human agency that one chooses, which might otherwise include acting carefully, calculatively, deliberately, carelessly, thoughtfully, or recklessly. By contrast, spontaneous action is better understood as the texture of action that obtains as an event of the motorsensory fabric. To think of it as sustained by the choices of an autonomous agent is to abstract movement out of its motor-perceptual embeddedness. Spontaneity is not an action attributable to a subject, but the feature of motion that obtains between a

---

87. One of the conceptual impasses in the emerging research on the "phenomenology of trust" is the self-defeating nature of willing trust. Several authors point out that trust is spontaneous and that if one attempts to will trust, that attempt is self-defeating, i.e. it is not a trusting act, it is a willingness to act despite a lack of trust. See A. Grøn and C. Welz, *Trust, Sociality, Selfhood.*

88. Merleau-Ponty, "Indirect Language and the Voices of Silence," 120.

89. Nishida, *An Inquiry into the Good*, 32.

mutually negated subject and world. Merleau-Ponty says it perfectly when he writes that "spontaneity consists in being in the mode of not-being."[90] Nishida's theory of expression is likewise based on negation:

> The principle of self-negation requires an articulation of the absolutely contradictory identity of that which forms itself expressively, that which is infinitely creative, and that which is created and creates, which is made and makes. The relation between creative and created is then a dynamic interface between that which is expressive (creative) and that which is expressed and which responds expressively (the created).[91]

Spontaneous expression is not a reckless or "anything goes" type of subjective indulgence. This would be to ignore the world's solicitations and the meanings already embedded in the world. When we see untrained spontaneous expression, we are mostly seeing a self whose actions are minimally part of the world's continuity of acts. To express oneself as such is implicitly to assert that I enter the world and change it and create it, but that the world does not enter me and make me. To express oneself meaningfully through spontaneous expression is not to indulge one's subjective desires, but to partially forego them by attuning oneself to the larger expressive desires of the sociohistoric world. "It is a question of knowing how the spontaneous and habitual actions of our bodies are at the same time functions within a system which binds our own expressivity to that of all the others, past, present, and future," writes Marratto.[92] All of our movements involve such a temporally expanded bind; expressive movements that seek to create artworks with new meaning must enact a more demanding task that does not entirely surrender one's own creative desires but allows the world to express itself in the motor-blind spot that punctuates one's own expression. To do so meaningfully requires training the body and the mind, honing movements and developing the ability to perceive and respond to minute details and to move in the subtlest ways. It is not untrained, like Cézanne's approach it is a study, it is to gain the most knowledge and reflective understanding possible, but at the moment of expression to let go

---

90. Merleau-Ponty, *The Visible and the Invisible*, 86.
91. Nishida, *Last Writings: Nothingness and the Religious Worldview*, 103.
92. Marratto, *The Intercorporeal Self: Merleau-Ponty on Subjectivity*, 181.

of everything promised by those endeavors, to have faith that the reflective intellect has done its work and that the body is then able to do its own work in concert with a motor-perceptual world whose contours and history cannot be represented. Expressing oneself in this way is to allow the world to work from inside the body, to guide movements in directions that could never be decided upon or even conceived of in advance. This is the wonder we feel when witnessing highly trained practitioners of spontaneous arts, of which the Japanese *Geidō* practices are paradigmatic. To allow oneself to be negated in the way they demand is potentially frightening because we cling to the idea of a visible and controllable self as the ground of our existence. Yet, as John Sallis writes, when the subject learns to get over "the supporting ground of his pretension to be self-grounding . . . [this] somehow reveals itself in such a way that in his response to it man can come to be sustained by a sustaining source of which he takes himself to be neither the creator nor the master."[93] The world is not inert motionless matter external to the self, nor is one's bodily motion strictly one's own. Motion, like existence, is a self-identity of contradiction. Nishida explains this ambiguity in terms of faith:

> In the depths of the self there is that which transcends the self. And yet it is not something merely external to the self, something merely other than the self. This is the dimension of existential contradiction, about which we are always going astray. Religious faith involves precisely this dimension wherein the self discovers itself as bottomlessly contradictory identity.[94]

In his *Last Writings*, Nishida considers the negation necessary for spontaneous action in the context of religious faith. "A true religion of other-power is required, and this can only be grasped in a logic of self-expression through self-negation."[95] Faith is the willingness to allow the body to be negated such that this other-power moves from within the body: not for other-power to overpower but to "line" self-power. Faith is not the choice of a self to believe in something; it is the structure of negation between self and world.

---

93. John Sallis, "Towards a Movement of Reversal: Science, Technology and the Language of Homecoming," in *Heidegger and the Path of Thinking*, ed. J. Sallis, 142.
94. Nishida, *Last Writings: Nothingness and the Religious Worldview*, 85.
95. Ibid., 102.

To move spontaneously is then not to be subjective, it is to immerse oneself in objectivity, in the sense discussed regarding Nishida. To do so is creativity as making while being made, expressing and being expressed. While one can try to deepen this faith, it is already at the foundation of all expression because, regardless of whether we recognize it, in Merleau-Ponty's decisive formulation, "every relation with being is simultaneously a taking and being taken."[96] We might consider the discipline of highly trained practitioners as aiming at the elusive balance between these two orientations within the world when they move toward spontaneous expressions in their chosen artform. Thus, the spontaneity that is nowhere more palpable than in the sweeping gestures of Sesshū's "Splashed Ink Landscape" evinces his taking as much as his having been taken by the landscape.

The Materiality of Spontaneous Expression: Bernard Leach and Pottery as Throwing-Thrown

Humans have forms of faith that can be elevated or diminished through decisions we make and efforts based thereupon. We seek heightened states of existence and exaltation through religious faith. It is unlikely that other animate beings have these particular kinds of faith, and they are certainly not characteristic of the inanimate world. The worship of deities, acts of religious piety, charity, meditation, prayer, or grace—these are religious practices that distinguish human life from the lives of animals and the world of matter. Prior to this distinction, however, and prior to any effort to accede to, or question faith, our bodies are already in communion with the mundane world. The motorsensory form of faith I have been discussing is, therefore, a feature that arises at the intersection of body and world, and it is thus more primordial than the division between human and non-human beings, or the division between the animate or inanimate world. Faith does not enter the world through humans; rather, it is a possibility given by a world that expresses itself through our bodies. A corporeal form of faith is implicated in the joint-materiality of our bodies and the world. Of course, upholding simple distinctions between the mental or the spiritual and the material will get in the way of appreciating the form of faith I am discussing; nevertheless, I would like to consider some of the dimensions of faith as they are revealed in the material world, if for no other reason than to counter the more prevalent tendency to assume that faith is a subjective disposition

---

96. Merleau-Ponty, *The Visible and the Invisible*, 266.

with little significance for the body or materiality. We are more familiar with faith as an orientation to the divine, toward transcendent beings, saints or bodhisattvas, whom we can worship and through whom we can attain heightened religious experience. But as bodies woven into the world, we also have a kind of faith that connects us to the world's mundane elements and materials: the light, the air, and gravity, as well as the earth and the mud from which we emerge and into which we return.

While spontaneity has been a grounding principle of East-Asian aesthetic practice for thousands of years, it has only been taken up relatively recently in the West. As Daniel Belgrad contends in his book *The Culture of Spontaneity*, the post-war American Avant-Garde attempted to resist the enormous psychological pressure to conform within growing rationalization, bureaucratization, capitalism, and neoliberal economics, by cultivating less constricted forms of subjectivity through spontaneous forms of expression.

Although Bernard Leach (1887–1979) might be one of the lesser-known figures of this movement, his work provides an intercultural opportunity for exploring the material side of faithful and spontaneous expression. Leach is interesting for the fame he achieved, given that he worked in a medium traditionally not included as a fine art in the West. Leach was a British potter, but his practice grew out of the Japanese Zen Buddhist traditions of pottery and tea ceremony, which have always been included within the Japanese canon of fine arts and practiced for their religious and philosophic import. Leach was born in Hong Kong, traveled extensively throughout Asia, and trained in Japan for eleven years. His practice was forged within the Japanese tradition, yet he developed his project in response to the concerns facing post-war America. Even after settling in the United States his practice continued to serve as a conduit for East–West dialogue. He would frequently visit and teach in Japan, and helped promote and exhibit the work of important Japanese potters (Sōetsu Yanagi, Shoji Hamada) whom he hosted and toured with in America. He also translated a collection of Yanagi's essays on aesthetics, which appears under its English title as *The Unknown Craftsman*. Leach was an important emissary of Japanese culture and helped initiate what remains an under-appreciated but considerable uptake of Zen Buddhist aesthetics by the American Avant-Garde.

Leach's life and practice offers not only an excellent example for exploring the material dimensions of spontaneous and faithful expression, further, it can be read according to Nishida and Merleau-Ponty's theories of faith and expression. Leach conceived of clay as a medium capable of recording the body's spontaneous impulses. The textures, markings, curvatures, and grooves of the plates and pots he threw were not just self-sufficient art qualities; they also expressed how his spontaneous body was brought to presence while interacting with clay. A positivist understanding of his body and the materials he worked with might assume that the potter enters and exits the studio more or less "as is," whereas clay is inert matter whose material form is transformed by the potter. This assumption, however, ignores the bidirectionality and reversibility of determination between body and world, and thereby mistakes the nature of expression. In interexpression, by contrast, the potter inhabits the clay's motor-perceptual negation while forming the clay's body, and at the same time the clay forms the potter's body by reaching into and inhabiting its negation. This is the "making-made" aspect of interexpression expounded by Nishida. The potter's body does not merely throw clay, but, we might say, it is actually thrown by the clay throughout a lifetime's work. The potter expresses himself through his work, but the clay also expresses itself through the potter's body. This is enabled according to Nishida's "predicate logic," where the potter's body becomes a predicate of the clay itself.

To overlook the ways in which clay forms the potter's body is to miss the reversibility of determination between body and world, and thereby mistakes the nature of expression. The etymology of the term "expression" (*exprimere*) suggests that something internal is "pressed out" into the "external world." Yet, as Schultz explains, "expression transpire[s] between the artist and the material medium, implying that the artist's subjectivity, as distinct from the so-called 'external world,' is not the sole origin of expression. Rather, the material the artist works with finds expression through its participation in the artist's vision."[97] Thus, in the context of a reversible inter-expressive relation, the potter makes the pot, but at the same time the pot, its very materiality, makes the body of the potter by way of its particular solicitations and motor-demands. It does so by constraining the movements in ways specific to its materiality. If a potter is too deliberative with her materials, if she thinks too much, hesitates, or tries to rework them, the clay instantly shows her through its body that it has been mistreated, and that the intertwinement has gone wrong. If the potter misses the appropriate balance between deliberation and spontaneity, the jug will tilt slightly to one side, look unbalanced or over-worked. This is not a verbal language, but is nevertheless the way materiality expresses itself. Because the wheel does not stop spinning, if one

---

97. Schultz, "Creative Climate Expressive Media in the Aesthetics of Watsuji, Nishida, and Merleau-Ponty," 64.

becomes too wrapped up in deliberative reflection, its revolutions count off the potter's hesitations. It thus demands a different balance of reflection and spontaneity than other materials would and elicits the appropriate orientation from the potter's body through its material language.

Learning to throw clay involves going through a long corporeal dialogue with the material, where one learns to read its motor-perceptual language and the requirements specific to its materiality. The way that clay needs to be treated, and the way these needs constrain the possible movements the material will accept, are the contours of the motorsensory negation clay affords the human body. As one learns how the material constrains the creation of a properly finished piece, the potter comes to know the way her movements correspond to how the clay interacts with gravity, the centrifugal forces of the wheel, the speed at which clay dries, how it holds itself up or bends or bows slightly while rotating, how it accepts some of the potter's interventions and rejects others. Gaining proficiency with clay involves not simply *knowing* these features, but allowing them to express one's own body. There is a term called "potter's body" that describes the posture and bodily idiosyncrasies of someone who has worked clay for a lifetime. The term perfectly captures the bodily side of taking-being-taken, expressing-expressed, making-being-made by the world that is essential for illuminating the bi-directionality of expression in both Nishida and Merleau-Ponty's philosophies. Although the potter's way of effecting clay is much more immediate, "potter's body" shows us that the human body becomes a medium for clay to express itself in the non-clay world.

If we consider clay in this inter-expressive context we can discern its motor-demands and its effects on the potter's body. Other materials might dry much faster and prevent any interaction altogether, whereas if they dried much slower they would not constrain the artist's movements enough, and might permit more deliberation, thereby not eliciting the artist's spontaneity. Clay has a very narrow tolerance for volitional orientations toward it, but is nonetheless still workable, and contrary to other mediums that allow for correction, erasing, and reworking, clay's very materiality functions in dialogue with the body to bring out a particular motor-perceptual orientation that other materials would not. As Belgrad writes, clay in particular is "an ideal medium for the enactment of a 'conversation' between the artist's will, the artist's unconscious, and the material environment, a guiding principle of the aesthetic of spontaneity."[98] As opposed to painting, certain forms of

---

98. Daniel Belgrad, *The Culture of Spontaneity: Improvisation and the Arts in Postwar America*, 165.

sculpture, drawing, and especially digital art—which allows for potentially infinite reworking—the particularity of clay reaches into the volitional negation the potter's body holds open, and occasions a spontaneous form of expression. It draws this orientation out of the body that engages it. In learning to listen to clay's materiality, that is, in going deeper into the mutual negation between body and clay, the potter is attuning himself to the particular way volition and faith take shape in this material. The properly turned pot is the mode of expression of clay indicating that the potter has achieved the volitional orientation clay demands. But because expression is more than a one-way determination, the clay also expresses the potter's body in a specific way. To become a potter over years of practice is to have faith to allow the motor demands of clay to determine the body. To do this for a lifetime is to strengthen certain muscles, elongate some tendons and tighten others; it is to give the body certain lines, a certain posture and a way of holding things in the hands, and it is to acquire specific sensorimotor habits toward material objects in general. The potter learns about more than her own body, her practice is wider than a study of clay; she becomes part of an inter-expressive event that takes shape when these two particular bodies move together through negation. The positivist describes this as expression—as the potter throwing clay. An account in tune with the dynamics of mutual negation would describe this as interexpression, as making while being made, throwing clay while being thrown by it.

The Fallacy of Motor-Perceptual Neutrality and Uni-Directional Expression

Part of the difficulty in appreciating how our body's relation to the world enacts a sensorimotor form of faith comes by way of that connection being so seamless and seldom interrupted that we do not notice this important feature of body–world relationality. If everybody were a potter from birth we would not notice "potter's body." But, what about our body as it is stylized by the everyday forces that express itself through our bodies? We do not notice how the body is expressed by the forces that are almost never foreign to it. It is easy enough to notice when we choose to use our bodies to express ourselves in the world but it is more difficult to discern how the particular world we are woven into expresses our bodies in particular ways. Further, the dominant Western worldview inclines us strongly toward conceiving of our connection to the world as being mental, rational, cognitive, or rational; not bodily and not faithful. Yet, by making visible some of the most basic features of our body–world relationality including light, even gravity, space and matter, we can appreciate how our bodies are determined by the specificities of the world we inhabit: how we are expressions of the world itself. Making this aspect shift to focus not on ourselves as the only expressive features of the world, to see how the everyday forces express us might make features of mundane terrestrial existence seem strange or alien, but if the thought experiment is successful, it could allow us to appreciate how faith is not incidental to the other take-for-granted forces that permeate our everyday world. Most important of all is that this view might disabuse us of a notion of freedom derived from our understanding space and light as non-motor-perceptual intervals or mediums, which ignores features of body–world relationality we are better to acknowledge if we want to grow and move in harmony with the natural world.

We are not free to move our bodies however we desire, nor can the artist choose whatever materials he wants in order to move or gesture spontaneously. One might think that an artist could make similar gestures with other materials or tools. That the hair of the beaver's pelt is just as good at outlining deciduous trees as strands from the marten's feathers. This, however, perpetuates the mistaken belief that action is the property of a subject against a material world that is volitionally neutral. Because bodily movement is an event of an inter-expressive fabric, the specificity of certain movements is only possible in conjunction with the peculiarities of certain materials. Thus, as the Chinese painting tradition develops amazing complexity, so too does its tools. And because all motion has a material aspect, because there is no motor-perceptual vacuum, the particular negation materials have dictates the body's range of possible motions.

Whether the paper is rough or smooth, how tightly woven the canvas or silk are, the length and rigidity of the brush hairs, the speed at which different inks dry, these are all particularities that demand different treatments, and thus evoke different bodily movements. Thus, van Briessen writes, "the material at hand forces the artist to adopt a particular technique through its limitations as much as through its qualities."[99] But, we can take this one step farther. Different materials also bring out different selves. The *Yujian* method, the tools and techniques it dictated, which Sesshū adopted, evoked a "voided selfhood" from the artist. To choose one's tools and one's paper is not inconsequential to the religious dimensions of expression. Referring to the Southern Song's preference for rough paper over fine silk, van Briessen writes that this "paper (this style, in other words) demands greater taste,

---

99. van Briessen, *Way of the Brush*, 183.

greater self-control—a sort of spiritual discipline, in fact."[100] To enable his spontaneous expression, Sesshū painted with a heavy, ink-filled brush, and chose rough, unsized paper rather than following the Chinese convention of using silk, a material that tended to evoke expression that appeared calculated and detailed. Sesshū's tools and materials were not insignificant to his chosen mode of expression. His paper did not simply "capture" his spontaneity as much as evoke it.

If one can allow that bodily movements are implicated in the materiality of objects in these ways, one might nonetheless assume that there is a type of movement free of material constraints. The idea could be that only when engaging with a foreign material—clay, paint, or marble—does matter dictate one's motions, and that one's everyday actions are not constrained in such a way because they are merely subject to gravity, space, or light. But this is to misconstrue the body's relation to the world, and to commit what we might consider as a fallacy of motor-perceptual neutrality.

We are immersed in a field of near uniform motorsensory forces from the time we leave the womb. Air, gravity, and light are for the most part constant throughout our lives. As a result, we do not notice how our bodies extend throughout our environments as an expression of *their* particularity; we can get through the day without having to take into account how we are entangled with the world of motion and perception. Just as light becomes invisible because the body intertwines with it to such an unadulterated extent, so air and gravity are also such all-encompassing mediums through which the ecstatic body seamlessly extends that they also become invisible and appear motor-perceptually neutral, as though they were inconsequential to how the body moves or grows. What we need to develop the notion of a bi-direction making-made form of expression is to consider the forces of light, gravity, and air as acts within a continuity of acts that include the body.

When I asked a class of studio artists what materials and tools they work with, no one mentioned light, gravity, air, space, or time, despite having named some of these as *themes* they worked on. Nor did any of them name their own body as one of their tools or materials. While overlooking the body as one of the artist's tools is understandable, the omission concerning light, gravity, air, etc., happens, I would argue, for similar reasons: because they are *features of* the body according to its phenomenal definition. As we have seen, once something is intertwined into the extended definition of one's corporeity, it becomes forgotten and invisible. Just as the body need

---

100. Ibid., 186.

not be specified, neither does the body's ecstatic reach through light and air or its being constrained by gravity. Part of the work of the artist, as Merleau-Ponty defines it, is to make these invisible aspects, through which the body extends, visible.

If we immerse ourselves in a field with a different density and motor-pull, one that might also obstruct motion and perception in different ways—if we jump in a pool, or out of a plane, fall in quicksand, or somehow experience weightlessness, for example—the new set of forces we would be immersed in would not remain invisible. If we were to remain in these fields as moving-perceiving bodies for long enough, their materiality and forces would express themselves through our bodies giving them a different form than those we have in our normal field of forces and matter. The key point is that to change to any of these different fields is not to go from a neutral or "natural" motor-perceptual vacuum to a modified "foreign" motor-perceptual medium: the body is always immersed in and dispersed throughout materiality. We simply do not recognize the everyday conditions of materiality we are normally immersed within as expressing the body and giving it its form just as we do not notice the tools such as the glasses on our face or the pen when writing. Yet, like tools, so do gravity, light, and air extend the definition of the body while determining its shape and capacities.

It is easy to think of the body as an expression of a strictly internal determinative principle, our DNA. Thus, the body develops and takes on its form as a uni-directional determination of our genetic material. Nishida's notion of inter-expression shows us that the body is also given its form as an expression of the material through which it extends, by the environment it lives in and how its particular forces constrain and enable certain motions. Any subjective orientation, faith included, is part of this inter-expressive relation and, thus, not a subjective imposition onto a motorperceptually neutral medium. Faith cannot arise in a human acting in the world unless it is—like perception and motion—an event transcending the boundaries between body and world. Just as the clay elicits a certain character of motion from our bodies, our everyday field of materials and forces also determines a way of moving that would be different if gravity were slightly stronger, if air were more dense, or if light did not travel so fast. To exercise faith, then, or to act spontaneously, is not a possibility that exists in the human body that is then introduced into the nonhuman or material world. All expression is made possible, constrained, and solicited by the character of the particular material medium through which the body extends. Because we are in an inter-expressive relation of making and being made, we would have different bodies if they were always immersed in fields of different material forces: if they were acts in a different continuity of acts. While the body ranges through air, light, and gravity so seamlessly, those materials and forces determine what kind of body we have and the character of its movements. Just as the potter has "potter's body" by way of interexpression after a lifetime of work, we might consider ourselves as having "air-density1.2kg/m^3—gravity 9.8m/s^2—light299792km/s-bodies" because we are in an interexpressive relation with an environment with these specific forces. To see different possible forms given to a body by its immersion in a different field of material forces, one can consider the different motions of bodies moving underwater, in outer space, or in the dark.

It would be a mistake to think that when we enter a foreign environment, the body goes from a prior motor-neutral position to a body that is only then constrained by the demands of a specific new medium. Nevertheless, we have names for the style of bodies we have in these different fields of material forces. We "swim" in water, "float" in space, and "navigate" through the dark, for example. Because the ecstatic negation of our normal field of material forces is so perfect and seamless, we do not have a word to refer to the body's "style" in its normal terrestrial mode. That mode is simply the "natural" or "human" way of being a body. One of the great things that Nishida and Merleau-Ponty offer is a better understanding of our bodies by bringing this invisible field of ecstatic materiality into visibility. If successful, one should be able to see and feel how one is immersed in a field of materiality, to feel oneself a part of a motor-perceptual fabric, just as one would realize this if they were all of a sudden immersed in water or propelled into outer space. By bringing one's ecstatic relation with this material field into focus, the faith the body has in the world also comes into relief.

It might seem reasonable to think that while people can be more or less faithful, the material world is inconsequential with respect to faith. However, just as humans can express themselves with greater or lesser degrees of faith, so too can the material world. To assume otherwise would require a kind of sensorimotor faith or spontaneity that exists independent of the material conditions through which the body extends. But we only have faith to the extent that the body pervades and is permeated by the material world. Certain materials are better at expressing how they elicit and manifest faith. To have achieved dexterity with paintbrushes, chisels, paint or paper is not simply to have acquired a set of intellectual skills that can be taken up or discarded at will; it is also to have allowed a material to embed its expressive particularities in one's body. This is not a possibility only for those who have chosen to engage with specific materials in art practice: despite appearing "natural" and not stylized in any particular way, our everyday body is also an inter-expressive entity, making and being made by its material surroundings. If somebody who grew up in a different motor-perceptual environment were to come to ours for the first time, she might notice that our movements are stylized by virtue of being co-constituted for a lifetime in the particular terrestrial conditions and uniform field of forces by which we grew up.

Just as certain humans are predisposed to particular forms of expression, more predisposed to allowing a certain material to pattern their bodies, so different materials are better or worse at bringing faith to a more heightened and visible expression. Clay, by way of its particular manner of negating and being negated by the body, brings faith to a greater visibility than, say, concrete or plastic. Materiality is not motor-perceptually neutral and is not simply something that we have faith *in*: the relation is intransitive—it goes both ways. Artists can read their body's faith through materials, tools, and a landscape that solicits particular gestures. If a painter must have faith in the world, then that world must be such that it can both accept what the artist puts into it, while through its own negation reciprocate with the worldly end required of that faith. What obtains is not purely the expression of human faith, but the interexpression of two bodies intertwining with each other, of two bodies entering into the negation each holds open for the other, which makes an imprint of this faith *on both bodies*. The pot could not have come about without the artist, but neither could the artist be this exact kind of artist if a particular material did not have a way of determining the body. Clay does not merely solicit a set of movements from inside the artist's body only when throwing the clay, but over time it actually gives the artist a particular body he or she will carry in all relations in the world. For the potter's body, clay remains present even in its absence, and so too for the artist and the pot. It might take less time for humans to throw a piece of clay, but the clay nevertheless throws the human body, just at a different scale, over a lifetime of practice.

There is no matter that is neutral concerning perception or motion, nor is it in relation to faith. Which is to say that there is nothing encounterable external to the motor-perceptual fabrics of flesh and *Basho*. When we do not have a good means of reading how our faith permeates the world, different kinds of matter can register that faith and present it back to us as evidence that our bodies relate to the world through reciprocal interexpression. Clay happens to be a particularly good medium to demonstrate how the body makes while being made, and although pottery is not considered the finest of the arts, it nevertheless shows that the most everyday and mundane material—not a divine or transcendent being, but even mud—enables the body's faithful communion with the world.

Spontaneity and the Temporality of Risk

To the extent that pre-determined artistic techniques prescribe movements for depicting objects, we can consider the authors of painting manuals as weaving the sensorimotor world of the artist with constraints, which might appear to limit spontaneity or reduce the need for faith. If there is a rule for depicting mountains and waters, to follow that rule is to reduce risk and, *ipso facto*, to reduce at least an ontic form of faith. With the enormous weight of tradition, with so many manuals dictating how expressive activity should be conducted, how difficult must it have been as a Chinese landscape painter to express himself with even a small measure of spontaneity? It would be almost impossible to find any aesthetic traditions with such a profound history. Before landscape painting was even a discipline in the West, the Chinese already had long-established institutions, meticulously codified practices, systems of apprenticeship, patronage, technical standards, conventions regarding symbolism, metaphor, as well as manuals that prescribed the minutiae of expressive techniques we have been discussing. While the art world evolved at a pace that makes innovation almost undiscernible, nevertheless, around the late eleventh century the so-called "literati" painters broke away from the Northern "academic" school to establish what we now know as the Southern Song School of Landscape Painting. Among artists such as Ma Yuan, Mi Fu, Wang Wei and Guo Xi, they began a tradition that departed from the Southern focus on accurate rendering of objects and cultivated spontaneous techniques aiming at a lyrical treatment of nature, using abstraction, and abbreviation for poetic effect. The painters of the "literati" tradition pursued a highly aestheticized life and their works evoke the transient beauty read in the great Chinese poetry of the time. The philosophical orientation informing their practice was equal measures Daoism and the Neo-Confucian philosophy of Zhu Xi, who advocated the ideal of a tranquil and detached mind free of defilements with the mundane world enabling one to respond naturally and spontaneously to its vicissitudes.

Although the distinction between the Northern and Southern schools would not have been well-known to Sesshū in Japan, nevertheless art historians have commented that while many of his paintings conform to Northern conventions, his "Splashed Ink Landscape" (see figure 3.1) is an exception in that it tends more toward the spontaneous poetic suggestion of the Southern school. Of course, this was not an anything-goes type of spontaneity. Sesshū would have remained constrained by Chinese conventions and innovated within exceedingly tight constraints. Van Briessen captures it well (and with a grammatical chiasm) when he describes Sesshū's practice as "spontaneous carefulness and careful spontaneity."[101]

The movements that we tend to notice and reflect upon are the more deliberative and careful rather than spontaneous actions. We act deliberatively and reflectively in the sense that when given a task, we often first decide how we will act—possibly by representing to ourselves how we would like the outcome to appear—before moving into the action we hope will bring about the best correspondence between desired and actual outcome. In this case, thought and action follow a sequential temporality. We first represent the outcome in thought, and then we act. A different temporal order occurs with spontaneous action. In spontaneity, thought and action are simultaneous. One of the better examples of spontaneous action—musical improvisation—exhibits a simultaneity of composition and expression. As one improvises, the *composition* of gestures, words, or notes occurs at the same time as their *expression*. An initial composition is not first formulated and then in the next instant an improvised expression follows. This would not be improvisation. To import an idea from an earlier moment takes the artist out of the present and out of the spontaneous mode of expression. As Merleau-Ponty explains, " '[c]onception' cannot precede 'execution.' "[102] Thus, to express oneself spontaneously is to relinquish a certain amount of control. To improvise successfully is to express oneself, but is equally to lend one's body as an instrument for the other musicians in the band. While improvising one is immersed in an environment of what Krueger calls "musical affordances," where musicians do not simply express what they desire, but through "musicking-in-listening" the composition arises beyond the circumscribable confines of any single body. Elberfeld, who speaks of a "musically extended body" explains that when performing "any reflection on the (musical) situation would disturb the liveliness of the event itself"[103] To reflect on or represent what will come of expression, in the next note or the

---

101. Ibid.

102. Merleau-Ponty, "Cézanne's Doubt," 184.

103. "Elberfeld, "*Handelnde Anschauung (kōiteki chokkan): Nishida und die Praxis der Künste*," 324.

next chord, signals an attempt to reduce risk. By contrast, in spontaneous expression the artist enters into a movement or gesture without knowledge or full control of what will obtain. Expression arises from the "musically extended" body. To express oneself from this ecstatic position is inherently risky because one cannot see where she is going before she gets there. Thus, another form of blindness punctuates expressive action. In *Ishiki no mondai* Nishida writes:

> Even in artistic intuition [the totality] is not merely suddenly given; it is not realized as it is. The artist goes through a process of seeing things step by step; a process of improving the totality. Therefore, we can say, with Bergson, that even the artist himself does not know how the work will turn out.[104]

Similarly, when elaborating the preconceptual inherence of the body in the world as "perceptual faith," Merleau-Ponty uses the language of trust to describe a similar blindness instituted by virtue of moving as part of a larger volitional totality. He writes: "we know neither what exactly is this order and this concordance of the world to which we thus entrust ourselves."[105] Trust is required because the blindness is such that we cannot know beforehand in full clarity "what the enterprise will result in, nor even if it is really possible,"[106] yet we still move, act, and express ourselves. Nishida's is not far from Merleau-Ponty when in *Art and Morality* he invokes a similar blindness in relation to the final outcome of spontaneous expression. When the artist is fully immersed in "the horizon of pure visual perception," Nishida contends, "he spontaneously moves the organs of his whole body and becomes one expressive movement. At this time, . . . the artist himself cannot foretell the direction and meaning of his own expressive act."[107] In such a situation, the artist "does not know what his creation will be . . . he sees through action."[108] Implicit in both Nishida and Merleau-Ponty's understanding of spontaneous expression is an element of risk. If artists or performers express themselves on the basis of a pre-given representation, they might achieve what they are aiming for, and it might even turn out better than expected;

---

104. Nishida, *Fundamental Problems*, 69.
105. Merleau-Ponty, *The Visible and the Invisible*, 39.
106. Ibid.
107. Nishida, *Art and Morality*, 48, 49.
108. Nishida, *Fundamental Problems*, 69.

nevertheless, to approach their art in such a way means that the body moves according to a temporality different from that which is operative in a spontaneous form of expression, and the pre-given representation seeks to reduce an aspect of risk. This temporal relation closes the artist off from the "infinite" that is accessible when they risk allowing an expressive body to intertwine freely with an expressive world.

It is not simply that one *does not know*, but that one *cannot know* what the painting will turn out like if one operates on the level of creating new forms of visibility and proceeding in acceptance of a constitutive motor-blindness. Art practice is true to the world not because one's reflective intellect knows what to expect, but instead, as Sallis writes, because the artist "plays an unknowing play [*unwissend Spiel*] with ultimate things, and yet it reaches them."[109] He further describes, quite beautifully, how Klee's practice risked expression within a temporal form of blindness:

> [I]n order to be successful, it is essential never to work toward an image already envisioned in advance. Rather, one must give oneself completely to the developing portion of the area to be painted. Here Klee makes it clear how decisively his sense of artistic creation differs from the ancient model of techne: in artistic creation it is not a matter of having the work in view—in the mind's eye, as we say—in advance so as then simply to materialize it in the actual artwork, which would thus come to be made precisely in the image of the paradigm envisaged in advance and directive throughout the creative process. It is not a matter of a vision prior to the production of the work but rather of a vision that only emerges as the work itself takes shape. Thus, artistic creation is not determined nor governed by a concept or image of what is to be created. An artwork is not simply a translation: artistic production does not merely translate into material form an idea of an image envisioned independently and in advance of the creative activity that brings the work forth.[110]

The blindness the artist must contend with exhibits the structure of *Fundierung* as Merleau-Ponty interprets in Husserl's philosophy. The artist

---

109. Sallis, *Paul Klee*, 19.
110. Ibid.

cannot see the artwork beforehand because she is not prior to that artwork but arises in the same moment. Accordingly, Merleau-Ponty proposes that "the originator is not primary . . . and the originated is not simply derived from it, since it is through the originated that the originator is made manifest."[111]

To express oneself artistically is to risk allowing composition to arise simultaneous with expression, and to allow the self as artist to arise simultaneous with the artwork. To do so involves foregoing the reflective intellect's propensity to ensure that action will correspond with a desired outcome. It is to launch oneself into an intertwinement with the motor-perceptual world such that action occurs as a negotiation between one's body and the world. Entering into any situation—be it expressive, ethical, or performative, to respond to the world's infinite demands, and act without a fully visible model of how action should manifest—demands a somatic faith where part of the action's initiation lies outside of the body in an invisible source of motion beyond one's ability to represent, to know, or to control. Faith is to move with this invisible volitional agent: "Faith," Merleau-Ponty writes, "is in things unseen."[112]

The Limits of Reflection and Doubt: The Pre-Reflective and the Necessity of Faith

To reflect upon or to doubt one's movements, one's choices, or one's gestures can be appropriate in many situations, in scientific, philosophic, and artistic expression. The extent to which the methodologies based on reflection and doubt are nearly beyond reproach, and so deeply engrained in our worldview, attests to the amazing advances they have enabled. Nevertheless, we must be very careful when these become the unquestioned foundation of philosophical inquiry. "A philosophy of reflection, as methodic doubt," Merleau-Ponty argues, is "a reduction of the openness upon the world to 'spiritual acts,' to intrinsic relations between the idea and its ideate."[113] While such a reduction might serve many important purposes, in the context of artistic expression a methodological reduction to reflection and doubt is "thrice untrue," according to Merleau-Ponty: "untrue to the visible world,

---

111. Merleau-Ponty, *Phenomenology of Perception*, 458.
112. Merleau-Ponty, "Faith and Good Faith," in *Sense and Non-Sense*, 176.
113. Merleau-Ponty, *The Visible and the Invisible*, 39.

to him who sees it, and to his relations with the other 'visionaries.' "[114] Implicit in visual experience as Nishida and Merleau-Ponty construe it are similar bids to go beyond doubt and reflection, beyond the mainstays of philosophic methodology to search out an appropriate deportment toward the pre-reflective moment of experience.

A danger of the reflective approach is that its amazing efficacy in limited domains can lead to the belief that not only is the world revealed by reflective intellection, but that the world also corresponds to its expectations and, therefore, solicits that particular approach. According to Merleau-Ponty, the "real" is not that which corresponds to the expectations of the reflective intellect, but is precisely that which exceeds those expectations. The real is the perceptual openness prior to affirmations and negations. It is, in Merleau-Ponty's words, "the prepossession of a totality which is there before one knows how and why."[115] At this level, where the body is first open to the world, before reflection intervenes is a world "whose realizations are never what we would have imagined them to be, and which nonetheless fulfills a secret expectation within us, since we believe in it tirelessly."[116]

Merleau-Ponty derives his notion of faith partly from Husserl's *Urdoxa*.[117] As Henry Maldiney explains, the real is not what is expected but is *para doxan*, that is, contrary to one's expectations: "The real is essentially what one does not expect, what transcends all that is possible, all recourse to the same. Each time, its appearance exceeds a lack of knowledge."[118] What is fully visible to the reflective intellect fools us into thinking it is entirely definitive of the real. But because the body is already continuously-discontinuous with nature prior to our reflecting upon it, once we articulate that relation, we are already adding something that occludes the relation. Our most primordial orientation is not as a reflective intellect cognizing a rational world that corresponds to our expectations, but rather as a body pervading the depths of nature, and an act caught up in a continuity of acts that always exceeds one's knowledge and expectations, and therefore demands a form of faith underlying unrestricted reflection and doubt.

---

114. Ibid.
115. Ibid., 42.
116. Ibid.
117. See Merleau-Ponty, *Husserl at the Limits of Phenomenology*, 165.
118. Henry Maldiney, "Flesh and Verb in the Philosophy of Merleau-Ponty," 56.

Faith is necessary for exploring the pre-reflective moment because of its counter-expectational character. Merleau-Ponty and Nishida seek to learn from artistic expression because it appears that some artists have worked out an appropriate non-reflective orientation to the aspect of reality that is unexpected and partially occluded. To remain within the reflective moment and explore it according to methodological doubt would be to drastically limit philosophy and put out of bounds the body's first and most fundamental truth. To turn one's back on this moment is to accept what Merleau-Ponty calls the "dogmatism of reflection" which "we know only too well where it goes, since with it philosophy concludes the moment it begins and, for this very reason, does not make us comprehend our own obscurity."[119] Artistic practice is, therefore, not just an aesthetic concern but a model for philosophic methodology because artists have advanced methodologies for bringing the body–world relation into relief as it obtains before reflection and as it appears prior to being submitted to doubt.

Merleau-Ponty uses several terms to refer to a philosophic mode of inquiry that finds its origins in this aspect of his analysis of artistic expression. "Hyper-reflection" (*sur-réflexion*), "radical-reflection" (*réflexion radicale*) and "interrogation" (*interrogation*)[120] are alternatives to the purely reflective approach to philosophic inquiry. Like artists, philosophers must risk beginning inquiry with the admission that they "do not even know in advance what

---

119. Merleau-Ponty, *The Visible and the Invisible*, 39.

120. "Interrogation" has a similar temporality in relation to expression as Merleau-Ponty's notion of "parole parlée." The distinction between "parole parlée" (spoken language) and "parole parlante" (speaking language) places language in the context of the temporality of expression being discussed. Parole Parlée is a way of speaking where one relies on language already spoken and meaning already developed. One has, we might say, a representation of the particular expression and its effects. A saying has been said before, and one re-presents that saying. It is less risky because one already has a sense of how expression will play itself out, having seen it already operate in the world. Parole parlante, which does not rely on already-spoken expression, does not have the luxury of knowing how this or that was said or heard in the past. In this case, there is no prior model or representation of an expression or its effects. This type of expression is "poetic," according to Merleau-Ponty. "It must be poetry; that is, it must completely awaken and recall our sheer power of expressing beyond things already said or seen." In this case, the speaker is oriented toward the future and engages with the act of creating meaning, rather than re-presenting it.

our interrogation itself and our method will be."[121] Alternatively, to be fixed ahead of time within the constraints of a positive methodology means that "[t]he manner of questioning prescribes a certain kind of response, and to fix it now would be to decide our solution."[122] That solution, rather than giving access to the real, actually blocks access to it, insofar as the real is constituted beyond its positivity and beyond what is immediately visible or representable. Like the artist, the philosopher too is caught up in this world and must evolve their methodologies beyond the limitations of reflection and doubt to include a practice of faith and even allow a measure of spontaneous expression into philosophy, or, more precisely, to acknowledge the measure of spontaneity that has always been there insofar as philosophy too is a mode of expression, one that is also worldly and thus operates beyond the philosopher's full control despite reflection and doubt leading us to believe otherwise.

Faith, Negation, and Volition in the Pre-Reflective

Although their philosophies problematize how we conceive of the relations between philosophy, art, and religion, neither Nishida nor Merleau-Ponty question whether we can or should continue doing philosophy *qua* philosophy. They focus on artistic expression because it uncovers elements of philosophic expression that are deeply problematic. The paradoxes of engaging the pre-reflective world beyond doubt, where the necessity of faith appears, raise a set of difficulties that Western philosophy has been reluctant to address until recently. To question the reflective approach, to attempt to theorize about or even sustain a pre-reflective orientation within the world appears to be self-defeating. If spontaneous or pre-reflective experience institutes this and numerous other problems, why not abandon them altogether and accept that philosophy has come up against a limit, and cannot be productively oriented toward the invisible, the negative, or the absent? Maybe the faith that would overcome these dilemmas is, properly speaking, non-philosophic, religious, or more appropriately left for artistic and poetic exploration. Merleau-Ponty intimates that this is

---

121. Merleau-Ponty, *The Visible and the Invisible*, 158.
122. Ibid.

his concern when he asks, "[s]ince the perceptual faith is a paradox, how could I remain with it?"[123] Yet, he does think philosophy can and should take up the challenge as art and literature have. He recognizes in Proust's "little phrase" an intimation of the paradoxes of expression: "[e]ach time we want to get at it immediately, or lay hands on it, or circumscribe it, or see it unveiled, we do in fact feel that the attempt is misconceived, that it retreats in the measure that we approach."[124] These questions are not merely a literary concern for Merleau-Ponty. His philosophy seeks to learn from the responses to the paradoxes encountered in literary or artistic expression. Since a purely intellectual approach can impede access to some of the most important valences of embodiment, of language, and of expression, philosophy must incorporate a methodological form of faith if it is to promote learning in any of these areas. To do otherwise is to ignore the absent and the invisible, to remain positivist, and to remain within the metaphysics of presence. It is to disregard the constitutive obstructions that limit motion and perception and thus also to forego the generativity that comes when thinking or artistic expression operates within their tension. Merleau-Ponty and Nishida are not willing to forsake the philosophical mode of inquiry, yet nor are they willing to remain positivist by turning their backs on the invisible, or remain merely "philosophic" by disregarding art and faith on a methodological level.

Whether philosophy can be productively oriented toward the pre-reflective is only a problem if there is a prior commitment to the notion of a pure philosophy as opposed to religion and art, and pure doubt unadulterated by faith: distinctions that might appear to protect the integrity of the discipline, but which actually significantly limit its meaning and scope. Nishida and Merleau-Ponty hold that philosophy cannot be so limited, and should accept the methodological ambiguities to engage the problematics of the negative and the orientation they demand, which includes dealing with the pre-reflective and accommodating a concept of faith within philosophic practice.

Faith might appear menacing to Western philosophy if it maintains a dualist metaphysics and sticks to a not entirely nuanced distinction between reflection and spontaneity. Many of the philosophers who theorize about the various paradoxes of expression—including Nishida and Merleau-Ponty, as

---

123. Ibid., 31.
124. Ibid., 150.

well as Heidegger and Dōgen—advocate thinking beyond this too simple dichotomy. Although its status is challenged, reflection does not have to be abandoned in the act of faith. The belief that we reject reflection in pursuing the pre-reflective marks one of the key difficulties in seeing how philosophy can approach the negative aspects of experience.[125] Yet, there is no pure reflection devoid of spontaneity. Reflection is not purely active. Even philosophers think and speak within a world that constrains and elicits what can be thought and said. Ideas come to us passively from a source that transcends us, and we string words together in complex patterns we could not achieve if we had to reflect on each word. Like movement, reflection is never a singularly human event performed by a wholly autonomous agent. Reflection is a worldly phenomenon too, solicited by other events, other minds, infused with randomness, never entirely under human control. Because reflection happens in a world, it too has a valence of spontaneity. On the other hand, even when we are in so-called "flow" experiences, the ideal spontaneous mode, we are still actively deliberating, calculating and making decisions. For Merleau-Ponty it is not just the artist who is out of control, but in all expression there is "a spontaneity which will not take orders, not even those which I would like to give myself."[126] Philosophy and science are not exceptions; they are possibly the two modes of expression, which more than any others have ignored the spontaneous core of reflection. What Merleau-Ponty calls "radical reflection" and "hyper reflection" are ways of being oriented to the full spectrum of what the world elicits from the body. "Radical reflection," he explains, "consists, paradoxically enough, in recovering

---

125. Toadvine, "The Silence of Nature and the Emergence of Philosophy." As Toadvine explains, reflection and the pre-reflective are not inimical to one another, and there is an approach within philosophy that makes room for both: "When Merleau-Ponty returns to this problem in the *Phenomenology of Perception*, it is posed in terms of reflection's relationship with the unreflective. On the one hand, reflection does not fail to make contact with the pre-reflective moment from which it opens, as our very ability to indicate and describe that pre-reflective moment attests. Yet, on the other hand, reflection never coincides with the pre-reflective or presents it transparently, since it necessarily transforms the structure of the pre-reflective in opening it to reflection . . . What Merleau-Ponty calls 'second-order' or 'radical' reflection in *Phenomenology of Perception* and 'hyper-reflection' in *The Visible and the Invisible* is this effort of reflection to account for its own foundation in a nature from which it emerges but that remains for it an unthematizeable past, a past that 'has never been present.'"

126. Merleau-Ponty, "Indirect Language and the Voices of Silence," 112. Emphasis added.

the unreflective experience of the world, and subsequently reassigning to it the verificatory attitude and reflective operations, and displaying reflection as one possibility of my being."[127]

Nishida likewise engages with the paradox of expression and the self-defeating nature of reflecting on the pre-reflective. He posits a version of reflection that does not oppose spontaneity. In his later works, where he focuses increasingly on the notion of "acting-intuition," he posits this as the foundation of reflection conceived beyond the distinction between active and passive intellection.[128] Because reflection includes spontaneity, engaging with the infinite does not have to involve completely discarding intellection. Thus, Sesshū does not have to deny the reflective connection he has to the Chinese tradition in order to innovate. As Dalissier points out, in Nishida there is a reference to reflection as "development" (*hansei sunawachi hatten* 反省即ち発展) where "one is operating in terms of an 'infinite' (*mugen* 無限, *endlos*) process of 'unification' (*tōitsusuru* 統一する, *Vereinigung*)."[129] This way of describing reflection is pertinent to the artist's expression as much as it is to our own regular experience as thinking, moving beings. Acting-intuition therefore incorporates reflection *and* spontaneity, allowing philosophy to develop an orientation toward the pre-reflective without abandoning reflection altogether, and allowing artists to create in forward-looking innovation without abandoning their traditions. Reflection and deliberative thought are, on this account, a surface manifestation of a non-dual relation between body and world that is ambiguously active-passive.

Merleau-Ponty is clear that philosophy should not reject reflection but instead "needs a contact with being prior to reflection;" such "a contact which makes reflection itself possible."[130] Before reflection does join the game there is still Sallis's "unknowing play" happening at the level of the negative. It is very apt for this question and the wider discussion that

---

127. Merleau-Ponty, *Phenomenology of Perception*, 280.

128. For an excellent discussion of the manifold meanings of Nishida's "reflection" (*hansei* 反省), the will (*ishi* 意志), and his idea of infinity as "infinity inside the finite" (*yūgen nonakani mugen* 有限の中に無限), see Dalissier, "The Idea of the Mirror in Nishida and Dōgen," 100. Here, he also refers to Nishida's use of the mirror metaphor to describe reflection and his notion of a two-way mirror (*yūgen nonakani mugen* 有限の中に無限) as a metaphor for a kind of reflection that does not reify the subject or object.

129. Ibid.

130. Merleau-Ponty, *The Visible and the Invisible*, 65.

Merleau-Ponty speaks of our apprehension of the moment prior to reflection as the "negintuition of nothingness," describing it as "the philosophical attitude that puts reflection and spontaneity in a sort of equivalence. If I really understand that nothingness is not."[131] Thus, as Nishida also believes, for philosophy to acknowledge its own limits—and how it is constituted in overstepping those limits into neighboring methodologies—the negative must be integrated.

Philosophy does not need to abandon reflection to find a constructive relation to the negative, or to have fidelity to its spontaneous origins. It need only recognize that reflection was never pure; it was never in complete opposition to the pre-reflective and the spontaneous. Just as movement is always punctuated by motionlessness, and the visible by the invisible, so the shift to incorporate the pre-reflective is not to add a foreign practice to philosophic methodology that was not already there, but is merely to recognize features that have always animated philosophic reflection and expression and even preceded methodological doubt. Pure reflection was a fiction of positivist metaphysics. Similarly, the pre-reflective and the access it affords to the negative are not unadulterated; they are lined with the visible, the active, and the reflective. Although philosophy is a particular means of expression, it is at the same time only one of many configurations coupling an expressive body and expressive world. Philosophic expression is interexpression, and it has always remained ambiguous with respect to activity, passivity, speech, silence, reason, and faith, as well as reflection and spontaneity. Methodological purity has never been one of its possibilities. Insofar as it is an expressive practice, philosophy contains an internal reference to what is outside of itself, to all other forms of expression, including religious and artistic expression.

Conclusion: Motor-Perceptual Faith between Philosophy, Religion, and Art

If comparing Nishida and Merleau-Ponty on the limits of reflection and doubt leads us to methodological forms of faith in both of their projects, then questioning strict boundaries between Eastern and Western philosophy, as well as between religion and art, is unavoidable in a dialogue between the two. While Western academia might dictate that such an intercultural

---

131. Ibid.

and cross-disciplinary claim is too broad to be a grounding assumption for philosophic methodology, we can appeal again to the fact that East-Asian thinking has no issues with the ambiguities between philosophy, religion, and art. As Parkes writes, "in the Chinese and Japanese traditions, philosophy is generally interfused with poetry and music, psychology and religion, as well as with training of the body and self-cultivation."[132] Nishida's philosophy evokes such disciplinary fluidity. Now that bridges have been built from similarities and key differences between the two philosophies regarding the numerous implications of their ontologies of mutual negation—and considering Merleau-Ponty's own dismissal of simple reason-faith binaries—little prevents us from continuing the dialogue with Nishida according to how he and his tradition construe the relations between philosophy, religion, and art.

Secularizing the Spiritual: Nishida's "Inverse Polarity" and "Interexpression"

To bring this last section and the study as a whole to completion, let us now return to the original matter regarding the sacred-secular binary and look more closely at how our philosophers in dialogue complicate the opposition. Now that the heavy conceptual lifting is done, we can shift gears to consider the larger scale implications of the dialogue.

Despite his prolonged and deep engagement with major figures of the Western intellectual tradition, Nishida's use of religious terminology—including references to the Christian "God," and notions of "faith" and "grace"—makes his position difficult to understand as straightforward philosophy in a Western sense. The religious concepts he borrows from Christianity, generally associated with transcendence and dualism, are hard to square with Eastern concepts of non-dualism, negation, and the identity of contradiction, to which Nishida is otherwise committed. Irrespective of whether he succeeds in developing a "world logic," Nishida did attempt to synthesize these seemingly irreconcilable traditions. This section explores how he attempts this reconciliation by employing Christian theology while discarding its dualist metaphysics, and thus secularizing its terminology by recasting it in accordance with Eastern principles.

For Nishida, God is not an anthropomorphic being standing outside the material realm, requiring a two-tier metaphysics to explain how he interacts with the world. God is not transcendent as opposed to immanent,

---

132. G. Parkes, *Composing the Soul: Reaches of Nietzsche's Psychology*, 1.

other-worldly as opposed to this-worldly, but is precisely the aspect of reality that unifies these seeming oppositions. God is, Nishida writes,

> independent, self-fulfilled, infinite activity. We call the base of this infinite activity God. God is not something that transcends reality, God is the base of reality. God is that which dissolves the distinction between subjectivity and objectivity and unites spirit and nature.[133]

In his *Last Writings: Nothingness and the Religious Worldview* (1945), Nishida expounds a notion of God (*kami* 神) or what he also refers to variously as "the absolute" (*zettai* 絶対) or "Buddha." Although not completely devoid of religious connotations, these terms are, in his use, more ontological than religious: "God," "Buddha," or "the absolute" are the most basic principles of reality or nature, which in Nishida's philosophy is the place of "absolute nothing" (*zettai mu no Basho* 絶対無の場所). Interestingly, Nishida often raises the issue of "God" in association with his notion of "inverse polarity" or "inverse respondence" (*gyaku-taiō* 逆対応): a concept that affords further comparison with Merleau-Ponty's concept "reversibility." "*Gyaku*" (逆) refers to something inverted or reversed, whereas "*taio*" (対応) means a correspondence relation between two things.[134] Thus, its etymology puts it in line with his later concept of continuity of discontinuity, while invoking the structure of the *kire* aesthetic, space as *ma* and the connecting-dividing dynamic of chiasm. The concept also accords with elements of his earlier idea of "self-identity of absolute contradictories" (*zettai mujunteki jikodōitsu* 絶対矛盾的自己同一), this time as applied to the relation between man and god. As his translators explain, "inverse polarity" describes how "absolute nothing negates itself (its own nothingness) to allow for the emergence of beings in their co-relativity and suchness. This also reminds us of the Mahāyāna notion of the 'emptiness of emptiness.' "[135]

Since our subject has been the artist and artistic expression, we have spoken mostly of negation at the level of the relation between painter and landscape, or body and tool. "Inverse polarity" would explain the bidirectional negation that obtains on those planes, but now Nishida's intention is to

---

133. Nishida, *An Inquiry into the Good*, 79.
134. Maraldo, "Nishida's Ontology of History," 408.
135. Krummel and Nagatomo, *Place and Dialectic*, 179.

describe not just objects or bodies as negated, but the fundamental principle of reality (God, "absolute," Buddha) as negating itself so that humans can be. As we can see, Nishida's conception of God is somewhat removed from the tradition he borrows it from. Although the notion of deific negation has a long history in negative theology (*Deus Absconditus, Deus Otiosus*) and in Eastern and Western mystical or apophatic traditions, these generally conceive of negation as unidirectional and decidedly nonambiguous. God negates himself to allow the world and humans to be; however, these accounts do not posit a symmetry where the world or humans reciprocate in mutual negation to allow God to be. In this context, humans are contingent upon God, but God is not contingent upon the humanity it creates. The expressive relation between God and humans would be, thus, discontinuous—a one-way negation. God might be the being that implements and maintains the metaphysical laws, but he remains outside of them. Nishida amends this and posits a relation between humans and God according to a mutually interpenetrative and reciprocally expressive continuous-discontinuity. He writes: "[t]he self exists in a relation of inverse polarity with the absolute." He goes on to claim that in the "paradox of God" there is a "face-to-face relation with the absolute in a dialectic of *mutual presence and absence*—there is the Zen celebration of ordinary human experience."[136] If it were not for the fact that God too was negating-negated, creation would be impossible. On this point Maraldo writes:

> only a God that includes self-negation within itself could be creator. God's self-negation is not an addition, a supplement, a self-alienation into something God lacks but needs. It is not, as Nishida writes, an "opus ad extra." God's self-negation "is" God, and since it is, God is not God. . . . [I]f God's very be-ing is creating, then God is not creating—not being God—at the same time."[137]

Like the body's relation to the world as flesh, man and God are in a chiasmatic mediation of mutual negation *and* mutual creation. This is the relation of "interexpression" that follows the earlier logic of his theory of expression as "from the created to the creating" (*tsukuraretamono kara*

---

136. Nishida, *Last Writings: Nothingness and the Religious Worldview*, 111. Emphasis added.
137. Maraldo, "Heidegger and Nishida: Nothingness, God, and onto-Theology," 371.

tsukurumono e 作られたものから作るものえ). Human creation does not simply emulate God's; creative expression is itself ambiguous regarding creator and created. "Because there is God as creator," writes Nishida, "there is the world as creatures, and because there is the world as creatures, there is God as creator."[138] This is Nishida's ontology of expression, and we find a similar intimation in Merleau-Ponty when he writes "Being is *what requires creation of us* for us to experience it."[139]

Thorough maintenance of ambiguity as an ontological principle requires accounting for negation in more than a singular direction: subject-qua-object implies object-qua-subject. The artist does not negate her body while the landscape remains purely positive, just as the believer does not remain posited while God negates to let them be. "Negation of the other," Krummel notes, "cannot happen without *self*-negation." Far from the notion of a god whose positivity is faced in transcendence, like Merleau-Ponty, Nishida posits a

> "transcendence-in-immanence"/"immanent transcendence" towards the absolute. It is the contradictory identity of objectivity and subjectivity, of the particular and the universal . . . [I]n this paradoxical structure of inverse polarity and biconditionality, the self faces the absolute by transcending itself outwardly, and, simultaneously, faces the absolute by transcending itself inwardly.[140]

We do not, therefore, only encounter this relation when we decide to enact a particular religious gesture, enter a sacred building, meditate, pray, or give thanks. Because we are always in a relation of mutual negation with the fabric of the world, we therefore "encounter the absolute as its inverse polarity, its mirror opposite, at each and every step of our lives."[141] Faith in God is not belief in a deity or religious dogma: faith is the practice of overcoming the false separation between self and world. One attains this faith by allowing the mutual negation to obtain between God and oneself. In the most basic sense, for Nishida, *the religious is the negative*. "Religion exists" Nishida writes, "where the self is absolutely negated, piercing through to its very source, in the self-realization of the self-contradiction of life."[142]

---

138. Nishida, *Nishida Kitarō zenshū*, 10: 316.

139. Merleau-Ponty, *The Visible and the Invisible*, 197. Emphasis added. For a more detailed consideration of this complicated issue in Merleau-Ponty, see R. Barbaras, 41–81.

140. Nishida, *Last Writings: Nothingness and the Religious Worldview*, 99.

141. Ibid., 96.

142. Nishida, *Nishida Kitarō zenshū*, 9: 145.

Faith is not just faith *in* negativity; it is faith in the sense of *being* negated with and by the world. As Dilworth writes, "The dynamics of religious conversion entail the reciprocal, but nondual, intentionality of God and the individual soul. 'Faith' and 'grace' are names for this dimension of mutual, and transpositional, revealment."[143]

I have returned throughout this study to the important connection between ontology and the various forms of linguistic expression in both Merleau-Ponty and Nishida, such as chiasmatic linguistic/grammatical structures and their use within a poetic idiom. The mutual negation between God and world is another ontological feature with direct consequences for expression. In Nishida's philosophy, as in Dōgen's, nature is an expressive fabric. God's teachings are, therefore, not only contained in books or given only at specific times and places. All of phenomenal reality expounds God's word. All beings, animate and inanimate, speak a natural language that one can learn to hear if one is able to go beyond the anthropocentric assumption that only human language is expressive. God, according to Nishida, is the nature of mutual negation that obtains between an expressive body and expressive world. The faithful relation between God and humankind is not teleological or mechanistic, it is a bidirectional interexpressive mutual determination:

> The absolute does not destroy the relative; it possesses itself and sees itself in its own absolute self negation. That which stands in relation to the absolute as its self-negation must itself be self-expressive through its own self-negation. Thus the relation between God and mankind is always to be understood as dynamically interexpressive based on the principle of self-negation.[144]

Conceiving of religious faith as mutual negation significantly problematizes the effort to achieve that faith. Part of the mediation between God and humankind is volitional; as such—and as already noted regarding the volitional paradox—a subject cannot solely augment their faith through an act of autonomous willing: being appropriately oriented within reversible ambiguity is arrived at by negating the will, and allowing God to express himself from the inside of one's own non-self, as other-power lining self-power, thus manifesting an inverse polarity between oneself and God. Nishida alludes to the dilemma: "People often confuse religious faith with subjective belief. In the worst extreme, they even consider faith to be grounded in the subjective

---

143. Nishida, *Last Writings: Nothingness and the Religious Worldview*, 35.
144. Ibid., 103.

power of the will."[145] Nishida looks to artistic expression to explore how philosophy can achieve this faith. Just as the artist discards her subjective desires and seeks their project within the objective, so too "religious faith pertains to something *objective*, some absolute fact of the self . . . Religious faith involves precisely this dimension wherein the self discovers itself as bottomlessly contradictory identity."[146] Faith is thus a co-originative event and, like artistic expression, has the ambiguous structure of making and being made: both the believer and the believed arise spontaneously at the same time, in the same act. The faithful relation between the divine and human—both religious and philosophical, augmented and made visible by the artist, but constitutive of all historical beings—is interexpression.

Religion is not simply the human act of opening up to the divine: "this opening," as Nishida puts it, is "a mutual opening—a co-originative event."[147] For one to be "religiously volitional," then, is not to reveal oneself to a being separate from oneself, but is to "open [oneself] up to the working of God or Buddha *within [one]self.*"[148] Most of us in the West have grown up in a culture that frames the individual as responsible for its well-being, as secured through the strength of one's autonomous will. By contrast, achieving Nishida's idea of faith is neither a simple heightening nor a diminishing of the will, but something more complex and subtle, a willing not to will. In his early thought, he writes, "It is not that faith is supported by knowledge and the will, but that knowledge and the will are supported by faith . . . If we exhaust our intellect and will, then we will acquire from within a faith we cannot lose."[149]

Like perception, motion, and expression, faith is more than a capacity of an individuated subject, but is an event that occurs beyond the body–world distinction. Faith as interexpression emerges from a body extending out beyond itself, a negated body in ecstasis, entering the world and being entered by it. God comes into being through human expression and *vice versa*. As Krummel writes, "God's working is expressed in man's working and man's working is supported by God's working."[150] The fabric of motor-

---

145. Ibid., 85.
146. Ibid. Emphasis added.
147. Ibid., 39.
148. Ibid.
149. Nishida, *An Inquiry into the Good*, 157.
150. John Krummel, "The Originary Wherein: Heidegger and Nishida on the 'Sacred' and 'the Religious,'" *Research in Phenomenology*, 394.

perceptual reality is therefore an interexpressive mediation between a mutually negated self and God. Creative and expressive activity is religious practice as much as it is philosophical. Faith in Nishida's philosophy is not ontic, and has nothing to do with a response to a scriptural demand; it is to learn a different language, the scripture of the world, or, for painters such as Cézanne and Sesshū, the sutra of mountains and waters. This language can manifest verbally, but also as the prevailing conditions of visibility and expressive movability. Faith is a texture of the infinite continuity of acts that is *Basho*. Actions that harmonize with the world's language are, therefore, religious, philosophic and possibly artistic acts of faith.

Because there is no outside of *Basho*, to unify with *Basho* is not to will oneself into a completely new religious-philosophic orientation one enjoys some time in the future. There is an eschatological element in Nishida's thought, but as read through his Zen tradition, it is stripped of its teleology. The site of religious significance is not in some far-off place or time, it is right here, always underfoot, in this time and this place in which we are em*placed*. Thus, "eschatological urgency here is not in light of a distant future; rather the *eschaton*, the 'end,' is now at *every moment* . . . Nishida's 'eschatology of the everyday' anchors the temporal shape of place in the present moment that envelops past and future in its placiality,"[151] writes Krummel. Religious experience is thus immanent-transcendence, not to some distant spiritual realm where we would hear the word of God, but to the "ordinary and everyday" (*byōjōtei*) of the Zen tradition, where the mundane fabric of existence is the expression of the absolute. Thus, one does not receive salvation in some time to come, rather, faith strips away the metaphysical illusions that prevent one from seeing that one is always already emplaced within the expressive world of the Absolute. If exercising faith required a jump from a non-negated to a negated way of relating with the world, this would contravene Nishida's conditions of continuous-discontinuity that otherwise prevail throughout the motor-perceptual fabric. To proceed from a non-faithful to a faithful embodiment would be a discontinuity if faith were ontic, the choice of a subject, but as an ontological structural quality obtaining by way of mutual negation, to act faithfully is to augment a feature that was always already in place and is to remain continuously-discontinuous with nature.

In adopting Western religious terminology and interpreting it through his Eastern roots, Nishida shows how all phenomenal reality is a site for the

---

151. Ibid., 399.

exercise of faith. In so doing, he secularizes the Western spiritual terminology he has appropriated, and creates a theory of expression that applies to religion, art, and philosophy alike. To enact religious faith in this sense is not to follow dogma or a spiritual code but to act in such a way that one risks moving with the motions of the world despite the obstructions that thwart one's attempt. "Faith means, not a subjective belief, but confronting the truth in which the historical world is grounded,"[152] he writes. Nishida's faith is, in a sense, purely formal. There is no specific religious content that one has faith in, and is therefore potentially, and actually infinite. The immanent is therefore spiritual, the secular is spiritual. Just as acknowledging our basic existential position involves recognizing the ineradicable self-contradictory unity of self and world, having religious faith for Nishida is to abide within the self-contradictory unity of self and God. This religious form of contradictory identity is one of several instantiations of his overarching idea of the self-identity of absolute contradictories. Although his discussion of faith is put forth with religious terminology, the negation that is required to form a contradictory identity is a negation Nishida believes obtains on all levels of *Basho*: from biological to animal, on the human and existential levels, and on the level of the *Basho* of being (*yū no Basho* 有の場所) and the *Basho* of nothingness (*mu no Basho* 無の場所). In this sense, despite his use of Christian terminology, there is nothing exclusively religious about Nishida's notion of faith. Faith is part of the texture of a self-contradictory unity as a general feature of our body's extension into the world through negation. A body and world in a relation of expressing-expressed. To practice Nishida's faith as interexpression is to achieve such a continuous ambiguity through painting, through meditation, religion, philosophy, or art.

Spiritualizing the Secular: Merleau-Ponty and "Anatheism"

Nishida's project was from the beginning an explicitly hybrid endeavor.[153] Merleau-Ponty's project, by contrast, did not appear to exploit the religious potential of his notions of faith, flesh, grace, nothingness, or communion. Despite any explicit attempt to do so, the space he makes for "non-philosophy"

---

152. Nishida, "The Logic of the Place of Nothingness and the Religious Worldview," 97.
153. For an analysis of multicultural aspects of Nishida's philosophy and Kyoto School Philosophy as "world philosophy," see Bret W. Davis, "Nishida's Multicultural Worldview: Contemporary Significance and Immanent Critique" and "Toward a World of Worlds: Nishida, the Kyoto School, and the Place of Cross-Cultural Dialogue."

nevertheless presents a powerful challenge to the self-conception of Western philosophy and its distinction from art, religion, and Eastern philosophy. Although Western philosophy tends to maintain clear and rigid boundaries between disciplines, Nishida's project demonstrates that these partitions need not be so clear-cut. Further, Merleau-Ponty's proximity to Nishida also suggests that such disciplinary divisions need not constrain philosophical thought conducted anywhere in the world, East or West.

Merleau-Ponty attains a similar religious-philosophic ambiguity as Nishida, but he arrives at it from the other way around, so to speak. He does not secularize already religious terminology, as Nishida did; instead, he tempers what we take to be secular with the sacred. He performs a "transformation of the quotidian into the sacred,"[154] as Richard Kearney calls it, whereby the fabric of everyday phenomenal experience is elevated to a site for the exercise of faith, grace, and communion.

Through his exploration of artistic expression, Merleau-Ponty sought a radically different context within which to understand fundamental aspects of the self and its relation to the world. He engages the foundational issues and interprets them through art practice, which had traditionally been a peripheral concern for philosophy, even seen as a hindrance to attaining truth as opposed to affording privileged access to it. Merleau-Ponty reaches down to the depths of what philosophy can tolerate, beneath intellectual and theoretical forms of knowing, to an aspect of the body–world relation he terms a "communion" with the world. "The sensible," Merleau-Ponty argues, does not just have a "motor and vital significance . . . [S]ensation is literally a form of communion."[155] He thus elevates this most elemental bond to the highest point within his phenomenology, to the very locus where truth is first revealed. What he finds is that the artist appears to have discovered better ways of being with the paradoxes and obstructions inherent to this realm, while the philosopher's methods inhibits her from understanding the pre-reflective communion of the body and world. Attaining truth at this level is simply to be continuous with the motor-perceptual fabric of the world, to be intertwined with "flesh" through reversible expression. Thus, Merleau-Ponty elevates the everyday and the profane, showing how all phenomenal reality is a potential site for what Kearney calls a "eucharistic" act of communion, which he claims is "no 'mere' metaphor: Merleau-Ponty

---

154. Kearney, "Merleau-Ponty and the Sacramentality of the Flesh," 153.
155. Merleau-Ponty, *Phenomenology of Perception*, 246.

requires this specific eucharistic act to present the complex intertwining of the finite and infinite, as 'communion' is intimately related to Merleau-Ponty's notion of a chiasmatic crossing of ostensible contraries."[156]

Through his "sacramental aesthetic," Merleau-Ponty designates the openness onto the profane world as the primary and highest form of truth and posits faith as one element necessary for expressing that truth. It is not surprising that this should appear threatening to Western philosophy. What becomes most philosophic is beyond or possibly below profound intellectual insight, it is the silent dialogue between body and world happening even when we are not paying attention, the thing we cannot turn off, a communion that even those with disfigured bodies, those without access to learning, even those with intellectual disabilities undergo; this is elevated to the highest form of truth. How these phenomenal aspects of embodiment can sit alongside reflection and doubt is not a simple question.

Kascha Semonovitch and Neal DeRoo introduce their volume *Merleau-Ponty at the Limits of Art, Religion, and Perception* by stating that Merleau-Ponty "argues for a certain sacramentalization of 'profane perception' that opens up the possibility of encountering divinity in our everyday experiences . . . [T]his new conception of divinity . . . is then used to challenge the dualistic conception of theism and atheism."[157] While secular Western philosophy would want to distinguish itself from philosophy of religion and theology, and therefore perpetuate the duality between theism and atheism, and between philosophy and religion, Merleau-Ponty's ideas of faith, sacramentality, and transubstantiation overcome these dualities in what Kearney calls an "anatheistic alternative to the endless doctrinal disputes between theism and atheism . . . [a] move beyond religious forms disfigured by otherworldly metaphysics to a faith in the divine potential inherent in the everyday secular life of action."[158]

By seeing faith as "communion" and non-duality with the everyday phenomenal world, Merleau-Ponty subverts the distinction between secular and religious philosophy, and thus takes a step outside of the Western tradition, bringing him closer to basic East-Asian religious-philosophical orientations. His explorations of art bring him further in line with East-Asian thought. He

---

156. Kearney, "Merleau-Ponty and the Sacramentality of the Flesh," 150.

157. K. Semonovitch and N. DeRoo, *Merleau-Ponty at the Limits of Art, Religion, and Perception*, 14.

158. Kearney, "Merleau-Ponty and the Sacramentality of the Flesh," 157.

sees the sacramental possibilities in all perceptual experience, and in artistic expression in particular. Artists have not been limited by methodologically pure conceptions of reflection and doubt and have developed practices that cultivate rather than cover over the body's relation to the sensible. Although challenging the distinctions between art, philosophy, and religion appears to be a lofty task, Kearney sees the "anatheistic" elements of Merleau-Ponty's thought on art practice as positioning philosophy between theism and atheism. Whether it is a question of "sacramentalizing the secular or of secularizing the sacred," Kearney suggests that "the anatheist paradigm may allow it to be *both at once*. Religion as art *and* art as religion."[159]

It might be too soon or too much to address all of the ramifications of integrating faith into philosophical methodology. Not to mention the more basic question as to whether faith is in fact an *innate* part of philosophy itself. All of these concerns take us far beyond Nishida and Merleau-Ponty's projects and far beyond my attempt to place the two in dialogue. Nevertheless, in shifting attention from reflection and doubt to the locus where body meets world, where motion and perception are woven into and out of flesh and *Basho*, if our practices to attain continuity at this level of existence meet obstructions that demand faith, then philosophy should not ignore the challenges that problematize its self-conception if that self-conception precludes facing those very issues. If artists have been cultivating an orientation within the fabric of sensible reality, possibly through a motor-perceptual form of faith, then part of defining what philosophy can be as a means of expression must involve listening to what other disciplines have to offer and thereby expanding the discipline by loosening the tight distinctions between philosophy, religion, and their possible expression through art.

Artists show us the irreducibility of faith as a feature of the body's relation to the world, and faith as a limit to the methodologies of reflection and doubt philosophy is otherwise grounded upon. This is not to suggest that philosophic methodologies or modes of expression should not be distinguished from religious or artistic expression. Yet, just as we have a body and encounter other bodies and the world while no positive boundaries separate us, likewise, as a discipline, there are no un-broken methodological

---

159. Ibid., 161.

boundaries cordoning off philosophy as a pure self-identical discipline. There are real and critical differences between the various disciplines, but they should not be divided according to the identity-difference logic used to distinguish objects when we take them to be self-identical and separate from each other: distinction is only possible where things are already encounterable and mutually constituting. According to this structure of relationality—the structure of chiasm and continuous-discontinuity—philosophy is not unambiguously distinct from religion and art, but can be delineated only insofar as they are part of a common expressive fabric. Philosophy differs from faith, from religion and art, but the cut that divides them is the one that joins. Intertwined with faith, and potentially expressed through art practice, philosophy can operate in excess of unambiguous methodological boundaries, overcoming the self-identity that would limit it and expanding by integrating the insights and practices of the non-philosophical—art and religion—into philosophy.

Works Cited and Bibliography

Abe, Maseo. "Nishida's Philosophy of Place." *International Philosophical Quarterly* 28 (Winter 1988): 355–371.

Addiss, Stephen. *Japanese Quest for a New Vision: The Impact of Visiting Chinese Painters, 1600–1900: Selections from the Hutchinson Collection at the Spencer Museum of Art*. Lawrence: Spencer Museum of Art, University of Kansas, 1986.

———. *Zenga and Nanga: Paintings by Japanese Monks and Scholars, Selections from the Kurt and Millie Gitter Collection*. New Orleans: New Orleans Museum of Art, 1976.

Alloa, Emmanuel. *Resistance of the Sensible World: An Introduction to Merleau-Ponty*. Fordham University Press, 2017.

Al-Saji, Alia. "The Temporality of Life: Merleau-Ponty, Bergson, and the Immemorial Past." *Southern Journal of Philosophy* 45, no. 2 (Summer 2007): 177–206.

Arata, Shimao. "'Haboku Sansui Zu' No Ga to Shi." *Tenkai Toga* 6 (2002): 32–46.

———. "Sesshū Tōyō No Kenkyū Ichi—Sesshū No Imeeji Senryaku." *Bijutsu Kenkyū* (January 1992): 196–213.

———. "Shiteki Sesshū Zō." In *Sesshū-Botsugo Gohyakunen Tokubetsuten*. Kyoto: Kyōto Kokuritsu Hakubutsukan, 2002, 218–225.

Aristotle. "Metaphysics: Book 4." Translated by J. Barnes. In *The Complete Works of Aristotle*. Princeton, NJ: Princeton University Press, 2014.

———. "Physics." Translated by J. Barnes. In *The Complete Works of Aristotle*. Princeton, NJ: Princeton University Press, 2014.

Barbaras, Renaud. *The Being of the Phenomenon: Merleau-Ponty's Ontology*. Bloomington: Indiana University Press, 2004.

———. "Les Trois Sens de la Chair." *Chiasmi International* 10 (2008): 19–32.

———. "Perception and Movement: The End of the Metaphysical Approach." In *Chiasms: Merleau-Ponty's Notion of Flesh*, edited by Fred Evans and Leonard Lawlor. Albany: State University of New York Press, 2012, 77–88.

Belgrad, Daniel. *The Culture of Spontaneity: Improvisation and the Arts in Postwar America*. Chicago: University of Chicago Press, 1999.

Bergson, Henri. *Creative Evolution*. La Vergne: Lightning Source, 2005.
Blanchot, Maurice. *The Work of Fire*. Stanford, CA: Stanford University Press, 1995.
Bowie, H. P. *On the Laws of Japanese Painting*. Redditch: Read Books Limited, 2016.
Brodskaya, Natalia. *Cézanne*. New York: Parkstone International, 2014.
Brubaker, D. "'Place of Nothingness' and the Dimension of Visibility: Nishida, Merleau-Ponty and Huineng." In *Merleau-Ponty and Buddhism*, edited by Jin Y. Park. Lanham: Lexington Books, 2009, 155–180.
Busch, Thomas W., and Shaun Gallagher. *Merleau-Ponty, Hermeneutics, and Postmodernism*. Albany: State University of New York Press, 1992.
Cahill, James. *The Lyric Journey: Poetic Painting in China and Japan*. Cambridge: Harvard University Press, 1996.
———. *Scholar Painters of Japan: The Nanga School*. The Asia Society Collection. New York: Arno Press, 1976.
Carbone, Mauro. *The Flesh of Images: Merleau-Ponty between Painting and Cinema*. Albany: State University of New York Press, 2015.
———. *The Thinking of the Sensible: Merleau-Ponty's A-Philosophy*. Evanston, IL: Northwestern University Press, 2004.
Cézanne, Paul, and P. Michael Doran. *Conversations with Cézanne*. Berkeley: University of California Press, 2001.
Chang, G.C.C. *The Buddhist Teaching of Totality: The Philosophy of Hwa Yen Buddhism*. Oxfordshire: Taylor & Francis, 2013.
Cheng, Maria. *Essential Terms of Chinese Painting*. Hong Kong: City University of Hong Kong, 2018.
Chouraqui, Frank. *Ambiguity and the Absolute: Nietzsche and Merleau-Ponty on the Question of Truth*. New York: Fordham University Press, 2013.
Cipriani, Gerald. "Merleau-Ponty, Cézanne, and the Basho of the Visible." In *Merleau-Ponty and Buddhism*, edited by Jin Y. Park. Lanham, MD: Lexington Books, 2009, 141–154.
Cleary, Thomas F. *Entry into the Inconceivable: An Introduction to Hua-Yen Buddhism*. Honolulu: University of Hawai'i Press, 1983.
Covell, Jon Carter. *Under the Seal of Sesshū*. New York: Hacker Art Books, 1975.
Dalissier, Michel. *Anfractuosité et Unification: La Philosophie de Nishida Kitarô*. Paris: Droz, 2009.
———. "The Idea of the Mirror in Nishida and Dōgen." In *Frontiers of Japanese Philosophy*, Vol. 1., edited by James Heisig. Nagoya: Nanzan Institute of Religion and Culture, 2006, 99–142.
Daly, Anya. *Merleau-Ponty and the Ethics of Intersubjectivity*. London: Palgrave Macmillan, 2016.
Davis, Bret W. *Heidegger and the Will: On the Way to Gelassenheit*. Evanston, IL: Northwestern University Press, 2007.
———. "Nishida's Multicultural Worldview: Contemporary Significance and Immanent Critique." *Nishida Tetsugakkai Nenpō* 10 (2013): 183–203.

———. "Provocative Ambivalences in Japanese Philosophy of Religion: With a Focus on Nishida and Zen." In *Japanese Philosophy Abroad*, edited by James Heisig. Nagoya: Nanzan Institute for Religion and Culture, 2004, 246–274.

———. "Toward a World of Worlds: Nishida, the Kyoto School, and the Place of Cross-Cultural Dialogue." In *Frontiers of Japanese Philosophy: Japanese Philosophy Abroad*, edited by James W. Heisig. Nagoya: Nanzan Institute for Religion and Culture, 2006, 205–245.

de Waelhens, Alphonse. "Merleau-Ponty: Philosopher of Painting." In *The Merleau-Ponty Aesthetics Reader: Philosophy and Painting*, edited by Galen A. Johnson. Evanston, IL: Northwestern University Press, 1993, 174–191.

Dillon, M. C. *Merleau-Ponty Vivant*. SUNY Series in Contemporary Continental Philosophy. Albany: State University of New York Press, 1991.

———. *Merleau-Ponty's Ontology*. Northwestern University Studies in Phenomenology and Existential Philosophy. 2nd ed. Evanston, IL: Northwestern University Press, 1997.

Dilworth, David. "The Initial Formations of 'Pure Experience' in Nishida Kitaro and William James." *Monumenta Nipponica* 24, no. 1/2 (1969): 93–111.

———. "Nishida's Early Pantheistic Voluntarism." *Philosophy East and West* 20, no. 1 (1970): 35–49.

———. "Nishida's Final Essay: The Logic of Place and a Religious World-View." *Philosophy East and West* 20, no. 4 (1970): 355–367.

———. "Postscript: Nishida's Logic of the East" in *Last Writings: Nothingness and the Religious Worldview*.

Dogen. *Moon in a Dewdrop: Writings of Zen Master Dōgen*. Translated by Tanahashi Kazuaki. New York: North Point Press, 1985.

———. *Treasury of the True Dharma Eye: Zen Master Dōgen's Shōbōgenzō*, 2 vols. Edited and translated by Tanahashi Kazuaki. Boston: Shambhala, 2010.

Dreyfus, H. L. *On the Internet*. Oxfordshire: Taylor & Francis, 2008.

Edgar, Orion. *Things Seen and Unseen: The Logic of Incarnation in Merleau-Ponty's Metaphysics of Flesh*. Cambridge: James Clarke and Co., 2016.

Elberfeld, Rolf. "*Handelnde Anschauung (kōiteki chokkan): Nishida und die Praxis der Künste.*" Translated by the author. In *Allgemeine Zeitschrift für Philosophie: Kitarō Nishida (1870–1945)*, 36:3, edited by Rolf Elberfeld. Stuttgart: Frommann-Holzboog Verlag, 2011.

———. *Kitarō Nishida: Moderne Japanische Philosophie und die Frage nach der Interkulturalität*. Amsterdam: Rodolpi Press, 1999.

———. "Komparative Ästhetik Eine Hinführung." Translated by the author. In *Komparative Ästhetik: Künste und Ästhetische Ehrfahrung zwischen Asien und Europa*, edited by Rolf Elberfeld and Günter Wohlfart. Köln: Editions Chora, 2000.

———. "Sensory Dimensions in Intercultural Perspective and the Problem of Modern Media and Technology." In *Technology and Cultural Values: On the Edge of *the Third Millenium*, edited by Peter D. Hershock, Marietta Stepaniants, and Roger T. Ames. Honolulu: University of Hawai'i Press, 2003.

Evans, Fred, and Leonard Lawlor, eds. *Chiasms: Merleau-Ponty's Notion of Flesh*. Albany: State University of New York Press, 2012.

Faure, Bernard. "The Kyoto School and Reverse Orientalism." In *Japan in Traditional and Postmodern Perspectives*, edited by Charles Wei-hsun Fu and Steven Heine. Albany: State University of New York Press, 1995, 245–282.

Field, S. L. *Ancient Chinese Divination*. Honolulu: University of Hawai'i Press, 2008.

Fielding, Helen A. "A Phenomenology of 'the Other World': On Irigaray's *To Paint the Invisible*." *Chiasmi International* 9 (2007): 221–234.

Flak, Valentina. " 'Dal Modello all'Archetipo!': Natura e morfologia fra Klee e Merleau-Ponty." *Chiasmi International* 4 (2002).

Fóti, Véronique, ed. *Merleau-Ponty: Difference, Materiality, Painting*. Amherst: Humanity Books, 2000.

———. *Tracing Expression in Merleau-Ponty: Aesthetics, Philosophy of Biology, and Ontology*. Evanston, IL: Northwestern University Press, 2013.

Frangi, Simone. "La matrice morphologique de la pensée esthétique de Maurice Merleau-Ponty." PHD diss. l'Università degli studi (Palermo, Italy, Italie), 2011.

Ghilardi, Marcello. *The Line of the Arch: Intercultural Issues between Aesthetics and Ethics*. Milan: Mimesis International, 2015.

———. "Soku 即 and Analogy in Nishida's Thought." In *The Line of the Arch: Intercultural Issues between Aesthetics and Ethics*. Milan: Mimesis International, 2015.

Gibson, J. J. *The Ecological Approach to Visual Perception*. Boston: Houghton Mifflin, 1979.

Gosetti-Ferencei, J. A. *The Ecstatic Quotidian: Phenomenological Sightings in Modern Art and Literature*. University Park: Pennsylvania State University Press, 2010.

Grilli, Elise, and Tanio Nakamura. *Sesshu Toyo*. Rutland: Charles E. Tuttle Company, 1957.

Grøn, A., and C. Welz. *Trust, Sociality, Selfhood*. Bristol: ISD, 2010.

Hamar, Imre. *Reflecting Mirrors: Perspectives on Huayan Buddhism*. Leipzig: Harrassowitz, 2007.

Heidegger, Martin. *Discourse on Thinking*. New York: Harper & Row, 1966.

———. *The Essence of Truth: On Plato's Cave Allegory and Theaetetus*. London: Bloomsbury, 2013.

———. " '. . . Poetically Man Dwells . . .' " In *Poetry, Language, Thought*. New York: HarperCollins, 2001.

———. "What Are Poets For?" In *Poetry, Language, Thought*. Perennical Classics, 2001.

Heisig, James. "Nishida's Deodorized *Basho* and the Scent of Zeami's Flowers." In *Frontiers of Japanese Philosophy: Japanese Philosophy Abroad*, Vol. 7, edited by James W. Heisig and Rein Raud. Nagoya: Nanzan Institute for Religion and Culture, 2010, 247–273.

———. *Philosophers of Nothingness: An Essay on the Kyoto School*. Honolulu: University of Hawai'i Press, 2001.

Herder, J. G. *J. G. Herder on Social and Political Culture*. Cambridge: Cambridge University Press, 1969.
Hiroshi, Ōnishi. *Sesshū Shiryō O Yomu*. 24 vols. Osaka: Nihon bijutsu kōgei, 1976–1978.
Hoover, Thomas. "Of Modes and Manners in Japanese Ink Painting." In *Zen Culture*. New York: Random House, 1977.
Huifeng, Shi. "Chiastic Structure of the Vessantara Jātaka: Textual Criticism and Interpretation through Inverted Parallelism." *Buddhist Studies Review* 32, no. 1 (October 2015): 146–159.
Husserl, Edmund. *The Crisis of European Sciences and Transcendental Phenomenology: An Introduction to Phenomenological Philosophy*. Evanston, IL:: Northwestern University Press, 1970.
Husserl, Edmund, Maurice Merleau-Ponty, Leonard Lawlor, and Bettina Bergo. *Husserl at the Limits of Phenomenology: Including Texts by Edmund Husserl, Maurice Merleau-Ponty*. Northwestern University Studies in Phenomenology and Existential Philosophy. Evanston: Northwestern University Press, 2002.
Ishihara, Yuko. "Later Nishida on Self-Awareness: Have I Lost Myself Yet?" *Asian Philosophy* 21, no. 2 (2011): 193–211.
Ishii, Kōsei. "Kegon Philosophy and Nationalism in Modern Japan." In *Reflecting Mirrors: Perspectives on Huayan Buddhism*, edited by Imre Hamar. Leipzig: Harrassowitz, 2007, 325–336.
Iwaki, Ken'ichi. "Nishida Kitarō and Art." In *A History of Modern Japanese Aesthetics*, edited by M. F. Marra., Honolulu: University of Hawai'i Press, 2001.
Jay, Martin. *Downcast Eyes: The Denigration of Vision in Twentieth-Century French Thought*. Berkeley: University of California Press, 1994.
Johnson, Galen A. *The Retrieval of the Beautiful: Thinking through Merleau-Ponty's Aesthetics*. Evanston, IL: Northwestern University Press, 2010.
Jones, Nicholaos John. "The Logic of Soku in the Kyoto School." *Philosophy East and West* 54, no. 3 (2004): 302–321.
Jullien, Francois. *The Great Image Has No Form, or On the Nonobject through Painting*. Translated by J. M. Todd. Chicago: University of Chicago Press, 2009.
Jung, Hwa Yol. "Revolutionary Dialectics: Mao Tse-Tung and Maurice Merleau-Ponty." *Dialectical Anthropology* 2, no. 1 (1977): 33–56.
———. *Transversal Rationality and Intercultural Texts: Essays in Phenomenology and Comparative Philosophy*. Athens: Ohio University Press, 2011.
Kasulis, Thomas. *Engaging Japanese Philosophy: A Short History*. Nanzan Library of Asian Religion and Culture. Honolulu: University of Hawai'i Press, 2018.
———. *Intimacy or Integrity: Philosophy and Cultural Difference*. University of Hawai'i Press, 2002.
———. "The Philosophical Truth: Comparative Speaking." Presentation delivered at University College Cork, 09/08/11.
———. *Zen Action Zen Person*. Honolulu: University of Hawai'i Press, 1981.

Kaushik, Ravi. "Lighten Up: Merleau-Ponty and Nancy on Light, Form and Intelligibility." *Chiasmi International: Thinking the Outside: Politics, Aesthetics* 19 (2017): 183–199.

Kazashi, Nobuo. "Bodily Logos: James, Nishida, and Merleau-Ponty." In *Merleau-Ponty: Interiority and Exteriority, Psychic Life and the World*, edited by D. Olkowski and J. Morley. Albany: State University of New York Press, 1999, 107–120.

———. L'intuition agissante et l'invisible chez Nishida, Kimura et Merleau-Ponty. In *Philosophes Japonais Contemporains*. Montreal: Les Presses de l'Université de Montréal, 2010.

Kearney, Richard. *Anatheism: Returning to God after God*. New York: Columbia University Press, 2011.

———. "Merleau-Ponty and the Sacramentality of the Flesh." In *Merleau-Ponty at the Limits of Art, Religion, and Perception*, edited by Kascha Semonovitch and Neal DeRoo. New York: Bloomsbury, 2010, 147–166.

Kim, Ha Tai. "The Logic of the Illogical: Zen and Hegel." *Philosophy East and West* 5, no. 1 (1955): 19–29.

Kim, Hee. Jin. *Flowers of Emptiness: Selections from Dōgen's Shōbōgenzō*. Lewiston, NY: Edwin Mellen Press, 1985).

Klee, Paul. *The Diaries of Paul Klee: 1898–1918*. Berkeley: University of California Press, 1964.

Koffka, Kurt. *Principles of Gestalt Psychology*. Oxfordshire: Taylor & Francis, 2013.

Kopf, Gereon. "Critical Comments on Nishida's Use of Chinese Buddhism." *Journal of Chinese Philosophy* 32, no. 2 (2005): 313–329.

———. "Is Dialectical Philosophy Tenable? Revisiting Hegel, Nishida, and Takahashi." *International Journal for Field-Being* 3, no. 1 (2006).

Krauss, Rosalind. *Passages in Modern Sculpture*. Cambridge, MA: MIT Press, 1981.

Krueger, Joel. "Affordances and the Musically Extended Mind." *Frontiers in Psychology* 4 (2013): 1–12.

———. "The Varieties of Pure Experience: William James and Kitaro Nishida on Consciousness and Embodiment." *William James Studies* 1 (2006).

Krummel, John. "Embodied Implacement in Kūkai and Nishida." *Philosophy East and West* 65, no. 3 (2015).

———. *Nishida Kitarō's Chiasmatic Chorology: Place of Dialectic, Dialectic of Place*. World Philosophies. Bloomington: Indiana University Press, 2015.

———. *Place and Dialectic: Two Essays by Nishida Kitarō*. Oxford: Oxford University Press, 2012.

———. "The Originary Wherein: Heidegger and Nishida on 'the Sacred' and 'the Religious.'" *Research in Phenomenology* 40, no. 3 (2010): 378–407.

Kullman, Michael, and Charles Taylor. "The Pre-Objective World." *The Review of Metaphysics* 12, no. 1 (1958): 108–132.

Landes, Donald A. *Merleau-Ponty and the Paradoxes of Expression*. Philosophy, Aesthetics, and Cultural Theory. New York: Bloomsbury, 2013.

Lau, Kwok-Ying. *Phenomenology and Intercultural Understanding: Toward a New Cultural Flesh*. New York: Springer International, 2016.
Lawlor, Leonard. *Early Twentieth-Century Continental Philosophy*. Bloomington: Indiana University Press, 2012.
Levin, D. M. *Sites of Vision: The Discursive Construction of Sight in the History of Philosophy*. Cambridge, MA: MIT Press, 1999.
Levine, Gregory. "Zen Art before 'Nothingness.'" In *In Inventing Asia: American Perceptions around 1900*, edited by Noriko Murai and Alan Chong. Boston: Isabella Stewart Gardner Museum, 2014.
———, and Yukio Lippit. *Awakenings: Zen Figure Painting in Medieval Japan*. New Haven, CT: Yale University Press, 2007.
Linde, Han. *Shítāo Yǔ "Huà Yǔlù" Yánjiū* 石濤与"画语录"研究. Nanjing: Meishu Chubanshe, 2000.
Lippit, Yukio. "Of Modes and Manners in Japanese Ink Painting: Sesshū's 'Splashed Ink Landscape' of 1495." *The Art Bulletin* 94, no. 1 (2012): 50–77.
Locke, John. *An Essay Concerning Human Understanding*. London: T. Tegg and Son, 1836.
Loughnane, Adam. "Merleau-Ponty and Nishida: 'Interexpression' as Motor-Perceptual Faith." *Philosophy East and West* 67, no. 3 (2017): 710–737.
———. "Merleau-Ponty and Nishida: The World's 'Self-Seeing' Through Painting." *European Journal of Japanese Philosophy*. Vol. 1. 2016: 47–74.
———. Böhler, Arno. Parkes, Graham. Performing Philosophy in Asian Traditions—Nishida Kitarō" *Journal of Performance Philosophy*. Vol. 1. 2015. www.performancephilosophy.org/journal/article/view/8
Mahendran, Dilan. "Optimal Grip, Préjujé Du Monde, and the Colonization of Being." In *Phenomenology Roundtable*. Philadelphia: Drexel University, 2010.
Maldiney, Henry. "Flesh and Verb in the Philosophy of Merleau-Ponty." In *Chiasms: Merleau-Ponty's Notion of Flesh*, edited by Fred Evans and Leonard Lawlor. Albany: State University of New York Press, 2012.
Maraldo, John. "Enaction in Cognitive Science and Nishida's Turn of Intuition into Action." In *Kitaro Nishida in Der Philosophie Des 20. Jahrhunderts: Mit Texten Nishidas in Deutscher Übersetzung*, edited by Rolf Elberfeld and Yoko Arasika. Welten Der Philosophie. Munich: Verlag Karl Alber, 2014.
———. "Heidegger and Nishida: Nothingness, God, and Onto-Theology." In *Japanese Philosophy in the Making: Crossing Paths with Nishida*. Nagoya: Chisokudō, 2017.
———. "Nishida and the Individualization of Religion." *Zen Buddhism Today: Annual Report of the Kyoto Zen Symposium* (November 1988).
———. "Nishida Kitarō." *Stanford Encyclopedia of Philosophy*. plato.stanford.edu/entries/nishida-kitaro/notes.html
———. "Nishida's Ontology of History." In *Japanese Philosophy in the Making: Crossing Paths with Nishida*. Nagoya: Chisokudō, 2017.

———. "Rethinking God: Heidegger in the Light of Absolute Nothing, Nishida in the Shadow of Onto-Theology." In *Religious Experience and the End of Metaphysics*, edited by J. Bloechl, 31–49. Bloomington: Indiana University Press, 2003.

———. "Self-Mirroring and Self-Awareness: Dedekind, Royce, and Nishida." In *Frontiers of Japanese Philosophy: Japanese Philosophy Abroad*, edited by James W. Heisig and Rein Raud. Nagoya: Nanzan Institute for Religion and Culture, 2010.

Marra, Michael. *Essays on Japan: Between Aesthetics and Literature*. Leiden: Brill, 2010.

———. *A History of Modern Japanese Aesthetics*. Honolulu: University of Hawai'i Press, 2001.

———. *Japanese Hermeneutics: Current Debates on Aesthetics and Interpretation*. Honolulu: University of Hawai'i Press, 2002.

———. *Modern Japanese Aesthetics: A Reader*. Honolulu: University of Hawai'i Press, 2002.

Marratto, Scott. *The Intercorporeal Self: Merleau-Ponty on Subjectivity*. Albany: State University of New York Press, 2012.

Matteo, Cestari. "Between Emptiness and Absolute Nothingness: Reflections on Negation in Nishida and Buddhism." In *Frontiers of Japanese Philosophy: Japanese Philosophy Abroad*, edited by James W. Heisig and Rein Raud, 320–346. Nagoya: Nanzan Institute for Religion and Culture, 2010.

Mazis, Glen. "Merleau-Ponty and the Backward Flow of Time: The Reversibility of Temporality and the Temporality of Reversibility." In *Merleau-Ponty, Hermeneutics and Postmodernism*, edited by Shaun Gallagher and Thomas Busch. Albany: State University of New York Press, 1992.

———. *Merleau-Ponty and the Face of the World: Silence, Ethics, Imagination, and Poetic Ontology*. Albany: State University of New York Press, 2016.

McMahan, David. *Empty Vision: Metaphor and Visionary Imagery in Mahayana Buddhism*. Oxfordshire: Taylor & Francis, 2013.

Meacham, Darian. "'Faith Is in Things Not Seen': Merleau-Ponty on Faith, Virtù, and the Perception of Style." In *Merleau-Ponty at the Limits of Art, Religion, and Perception*, edited by K. Semonovitch and N. DeRoo. New York: Bloomsbury, 2010.

Merleau-Ponty, Maurice. "Cézanne's Doubt." Translated by Galen Johnson. In *The Merleau-Ponty Aesthetics Reader: Philosophy and Painting*. Evanston, IL: Northwestern University Press, 1993.

———. "Eye and Mind." Translated by Galen Johnson. In *The Merleau-Ponty Aesthetics Reader: Philosophy and Painting*. Evanston, IL: Northwestern University Press, 1993.

———. "Eye and Mind." Translated by T. Toadvine and L. Lawlor. In *The Merleau-Ponty Reader*. Evanston, IL: Northwestern University Press, 2007.

———. "Faith and Good Faith." In *Sense and Non-Sense*. Chicago: Northwestern University Press, 1964.
———. *Husserl at the Limits of Phenomenology*. Evanston, IL: Northwestern University Press, 2002.
———. *In Praise of Philosophy*. Northwestern University Studies in Phenomenology and Existential Philosophy. Evanston, IL:: Northwestern University Press, 1963.
———. "Indirect Language and the Voices of Silence." Translated by Galen Johnson. In *The Merleau-Ponty Aesthetics Reader: Philosophy and Painting*. Evanston, IL: Northwestern University Press, 1993.
———. *Institution and Passivity: Course Notes from the Collège De France (1954–1955)*. Evanston, IL: Northwestern University Press, 2010.
———. *Les Philosophes Célèbres*. Paris: Edition d'art Lucien Mazenod, 1956.
———. *Le Visible Et L'invisible: Suivi De Notes De Travail*. Collection Tel 36. Paris: Gallimard, 1979.
———. *Nature: Course Notes from the Collège De France*. Evanston, IL: Northwestern University Press, 2003.
———. *Parcours Deux, 1951–1961*, Ed. Jacques Prunair. Lagrasse, France: Verdier, 2000.
———. *Phenomenology of Perception*. New York: Routledge, 2002.
———. *The Primacy of Perception: And Other Essays on Phenomenological Psychology, the Philosophy of Art, History and Politics*. Chicago: Northwestern University Press, 1964.
———. *Prose of the World*. Evanston, IL: Northwestern University Press, 1973.
———. *Sense and Non-Sense*. Chicago: Northwestern University Press, 1964.
———. *Signs*. Chicago: Northwestern University Press, 1964.
———. *The Structure of Behavior*. Boston: Beacon Press, 1963.
———. *The Visible and the Invisible: Followed by Working Notes*. Translated by Claude Lefort. Evanston, IL: Northwestern University Press, 1968.
———. "What Is Phenomenology?" Translated by T. Toadvine and L. Lawlor. In *The Merleau-Ponty Reader*. Evanston, IL: Northwestern University Press, 2007.
Minoru, Watada. "Sesshū Nyūmin-Hitori No Gasō Ni Okotta Tokushu Na Jiken." *Bijutsu Kenkyū* 318 (March 2004): 209–232.
Moeller, Hans-Georg. *Daoism Explained: From the Dream of the Butterfly to the Fishnet Allegory*. Chicago: Open Court, 2004.
Munson, Thomas N. "The Pre-Objective Reconsidered." *Review of Metaphysics* 12, no. 4 (1958): 624–632.
Nietzsche, Friedrich. *On the Genealogy of Morals*. Translated by W. A. Kaufmann. New York: Vintage Books, 1989.
Nightingale, A. W. *Spectacles of Truth in Classical Greek Philosophy: Theoria in Its Cultural Context*. Cambridge: Cambridge University Press, 2004.
Nishida, Kitarō. *Art and Morality*. Honolulu: University Press of Hawai'i, 1973.

———. "Basho." Translated by John Wesley Megumu Krummel and Shigenori Nagatomo. In *Place and Dialectic: Two Essays*. Oxford: Oxford University Press, 2012.

———. *Fundamental Problems of Philosophy: The World of Action and the Dialectical World*. Translated by D. A. Dilworth. Tokyo: Sophia University Press, 1970.

———. "The Historical Body." Translated by David Dilworth, Valdo Viglielmo, and Agustin Jacinto Zavala. In *Sourcebook for Modern Japanese Philosophy*, edited by David Dilworth, Valdo Viglielmo, and Agustin Jacinto Zavala. Westport, CT: Greenwood Press, 1998, 37–53.

———. *An Inquiry into the Good*. New Haven, CT: Yale University Press, 1992.

———. "The Intelligible World." In *Intelligibility and the Philosophy of Nothingness*. Westport, CT: Greenwood Press, 1973.

———. *Intuition and Reflection in Self-Consciousness*. Translated by Valdo Viglielmo. Albany: State University of New York Press, 1987.

———. *An Inquiry into the Good*. New Haven, CT: Yale University Press, 1990.

———. "Ishiki No Mondai" (Unpublished translation). Translated by Valdo Viglielmo.

———. *Last Writings: Nothingness and the Religious Worldview*. Translated by D. A. Dilworth. Honolulu: University of Hawai'i Press, 1993.

———. "Logic and Life." Translated by John Wesley Megumu Krummel and Shigenori Nagatomo. In *Place and Dialectic: Two Essays*. Oxford: Oxford University Press, 2012.

———. "The Logic of the Place of Nothingness and the Religious Worldview." Translated by D. A. Dilworth. In *Last Writings: Nothingness and the Religious Worldview*. Honolulu: University of Hawai'i Press, 1993.

———. *Nishida Kitarō zenshū*. Vol. 1–24. Tokyo: Iwanami Shoten, 1965.

———. *Place and Dialectic: Two Essays*. Translated by John Wesley Megumu Krummel and Shigenori Nagatomo. Oxford: Oxford University Press, 2012.

———. "Sho no bi"「書の美」. In *Nishida Kitarō Zenshū*, Vol. 7, 331–332. Tokyo: Iwanami Shoten.

———. "The Standpoint of Active Intuition." In *Ontology of Production: Three Essays*. Durham, NC: Duke University Press, 2012.

———. "World as Identity of Absolute Contradiction." In *Sourcebook for Modern Japanese Philosophy*, edited by David Dilworth, Valdo Viglielmo, and Agustin Jacinto Zavala. Westport, CT: Greenwood Press, 1998, 54–72.

———. "歴史的形成作用としての芸術的創作 Rekishi-Teki Keiseisayō Toshite No Geijutsu-Teki Sōsaku." In *Nishida Kitarō Zenshū*, Vol. 9, Tokyo: Iwanami Shoten, 2003.

Nishijima, G. W., and C. Cross. *Shōbōgenzō: The True Dharma-Eye Treasury: Volume 1*. 4 vols. Berkeley, CA: Numata Center for Buddhist Translation and Research, 2008.

Nitta, Y., and H. Tatematsu. *Japanese Phenomenology: Phenomenology as the Trans-Cultural Philosophical Approach*. Dordrecht: Springer Netherlands, 2012.
Noe, Keiichi. "Phenomenology in Japan: Its Inception and Blossoming." In *The Bloomsbury Research Handbook of Contemporary Japanese Philosophy*, edited by Michiko Yusa. New York: Bloomsbury, 2017.
Noma, Seiroku. *Artistry in Ink*. Tokyo: Tōto Bunka Co., 1958.
Odin, Steve. *Artistic Detachment in Japan and the West: Psychic Distance in Comparative Aesthetics*. Honolulu: University of Hawai'i Press, 2001.
———. *Process Metaphysics and Hua-Yen Buddhism: A Critical Study of Cumulative Penetration vs. Interpretation*. Albany: State University of New York Press, 1982.
———. *The Social Self in Zen and American Pragmatism*. SUNY Series in Constructive Postmodern Thought. Albany: State University of New York Press, 1996.
Olkowski, D., and J. Morley. *Merleau-Ponty: Interiority and Exteriority, Psychic Life and the World*. Albany: State University of New York Press, 1999.
Orsborn, M. B. "Chiasmus in the Early Prajñāpāramitā: Literary Parallelism Connecting Criticism and Hermeneutics in an Early Mahāyāna Sūtra." Hong Kong: University of Hong Kong, 2012.
Ōta, Asaoka. *Zōtei Koga Bikō*. Vol. 2. 4 vols. Tokyo: Yoshikawa Kōbunkan, 1904.
Park, Jin Y. *Buddhism and Postmodernity: Zen, Huayan, and the Possibility of Buddhist Postmodern Ethics*. Lanham, MD: Lexington Books, 2008.
———, and Gereon Kopf. *Merleau-Ponty and Buddhism*. Lanham, MD: Lexington Books, 2009.
Parker, Joseph D. *Zen Buddhist Landscape Arts of Early Muromachi Japan (1336–1573)*. SUNY Series in Buddhist Studies. Albany: State University of New York Press, 1999.
Parkes, Graham. *Composing the Soul: Reaches of Nietzsche's Psychology*. Chicago: University of Chicago Press, 1996.
———. "Dōgen's 'Mountains and Waters as Sūtras.'" In *Buddhist Philosophy: Essential Readings*, edited by William Edelglass. Oxford: Oxford University Press, 2009, 83–92.
———. "The Role of Rock in the Japanese Dry Landscape Garden." In *Reading Zen in the Rocks: The Japanese Dry Landscape Garden*. Chicago: University of Chicago Press, 2000.
Parkes, Graham, and Adam Loughnane. "Japanese Aesthetics." *Stanford Encyclopedia of Philosophy*. plato.stanford.edu/entries/japanese-aesthetics
Phillips, Q. E. *The Practices of Painting in Japan, 1475–1500*. Stanford, CA: Stanford University Press, 2000.
Rodin, Auguste, and Paul Gsell. *Art: Conversations with Paul Gsell*. Berkeley: University of California Press, 1984.
Sallis, John. *Paul Klee: Philosophical Vision: From Nature to Art*. Chicago: University of Chicago Press, 2012.

———. "Towards a Movement of Reversal: Science, Technology and the Language of Homecoming." In *Heidegger and the Path of Thinking*, edited by John Sallis. Pittsburgh, PA: Duquesne University Press, 1970, 138–168.

Sartre, Jean-Paul. *Being and Nothingness: An Essay on Phenomenological Ontology*. New York: Philosophical Library, 1956.

Schreyach, Michael. "Pre-Objective Depth in Merleau-Ponty and Jackson Pollock." *Research in Phenomenology* 43, no. 1 (2013): 49–70.

Schultz, Lucy. "Nishida Kitarō, G.W.F. Hegel, and the Pursuit of the Concrete: A Dialectic of Dialectics." *Philosophy East and West* 62, no. 3 (2012): 319–338.

———. "Creative Climate Expressive Media in the Aesthetics of Watsuji, Nishida, and Merleau-Ponty," *Environmental Philosophy* 10, no. 1 (2013): 63–82.

Semonovitch, K., and N. DeRoo. *Merleau-Ponty at the Limits of Art, Religion, and Perception*. New York: Bloomsbury, 2010.

Shriver, Ryan. "From the Depths of Aesthetic Expression: Nishida, Merleau-Ponty, and the Body." Presentation at 6th Annual Meeting of The Comparative & Continental Philosophy Circle. Cork, Ireland. March, 2011.

Simpson, Christopher. *Merleau-Ponty and Theology*. New York: Bloomsbury, 2013.

Sinha, Pawan. "The Newly Sighted Fail to Match Seen with Felt." *Nature Neuroscience* 14, no. 5 (2011): 551–553.

Smith, N. S., and L. Nelson. *Contact Quarterly's Contact Improvisation Sourcebook: Collected Writings and Graphics from Contact Quarterly Dance Journal, 1975–1992*. Boston: Contact Editions, 1997.

Soetsu, Yanagi. *The Unknown Craftsman: A Japanese Insight into Beauty*. Tokyo: Kodansha International, 1989.

Stevens, Bernard. "Self in Space: Nishida Philosophy and Phenomenology of Maurice Merleau-Ponty." In *Merleau-Ponty and Buddhism*, edited by Jin Y. Park and Gereon Kopf. Lanham, MD: Lexington Books, 2009, 133–140.

Stewart, Jon. *The Debate between Sartre and Merleau-Ponty*. Northwestern University Studies in Phenomenology and Existential Philosophy. Evanston, IL: Northwestern University Press, 1998.

Tadashi, Ogawa. "The Kyoto School of Philosophy and Phenomenology." *Analecta Husserliana: Japanese Phenomenology: Phenomenology as the Transcultural Philosophical Approach* 8 (2012): 207–221.

Takeuchi, Melinda. *Taiga's True Views: The Language of Landscape Painting in Eighteenth-Century Japan*. Stanford, CA: Stanford University Press, 1994.

———. " 'True' Views: Taiga's Shinkeizu and the Evolution of Literati Painting Theory in Japan." *The Journal of Asian Studies* 48, no. 1 (1989): 3–26.

Taminiaux, Jacques. "The Thinker and the Painter." In *The Merleau-Ponty Aesthetics Reader: Philosophy and Painting*, edited by Galen Johnson. Evanston, IL: Northwestern University Press, 1993, 278–292.

Tanaka, Ichimatsu. *Japanese Ink Painting: Shubun to Sesshu*. Tokyo: Heibonsha, 1974.

Tapié, Michel, and Tōre Haga. *Avant-Garde Art in Japan.* New York: Harry N. Abrams.
Toadvine, Ted. "The Silence of Nature and the Emergence of Philosophy" (Unpublished). Presented at Nature, Freedom, History: Merleau-Ponty after Fifty Years, Inaugural Conference of the Irish Phenomenological Circle, May 24, 2011, University College Dublin.
Tremblay, Jacynthe. "Présent absolu et avenir absolu." *Théologiques* 17, no. 2 (2009): 245–263. doi:10.7202/044071ar
Trigg, Dylan. "The Role of the Earth in Merleau-Ponty's Archaeological Phenomenology." *Chiasmi International* 16 (2014): 255–273.
Valvo, Alberto, Leslie L. Clark, Zofja S. Jastrzembska, and American Foundation for the Blind. *Sight Restoration after Long-Term Blindness: The Problems and Behavior Patterns of Visual Rehabilitation.* New York: American Foundation for the Blind, 1971.
van Briessen, Fritz. *Way of the Brush: Painting Techniques of China and Japan.* Clarendon: Tuttle, 2000.
Welch, John W. *Chiasmus in Antiquity: Structures, Analyses, Exegesis.* Provo: Research Press, 1999.
Wilkinson, Robert. *Nishida and Western Philosophy.* Farnham: Ashgate, 2009.
Wiskus, Jessica. *The Rhythm of Thought: Art, Literature, and Music after Merleau-Ponty.* Chicago: University of Chicago Press, 2013.
Wong, Aida-Yuen. "A New Life for Literati Painting in the Early Twentieth Century: Eastern Art and Modernity, a Transcultural Narrative?" *Artibus Asiae* 60, no. 2 (2000): 297–326.
Wrathall, Mark. "The Phenomenological Relevance of Art." In *Art and Phenomenology*, edited by Joseph D. Parry. New York: Routledge, 2011, 9–30.
Yuasa, Yasuo. *The Body: Toward an Eastern Mind-Body Theory.* Translated by T. P. Kasulis. Albany: State University of New York Press, 1987.
Yusa, Michiko. *Zen and Philosophy: An Intellectual Biography of Nishida Kitarô.* Honolulu: University of Hawai'i Press, 2002.
Zahavi, D. *Husserl's Phenomenology.* Stanford, CA: Stanford University Press, 2003.
Ziporyn, Brook. *Being and Ambiguity: Philosophical Experiments with Tiantai Buddhism.* Chicago: Open Court, 2004.
———. "How the Tree Sees Me: Sentience and Insentience in Tiantai and Merleau-Ponty." In *Merleau-Ponty and Buddhism*, edited by Jin Y. Park and Gereon Kopf, ix. Lanham, MD: Lexington Books, 2009.

Index

Abe, Maseo, 186
absence, xxxvi, xlv, 19, 31–32, 35, 37, 41, 44, 65–67, 74, 84–85, 96–97, 108–109, 123–124, 127, 129–130, 136, 139, 157, 160, 212, 215, 257, 259, 270, 278, 303, 316, 324–325, 331; of color, 257–259; in hasegawa, 67–69; of knowledge (*see* agnosia); of obstructions in Nishida, 19, 141–144, 270, 278; of self, 37; in Sesshū, 160. *See also* ambiguity of absence and presence; presence
absolute, xvii, 2, 8, 10, 16, 24–25, 32, 35–36, 38–42, 47, 66, 145, 164, 166, 172, 175, 186–187, 200, 202, 207, 226, 248, 253, 272–275, 300, 330–336; God as, 2, 331; nothingness" (*nullité absolue*) in Sartre, 34–38; positivity and negativity, 166, 217; present, xiii, 202; and pure philosophy, xvii
absolute negation (*zettai hitei* 絶対否定), xxvii, xl, 8, 20, 23–24, 36–41, 202, 273. *See also* mutual negation; negation; *nullité absolue*
absolute negation-*qua*-affirmation (*zettai no hitei soku kōtei* 絶対の否定即肯定), 23. *See also* identity-difference thinking; negation

absolute nothingness (*zettai mu* 絶対無), xiii, xxvii, xl, 16, 35, 39, 55, 185, 259, 272–274
absolute other (*zettai ta* 絶対他), 41
absolute present (*zettai genzai* 絶対現在), xiii, 202
absolutely contradictory self-identity (*zettai mujunteki jikodōitsu* 絶対矛盾的自己同一), 8, 275, 330. *See also* self-identity, logic of absolutely contradictory self-identity
abyss, 36
acting-intuition (*kōiteki chokkan* 行為的直観), 9, 25, 202, 244–248, 250, 327; reflection and spontaneity in, 327
action, activity, act of faith, 285, 326; artist's, 171, 174; at a distance, 130, 135; infinite, 185, 296, 330; invisible background of, 188; and motionlessness, xli, 163, 170–171, 175, 180, 184, 190, 192, 229, 257; motor-perceptual continuity of act and act, xli, 178–179, 187–189, 193, 197, 209–210, 212, 217, 229–230, 234, 289, 297; multi-volitional, 180, 208–209; new continuity of act and act, 189, 197, 230; pure, 186; temporality of spontaneous, 318;

action, activity, act of faith *(continued)* visual, 181, 242; without an actor, 187, 209; world's continuity of, 305. *See also* non-action; motion

active self (*hataraku jiko* 働く自己), 246. *See also* non-action

aesthetic(s), *aesthetikos*, xliv; of accident, 162; constraints, 195, 218, 232, 238, 256, 265, 282, 288–290, 313, 317, 324; creation, 41, 157, 160, 200, 213, 226, 237–239, 248, 277, 310, 319–320, 331–332; daoist, 62, 65–70; ideals, xxxv, 93, 154, 157; of inebriation, 162; judgment, xxxvi–xxxvii, xliv; judgments of the beautiful, xliv; logic, correspondence-based, 280; practice, zen religious, 62, 151, 156–157 (see also *Geidō* practices; Sesshū Tōyō); sacramental, 338; theory of beauty, xxxv; of transparent mediality, 121–123, 139

affirmation of absolute negation (*zettai hitei no kōtei* 絶対否定の肯定), xl, 23, 41. *See also* negation; absolute negation

affordances, xiv, xxix, 13, 53, 76, 93, 106, 121–122, 125, 147, 199, 210, 215, 242, 256, 276, 310, 318, 328, 330, 337; musical 318. *See also* Gibson, J.J.; solicitations

agency, xxxiv, xliii, 160, 173–174, 178, 186, 196, 209, 216–217, 225, 230, 246–247, 256, 284, 291, 301–302, 304. *See also* will; volition

agnosia, 127–128, 133

air, 101, 121, 123–124, 291, 293, 308, 313–315

Al-saji, Alia, 181, 203–204

alienation, 74, 331

Alloa, Emmanuel, 122, 124

alterity, 74. *See also* absolute other

ambiguity, attempt to eliminate, reduce, 12; of ambiguity, 94 (*see also* emptiness of emptiness [*śūnyatāyāh śūnyatā*]); between distance and proximity, 112–120; between "there is" and "there is not," 66–68, 162, 165, 253 (*see also* Jullien, Francois); continuous-discontinuous, xl, 8, 24–25, 31–32, 46, 71, 76, 80, 87, 109, 146, 161, 189, 226, 250, 275, 322, 335 (*see also* chiasm); gripped and being gripped, 218; logic of, 8 (*see also* A and not-A; *sokuhi* logic); of motion and motionlessness, xli, 163, 170–171, 175, 184, 190, 192, 229, 257; moving-moved, 174; obstructing-revealing, 123, 125, 129, 132, 134; of past, present, and future, 79; of philosophy and religion, xxi–xxvii, 329–339; of physiology, 29–30; of positive and negative, 22–23, 26, 32, 36–37, 64, 166–168, 171, 264; relational, xxxviii, xl, 33; of skin and bones, 87–88, 90, 94–95, 181; subjective-objective, 277; of surface and depth, xl, 87, 89–90, 95, 100 (*see also* box example, Nishida); throwing-thrown, 307; turning while being turned, 228; of visible and invisible, xl, 6–7, 13, 32, 65–67, 69, 74, 80, 90, 163, 171, 281, 294; visual-tactile, 53, 100, 117–118, 120–121, 140, 240. *See also* unambiguous

ambivalence, xxiv, xxvii, xlv, 36, 264, 269–270

American avant-garde, 308

anatheism, 336, 338–339. *See also* Kearney, Richard

anatomy, 27, 29–30, 51, 88. *See also* chiasm

INDEX

angle of totality, 61–62, 65. *See also* Guo Xi; multi-perspectivalism
animate, 92, 106, 151, 155, 175–180, 185, 221, 307, 328, 333; bodies, 94, 175–176, 178; -inanimate distinction, 176; and inanimate world, 175–176, 179, 307, 333. *See also* inanimate
anonymity, 74, 94, 205, 250, 284; agency, 205, 284; *anonymat inné de moi-même*, 74; and narcissism of vision, 74, 94; reversible, 74; vision, 250. *See also* non-self
anti-foundationalism, 40
antinomy, 111, 172
apophaticism, xxi, 12
aporia, 290
appearing-disappearing, 68
Arata, Shimao, 155
architecture, Japanese, 32, 159
Aristotle, 11–12, 21–22, 31, 43, 57, 59, 123, 131, 135, 175, 197–199; causation, 13, 198; grammar, 22, 24 (*see also* non-contradiction, laws of); logic, 16, 22, 24, 197; motion and *energeia*, 175–176; object-based logic, 21; ontology, 11–13; transparent-qua-transparent, 123, 131. *See also* diaphanous; separation (*chōriston*)
art history, 51, 60, 93, 122, 168, 190, 220, 233. *See also* Jullien, Krauss, Levine, Lippit, Takeuchi
artistic genius, 157, 213, 238. *See also* originality, myth of
Ashikaga Academy, 156, 159, 220, 257
asymmetry, 51
asymptote, 42, 189, 261; *asumptōtos*, 42
atheism, xxvi, 338–339; sacred-secular ambiguity, xiv, 4, 150–151, 156, 329–339. *See also* anatheism, religion
Augustine, xxi

aural, 117
authenticity, 155, 221
autonomy agency, 183, 185, 229, 291, 302, 304, 326; expressive self, 296; motor-neutrality, 190; substantial, 198–199; will/willing, 185, 333–334. *See also* positivity and selfhood

Bach, Johann Sebastian, 221
background, 178, 182–183, 188–190, 210, 212, 215, 224, 231, 267, 304; of acts, invisible, 188; motor-, 178, 191, 209, 215–216, 228–229, 290; of motor-demands/solicitations, 182–183, 188–190, 210, 212, 215, 224, 231, 267, 304; in Nishida as (背後), 184, 188; set of motions, 184, 190; temporally extended, 191. *See also* affordances; solicitations
bamboo, 38, 70, 105, 163, 171, 192, 230
Barbaras, Renaud, 3, 35, 37, 177, 203, 266, 332
Basho (場所), body's continuity with flesh or, 71; logic of place (*basho no ronri* 場所の論理, *bashoteki ronri* 場所的論理), 20; motorsensory continuum of flesh and, 250; /place of being (*yū no basho* 有の場所), 6, 336; /place of nothingness (*mu no basho* 無の場所), 6, 336; /place of true nothing (*shin no mu no basho* 真の無の場所), 22; self-seeing of, 263, 271, 274, 277, 285. *See also* field; ontology; relational ontology; place

beauty, xxix, xxxiii–xxxiv, xxxvi, xliv, 5, 30–32, 91, 155–156, 166–167, 184, 189, 206, 230–231, 234–235, 284, 292, 296, 317, 320. *See also* aesthetics

becoming object (*kyakkanteki naru* 客観的なる), 223. *See also* practice, artist's
begegnung, 8. *See also* encounter
being-for-itself, 35
Belgrad, Daniel, 308, 310
Benjamin, Walter, 281
Bergson, Henri, xxiii, 35, 166, 170, 181, 203–204, 319
Bernard Leach, xliii, 307–308
Bernard, Emile, 165, 253
Bhagavad ghita, 292
bi-directional(ity), 231, 256, 333; determination, 213; expressive determination between body and world, 171, 195; form of expression, 207, 310; making-made reciprocity, 199, 246; Merleau-Ponty's "expressing-expressed," 199; negation, 330; relation between painter and tradition, 231; and reversible body-world determination, 309. *See also* mutual negation; reciprocity
Bible, 28
black and white, 70, 252, 255, 258. *See also* monochrome
black(ness), 56, 66–67, 166, 251, 257–259, 262; expressed as whiteness, 258; of milk, secret, 259
Blanchot, Maurice, 237, 281
blind spot, xlii, 98, 244, 264–268, 271–272, 277, 280–281, 283–284, 289, 299, 305; dynamic and elusive quality of, 266; motor-, 265, 267–268, 281, 305, 320; motor-perceptual, 265, 267, 271, 280, 283; *punctum ceacum*, 98, 264. *See also* obstruction; opacity; resistance of the sensible
blindness, xli–xlii, 53–54, 58, 106–110, 115, 121, 123, 125–130, 133–134, 138, 255, 265–266, 269, 271, 277–278, 282, 294, 301, 319–320; blind person's cane, 53–54, 106–110, 115–116, 121, 127–130, 133–135, 138–140; motor-, 265, 320; newly blind person, 127–129, 134; partial, 294; philosophic or religious, 55
Boccioni, Umberto, 60
bodhisattvas, 308
body, -tool dynamic, 105–106, 109, 129; artist's, xxvi, xlii, 24, 106, 121–122, 146, 149, 150, 163, 171, 174, 183–184, 188–189, 193, 205, 208, 211, 240, 302, 316; auxiliaries, 109; color-neutral, 261; continuity with flesh and *Basho*, 71; Cézanne's, 163, 243; ecstasis, 130, 206; ecstatically temporal dimension, 210; expansion through/as light, 131; expressive, 320, 328, 333; extensions, 104, 109; fetishization of transparent mediation between world and, 122; forces of light on, 139; historical, 17, 25, 186–187, 191, 193–196, 199–202, 205, 208, 210, 233, 245, 247, 270–271, 274–275, 277; historical body (*rekishiteki shintai* 歴史的身体), 25, 193–194, 274; idealized human, 51; motor-neutral, 183; movement, 144, 174, 185–186, 188, 208, 217, 253, 267, 271, 303, 312; musically extended, 319; non-color-inflected, 255; obstructing expressive possibilities of, 150; perfect, 51; positivist definition of, 103, 114; postures, 153; potter's, 310, 315; "re-membering" of, 206; relation to light, 53, 100, 103, 113, 122–123; relation to tools, 53, 100, 116, 145; reversible determination between world and, 309; sociohistoric

determination of, 288; solicitations that constrain-enable artist's, 211; temporal, 205; temporality of, 206; light's relation to, 122; tools relation to phenomenal, 110; volitional, 216, 219; volitionally ecstatic, 210, 230, 239, 241; -world bidirectional expressive determination, 171, 195; -world interdetermination, 199; -world relationality, xxxv, 105, 199, 311–312

Boehme, Jakob, xxi

Bogaard, Paul, 59

bonelessness, 105, 162. See skin and bones; surface and depth

bones, xl, 83, 87, 89–90, 92–94, 105, 162, 236; of body, 83, 87–90; of landscape, 90–95. See also Taiga, Ike no; skin and bones; surface-depth binary

Borges, Jorge Luis, 292

Botticelli, Sandro, 60

Bowie, H.P., 105

box example, Nishida, 83–84, 86, 94, 102. See also internal-qua-external perception; ambiguity of surface and depth

Brâncuși, Constantin, 89

Braque, Georges, 60

breathing, 136–138

Brodskaya, Natalia, xxix

Brubaker, David, 3, 18, 21, 25, 195, 269, 273, 275

Brunelleschi, Filippo, 279

brush, xxx, xxxii, xxxiv–xxxv, xxxvii, 70–71, 104–106, 109, 112, 121, 143, 153–154, 158, 160, 169, 171, 193, 198, 218, 220–222, 231, 257, 291, 304, 312–313. See also ecstatic body; distal sensitivity; "have brush" (*yu pi*), 104; tool use

brushmaking, 105

brushstroke, 92, 153, 162, 169, 180, 192, 216, 219–220, 243, 293, 295, 298. See also gesture

brushwork, xxxv, 153, 216, 220–221; *gyōsho* chinese painting style, xxxv, 162, 251; *kaisho* style, xxxv of Northern and Southern Song schools, 92; *p'o mo* style, 162. See also broken ink; splashed ink

Buddha, 19, 28, 54, 176–177, 292, 330–331, 334; Dainichi, 292; -nature, 175–176

Buddhism, and Daoist themes, paintings of (*doshakuga*), 154; Buddhist practice, xxii, xxxvii, 14, 158, 176; Ch'an, xxxiii, 15, 156, 158; dharma, 176–177; grammar, 14 (see also *sokuhi* logic); Huayan, xlii, 15–19, 22, 24, 109, 276, 293; Indian, 13, 15, 54, 56; Kegon, 17, 292; Madhyamaka, 14; Mahāyāna, xxiv, xl, 13, 15–16, 21, 28, 39–40, 54, 56, 59, 330; meditative discipline, 158; ontology, 14; philosophy, xxxvi; Pure Land, xxii; Rinzai, 31, 155; Tiantai, 15, 77, 98, 198, 210, 227–229, 259, 292; Yogācāra, 228; Zen, xxi, xxiii–xxiv, 62, 151, 155–158, 168, 308

Busch, Thomas, 207

Bushidō, xxxiii

calligraphy, xix, xxviii, xxxiv–xxxv, 90, 151, 155–156, 162, 221, 233, 251, 258; Nishida and, xxxiv; "The Beauty of Calligraphy" (*Sho no bi* 書の美), xxxiv, 155. See also *Geidō*; aesthetics, Zen practice

camera model of perception, 133, 170; technology, 43–44, 128, 133, 170, 280, 287–289. See also coherent deformation

cane, xli, 53–54, 106–110, 115–116, 121, 127–130, 133–136, 138–140. *See also* ecstatic body; non-object; tool use; transparency
Canova, Antonio, 60
Carbone, Mauro, 122, 203, 265
Catholicism, xxv, xxix; and existentialism, xxv
cause(s), causality xxvii, 12–13, 114, 123, 135–137, 143, 198–199, 208, 241, 249; Aristotelian, 13, 198; diachronic and synchronic, 67; force, 136–139, 174; mechanical, 135–137, 139, 193; mechanical, differences between visual and tactile, 135–141; mediated, 137; plurality of, 13; reversibility, 138, 140; similarities between the visual and tactile, 137; through medium of light, 135–141; visual, 137
Cestari, Matteo, 16
Cézanne, Paul, color between positivity and negativity, 166–167; concept of "nature," 166; critique of Impressionists, 166–167; as "doorway between East and West," xxix; and motor-solicitation, 183–184; multi-perspectivalism, 168; and religion, 163–164; "suicide," 253; visual-tactile ambiguity, 120. *See* landscape painting
Chang, G.C.C., 151, 252
Cheng, Maria, 105
Chengguan, 17–20, 109. *See also* Huayan; non-obstruction
chiasm, anatomical, 29–31; continuous-discontinuity, xl, 8, 24–25, 31–33, 38, 46, 71, 76, 80, 87, 93, 109, 145–146, 161, 189, 226, 250, 275, 322, 335; chiasma, 25–26; chiasmatic temporal negation, 76; *chiasme*, xl, 26; chiasmus, 27–28; chiastic structure, 27–28; connecting-dividing dynamic of, 330; grammatical, 27; and Greek letter X (chi), 27; muscle-tendon, 31; and negation, 24, 28, 34, 74–76, 80–82, 161, 202–204; non-chiasmatic discontinuous relation, 33, 43, 266; optic, 29–30; relationality, 24, 27–28, 30, 81, 120, 246; and temporal negation, 76; time as, 75, 203–204. *See also* ambiguity; intertwining; relational ontology; continuity of discontinuity
China, xvii–xix, xxxii–xxxv, xxxix–xl, 15–16, 38–39, 48, 51, 62–63, 66, 68, 70, 90–92, 104–105, 113, 151–154, 156, 158–159, 162, 165, 179–180, 195, 219–223, 230, 233–235, 237, 251–252, 255, 277, 280–282, 312–313, 317, 329
Chinese masters, 92, 154, 159
Chinese painting, 70, 155, 160, 236, 238, 327; conventions, 155, 318; *Gyōsho* style, xxxv, 162, 251; *kaisho* style, xxxv; literati (文人畫 *wenrenhua*), 90–92, 160; as musical score, 221; Northern Song School, 179; *p'o mo* style, 162; Song landscape painting, 62; Southern Song school of landscape painting, 92, 154, 312, 317; techniques, 159. *See also* Guo Xi; Shitao; Jullien, Francois
chisel, 104, 107, 112, 171; eye at end of, 104. *See also* ecstatic body; tools as non-object
chōra (χώρα), 4, 20
chōrismos, 11
chōriston, 11, 13–14, 22, 25, 46, 55, 107, 140, 145, 178, 198, 201
Chouraqui, Frank, 5, 32, 41–42, 166–167, 189

Christianity, xxi, xxv, xxvii, xxxiii, 2, 223, 329, 336; doctrine, xxi; mysticism, xxi, 268, 270, 331. *See also* de Cusa, Nicolaus; Eckhart

chromatic, xlii, 252–254, 257–259, 261–262; acts, continuity of motor-, 262; motor-, xlii, 252, 254, 262; neutrality, 254; painting, 253. *See also* black and white; black(ness); color; ink; monochrome

cinema, 32, 170, 265

Cipriani, Gerald, 25, 279

circumferenceless circle, xiii, 270. *See also* de Cusa, Nicolaus; Hermes Trismegistus; Pascal, Blaise

circumscribability, xxvi, 11–12, 22, 30, 34, 44, 48, 70, 79, 104, 107, 109, 114, 140, 162–163, 166, 184, 188, 193, 227–228, 236, 252–253, 266–268, 282, 284, 294, 318, 325; *circumscribere*, 11, 167; of negativity, 204; of objects, 12, 22, 44, 64, 113. *See also* non-circumscribable; non-obect; object

Cleary, Thomas, 18

cognition, 77, 82, 115, 138, 182, 223, 233, 245, 311, 322; cognition, 77, 82, 138; *res cogitans*, 116

coherent deformation (*déformation cohérente*), 71, 144, 285, 287–288, 290. *See also* conditions of visibility; "Epsom Derby"; photographic depiction

color, xlii, 105, 127, 131, 165–167, 169, 171, 211, 213, 216, 239, 251–262, 278, 293, 295; absence of, 257–259; abstract, 261; and attributes of, 254–255; -based solicitations, 256; and bodily motion, 254; cognition of, 255; and colorlessness, 253, 257–259, 262; continuity of motor-chromatic acts, 262; Cézanne's use of, 166–167; expressed in black and white, 251–252, 257–258; field, 253–255; in-itself, 261; -inflected motion, 255–257; intentionality motor-tuned to, 257; metaphysics of, 251; monochrome, 252–253; motor-dynamics of, 252, 254; motor-reality of, 252; negated color, 259; -neutral agent, 261; -neutral body, 261; non-color-inflected body, 255; in pure positivity, 260; saturation, 255. *See also* chromatic; black and white

colorlessness, xlii, 251, 253–254, 257, 259. *See also* monochrome; color

comparison, xiii, xv, xviii–xix, xxi, xxviii, xxx, xxxii–xxxiii, xxxviii–xl, xlii, xliv–xlv, 1–2, 4, 8, 10, 16–17, 20, 25, 34, 39, 55, 76, 82, 86, 96, 98, 110, 137, 144, 149, 150, 161, 179, 210, 233, 239, 251–252, 274, 283, 328, 330. *See also* circumferenceless circle; intercultural; transversality

Conatus, 175

Condillac, Étienne, 141

conditions, of motor-visibility, 235, 238, 278, 280, 283; of movability, 239, 242, 249; of new visibility, 193, 237, 243, 247, 281; of visibility, 149, 190, 193, 218, 235, 237–239, 242–243, 249, 277, 281–283, 285, 288–289, 293, 335; of visibility instituted by past artists, 193; of visibility of a tradition, 218; of visibility, prevailing, 190, 218, 237, 281, 283, 285, 288–289, 335. *See also* coherent deformation

Confucianism, xix, xxii, xxxiii, 13

continuity, of-discontiniuty, 24, 26, 31–34, 37–38, 69, 71, 76, 80, continuity, of-discontiniuty *(continued)* 87, 93, 109, 129, 131, 139, 145, 161, 174, 188–190, 226, 250, 275, 331, 335; absolute, 45; of "act and act," xli, 178–179, 187–189, 193, 197, 209–210, 212, 217, 229–230, 234, 289, 297; of acts, world's, 305; becoming continuous, 151, 158; continuum, 11, 168, 250, 261; of discontinuity (*hirenzoku no renzoku* 非連続の連続), xxii, xl, 8, 24–25, 32, 46, 54, 90, 146, 186, 330; -discontinuity negation, 87; of motor-chromatic acts, 262; unambiguous, 26, 45, 109, 266. *See also* discontinuity

continuity of discontinuity (*hirenzoku no renzoku* 非連続の連続), xl, 8, 24–25, 46, 146, 275. *See also* chiasm; intertwining

contradiction, xxxii, 8, 10, 12, 15, 19, 21, 23, 25, 29, 37, 126, 187, 200, 226, 230, 248–249, 275, 303, 306, 330, 332, 336

contradictory identity, 271, 300, 305–306, 332, 334, 336

copy, 48, 90–92, 113, 154, 159, 165, 193, 220–221, 223, 236, 243, 258, 282–283, 297; copying great artists of one's tradition, 227; copyist, 221; and original, 159, 219–220; the works of the masters, 219. *See also* originality, myths of; representation; *shinkeizu*

corporeity, 107, 110, 140, 182, 240, 265, 310, 313. *See also* body

Correspondence, 8, 48, 55, 280, 287, 293–294, 318, 330; -based aesthetic logic, 280; -based expectations, 294; -based measures, 282; inverse correspondence (*gyakutaiō* 逆対応), 8; notion of truth, 288

Coulomb's Law, 113

Covell, Jon Carter, 155, 159, 220

Cranach the Elder, 60

created-creating/making-made (*tsukurareta mono tsukuru mono* 作られたもの 作るもの), 3, 8, 23, 194, 199, 210, 231–232, 248, 309, 331. *See also* interexpression; non-action

creation, aesthetic, 41, 226; blindness of, 319–320; created-creating, 8; and deformation of visible, 193; desire, 230, 305; *ex-nihilo*, 213; genius, 217. *See also* created-creating/making-made; interexpression

creativity, and originality East and West, 219; of the individual, 3, 157; inherent risk of, 237; modern idea of, 238. *See also* originatility, myth of

Cross, Chodo, 27, 29, 80, 117, 150, 194, 329, 336

Cubism, 60, 64, 66

cut-continuance (*kire-tsuzuki* 切れ続き), 31, 46, 69, 108, 117. *See also* *kire* (切れ); *ma* (間)

Dalissier, Michel, 18, 39–40, 48, 55, 185, 258–259, 295, 327

Daly, Anya, 10

dance, 136, 138–139, 143, 192. *See also* ambiguity of motion and motionlessness

Daoism, xix, xxxiii–xxxiv, xl, 13, 62, 66–69, 92, 161, 175, 179, 223, 234, 303, 317; aesthetics of, 62, 66 (see also *Geidō* practices); classics of, xxii; continuity with the Dao, xxxvii; iconography of, 66; non-action (*wuwei* 無為), xxxiv, 13, 276; paintings of themes in, 154; philosophy of, 61, 66–67; and Sesshū, 161–162; visible and

invisible in. *See* Hasegawa; Jullien; 65–72; yin-yang, 66–68
darkness, 12, 55, 66–67, 167, 169, 238, 283, 315
das Gleiche (and *das Selbe*), xlv. *See also* comparison; identity-difference thinking
Davis, Bret, xxi–xxiv, xxvii, 97, 269, 336
de Cusa, Nicolaus (Cusanus), xiii, xxi, 270
dependent origination (*Pratītyasamutpāda*), 13–14
de Waelhens, Alphonse, 282
de-substantialize, xli, 22
death, xxiv–xxv, 38, 81, 90, 156, 195, 237, 294; and being born, 202; of consciousness, 38; live by dying, 81, 83
Dedekind, Richard, 271, 278, 295
deformation, xlii, 93–94, 114, 243, 285, 287–290
Deleuze, Gilles, 179, 281
Democritus, 123
depth, xxxvii, xl, xliv, 2, 13, 29, 40–41, 48–49, 65–66, 68, 71–73, 76, 81, 83, 87–90, 94–95, 100, 102, 106, 131–132, 150, 167, 179, 181, 195, 203, 205–207, 224, 259, 273, 287, 306, 322, 337; historical, 193, 202, 205, 211–212, 274, 290; spatial, 76; -surface binary, xl, 83, 87, 89–90, 95, 100; temporal, 76, 82, 86, 150, 172, 192, 258. *See also* bones; skin and bones; surface
DeRoo, Neal, 338
desire, xxi, 20, 30, 42, 98, 106, 165, 167, 170, 196, 220, 228, 290–291, 293, 312, 318, 321; constraining expressive, 227; creative, 230, 305; embedded within motor-perceptual fabric, 197; expressive, of the historical world, 196; for originality, novelty, progress, 173; partial negation of, 201; subjective, 224, 305, 334. *See also* non-willing
determination, xxii, 21, 23–24, 35, 38, 41, 46, 130, 132–133, 139, 141, 143, 173, 185, 190, 194–196, 199–201, 207–208, 232, 256–257, 260–262, 266, 269, 271–275, 278–279, 291, 304, 309, 333; Aristotle's uni-directional, 195, 198, 311; body's sociohistoric, 288; body-world, bi-directional, 171, 213; craving for determinacy, 42; determinacy, 37–38, 42, 46, 70, 189; inter-, 21–23, 133–134, 173, 273; inverse determination (*gyakugentei* 逆限定), 199; motor-perceptual, 24; objective, 261, 273; one-way/uni-directional, 198, 213, 311, 314; point of view, 272, 277; reciprocal, 13, 23, 81, 139, 171, 194–195; unambiguous, 35, 42, 115, 284
determination without determiner (*genteisurumononaki gentei* 限定するものなき限定), 173. *See also* mutual negation
Deus Absconditus, Otiosus, 331
Dharma, 54, 80, 161, 176–177
Dharmakāya, 176
dialectic, xvii, xxx, xxxix, 9, 17, 23, 25, 28, 35–37, 39–40, 81, 96, 99, 109–110, 142, 146, 172, 186, 194–196, 226, 242–243, 246, 248, 250, 330–331; *benshōhō* 弁証法, 8; Hegelian, 40; hyper-, 7, 40; Nishida's, 40
diaphanous. *See* transparency; transparent-qua-transparent
dichotomy. *See* duality/binarity
Dillon, M.C., 35, 206

Dilworth, David, xxi, xxx, 15, 17, 21, 195, 209, 333
Dionysius the Areopagite, 12
direct consciousness (*chokusetsu ni ishiki* 直接に意識), 84. *See also* box example, Nishida; internal-qua-external perception
direct experience (*chokusetsu keiken* 直接経験), 83. *See also* box example, Nishida; internal-qua-external perception
discipline, academic, xvi, xx–xxi, xxiii–xxiv, xxvi, xxviii, 12, 157–159, 307, 313, 317, 325, 337, 339–340; disciplinary, xvi, xix, xliii, xlv, 329, 337; disciplinary fluidity, 329; interdisciplinary, xxvii
discontinuity, xvi, xx, xxxviii, 25–26, 30–33, 37, 41, 43, 45–46, 71, 80–81, 108–109, 116, 119, 131, 141, 145–146, 157, 174, 188, 205, 220, 226, 235–236, 266, 270, 275, 322, 331, 335; between perceiver and perceived, 43; mere/unambiguous/simple/full, 37, 45, 174, 188, 275 (*see also* separation; *chōriston*); and obstruction, 145; partial, 275; physiological, 30. *See also* continuity; continuity of discontinuity
distal, 54, 108, 112–113, 118, 128–130, 135, 141, 229, 240; end of visual reach, 54, 118, 128, 130; extremity of brush, 112; extremity of cane, 108; organs, 240; solicitations, 191; solicitations, temporal, 191; source of motion, 229 (*see also* affordances; solicitations); stimuli, shift from proximal to, 107, 128–129, 141; stimulus, 107. *See also* ambiguity between distance and proximity; Koffka; proximal
distance, xiii, 11, 32–33, 36, 42–44, 54–56, 69, 73, 77, 103–104, 112, 114, 116–121, 135, 137, 141, 145–146, 207, 215, 240; action at a, 130, 135; binding-at-a-, 139; and distancelessness, 56, 69, 119, 131, 140, 144–146, 301; -proximity binary, 104, 121; and proximitiy, unambiguous, 32, 43, 56, 113, 118–119, 121, 240; and touch, 49, 114; and touch ambiguity, 114; non-perceptual, 119; relation at a, 137, 145; space and, 103, 112–113, 240; spectatorial, 43, 58. *See also ma* (間); proximity
distanceless distance, 56, 69, 116, 119, 131, 140, 145, 301. *See also ma* (間)
distant will, xlii, 224, 229, 257. *See also* Klee, Paul
DNA, 292, 314. *See also* holography
Dōgen, xxxv, 55, 79–80, 156, 175–177, 185, 228, 295, 326–327, 333
double belonging, 116. *See also* chiasm
doubt, xix–xx, xxiii, xxvi–xxix, xxxi–xxxii, xliii, 43, 101, 133, 139, 157, 164–168, 171, 173, 176, 178, 190, 211, 221–222, 253, 261, 277, 288, 291, 293, 295–297, 318, 321–325, 338–339. *See* faith; trust
dragon veins, 65, 70–71, 179; in landscape, 70, 179; in painting, 70. *See also* Daoism; Daoist aesthetics; *Fengshui;* invisibility of motor solicitations
drawing, xiii, xxxi, xxxvi, xlv, 11, 57, 84, 142, 167, 171, 205, 207, 209, 268, 271–272, 285, 287, 301, 311; from life (写生 *shasei*), 159

Dreyfus, Hubert, 212–213, 280
duality/binarity, xiv, xxxviii–xxxix, 1, 7, 25, 27, 36, 39–41, 66–67, 144–145, 158, 175, 197, 225, 297, 325, 329, 338; of chromatic/non-chromatic, xlii, 251–254, 257–259, 262; of distance/proximity, 104, 112–121; of identity/difference, xvi, xx–xxi, xxiv, xlv, 30, 80, 145; of in-itself/for-itself, 203; of internatlity/externality, 83–87, 89, 94–95, 175, 180–181, 215 (see also box example, Nishida; skin and bones); of motion/motionlessness, xli, 163, 170–171, 175, 180, 184, 190, 192, 229, 257; of negative/positive, 22–23, 26, 31–32, 36–37, 64, 69, 166–168, 171; of presence/absence, 66–69, 259, 331; of reason/faith, xxvi, 328–329; of sacred/secular, xiv, 4, 150–151, 156, 329–339; of subject/object, xliv, 2, 20–21, 25, 45, 53, 55–56, 59, 107, 111, 238, 245, 269–270; of surface/depth, xl, 87, 89–90, 95, 100; of the positive and negative, 31; of visible/invisible, xl, 6–7, 13, 32, 65–67, 69, 74, 80, 90, 163, 171, 281, 294; surface-depth binary, 90

"Early Spring" (Guo Xi), 57, 62–63. See also angle of totality; Chinese painting; landscape painting; multi-perspectivalism; negative space
Eckhart, Meister, xxi
ecstasis, 120, 141, 146, 149, 183, 245, 257, 261, 334; bodily, 130, 206; body's expansion through/as light, 131; light-based, 131; and materiality, 315; motor-, 229; of motor-perception in chromatic world, 261; of motor-perceptual gestures, 163; and mutual negation with cane/brush, 125; and the present, 78, 226; temporal dimension of body, 210; and temporality, 75, 78; and time, 79; and time consciousness, 80; time consciousness (Husserl), 76; tradition as historical-volitional, 228; visual, 112–113, 131, 255; visually ecstatic body, 112–113; volitionally ecstatic body, 230, 239, 241. See also ecstatic body
ecstatic body, perceptual, 78, 110, 112–113, 130–131, 163, 206, 210, 228–229, 239, 255, 261; tool use, 53, 100, 109, 116, 145; volitional, 230, 239, 241. See also ecstasis
Edo-period, xxxiv, 90, 92, 153
ego, 163, 222. See also self; non-self
Einstein, 184
élan vital, 303
Elberfeld, Rolf, xxxiv, xlv, 8–9, 55, 318
electromagnetism, 30, 114–118, 137; and difference from electrostatics, 115; interval as "distanceless distance" and cut-continuance, 116–117; and visual physiology, 30; divide, 117. See also Coulomb's Law; electrostatics
electrostatics, 114–115, 117; difference from electromagnetics, 115; expansion of the body, 114; outer layer of body, 114; repulsion, 113–115. See also Coulomb's Law; electromagnetism
embodiment, xxix, xxxviii, xli–xlii, xliv, 2, 14, 82, 102, 115, 151, 160, 168, 170, 273, 278, 291, 299, 325, 335, 338. See also body; motion; motor-perception; perception

Empedocles, xiii, 175
Empiricism, 10, 59, 126, 197
Emptiness (*Śūnyatā*), xl, xlv, 13–17, 19, 21, 40, 47–48, 54, 59, 67–69, 114, 121, 123, 145, 177, 183, 330
emptiness of emptiness (*śūnyatāyāḥ Śūnyatā*), 14–15, 40, 330. See also relational ontology
encounter, *Begegnung*, 8; encounterability, 23, 35–36, 40–42, 117, 133, 161, 259, 316, 340; intercultural, xiii, xviii, 34; phenomenal, xliv, 24, 33, 36, 38, 109, 251, 278. See also obstruction; non-obstruction
end-Forms, 278, 281
energeia, 175
enlightened mind, 151, 157–158, 292
enlightenment, xvii, xxii, 54–56, 158
ens extensum, 11
entrainment, 256. See also affordances, musical
enveloped-enveloping, 75, 204. See also reciprocity; bi-directional determination
enveloping (*fukumu* 含む), 6
epistemology, xxxi, xxxv, 3, 9, 20–22, 35, 43, 55–57; epistemological panopticon, 55; platonic, 57; *epistêmonikon*, 12; spectator theory of knowledge, 59
"Epsom Derby" (Gericault), 286–287. See also coherent deformation
equipmentality (*Zeughaft*), 106
Ereignis, 9
eschatology, xxi, 335
essence, 13–14, 23, 25, 93, 185, 188, 191, 227; *sabhāva* 14
essentialism, xxii, xxxiii, 14, 157, 160
eternal now (*eien no ima* 永遠の今), 81. See also negation and time
ethics, xxxi, xxxv, xxxvii, 3, 9–10, 15–17, 19, 321

etymology, 25–27, 39, 78, 123, 245, 273, 309, 330
eucharist, 337–338
Eurocentrism, xvi, xviii, 55–56
Europe, xvii, xxi–xxii, xxx, 168, 253, 277, 285
everything-touching-everything, 146. See also nothing touches anything; touch
existentialism, 8, 265, 306, 336; and Catholicism, xxv
expression, and control, 296; anthropocentric conceptions of, 178; artistic, xiv–xvi, xxv–xxxii, xxxiv, xxxvi, xxxix, xli, xliii–xliv, 1–2, 7, 10, 23–24, 29, 33, 48, 52, 91, 100, 106, 122, 136, 146, 161, 165, 169, 171–174, 185, 188, 190, 198, 201, 219, 223, 227, 230, 238–239, 244, 248, 265, 277, 284, 290, 298, 321, 323–325, 328, 330, 334, 337, 339; bi-directional, 207, 310; constitutive risk of, 15, 277, 283; desires, constraints of, 227; expressing-expressed, 199, 277, 310, 336; expressive world, 188, 197, 201, 320, 328, 333, 335; *exprimere*, 309; faithful, xxxii, xliii, 251, 308; freedom of, 196, 304; God's un-expressibility, 12; history of, 288; infinite form of, xlii interexpression, xliii, 17, 195, 198, 333, 335; materiality of spontaneous, 106, 307; and motion, 99; Nishida's theory as "from the made to the making," 294; ontologies of, 3, 175–176; paradox of, 3, 199, 325, 327; philosophic, xxx–xxxi, xliii, 12, 15, 324, 328; in positivist account of motion and volition, 230; reciprocity, 246, 302; reversible mode of, 194; risk of, 15, 277,

283; spontaneous expression, xliii, 106, 160, 163, 303, 305, 307–308, 313, 319, 324; techniques of, 317; theories of, xv, xxxi–xxxii, xliii, 3, 15, 26, 40, 80, 149, 194, 199, 223, 245, 285, 294, 296, 305, 331, 336; uni-directional, 311; without an artist, 173. *See also* creativity, creation

expression as "motor-perceptual faith," xli, xlv, 4, 23, 263, 265, 290, 328. *See also* expression, artistic

expressionism, 166

external organs (*gaibu kikan* 外部機関), 240. *See also* affordances; ecstasis; ecstatic body; solicitations

external perception (*gaibu chikaku* 外部知覚), 65. *See also* box example, Nishida; ecstasis; ecstatic body; internal perception

externality, xxviii, xxxiii, xl, xlv, 5, 11, 13, 15–16, 22, 38, 43, 46, 65, 81, 83–84, 86–87, 90, 94–95, 108, 140, 174–175, 180, 183, 194–195, 212, 215–216, 225, 228–229, 240–242, 248–249, 262, 272, 282, 306, 309, 316

experience, *keiken* (経験), 4, 21

Eyes, at end of chisel/brush, 104; palpation with, 68, 109, 112–113, 117, 121, 128–131, 135, 138, 140, 142–143, 214; synchronicity, hand-, 142–143; touching light, 128, 130; touching with, 112–113, 128, 130, 134

fabric, motor-perceptual, desires embedded within, 197; *étoffe*, 5 expressive, 176, 312, 333; inter-expressive, 312; metaphor, 4, 6–8, 27, 30, 33, 194, 284; motor-perceptual, 1, 7, 52, 93, 139, 147, 149, 150, 158, 180, 184, 188, 190, 193, 197, 199, 208–210, 212–213, 217, 248, 252–253, 262–264, 268, 274, 276, 279, 284, 315–316, 335, 337; motorsensory, 147, 172, 174, 188, 190, 192, 212, 218, 228, 231, 235, 247, 252, 256, 260, 265, 267–268, 304; ontological, 8, 33, 93, 115, 121; perceptual, 1, 5, 7, 34–35, 46, 51–52, 61, 68, 71–72, 80, 84, 93, 96, 98, 101, 111, 113, 119, 130–133, 139–140, 145, 149, 150, 153, 155, 157, 159–161, 163, 165, 167, 169, 171, 173, 175, 177, 179–181, 183–185, 187–191, 193, 195, 197, 199, 201, 203, 205, 207–213, 215, 217, 219, 221, 223, 225, 227, 229, 231, 233, 235, 237, 239, 241, 243, 245, 247–249, 251–253, 255, 257–259, 261–264, 266, 268, 273–274, 276, 279, 284, 315, 335, 337; of reality, xxvii, xxxv, 6, 116; texture of the motorsensory, 192, 265; visual, 73; volitional, 248

faith, -reason binaries, xxvi, 328–329; act of, 285, 326; bodily form of, xxvii, xliii–xliv, 42, 71, 208, 227–228, 277, 291; as communion, 338; in expression, xxxii, xliii, 251, 308; *foi perceptive*, xiv; methodological form of, 325, 328; motor-perceptual form of, xv, xli, xliii, xlv, 3–4, 23, 173, 239, 244, 263, 265, 267, 269, 271, 273, 275, 277, 279, 281, 283, 285, 287, 289–291, 293, 295, 297, 299, 301, 303, 305, 307, 309, 311, 313, 315, 317, 319, 321, 323, 325, 327–329, 331, 333, 335, 337, 339; motor-perceptual, expression as, xv, xli, 4, 23, 173, 239, 263, 290, 328, 339; non-transitive form of, 2, 4; ontic form of, 317; in perception, 2;

faith *(continued)*
intransitive, 2, 290; perceptual, xv, xx, xxvii, xxix, xli, xlv, 2, 4, 7, 23, 73, 263, 265, 267, 269, 271, 273, 275, 277, 279, 281, 283, 285, 287, 289–291, 293, 295, 297, 299, 301, 303, 305, 307, 309, 311, 313, 315, 317, 319, 321, 323, 325, 327–329, 331, 333, 335, 337, 339; primary, 298; religious, xiv, xxvii, 300, 306–307, 333–334, 336; *shinnen* 信念, xiv; somatic, 321; and spontaneous expression, 308. See also *Urdoxa*

famous spots (*meisho* 名所), 91, 159

Faure, Bernard, 3

feminine, 55, 67

fengshui (風水), 179–180

Fichte, Johann Gottlieb, 186

Fiedler, Conrad, 141–143, 239, 241, 258, 295

field, color, 253–255; of consciousness (*ishiki no ba* 意識の場), 21; of invisible ecstatic materiality, 315; multi-volitional, 209; non-obstructive, 24; perceptual, 4, 190, 259; pre-reflective, 9; visual, 78, 82, 120, 139, 182, 208, 213, 243, 253, 255, 295; warp and weft of perceptual, 4, 7, 34, 150, 190. See also *Basho*, flesh

field of consciousness (*ishiki no ba* 意識の場), 21

Field, S.L., 179

Fielding, Helen, 30

figurative, 30, 104

figure-ground shift, 215, 267

first-person, 9

Five Great Temples of China, 154

Five Mountain Art Academy, 220

Flak, Valentina, 142

Flesh (*chair*), activity and passivity, 171–173; and motor-perceptual fabric metaphor, 158–160, 171, 191, 252, 264, 268, 282, 316; and mutual negation, 18, 161, 274; and negated objectivity, 75; and perceptual fabric metaphor, 5–7, 115, 121, 135; as principle of motion, 176–177; as relational ontology, 102–103; of time, 75, 203–204. See also *Basho;* relational ontology

flexous line (Leonardo), 167

floating perspective (Guo Xi), 62, 168. See also multi-perspectivalism

foi perceptive. See perceptual faith

fold, 4–5, 199, 217, 280. *See* fabric metaphor

force, 53, 69, 90, 136, 138–139, 155, 175, 184, 186, 191, 229, 241, 261; formative forces, 278, 281; material, 315; mechanical, 136; of habit, 231; of historicity, 231; of tradition, 213, 285

foreshortening, 279

form, of the formless, xxxvi; is emptiness, emptiness is form, 28; vision of, 129. See also formlessness

formlessness, 162, 301; vision of, 129

Fóti, Véronique, 3

Foucault, Michel, 281

Frangi, Simone, 142

freedom, 136, 157, 195, 217–218, 224, 265, 304, 312; creative, 265; motor-perceptual, 218; of expression, 140, 196, 304; of motion, 140, 217

Fuji, 159, 236

fullness (*you* 有), 67. *See also* emptiness; presence

Fundierung, 7, 320

Fur Lined Teacup, 232–233

Gallagher, Shaun, 9, 207
Gegenstand, 197
Geidō practices, xxxiv–xxxv, 233, 306. See also Daoist aesthetics
Geijutsu, 104, 297
Gelassenheit, 191
generativity, 325; of the identity of opposites, 70; and the resistance of perceptual obstruction, 122
genitive, double, xxiv
geometry, xiii, 34, 42, 118, 168, 264. See also circumferenceless circle
geophilosophy, 179
geophysical, 70
Géricault, Théodore, 286–287
Gestalt psychology, xxv, 107
Gesture, artist's, as "lined" by landscape's motor-demand, 194; blindness of, 294; calligrapher's, xxxv; codified in Chinese manuals, 153, 192; color-inflected, 252, 256, 261–262; copying, 221; everyday, mundane, 3, 209; expressive, xliii, 16, 82, 93, 99, 120, 136, 139, 182, 190, 236, 293, 302; infinite, 295–296; motor-perceptually ecstatic, 163; painter's, 91, 121, 206, 217; religious, 332; solicited, 91, 190, 304, 316; spontaneous, 160, 164, 307, 312, 318; temporality of, 210, 293; temporally ecstatic, 210. See also movement, artistic
Ghilardi, Marcello, 15–16, 32, 39, 48, 68, 93, 221
Gibson, J.J., 123, 287
God, xiii, xx, xxv–xxix, 2, 12, 17, 23, 40, 270, 329–336; Christian, 329–330; creation, 332; -eye view, 97; *Gotheit*, xxi *kami* 神, 330; -human negation, 331–334; interexpression between man and, 16, 335; paradox of, 331; personalistic and transcendent, xxvii; self-contradictory unity of self and, 336; un-expressibility of, 12. See also anatheism; *Gotheit;* interexpression
Gosetti-Ferencei, J.A., 183
Grammar, xxxii, 2, 4, 7, 9–10, 12, 22, 24, 27–28, 30, 75, 246, 304, 318, 333; Aristotelian logic and, 24; and *Basho*, 22; Buddhist practice and, 14; and chiasm, 27–28, 75, 246, 333; of substance ontology, xxii, 2, 15, 22; subject-verb-object, 15, 28. See also A and not A; contradiction; Law of non-contradiction
gravity, 156, 216, 308, 310–311, 313–315
Greece, xvii, xix, xxxiii, xl, 11, 14, 27, 42–43, 51, 57, 175, 223; ancient, 27, 54, 56, 127
groundless ground, 14–15, 21, 23
Guernica, (Picasso) 288–289. See also camera technology
Guo Xi, xl, 3, 52, 57, 60–66, 79, 92, 103, 165, 168, 219, 251, 317

habit, 58, 107, 119, 230, 305, 311
Haboku Sansui (Splashed Ink Landscape), xxxiii, 150–152, 157, 160–162, 216–217, 251, 282, 285, 307, 318. See also *Hatsuboku Sansui*; Sesshū; landscape painting
haiku poetry, xix, 32, 157
Hamada, Shoji, 308
hand-eye synchronicity, 142–143
harmony, 3, 67, 87, 142, 179, 312, 335
Hasegawa, Tōhaku, 68–69
Hatsuboku Sansui, See *Haboku Sansui*
"have brush" (*yu pi*), 104. See also ecstatic body; too use; tool as non-object

"have ink" (*yu mo*), 104. *See also* ecstatic body; ink, agency of
hearing, 30, 117
Hegel, xvii, xxii–xxiii, 15, 39–40, 55–56
Heian period, xxxv, 234
Heidegger, Martin, xxxvi, xlv, 8–9, 27, 78, 106, 191, 276, 281, 306, 326, 331, 334
Heisig, James, xv, xxi, 15, 184, 199, 245, 250, 271
Heraclitus, xix
Herder, J.G., 56
hermeneutics, 19, 28, 207
Hermes Trismegistus, xiii
Hiroshi, Ōnishi, 155
historical body (*rekishiteki shintai* 歴史的身体), 25, 193–194, 274. *See also* body
historical world (*rekishiteki sekai* 歴史的世界), 17, 25, 99, 191, 193–196, 199–202, 205, 208, 245, 247, 271, 274, 277, 336
history, art, 51, 60, 87, 93, 113, 122, 156, 168, 190, 220, 222, 233, 237; historiography, 155; of motion, 190; of motor-visibility, 278; Nishida's philosophy of, 274–276; of expression, 288; of other's expressions, 284, 288; pre-, 205, 209; pull of, 191; thickness of, 207. *See also* historical body, historical world
Hokusai, 232
holographic model, 290, 292, 294
Hoover, Thomas, 154, 257
horizon, 5, 20, 76–78, 87, 143, 187, 203, 208, 212, 215–216, 260, 288, 319; of intentionality, 76, 203 (*see also* protentions [and retentions]); internal, external, 87, 215–216, 260; of motorsensory demands, 232; temporal, 76–78, 288

hōronriteki, 6
hosshin-seppō (法身説法), xxxv, 176. *See also mujō-seppō* (無情説法); language
Huayan Buddhism, xlii, 15–19, 22, 24, 109, 276, 293. *See also* Kegon
Huifeng, Shi, 28
Huineng, 21
humanism, xx, xxvi
Husserl, Edmund, xvii, xxiii, 8–9, 76–79, 85, 115, 119, 184, 202–204, 206, 242, 320, 322; account of time, influence on Merleau-Ponty, 77; consciousness, ecstatic, 76; divergence with Merleau-Ponty, 79; ecstatic temporality, 77; motor-intentionality, 184; protentions (and retentions), 203; time consciousness, 76
Hylomorphic Theory (Aristotle), 11
hyper-dialectic (*hyper-dialectique*), 7, 40
hyper-realism, 71. *See also* representational positivism
hyper-reflection (*sur-réflexion*), xxvii, 8, 301, 323, 326. *See also* reflection; paradox of reflecting on the pre-reflective

I-thou (*watashi to nanji* 私と汝), 38, 40. *See also* non-self
idealism, 10, 20, 111, 304
identity, 23, 25, 36, 46, 81, 156, 167, 187, 200, 248, 284
identity and difference, xvi, xx–xxii, xxiv, xxvi, xxxviii, xlv, 14, 25, 30, 35, 44, 46, 80, 145, 264, 340. *See also* A and not A; substance ontology language
identity of contradiction, 195, 306, 329. *See also* absolutely contradictory self-identity
identity-difference thinking, xxii, xlv
ikebana, 32. *See also kire* (切れ); *Geidō*

image, xxix, xxxiii, 16, 30, 43, 55, 62, 64, 66–69, 122, 155, 160, 217, 220–222, 232, 239, 265, 271, 287–288, 293–294, 320; infrared, 131; thermal, 131; x-ray, 131

imitation, 185, 220, 279. *See also* copy; copy and original; representation; *shinkeizu*

immanence, xxvii–xxviii, xli, 51, 111, 183, 203, 241, 276, 329, 332, 335–336

immateriality, 7, 46. *See also* materiality; matter; non-sentient matter

immediacy, 4, 37, 39, 76, 122, 125, 128–129, 134–135, 137, 150, 162, 173, 182, 188, 203, 208, 241, 285, 297, 310, 324–325. *See also* mediation

impermanence, 13, 51, 79, 172

Impressionists, 165–167, 253
  Cézanne's critique of, 166–167

improvisation, 192, 310, 318; musical, 318. *See also* spontaneous expression

inanimate, 106, 175–176, 178, 307, 333; and inanimate nature/world, 175–176, 179, 307, 333; matter, 175; sculpted bodies, 94

incarnation, xxvii, 132

incomensurability, 118, 264

incompleteness, constitutive, 266

indirect consciousness (*Kankaku-teki ishiki ni chokusetsudenai* 感覚的意識に直接でない), 84. *See also* box example, Nishida

indirect experience (*kansetsu keiken* 間接経験), 83. *See also* box example, Nishida

individual, xxii, 11–12, 17–18, 24–25, 38, 46, 187, 195, 198–200, 208, 222–223, 229, 237, 254, 273, 275, 284, 333–334

individualism, xxxiv, 3, 222, 224

Ineinander, 75, 80, 204. *See also* enveloped-enveloping

inertia, 11. *See also* material objectivity, reductionism

infinite, activity, 185, 296, 330; activity of God, 330; angle, 270; artist's gesture, 295; circle without circumference, xiii, 270; faith, 336; form of expression, xlii, 290; limited-yet-, xliii; *mugen* 無限, 327; logos, 295; reflecting mirrors, 270; task, 208, 243; vision, 278; world's demands, 321. *See also* risk, attempt to reduce

infinite continuity of acts (*sayō no mugen renzoku* 作用の無限連続), 184, 187, 190, 191, 228, 267, 276, 304, 335. *See* affordances; background motor solicitations

ink, xxxiii, 69, 104, 151–154, 160, 162–163, 216–217, 251–252, 257–258, 262, 312–313; agency of, 216–217; black, all colors within, 252, 257–259; inkwork, 217; landscape painting, xxxiii, 150–152, 157, 160–162, 216–217, 251, 282, 307, 318; painters, 259; painting (*shigajiku* 詩画軸), 155; *sumi* (墨), 151; technique of splashed-, 162–163. *See also* "have ink" (*yu mo*)

innovation, xliv, 9–11, 52, 79, 89, 94, 100, 109, 150, 154–155, 160, 168–170, 173, 199, 218–223, 231–232, 234–235, 253, 278–280, 282–283, 289–290, 317–318, 327. *See also* novelty; originality, myth of

insentience, 14, 77, 98, 176, 210

institution (*fundierung*), xxxvii, 7, 320. *See also* interexpression

intercultural encounter, xiii, xviii, 34. *See also* comparison

interdependence, 17, 70, 172, 249. *See also* dependent origination interdisciplinary, xxvii. *See also* ambiguity philosophic-religious; discipline, academic

interexpression (*hyōgen-teki kankei* 表現的関係), xliii, 3, 8, 10, 16–17, 25, 153, 195, 198, 309, 311, 315–316, 328–329, 331, 333–336; between body and world, 195, 315; between God and man, 16, 335; and faith, 334–336; god-human negation, 331–334; as making-made, 261, 309, 311, 331; and negation, 16, 316, 333, 335; and sokuhi logic, 16. *See also* created-creating; making-made reciprocity

interiority and exteriority, 83, 86, 88–89. *See also* box example, Nishida; skin and bones

intermediary, 123, 137, 139, 288–289; deformations, 289. *See also* mediation; obstruction; opacity; transparency

internal organs and external organs, 240. *See also* ecstatic body

internal perception (*naibu chikaku* 内部知覚), 65, 83. *See also* box example, Nishida; ambiguity of surface and depth

internal perception-*qua*-external perception (*naibu chikaku soku gaibu chikaku* 内部知覚即外部知覚), 66, 81–83, 181. *See also* ambiguity of surface and depth; box example, Nishida

internality, 86, 95, 180; -external binary, 83, 87, 94; and external horizons, 216; and external sources of motion, 175; and external structures, 87; muscular perception, 241; principle of motion, 175. *See also* externality

interpenetration, 33, 67, 331. *See also* chiasm, continuity of discontinuity

interrogation (*interrogation*), 323

intersubsumption, Tiantai concept of, 98, 198. *See also* negation unambiguous; non-obstruction, full

intertwining (*entrelacs*), xxxvi, xxxviii, 7, 25, 33, 46, 66, 80, 102, 104, 109, 183, 189, 216, 231, 239, 303, 316, 338. *See also* chiasm; continuity of discontinuity

interval, 32, 52, 54, 75, 116–117, 119, 121, 131, 136, 312. *See also* distance, *ma* (間)

interweave, xxxviii, 22, 25, 27, 31, 33, 45, 52, 71, 174, 192, 267. *See also* intertwining; fabric metaphor

intransitivity, 290, 316; form of faith, 2, 290. *See also* ambiguity of subject and object; transitivity

intuitionism, 186

intuitions, 100, 103, 114, 121, 137

inverse correspondence/polarity (*gyakutaiō* 逆対応), 8, 329–333

inverse determination (*gyakugentei* 逆限定), 199. *See also* determination

inverted parallelism, 27–28. *See also* chiasm, grammatical

invisibility, 5–7, 13, 32, 44, 66–67, 140, 163, 171, 189, 265–266, 281, 290; ambiguity of visibility and, 6, 13, 32, 66–67, 74, 80, 266, 281, 294; of artist's expressive movements, 171; of artist's style, 284; of background acts, 188; and field of ecstatic materiality, 315; irreducible, 290; of kimono's lining, 6; of motor solicitations, 179; lining of, 5–6, 27, 65, 207, 266; of motor-perceptual medium, 53, 130–132; of motor-world's demands on body, 189; of perceptual medium, 123, 132; partial, 140; pure (unambiguous), 70; reversibility of visibility and, 71; and visibility in Daoism, 65–72;

visible-invisible binary, 27, 34, 257. *See also* opacity; *punctum ceacum*; visual obstruction
Ireneus, 11
Ishihara, Yuko, 8–9, 269
Ishii, Kōsei, 17
Iwaki, Ken'ichi, 186, 188

Japanese philosophy, xxi, xxiii–xxiv, xxvii, 8, 186, 269, 271, 292. *See also* Kyoto School
Jay, Martin, 54–55, 59
jemeinigkeit, 276
Johnson, Galen, 5, 10, 30, 207, 282, 284
Jones, Nicholaos John, 15
Josetsu, 220
Josui Sōen, 161
judō, xxxiv. See also *Geidō*
Jullien, Francois, 62, 64, 66–67
Jung, Hwa Yol, xvii–xviii, 34, 55, 179

kadō, xxxiv. See also *Geidō*
kaisho ("formal") Chinese painting style, xxxv. *See also* Chinese painting
Kant and Kantianism, xxii–xxiii, 8, 21–22, 43, 55–56, 197
karate, xxxiv
Kasulis, Thomas, xlv, 196, 292
Kata, xxxiv. See also *Geidō*
Kaushik, Ravi, 264
Kazashi, Nobuo, 20–21, 25, 208, 246
Kearney, Richard, 337–339
Kegon Buddhism, 17, 292. *See also* Huayan Buddhism
Kells, Book of, 27
kendō, xxxiv. See also *Geidō*
kenosis, xxi
kenshō, 54
Kierkegaard, Søren, xxi
Kim, Ha Tai, 15, 228
kimono, 6. *See also* invisibility; lining
King, Philip, 89

kire (切れ "cutting"), 31–32, 46, 54, 69, 75, 330. *See also* cut-continuance
Klee, Paul, xlii, 3, 141–142, 224, 228–229, 278–279, 281–282, 320
kōan, xxiii
Koffka, Kurt, 107
Kopf, Gereon, xxi, xxxix, 15–17, 39, 279
Krauss, Rosalind, xl, 87–90, 93
Krueger, Joel, 210, 256, 318
Krummel, John, xxi, 17–18, 25–26, 28, 39–40, 81, 96, 145–146, 197, 202, 246, 249–250, 269, 278, 334–335
Kūkai, xxxv, 156, 176, 278
Kullman, Michael, 167
künstlerische Tätigkeit, 248
Kyoto School, xiii, xxi–xxii, 3, 8, 15, 155, 184, 250, 336. *See also* Japanese philosophy
kyudō, xxxiv. See also *Geidō*

Landes, Daniel, 3, 199
Landscape, artist's gestures "lined" by motor-demand of, 194, 231; dragon veigns of, 70, 179; expressive impulse embedded within, 240; motor-perceptual demands of, 112, 141, 183; as non-object, 2, 48, 62, 68, 242; as object, 4, 163; skin and bones of, 90, 95
landscape gardening, dry, 156
landscape painting, xix, xxxv, 7, 32, 62, 70, 104–105, 162, 192, 218–219, 221–222, 231, 233–234, 251, 317; artist, xvi, 66; broken ink, 162; Chinese, 62, 192, 218–219, 222, 231; *Haboku Sansui* (Splashed Ink Landscape), xxxiii, 150–152, 160–162, 216–217, 251, 282, 307, 318; *Hatsuboku Sansui*, 285; ink, xxxiii, 15–152, 157, 160–162, 216–

landscape painting *(continued)* 217, 251, 282, 307, 318; *Nanga* school (南画), 90, 93, 153, 155, 159, 219; Northern Song School of, 179; Song Chinese, 62, 154, 159, 317; Southern Song School of, 312, 317; splashed ink, 151, 160–163, 216–217, 251, 282, 307, 318; tradition of monochrome (*sansuiga* 山水画), 251

Language, and chiasm, 31–32 and ontology, 5, 9–12, 23, 28, 167, 246; anthropocentric notion of, 177; of materiality, 309–310; motor-perceputal, 310; nature's, 158, 177. See also *hosshin-seppō* (法身説法); *parole parlante* and *parole parlée*, 323

Lascaux, 194, 218, 280. *See also* conditions of visibility

lateral universal, xviii. *See also* comparison; intercultural encounter

Lau, Kwok-Ying, xviii

Lawlor, Leonard, 97, 101

Léger, Fernand, 60

Leibniz, Gottfried Wilhelm, 3, 264, 270; view from nowhere, 270

Leonardo, da Vinci, 167, 279

Levin, D.M., 54–55, 59

Levine, Gregory, xxxiii, 155

Light, -based ecstasis, 131; -based illumination, 131–132; -based mediation, 125; -based metaphors, 56. *See also* ocularcentrism; achieving partial transparency, 130; -based mutual negation, 131; -based obstructing-revealing dynamic, 125; -based vision, 52, 103, 127, 135–136; body's expansion through/as, 131; body's relation to, 53, 100, 103, 113, 122–123; causation through medium of, 135; energy of (*hikari no enerugi* 光のエネルギー), 48; forces of, 139; as inherently non-obstructive, 53; as inherently obstructive, 53; as inherently transparent medium, 121; intermediary of, 127–128, 136, 138–139; luminosity, 55; as not inherently transparent medium, 53; obstructive features of, 122, 125, 127, 129–132, 134–135, 139, 141 (*see also* resistance of the sensible); and ontology of negation, 53; period of learning to intertwine with, 126–129, 133–135; positivist conception of, 52; -related tools, 125; reversibility of, 135; semi-transparency of, 134; sensation of (*kankaku* 感覚), 48; tool-like features, 56, 113, 121–130, 133–136, 140–141, 149; visibility of, 130; -waves, 138, 206

Linde, Han, 292

lining, 73, 77, 81, 194, 208, 230, 266; *doublure*, 5; of invisibility, 5, 27, 65, 207; of a kimono, 6; of negative in positive of motion, 172; of passivity in activity, 187, 216; perception, 182; of self-power within other-power, 333; *tapiss*, 5; the visible, 65; 裏付ける, 5–6

Lippit, Yukio, xxxiii, 69, 155, 160, 162, 216–217

literati (文人畫 *wenrenhua*), 90–92, 160. *See also* Chinese painting

literature, xxi, 27–28, 56, 91, 142, 155, 183, 237, 325

little phrase (Proust), 325

live by dying, 81, 83

Locke, John, 43, 126

Logic, xvi, xxvi, xxx, xxxii, 2, 6, 15–16, 21–23, 25, 36, 44, 64,

95, 109, 113, 119, 142, 145, 194, 196–199, 243, 262, 292–293, 340; Aristotelian subject-based, 197–199, 270; correspondence-based aesthetic, 280; Eastern, 197; holographic, 293; logos, xx, 20, 196, 200, 208, 295; Mahāyāna *sokuhi*, 21; Nishida's predicate, 248, 270; object (*taisho ronri* 対象論理), 21; peri-logical (*hōronriteki*), 6; of place (*basho no ronri* 場所の論理, *bashoteki ronri* 場所的論理), 20; predicate-based, 197–198; of *sokuhi* (*sokuhi no ronri* 即非の論理), 15–16; *sokuhi* logic, 15–16, 18, 21, 23; subject logic (*shugoteki ronri* 主語的論理), 21; subject-based, 197–199, 270; world (*sekai no ronri* 世界の論理), xxiv, 329

logic of absolutely contradictory self-identity (*zettai mujunteki jikodōitsu no ronri* 絶対矛盾的自己同一の論理), 22

Lotus Sūtra, 154

Ma (間), 32, 54, 69, 75. *See also* ambiguity of distance and proximity; distanceless-distance

Ma Yuan, 162, 220, 317

Madhyamaka Buddhism, 14

Mahāyāna Buddhism, xxiv, xl, 13–16, 28, 39–40, 54, 56, 59, 61, 330

Mahendran, Dilan, 214, 216, 242

making and being made (*tsukuraretamono kara tsukurumono e* 作られたものから作るものえ), 3, 23, 194, 199, 231, 248, 309, 331. *See also* ambiguity; creation; interexpression

Maldiney, Henry, 322

Malebranche, Nicolas, xxx, 43

Mandala, 150, 292

maps/mapping, 120, 242, 271–272, 283; map, perfect (Josiah Royce), 271; mapmaker, 271–272; mapping, 270, 272. *See also* representation

Maraldo, John, xxi–xxiii, 8–9, 18, 25, 39, 194–195, 200, 202, 223, 245–246, 249, 269–272, 276, 278, 295, 297, 330–331

Marra, Michael, 142

Marratto, Scott, 174, 199, 210, 256, 305

Marxism, xxv

material, xxxvii, 105–106, 114, 153, 169, 212, 214, 233, 251, 308–310, 312–316; agency of artist's, 216; constraints on artist, 106, 310; circumscribability, 114; inert, 175; invisible field of ecstatic, 315; lining, 73, 77, 81, 194, 208, 230, 266; of a kimono, 6; motionless, 287–288; non-sentient, 106; objectivity, 68, 75, 110; obstruction, 124; reductionism, 178; of representation, 287; and spontaneity, 312; of tools, 102, 125, 139. *See also* immateriality; lining; warp and weft of perceptual

materialism, 6, 111

materiality, xliii, 4, 6, 19, 116, 207, 288, 304, 308–311, 313–316; and ecstasis, 315; and faith, 314, 316–317; invisible ecstatic, 315; invisibility and field of ecstatic, 315; joint-materiality of body and world, 307; of representation, 287; of spontaneous expression, 106, 307–308

Matisse, Henri, 163, 295

maximum clarity/sharpness, 213–215

Mazis, Glen, 204–206

McMahan, David, 54, 59

Meacham, Darian, 207
media, 209, 309
mediality, xxvii, 122, 124, 136, 141. *See also* of transparent mediality
mediation, xlii, 6, 22, 25–26, 35–36, 42, 55, 108, 116, 118, 124, 131, 137–138, 146, 200, 268, 331, 333, 335
meditation, xix, xxiii, xxix, xxxvii, 55, 143, 150, 157–158, 172, 189, 191, 242, 249, 304, 307, 336; Cézanne's "germinations," 163; motionlessness, xli, 163, 170–171, 175, 180, 184, 188, 190, 192, 229, 249, 257; Sesshū, 157, 172; and visual stillness, 249; zazen, xxiii, 158. *See also* ambiguity of motion and motionlessness; Buddhist practice; Nishida's practice; practice, zen religious; religious practice
medium, 22, 43, 52–53, 60, 121–124, 128–131, 137–140, 160, 196–197, 238, 257, 287, 308–310, 312–316. *See also* distance; distanceless-distance; mediation
Meiji-era, xxi–xxii
memory of the world, 207
metaphor, xxv, 4, 6, 16, 43, 54–56, 59, 69–70, 99, 112–113, 116, 137, 164, 171, 180, 223, 250, 272, 317, 327, 337; dragon, 70; of fabric, 4, 6–8, 27, 30, 33, 194, 284; light-based, 54, 56. *See also* ocularcentrism; of self-mirroring, 271; religious, xxv; vision-based, 54–56
metaphysics, and grammar, 2, 4, 10; of color, 251; of copy and original, 219; dualist, 325, 329; part-whole, 291–293; part-whole and temporality, 291; Plato, 57; positivist, 109, 169, 174, 228,

328; of presence, 109, 169, 325; of representation, 42, 59; subject-object, xliv, 53, 55–56, 107; transitive, 10; of vision, xl, 61
methodology, xiv, xix–xx, xxvii–xxviii, xxx, xxxii, xxxvii, xliii, xlv, 277, 291, 298, 323–324, 328, 339; and ambiguity, 325; based on reflection, 321; comparative, xliv–xlv, 34; of doubt and reflection, 290; of faith, 325, 328; methodological doubt, 291, 297, 323, 328; phenomenological, xxxvi; philosophic, xiv, xvi, xix, xxviii, xxxii, xxxvi–xxxvii, 4, 14, 303, 322–323, 328–329; purity, 328; religious, xxx; *shinkeizu* (真景図) painting, 93, 219
Mi Fu, 317
Michelangelo, 157, 211
middle voice, 34, 123. *See also* ambiguity, subject-object
middle way, 14, 167. *See also* Madhyamaka; Mahāyāna
mind, xv, xx, xxx, xxxiv, xliv, 4, 7, 14, 29, 41–44, 55, 60, 69, 76, 78, 86, 111, 115–116, 124, 134, 138, 141–142, 150–151, 194, 196, 210, 237–238, 255, 257, 264, 305, 317, 320
Ming Dynasty, 154, 159
minimalism, xxxvi
Minoru, Watada, 155
mirror, 10, 55, 72–73, 94, 181, 185, 270–272, 280, 295, 327, 332
mirroring, 270–271, 297 self-, 271
modernist, 122, 166
modernity, 91, 175
Moeller, Hans-Georg, 67
Molyneux's Problem, 125
Molyneux, William, 125–127, 129, 132–135

monism, 10, 111, 144–145, 248
monochrome, 251–253, 257–259, 262; color expressed in, 251–252, 257–258; ink painting, 156; landscape painting (*sansuiga* 山水画), 251; and negation, 259. *See also* black and white; ink
Mont Sainte Victoire, 163–165, 200, 216, 218, 236, 244, 282, 302. *See also* Cézanne; landscape as non-object
morphology, 26–28, 92, 142 skeletal, 87
Morris, Robert, 89
motion, ambiguity of motionlessness and, xli, 163, 170–171, 175, 180, 184, 190, 192, 229, 257; background of, 184, 190; of color, 254–255, 261; color-inflected, 255–257; freedom of, 140; invisibility, 262, 321; and negation, 172, 226, 267; ontological source of, 175–177, 186; origin of, 228; and perception (*see also* motor-perception); positivist account, 174, 183; relative motion (Einstein), 184; reversibility of, 264; and risk, 268; time and, 146, 149, 150, 170; as vision, 240–251. *See also* background motor-solicitations; motor-perception
motionlessness, xxxvii, xli–xlii, 150, 157–158, 163, 169, 171–172, 175, 182, 184, 188–192, 228–230, 242, 251, 253–255, 257, 259, 261–262, 287, 306, 328; ambiguity of motion and, xli, 163, 170–171, 175, 184, 190, 192, 229, 257. *See also* motion
motor-, background, 178, 191, 216, 229; chromaticity, 252, 254; continuity, 236; demand, 82, 163, 182, 193–194, 242; entwined position, 231; intentionality (Husserl), 184; negation, xli–xlii, 180, 192, 210, 240; neutrality, 182–183, 185, 190, 212, 231–232, 254, 257, 261, 268, 302, 315; pull, 314; sensory, 160–161, 170, 183, 190, 205, 208–210, 221, 231, 244, 250, 290, 307, 313; visibility, conditions of, 235, 238, 278, 280, 283. *See also* motor-perception
motor-perception/ual, and time, temporality, 78; background motor-solicitations, 182–184, 188–189, 191, 212, 215, 224, 231, 267, 304; background of motor-demands, 183, 216, 228; blind spot, 265, 267, 271, 280, 283; continuity, 48, 80, 91, 142, 168, 212, 291; continuity of act and act, xli, 178–179, 187–189, 193, 197, 209–210, 212, 217, 229–230, 234, 289, 297; continuity with landscape, 48, 80, 91; demand, 24, 196, 207, 238, 244; desires, 196; determination, 24; directive from the landscape, 112; disciplines, 157; ecstasis in chromatic world, 261; ecstasis, 146, 163, 261; externality, 282; fabric, 1, 7, 52, 93, 139, 147, 149, 150, 158, 180, 184, 188, 190, 193, 197, 199, 208–210, 212–213, 217, 248, 252–253, 262–264, 268, 274, 276, 279, 284, 315–316, 335, 337; fabric, expressive desires of, 197; field, 138, 149, 182, 191, 240; form of faith, xv, xli, xlv, 4, 23, 173, 239, 263, 265, 267, 269, 271, 273, 275, 277, 279, 281, 283, 285, 287, 289–291, 293, 295, 297, 299, 301, 303, 305, 307, 309, 311, 313, 315, 317, 319, 321, 323, 325, 327–329, 331, 333, 335, 337, 339; freedom, non-intertwined, 218; historicity

motor-perception/ual *(continued)* of objects, 233; innovations, 168; language, 310; -neutral visual position, 254; negation, xlii, 24, 146, 161, 174, 180, 188, 205, 241, 251, 309; neutrality, 313, 316; neutrality, fallacy of, 311, 313; obstruction, 267, 277, 284 performance, 221; practices, 3, 103; pull, 231, 314; reversibility, 242; risk, xliii, 227, 294; solicitations, 201, 233, 294; vacuum, 250, 312, 314, 316

motor-visibility, 235, 238, 278, 280, 283; conditions of, 235, 238, 278, 280, 283; history of, 278. *See also* motor-perceptual; vision

motorsensory, continuum of *Basho* or flesh, 250; demands, horizon of, 232; expectations, 235; externality, 150, 191, 291; form of faith, xv, xliii, 3, 244, 311, 315; limits and obstructions, 20; torsion, 235. *See* motor-perception

Mounier, Emmanuel, xxv

mountain, xxx, xxxv, 16, 26, 32, 34, 41, 51, 62, 64, 70, 79, 99, 105, 117, 121, 123, 153, 161–163, 165, 169, 175–177, 179, 192, 200, 216, 218, 230, 232, 234–236, 240–242, 253, 258, 292, 302, 317, 335. *See also* landscape; landscape as non-object; Mont Sainte Victoire

movement, and risk, 210, 228; artistic, 52, 62, 147, 163, 189, 295, 310; bodily, 144, 174, 185–186, 188, 208, 217, 253, 267, 271, 303, 312; of chromatic world, 262; constitutive risk of, 228; constrain and enable, 212, 309; control of, 227–228, 267, 290; deliberative, 304; expressive, 120, 142, 171, 189, 192, 208, 217, 238–239, 244, 247–248, 265, 293, 296, 305; eye, 142, 144; freedom of, 140; hand, 142–144; of hand guided by the visual, 143; of nature, 163, 176; religious, 150; solicitation, 1, 82, 196, 212, 217, 221, 230, 236, 256; spontaneous, 144, 160, 303–310, 317–320; time, temporality, 169, 204, 305, 316; as vision, 239–251, 264; vision and, 239–240, 264; without a mover, 263–264. *See also* background; conditions of; motion; motor-; motor-perception

moving without a mover, xv. *See* negation, motor-; non-action

moving-moved, 174. *See also* bi-directionality; reciprocity

mujō-seppō (無情説法), 176. *See also hosshin-seppō* (法身説法)

multi-Perspectivalism, xl–xli, 49, 51, 54, 57, 60–62, 64–65, 72–73, 76–77, 80–82, 87, 95–97, 100, 168, 180, 192, 208–209, 229, 264, 268–269, 272–273, 278; achieved rather than given, 60; and depth, 65, 73, 80–81; in Guo Xi's "Early Spring," 57, 79; in Ike no Taiga, 87; and "infinite vision"/omni-perspectivalism, 278; as "internal-qua-external" perception, 82, 272; and negation, 61–62, 65; obstructions, 97; and ocularcentrism, 54; and perception, 57; and reversibility, 73; as "seeing without a seer," 96; simulating, 65; with Cézanne, 168; with "Three Graces," 61–62, 65

multi-stability, xxxix, 7, 229. *See also* figure-ground shift

Munson, Thomas, 167

Muromachi Period, 62, 153–154, 156, 160, 168

muscular sensation, 181, 229, 240–241
music, 111, 139, 210, 221, 256, 318, 329; affordances, 318; Chinese painting as musical score, 221; improvisation, 318; musical instrument as foreign object, 111; musically extended body, 319; musicking-in-listening, 318
mutual negation, Huayan, 22; and obstruction, 134, 275–276; "absolute negation" (*zettai hitei*) as, 39–40, 202; between "historical body" and "historical world," 195; between artist and landscape, 192; body-tool, 105–106, 129; color and, 261; fabric analogy, 33–34, 46; faith and, 265, 333, 335; flesh, 274; god-human, 331–333; and interexpression, 311; I-thou, 40; light-based, 131; ontologies of, 146, 180, 217, 263, 274–275, 329; physiological, 29, 33; relationality as, 20, 149, 252, 278; reversibility of, 133, 143; and time, 75–76, 204; two-way, partial, 38; volitional, 226. See also *Basho*; chiasm; continuity of discontinuity; flesh
Muybridge, Eadweard, 286–287
mystical and apophatic traditions, East and West, 331

Nāgārjuna, 14
Nanga school (南画), 90, 93, 153, 155, 159, 219. See also landscape painting
narcissism, fundamental (*narcissisme fundamental*), 74
narcissism and anonymity, 74, 94; narcissism and anonymity of vision, 74, 94; narcissistic perception, 74, 94. See also self; non-self
nature, xx, xxvi, xxxv, xxxvii, 2, 9, 13–14, 19, 25, 34, 54, 66–67, 69, 92, 99, 104, 153, 157–159, 163, 165, 175–177, 184, 193, 198, 200, 202, 216–217, 220, 224–225, 227, 230, 250–251, 258, 274–275, 279, 281–282, 284, 292, 296–297, 303–304, 309, 317, 322, 326–327, 330, 333, 335; Cézanne's concept of, 166. See also objectivity
negation, affirmation and, 22, 41, 301; ambiguity, xxxvii, 116, 144; beyond affirmation and, 22; chiasmatic, 24, 28, 34, 74, 80–82, 161, 202; of color, 259–262; of consciousness, 35; continuously-discontinuous, 87, 129, 275; deific, 331; dynamics of, 21–22; and emptiness, 40; expressing-expressed, 2, 305; and faith, 2, 306, 324, 329; and God, 331–333, 336; historic, 205; and light, 131; limits, obstructions to, xli, 100, 129, 134, 278, 284; materiality of, 312; motor-, xli–xlii, 180, 192, 210, 240; motor-perceptual, xli–xlii, 24, 146, 161, 174, 180, 188, 205, 241, 251, 309; motorsensory, 24, 310; and multi-perspectivalism, 82, 192; multivalent, 41; and narcissistic vision, 94; negated subject, 2, 41, 45–46, 161, 269, 284, 305; negating-negated, 68, 331; non-object, 75, 161; and *sokuhi* logic, 16; of object, 2, 44, 46–48, 107, 163, 167–168; of object, full/complete/unambiguous, 98, 166–167; of one's desires, 201, 224; one-sided, 41, 331; ontology of, 52–53, 69, 146, 180, 252 (see also *Basho* (場所); flesh); ontology of negation regarding light, 53; partial, 201, 226, 274; perceptual, xl, xlii–xliii, 16, 41, 45, 71, 74, 94, 109, 146,

negation *(continued)*
160–161, 180, 188, 192, 251, 259; reciprocal, 33, 161, 316 (*see also* bi-directional(ity)); relationality, xxxviii, 14, 19–20, 104, 116, 274; reversibility, 133, 143; risk of, 284; self-negation, 160, 202, 222–223, 305, 332–333; self- (*jiko hitei* 自己否定), 16, 22, 25, 38–39, 109, 160, 202, 226, 305–306, 331–333; sponteneity and, 161; structure of, 4, 26, 42, 48, 306; of subject, xiv, xxiii, 2, 36, 41, 45–46, 161, 225, 260, 269, 284, 305; of subject, full/complete/unambiguous, 36, 98, 157, 247, 263, 269–270, 273–274, 276–278 (*see also* nothingness" [*nullité absolue*] in Sartre); temporality, time and, xl, 75–76, 79, 81–82, 202, 204, 209, 274; theories of, xxxviii, 20, 24; volitional, 187, 226, 236, 248, 250, 262, 311; with landscape, 161, 163, 192, 330. *See also* absolute nothingness (*nullité absolue*) in Sartre; mutual negation
negative theology, 331
negativity, xxxviii, 13, 18, 22–23, 32, 36–38, 42, 44, 46–48, 70, 79, 166, 168, 204, 265, 333; absolute, 36, 166, 217; circumscribed, 204; consciousness-as-pure-, 47 (see also *nullité absolue*); constitutive role of, 145; faith in/as, 333; focuses of, 48; full, 36, 40; in Hasegawa's painting, 70; interweaving of positivity and, 22, 26; mode of depiction between positivity and, 167, 253; positivity and, 16, 23, 26, 32, 36–38, 166–168, 253; pure, 36; subjective, 37
negintuition of nothingness, 328
Nelson, L., 192

Neo-Confucianism, xxii, 317
Neo-Kantian, xxiii, 21, 197
nerve fibers, 115, 137
Nicephorus, 11
Nietzsche, Friedrich, xix, 32, 59, 175, 196, 329
Nightingale, A.W., 59
nihilism, 14
Nishida, Kitarō, conception of God, xxvii, 17, 329–336 (*see also* interexpression); dialectics, 40, 81, 248, 331; notion of temporality, 79; ontology, xxiii, xxvi, 1, 6, 8, 39, 175, 195, 202, 246, 274, 276, 330, 332; phenomenology, 8–10; philosophy of history, 274; predicate logic, 248, 270
Nishijima, G.W., 80
Nishitani, Keiji, xxiii, 17
Nō drama, 32, 156
Noe, Keiichi, 8
Noma, Seiroku, 258
non-action (*wuwei* 無爲), xxxiv, 13, 276. *See also* improvisation; negation, volitional; non-self; spontaneity
non-circumscribability, 12. *See also* circumscribability; formlessness
non-contradiction, laws of, xxxii, 9, 11–12, 15, 21–22, 29–30. *See also* substance ontology, language of
non-duality, 10, 333. *See also* ambiguity; duality/binarity
non-object, 2, 13, 38, 41, 45–46, 48, 62, 68, 75, 101, 139, 161, 163, 167, 180, 242, 245, 259; and color, 259; landscape as, 2, 48, 62, 68, 161 (*see also* Guo Xi; Hasegawa, Tōhaku; Jullien, Francois; Sesshu Tōyō); in Merleau-Ponty, 44–45; motor-demand of, 163, 180, 192,

242; negated, 75, 161; negation and, 38, 41, 48, 75, 101; tools as, 104–105, 109, 139
non-obstruction (*wuai* 無礙; *muge*), 10, 17, 19, 22, 24, 53, 111, 130–131, 133, 150, 226, 248, 272; between body and instrument, 121; between phenomena and noumena (*lishi wuai* 理事無礙), 16; between phenomena and phenomena (*shishi wuai* 事事無礙), 17; body-world relation, 150, 226, 238; field of, 24; as full reversibility, 97–98; full, unambiguous, 20, 97–98, 130, 140, 271, 277–278. *See also* intersubsumption, Tiantai concept of, 98, 198; Huayan concept of, xlii, 16–17, 22, 98; Huayan limits to, 24, 264. *See also* Chengguan light and, 53, 131, 134; limits to, 18–19, 24, 97, 109, 263; relationality, 111; sensorimotor, 17; tools and, 134; vision, 96, 140, 272. *See also* obstruction; phenomenal encounter
non-perceptual, 43–44, 49, 52–54, 82, 84–85, 99, 101–102, 113, 115, 117, 119, 121, 131, 136, 140, 145, 247; distance, 119; entity, 44, 102; matter, 99, 115; medium, 43, 53; object, 84, 181; past as, 85; perceptual and the, 44–45, 48; rift, 113; space, 54, 115, 140, 145; space, interval between objects as mere empty, 121; space, interval, rift, gap, 52, 54, 113, 119, 121, 131, 136, 140, 145; void, 101, 117. *See also* material reductionism
non-perspectival seeing, 97, 272. *See also* omni-perspectivalism; view from nowhere

non-philosophy, xvi–xviii, xx, xxv, xxviii, 324, 340. *See also* ambiguity of philosophy and religion
non-present, 85–87, 95. *See also* absence; presence
non-subject, 2, 38, 41, 46, 101, 245, 259; artist as, 2; negation, 101; and non-object, 41, 46, 101, 109, 245, 259. *See also* non-self
non-substantial, 22, 24, 34; medium, 22. See also *Basho*; field; flesh; obstruction
non-substantiality (*mukitei* 無期底), 21
non-Western thought, xlv
non-willing, 191, 303. *See also* negated volition; non-action; paradox of actively willing passivity
Northern "academic" school, 154, 179, 317–318. *See also* Chinese painting
nothingness (*mu* 無), xxiv, xxxviii, 3, 5–6, 13, 15, 21, 28, 35, 37, 47, 67, 120, 145, 184–186, 199, 245, 248, 250, 270, 273, 275, 300, 305–306, 328, 330–333, 336. *See also* negation; *nullité absolue*; relational ontology
nothingness of nothingness (*mu no mu* 無の無), 40
noumenal, 18–19; in Huayan; noumena (*li* 理), 16–19. *See also* phenomena (*shih* 事)
novelty, new art, 149, 196, 217–219, 223, 225, 227, 230, 243, 279–281; new continuity of act and act, 189, 197, 230; new legibility, 196; new motor-orientations, 238; new object, 212; new solicitations, new continuity of act and act, 230; new subjectivity, 225; new visibility, 193, 237, 243, 247, 281; new ways of moving, 155, 160, 236,

novelty *(continued)* 243; newly blind person, 128–129; newly sighted, 126–130; renew the landscape's, 237. *See also* creativity; deformation; originatity, myth of

Nullité Absolue, xl, 34–35, 40. *See also* negation; negativist philosophy; self-negation; unambiguous negation

object (grammatical), subject-verb-, 15, 28; relation between grammatical subject and, 22. *See also* language; substance ontology, language

object (thing), -as-pure-positivity, Sartre, 36, 47, 260; becoming object (*kyakkanteki naru* 客観的なる), 223; circumscribed, 12, 22, 44, 64, 113, 140; dissolution of, 166; fragment or multiply, 60, 64 (*see also* Cubism; "Three Graces," "Three Shades"); full negation of, 98, 166–167; historical, 233; historicity, 231, 234; Impressionist dissolution of, 166; landscape-, 4, 163; logic (*taisho ronri* 対象論理), 21; motor-negated, 192; motor-neutral, 190, 212, 232; negated, 2, 44, 46–48, 107, 163, 167–168 (*see also* non-object); new, 212; non-negated, 107; opaque, 107; perceptual, 36, 43, 48, 61, 76, 237; positive, 38, 45, 108, 166; representational, 161; secondary attribute of, 254; -subject dualism, xliv, 2, 20–21, 25, 45, 53, 55–56, 59, 107, 111, 238, 245, 269–270; surface of, 49, 252; temporally ecstatic, 79; transmissive, 162; volitional (*ishitaishō*, 意志対象), 185, 227. *See also* negated object; non-Object

object logic (*taishō ronri* 対象論理), 21. *See* Aristotle

objective, xxiv, xliii, 9, 21, 41–42, 47, 59, 64, 104, 111, 116, 143, 153, 167–168, 175, 185–188, 195–196, 212, 223–228, 238, 245, 252, 260–261, 273–274, 277, 279, 287, 294, 300, 334; objective (*fūkeiga*), 92; purification, 225

objective artist (Nietzsche), 196

objectivity, 2, 42, 44, 68, 75, 103, 105, 110–111, 116, 118, 163, 175, 186–187, 189, 200, 221, 223–227, 230, 238, 247, 261, 276–277, 304, 307, 330, 332; *kyakkansei* 客観性, 223; positivist, substantialist accounts of, 22; pure objectivity (*jun naru kyakkan* 純なる客観), 225; pure, immersing onesel within, 224; self conforming to, 225

obstruction/ing -enabling, 134–135; artist's motion, expression, 150, 198–199; between temporal orders, 85; body-tool, 107–109; dynamic, 265, 268, 272; expansion through, 124; faith, 336, 339; of foreign object, 111; generativity of perceptual, 122; independent volition, 304; irreducible, 123; of light, 125, 127–130, 141; limits, xxxvi, xxxviii, xli, 11, 20; of matter, 116, 314; and mediality, 124; motor-, 267; motor-visual, 277, 284, 325; mutual, 33, 36, 38, 40, 106, 204, 225–226; mutual, or temporal orders, 204; obstructed-obstructing, 275; ontological, 198; originating in the objective, 238; originating in the subjective, 238; partial, 129, 132, 264, 275–276; perceptual, xlii, 98, 100, 103, 122, 276; of positive selfhood, 41; reflection and, xxxii; resistance of, 125; -revealing dynamic, 125, 132, 134–135;

-revealing of tools, 107, 129;
revealing and obstructing quality,
123; sensorimotor limits and, 20;
solicitations, 217; unambiguous/full,
127–128, 189, 276; valence of, 120,
127, 132, 139; visual, 44, 90, 97,
132, 271, 273, 294. See also blind
spot; non-obstruction; opacity
ocularcentrism, xl, 54, 56–57, 59,
122; bias, 55. See also metaphor,
vision-based
Odin, Steve, 82
omni-perspectivalism, 278. See also
multi-perspectivalism; vantage point,
positionless; view from nowhere
omnicentrism, 198. See also non-
obstruction; Tiantai
ontology, and language, 5, 9–12,
23, 28, 167, 246; and language/
grammar, 28, 246; of negation,
52–53, 69, 146, 180, 252;
perceptual, 96, 102; relational, 10;
source of motion, 186; substance,
xxxii, 5, 10, 15, 28, 167. See also
ambiguity; Basho (場所); flesh;
mutual negation
opacity, 103, 116, 122, 124, 127–128,
130, 132, 140. See also blind spot;
obstruction, visual; transparency
Oppenheim, Méret, 232–235
optical, 29–30, 115, 128
optimal grip, 213–214, 216, 229, 256.
See also pre-reflective solicitations
ordinary and everyday (byōjōtei), 335
ordinary mind (byōjōshin 平常心), xxxvii
Orientalism, 3
originality, myths of, 217. See also
novelty
Orsborn, M.B., 28
Ōta, Asaoka, 291
other-power, 306, 333. See also self-
negation; non-action

p'o mo (sōsho) painting style 162. See
also Chinese painting
painless-pain, 181
paint, xxx, xxxii, xxxvii, xlii, 23, 26,
30, 34, 38, 41, 64, 66–68, 74, 80,
95, 98–99, 103, 105–106, 112,
121, 141, 151, 159, 165, 167–169,
182, 190, 193–194, 198, 207–208,
218, 220–221, 224, 230, 232, 244,
252–253, 258, 284, 287, 289, 297,
313, 315
painter, "academic," 158–159; Chinese,
62, 66, 68, 192, 218–219, 222,
231, 252, 317; Japanese, 150–
151, 220; Japanese modal, 113;
landscape, xxix–xxx, xxxv, xl, 62, 68,
100, 106, 122, 141, 159, 181, 219–
221, 251–252, 254, 317; "literati"
(文人畫 wenrenhua), 90–91, 317;
outside the academy, 220; -subject,
4, 163. See also painter-priest
painter's brush, xli, 53–54, 107–108,
117, 121, 129, 135, 140–141, 315.
See ambiguity, visual-tactile; ecstasis;
relationality of body to tools; tool as
non-object
painter-priest, xvi, 151, 156–158.
See also artistic practice; devotional
practices; practice, zen religious;
religious and aesthetic practice
painting, 48, 156, 162; black-and-
white, 251–253, 257–259, 262;
broken ink landscape, 151, 162;
Chinese landscape, 62, 192,
218–219, 222, 231; of Daoist and
Buddhist themes (Doshakuga), 154;
kara-e (唐絵 "Chinese painting"),
154; landscape, xix, xxxv, 7, 32, 62,
70, 104–105, 162, 192, 218–219,
221–222, 231, 233–234, 251, 317;
monochrome, 257–258, 262;

painting *(continued)*
    monochrome ink, 156; Mustard Seed Garden Manual of, 282; Northern Song School of Landscape, 179; *shinkeizu* (真景図) "true view paintings," 90–93, 159–160, 219; Southern Song School of Landscape, 92, 154, 312, 317; Sung and Yuan (*sougenga* 宋元画), 153; tradition, monochrome landscape (*sansuiga* 山水画), 251; *yamato-e* (大和絵 "Japanese painting"), 154
pantheistic voluntarism, 209
paradox, xxx–xxxii, xxxvi, xliii, 9, 15, 158, 253, 258, 290, 295, 303, 324–326, 332, 337; of actively willing passivity, 303; of expression, 3, 199, 325, 327; of God, 331; part-whole, 295; of perceptual faith, 15, 325; of radical reflection, 326–327; of reflecting on pre-reflective, 9, 324; of self-negation, 303; of willing spontaneity, 304; volitional, 333
paragone, 60. See also multi-perspectivalism
Park, Jin Y, 19, 195, 279, 293
Parker, Joseph, 160
Parkes, Graham, xxxv, 32, 176, 179, 329
parole parlante, parole parlée, 323
part-whole, 291–294, 296; dichotomy, 291; metaphysics, 291–294; temporality, 291. *See also* holographic model
Pascal, Blaise, xiii
passivity, xxxiv, xli, 7, 13, 44, 74, 158, 170–173, 178, 189, 191–192, 197, 210, 241, 246, 249, 262, 267–268, 276, 290, 303–304, 328; -activity ambiguity, xli, 7, 13, 44, 158, 172–174, 185, 191, 210, 245, 268; full reversibility of activity and, 174; lining activity, 187, 216; and matter, 183; paradox of actively willing, 303; unambiguous form of, 189, 191, 202
pensée de survol "high-altitude thinking," 58, 97
perception, activist theory of, 59; camera model of, 133, 170; critique of representational model of, 64, 285; de-localized, 99; expansion of, 83; external perception (*gaibu chikaku* 外部知覚), 65; faith in, 2; internal muscular, 241; internal perception (*naibu chikaku* 内部知覚), 65, 83; internal perception-qua-external perception (*naibu chikaku soku gaibu chikaku* 内部知覚即外部知覚), 66, 81–83, 181; mineness of, 97; motion and, xv, xxxvii, xliv, 18, 53, 106, 121, 169–170, 173, 239–240, 249, 263–264, 276, 290, 313, 325, 339; narcissistic, 74, 94; negation, xl, xlii–xliii, 16, 41, 45, 71, 74, 94, 109, 146, 160–161, 180, 188, 192, 251, 259; non-internalist account of, 95–96; Plato's and Aristotle's accounts of, 59; positivist model of, 133; pure visual perception (*junsui shikaku* 純粋視覚), 247; representational model of, 42, 45, 47, 55, 136, 255, 285; reversibility of motion and, 245, 264. *See also* motor-perception
perceptual data, 95
perceptual faith (*foi perceptive*), xv, xx, xxvii, xxix, xli, 2, 7, 73, 290, 297, 319, 325. *See also* motor-perceptual faith
perceptual ontology, 96, 102. See also *Basho*, flesh

INDEX 385

perfect map (Josiah Royce), 271
performance, xxxi, 9, 93, 122,
  136–139, 141, 182–184, 189, 192,
  210, 215, 221, 224, 233, 245, 288,
  301, 321, 326, 337
perigraptos, 11, 167. *See also* substance
  ontology; *circumscribere*
personality, artist's, 93, 221. *See also*
  untrammeled personality (*yipin* 逸品)
perspectivalism, 59, 65, 79. *See*
  multi-perspectivalism
perspective, 19, 30, 33, 58–62, 64–65,
  68, 72–73, 76–77, 79, 81, 83, 92,
  98, 100, 110, 143, 145, 167, 208,
  213, 222, 242, 250, 261, 264, 266,
  273–274, 277–279, 298; floating,
  62, 168 (*see also* Guo Xi; Jullien,
  Francois); lived, 168; multiple, as
  achievement, 61; non-perspectival
  (Platonic forms), 58; perspectiveless,
  97, 264; *phainestai*, 123; single, 57,
  64, 76–77. *See* multi-perspectivalism
Phenomenal encounter, xliv, 24, 33,
  36, 38, 109, 251, 278. *See also*
  Begegnung, entities, 109. *See also*
  obstructions
phenomenology, xvii, xxxix, xliv, 9–10,
  35, 77, 89, 100, 102, 107, 116,
  121, 133, 136, 140, 142, 169, 180,
  183, 212, 250, 252, 259, 303;
  account of time, Husserl's influence
  on Merleau-Ponty, 77; Husserl's, 8;
  Merleau-Ponty's, xxxvi, 122, 135;
  naturalizing, 115; Nishida's, 8–10
philosophy and art, xxxvii, 61
philosophy of art, xxviii, xliv, 1
photographic depiction, 287. *See also*
  coherent deformation; Gericault;
  materiality of representation;
  Muybridge
photoreceptors, 115, 133, 138

Picasso, Pablo, 60, 89, 288–289
"Pine Trees" (Hasegawa), 32, 67–70,
  149, 232
place, of absolute nothing (*zettai mu
  no basho* 絶対無の場所), 22; of
  being (*yū no basho* 有の場所), 6; of
  nothingness (*mu no basho* 無の場
  所), 6; of true nothing (*shin no mu
  no basho* 真の無の場所), 22. *See also*
  Basho (場所); field; non-obstruction
place of nothingness (*mu no basho* 無
  の場所), 6
Plato, 11, 27, 53, 57–60, 130, 191,
  200, 249
Platonism, xl, 51, 58–59, 62, 64, 66,
  175
Plotinus, xix
poetry, xxxv, xlv, 91, 233–235, 317,
  323, 329
Pollock, Jackson, 167
polychrome, 257. *See also* color;
  monochrome
positivism, 35, 57, 60, 75, 116, 166,
  275; and artistic expression, 230;
  Bergson, 35; and camera model of
  perception, 133; and conceptions
  of light, 52; definition of the body,
  103, 114; representational, 49, 57,
  62; and substantialist accounts of
  objectivity, 22
positivity, 13, 22–23, 26, 32, 35–38,
  44–45, 47–48, 57, 67, 70, 94, 98,
  105, 109, 113, 145, 166–168,
  189, 260, 267, 269, 324, 332;
  between negativity and, 16, 36, 64,
  253; color in pure, 260; depiction
  between negativity and, 253; "hard-
  core" of, 44; -negativity binaries,
  31, 69; and negativity, painting the
  object between, 167; and object, 38,
  45, 108, 166; of the present,

positivity *(continued)*
79, 204; pure/full/unambiguous, 18, 35–36, 40–41, 217, 260–261, 266, 276; Sartre's object-as-pure-positivity, 47; and selfhood, 41; and the sensual, 85. *See also* negativity

post-war America, 308

pottery, xliii, 307–311, 315–317. *See also* Leach, Bernard; materiality of spontaneous expression; throwing-thrown

practice, art, xxxvii, xl, 51, 57, 60, 136, 144, 156–157, 160–161, 199, 220, 293, 299, 316, 320, 337, 339; artists' expressive, xxxvi, 141; artists' sensorimotor, 122; Buddhist, 14, 176; contemporary dance theory and, 192; *Geidō*, xxxiv–xxxv, 233, 306; meditative, xix, xxiii, xxix, xxxvii, 55, 143, 150, 157–158, 172, 189, 191, 242, 249, 304, 307, 336; mundane, 151; philosophic-religious, 156; religious, xxii, 158, 161, 234, 335; secular, xxvii studio-based, 219; Zen artistic, 168. Zen religious, 157. See also *Geidō*, Sesshū Tōyō

Prajñāpāramitā sūtras, 28

Pratītyasamutpāda. See dependent origination; Mahāyāna; relational ontology

pre-personal tradition, 209. *See also* historical body; historical world; expression of the historical world

pre-reflective, xxxi–xxxii, xxxv–xxxvi, 9, 24, 234, 298–299, 321–328, 337; bodily expectations, 234; and faith, 325–326; field, 9; grounds, 298; opening to the world, 9; paradox of reflecting on, xxxvi, 9, 298, 324, 327; solicitations, 256; spontaneity, 324, 328; willing the, 324. *See also* hyper-reflection; reflection

predicate, 197–198, 200, 270, 304

predicate logic, 248, 270

préjugé du monde, 115, 214, 216

presence, 38, 44, 51, 66–67, 83, 89, 130–131, 136, 160, 183, 190, 201–202, 206–207, 216, 234, 251, 255, 257–259, 272, 280, 295, 309, 331; -absence binary, 66, 69; absolute, 35, 202; body's, 51, 130; deep, 193, 202; fullness (*you* 有), 67; indeterminacy between absence and, 68; metaphysics of, 325; non-presence, 81; non-representational, 206; pure, 83. *See also* absence

priest, xvi, 151, 157–158, 161. *See also* devotional practices; practice, zen religious; religious and aesthetic practice

primal impression, 77

productive ambivalence, xxiv, xxvii, xlv, 278. *See also* comparison; intercultural encounter

protentions (and retentions), 203. *See also* ecstatic time consciousness

purity, consciousness-as-, pure-negativity, 47; activity, 186; doubt, 325; free will, 188; invisibility, 70; *junsui* 純粋, 247; nothingness, 36; objective, 224–225; objective purification, 225; objectivity, immersion in, 224; objectivity (*jun naru kyakkan* 純なる客観), 225, 277; philosophy, xix, 325; positivity, 36, 260, 332; positivity of color, 260; present, 77–78; reflection, 326, 328; Sartre's object-as-pure-positivity, 47; seer, 37; subject as "pure consciousness," 168 visual perception, 247, 296, 319. *See also* ambiguity

pure objectivity (*jun naru kyakkan* 純なる客観), 225

pure visual perception (*junsui shikaku* 純粋視覚), 247

qi "ki" (気), 179–180. *See also* dragon veigns; fengshui; ontological source of motion

radical reflection (*réflexion radicale*), 323. *See also* reflecting on pre-reflective

Raphael, xl, 52, 57–58, 60, 64, 163, 279

realism, 20, 90, 92, 154, 167, 203, 285, 288

reciprocity, 74, 195, 200, 316, 331; of determination, 13, 23, 81, 139, 171, 194–195 expression between oneself and color, 261; expressive, 231, 246, 302; expressive structure, 231; making-made, 199, 210, 232, 246; and negation, 33. *See also* bi-directionality

reflection, act of, 77, 82–83; and faith, 297, 326; critique of, 299; deliberative, 296; as development (*hansei sunawachi hatten* 反省即ち発展), 327; dogmatism of, 323; *hansei* 反省, 55, 268, 295, 297, 327; infinite, 272; and intellect, xx, xxxi, xxxvi, 9, 41, 158, 208, 291, 296–297, 299–301, 303, 306, 320–322; limits of doubt and, 321, 328; methodologies based on, 321; methodologies of doubt and, xx, xxvi, xxviii, xxxi, 277, 290, 296, 321–322, 324, 338; philosophic, philosophy of, xxviii, xxxii, xxxvii, 172, 299, 321, 328; on the pre-reflective, xxxvi, 9, 298, 324, 327; pure, 326, 328, 339; radical, 326; and spontaneity, 310, 325–328; and spontaneity in acting-intuition, 327; *utsusu* (写す), 297. *See also* mirroring

relation, as mutual negation, 20, 149, 252; of artist to past, to tradition, 193; of blind person to cane, 53–54, 106–110, 115, 121, 127–130, 133, 135, 138–140; of body to light, 53, 100, 103, 113, 122–123; of body to tools, 53, 100, 116, 145; body-world, xxxv, 105, 199, 311–312; chiasmatic, 24, 27–28, 30, 81, 120, 246; at a distance, 137, 145; horizontal, 17; mutually expressive, 194; non-chiasmatic discontinuous, 43; texture of, 23, 26, 30, 226; vertical, 17. *See also* ambiguity; dependent origination; mutual negation; non-obstruction; relational ontology

relational ontology, xxxviii, 10, 13; substance ontology and, 10. *See also* dependent origination; negation; non-obstruction; obstruction; substance ontology; relation

religion, xiii–xiv, xvi, xix–xxvii, xxxiii, xliii, xlv, 12, 54, 156, 160, 168, 265, 268–269, 271, 296, 306, 324–325, 328–329, 332, 334, 336–340; discipline, xxix, 156; gesture, 332; nonreligious, xxix; of other-power, 306; and philosophy, xxvi–xxvii, 160, 268, 296, 338–339; philosophy of, xxiv, xxvii–xxviii, 269, 338; philosophy of religion (*shūkyōtetsugaku* 宗教哲学), xxiv; practice, xv, xxii, 156, 158, 161, 234, 307, 335; religious experience, xxiii–xxiv, 20, 308, 335; terminology, xxvii, 329, 335–337; religiously volitional, 334. *See also* faith

Renaissance, 60, 153, 157, 278–280

representation, accuracy, 288; absence, 73, 78, 86, 93, 208; artistic, 60, 65, 92, 220, 236, 238, 243, 282, 285, 287–288, 318–320; color and, 252–253; conventions of, 243; critique of, 64, 285; dynamic obstruction to self-, 272; materiality of, 287; metaphysics of, 59; model, 42–45, 53, 57, 59, 73, 110, 113, 119, 144, 165, 254, 294–295; non-representational, xxix, xxxii, 56–57, 62, 181; non-representational presence, 206; object, 161; positivism, 49, 62; risk, 244, 250; self-, 272; system of self-, 271; temporality of, 294; verisimilitude, 162

resistance of the sensible, 122, 124. *See also* obstruction; opacity; transparency; transparent mediality

reversibility (*reversibilité*), activity and passivity, 174; and anonymity, 74; between internal and external organs, 242; causal, 138, 140, 199; and expression, 194, 337; flesh, 205; full, non-obstructed, 20, 97–98, 141, 278; limits to, 98, 264, 276, 278. (*See also* of action-intuition, 245, 247, 264); of activity and passivity, 174; blind spot; of body and light, 135; of body and tool, brush, 135, 140; of body-world determination, 309; of causal forces, 138; of interexpression, 309; of motion and perception, 245, 264; multi-perspectival, 73; mutual-negation, 143; non-reversible, 141, 198; obstruction; motor-perceptual, 73, 242; past and present, 204; of reversibility, 98; seeing-seen, 200; temporality, 249; of the visible and the invisible, 71, 170; of the visual and the tactile, 130, 133, 141; with landscape, 207. *See also* bidirectionality; created-creating/making-made; reciprocal expression

reversibility of reversibility, 98

risk, 2 attempt to reduce, 283–284, 291, 293, 317, 319–320; constitutive lack of control, 268; creativity that is inherently risky, 237; of deforming conditions of visibility, 285; existential, associate with negative, 42; of expression, 15, 277, 283; impinging upon expressive motion, 228; of indeterminacy, 42; motor-perceptual, xliii, 227, 294; of movement, 228; of negation, 284; spontaneity and, 317; temporality of, 281, 317. *See also* faith

rock gardening, xix, 32. See *Geidō* practices

Rodin, Auguste, xxviii, xxxvii, xl, 60, 83, 87–89, 93–94, 100, 103, 149, 181–182, 211

Royce, Josiah, xxiii, 270–272, 278, 295

Rubens, 60

sabhāva (essence), 14
Sacks, Oliver, 133
sacramentality, xxv, xxvii, 337–339
sacred, xiv, xxiv, xxvii, xxxv, xliii, 70, 150, 161, 176, 234, 265, 332, 334, 337, 339. *See also* ambiguity of sacred and secular
Sallis, John, 279, 281, 306, 320, 327
Sartre, Jean-Paul, xxv, xl, 34–36, 39–41, 47, 56, 119, 217, 275; absolute other, 35–39, 41; consciousness as "absolute negation," 37; Merleau-Ponty's critique of, 34–38; object-as-pure-positivity, 47
Scheler, Max, xxv

Index

Schreyach, Michael, 167
Schultz, Lucy, 40, 209, 309
scoptophilia, 54–55
scriptural demand, 335
scripture of the world, 335
sculpture, 60, 87, 89, 94, 113, 143, 211, 223, 303, 311
Secular, xiv, xix, xxi, xxiv, xxvii, xxxvii, xliii, 150, 265, 336–339. *See also* ambiguity of sacred and secular; ordinary and everyday (*byōjōtei*); ordinary mind (*byōjōshin* 平常心)
seeing, formless light, 129; productive, 143; seeing-seen, 7, 37, 51, 74, 82, 174, 229; without a seer, xv, xl, xlii, 20, 96, 98, 173, 198, 245, 248, 250, 263–264, 268–270, 272–278; world's self-, xlii, 20, 96–97, 250, 263, 271, 274, 277. *See* ambiguity of visual and tactile; motor-perception. *See also* motor-perception
seeing without a seer (*mirumono nakushite miru koto* 見るものなくして見ること), /, xv, xl, xlii, 20, 96–98, 173, 198, 245, 248, 250, 263–264, 268–278. *See also* anonimity and vision; negation and vision
seer, 5, 43, 74, 96–97, 101–102, 132–133, 165, 198, 209, 250, 264, 271–278; individuated seer, 208, 263, 274; *seinlassen*, 191. *See also* seeing without a seer
self, -awareness, 8–9, 21, 28, 222, 270–271, 278, 295; active self (*hataraku jiko* 働く自己), 246; alienated, 301; autonomous expressive, 296; erasure of, 157; *jikaku* (自覚), 270; -mirroring, 268, 270–272, 278, 295, 297; negated selfhood as a threat, 42; negation of, 223; positive, 41; reified, 157; -seeing, xlii, 20, 96–97, 250, 263, 271, 277; self-power and other power, 306; selfless, 14, 160, 275; voided, 312. *See also* alterity; non-self (無我)
self mirroring (*jiko shazō* 自己写像), 268, 270–271; metaphors of, 271. *See also* self-representation
self-awareness (*jikaku* 自覚), 21, 270–271
self-identity, xxviii, 8, 10, 16, 22–23, 25, 42, 226, 275, 306, 330, 336, 340
self-identity of absolute contradictories (*zettai mujunteki jikodōitsu* 絶対矛盾的自己同一), 8, 10, 22, 25, 306, 330, 336
self-identity of opposites (*sōhansurumono no jikodōitsu* 相反するものの的自己同一), 23; self-seeing (*jiko jishin wo miru* 自己自身を見), xlii, 20, 96, 97, 99, 250, 263, 271, 274, 277, 285. See also *Basho*; reflection, *utsusu*
Semonovitch, Kascha, 338
sensation, 12, 48, 82, 85–86, 93, 129, 134, 142, 167, 181, 229, 240–241, 255, 259, 264, 287, 299
sensationalism, 86
sensationalist fallacy, 86
sensitivity, xvii, xxxiii, 47, 107–108, 113, 128, 133, 145, 162; distal, 107, 128–129; muscular, 181, 229, 240–241; proximal, 128; shift from a proximal to distal, 128
sensory, xlii, 3, 52, 84–86, 126, 142, 179, 215, 247, 256; sensory data, 43, 59, 75, 77, 84, 90, 181, 241, 258–259
separation (*chōriston*), 10–11, 13–14, 22, 25, 46, 55, 107, 140, 145, 178, 198, 201. *See also* substance ontology

Serra, Richard, 89
Sesshū Tōyō, as Zen artist, 155–156; "boneless" style, 105; Chinese influence, 153–155; negated subjectivity, 160–161; meditative practice, 157–159; Nishida, interexpression and, 153; as priest-painter, 157; *shinkeizu* style, 160; Splashed Ink Landscape (*Haboku Sansui*), 161–163; travels to China, 154; trope of "Zen" artist, 155; Zen discipline, 157–158. *See also* artistic practice; Buddhist practice; *Geidō* practices; practice, Zen religious; religious and aesthetic practice
shadow, 66, 128, 157, 169
shasei "sketching from life," 90–92
shibari, 181
shinkeizu (真景図) "true view paintings," 91–93, 159–160, 219. *See also* copy; deformation; representation, artistic
Shintoism, xix, xxxiii, 292
Shinzinger, Robert, 6
Shitao, 68, 291–292
Shizuteru, Ueda, 270, 272
Shūbun, 158–159, 220
sight, 37, 53–56, 62, 68, 96, 108, 111–112, 126–128, 130, 133–134, 136, 168, 241, 266, 269, 278, 296. *See also* motor-perception; seeing; vision; visual
silence, 185, 207, 215–216, 231, 234, 239, 262, 284, 295–296, 299, 302–304, 326, 328, 338
Sinha, Pawan, 127
skin and bones, 87–88, 90, 94–95, 181; with Ike no Taiga 87, 90–95; with Rodin 87, 88–95, 181. *See also* ambiguity of surface and depth; interiority and exteriority; internal-qua-external perception; "Three Shades"
Smith, N.S., 192
Sōkoku-ji monastery, 156
sokuhi logic, 15–16, 18, 21, 23
solicitations, 71, 91, 182, 189, 206, 212–215, 217, 221, 230–231, 233, 236–238, 252, 256, 258, 262, 290, 295, 314, 316, 322, 326. *See also* affordances; distal source of motion; distant will; dragon veins; external organs; unity of act and act
Song China, 62, 77, 154, 159, 179, 222, 234, 252, 312, 317
soteriology, 79, 178
space, and distance, 103, 112–113, 240; empty, 114, 117; extension, 19; *ma* (間), 32, 46, 54, 69, 75, 83, 330; negative, 32, 67–68, 70. *See also* Hasegawa, Tōhaku; non-perceptual, 54, 115, 121, 136, 140, 145. *See also* distance; ambiguity of distance distanceless
spectator theory of knowledge, 59
speculation (*shisaku* 思索), 55
Spinoza, Baruch, 175
spirit resonance (*ch'i yun*; *kiin*), 91
splashed ink, 151, 160–163, 216–217, 251, 282, 307, 318. See also *Haboku Sansui*; *Hatsuboku Sansui*; ink, agency of; landscape painting; Sesshū Tōyō; spontaneity
"Splashed Ink Landscape" (Sesshū) (*Haboku Sansui*), xxxiii, 150–152, 160–162, 216–217, 251, 282, 307, 318. See also *Hatsuboku Sansui*; landscape painting; Sesshū Tōyō
spontaneity, aesthetics of accident, 162; aesthetics of inebriation, 162; aesthetics of, 310; anything-goes, 318; artist's, 310; arts, 306

(see also *Geidō* practices); core of reflection, 326; deliberation and, 309; and expression, xliii, 106, 160, 163, 303, 305, 307–308, 313, 319, 324; expression, materiality of, 106, 307; and faith, 314–315, 317; and faithful expression, 308; grammatical conventions, 304; movement, 144, 160; and negation, 161; organization, 168; reflection and, 310, 325–328; and reflection in acting-intuition, 327; and risk, 319–320; and self-defeating will, 304; and temporality, 318; un-trained, 202. *See also* negated volition; non-action

standpoint, 14, 35, 99, 140, 188, 208, 223, 245, 253; standpointless standpoint, 263

Stevens, Bernard, 8, 25, 269–271

Stewart, Jon, 35

stimulus, distal, 107, 113, 128–129; proximal, 107, 113, 128–129, 141; sequence theory, 287. *See also* Gibson, J.J.

Style, xxi, xxiii, xxx–xxxi, xxxv, 64, 90, 92–93, 105, 131–132, 151–155, 159, 162–163, 207, 222, 244, 281, 283–285, 291, 302, 311–312, 315–316; invisibility of artist's, 284. *See also* obstruction, motor-visual

subject, -based logic (Aristotle), 197–199, 270; active, 173, 186, 246–247; as "pure consciousness," 168 (*see also* Sartre, Jean-Paul); autonomous, 198–199; decentering, 178, 197; of faith, 2; individuated, 96–97, 168, 172, 185, 199, 334; negated, xiv, xxiii, 2, 36, 41, 45–46, 161, 225, 260, 269, 284, 305; non-negated, 225;

and object, grammatical, 22; -object metaphysics, xliv, 53, 55–56, 107; -object opposition, 21, 56; painter-, 4, 163; partial, 189; perceiving, 36, 43, 45–46, 48, 59, 96, 263; positive, 35, 42, 189; reification of, 3, 97, 111, 246, 264, 327; as time, 75; visual, 45, 98, 263, 269–270, 273–276, 278; volitional, 209. *See also* ambiguity between subject and object; non-subject

subjectivity, artist's, 223, 309; de-subjectivized, 97; evacuation of, 160; negated, 2–3, 161, 275; new, 225; -objectivity ambiguity, 277; positive, 189; -qua-objectivity, 82, 116, 273, 276–277; visual, 2, 161, 275, 277. *See also* objectivity

substance, 10–13, 15, 22–23, 25, 30, 68, 73, 89, 94, 99, 109, 145, 175, 178, 181, 188, 197–198; de-substantialized seer or mover, 264; dualism, 144, 175; dualism and monism, 10, 111, 144–145, 248; ontological tradition, ontology, Western, 145; ontology, xxxii, 5, 10–12, 15, 22, 25, 28, 30, 145, 167, 178, 188; Primary (*protai ousiai*), 11; and relation ontologies, xxxii, 5, 10, 15, 28, 167. *See also* Aristotle; *circumscribere*; *perigraptos*; separation (*chōriston*)

substratumless (*mukiteiteki* 無基底的), 21. *See also* emptiness; groundless ground

sumi (墨), 151, 258. *See also* agency of; broken ink; "have ink" (*yu mo*); ink painting; monochrome ink; splashed ink

surface, 11, 49, 68, 83, 87–90, 93–95, 100, 102, 104, 106, 123, 127, 144,

surface *(continued)*
206, 211, 268, 327; ambiguity of depth and, xl; -depth binary, xl, 83, 87, 89–90, 95, 100; -depth (Krauss, Rodin), 87–90, 94–95; depth and, xl, 83, 87, 89–90, 95, 100; external, 93; landscape's, 206; object's, 11, 49; outer extremity of the skin, 104, 113; of painting, 68; skin's, 114, 137; skin-bones binary, 93; surface of objects, 49, 252. *See also* depth of; skin and bones

Sūtra, xxxv, 15, 28, 176–177, 335

Suzuki, D.T., xxiii, 15–17, 155

svabhāva, 14

Tadashi, Ogawa, 8

Taiga, Ike no, xxxvii, xl, 83, 87–94, 100, 153, 155, 159, 193, 201, 219, 234–236. *See also* skin and bones; True View of Mr. Asama (*Asamadake shinkei-zu* 朝熊嶽真景図)

Takeuchi, Melinda, xl, 92, 155, 159

Taminiaux, Jacques, 38, 207, 218, 230

Tanabe, Hajime, 28

Tanaka, Ichimatsu, 151, 154

tea ceremony, xix, xxxv, 156, 233, 308; cup, 233, 235; Fur Lined Teacup, 232–233. See also *Geidō*

temporal(ity), ambiguity past, present, and future, 79; blindness, blind spot, 283, 289, 320; body, 205–206; body's ecstatic, 210; chiasmatic negation, 76, 206; chiasms of, 206; depth, 76, 82, 86, 150, 172, 192, 203–204, 258; dislocation, 288; distal solicitations, 191, 209, 218; ecstasis, 75, 78, 191, 210; ecstatic object, 79; ecstatic set of motions, 191; extended background, 191; horizon, 76–78; horizon of, 77 (*see also* protentions [and retentions]);

negation, 76, 81–82, 274; and negation, xl, 79, 81–82, 202, 204, 209, 274; Nishida's notion of, 79; orders, mutual obstruction, 204; of part-whole metaphysics, 291; of representation, 294; of risk, 281, 317; of risk and spontaneity, 281–283, 294, 317–318; of spontaneous action, 318. *See also* Time

Tenzo, 228

Theatetus, 59, 191

theology, xx, 12, 329, 331, 338

theoria (θεωρία), 43

theoros (θεωρός), 43

Theravadin Buddhism, 28

"there is" and "there is not," 67, 162, 165. *See also* Jullien, Francois

"Thirty-Six Views of Mount Fuji," (Ike no Taiga), 232

"Three Graces," (Raphael) 57–58, 60–62, 65–66, 77–78, 88, 92. *See also* multi-perspectivalism; sculpture

"Three Shades" (Rodin), 88, 93–94. *See also* sculpture; skin and bones

throwing-thrown, 307. *See also* bi-directional(ity); expressing-expressed; Interexpression; making-made reciprocity

Timaeus, 27, 59

time, and expression, 197, 207–208; as chiasm, 75–76, 202–204; before time, 204; being-time/existence-time (*uji* 有時), 79 (*see also* Dōgen); causation of, 193; consciousness, ecstatic (Husserl), 76–77, 79–80; flesh of, 204; Merleau-Ponty's relation to Husserl, 77; Merleau-Ponty theories of, 169, 194–195; and motion, 26, 146, 149, 150–151, 170; and negation, xl, 75–76, 79, 81–82, 175, 202, 204, 209, 274; Nishida, phenomenological account of motion and, 170; positivist view of, 169–170; realist conception of, 194; transcendental conception of, 194. *See also* temporal(ity)

Toadvine, Ted, 326

tool(s), -like features of light, 56, 101, 113, 121–130, 133–136, 140–141, 149; artist's, 104–105, 124, 138, 313; body's relation to, 25, 53, 100, 109, 116, 145; equipmentality (*Zeughaft*), 106; light as, 56, 113, 121–130, 133–136, 140–141, 149; light-related, 125; -like mediation, 101; as non-object, 104–105, 109, 139; obstruction-revealing of, 123, 125, 129, 132, 134; semi-transparency of light and, 134; use, 106, 110, 113, 121–122, 124–126, 128–129, 135, 229; -use analogy, 103. *See also* ecstatic body and tool use; external organs; intertwining

topography, 193, 199–200, 268 *topoi*, 4, 20

topos, 249. See also *Basho* (場所)

touch, xxxvii, 7, 54–55, 100, 103–104, 108–110, 112–120, 126–131, 133–134, 136–138, 142, 144–145, 182, 200, 211–212, 214, 224, 234; ambiguity between vision and, 53, 56, 100, 103, 117–121, 126, 140, 240; ambiguity regarding distance and, 114; distance and, 49, 114, 141; everything-touching-everything, 146; landscape through vision, 112–113; of light on eye, 128, 130; as "mere contact," 137–138; nothing touches anything, 145–146; reversibility of vision and, 134; touching-touched, 30, 133, 135, 140, 200; vision and, 44, 55, 100, 104, 108, 112, 115, 117–118, 126, 134, 137, 140, 144, 240; vision as, 56, 100, 103, 119–120, 126, 131. *See also* motor-perception; seeing

tradition, monochrome landscape painting, 251; artist's, 218, 224, 278; artist's relation to, 193; conditions of visibility of, 218; copying great artist of one's, 227; force of, 213, 285; as historical-volitional ecstasis, 228; mystical and apophatic, 331; pre-personal, 205; Song Chinese landscape painting, 62; weight of, 150, 192, 317. *See also* historical body

transcendence, xxvii, xxix, 14, 51, 172, 228, 274, 308, 317, 329, 332, 335

transdisciplinary, xx. *See also* discipline, academic; interdisciplinary; methodology

transitive, 1–3, 7 metaphysics, 10. *See also* intransitivity; unambiguous subject and object

translation, xlv, 5–6, 32, 36, 39, 41, 47, 127, 176, 179, 184, 195, 201, 245–246, 259, 292–293, 308, 320

transparent, xxxi, 107, 116, 122–124, 128–133, 136, 140, 216–217, 266, 326; of air, water, or other solid bodies, 123; accomplished, 129; of cane, 129; contingency of, 140; *diaphanés* διαφανής, 123; invisible medium, unambiguous, 53, 130–132; light as contingently, 53; light as inherently, 116, 121–124, 129, 131–132, 145; mediality, aesthetics of, 121–123, 139; mediation, fetishizing the notion of, 122; medium, 53, 103, 120–123, 129, 132, 141, 145; non-objective, 122; partial, semi-, 129–130, 134; qua-transparent, 123; see-through intermediary, 123; tool or light,

transparent *(continued)*
  semi-, 134; unambiguous/full/inherent/perfect, 53, 116, 121, 129, 131–132, 140–141. *See also* non-obstruction; opacity
transversality, xviii, 34, 55, 179. *See also* comparison; intercultural encounter
Trigg, Dylan, 203
"True View of Mt. Asama" (*Asamadake shinkei-zu* 朝熊嶽真景図), 91–92
true view pictures (真景図 *shinkeizu*), 159
trust, 304, 319. *See also* faith
truth, xxxi, xxxiii, xxxvii, 21, 32, 54–55, 59, 92, 114, 191, 237, 258, 295, 301, 323, 336–338

unambiguous, xliii, 6, 16, 49, 75, 77, 82, 112, 115, 144, 162, 208, 225, 250, 254; activity, 189; chromatic neutrality, 254; distance, 32, 43, 56, 113, 118–119, 121, 240; distance or proximity, 49, 119; identity, 19; identity and difference, 19; motionless, 184; negation, 162; passivity, 189, 191, 202; positivity, 276; present, 77–78, 183, 208; proximity, 112, 144; subject and object, 82, 225; vision, 6, 250. *See also* ambiguity; duality/binarity; dichotomy
uni-perspectival, xl, 49, 60–61, 65. *See also* multi-perspectivalism; perspectival
unification (*tōitsusuru* 統一する), xxv, 327
unity, xviii, xxxvii, 68, 77, 81–82, 124, 134, 185, 197, 207, 226, 294–295, 297. *See also* unity of act and act
universal, xviii, 16–18, 23, 54, 56, 95, 332

unseen, 44, 61, 170, 181, 207, 218, 244, 321; position, 272. *See also* perfect map (Josiah Royce)
unwissend Spiel, 320
Urdoxa, 322. *See also* faith; Husserl

Valéry, Paul, 259
Valvo, Alberto, 126
van Briessen, Fritz, xxxiv, 71, 154, 218, 221–222, 231, 312, 318
vantage point multiple, 64, 76; positionless, 271; single, 61, 64, 83, 86, 92. *See also* "infinite vision"; multi-perspectival; omni-perspectivalism; view from nowhere
view from nowhere (Leibniz), 97, 264, 269–270. *See also* "infinite vision"; omni-perspectivalism; vantage point, positionless
vinculum, xxvi
visible, -invisible ambiguity, 74, 80, 281, 294; create/modify/deform the, 193, 199, 243, 285, 287; -invisible binary, 27, 34, 257; and Invisible in Daoism, 65–72 (*see also* Jullien, Francois); light as, 122, 125, 127, 129–132, 134–135, 139, 141; lined by invisible, 5–6, 27, 65, 207, 266; reproducing the, 238 (*see also* copying); reversibility of invisible and, 71, 170; reversibility of tactile and, 53, 100, 117–118, 120–121, 130, 133, 140–141, 240. *See also* visible-invisible binary
vision, -based metaphor, 54–56 (*see also* ocularcentrism; scoptophilia); ambiguity between touch and, 118; anonymous, 250; causality of, 137; of formlessness, 129; as highest of senses, 55; infinite, 278; irreducible perspectival nature of, 272; light-based, 53, 103, 127, 135–136;

mechanical causality and reversibility of, 135; as "mere contact," 137–138; movement as, 239–240, 242, 264; narcissism and anonymity of, 74, 94; non-representational approaches to, 56; non-tactile, 118; perspectivaless, 97, 264; phenomenological theory of, 134; theoretical, 58; thermal, 132; tool-like features, 56, 101, 113, 121–130, 133–136, 140–141, 149; and touch, 44, 55–56, 100, 104, 108, 112, 115, 117–118, 126, 134, 137, 140, 144, 240. *See also* motor-perception; multi-perspectivalism; seeing

visual, -motor obstructions, 277; act, 181, 242; causal similarities between tactile and, 137; data, 29, 62, 65, 76, 84, 86, 95, 110, 133, 258; ecstasis, 112–113, 131, 255; field, 78, 82, 120, 139, 182, 208, 213, 243, 253, 255, 295; hand movement guided by, 143; intertwinement of tactile and, 120; motor-neutrality, 254; obstruction, 44, 90, 97, 132, 271, 273, 294; pure visual perception (*junsui shikaku* 純粋視覚), 247; resistance of, 40, 122, 124; reversibility of tactile and, 141; -tactile independence, 134; -tactile reversals, 127, 130; -tactility, 130; technologies, 43–44, 170, 289. *See also* fabric

volition(al), -body, 216, 219; artistic expression in positivist account of, 230; character of the World, 170-ecstasis, tradition as historical, 228; -fabric, 248. *See also* ecstatic body, 239; ecstatic body, 230, 239, 241; field, multi-, 209; multi-, 180, 208–209, 229; objects, 185, 227; paradox, 333; religiously, 334;

solicitation; unity of act and act; volitional negation, 187, 226, 236, 248, 250, 262, 311; volitional objects (*ishitaishō*, 意志対象), 185, 227. *See also* will

volitional objects (*ishitaishō*, 意志対象), 185, 227

Voltaire, xiii

voluntary/ism, 183, 185–187, 209, hyper-voluntarism, 186. *See also* volition(al); will

Wang Wei, 219, 317
ways (*michi* 道), 156
Welz, Claudia, 304
wild being (*l'être sauvage*), 5
will, 227, 310; autonomous, 185, 333–334; "distant will," xlii, 224, 229, 257 (*see also* solicitation; unity of act and act); heightening, diminishing, 334; and faith, 334; hyper-voluntarism, 186; of an individual, 229; *ishi* 意志, 186; negating, 333; objective, 185, 227; paradox of actively willing passivity, 303; and the pre-reflective, 324; pure free, 188; spontaneity and self-defeating nature of, 304; subjective power of, 333–334. *See also* non-willing; volition(al)
will to power, 175
William Blake, 292
Wittgenstein, Ludwig, xix
Wong, Aida-Yuen, 91
world logic (*sekai no ronri* 世界の論理), xxiv, 329
world philosophy, xvi, xviii, 336
wrapping (*tsutsumu* 包む), 6. *See also* metaphor of fabric

Yanagi, Sōetsu, xxix, 308
Yuasa, Yasuo, 82, 196, 201; *yūgen*, 327

Yujian style, 162, 216, 312. *See also* Chinese painting
Yusa, Michiko, xxiii

Zahavi, Dan, 9, 242
Zen, xxi–xxiv, xxvii, xxxi, xxxiii–xxxiv, xxxvi–xxxvii, 15, 19, 23, 62, 80, 82, 151, 154–158, 160–161, 179, 257, 308, 331, 335; aesthetics, xxxiii, 62, 155–158, 308; artistic practice, 168 (see also *Geidō*); Daoist influence, xxxiv, 62; gardens, 156; meditative practice, xxxvii, 158; Nishida's practice, 22–24 (*see also* Suzuki, D.T.); philosophy, xxi; priest, xvi, 151, 156, 158, 161 (*see also* Buddhist practice and; *Geidō* practices; religious practice; Sesshū Tōyō); religious and aesthetic practice, xxxiv, 151, 157, 168; religious' artist (*ebushi*), 155
Zhu Xi, 317
Ziporyn, Brook, 77, 98, 198, 210, 227–229, 259, 264

www.ingramcontent.com/pod-product-compliance
Lightning Source LLC
Chambersburg PA
CBHW020257240426

43673CB00039B/625